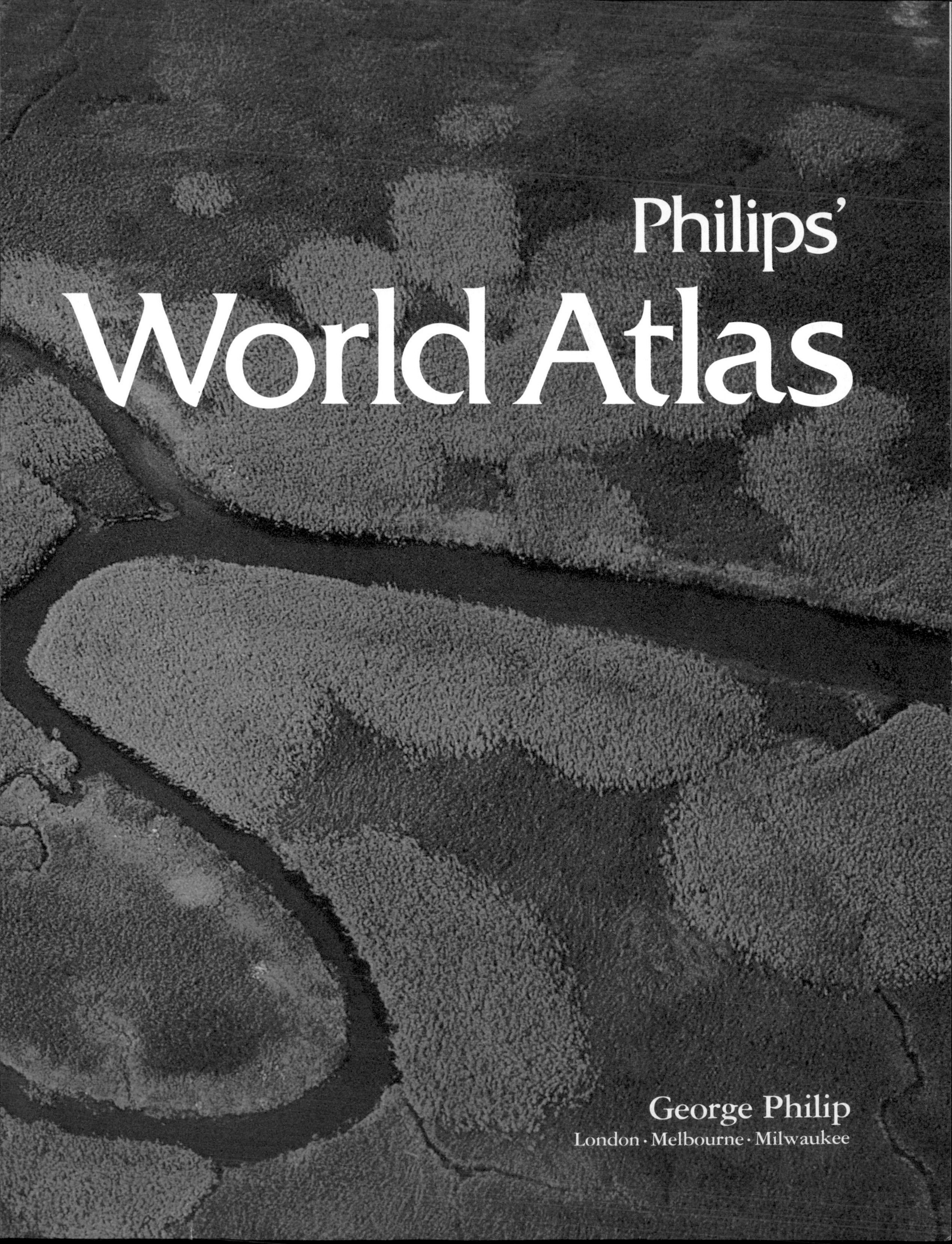

Philips'

World Atlas

George Philip

London · Melbourne · Milwaukee

Edited by
B.M. Willett
Cartographic Editor

THE WORLD TODAY

Contributors
John Chesshire, Science Policy Research Unit, Sussex University; Dr Richard Crockett, Institute of Geological Sciences; Arthur Kilgore, Gordon MacKerron, Science Policy Research Unit, Sussex University; Pauline Marstrand, Science Policy Research Unit, Sussex University, Professor J.H. Paterson, Department of Geography, Leicester University; John Rowley, Editor of *People*, the journal of the International Planned Parenthood Federation; Howard Rush, Science Policy Research Unit, Sussex University; Robert Stewart.

Illustration Acknowledgements
The publishers would like to thank the following individuals and organizations for their kind permission to reproduce the photographs in this section; Ardea, London; Paul Brierley; Camera Press Ltd.; Bruce Coleman Ltd.; *The Daily Telegraph;* Susan Griggs Agency Ltd; Maldwyn Glover; The John Hillelson Agency Ltd.; Alan Hutchison Library; Picturepoint Ltd.; Rex Features Ltd.; John Topham Picture Library; Transworld Feature Syndicate; Zefa Picture Library.

Illustrations on preliminary pages
Half-title: sand and sea at Brighton on the south coast of England *(Bruce Coleman)*; *title:* mangrove swamp on the Caribbean coast of Panama *(Susan Griggs)*; *contents:* harvesting sea salt near Cabo Frio, Brazil *(Bruce Coleman)*; *foreword:* Bora-Bora, an oceanic island fringed with a coral reef in French Polynesia *(Bruce Coleman)*; New York *(Bruce Coleman)*.

First Edition September 1979
Fifth Edition 1985

British Library Cataloguing in Publication Data
Philips' world atlas. –5th ed.
1. Atlases, British
912 G1021

ISBN 0 540 05499 2

Printed and bound in Italy
by L.E.G.O., Vicenza.

Contents

The World Today
1 General Reference
World: Physical 1:150M
2–3 World: Political 1:80M
4 Europe: Physical 1:20M
5 Europe: Political 1:20M
6–7 England and Wales 1:2M
8 Scotland 1:2M
9 Ireland 1:2M
10 Great Britain & Ireland: Administrative 1:4M
11 Netherlands, Belgium and Luxembourg 1:2·5M
12 France 1:5M
13 Spain and Portugal 1:5M
14–15 Central Europe 1:5M Central Europe Political 1:25M
16–17 Mediterranean Lands 1:10M
18–19 Italy and the Balkan States 1:5M
Malta 1:1M South East Europe Political 1:25M
20–21 Scandinavia and the Baltic Lands 1:5M
Iceland 1:5M
22–23 U.S.S.R. in Europe 1:10M
24–25 U.S.S.R. 1:20M
26 Asia: Physical 1:50M
27 Asia: Political 1:50M
28 Israel and West Jordan 1:1M
29 Arabia and the Horn of Africa 1:15M
30–31 The Near and Middle East 1:10M
32–33 South Asia 1:10M
34–35 East Indies 1:12·5M
Java and Madura 1:7·5M

36 Japan 1:10M
Central Japan 1:5M
37 China 1:20M
38–39 Eastern China and Korea 1:10M
40–41 Australia 1:12M
Australasia: Political 1:80M
42–43 Eastern Australia 1:8M
44–45 Western Australia 1:8M
46 Southeast Australia 1:4·5M
47 New Zealand 1:6M
New Zealand and Dependencies 1:60M
Samoa Is., Fiji and Tonga Is. 1:12M
48 Africa: Physical 1:40M
49 Africa: Political 1:40M
50–51 Northern Africa 1:15M
52 East Africa 1:7·5M
53 Nigeria and Ghana 1:8M
54–55 Central and South Africa 1:15M
Madagascar 1:15M
56–57 Southern Africa 1:8M
Madagascar 1:8M
58–59 North America: Physical 1:30M
North America: Political 1:70M
60–61 Canada 1:15M
Alaska 1:30M
62–63 Eastern Canada 1:7M
64–65 Western Canada 1:7M
66–67 United States 1:12M
Hawaii 1:10M
68–69 Eastern United States 1:6M
70–71 Middle United States 1:6M
72–73 Western United States 1:6M
74 Mexico 1:12M
Panama Canal 1:1M
75 West Indies 1:12M
Bermuda 1:1M
Leeward Is., Windward Is., Jamaica, Trinidad and Tobago 1:8M
76 South America: Physical 1:30M
77 South America: Political 1:30M
78–79 South America: North 1:16M
80 South America: South 1:16M

Index 1–57

Climatic Statistics 58–61

Population of Cities 62–63

Population of Countries 64

Foreword

Philips' World Atlas presents the reader with two complementary views of the world. The maps and index are a detailed source of reference on the world as it is today while the introductory essays describe many of the important aspects of life on this planet at the end of the twentieth century, and consider what the future may bring in a world where changes take place at an accelerating pace.

The maps are designed to show where places are and to make available a large quantity of information about them.

The Idea of Location There are two related but really quite different kinds of location – absolute and relative. By absolute location is meant the identification of a point on the surface of the earth by reference to a network of lines composed of parallels of latitude and meridians of longitude. The numbering of parallels begins at the Equator and continues as degrees of a quarter circle to the Poles (90°), both North and South. The meridians are numbered from the Prime Meridian, which passes through Greenwich, England, to 180° either East or West.

Relative location means the identification of a place in relation not to the network just described, but to other places or areas. For example, Greenwich is (relatively) located in Great Britain, in England, near the mouth of the River Thames, about 10 miles East of London. If you ask where Greenwich is, any of these answers could be appropriate.

Regional Maps There are 65 pages of regional maps in the atlas, containing a wealth of detail. Information given includes landforms and drainage features and selected aspects of human occupation such as settlements, railways, highways, canals, pipelines, and political boundaries. Surface relief is brought out by combining contours with layer-colouring and relief-shading.

Layer-colouring serves to mark off one range of elevation from the next, and each map contains in its margins an altitude scale which indicates in metres the values of the contours employed. The layer-colouring also extends below sea-level, and shows the continental shelf.

Relief-shading serves to emphasize changes in elevation, and, in addition, contributes a three-dimensional quality to the land surface.

Other natural features such as drainage – rivers, lakes, reservoirs and canals – are shown in conventional blue, and transportation is shown in black for railways, in red for major highways.

The settlements shown on the maps have been classified into nine categories, reflecting size of population and importance.

The regional maps are both physical and political in character. All international boundaries are reinforced with red for clarity and emphasis, and provincial and other sub-national boundaries are shown for a number of major countries.

World and Continental Maps Physical and political maps of the world introduce the atlas and each continental section similarly begins with summary physical and political maps.

Scale The importance of scale, and of distinguishing between maps at different scales, cannot be overestimated. Thus, the map of the continent of Africa (page 48) is shown at a scale of 1:40,000,000, whereas the map of East Africa (page 52) is drawn at a scale of 1:7,500,000. A larger-scale map means that very much more can be shown of terrain, of settlement, of transportation and other features and such scales are used for parts of the world where the users' interests are likely to require them.

The Spelling of Place Names In this atlas, the principle followed is that, for settlements at least, and where the Roman alphabet is employed, the indigenous spellings are used, except for a relatively few places which are so well known that the indigenous spelling would be confusing to the reader. For many of the names in this latter group alternative spellings are also given.

In cases where the Roman alphabet is not employed in the native language, transliteration and romanization are required. In these cases, the recommendations of the U.S. Board on Geographic Names and the U.K. Permanent Committee on Geographical Names are followed wherever possible.

Index The index at the back of the atlas contains over 20,000 place names. Reference is given to the largest-scale map on which the place appears, and this is followed by a description of the absolute location of the place in terms of latitude and longitude.

Statistical Information On pages 58-61 (following the index) climatic statistics are given of monthly temperature and rainfall for over 80 places in the world. These figures allow the reader to form some idea of the average weather to be expected there.

On pages 62-64 are tables of areas and populations for the countries of the world and for the populations of major towns and cities.

The World Today

The planet earth 2–3
A crowded planet 4–5
Environment in danger 6–7
Feeding the world 8–9
What kind of food production? 10–11
Man's quest for energy 12–13
Energy alternatives 14–15
The earth's mineral wealth 16–17
A conserving future 18–19
Economic trends 20–21
The politics of possession 22–23
Transport and communication 24–25
Industry and technology 26–27
The quality of life 28–29
One earth 30–31
Earth data 32

The planet earth

THE earth was formed approximately four-and-a-half billion years ago, although some of the materials that form its surface today may have been laid in place, by the action of rivers for example, only yesterday. By contrast to the age of the planet, the history of man on earth dates back only one million years, and the period of man's occupance of which we have any direct knowledge represents only a minute fraction of this shorter span of time.

During this short period of time, nevertheless, human beings have developed a remarkable variety of races, languages and cultures. Since the earth is a sphere, natural conditions of temperature, landscape and fertility range widely between polar and tropical, and some of the variety of mankind's development is clearly due to this variety in nature. Man has adapted to living in both hot and cold climates, and not only his lifestyle but some of his institutions, such as religion, reflect this adaptation. Yet there is a much greater variety in human life-forms and customs than can be accounted for by environment alone. For one thing, members of the same race, or language group, may be bitterly opposed to one another on political or religious grounds. For another, a sense of belonging draws people together in national or tribal groupings, which develop their own particular means of cultural expression.

Basic resources

Man's primary need is his own life support. Alone among the planets, as far as we know, the earth provides the conditions necessary to sustain life. These conditions we know as resources. Fundamental to the resource structure of the earth is the energy of the sun: it is the power plant that drives all other systems. At a secondary level are the mineral deposits, soils and water on the earth; and thirdly, there are the plants that support animal life, and those animals which exist by preying, species upon species. All these can be classed as the earth's natural resources.

At the highest level, where man exists in total isolation from the natural world, there is a further resource component: what is normally referred to as human resources. These are represented by the ability of man to think, work, invent and find uses for natural materials; to apply skill or power to these materials and transform them. Many animals can build themselves a home in ways that display great engineering skill. Most creatures, however, can only build one kind of structure. Man can build a whole range of structures and design new forms to suit his needs as he anticipates them.

Unequal distribution

The distribution of natural resources over the earth's surface is far from even. The whereabouts of mineral deposits depend on random events in a remote geological past; patches of fertile soil depend on events more recent but, to man, equally capricious — the flow of rivers or the movement of ice. When it comes to agriculture, the activity that has been basic to the survival of man and his increase in numbers, we find that, in round figures, 20 per cent of the earth's surface is barred to him by ice or perennially frozen soil; 20 per cent is composed of highlands too cold, rugged or barren for the cultivation of crops; 20 per cent is arid or desert, and between five and 10 per cent of the remainder has no soil, either because it has been scraped by ice or because it is permanently wet or flooded. This leaves only 30-35 per cent of the land surface where food production is possible, together with the oceans and whatever resources may be obtained from that source.

We can think of these natural resources as forming a cover, or coating, of varying thickness over the earth's surface: in some places it is deep and rich; in others it is for all practical purposes non-existent. In the same way, observation shows that human resources vary in quality from place to place. What, in fact, we are observing are different levels of technical ability and equipment among different peoples. Whereas, however, we can accept that natural resource distribution is either random or climatically determined, and therefore unchangeable, the explanation for different development levels of human resources is a much more complex matter.

Why have some nations or groups advanced more rapidly than others in technology? Why have some lost the lead they once had? A number of explanations have been offered in order to answer these questions. One of these is climatic — that some environments are more stimulating to effort and inventiveness than others. Some are racial — and may, in due course, become racist — arguing that one race is more gifted than another. Yet others focus on the structure of society, and the opportunities it affords for the use of individual talents and the freedom to innovate.

The key to exploitation

Each of these theories in isolation can be disproved, simply by pointing out the exceptions to it. Whatever the explanation, however, the fact is clear: that the ability to make use of what nature has provided in the way of resources varies critically from society to society, and that a high level of human resource input can provide a good living for people in areas, such as Scandinavia, where the natural endowment is meagre, while people may live on top of a veritable treasure chest of natural riches, as, it would appear, the Brazilians do, without necessarily obtaining the benefit of them. It is, after all, only a few years since the oil states of the Middle East were among the world's poorest nations. If we think of the earth as a storehouse of natural wealth, then it is human ingenuity — the human resources represented by technical skills — which provides the key to open it.

Fortunately, no nation today possesses a monopoly of these skills, or is, for that matter, debarred from acquiring them. It is a slow process to do so, but one that can be speeded up if those societies which are relatively advanced will help those that are only at the beginning. Human resources have transformed parts of this planet once judged to be too cold, or too dry, or too poor to support the dense populations, either on the land or in the great cities, that now occupy them.

▲**The earth in space** *was an unfamiliar view we obtained when man first ventured beyond his natural environment: a small, rocky*

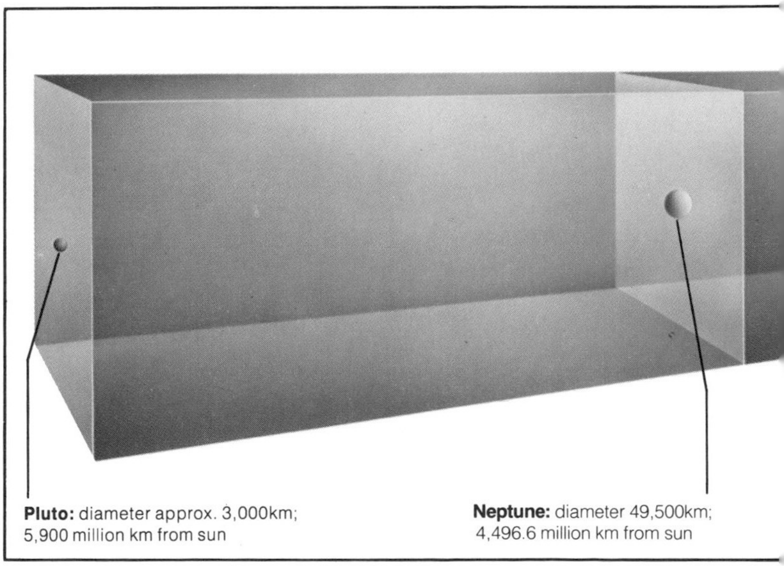

planet with much surface water and a dense atmosphere.

200 million years ago

135 million years ago

Present day

150 million years' time

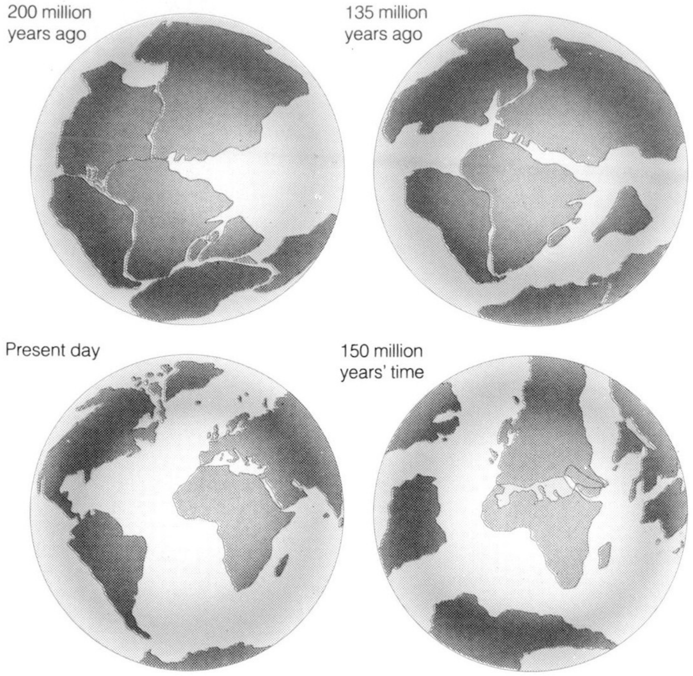

Plate Tectonics
The migration of the continents is a feature unique to Planet Earth. The complementary, almost jigsaw-puzzle fit of the coastlines on each side of the Atlantic Ocean inspired Alfred Wegener's theory of continental drift at the beginning of the twentieth century. The theory suggested that an ancient supercontinent, which Wegener named Pangaea, incorporated all of the earth's land masses and gradually split up to form the continents we see today. The modern theory of plate tectonics attributes continental drift to movements in crustal plates underlying the oceans as well as the continents. These movements are caused by the slow but continuous welling-up of material from deep within the earth along a series of mid-ocean ridges. Geological evidence that the continents once formed a single land mass is provided by distinctive rock formations that can be assembled into continuous belts when Africa and South America are lined up next to each other. Distribution of some plants and animals in the past, as well as ancient climatic zones, can only be explained by the theory of plate tectonics.

Uranus: diameter 51,800km; 2,869.6 million km from sun

Saturn: diameter 120,000km; 1,427 million km from sun

Jupiter: diameter 142,800km; 778.3 million km from sun

Mars: diameter 6,787km; 227.9 million km from sun

Mercury: diameter 4,800km; 57.9 million km from sun

Venus: diameter 12,104km; 108.2 million km from sun

Earth: diameter 12,756km; 149.6 million km from sun

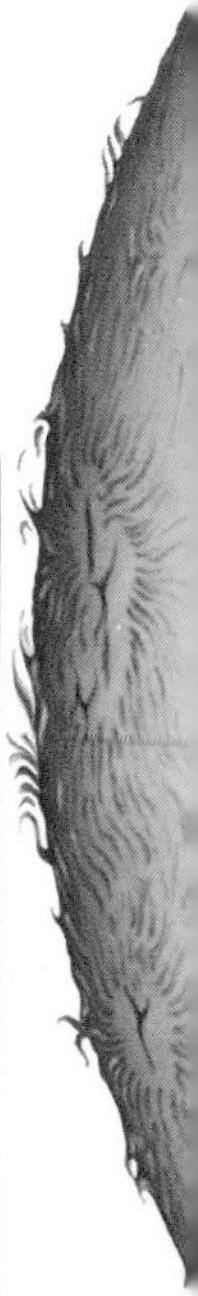

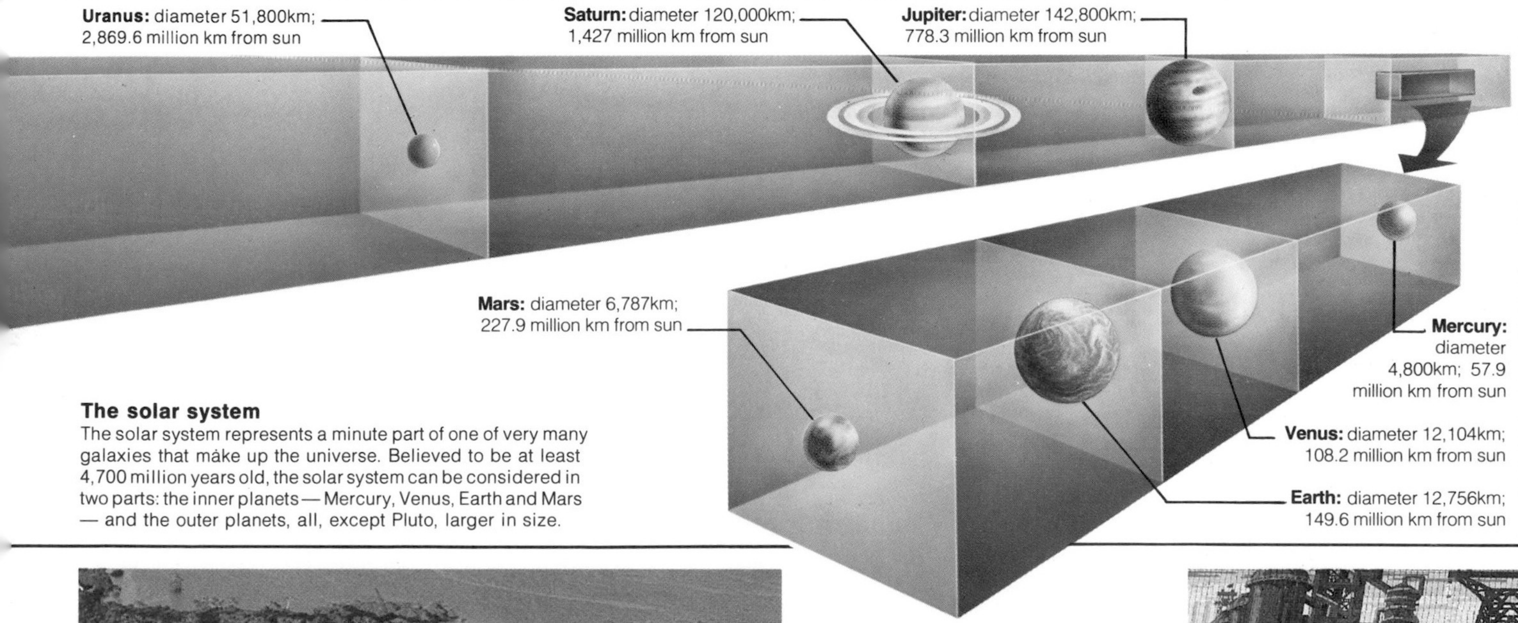

The solar system
The solar system represents a minute part of one of very many galaxies that make up the universe. Believed to be at least 4,700 million years old, the solar system can be considered in two parts: the inner planets — Mercury, Venus, Earth and Mars — and the outer planets, all, except Pluto, larger in size.

▶ **The evolution of man** *as a unique social and cultural animal has produced a variety of races, languages, religious and social systems. A political rally in China illustrates one aspect of culture.*

◀ **The Amazon basin** *is one of the few remaining wildernesses on earth. Such vast areas of forest play a vital role in global ecology — by helping to maintain the balance of oxygen in the atmosphere.*

▶ **Throughout history** *man has found various ways of expressing his beliefs in supernatural powers. Here, monks follow the teachings of the Dalai Lama in a temple in Tibet — one facet of religion today.*

3

A crowded planet

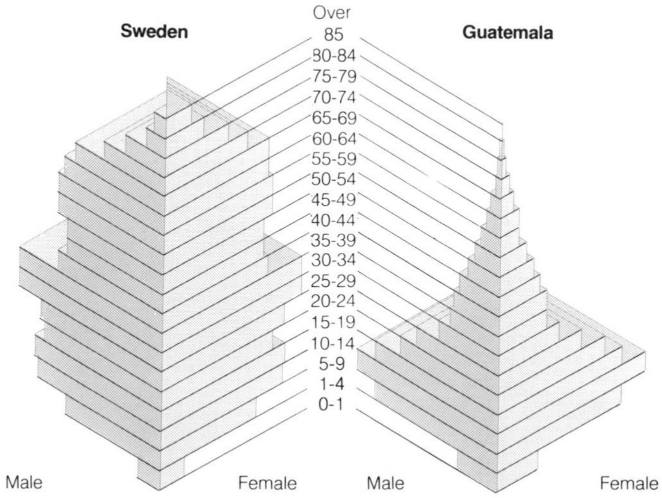

FROM man's earliest ancestors on the planet earth, more than one million years ago, until the beginnings of settled agriculture some 10,000 years ago, the number of human beings alive at any one time did not exceed five million. By 1800 the world was home to one billion people. The second billion was reached by 1930, the third by 1960 and the fourth billion by 1970. The likelihood is that the fifth billion will be reached by 1987 and that a sixth billion will be added by the end of the century, when United Nations demographers estimate that the earth will "carry" 6,250,000,000 human beings.

The key to population growth
What happens after that depends on the speed at which the rate of population growth slows down over the coming decade. The annual growth rate is believed to have peaked at about two per cent in 1970, declining to between 1.7 and 1.8 per cent today. This deceptively small statistic is adding some 80 million people to the world's population each year and, because the world's total population includes such a high proportion of young people who have yet to grow up and have children, it is going to take a long time for the population to stabilize at somewhere between eight and 15 billion, some time in the twenty-first century.

The cause of this extraordinary explosion in human numbers over the past 200 years lies essentially in declining death rates rather than in increasing birth rates. Medical advances and improved conditions of life first cut death rates in Europe. The subsequent explosion in the numbers surviving was partly masked by the massive exodus to new countries, with some 60 million migrants travelling to the Americas and elsewhere before World War II. An even greater and faster increase in numbers began in the developing countries of Asia, Africa and Latin America before World War II as a much more rapid drop in death rates followed the spread of scientific technology to prevent and control disease and improvements in the availability of food.

As death rates declined in Europe birth rates also slowly came down, and today population growth in all modern industrialized countries is low or non-existent. In a few cases, such as West Germany and Austria, the population has even begun to decrease. But less than one-third of the world's population lives in these developed regions, and it is among the two-thirds in the developing countries that population is growing fast. Although the rates of growth have begun to fall in many countries, the proportion of the world's population in the developing countries of Asia, Africa and Latin America will continue to rise until the year 2000.

The distribution of people
At the moment Europe remains the most densely populated area of the globe, with an average of 90 people per square kilometre. The vast territories of southern and eastern Asia are, however, not far behind, and within the next 100 years they are likely to have three times the density of present-day Europe, according to United Nations estimates. In Asia as a whole, population is likely to increase from 2.5 billion to 3.6 billion in the next 20 years. Africa, by contrast, is relatively lightly populated at present, though individual countries such as Egypt, Rwanda and Lesotho have high populations in relation to productive land. The African continent is likely to add another 400 million people to its 1979 population of 455 million by the turn of the century, while Latin America's population will grow from 360 million to some 600 million in the same period.

Of more concern to many governments than overall density of population is the distribution of population within national boundaries. The growth of cities is one of the most striking features of our time. At the beginning of this century there were only 250 million city dwellers in the world. Today 1,500 million people live in urban areas and by the year 2000, it is believed, more than half the world's population, or some 3,000 million people, will be living in towns and cities.

The call of the city
The growth of cities is partly the result of natural increase, but more significantly the result of migration from the countryside, where population growth often coincides with rural stagnation and a shortage of work. Unlike the situation in the nineteenth century, there are few unused fertile areas left in the world. And the only job opportunities are those which appear to beckon from the growing cities. Already one-third of the urban inhabitants in less-developed countries are squatters living on the fringes of cities such as Djakarta, Bombay, Calcutta, Rio de Janeiro, Manila and Mexico City. These are among the fastest growing settlements in the world today.

Taking both rural and urban areas of the developing world together, more than 40 per cent of the population is either unemployed or underemployed, two billion are continually undernourished and some 1,400 million are illiterate. The causes of such problems are complex, but rapid population growth makes all of them more difficult to solve. As a result, four-fifths of the developing world's population now live in countries which have adopted policies aimed at slowing down the rate of population growth.

Since the world conference on population in Bucharest in 1974, governments have increasingly come to realize that such policies stand the best chance of success if they involve social and development policies which create a wish for smaller families, as well as access to family planning information and services. The motivation for small families involves the reduction of infant and child mortality, the expansion of basic education, especially for girls, an increase in the income of the rural poor, a more equal distribution of wealth and — of particular importance — the improvement of the status of women in society. Where such measures have been taken along with the provision of family planning services, including access to early abortion and a range of fertility control methods, rapid declines in fertility have taken place. The most spectacular example in recent years has been China.

Millions of people in the developing world, however, have no access to modern birth control methods and, indeed, some governments, on religious grounds or for strategic reasons, actively discourage family planning programmes. With greater pressures being put upon the earth's limited resources, from agricultural land to mineral wealth, and the ever-increasing impact of man's activities on the environment, the prospect of further population growth poses many and varied problems.

▲ **Most of the world's poor** *live in appalling conditions. Having migrated to the cities in the hope of greater opportunities, many people find themselves in even worse* surroundings. Shanty towns, such as this one in Sao Paulo, are home to a large proportion of the inhabitants of the world's fastest-growing cities.

Age/sex structure

Age pyramids illustrate the differences in population structure between developed and developing countries. The broad base of the pyramid for Guatemala shows that the country's population is increasing rapidly. In general, as birth and death rates decline, such a diagram loses its pyramid shape and becomes barrel-shaped. This indicates an increasing number of old people in the population.

Sweden | Guatemala

Over 85 / 80-84 / 75-79 / 70-74 / 65-69 / 60-64 / 55-59 / 50-54 / 45-49 / 40-44 / 35-39 / 30-34 / 25-29 / 20-24 / 15-19 / 10-14 / 5-9 / 1-4 / 0-1

Male | Female | Male | Female

▲ **India,** *with the second-largest population in the world, has introduced many birth control methods. At this sterilization clinic many vasectomies are carried out at one session.*

▶ **The status of women** *in a society affects attitudes to population control. In China women are considered to be an essential part of the work force and birth control is encouraged.*

▲ **Birth rates remain high** *in many of the less-developed countries. Large numbers of children are very often encouraged by the societies, for religious, economic and political reasons.*

World population in 1500

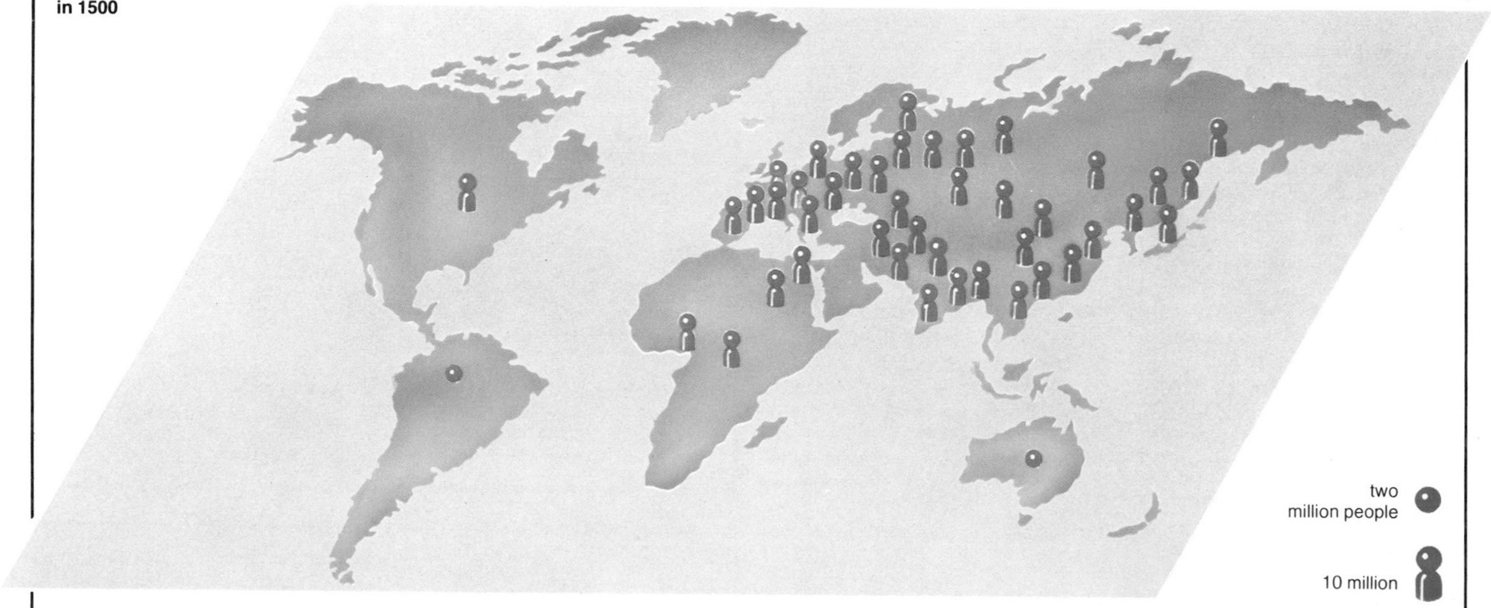

Present day population and projected population for the year 2000

By about 8000 BC there were approximately five million people on earth. From then on, numbers increased by between 0.04 and 0.06 per cent a year until about 1650. The "doubling time" of human numbers had been reduced from 1,500 to 200 years by 1800, by which time world population had reached one billion.

Environment in danger

ALL life on our planet is confined to a thin skin of earth, air and water that is no more than 10 kilometres thick. It depends for its healthy existence on green vegetation which turns sunlight into chemical energy and maintains the balance of oxygen and carbon dioxide in the atmosphere. On this process are based the complex food chains made up of many thousands of plant and animal species, all of which are vulnerable to the activities of man.

The mounting impact of man on the environment is partly the result of his increased numbers. It is also due to the enormous increase in industrial activity and consumption of the earth's resources, particularly in the countries of the northern hemisphere. A two per cent annual increase in population since the middle of this century has been accompanied by a four per cent annual increase in consumption, a rate of growth which, if maintained for a century, will increase consumption 50 times and create an even greater impact on the biological environment.

The impact of man

The oceans, grasslands, croplands and forests have all felt the impact of man's rapidly increasing exploitation of these resources for food, fuel and living space. Forests play a vital role in maintaining the ecological status quo, preserving watersheds, preventing soil erosion and the silting of dams, moderating climate and providing fuel, building materials and paper. But the destruction of trees for farmland and firewood has a long history, and by the middle of this century between one-third and one-half of the earth's original forest cover had gone.

Forest management in western Europe, the Soviet Union and North America now shows an awareness of the need to conserve existing woodland, while China is striving to undo the destruction of past generations. Almost everywhere in the developing world, however, the remaining tree cover is under pressure as the growing population increases the demand for firewood supplies and farmland. Serious deforestation is occurring in the Himalayas, causing erosion and flooding in the plains below, and similar problems are reported from eastern India, Pakistan, Thailand, the Philippines, Malaysia, Tanzania and elsewhere. The tropical forests of southeast Asia, central and west Africa and Amazonia are also severely threatened, and with them the earth's richest store of rare plants and animals.

The loss of farmland

Arable land, which makes up one-tenth of the earth's land surface, is also under great pressure. The area of cropland is being reduced by serious erosion and conversion to non-agricultural use at a faster rate than new land is brought under the plough. Japan, for example, lost six per cent of cropland in the 1960s.

The oceans, too, have recently been exploited more intensively than ever before: the fish catch trebled from 21 to 72 million tonnes between 1950 and 1980. As a result, many areas have been overfished, particularly in the North Atlantic, where there have been sudden declines in catches of cod, haddock, sole and herring. The Peruvian anchovy has been grossly overfished and several species of whale have been hunted almost to the point of extinction.

The oceans are suffering also from another consequence of man's escalating consumption: the generation of excessive and dangerous wastes. The seas, which cover two-thirds of the earth's surface, have become a dustbin for oil, chemicals, radioactive materials, sewage, junk metal, pesticides and detergents, among many other products. Approximately one million tonnes of oil seep into the sea from ships and drilling rigs each year, and many inland seas and estuaries are now so heavily polluted that fish, if they survive at all, are not safe to eat. Pollution is also having its effect on human health through the air we breathe and the food and water we consume. Some 600,000 different chemicals are in daily use and every year several thousand new ones enter into significant use. Among the illnesses they have produced are parasitic infections, emphysema, heart disease and some cancers. With polluted rivers running across national frontiers and acid rain falling over a wide area of Europe, pollution can now be considered an international problem.

A growing concern

The long-term effects of some of man's activities are uncertain. There is considerable concern about the fluorocarbons contained in aerosol cans. Half a million tonnes of these chemicals are released into the atmosphere each year, and it is thought they may be destroying the ozone layer which filters out the harmful ultraviolet radiation from the sun. The result of this could be an increase in the incidence of skin cancer, damage to crops and even a change in climate. The ozone layer may be threatened also by the release of nitrous oxides from nitrogen fertilizers, on which man depends for greater crop yields.

Of more immediate concern is the environmental stress caused by rapid urbanization. By the end of the century more than half the world's six billion people will be city dwellers if present trends continue. The lack of basic services in many cities and the crowding and stress suffered by the majority of urban dwellers in the less-developed countries pose a great environmental problem, albeit local in effect.

There is a rapidly increasing awareness of the environmental impact of man's activities. It is, however, often difficult to put a price on the conservation of nature and the protection of our vulnerable environment.

Environmental pollution

The possibility that the earth's climate may be changing has been a subject much discussed in recent years. Untypical, "freak" weather during the 1970s may well be the result of natural trends of cooling and warming that the earth has experienced throughout its history, but there are suggestions that the activities of man may fundamentally alter the world's climatic patterns. A manifestation of this is what is known as the "greenhouse effect". Carbon dioxide in the atmosphere is transparent to the shortwave infra-red heat radiation from the sun, but opaque to longwave infra-red radiation emitted from warm objects on earth. What this means, in effect, is that heat can get in but it cannot get out as easily. Measurements show that the level of carbon dioxide in the air has increased significantly during this century, possibly by as much as 15 per cent. The combustion of fossil fuels produces carbon dioxide and is the chief culprit, but ploughing land also releases large amounts of soil-held gas into the atmosphere.

Industrial effluent and untreated sewage are the most common pollutants of water, but the increasing use of fertilizers in food production means that larger amounts of nitrates and phosphates are leached into river systems. The over-abundance of chemicals such as phosphates in lakes and coastal waters produces an increase in algae on the surface, which blots out the light necessary for plant life. This, in turn, reduces the oxygen content and, ultimately, marine life. More and more water systems are "dying" as a result.

▲ **The world is in danger** *of losing some of its rarest fauna as a result of man's activities. Such animals are either hunted into extinction or their habitats are ruined by human encroachment.*

▼ **Road vehicles** *consume vast amounts of oil and other raw materials, pollute the air and eat up land space for roads and car parks.*

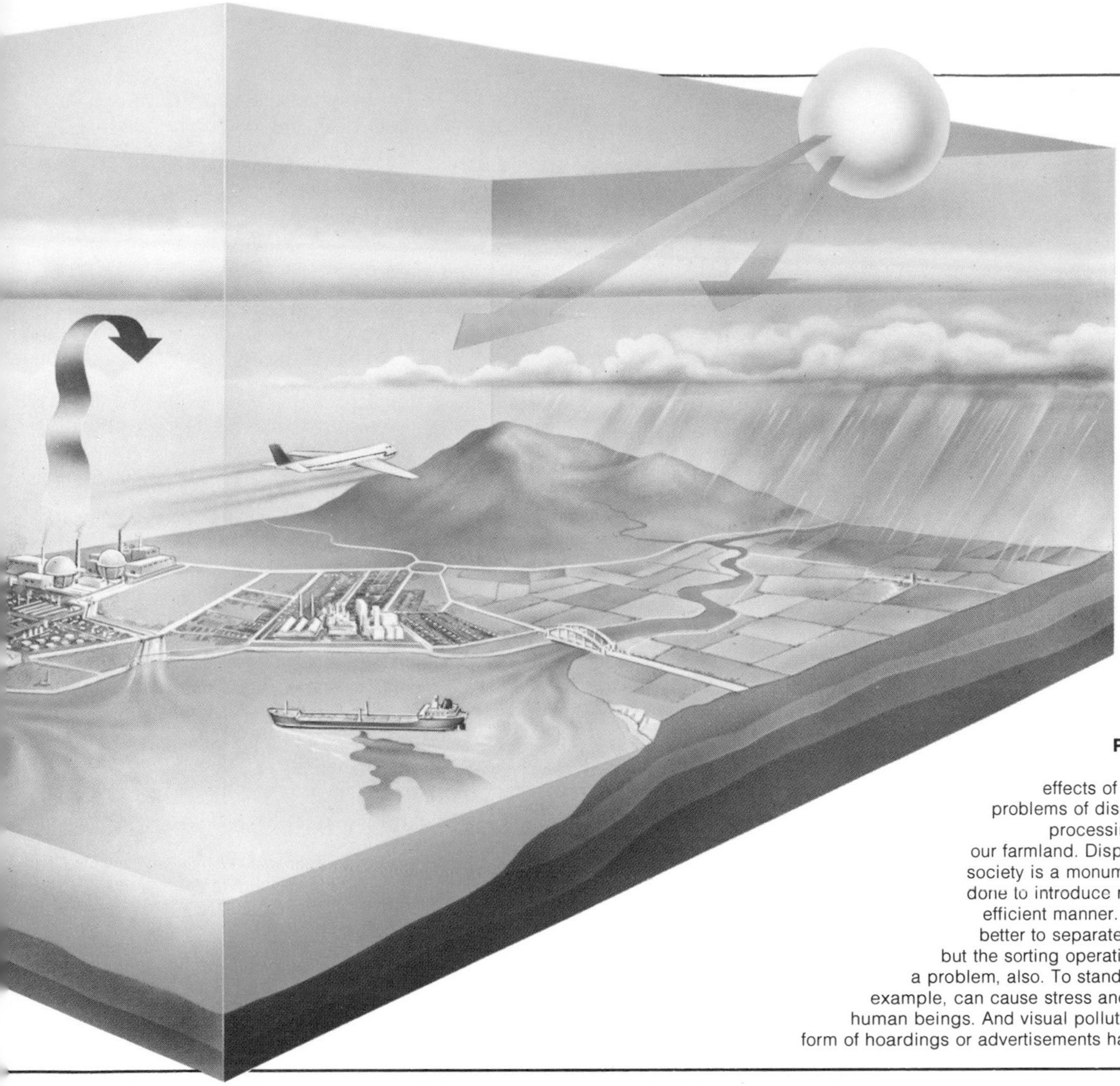

Pollution of the air can take the form of smogs — for which London was notorious before the 1950s — produced by the accumulation in the air of sulphur dioxide, sulphuric acid and smoke from industry, and the photochemical hazes produced largely by car exhaust fumes. Ironically, clean air acts that have reduced the smoke content of the air have furthered the photochemical reactions which are initiated by the sun's energy. It is argued by some experts that pollution of the air increases the cloud cover — particles provide a nucleus around which cloud droplets can condense — which reflects solar radiation back into space and which would therefore lower temperatures on earth. The problem of pollution is certainly not a localized one: as a result of air currents and winds, "acid rain" now falls over parts of western Europe that are not themselves industrialized regions, inhibiting forest growth.

Pollution of the land in its most obvious form is all too familiar: the devastating effects of open-cast mining on the landscape; the problems of disposing of waste products from industrial processing; and the scattering of chemicals over our farmland. Disposing of the waste produced by modern society is a monumental problem and so far little has been done to introduce recycling on a large scale or in the most efficient manner. Before burning refuse, for example, it is better to separate the glass, metal or plastic constituents, but the sorting operation is a costly one. Noise is increasingly a problem, also. To stand within a few metres of a heavy lorry, for example, can cause stress and, after a time, damage to the hearing of human beings. And visual pollution, especially for urban dwellers, in the form of hoardings or advertisements has become a common feature of society.

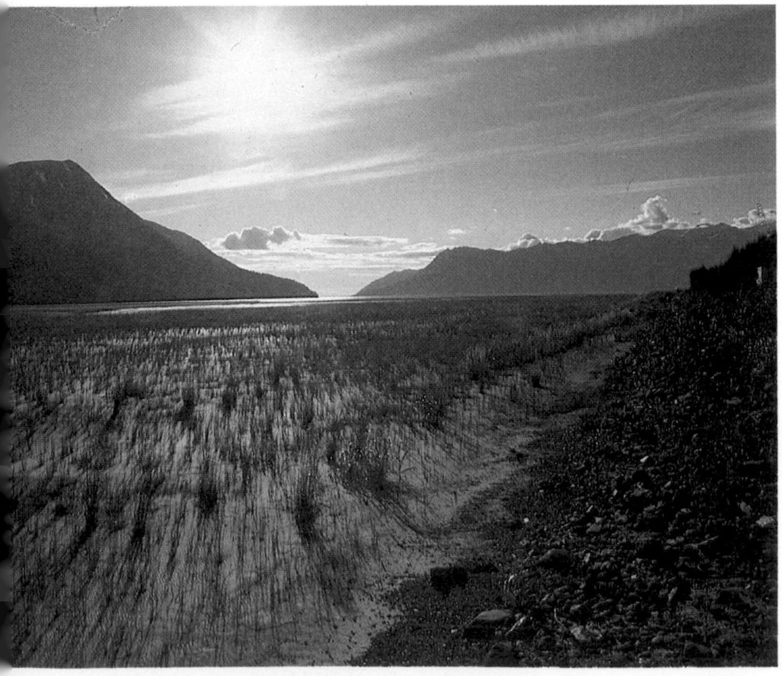

▲ **The air is still clear** *and the land unscarred in regions of the earth that are apparently remote from the industrialized world. Studies of tissues from certain animals in the far northern and southern latitudes, however, shows evidence of pollution in the form of insecticides and other man-made chemicals that are carried to all parts of the globe by the earth's wind and water systems.*

► **Pollution of the air** *can be manifested in what is known as a photochemical haze, seen here lingering over a Californian beach. Car exhausts provide many of the raw materials needed for the atmospheric reactions: nitrogen dioxide, hydrocarbons and other organic compounds. Reactions are initiated by the sun's energy.*

▼ **The destruction of tree cover,** *overgrazing and overcropping contribute to the spread of deserts. The Sahara has crept both north and south – as in the Sahel region shown here – at a rate of almost 100 kilometres in the last 17 years, with the recent loss of 650,000 sq kilometres of productive land.*

Feeding the world

WORLD food supplies have been increasing steadily and, in spite of predictions of impending disaster, have not yet been outstripped by population growth. Although current methods for determining accurately either world population or global food production figures are woefully inadequate, official United Nations statistics estimate that the earth's population has been increasing at less than two per cent annually while food production is growing at 2.9 per cent. While these figures are encouraging they do mask a high level of malnutrition,

which is thought to affect between 60 and 400 million people. The cause of this problem is poverty created by an unequal distribution of land, wealth and opportunity rather than actual food shortages.

Nutritional requirements

Over the past two decades, as the young science of nutrition gathered more information, our understanding of nutritional requirements has become more exact. Figures on how many people were inadequately fed were previously based on the assumption that each person needed at least 3,000 kilocalories, including 90 grams of protein, a day. More recent findings have had the effect of revising these figures downwards to 1,990 kilocalories a day for developing countries and 2,320 kilocalories a day for developed countries. These figures are still only an average. Individual nutritional requirements vary, depending on age, sex, level of physical activity and even the climate of the region in which one lives. For example, the range extends from 820 kilocalories for a female child of less than one year to 3,100 kilocalories for a teenage boy.

The new recommended kilocalorie requirements mean that, on average, every individual needs the equivalent of 250 kilograms of grain a year. If the marketed supplies of food could have been equally distributed, then during the early 1970s, when concern about the amount of food available was so high, every person could have had 2,240 kilocalories a day, which is more than enough to engage in a

healthy and active life. By the end of the 1970s approximately 1,300 million tonnes of food were reaching the market each year. That would have been enough to feed almost 5,200 million people, more than 1,000 million more than are on earth at the present time.

How much land is available?

During the same period in which nutritional requirements have been revised, our knowledge of how much food can be produced has also improved. Findings based on detailed studies of soil conditions, water availability, climate and crop characteristics indicate that there is the physical capability to produce enough food for even the highest estimate of population in the next 100 years. Studies show that a great deal more land is suitable for agricultural use than was previously believed. In southeast Asia, for example, only about 75 per cent of land which could be put under production is presently farmed.

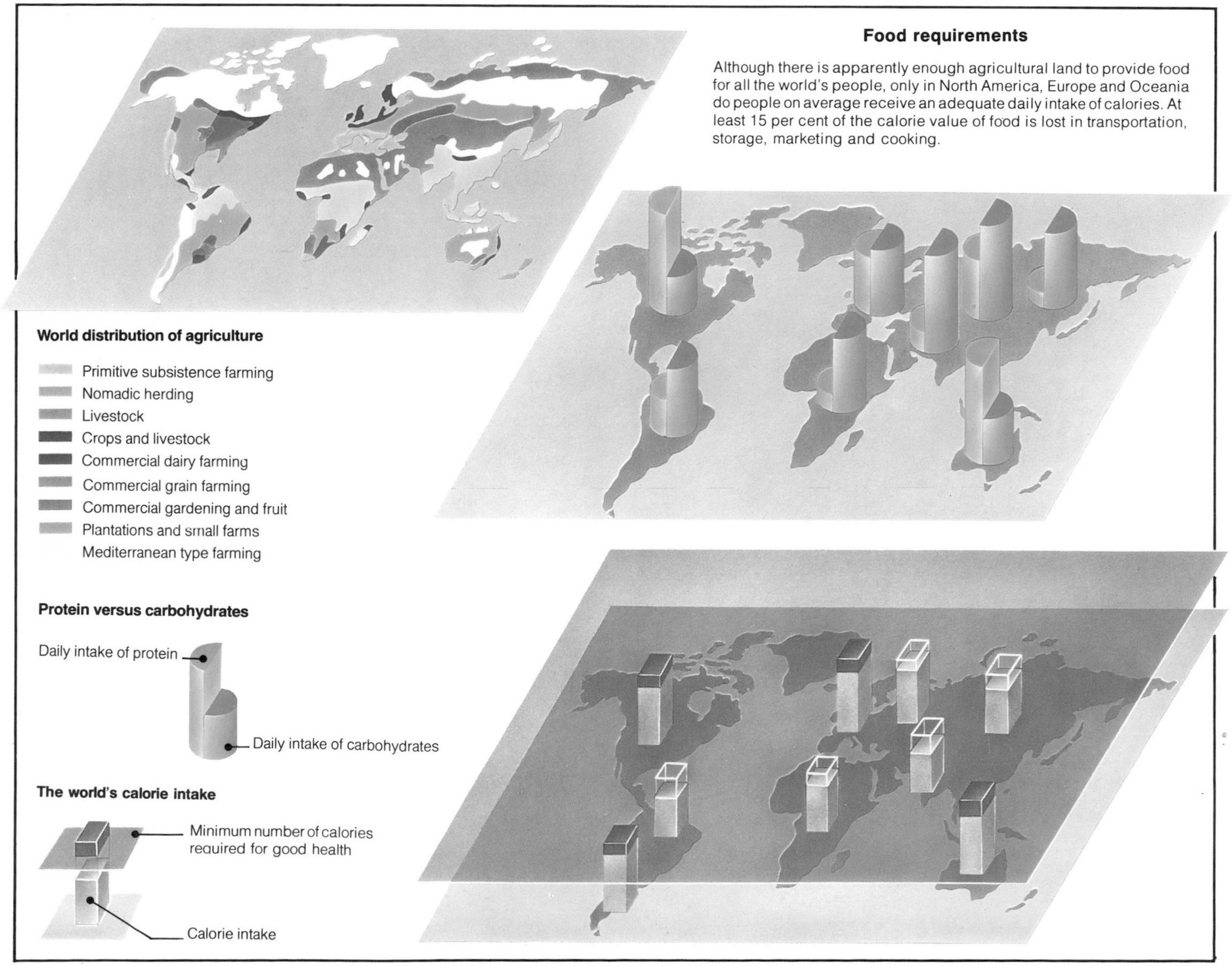

Food requirements

Although there is apparently enough agricultural land to provide food for all the world's people, only in North America, Europe and Oceania do people on average receive an adequate daily intake of calories. At least 15 per cent of the calorie value of food is lost in transportation, storage, marketing and cooking.

World distribution of agriculture

- Primitive subsistence farming
- Nomadic herding
- Livestock
- Crops and livestock
- Commercial dairy farming
- Commercial grain farming
- Commercial gardening and fruit
- Plantations and small farms
- Mediterranean type farming

Protein versus carbohydrates

Daily intake of protein

Daily intake of carbohydrates

The world's calorie intake

Minimum number of calories required for good health

Calorie intake

From the use of United Nations soil maps and studies of crops by the International Biological Programme it is estimated that there are 3,714 million hectares of land suitable for farming. Of these, 1,900 million have the potential for irrigation, a technique which can improve crop yields dramatically. Of course, competing uses for this land and the inability, for social and economic reasons, to gain access to "best-practice" techniques will mean that not all of this area is used to the fullest of its potential. If, however, only 1,208 million hectares were to be irrigated and crop yields were to reach 65 per cent of their potential, then 32,390 million tonnes of grain could be produced each year. That would be enough to feed 30 times the number of people on earth today.

Animal and plant resources

In addition to availability and productivity of land, food production depends on effective utilization of animals and plants. Plant-eating mammals and birds are all potentially edible. There are also numerous other animals, fish, insects and crustaceans which are eaten in some parts of the world but not in others. Many of these are in serious danger of elimination if industrial development takes place without consideration for the environmental requirements of these creatures. We need a world inventory of edible species so that these food sources are not lost by accident and not reduced without replacement.

Many of the hoofed animals thrive better in their home countries than imported sheep and cattle. They can be managed as wild herds by culling a calculated proportion each year for food. A further development would be domestication, as was performed on the original wild cattle of Europe. With modern knowledge of genetics animal breeding programmes could achieve targets in shorter periods than were necessary for the familiar breeds, and such animals as the eland and saiga antelope could be improved to meet the desired characteristics of meat, milk and hides that have been developed successfully in familiar domestic breeds.

More plants to eat

Just as the animal resources of most of the world are hardly yet developed, so too are indigenous plants in many regions where it is urgent that more food is produced locally. The International Biological Programme of 1963-74 identified several hundreds of plants which can fix nitrogen and, therefore, do not need nitrogen fertilizers. Many of these plants produce edible parts and could be improved by selection to become crops. Social anthropological studies show that people eat a much wider variety of plants and parts of plants than is generally supposed. An inventory of these would indicate which have the widest degree of acceptance and these could then be the subject of deliberate programmes of improvement to increase production.

The third factor in food production is technology, and its suitability to the societies that adopt it. So far, wherever a new technology has been introduced into a society where land and other resources are unequally distributed, the effect has been to increase the gap between rich and poor. Even when more food has been produced, poor people seldom get more of it, and there are many documented instances when they have got less.

The future of food production raises many issues, but the overriding aim should be to increase the food supplies available to the millions of people who still go hungry. The problem is to try to ensure that technical advance will for the present keep pace with population growth, and will in the long run overtake it so that those millions can have an adequate diet in the future. The question is what kind of food production is most suitable.

▲ **The rolling plains** *of the North American continent have made the United States the granary of the world, on which millions of hungry mouths depend. (The USSR is actually the largest grain producer, but also the greatest consumer.) A series of bad harvests in the 1970s reduced world grain reserves to a few days' supply.*

▲ **Nomadic pastoralism** *is practised on marginal lands where extremes of temperature or lack of water make cultivation virtually impossible. Subsistence farming makes no impact on world food markets, but half the world's population lives off the land and produces little or no surplus.*

▶ **The dire conditions** *of most of the world's poor — here typified by a mother and her children in the slums of an Indian city — do not offer much opportunity for an adequate diet.*

▼ **It is claimed** *that half the food bought in the United States ends up in the waste bin. We are constantly encouraged to buy more even though obesity is an extensive problem in the western world.*

▲ **Commercial livestock ranching** *is big business, especially in North America. It is often argued that we do not need as much meat as we eat and that cattle consume too much grain.*

What kind of food production?

WITH the world's population increasing by 70 or 80 million each year, and with many of the present population living off a totally inadequate diet, there can be little doubt about the urgency of increasing available food supplies. Nor is there any question about the two principal ways of doing so. They are to increase the area at present cultivated or grazed by farmers, and to obtain higher production per unit area from the existing farmlands.

In certain respects, these two objectives overlap. The effective area of cultivation will be doubled, for example, if a single, annual crop can be replaced by double-cropping. To obtain two crops in place of one, however, will probably require either a new breed of plant, which will mature faster, or an addition to the water supply, probably by irrigation, to provide enough water for double-cropping.

Extending the farming frontier
The principal methods by which the cultivated or pastured area can be extended are by clearance of forest, by irrigation, by drainage, by breeding hardier stocks and by removing the barriers presented by disease. The first three date back to antiquity. Irrigation was the basis of the Egyptian, Mesopotamian and some Central American civilizations, while in Europe, where nearly 90 per cent of the potentially arable land is cultivated, forest clearance has historically been the main method of extending the farming frontier, just as it has been for the past three centuries in eastern North America. Forest clearance assumes that the need for, or value of, land under agriculture is greater than the value of land under trees, an assumption that could realistically be made in medieval Europe, but that has ceased to hold good, for example, along the Canadian margins of agriculture. It is probable, in fact, that worldwide at present the forest is advancing on the farmland rather than the reverse. The potential for extra cropland, however, does exist in many areas of the world.

Irrigation and drainage both involve re-directing natural water supplies, and together they have already transformed great areas of Asia (the continent with by far the largest irrigated area, and where the Chinese have been using valley and delta drainage for millennia), the Middle East and North America. The Mississippi Valley and the Central Valley of California are today two of the world's most productive farming regions, yet a century ago one was a tangle of swamps and trees, and the other an area of desert and salt pans. Irrigation and drainage hold out good prospects for further increasing the area of farmland, but the capital costs are enormous, and the more irregular the water supply, the higher those costs become.

The breeding of hardy and quick-maturing plants has already served to push back frontiers by permitting the use of land formerly unsuitable for cultivation because of low temperatures or a short growing season. It is by this means that the great cereal areas of the Canadian prairies and the Soviet steppes have been enlarged still further.

The removal of barriers raised by disease would open up other great areas to the food producer. Africa, one of the most seriously food-deficient regions of the world, would be the principal target in this respect: only 22 per cent of its potentially arable land is cultivated, and much of it is unproductive because of diseases such as sleeping sickness.

A green revolution
The other main method of producing more food is by increasing yields per hectare. If yields worldwide were at the level of those in northwest Europe or the American Midwest, then every hectare of the world's farmland could support between 15 and 20 people on average, instead of the present global figure of between 2.8 and 3.0. The problems are not those of technology, but of supply, economics and education.

On the technical side, the major contribution so far has been made by the plant breeders. The heart of the so-called green revolution of the past four decades has been the scientific creation of high-yielding strains of corn, wheat, rice and other crops, together with improved breeds of livestock. A series of international institutes, most of them located in less-developed countries, now provide a focus for this work. Sometimes the development concerns the period necessary for the plant to mature: a rice that matures in 120 days instead of 160 may permit two crops to be grown each year instead of one. Sometimes it is a case of altering the density of planting: it is possible by scientific breeding to double the number of plants per square metre without overcrowding or loss of growth. Alternatively, the actual structure of the plant may be involved: it must have a shorter stem, for instance, in order to be able to support a heavier head.

Other areas of technical innovation are in the use of chemical fertilizers and pesticides, and in educating the farmer in a wider range of expertise, thus encouraging him to make more innovations. There is, however, the limitation imposed on adopting the new farming techniques by economics. Not only are supplies of seed for the new "wonder crops" limited at present, but the additional fertilizer input and the equipment to harvest and store larger crops have to be paid for. And this cost is not purely financial. Chemical fertilizer production involves far greater energy inputs than the additional food energy yielded by their use. It is necessary, therefore, to possess the raw materials, whose price has been soaring, and to consume other resources, before the farmer can produce more food. It is small wonder that many farmers cling to traditional methods.

Certainly, improvements in food supply can be made: by cutting down losses due to pests and disease; by mariculture, or farming the sea for food; by organizing the marketing of products through co-operatives and re-organizing the tenure of land; and in the future, perhaps, by the development of synthetic food stuffs. Most of these, however, are long-term projects and, like the cross-breeding of plants, cannot be hurried.

Textured vegetable protein

Textured vegetable protein is thought by many experts to be the answer to our food shortage problems. Food processing is now such that we can eat what appears to be meat but is in fact Kesp, a textured vegetable protein meat substitute that is manufactured from soya beans, as shown below.

Soya beans grown and harvested protein content: 40%

Oil extracted and solid residue milled into flour

Soya flour protein content: 50%

Extraction of carbohydrate and washing process to isolate protein

Isolated soya protein protein content: 95%

Oils, flavouring and colouring added

Spinning process

Spun protein food products

Beef chunks

Beef mince

Chicken chunks

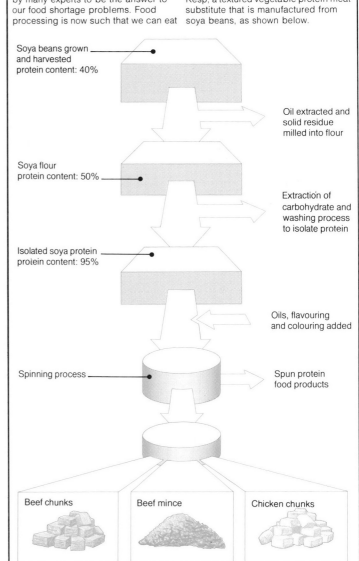

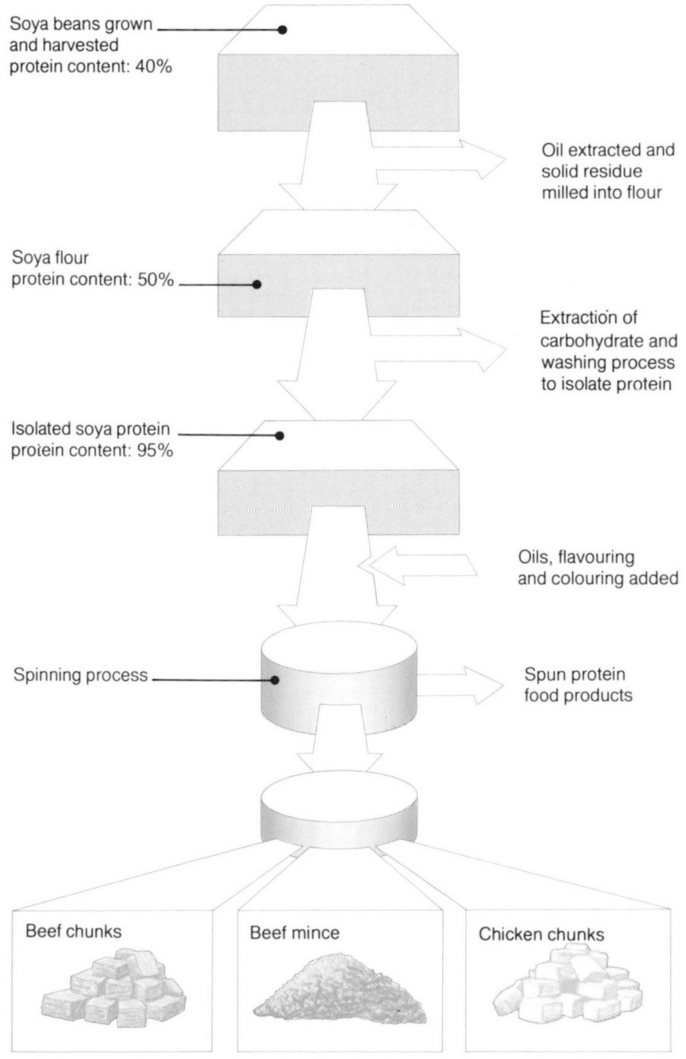

▲ **Deserts** *are not necessarily infertile regions and, once water is supplied, they can be transformed into highly productive areas, as in the Algerian Sahara. Water can be pumped from underground reservoirs, or basins can be dug so that the root systems of crops can reach groundwater supplies. Fences protect crops from sand.*

▼ **The world fish catch** *reached more than 60 million tonnes a year in the 1970s as a result of greater efficiency and better technology. Some species have been seriously overfished. Attention is now being paid to aquaculture — the artificial culturing of fish — and fish farming, which increases natural stocks in the open sea or seawater tanks.*

▲ **Terracing** *is the traditional method of cultivation on the densely populated island of Bali in Indonesia and is being usefully employed in other regions where land is in short supply. In contrast to the terraces shown here, however, modern schemes often involve mechanized excavations and produce non-irrigated crops.*

▶ **Sorghum** *could be grown as an energy crop as well as for food. It has a high concentration of carbon dioxide around its green pigment and can convert solar energy 10 times as efficiently as other crops.*

Nutrient film technique

Technology has come to play an increasingly important role in modern agriculture and one new method — the nutrient film technique — means that the farmer can actually grow crops without any soil. This is done with the aid of the device shown here, whereby crops are planted, either outdoors or in greenhouses, in plastic trays. A solution containing all the vital nutrients the plant needs is constantly circulated through the trays. This method — first developed by the Glasshouse Crops Research Institute in England — has proved highly successful and is used in many parts of the world.

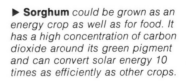

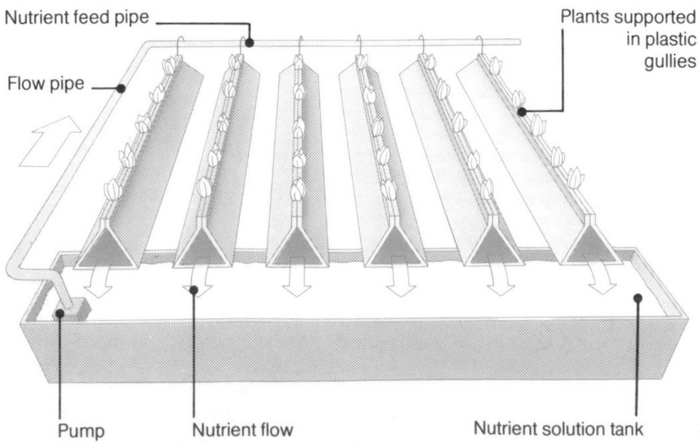

Man's quest for energy

SINCE the Industrial Revolution there has been a close relationship between economic activity and world energy use. For many years a one per cent increase in economic growth has been matched by a similar increase in energy demands. Because of this close, historic relationship, and given fears of impending resource scarcity, energy is very much at the centre of the debate about man's future. Energy underlies everyday life: it heats and lights homes, offices and factories, drives machinery and raises steam for industrial processes, fuels transport systems, and is a key requirement for food production — directly for tractors and food processing and indirectly for the production of fertilizers and pesticides.

Since man learnt to utilize fire, the quest for energy has been a key feature of every civilization. Humans, animals, wood, wind and water were harnessed and the availability of such sources of energy set the limits to economic activity within societies.

First use of fossil fuels

Since the process of industrialization and urbanization began, man has increasingly supplemented the use of renewable sources of energy by exploiting the depletable fossil fuels. At first coal was mined at or near the surface, but as demand grew and technology improved, underground mining complexes were developed. Coal was used in boilers, steam engines and locomotives and in open fires to heat homes; converted to coke it fuelled a breakthrough in iron and steel production, and as gas it supplied street lighting and domestic heating; some was used to make chemicals, dyes and explosives.

Coal dominated world energy supplies until the 1950s, although oil and natural gas were by then widely used in the United States. In 1900, coal accounted for 94 per cent of the world's use of commercial fuels, oil four per cent and natural gas one per cent, and wood and hydroelectric power for the remainder. By 1950, these percentages had changed to 62, 25 and nine respectively, and in 1974, the year after the oil crisis, to 32, 45 and 21. Today oil and natural gas account for more than two-thirds of world fossil fuel supplies.

The other dramatic development since the beginning of this century has been a change in the scale of demand for energy. World consumption of fossil fuels increased ten-fold between 1900 and 1980 from 760 million tons of coal equivalent (tce) to 8,500 million tce. The western industrialized economies, mainly North America, Western Europe and Japan, consumed 60 per cent of the total, the USSR and Eastern Europe 23 per cent, and the poorer, less-developed countries (including those with large populations such as India and China) only 17 per cent of the total.

World energy supplies

Coal production reached 3,740 million tonnes in 1980 and is forecast by the World Energy Conference to double by the year 2000. The main producers are the USSR, USA,

World energy consumption

A continuation of current trends of energy consumption for 75 years would lead to an annual world consumption of about 80,000 million tce in the year 2050: today's poor countries, with 75 per cent of the world's people, would still account for only one-third of total energy consumption.

► **Large pipelines** — *used here to carry oil across the desert in Qatar — have higher capital costs but lower running costs than other forms of transport. They also raise international political issues.*

◄ **Modern, industrialized society** — *epitomized by the New York skyline — is dependent upon vast supplies of energy. In 1981 the total amount of energy produced commercially was the equivalent of 2.1 tonnes of coal per person.*

China, Poland, the UK and West Germany. Amongst developing countries, India is the major producer. Ultimately recoverable resources are vast — more than one million, million tonnes.

Oil production rose to 4,330 million tce in 1980, the major producers being the USSR, USA, Saudi Arabia, Iran, Venezuela and Iraq. A major recent development has been the exploitation of offshore oil resources. Ultimate crude oil reserves are estimated at between 250 and 300 thousand million tonnes, with a similar quantity in unconventional forms such as oil shales, tar sands and synthetic oils, exploitable at higher costs. Natural gas has become a major world fuel only relatively recently. Proved reserves are estimated at between 70 and 90 thousand million tce, but this is thought to be conservative.

Nuclear power is based on the fission (or splitting) of uranium atoms in a range of reactor types, the dominant categories being water-cooled (mainly in the USA, France, West Germany and Japan) and gas-cooled (mainly in the UK). Future reactor types include fast breeders based on a mixture of uranium and plutonium fuel and the high temperature reactor. Nuclear power at present provides about four per cent of world electricity requirements but a substantial increase is planned by 2000. The extent of uranium reserves is subject to considerable uncertainty and this also applies to thorium, which may prove a suitable alternative fuel, although no commerical thorium reactors have been put into operation yet.

Only about 14 per cent of world hydroelectric potential is exploited at present, mainly at sites in industrialized countries. The capital costs of major hydro schemes are often beyond the reach of developing countries unless aided by massive financial assistance.

Industry is the largest consumer of energy in the developed world, accounting for 35-40 per cent of total demand. Those industries concerned with processing of materials — iron and steel, chemicals, aluminium, bricks — account for two-thirds of this total. Technical changes in industrial processes have led to improved energy efficiency and recent fuel price increases will encourage this further. Increased recycling of materials will also reduce the energy demand per unit of output. Public and private services account for 10-15 per cent of energy demands in the developed countries, mainly for heating and lighting.

Energy use in the home

Domestic use accounts for 20-25 per cent of energy demand. Of this about 60 per cent is used for space heating and air conditioning; 20-25 per cent for water heating; 10 per cent for cooking and between five and 10 per cent (almost entirely as electricity) for appliances such as washing machines, televisions and so on. Many appliances, for example hi-fi, use little electricity, but others such as tumble driers and dishwashers may be key future growth areas. Improved insulation of buildings could reduce domestic energy demands.

Transport accounts for 25 per cent of energy demand in the USA and 20 per cent in Western Europe. The largest proportion is used by road transport, especially the private car. A range of new technologies might reduce fuel consumption per mile by 20-40 per cent in the coming decades and there is scope for improving the efficiency of public transport systems.

Over the next 20-30 years, the world will experience a transition from a dependence on oil and gas towards greater use of coal, nuclear power and renewable energy sources. Major technical changes will be necessary and will require a considerable developmental period before widespread application is possible.

How one nuclear reactor works

Certain atoms of uranium break into fragments when a neutron is added to the nucleus. If this occurs, the uranium atom is split into two and energy is released in the form of heat. At the same time neutrons are given off and they continue the process by splitting other nuclei. This is called a chain reaction and it forms the basis of the generation of nuclear power. In a nuclear reactor the chain reaction is kept going at a steady rate and the heat is used to produce steam to drive electricity generators. In order to maintain a steady rate the number of neutrons that continue the reaction has to be controlled. This is done by absorbing excess neutrons in control rods made of boron. If neutrons produced by the reaction are slowed down they can split the nuclei more easily. The slowing down is achieved by surrounding the fuel with a moderator — so-called because it moderates the speed of the neutrons. The reactor is protected by a concrete shield to prevent the escape of dangerous radiation. In a gas-cooled reactor, such as the one shown here, the heat produced by the reaction is removed by circulating carbon dioxide gas. Alternatively, the heat can be removed by circulating water through the system. The heat is used to convert water to steam.

Reactor — Control rod, Charge tubes, Graphite moderator, Fuel element, Concrete shield

Heat exchanger — Hot gas, Steam, Water, Gas blower, Cold gas

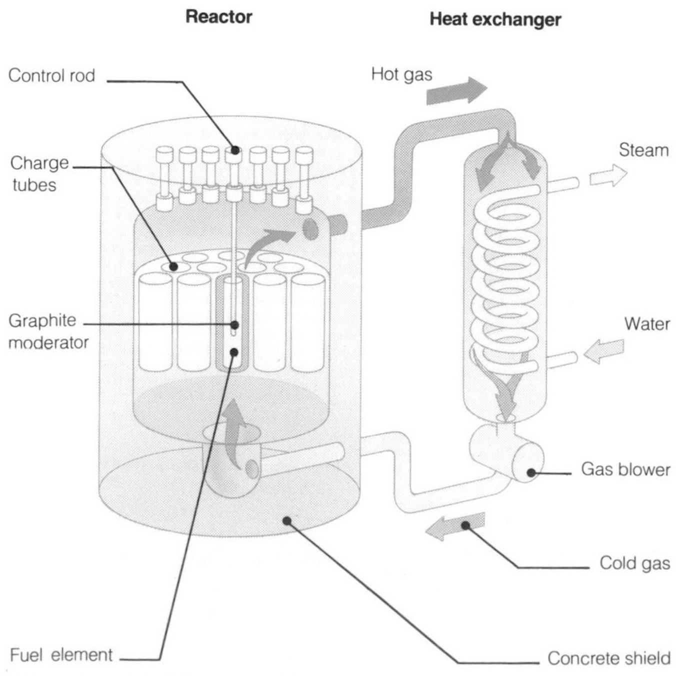

▲ **Natural gas** was once considered to be a useless by-product of drilling for oil and was burnt off. Today, however, technical developments, such as liquefied natural gas tankers and large pipeline networks, have enabled a rapid growth in its use. Deposits are found in association with oil or on their own, as in this Iranian field.

▶ **Millions of people** in the less-developed countries are dependent for energy on what nature supplies, mainly firewood and dung. Non-commercial consumption of energy is difficult to assess accurately, but is probably in the region of 1,500 tce. Such energy sources are steadily being replaced by fossil fuels, however.

▶ **Recoverable coal reserves** are vast enough to last for almost 3,000 years at current rates of consumption. Greater concern for the environment may affect production techniques, however. Open-cast mining — seen here in West Virginia — is one of the most economical mining methods but it usually has a devastating effect on the landscape.

Energy alternatives

AT PRESENT the world depends almost entirely on non-renewable sources for its energy. More than 90 per cent of our energy is derived from the major non-renewable fossil fuels: coal, oil and natural gas. A high proportion of the rest, especially in countries of the Third World, comes from wood which, although renewable in principle, is being rapidly depleted. We are never likely to run out of any of these resources completely, but we are already experiencing large increases in the cost of obtaining each unit of fossil fuel. This trend will continue and will impose an ever-increasing strain on the world's systems of production and the societies built on them.

We are at the moment ill-equipped to deal with this eventuality: none of the possible renewable sources of energy are anywhere near ready to start replacing fossil fuels. Moreover, the processes of developing and commercializing major new technologies are extremely difficult and lengthy. Nuclear power, for instance, has been under intensive and massively funded development for more than 30 years, and yet it is still far from being a mature technology and supplies only one per cent of the world's energy demand. Renewable energy, by which we mean direct solar, geothermal, hydroelectric, wind, wave and tidal power, biomass fuels and nuclear breeding and fusion, will require a similar, if not greater, volume and intensity of effort if it is to make a substantial impact on world energy supplies in 50 years' time.

Renewable energy and lifestyles
Renewable energy sources (with the exception of nuclear) are often called "alternative" energy. Alternative energy tends to be linked with the idea of alternative culture — implying a radical change in lifestyle both at an individual level and in the political, economic and social spheres. It is perhaps unfortunate that practitioners of 'alternative culture' in the West are rarely good advertisements for the advantages of their lifestyle but it is certainly true that at their existing (mainly rudimentary) stage of development, most renewable energy sources are most compatible with a low energy-using, rural society with limited industrialization. This is because the majority of renewables provide only diffuse, low-grade energy, which is subject to considerable variability in supply.

Much of the development effort in renewable energy must, therefore, be concentrated on making it as compatible as possible with urban, industrial society. The difficulties of achieving this (through effective storage and the up-grading of low-grade heat, for instance) are what makes the development of renewable energy sources so expensive. In the long term, therefore, widespread reliance on renewable energy will probably not require major and fundamental changes to existing lifestyles. Renewable nuclear sources (breeders and fusion), on the other hand, are specifically designed to fit existing industrial societies and their development in the future may well be compatible only with even more centralized and interdependent societies than exist at present.

Sources of renewable energy
Direct solar energy is the most obviously attractive source because of its abundance. The major problems in its development (common to a number of renewables) concern its low efficiency and its variability, which requires the development of storage technologies. High yields of useful energy from the sun are therefore likely to need heavy capital investment. Domestic space heating technology is reasonably well developed and electricity production from direct solar sources has been demonstrated, but enormous problems remain to be solved.

Hydroelectricity is the only renewable source in significant commercial use, and it provides more than one-fifth of the world's electricity. Its main problems are that it is not a genuinely renewable source in the long term (because of reservoir silting) and that most sites suitable for large-scale development have already been used in

▲ **Wind power** *was used traditionally for pumping water or grinding corn and modern wind power generators have been built in some areas, such as the Orkneys. Wind is an attractive energy source since its use produces no extra heat load on the environment.*

◀ **The world's largest solar furnace,** *at Odeillo in the French Pyrenees, uses a large concave mirror to focus the sun's rays. In regions where there is strong sunshine during the day, solar energy can be used for space heating or to supply hot water to homes or larger buildings that have a low requirement for hot water.*

many industrialized countries. Geothermal sources make use of the earth's internal heat to supply either heat or electricity. Limited commercial development has already taken place. Diffuseness is again a major developmental problem.

Wind power has improved significantly since the heyday of traditional windmills. It may well prove extremely suitable for rural use (pumping and electricity) where climatic conditions are suitable. Wave power could in principle supply large amounts of electricity, but has not yet been substantially demonstrated, and its development faces major technical and economic problems. Tidal power has already been demonstrated on a fairly large scale, but there are few suitable sites in the world.

Biological sources of energy (wood, dung, wastes and crops) are already of vital importance to the Third World, though there are major problems of depletion. The main long-term problem for biomass fuels is competition with food production for the use of land.

The future of nuclear power

Fast breeder nuclear reactors — which "breed" their own fuel in the form of plutonium — and fusion reactors — in which common light elements fuse and release energy — can be considered as renewable sources. Breeders are being built on a commercial scale, but technical, safety and environmental problems remain to be solved. They are, nevertheless, a long-term possibility for electricity production and have massive government backing in both capitalist and communist countries as the main "technical fix" for fossil fuel scarcities. Nuclear fusion is an attempt to reproduce on earth the fusion reaction of the sun, and it would mean an end to the world's energy problems. Fusion occurs, however, at temperatures of about 100 million degrees and the problems of holding the resulting "plasma" stable and then safely extracting energy are currently well beyond our technical capabilities.

The obvious and enormous difficulties that still need to be overcome before renewable energy can by widely used, together with the ever-rising costs of non-renewable sources, lead to two main conclusions: that there is a critical need to promote energy conservation as a way of reducing demand and buying time; and that we will almost certainly need to rely on a combination of a large number of renewable energy sources.

▲ **A considerable number** of sites suitable for hydroelectric power schemes remain unexploited in less-developed countries, but constructing a dam such as the Kariba poses enormous financial, technical and political problems for the developing nations.

Solar power

Solar collectors operate in much the same way as a greenhouse. Air inside a metal-backed box with a transparent lid of either glass or plastic is heated by the sun. The glass traps the infra-red radiation and so the box becomes a collector for the heat. Another version has copper pipes in which water is heated instead of air. A solar system can only be effective if the heat can be stored for release when the house needs warming. This is done by means of the heating of a rock store, usually placed beneath the house, or by heating water in a storage tank.

Sunlight — Glass plates — Water in pipes heated by sunlight — Insulation

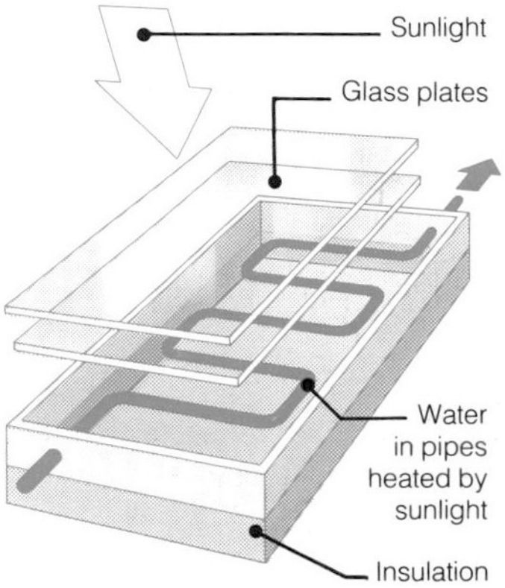

▲ **Power from geothermal sources** makes use of heat stored in the earth in volcanic regions or deep sedimentary basins. Electricity can be generated from turbines driven by the pressure of underground streams of hot water and steam. Geothermal power is produced commercially in Iceland, the USA, Italy and New Zealand.

Power from the sea

One wave power converter consists of a "duck" that rocks backwards and forwards on a spindle and can extract up to 90 per cent of the energy contained in a wave that it intercepts. No commercial wave power station has yet been built, but to produce power in quantity a long series of ducks in concrete rafts would be needed. They would drive a generator within the axle linking them. It is agreed that, for greatest efficiency, wave power stations should be designed to extract energy not from the biggest waves that occur only a few times a year but from the average-sized waves that flow all the time. The stations will still have to withstand powerful storm waves, however. The average Atlantic wave can produce a power equivalent of about 70 kilowatts per metre. That is enough to heat seven medium-sized houses in a temperate climate for an hour. In a tidal power scheme a basin reservoir is created by constructing a barrage across a tidal estuary. Seawater enters and leaves the basin through ducts containing turbines that power generators. Such schemes are restricted to estuaries whose tidal range between high and low water is extremely large, such as the Rance estuary in northwestern France. The Severn estuary in England is a possible site for the future development of tidal power.

Tidal power

Incoming tide — Turbine — Outgoing tide — Turbine

Wave power

String of floating ducks — Oncoming wave — Power take-off

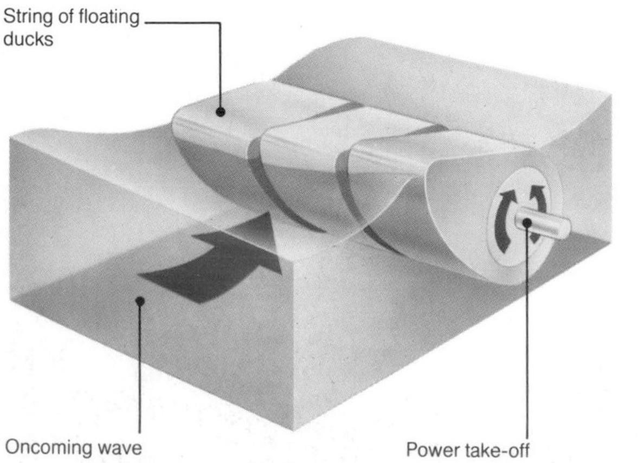

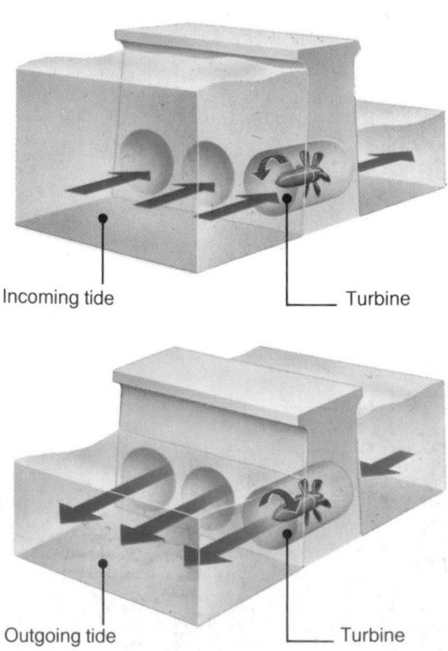

The earth's mineral wealth

MODERN industrial society is dependent upon an assured supply of a wide variety of mineral commodities besides those that are used as a source of energy. Very few countries are totally devoid of all nonfuel minerals but, conversely, even the few exceptionally mineral-rich nations, such as Australia, Canada and South Africa, usually need to import at least one critically important commodity.

Bulk minerals used for construction purposes, for example crushed stone, sand, gravel, cement and clay, are widely distributed geographically and are therefore unimportant in terms of international trade. Moreover, although they are consumed in large quantities, they have a low intrinsic value and can rarely be transported economically for any great distance even within their countries of origin.

Of other important mineral commodities, some, such as iron ore and bauxite (the raw material of the aluminium industry), are mined and consumed in vast quantities, but because of an unequal global distribution of resources, the considerable cost of transportation has to be borne by the many consumer nations. At the other extreme, minerals such as the various precious metals, diamonds, cobalt, chromium and many others have a high intrinsic value, are not consumed in vast tonnages and, in their case, transportation costs have relatively little significance.

Three categories
When considered in terms of their end-use, the minerals entering international trade fall broadly into three categories. Minerals required as raw materials for the iron and steel industry include, in addition to the iron ore itself, the ores of the alloying metals such as tungsten, nickel, manganese and chromium and sometimes special grades of limestone for smelting purposes.

Non-ferrous metals used in their own right and not mainly as an adjunct to the iron and steel industry form a distinct category of their own. These include the base metals such as copper, lead, tin and zinc and also the precious metals.

A third category includes those substances that are loosely termed industrial minerals, and embraces those which are not utilized as a source of metal. Some, like phosphate rock, fluorspar and potash, are essential raw materials in the large-scale manufacture of important chemicals. Others, like ceramic and refractory clays, asbestos, talc and mica, are sought because of certain distinctive physical and chemical properties.

The growth and survival of the world's mineral industry demands considerable expertise at all levels of exploitation, including prospecting, mining, processing and utilization. The widespread search for minerals on and beyond continental limits requires much investment in geological, geophysical and geochemical exploration methods, and reflects the reality that mineral resources are far from being randomly or equally distributed.

A geological revolution
An intellectual revolution in the earth sciences in the last two decades has led to a better understanding of how continental segments or "plates" have evolved and moved relative to each other through more than three billion years of planetary history. In turn, this wider understanding of geological processes has encouraged a broader insight into the mechanism of formation and the reasons for the distribution of many key mineral commodities. For example, the presence of many large copper-bearing ore bodies of the so-called porphyry type along the geologically active western margins of both North and South America can be related to the present-day seismic and volcanic activity in those regions. This kind of correlation provides guidelines for the location of analogous ore bodies in much more ancient terrains.

Other major mineral resources, well exemplified by the major iron ore deposits of Australia, Brazil and South Africa and bauxite in several tropical countries, have a distribution related not so much to deep-seated crustal processes as to climatic or other physical conditions that were prevalent at specific periods in the earth's history. The recognition of the role that such palaeo-environmental factors have had on the formation of these ores serves to focus the search for further mineral deposits.

Exploration for new mineral deposits is also assisted by increasingly refined methods of detection. Discovery of such deposits is now rarely dependent upon the recognition of visible traces of ore but instead requires detection of the subtle physical and chemical effects which may be the only tangible manifestation of important ore bodies concealed beneath considerable thicknesses of barren rock. Such improvement in prospecting techniques owes much to modern methods of rapid chemical analysis, complex electronic circuitry in geophysical instruments, automatic data processing and remote sensing, using both aircraft and satellite-borne detection devices.

A success story so far
In the fields of mining, handling and milling of ore, economies resulting from the increasingly larger scale of operation have enabled the mining industry to keep pace with ever increasing demand for most commodities. The development of large and highly mechanized open-cast mining operations at the expense of labour-intensive underground methods has resulted in a significant reduction of the economic ore cut-off grade. Further developments in the processing of low-grade ores, for example by chemical and bacterial leaching, suggest that the process of technical improvement may continue. Mining of sub-sea mineral resources can also be expected to commence in the near future, although there the barriers are of a political nature.

Despite the continuing success of the mining industry, demand for most commodities continues to rise. Investigation of the potential resources that, it is hoped, will provide the necessary margin of reserves ahead of production must therefore be pursued vigorously. Although this search has so far proved successful, some alarm has been expressed that shortages may soon appear in the supply of some key mineral commodities.

Where economic minerals occur

The distribution and concentration of minerals of economic significance is controlled by the major geological processes of magmatism (the melting, movement and solidification of volcanic and other igneous rocks), metamorphism (chemical and physical changes to rocks brought about by heat and pressure below the zone of weathering) and sedimentation (the transport and deposition of material derived from the weathering of other rocks).

Folded mountain belts containing a wide variety of igneous and metamorphic rocks are home to some of the most important deposits of copper and other metals.

Weather-resistant minerals such as gold, diamonds and tin ore are concentrated in alluvial deposits.

Limestone penetrated by hot solutions is a host to important deposits of lead, zinc, silver and fluorspar.

Hydrothermal veins containing the ores of tin, copper and tungsten may be found in rock surrounding magmatic intrusions.

Pegmatite veins at the extremities of igneous intrusions contain rare commodities like lithium, tantalum and emerald.

Concentrations of titanium minerals in beach sands are a most important source of this metal.

Sedimentary rocks are important sources of iron, dolomite, gypsum, potash and others.

Ancient metamorphic rocks are host to many economic minerals; for example, gold, nickel, iron, asbestos.

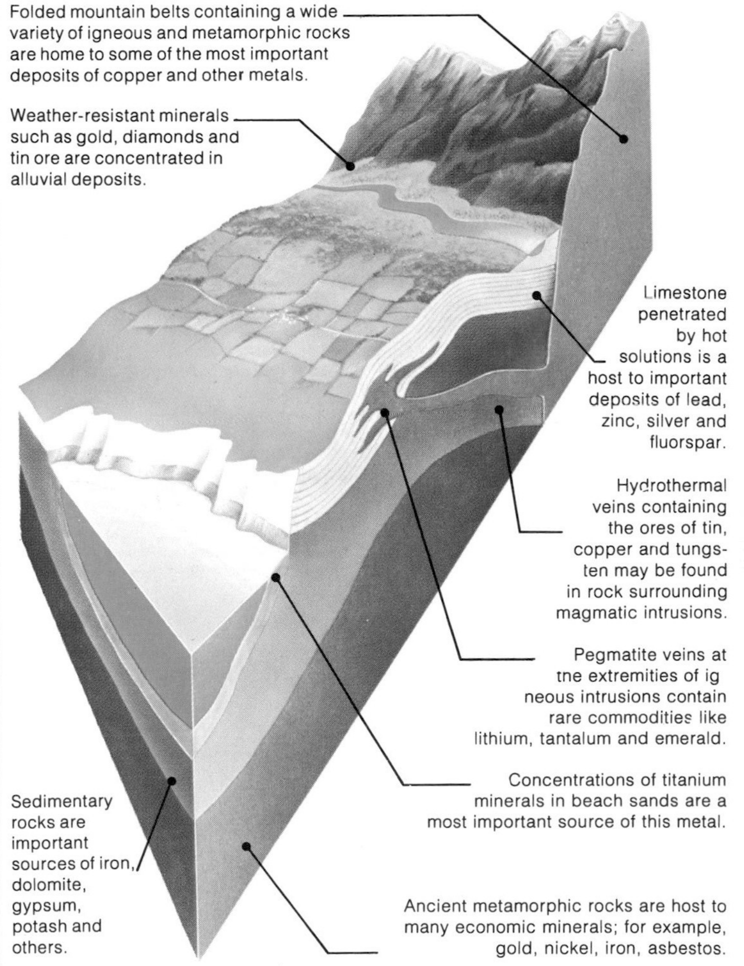

▲ **More than two-thirds** *of the world's metallic mineral output is produced by open-cast methods which are cheaper and easier now that technology is available to remove thick overburden.*

▲ **Satellite surveying** *includes taking photographs that emphasize certain bands of the light spectrum and reveal many large-scale geological features that would be unrecognizable from the ground. Satellite-borne detection devices have reduced the time and increased the efficiency of mineral prospecting on the ground.*

► **The precious metals,** *long valued as a store of wealth, are of increasing importance to industries such as electronics, dentistry, photography and aerospace.*

Major mineral deposits

Relatively few mineral deposits are of economic value, and of those the metals are the most important. Iron, the fourth most abundant element in the earth's crust, occurs widely and 500 million tonnes are produced annually. Aluminium is the most common metal, but only 18 million tonnes are produced a year. Tin deposits are restricted to a few areas which makes it an expensive metal (production: 210,000 tonnes). Other major metals include copper (7.7 million tonnes), gold (less than 1,500 tonnes), silver (about 10,000 tonnes), uranium (38,000 tonnes) and lead and zinc, which usually occur together (4.4 and 6 million tonnes respectively). The distribution of major deposits of the world's most valuable minerals is shown on the map below.

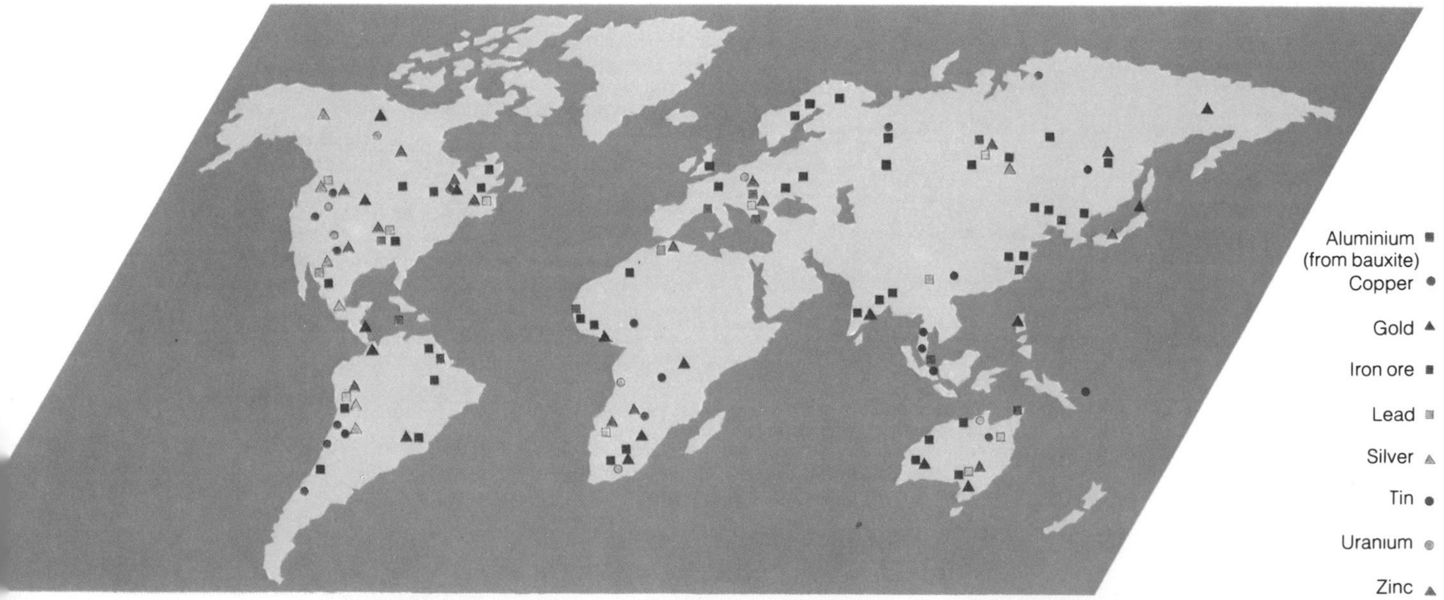

Asbestos (chrysotile)

Mercury (cinnabar)

Uranium (autunite)

Iron (haematite)

Copper (bornite)

A conserving future

IN THE context of an ever-increasing world population and the consequent rise in demand for living space, food and raw materials, it has been predicted by some economic forecasters that a crisis in the supply of our most important mineral resources is imminent. Although the mining industry has been successful in continuing to discover new resources ahead of demand, it is suggested that the number of new discoveries of ore yet to be made must be finite and that sooner or later mankind will be faced with an absolute shortage of many key commodities which are essential to an industrial society.

The question of conservation

At the simplest level of argument, conservation of minerals is proposed as a desirable object of international co-operation simply to delay for as long as possible the point at which society can no longer rely on supplies. A diametrically opposed view is, however, often supported, not least by the mining industry itself. This argues that the efficient utilization of all resources that are available and can be extracted economically at the present time, far from being discouraged, should be vigorously pursued. Only this will give an innovative society the economic encouragement that it needs to discover technical solutions to the problems of raw material shortages that may occur in the near future.

Expressed in this way, arguments for and against mineral conservation appear to be somewhat academic. However, recent history has shown that for two reasons, political and environmental, conservation or, more accurately, the efficient utilization of mineral resources is a desirable end. In the political sphere, the growth of producer cartels such as OPEC (petroleum), CIPEC (copper) and the IBA (bauxite) may well have the effect of encouraging countries which are net importers of the commodities concerned to examine more closely the efficiency with which those commodities are utilized.

The growing pressure of mining on the environment is partly the result of increased demand requiring bigger mines, but it can also be attributed to the exhaustion of high-grade ore deposits, resulting in a shift of emphasis towards large-scale extractive operations that are able to work vast low-grade deposits at a profit.

Political and environmental pressures, although fundamental in encouraging the efficient use of non-renewable resources, can often act indirectly. For example, the increases imposed for political reasons upon the price of crude petroleum not only encourage less wasteful use of the refinery products themselves but also, at second hand, the efficient use of, say, metals produced in smelters dependent upon oil-based energy.

How to improve efficiency

The efficient use and therefore, ultimately, the conservation of mineral resources involves a critical examination of the way in which they are utilized at all stages from their removal from the ground, through processing, fabrication, usage and recovery as scrap.

At the point at which minerals are mined there is often scope for improvement in recovery ratios. Open-cast mining often permits the recovery of almost 100 per cent of the ore available, but such favourable recoveries are rarely attainable with underground mining. And it must be admitted that in some cases the installation of mechanization to improve the economic performance of underground mining results in a concomitant reduction in the attainable reserves available. Mechanical cutters on longwall faces, for example, can only work on seams that are more than a minimum thickness.

The processing and fabrication stages in the conversion of raw material to finished product offer the opportunity for resource conservation in the way in which energy is used and also in terms of the way in which the final products are designed. Nevertheless, scrutiny of the energy input of manufacturing processes demands a sophisticated degree of analysis. For example, the use of the light metals aluminium and magnesium in automobile components can only be justified if the amount of fuel saved during the lifetime of the vehicle more than offsets the higher energy cost of smelting these substitute metals.

Substitution of many important commodities to meet specific shortages can be envisaged. A good example is aluminium which can substitute for copper as an electrical conductor or for steel in the construction industry. But the physical properties of substitutes are never identical, and in some cases substitution does not appear to be a realistic possibility. Silver, for example, is probably irreplaceable for photographic purposes.

Recycling

It is probable that in the short term recycling of scrap and waste will create more impact than substitution on resource conservation. Once again, however, the trade-offs have to be considered. While little energy input is involved in collecting high-quality process scrap from the floor of a machine shop, the same is not necessarily true if useful materials have to be separated at great expense from general industrial waste. There also tend to be restrictions on the uses to which recovered material can be put. Scrap aluminium usually contains some silicon and can therefore be used for making castings but not for many fabrication purposes. The total efficiency of scrap recovery is closely related to the purpose to which the material is put.

The technical aspects of mineral conservation appear to be fairly well understood. Encouragement for their implementation requires social and political initiative although the operation of the simple law of supply and demand will be effective in time.

The life-span of minerals

World demand for the 20 minerals most vital to modern society is expected to double by 1988 and treble by 2000. This will greatly reduce the life-span of world reserves of the major minerals. Shortages of minerals in the future will inevitably raise market prices. This will mean that deposits uneconomical at present will become workable which will, in turn, encourage exploration. A price rise will also encourage the further use of scrap metal. Scrap materials containing scarce minerals will also rise in price and the recycling market will increase.

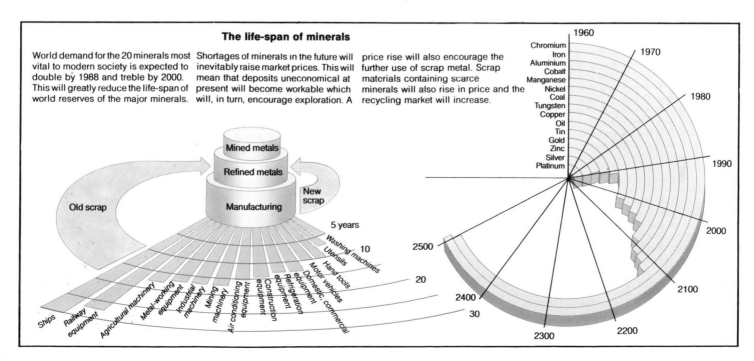

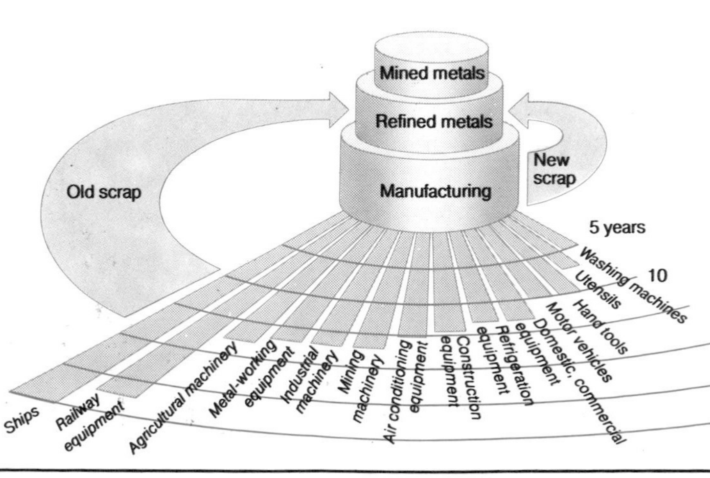

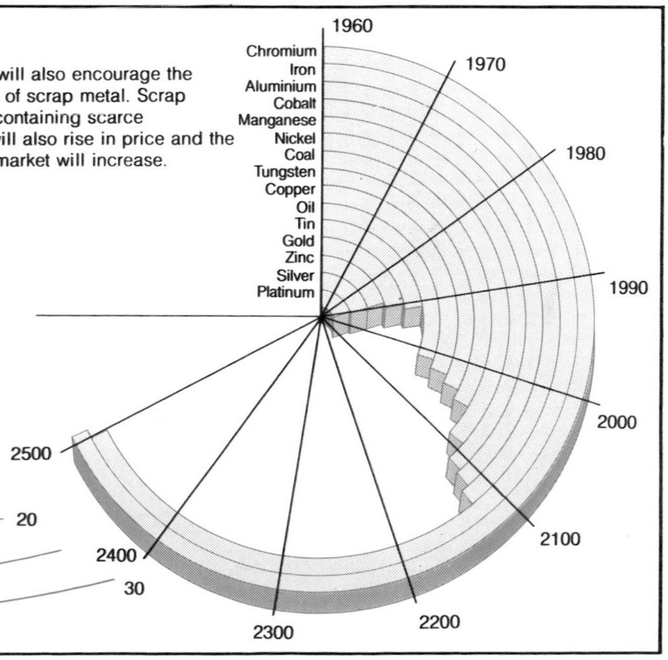

▲ ***Iron,** and its principal alloy, steel, are the most important and widely used metals. Iron and steel mills, consuming vast quantities of energy and water as well as raw materials, and the steel-consuming industries such as ship-building represent more than anything else the road to industrialization for the less-developed world.*

◀ ***Bridges** constructed from reinforced concrete as opposed to metal are another step towards the conservation of minerals.*

▲ ***If more motor vehicles** could be produced economically from substitute materials such as glass reinforced plastic, a significant saving of metals would be made.*

▶ ***More and more** food and drink is sold in non-returnable containers, especially bottles and cans, which create mountains of litter. Aluminium cans, for instance, are no good for composting, they do not degrade and therefore have to be removed. They can be recycled but separation is a costly process.*

▲ ***Millions of cars** are dumped each year when they could be recycled. Since they contain plastic, rubber and other metals as well as steel the end-product from crushing has to be refined before it can be re-used.*

▼ ***Manganese nodules,** found beyond depths of about three kilometres below the surface of the oceans, may be commercially dredged in the future. The origin of these nodules is uncertain, but they may prove an invaluable source of heavy metals as land deposits become increasingly depleted.*

Marine mineral deposits

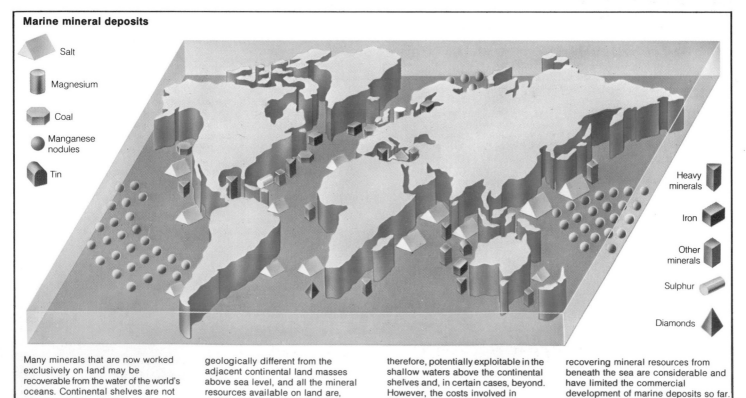

Many minerals that are now worked exclusively on land may be recoverable from the water of the world's oceans. Continental shelves are not geologically different from the adjacent continental land masses above sea level, and all the mineral resources available on land are, therefore, potentially exploitable in the shallow waters above the continental shelves and, in certain cases, beyond. However, the costs involved in recovering mineral resources from beneath the sea are considerable and have limited the commercial development of marine deposits so far.

Economic trends

THE object and function of international trade is to make the world as a whole richer in the supply of material goods, whether they be raw materials (including food) or manufactured products. Two countries will engage in trade only if each of them gains by it, except in circumstances which allow one country to exercise compulsion over the other.

Growth of world trade

In the last 20 years the value of world trade has increased about twenty-fold (although inflation magnifies the real extent of this expansion). In 1948 the value of imports stood at US $62,700 million and exports were valued at $57,000 million. In 1980 the corresponding totals (in millions) were $2,045,800 and $2,001,700. Nevertheless, the continuing growth of international trade has done little to bring about a more equal distribution of wealth among the nations of the world. With a few exceptions, such as Australia, New Zealand and Denmark, those countries that have concentrated in the last 100 years or more on developing their manufactures have come to appropriate a disproportionate share of the world's wealth.

In the nineteenth century, the influential German economist Friedrich List argued strongly that only when a country had developed its own national industries could it share in the profits that were the reward of the international division of labour. He went even further and gave his opinion that only a country that exported manufactured products and imported food could rise in the international wealth tables. His influence is still felt today. Most leaders of Third World countries are engaged in an effort to industrialize their economies. Yet it may well be that many of them would profit more from international trade if they ceased to identify prosperity and national pride with steel mills and oil refineries.

A Third World

About 140 countries comprise what has come to be called the Third World. These countries are variously described as "less-developed", "under-developed" or "developing", names that assume Western patterns of development and industrial growth as norms, and desirable norms at that. The people of the Third World, comprising some two-thirds of the world's population, live, for the most part, in dire poverty. National per capita income figures for the seven major regions of the globe show how marked is the divide between the standard of living enjoyed by those living in developed countries and that of the rest of the world. In 1978 annual per capita income was £4,187 in North America, £3,149 in Europe, £2,834 in Oceania. In stark contrast were the figures for the Middle East (£1,013), Latin America (£684), Africa (£276) and Asia excluding Japan (£138). In the 1970s the national income of some oil-producing countries of the Third World has risen dramatically, but there is no guarantee that their present prosperity will survive the depletion of their oil resources.

It is rare for more than 10 per cent of the gross national product of a Third World country to consist of manufactures. Most developing economies lack the required capital and trained skills for large-scale industry. Their chief preoccupation is with providing enough food for their people. As a result they contribute only a small part of the total volume of world trade. Again, 1980 import/export figures (in millions of US dollars) reveal large discrepancies between North America (319,359/238,879) or Europe (1,014,128/895,062) and, for instance, Africa (85,513/95,875) or Central and South America (113,824/105,099). The same point is made by comparing the figures for Australia and New Zealand (27,864/27,308) with those for less-developed Oceania (3,539/2,439).

Patterns of trade

A breakdown of world trade figures reveals a number of trends that have become apparent in recent years. Although the developed market economies of the West retain the lion's share of world trade, the volume of their international trade has been growing at a slower rate than that of the Third World and the centrally planned economies (the Soviet bloc members of COMECON and China). Between 1970 and 1976 the volume of world trade rose by 21.2 per cent. The rate of growth in the developed market economies was only 16.7% in the second half of the decade but increased to 22.9% in 1978–9. The comparative figures for the Third World countries were 18.5% and 39.1%.

This dramatic shift in trading patterns reflects, of course, the oil boom enjoyed by those members of OPEC, whose exports rose by 48.2 per cent between 1973 and 1976. That rise is almost entirely explained by exports of oil and was not shared by the rest of the Third World. It does not, therefore, represent a permanent shift in the patterns of international trade.

More important, in the long run, may be the perceptible rise in the Third World's share of the trade in manufactured goods. World exports of machinery and transport equipment, for example, rose by 19.3 per cent between 1970 and 1979. The developing economies increased their exports of these goods by 35.2 per cent in the same period. Their exports of primary materials and food, on the other hand, moved at exactly the same rate as those of the world as a whole — increasing by about 16 per cent. In time, if this trend continues, the relative wealth of the industrialized West and its partners may decline.

The cry for a new international economic order is an attempt by developing countries to strengthen and realize the potential of their resources and at the same time mitigate the relations of dependency that have characterized their integration into the international economic order. Moves have already been made to stabilize export earnings, increase the flow of aid and technology from the developed to the developing world, and gain favourable trading privileges. But such developments have yet to make a truly significant mark on patterns of international trade and the overwhelming dominance of the Western world in the global economic system.

GNP and world trade

Gross national product and patterns of export trade reveal much about the world economy. The nations with the largest GNPs are those which dominate international trade, and have done so for at least a century. The most apparent feature of patterns of international trade is the fact that approximately 75 per cent of it flows between developed, capitalist countries. Since the distribution of resources is uneven across the globe, the production of goods varies from one region to another and gives some a "comparative advantage". Such differences in the cost of production of goods leads, through the development of trade, to specialized areas of production. Some experts argue, however, that this is the result of relationships between developed and under-developed economies. Wealth is extracted from less-developed countries and accumulated in the economic capitals of the developed world. This reflects the free trade philosophy of the nineteenth century when what we now know as the Third World supplied primary products for industrial centres in the Western world. Resource-rich countries, however, have come to command rather more respect in trading agreements today.

▲ The London stock exchange *epitomizes the sophistication and the dominance of developed countries in the world of finance and trade. Bidding and counter-bidding in stock and commodity markets reflect the economic climate of the world.*

▼ In many parts *of the developing world, goods are traded in relatively primitive market conditions, such as here in Morocco. For most people economic activity does not extend beyond the local market place.*

North America

Europe, USSR, Asia, Japan, Middle East, South America, Africa, Oceania

North America, USSR, Asia, Japan, Middle East, South America, Africa, Oceania

Europe

North America, Europe, Asia, Japan, Middle East, South America, Africa, Oceania

USSR

North America, Europe, Asia, Japan, Middle East, S. America, Africa, Oceania

Japan

N. America, Europe, USSR, Japan, Middle East, South America, Africa, Oceania

Asia

North America, Europe, USSR, Asia, Japan, Middle East, Africa, Oceania

Middle East

North America, Europe, USSR, Asia, Japan, Middle East, Africa, Oceania

Africa

South America

North America, Europe, USSR, Asia, Japan, Middle East, Africa, Oceania

Oceania

North America, Europe, USSR, Asia, Japan, Middle East, South America

Over US$2000 million
US$500-1000 million
US$250-500 million
Under US$250 million

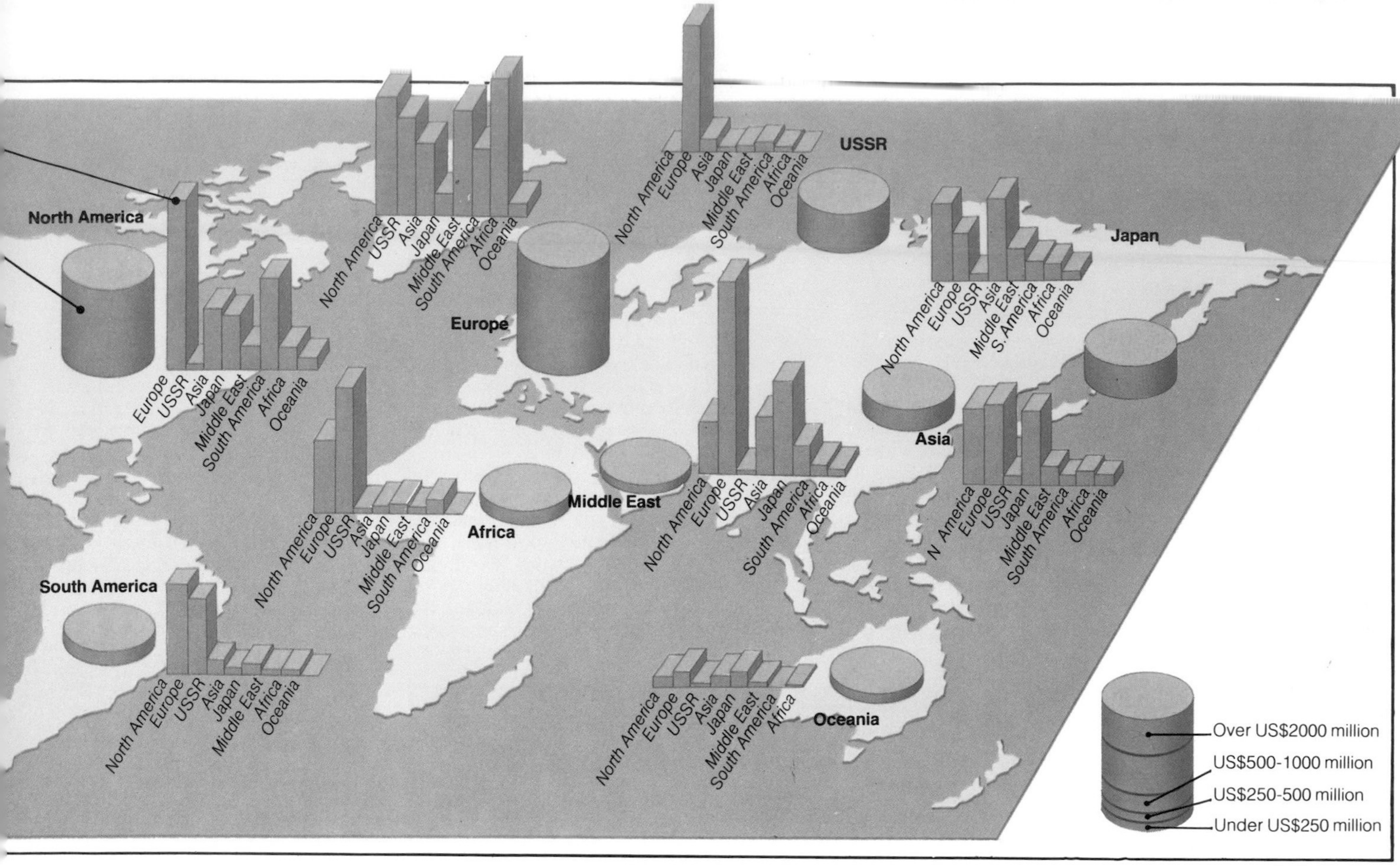

The multinationals

The emergence of vast multinational companies is of more than economic and industrial significance. The activities of such organizations affect governmental policy and the relationships between nations. The operations of multinationals span the earth and represent a startling example of international co-operation. Many have annual sales exceeding the gross national product of a small nation.

total sales

profit as proportion of sales (% below)

Exxon 5.5%	Royal Dutch Shell 6.7%	Mobil Oil 5.5%	General Motors 1.3% loss	Texaco 5.2%
British Petroleum 6.9%	Standard Oil (Chevron) 5.9%	Ford 4.2% loss	Gulf Oil 5.3%	IBM 13.6%
General Electric 6.1%	Unilever 2.8%	Renault 0.9%	ITT 4.8%	Philips 0.9%

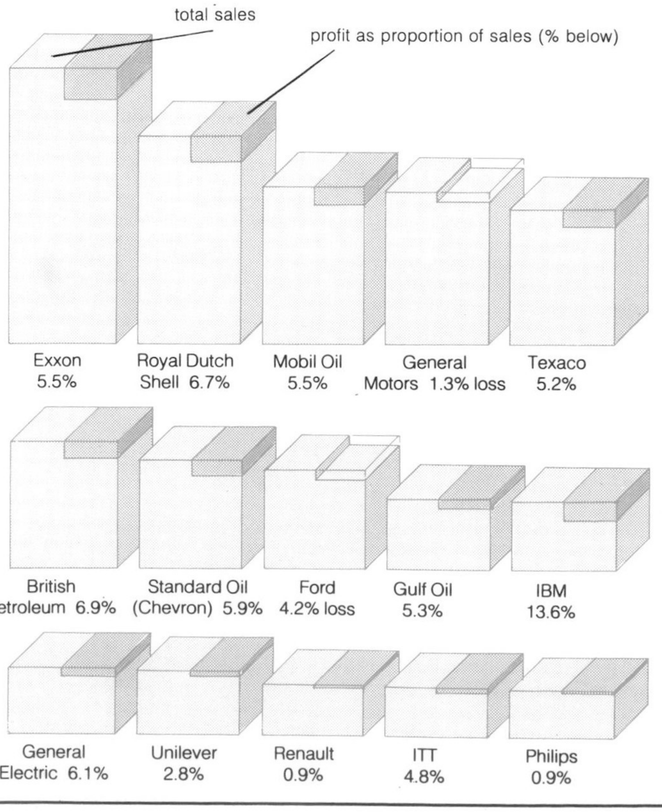

▲ **The export of luxury goods** *such as motor cars is obviously important for a healthy balance of payments. Another characteristic of developed economies is the export of what is known as "capital" goods — equipment and machinery used in the production of other items, such as farm implements.*

▶ **Regional trading groups** *are formed to stimulate production and trade, but can produce economic anomalies. Certain products can be over-priced because prices are maintained by government subsidies. This leads to wastage. Here French farmers protest against Common Market policies.*

The politics of possession

WHEN the various resource categories — people, land, minerals and energy — are examined in relation to one another, we discover their full political significance. The resources possessed by a nation combine to form the resource structure on which economic and military strength are based. Agriculture, for instance, is essential for a healthy and productive labour force, while substantial energy inputs are required to exploit and develop mineral resources and increase agricultural production.

Resources and power

The power base that is formed by the multifarious links between resources defies the temptation to make a direct correlation between the possession of a single resource and political power. In the case of population, for example, what are regarded as the three most powerful countries in the world — the USA, the USSR and the People's Republic of China — are among the four most populous countries in the world. When one looks to India and Bangladesh, however, with the second- and eighth-largest populations respectively, any direct correlation between power and the size of population breaks down. Quite clearly, the population in these latter countries is out of all proportion to the possession and development of other resources. The access that a population has to other resources, including capital and knowledge, will determine how much it will add to or detract from the political power of the state.

In isolation one can observe the political importance assigned to the categories of resources as links in the power base of a state. In a pariah state such as Israel, self-sufficiency in agriculture is of strategic importance, enabling the country to resist external pressures.

Energy is an increasingly important component of the resource structure, driving countries such as the United Kingdom, France, Brazil and India to develop politically unpopular nuclear power programmes. Industrialized countries such as the United States hold strategic stockpiles of the most important minerals to mitigate any interruption in supply that could arise during political conflicts.

It is bordering on a truism to state that an optimal mix of resources enhances the power of a state while the greater the sum total of that mix, the stronger will be the base from which a state exercises power. The USA and the USSR, as superpowers, derive much of their power from the possession of large amounts of all categories of resources. Saudi Arabia, a country with a sparse population and few agricultural and mineral resources, stands as an

▲ **International conventions,** whether they be conferences on population or desertification, or political gatherings such as this International Socialist Convention, are a feature of the modern world.

◄ **Rockets on display** in Moscow's Red Square during May Day celebrations in fact, through the media, show off the Soviet Union's military might to the world.

The Arab-Israeli conflict is a serious threat to world peace. This picture was taken when Israeli-occupied territory extended to the Suez canal.

Political organizations

- British Commonwealth
- French Community
- Arab League

- USSR
- Other communist states
- People's Republic of China

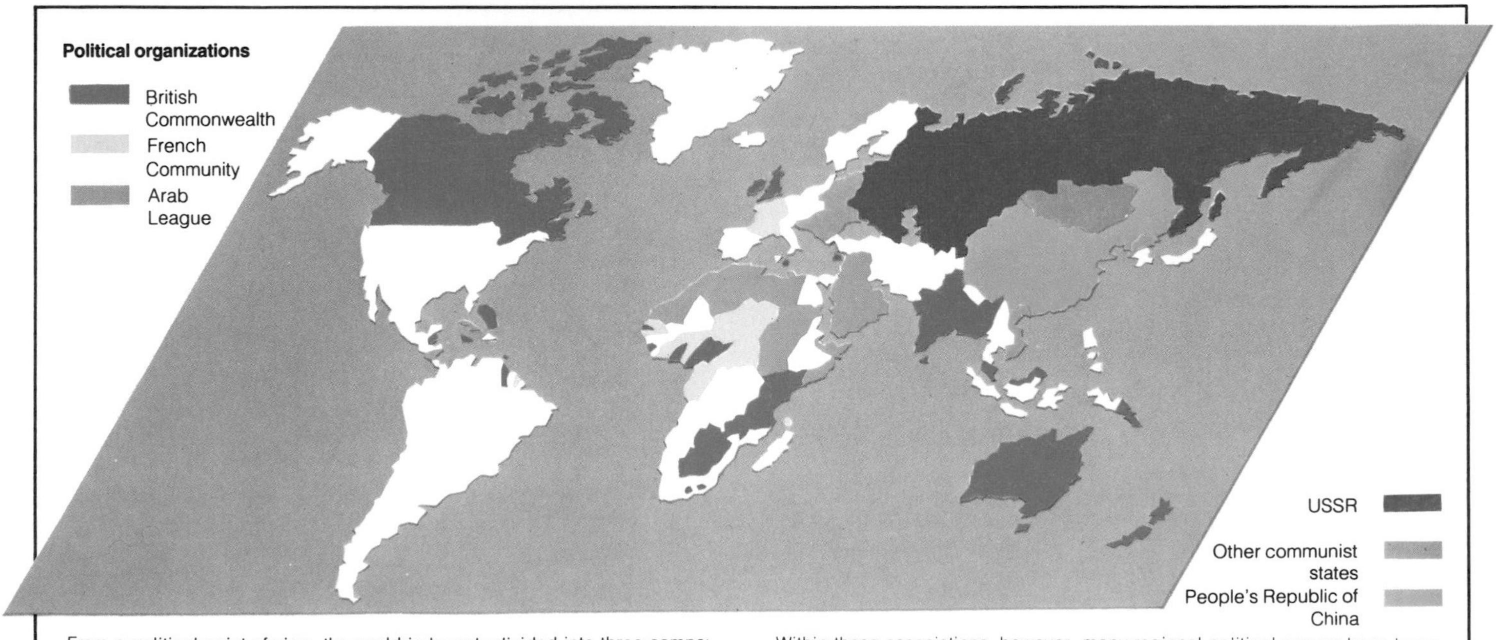

From a political point of view, the world is loosely divided into three camps: the capitalist, Western bloc, the socialist states and the so-called "Group of 77".

Within these associations, however, many regional political groups have been formed since World War II.

aberration to this pattern. As the world's largest exporter of oil, Saudi Arabia is able to exercise power in world politics far beyond the capability of other single resource states — a power that belies the country's scarcity of resources.

Dependency and power
An abundance or lack of resources is also critical to the dependency structure. A country that is deficient in certain resources often becomes reliant upon external sources. This dependence on external sources for resources is reinforced when a country depends on foreign exchange to finance development and when that foreign exchange is earned primarily by the export of a few commodities. Such nations are forced to look to external sources for aid in financing development and in turn become politically vulnerable as aid is tied to exports

from the donor country or preconditions set by lending institutions.

It is contended by some observers that today's world is one of interdependence, where even the most self-reliant countries such as the USSR and China depend on imports of wheat and high technology from the West, while the West's own power is diminished because of its dependence on developing countries for raw materials.

The lessons of World War II altered the utility of war as a political tool by which a state could seize resources. Total war had become exceptionally costly in terms of the drain on resources and the destruction wrought by modern warfare. What emerged from the War was a bipolar political world characterized by two distinct blocs, with two resource-rich superpowers, the USA and the USSR, serving as respective leaders of each bloc.

The West sought to reduce competition over resources and institutions such as the General Agreement on Tariffs and Trade (GATT) and the International Monetary Fund (IMF) were founded to encourage free trade and stable monetary relations at an international level. The socialist bloc sought a system in which states were to be as self-reliant as possible, with centrally planned economies.

Recent political trends
Two apparent trends have led some to believe that the rift between East and West is diminishing. The first is the disintegration of both political blocs. In 1971 the USA ceased to exchange gold for dollars, marking an end to the post-war monetary system and America's unchallenged leadership of the West. And the socialist bloc has developed rifts within itself. The second trend

is that of convergence between East and West. Western countries such as the UK and Denmark often include a high degree of central planning in their economies, while socialist countries rely on trade with the West to obtain many products.

The rise of a new political bloc of developing countries, otherwise known as the Group of 77, has recently given prominence to a new confrontation over the allocation of resources — the "North-South dialogue". In the mid-1970s the United Nations General Assembly adopted resolutions calling for the transfer of real resources from developed (both capitalist and socialist) to developing countries.

The preoccupation of all countries with political self-interest where ownership and control of resources is concerned shows that resources remain inseparable from the achievement of political ends.

▲ **The education gap** *between developed and less-developed countries is of great significance in a world where an educated population is considered to be a vital resource. Practical training rather than theoretical learning is perhaps the most crucial element of education in the Third World.*

Sweden – a developed country

Income: US$9,274

Doctors per 100,000 people: 178

Hospital beds per 100,000 people: 1,496

Hospital beds per 100,000 people: 187

Doctors per 100,000 people: 40

Income: US$749

Guatemala – a developing country

Electric power (kilowatt hours per person): 22,097

Roads (kilometres per 100,000 people): 2,209

Literacy: 99%

Literacy: 47%

Roads (kilometres per 100,000 people): 235

Electric power (kilowatt hours per person): 177

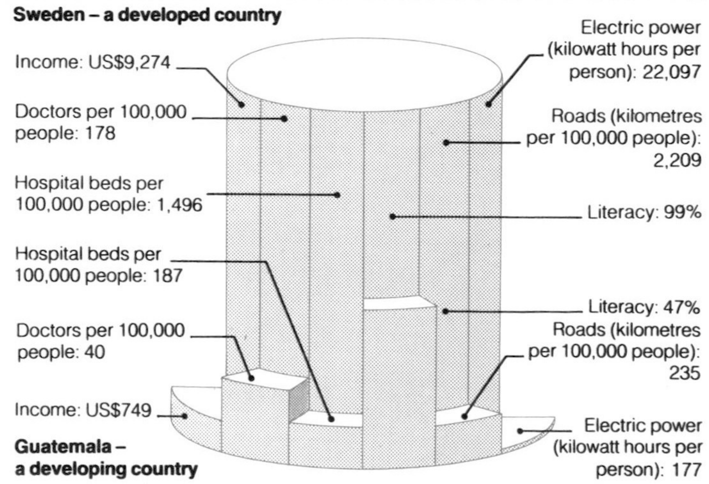

The North/South dialogue
The "haves" versus "have-nots" debate concerning the differences in standards of living or opportunities between the developed and Third worlds has become polarized in what is known as the "North-South dialogue". This is what amounts to a confrontation over the allocation of resources and is an attempt on the part of developing countries to take full advantage of the resources they possess and, at the same time, do away with their dependence on the developed countries which has been a feature of their integration into the international economic system so far. Their goal can only be reached when they have true economic as well as political independence.

Military organizations

NATO

Warsaw Pact

OAS

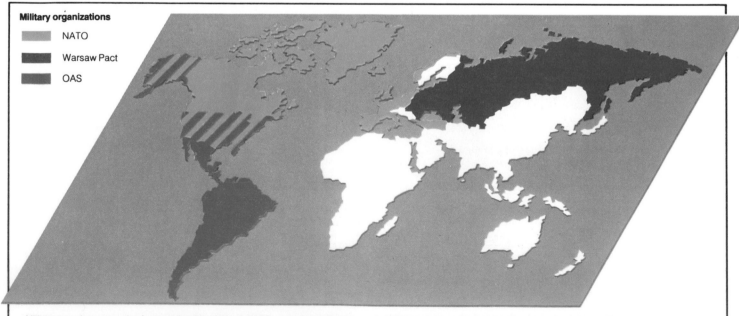

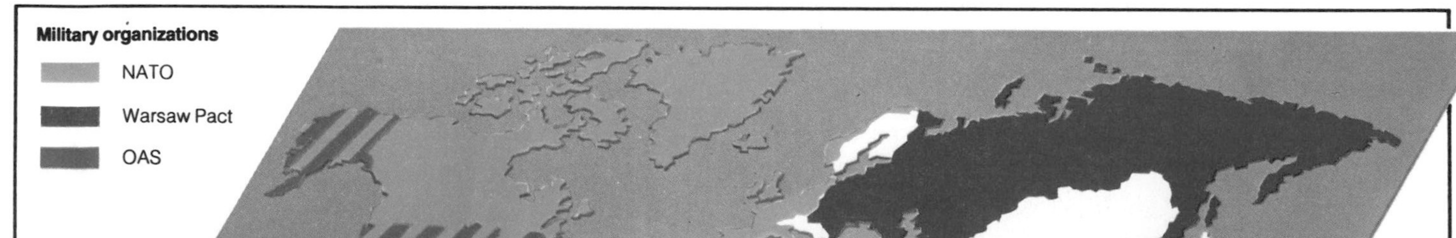

Military groupings were also formed after World War II. NATO, or the North Atlantic Treaty Organization, for example, is a Western defensive alliance that was formed in 1949 to promote military aid and co-operation between Europe and North America during peacetime.

Transport and communication

TWO hundred years ago there began a revolution in the speed, availability and cost of transport. For centuries prior to the end of the eighteenth century, speeds had been limited to those of the horse on land and the sailing vessel at sea, while the carriage of heavy goods was prohibitively expensive and restricted in practice to movement by water. The period since then, however, has seen one transforming event after another — road improvement, canal building, railway construction, the steamship, pipeline, aeroplane and hovercraft. Men who sailed before the mast on the old clipper ship have lived to travel by supersonic jet. Modes of transport have superseded one another rapidly. Since World War II an extensive network of motorways has been built in Britain and much traffic that used to be carried by rail now goes by road, despite the fact that road transport uses energy less efficiently.

The transport revolution

The revolution in transport, in turn, made other changes possible. The Industrial Revolution of the nineteenth century involved, among other things, the assembly of huge quantities of raw materials, such as coal or iron ore. It involved also the transfer of other materials, such as cotton or rubber, from distant parts of the world to the new industrial areas, and the new industry necessitated the concentration of workers near to mines or factories in regions that may previously have had only a sparse population. Basic to all these changes was a transport system that could ensure rapid, predictable flows of traffic to keep industry supplied.

Transport was a key factor also in the "urban revolution" of the same period, as population drained away from the countryside and into the new industrial towns. These new townsmen no longer produced their own food: they had to be supplied from farms elsewhere, and supplied as cheaply as possible. As the nineteenth century drew to a close, the cheapest sources of food were found, on the whole, in countries thousands of miles away from the city markets — in the Americas and Australasia.

Such rapid changes in transport technology have inevitably meant that its development has seen a good deal of waste: waste of capital invested in quickly-outmoded facilities, and waste in the construction of competing routes. Scarcely had the canals in Britain been built when they were superseded by the railways and, in regions such as Britain and North America, not only by one railway but by two or three. Every day, hundreds of empty seats cross the Atlantic in aircraft which fly not so much because there are enough passengers to fill them as for reasons of prestige or competitive pressure. New types of plane, car or train are outdated almost before they can complete the transfer from drawing board to assembly line. A rational transport policy, whereby everybody and everything travelled by the most economical transport mode available, would represent a huge saving in world resources of capital and energy. At present, however, no such policy for transport is in sight.

On land the railway dominated the nineteenth century as road transport has dominated the twentieth. Railways are still being built here and there, but almost exclusively either to tap a particular mineral deposit or for strategic purposes. Some regions have never seen the railway and probably never will. By contrast, every year sees the extension of road networks to accommodate some 350 million motor vehicles that now use them.

This last figure indicates another aspect of the transport revolution. There was a time when travel was the privilege of a few: most people never had the opportunity to travel for pleasure. It is estimated today, however, that there are 300 million tourists worldwide each year: that is, one in 14 of the world's population makes a journey purely for pleasure. Travel has truly been democratized.

Economy of scale

Technical changes in transportation continue, and economies are being made in what has been, in the past, a wasteful industry. The most dramatic of these economies is represented by the rise of the supertanker, the bulk carrier and the jumbo jet — the economies of scale in using a large vehicle. Economies have been made also in loading and unloading techniques as a result of the "container revolution", which has placed small cargoes in easily-handled modules of standard size, and produced the roll-on, roll-off vessel that cuts out transshipment of cargo altogether. These changes have been necessary if only because of the great increase in international waterborne commerce — from some 900 million tonnes in 1955 to 3.8 billion tonnes in 1979, the bulk of this increase accounted for by the movement of oil.

▲ **"Containerization"** *has been the major development in the transport of goods in the last two decades. Containers are all of an internationally agreed size and can be quickly loaded into purpose-built vessels.*

◀ **Road transport** *has benefited in the last half-century by the investment by governments in motorway systems. It is, however, not as efficient as rail transport in terms of energy consumption, and threatens the environment.*

Communications

If the past two decades have seen revolutionary changes in transport, there have been equally striking developments in communications. These began in 1843 with the transmission of messages by key and code down electric wires: they continued with the telephone, the radio (or wire-less), television and the satellite, and have reached their present degree of sophistication with the involvement of computers, data storage and instant electronic recall of information.

It seems clear that the impact of these changes has still to be fully felt. Already, however, we can see how business structures and, indeed, whole industries, can be transformed by electronics. Branch offices, for example, have immediate access to central records; executives can "sit in on" conferences at which they are not physically present; and machines are built by other machines rather than by human hand.

The contribution of satellites to the development of communications systems has been particularly dramatic. A number of tasks which previously involved the presence on the ground of a human agent — for example, to map land use or military installations — can now be done much faster and just as effectively from the sky. Satellite pictures help weather forecasters and mineral prospectors, and people across the world can watch an event on television as it happens, instead of the next day or even the following week.

All these developments — whether in transportation or communications systems — are a far cry from the relatively recent days when news was conveyed by runners, goods were moved by barge and empires were administered by issue of orders which could take years to be received and even longer to be implemented.

Agriculture

Coastal features

Earth tides

Marine life

Mineral deposits

Weather forecasting

Glacial features

Seismic activity

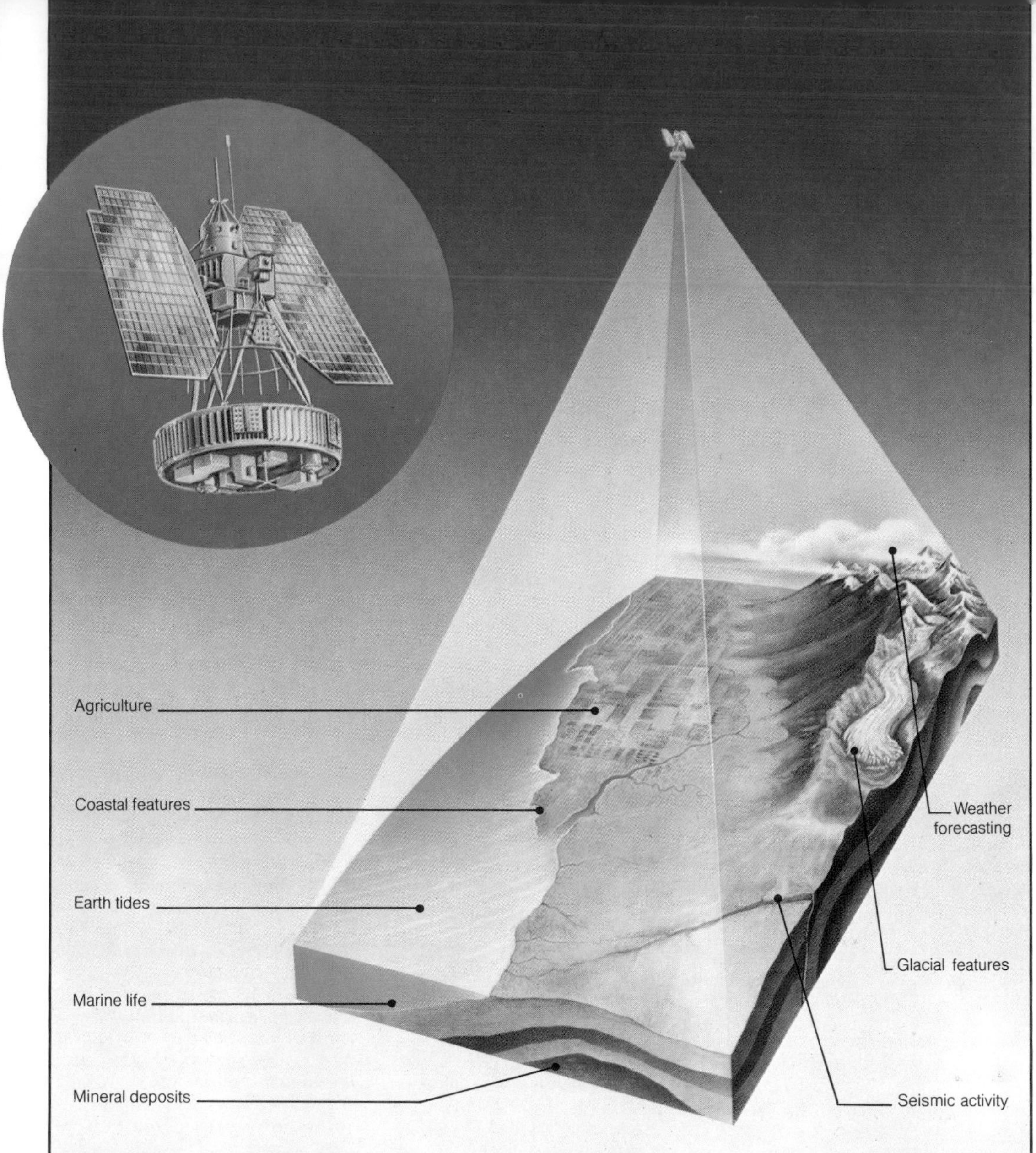

The first satellites for meteorological purposes were launched in the early 1960s. By means of multi-band cameras and infra-red and microwave sensors that can discriminate conditions on earth far better than the human eye, satellites now provide a wealth of information from their constant surveillance of much of the globe. Satellites can also be used for defence purposes. Sophisticated infra-red sensors can detect exhaust plume emissions from missiles as they are launched and thus give an early warning of possible attack.

▲ **Supertankers** *can be loaded and unloaded quickly with the aid of specialized port facilities and they require few crew members.*

▼ **Transport by air,** *especially of passengers, has increased enormously in the last 30 years, particularly over long distances.*

▲ **Traffic flow** *through the city centre can be monitored from the traffic control room by means of close circuit television cameras mounted in strategic places throughout the city. Details are then relayed to the traffic police in the streets. Highly sophisticated communications systems have revolutionized many industries.*

The shrinking world

As with other aspects of man's activities, from consumption of the earth's resources to the increase in human numbers, the development of transport systems has shown an exponential growth in the speed of the various modes of travel since the take-off point in the nineteenth century. But what of the future of transport? Since social and commercial life depends upon an efficient transport system and as concern for increasingly depleted resources and a threatened environment grows, governments are playing an ever greater role in decision-making within the transport sector. Support for public transport systems, for instance, could see the future development of extensive and rapid mass-transit systems at the expense of private transport which is being made to carry an ever heavier burden of taxation.

1500-1850
Best average speed of horse-drawn coaches or sailing ships was 10 miles per hour

1850-1930
Average speed of the fastest steam trains was 65 mph and of the fastest steam ships 36 mph

1950s
Average speed of propeller aircraft was between 300 and 400 mph

1960s
Average speed of jet passenger aircraft was between 500 and 700 mph

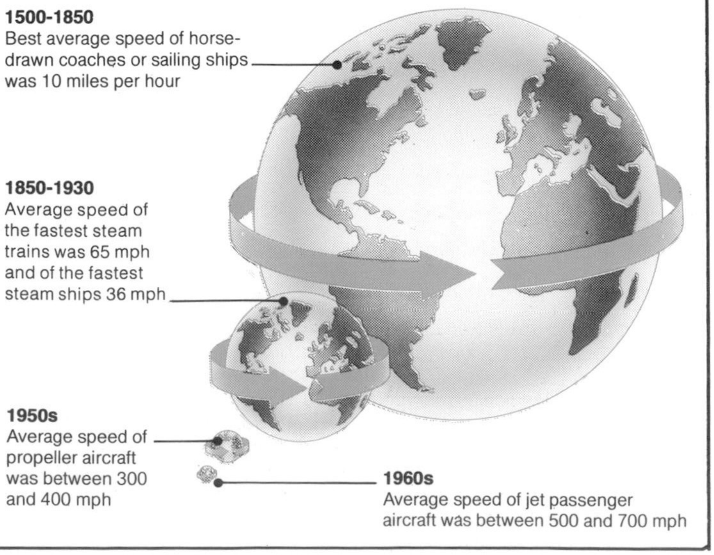

Industry and technology

WITHIN the last 30 years there have been a number of changes in the overall pattern of world industry or, at least, of industrial science and technology, which are the mainsprings of industrial advance. Before World War II most industrial research was carried out in university laboratories, supported by meagre funds. The technological fruits of that research were, in turn, developed by private companies with their own capital. In both fields — scientific research and technological development — the countries of Western Europe maintained the lead which they had established in the nineteenth century. In the 1950s and 1960s, however, three major changes took place.

Significant developments

In the first place there was an explosive growth in the amount of scientific and technological knowledge and output. Second, there was a massive assumption by government departments and agencies of responsibility for supporting industrial research and development. Third, the United States became the pre-eminent centre of world industry, both in its role as the discoverer of new technologies and in the command which it has come to exercise over worldwide industrial empires. By 1970 the United States was spending 3.5 per cent of its gross national product — about $30 billion, or more than twice the total investment of the rest of the western world — on industrial research and development. This massive capital investment by the government has given the USA its present dominance of industries such as electronics and aerospace.

There have also been changes of direction in other areas. In industries such as chemicals, transport, steel and paper production, there has been a shift away from the simple search for "bigger and better" products. Industry has begun to direct its attention to finding safer chemical products, quieter industrial plants and goods which are both destructible and made from synthetic materials. In such ways industry is beginning to respond to the need for a reduction in the consumption of the earth's natural resources and to the concern of the public that the environment should be protected.

Several trends have manifested themselves in the organization of industry. There has been a move away from adapting organization to technological requirements and towards adapting technology to human and organizational needs. There has been a shift away from plants of maximum size to medium-sized and small units which are more responsive both to market changes and to technological changes in production methods. This change has been especially noticeable in the chemicals and electronics industries and in mechanical engineering works.

In the last 20 years it has been the low-income countries (annual per capita income of less than US $250) and the middle-income countries (more than US $250) that have shown an increase in manufacturing as a percentage of gross domestic product. For all countries, however, the rate of industrial growth has slowed down during the 1970s. A growth rate of 6.7 per cent in low-income countries between 1960 and 1970 fell to 4.5 between 1970 and 1976. In industrial states for the same periods the growth rate fell from 5.7 to 3.2 per cent.

Energy and industrial growth

Undoubtedly, the major cause of this trend has been the increasing cost of energy. Industry will not take strides forward again until alternatives to non-renewable sources of energy (chiefly oil and natural gas) are developed. The high cost of energy in the 1970s is only partly the result of the decision of the oil-exporting countries to raise their prices. It is in the very nature of a non-renewable commodity that the more it is used, the more expensive it becomes. As the most easily exploitable oil fields become exhausted, the cost of developing less accessible and smaller resource deposits automatically rises. This cost is passed on to the major consumer items: housing (fuel and electricity), clothing (synthetic materials based on petroleum) and food (fertilizers and pesticides made from petroleum and natural gas).

This steady and irreversible rise in the price of non-renewable energy sources leads necessarily to industrial stagnation. It produces inflation, a shortage of capital and an unwillingness to invest in high-risk manufacturing enterprises (because the basic cost of energy is so unstable). The future of industry depends upon the current search to find marketable ways of exploiting alternative sources of energy, and the making of plans today for using alternative energy tomorrow.

Technological breakthrough

Two developments, pioneered in the United States, represent a startling technological advance. One is the manufacture of integrated circuits — postage stamp sized chips containing electric currents sufficiently elaborate to operate complex computer systems. Production began in the early 1960s and the results have been successful enough for the product to enter the mass market in the form of digital watches and pocket calculators.

A more recent and equally important development is the photovoltaic cell. This is a thin, chemically-treated slice of silicon, mounted on a metal base. When light hits it, an electric current is generated. This development could eventually provide the answer to a substantial proportion of our electricity demands. The difficulty is to create a market large enough to reduce costs to the point where the cells could be made in large quantities.

Creating a demand

A vicious circle is in operation: because the demand for photovoltaic cells is at present too low to support an efficient scale of production, the cost of the cells remains too high for them to compete on the energy market. The demand has therefore to be created and only governments have the resources to create such a demand. It was huge orders from the American defence department, placed deliberately in order to stimulate production, that made integrated circuits competitive. If any new commodity is to have the same degree of success, a similar stimulation from governments — on a scale that private industry cannot meet — will have to be provided.

This final point helps to explain why, when one looks globally at industrial and technological development, and despite intense efforts in recent decades to transform many Third World countries from subsistence-level, agricultural economies to industrialized, manufacturing economies, the world remains divided into a relatively rich, industrial north and a relatively poor, agricultural south.

▲ **The North American farmer** *has tended to become a small link in a vast agricultural production line that has earned itself the title of agribusiness. Investment in the farm is massive and trends in food production are dictated by the large food corporations.*

The labour shift

The growth of service industries has been the most significant development within the economic structure of developed countries since World War II. More than 60 per cent of all workers in the United States are employed in the service sector. A service industry is distinguished from other industries in that it supplies the needs of industry or the consumer in the form of such things as banking and insurance, entertainment, education, transport and communications, legal or financial advice, medical and social services, government and the distribution and sale of goods by wholesalers and retailers. The increase in services reflects greater per capita income levels. As people earn more than is required to meet their basic needs they desire and can afford more services. The growth of services does not necessarily reflect a proportional increase in demand. Service industries are labour-intensive and output per worker is not as great as in other sectors. Service industries (personal servants excepted) are of much less significance in developing countries where most growth has been in the retail trade.

▲ **Assembly line work,** *such as this Ford production line in Detroit, represents for many workers a sophisticated form of drudgery. Wages are high to compensate for the repetitiveness of the work.*

◄ **Textiles** *have played a pioneer role in the economic development of Third World countries. Mechanization exacerbates already high levels of under-employment.*

► **Since the advent** *of the transistor radio, electronic devices have become more diverse and increasingly sophisticated. The range of their application today extends from telecommunications to data processing and automatic control. The latter raises serious questions about possibly greater unemployment in the future.*

Services · Commerce · Transport and communication · Construction · Manufacturing · Mining · Agriculture

1700

1800

1970

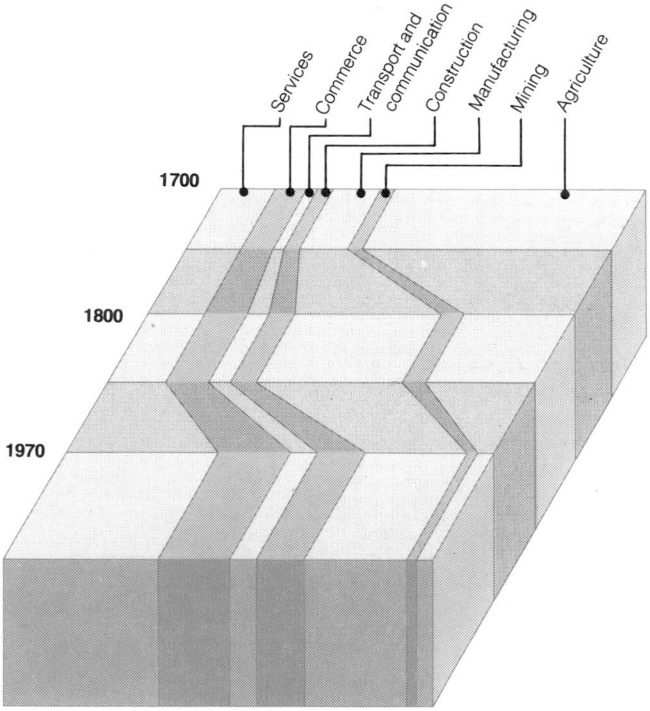

Industrial relations

Good industrial relations have become an increasingly important ingredient for the economic well-being of a nation. The purpose of trade unions is to represent the interests of workers and unions now exist in most countries of the world. The level of organization, however, varies enormously from one country to another. It depends, for instance, on social attitudes, political policies and the economic framework of the country. Disputes and strikes are an inevitable part of a democratic system of industrial relations. Britain does not fare too badly within a league of developed countries, but strikes in Britain differ from many other countries in one important respect: a large proportion of them are unofficial, that is, they are in breach of union rules.

Japan .13 hrs

France .576 hrs

United Kingdom 3.63 hrs

Switzerland .015 hrs

Time lost as a result of industrial disputes (working man . . . per year)

Working population

Sweden 8.39 hrs

West Germany .037 hrs

Australia 4.37 hrs

Canada 6.38 hrs

United States 2.54 hrs

10 20 50 100 million

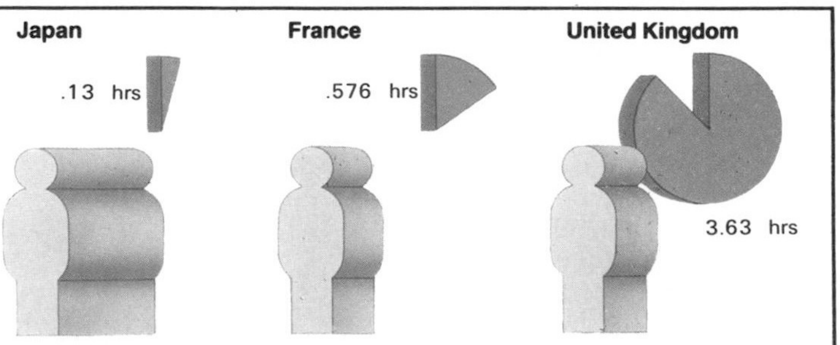

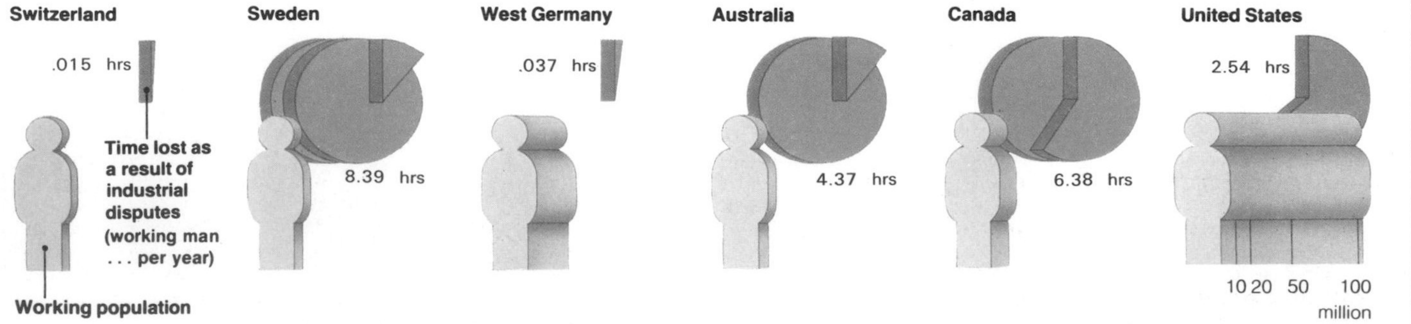

The quality of life

THAT people should wish for an improvement in the quality of life for themselves and their children seems to most of those people who live in the world's developed countries both reasonable and "normal". For them change is constant and advance is taken for granted. It is important to realize, however, that this state of affairs is relatively recent in the history even of the developed world, and it does not apply, even today, to millions of inhabitants of the developing countries.

The element of choice

What underlies an improvement in the quality of life is the idea of choice: the freedom of human beings, either individually or as communities, to choose among several possibilities the one that best serves their own interests, whether it be type of work, location and kind of dwelling, or use of leisure time. In a society where the dawn to dusk efforts of every single member of the community are required merely to keep starvation at bay, there are no such choices. Everybody must live wherever the work is, in whatever kind of shelter is available, and there is little opportunity for leisure activities.

Sometimes, of course, the absence of choice is imposed not by economic necessity but by political and social restraint. In the feudal society of medieval Europe, for example, most of the population were tied to the soil: they had no right to move from their birthplace, or to withhold their labour when it was required by their overlord. For many centuries, in fact, the only changes that occurred were almost always disastrous — the passage of marauding armies, or the withdrawal of common rights by the landlord. In any totalitarian society, choice is the privilege of those who rule that society.

Industrialization and choice

In the developed world, freedom of choice broadened gradually with the breakdown of feudalism and serfdom, with a growing diversity of work opportunities (especially after the onset of industrialization), with an increasing margin in the economy above the level of mere survival, and with the coming of cheap and rapid movement by public transport. Even so, change was no friend to the first generation or so of the new, freer society. Craftsmen were rendered unemployed by factory-based machines, and small farmers were dispossessed. Thousands of country people found themselves in the new slums of the industrial cities, their only "choice" being to starve on the land or work 12- or 16-hour days in the factories. It has taken time for choice to percolate down through society so that today even the most poorly paid worker has some choice about where he lives or how he spends his leisure hours.

Improvement of the quality of life is a goal also in the centrally planned economies of the Communist world no less than in Western Europe or North America, although the emphasis is on improvement for the community as a whole, rather than for its individual members. Even in these countries, however, it is impossible in practice to eliminate the idea of personal incentive and achievement: in sport, in recreation, in striving for a better job, or in the rewards that come with higher output per worker.

What of the less-developed world, however? There is no reason to suppose that, given the opportunity, millions of inhabitants in developing countries would not welcome the same range of choice that is enjoyed by others. At the moment, most of these people are tied to particular patches of earth which afford their only means of subsistence, and if and when they have the opportunity and the courage to break away, they are as likely as not to find themselves in the shanty towns that have grown up on the outskirts of many large cities in less-developed countries. There they live in appalling conditions and experience great deprivation.

A standard of living

The term normally used to identify differences in the quality of life is standard of living, although the two concepts are subtly different in character. Standard of living is generally expressed by the level of income per person. If we compare nation with nation in this respect, the differences in standards are enormous: $14,044 per person in Switzerland (1979 figures) compared with $192 in India, $218 in Sri Lanka, or $200 per person in Rwanda. Within these countries, needless to say, the range variation about the average figure is great. In many Latin American countries, for example, the idea of an "average" standard of living is meaningless.

Nevertheless, it is the policy of more or less every government, whatever its political complexion, to raise the standard of living of its people. Standards may rise, however, without a corresponding improvement in the quality of life. In general we can say that advance in either will be accompanied by certain signs of change within the society or economy that reflect the improvement of living standards.

Indications of change

As the standard of living rises, it will probably be marked by a decrease in the proportion of the population engaged in primary production — in working on the land, or in forestry, fishing or mining — which implies a broadening variety of other forms of occupation — in manufacturing, transport, education and other service industries. In other words, the society requires fewer people to supply its basic needs. In the United States today only three workers out of ten actually produce anything at all, by farming the land or manufacturing goods.

Another indicator is an increase in the volume of circulation, whether of goods or of people, within society. This implies a greater and wider range of demand for commodities beyond those produced locally, and a greater freedom, financial and personal, to come and go at will. Finally, an improvement in the quality of life will be marked by the increased allocation of resources, especially of land, to leisure pursuits, from golf courses and waterfronts to national parks, in some cases the size of a small country. This involves setting aside some part of land resources from ordinary productive use, and expresses a growing concern for the facilities available to the population when they are not working in offices or factories.

There is an increasing awareness now, however, that the path to industrialization and a higher standard of living in the past will not lead to an improvement in the quality of life in the future. That improvement may well necessitate a fourth indication of change within society — the conservation of the earth's limited resources and the protection of the natural and our man-made environment.

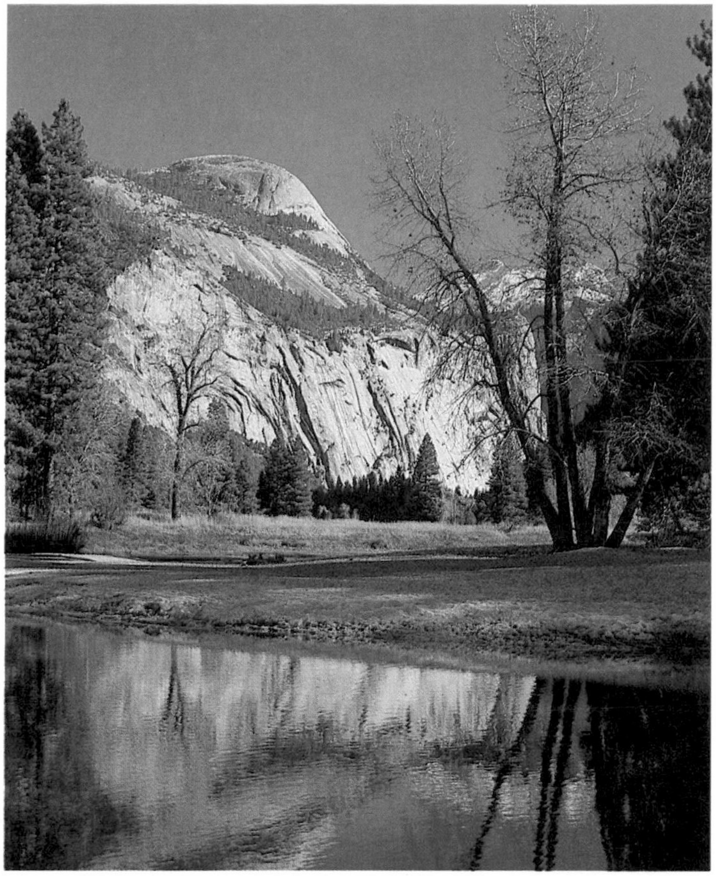

▲ **The clamour** *for extensive, unpolluted open spaces in which to spend our leisure time has meant that millions of hectares in the form of national parks or game reserves have been put aside for just that purpose. Areas of outstanding natural beauty are now protected by law from human encroachment that could damage the environment.*

Labour migration

The migration of people has been a recurrent theme throughout history, but a high degree of individual mobility is a characteristic of recent times. Migration has been an essential part of the processes of urbanization and industrialization. To a large extent this has reflected the greater job opportunities and higher income levels in urban centres. For similar reasons, rural-urban migration has been on the increase in less-developed countries. Migration represents one way by which people can improve their standard of living. On the other hand, the post-war prosperity of Europe, for example, has been increased by a vast pool of immigrant labour. The economic recession of recent years, however, has meant that many countries have closed their doors to unlimited foreign labour and only let migrant workers in according to the needs of the country. To some extent, therefore, a migrant workforce may shield the native workforce from the effects of a recessionary period as a contraction in employment will result in fewer migrant workers being admitted or allowed to stay in the host country. In times of growth, on the other hand, immigrant workers will help support economic expansion.

Total work force with percentage of immigrant labour

Great Britain 7%

Netherlands 3%

Ireland

France 8%

Caribbean India and Pakistan Africa

Portugal

Switzerland 35%

Spain

Morocco Algeria Tunisia Sicily

Africa

Sweden 6%

Finland

West Germany 9%

Austria 10%

Yugoslavia

Italy Greece Turkey

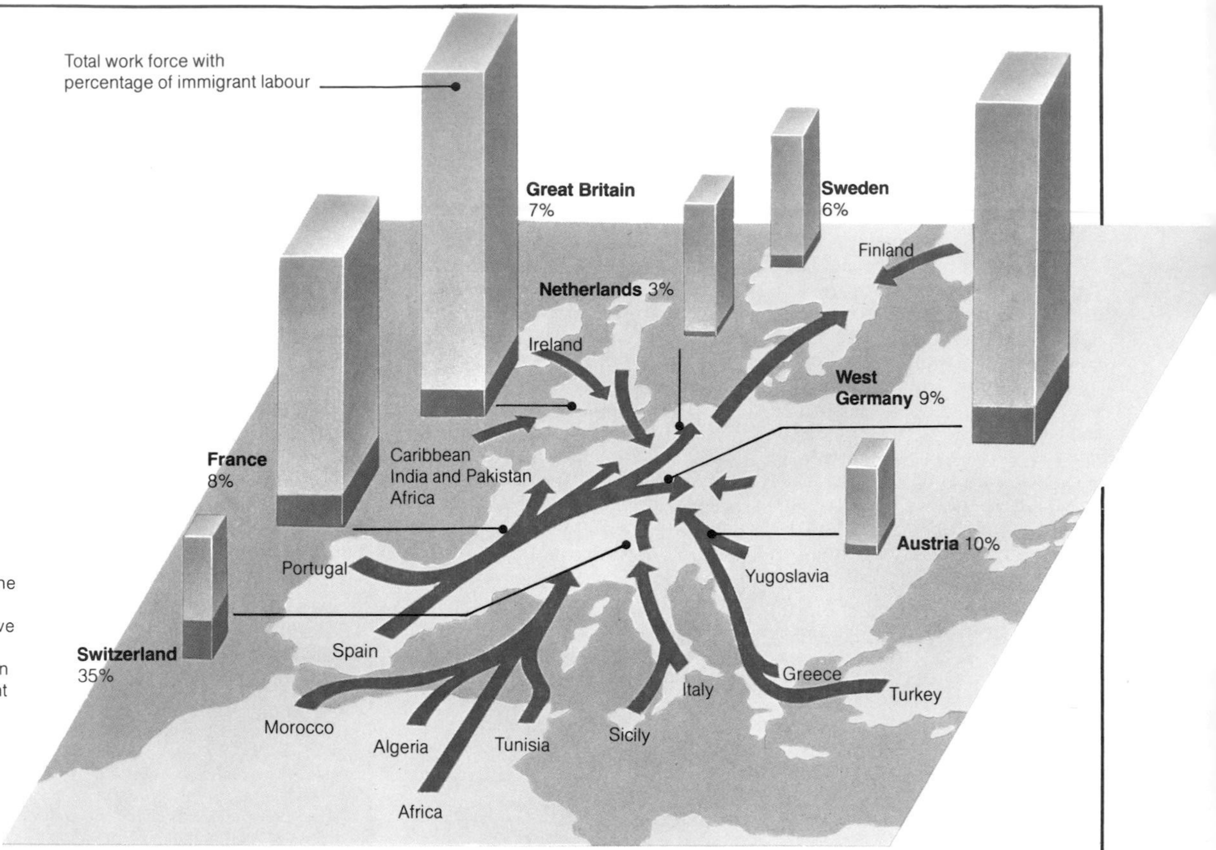

▶ **The greater opportunities** *for migrant workers in post-war Europe has meant an escape from poverty for, for example, millions of Turkish factory workers in West Germany.*

▼ **In the West** *we tend to take social improvement for granted, but for the underprivileged in New York's Bowery, life in the developed world offers little opportunity.*

▼ **An ever-shorter** *working week and more leisure time leads to increasing demands for leisure facilities. Many sports, such as American baseball, are now big business ventures.*

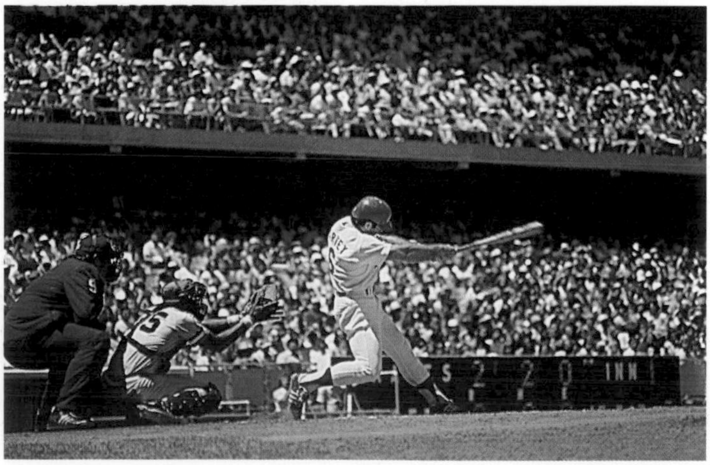

Life expectancy

Not only do we expect better opportunities in life and an ever-higher standard of living, we also expect a healthier and longer life than did our forebears. With the advances of medical science, the length of life the average new-born baby in the developed world can expect has more than doubled in the last two centuries to about 70 years today. Although death rates in many Asian and South American countries have been dramatically reduced, death rates in parts of the African continent have only just begun to decline and remain very high.

72.0 67.0 68.9 57.8 45.7 42.7 69.5

High income Upper middle income Lower middle income

Middle income Low income

Developing countries

Industrialized countries

Centrally planned economies

29

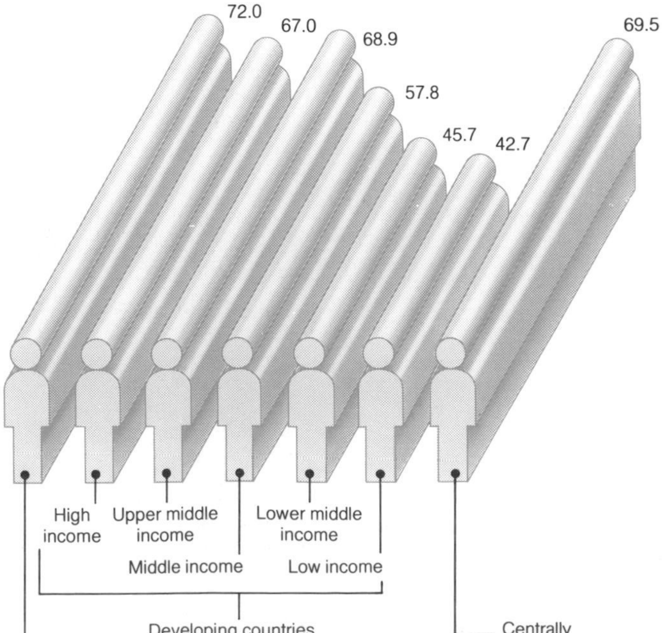

One earth

WITH people everywhere, both in less-developed and developed countries, clamouring for an improved standard of living, it is necessary to appreciate what this implies for an earth whose resources are finite. One way of defining standard of living is as the total amount of resources consumed in a year by the average person in a nation or community. At present, people in countries with a high standard of living are consuming huge and varied quantities of materials derived, in one way or another, from the earth — not only more food per person than their bodies actually require,

but steel and petrol for their cars and a whole range of goods, in fact, that are part of everyday life. Such a community leaves behind it mountains of waste. By contrast, the total resource consumption in a poor community may be represented by small amounts of food and clothing.

Between these levels of consumption there is manifestly no comparison. Yet if we are to visualize that, in the course of time, all living standards will rise and converge upon the highest level we now know, then that implies a colossal drain on the earth's resources. To envisage all of mankind living as North Americans or

Western Europeans currently do, in the present state of our knowledge and technology, is an extremely daunting prospect.

Resources and technology
In past eras, inequalities in living standards were confronted very simply: groups preyed on one another, and the strong grew rich while the poor starved. Not only is this unacceptable by present-day standards, but a new factor has been introduced into the competition for resources — the technical ability to use them. A community with a high level of technology can, in practice, reach out and tap the resources of others: by contrast, a country richly endowed with natural resources may not have the technical expertise to exploit them, and so may have to bring in outsiders and share its wealth with them in return for their assistance. All this means,

however, is that, without resorting to force, the rich grow richer, often at the expense of the poor.

There are several possible remedies for this situation. One is to set up a world organization with sufficient power to introduce some form of international rationing. However, not only would it be exceedingly difficult to decide what constituted "fair shares" for nations with entirely different needs and lifestyles, but such an arrangement could, in practice, only be introduced with the consent and help of the most wealthy nations, and they would naturally be the losers by it.

A question of distribution
The second possibility is that the largest consumers of resources should limit their usage and leave more for the rest of mankind. It has even been agreed that the living standards of the rich would not

▲ **The rehabilitation** of land spoiled by man's activities has become an exact science. Here in Wales colliery spoil is spread over toxic metal waste and planted with a special strain of grass whose short root system does not reach the toxic soil beneath the top layer.

The United Nations

The United Nations was established in 1948 by 50 nations. It now has three times as many members and stands as a symbol of world unity. The political sector of the UN is the General Assembly and the Security Council. The Economic and Social Council, under the supervision of the General Assembly, co-ordinates the economic and social work of the UN

and 14 specialized agencies. The Trusteeship Council was set up to supervise the affairs of 11 territories all of which except one, the Pacific Islands, are now independent. The International Court of Justice is the principal judicial body and the Secretariat services all other departments and is responsible for implementing their policies.

General Assembly — 1

Security Council — Secretariat — Economic and Social Council — Trusteeship Council — International Court of Justice

2 3 4 5 6 7 8 9

IMF International Monetary Fund	IDA International Development Association	ITU International Telecommunications Union
WHO World Health Organization	IBRD International Bank for Reconstruction and Development	WMO World Meteorological Organization
FAO Food and Agriculture Organization	IFC International Finance Corporation	GATT General Agreement on Tariffs and Trade
ILO International Labour Organization	Universal Postal Union	IMCO Inter-Governmental Maritime Consultative Organization
UNESCO Educational, Scientific and Cultural Organization	ICAO International Civil Aviation Organization	

IAEA International Atomic Energy Authority
Peace keeping forces/Military observers
Disarmament Commission

1 UNCTAD Conference on Trade and Development
2 UNIDO Industrial Development Organization
3 UNITAR Institute for Training and Research
4 UNHCR High Commission for Refugees
5 UN Capital Development Fund
6 UNDP Development Programme
7 Trade and Development Board
8 UNICEF Children's Fund
9 UN-FAO World Food Programme

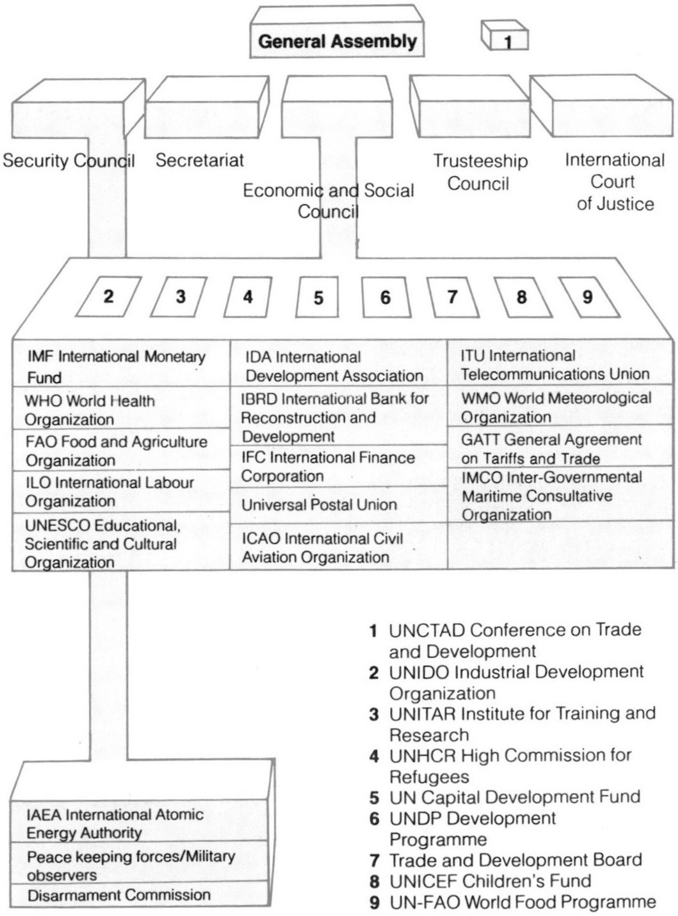

necessarily fall. Their present consumption patterns are so wasteful of resources that any loss in supply could be recouped by the proper use of the resources they still possessed. By eliminating waste, improving efficiency and recycling materials, the developed countries could live on a lot less.

All this is true, and there is no doubt that the average consumer in the developed world today has a far more tender conscience, and a far greater awareness of the needs of others, than was the case a few decades ago, thanks in part to the development of communications and the immediate coverage of famine, catastrophe and living conditions worldwide. Reduced consumption by the well-to-do will not, however, solve the problem of transferring the resources saved by one country in order to supply the needs of another. If the United States were to reduce its consumption of petroleum, this would not necessarily make it cheaper or easier for a poor and oil-less state such as Bangladesh to obtain petroleum. The connection between supply and demand is not that simple. While there is, therefore, an obvious argument that there should be fairness for all, the machinery for achieving this has yet to be created, at least on an international level.

The provision of aid
The only workable alternative to these two ideas, and one which has received a lot of attention in the years since World War II, is that of giving technical aid. Since it is the difference in technical standards and capacities which chiefly distinguish the rich nation from the poor one, a levelling up of those standards ought to lead directly towards an equalization of living standards. Furthermore, it should be possible to do this with a minimum of disturbance to ordinary trade relations, and without the need to move large quantities of food and materials from one place to another. By upgrading the poor nation's ability to make use of its own resources, the poor may gain much and the rich will lose little, at least in the short term. Over a longer period, however, the technically-advanced nation is creating competitors for its own producers. But it is reasonable to expect that, by the time that happens, the advanced economy will have moved on again to different levels of technology.

Experience has shown, however, that aid from the developed countries to the developing has been double-edged. Much of the aid has been in the form of loans, on which interest has to be paid, or there are strings attached, such as the demand that purchases of equipment for the developing economy shall be made only from the aid-granting country. Sometimes technical aid to agriculture benefits only the large farmers and makes life more difficult for the small operator, and industries are established which are not only controlled but also staffed largely by technicians from abroad, so that their presence makes little impact on unemployment in the area.

What this means is not that aid should be stopped, but that it should take carefully chosen forms, and that the basic objective of every aid programme should be to give the maximum assistance to those most in need. In the world today, it is not by the condition of the average man, and certainly not by the wealth of the richest, but by the circumstances of the most needy that future generations will judge us.

▲ **The most constructive form** of aid to less-developed countries is education and the introduction of a technology that is best suited to their requirements.

◄ **Massive foreign aid** *is granted to developing countries each year. Aid at times of catastrophe is widely publicized — less well known is the work of the United Nations and other international organizations in assisting economic development in the less developed world.*

▶ **Proponents of an alternative society** *advocate a return to a pre-industrial way of life in which men live more simply and without generating the problems of modern times. The Amish of Pennsylvania, however, have never succumbed to the pressures of American society and have lived in relative seclusion for the past two centuries.*

World models

World models are an attempt to predict the future behaviour of a dynamic system (the earth) given a number of variables such as population growth, industrial output and food production. Such models are criticized for their generalization and the incomplete, sometimes unrepresentative nature of the data they use. *The Limits to Growth* is one of the best-known projections. A number of computer runs at the Massachusetts Institute of Technology all predicted the eventual collapse of society as we know it now.

Adequate resources, good pollution control and complete birth control

Standard run

Natural resources

Pollution

Industrial output

Population growth

Food production

Time

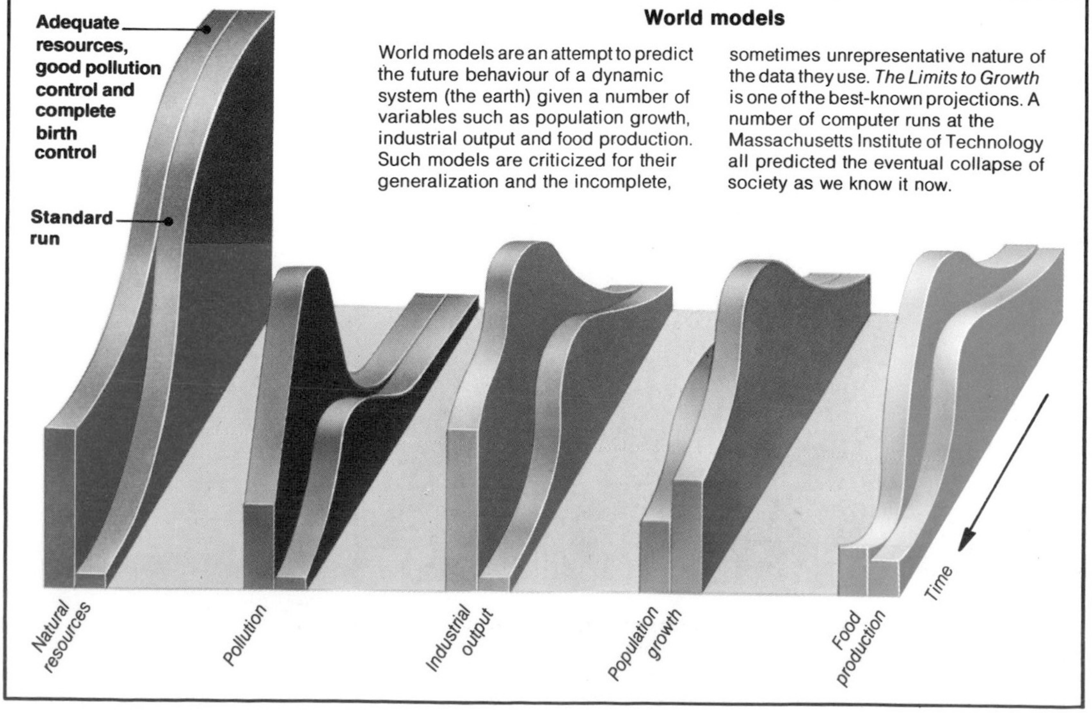

Earth data

The earth's dimensions

Superficial area	510,000,000km²
Land surface	149,000,000km²
Land surface as % of total area	29.2%
Water surface	361,000,000km²
Water surface as % of total area	70.8%
Equatorial circumference	40,077km
Meridional circumference	40,009km
Equatorial diameter	12,757km
Polar diameter	12,714km
Volume	$1,083,230 \times 10^6$km³
Mass	5.9×10^{21} tonnes

The earth's surface

Highest point (Mount Everest, Tibet-Nepal border)	8,848m
Lowest point (Dead Sea, Israel-Jordan)	395m below sea level
Greatest ocean depth (Challenger Deep, Mariana Trench)	11,022m
Average height of land	840m
Average depth of sea	3,808m

The largest oceans and seas

Pacific Ocean	165,721,000km²
Atlantic Ocean	81,660,000km²
Indian Ocean	73,442,000km²
Arctic Ocean	14,351,000km²
Mediterranean Sea	2,966,000km²
Bering Sea	2,274,000km²
Caribbean Sea	1,942,000km²
Mexico, Gulf of	1,813,000km²
Okhotsk, Sea of	1,528,000km²
East China Sea	1,248,000km²

The longest rivers	LENGTH	LOCATION
Nile	6,669km	Africa
Amazon	6,516km	South America
Mississippi-Missouri	6,050km	North America
Yangtze-Kiang	5,989km	Asia
Ob-Irtysh	5,149km	Asia
Amur	4,666km	Asia
Zaire	4,373km	Africa
Hwang Ho (Yellow River)	4,344km	Asia
Lena	4,256km	Asia
Mackénzie	4,240km	North America

The largest lakes and inland seas	AREA	LOCATION
Caspian Sea	393,896km²	Asia
Lake Superior	82,413km²	North America
Lake Victoria	69,484km²	Africa
Aral Sea	68,681km²	Asia
Lake Huron	59,596km²	North America
Lake Michigan	58,015km²	North America
Lake Tanganyika	32,893km²	Africa
Great Bear Lake	31,792km²	North America
Lake Baykal	30,510km²	Asia
Lake Nyasa	29,604km²	Africa

The highest mountains	HEIGHT	LOCATION
Everest	8,848m	Tibet-Nepal
K2 (Godwin Austen)	8,616m	Kashmir
Kanchenjunga	8,591m	Nepal-Sikkim
Makalu	8,481m	Tibet-Nepal
Dhaulagiri	8,177m	Nepal
Nanga Parbat	8,131m	Kashmir
Annapurna	8,078m	Nepal
Gasherbrum	8,073m	Kashmir
Gosainthan	8,019m	Tibet
Nanda Devi	7,822m	India

The largest islands	AREA	LOCATION
Greenland	2,175,000km²	Atlantic
New Guinea	885,780km²	Pacific
Borneo	743,330km²	Pacific
Madagascar	587,045km²	Indian
Baffin	476,070km²	Arctic
Sumatra	473,600km²	Indian
Honshu	230,540km²	Pacific
Great Britain	218,050km²	Atlantic
Ellesmere	212,690km²	Arctic
Victoria	212,200km²	Arctic

The continents	AREA
Asia	44,250,000km²
Africa	30,264,000km²
North America	24,398,000km²
South America	17,807,800km²
Antarctica	13,209,000km²
Europe	9,906,000km²
Australia and New Zealand	8,842,400km²

The greatest waterfalls	HEIGHT	LOCATION
Angel	980m	Venezuela
Tugela	853m	South Africa
Mongefossen	774m	Norway
Yosemite	738m	California
Mardalsfossen	655m	Norway
Cuquenan	610m	Venezuela
Sutherland	579m	New Zealand
Reichenbach	548m	Switzerland
Wollomombi	518m	Australia
Ribbon	491m	California

Notable volcanoes	HEIGHT	LOCATION
Etna	3,340m	Sicily
Fuji	3,778m	Japan
Mauna Loa	4,160m	Hawaii
Ngaurone	2,290m	New Zealand
Njamiagira	3,059m	Zaire
Nyiragongo	3,472m	Zaire
Pacaya	2,546m	Guatemala
Popocatepetl	5,456m	Mexico
Saint Helens	2,744m	USA
Stromboli	927m	Italy
Tristan da Cunha	2,026m	Atlantic Ocean
Vesuvius	1,278m	Italy

GENERAL REFERENCE

Abbreviations of measures used — ft Feet; mm { Millimetres / Millimeters ; cm { Centimetres / Centimeters ; m { Metres / Meters ; Km { Kilometres / Kilometers ; mb Millibars

City and Town symbols in order of size

Sites of Archæological or Historical Importance

International Boundaries

International Boundaries (Undemarcated or Undefined)

Internal Boundaries

Principal Roads

Tracks, Seasonal and other Roads

Road Tunnels

Principal Railways

Other Railways

Railways under construction

Railway Tunnels

Principal Canals

Principal Oil Pipelines

Principal Airports

3386 Principal Shipping Routes (Distances in Nautical Miles)

Perennial Streams

Seasonal Streams

Seasonal Lakes, Salt Flats

Swamps, Marshes

Wells in Desert

Permanent Ice

Passes

▲ 8848 Height above sea-level
▼ 8050 Depth below sea-level } in metres
1134 Height of lake-level

CONVERSION SCALE

ft	m
30 000	9000
	8000
24 000	7000
	6000
18 000	5000
	4000
12 000	3000
9000	2000
6000	1000
3000	500
Sea-Level 0	0 Sea-Level
	500
	1000
1000	2000
	3000
2000	4000
	5000
3000	6000
	7000
4000	8000
	9000
5000	10 000
6000	11 000
	12 000
7000 fathoms	m

THE WORLD
Physical
1:150 000 000

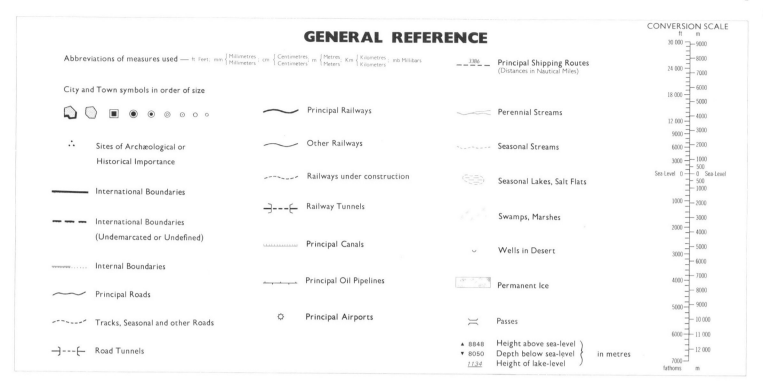

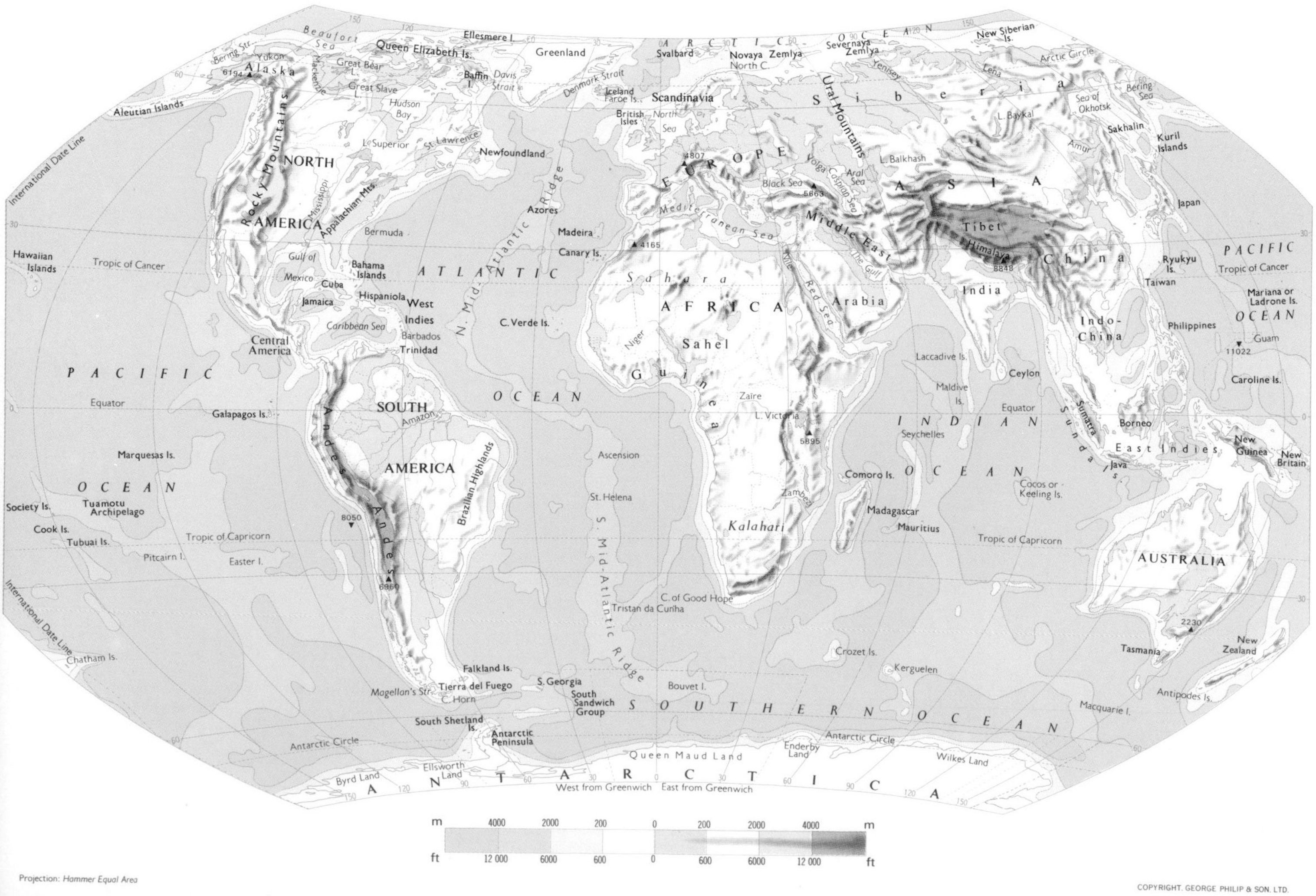

Projection: Hammer Equal Area

THE WORLD : Political

Projection: *Hammer Equal Area*

ARCTIC OCEAN
Zemlya Frantsa Iosifa
Novaya Zemlya
Barents Sea
Nord Kapp
Murmansk
Kara Sea
Severnaya Zemlya
Laptev Sea
New Siberian Is.
East Siberian Sea
Arctic Circle
Tiksi
Nizhne-Kolymsk
Ust Port
Verkhoyansk
Anadyr
Yenisey
Lena
Vilyuysk
Yakutsk
Narvik
Arkhangelsk
Salekhard
UNION OF SOVIET SOCIALIST REPUBLICS
RUSSIAN SOVIET FEDERATIVE SOCIALIST REPUBLIC
Okhotsk
Bering Sea
Sea of Okhotsk
Kamchatka
Petropavlovsk-Kamchatskiy
C. Lopatka
FINLAND
SWEDEN
Helsinki
Stockholm
Leningrad
Yaroslavl
Perm
Sverdlovsk
Novosibirsk
Tomsk
Krasnoyarsk
L. Baykal
Moskva
Kazan
Ufa
Chelyabinsk
Omsk
Novokuznetsk
Barnaul
Irkutsk
Ulan Ude
Sakhalin
Komsomolsk
Khabarovsk
Kuril Is.
Amur
POLAND
Warszawa
Minsk
Kuybyshev
Voronezh
Kiyev
Saratov
Orenburg
Karaganda
Irtysh
Ulaanbaatar
Berlin
Kharkov
Volga
Volgograd
Ural
KAZAKHSTAN
L. Balkhash
MONGOLIA
Harbin
Ch'angch'un
Shenyang
Vladivostok
Sapporo
Hakodate
Praha
Wien
Budapest
ROMANIA
UKRAINE
Odessa
Rostov
Astrakhan
Aral Sea
Caspian Sea
Milano
Beograd
YUGOSLAVIA
Bucuresti
BULGARIA
Black Sea
Grozny
Tbilisi
UZBEKISTAN
KIRGIZIA
Alma Ata
Tashkent
N. KOREA
Sea of Japan
Pyongyang
JAPAN
Tokyo
Yokohama
Roma
Napoli
Sardinia
Sofiya
GREECE
Istanbul
Yerevan
Baku
Samarkand
TURKMENISTAN
Dushanbe
CHINA
Peiping
Tientsin
T'aiyüan
Tsinan
Lu-ta
Tsingtao
Soul
S. KOREA
Kyoto
Nagoya
Osaka
Kobe
Pusan
Kitakyushu
Mediterranean Sea
Sicily
Athinai
MALTA
Crete
Izmir
TURKEY
Tabriz
Ashkhabad
Mashhad
AFGHANISTAN
Tehran
IRAN (PERSIA)
Lanchow
Sian
Hwang Ho
Nanking
Shanghai
TUNISIA
Tarabulus
Banghazi
CYPRUS
Halab
SYRIA
Dimashq
LEB.
Bayrut
Tel Aviv-Yafo
ISR.
Amman
JORDAN
Jerusalem
Baghdad
IRAQ
Esfahan
Abadan
Shiraz
Kabul
Rawalpindi
Srinagar
Lahore
Indus
TIBET
Lhasa
Chengtu
Chungking
Wuhan
Yangtze Kiang
East China Sea
El Iskandariya
El Qahira
Bur Said
KUWAIT
The Gulf
PAKISTAN
Delhi
NEPAL
Katmandu
Agra
Kanpur
Lucknow
Ganges
BHUTAN
Ch'angsha
Foochow
Taipei
Ryukyu Is.
PACIFIC OCEAN
LIBYA
EGYPT
Nile
Aswan
BAHRAIN
QATAR
Ar Riyad
SAUDI ARABIA
U.A.E.
OMAN
Karachi
INDIA
BANGLADESH
Dhaka
Calcutta
BURMA
K'unming
Kwangchow
TAIWAN (FORMOSA)
Tropic of Cancer
Ahmadabad
Arabian Sea
Bombay
Pune
Nagpur
Bay of Bengal
Mandalay
Hanoi
Hong Kong (Br.)
Hainan
VIETNAM
South China Sea
Northern Marianas (U.S.)
Wake I. (U.S.)
Makkah
Red Sea
SOUTH YEMEN
YEMEN
Hyderabad
Rangoon
Vientiane
LAOS
THAILAND
Bangkok
Manila
PHILIPPINES
OCEAN
NIGER
CHAD
L. Chad
Ndjamena
SUDAN
Omdurman
El Khartum
Asmera
Blue Nile
White Nile
Aden
Gulf of Aden
DJIBOUTI
Socotra (S. Yemen)
Bangalore
Madras
Andaman Is. (India)
CAMBODIA
Phnom Penh
Phan Bho Ho Chi Minh
Guam (U.S.)
TRUST TERRITORY OF THE PACIFIC ISLANDS (U.S.)
Marshall Is.
Yap
Truk
Caroline Is.
Ponape
NIGERIA
CAMEROON
CENTRAL AFRICAN REPUBLIC
Addis Abeba
ETHIOPIA
SOMALI REP.
Lakshadweep Is.
SRI LANKA (CEYLON)
Colombo
Nicobar Is. (India)
Dondra Hd.
Cebu
Douala
Yaounde
Bangui
MALDIVES
MALAYSIA
BRUNEI
SABAH
Medan
Kuala Lumpur
PEN. MALAYSIA
Kuching
SARAWAK
SINGAPORE
L. Turkana
Kisangani
UGANDA
Kampala
KENYA
Mogadishu
Equator
Borneo
Maluku
KIRIBATI
NAURU
GABON
CONGO
Zaire (Congo)
ZAIRE (CONGO)
Victoria
RWANDA
BURUNDI
Nairobi
INDIAN OCEAN
Sunda Islands
Sumatera
Palembang
Banjarmasin
Sulawesi
INDONESIA
Irian Jaya
PAPUA NEW GUINEA
New Ireland
Rabaul
New Britain
SOLOMON IS.
TUVALU
Brazzaville
Kinshasa
CABINDA
Kananga
Mombasa
Zanzibar
Dar es Salaam
L. Tanganyika
TANZANIA
Amirante Is.
SEYCHELLES
Chagos Arch. (Br.)
Diego Garcia (Br.)
Jakarta
Bandung
Jawa
Ujung Pandang
Surabaya
Timor
Arafura Sea
Timor Sea
Port Moresby
Louisiade Arch.
Santa Cruz Is.
Luanda
ANGOLA
Benguela
Lubumbashi
MALAWI
Malawi
ZAMBIA
Lusaka
Zomba
Aldabra
COMORO IS.
Cocos (Keeling Is.) (Australia)
Christmas I. (Australia)
Darwin
C. York
ZIMBABWE
Harare
MOZAMBIQUE
Mozambique Chan.
MADAGASCAR
Antananarivo
Rodriguez
MAURITIUS
Réunion (Fr.)
NAMIBIA
Windhoek
BOTSWANA
Bulawayo
Gaborone
Pretoria
SWAZILAND
Maputo
Johannesburg
SOUTH WEST AFRICA
SOUTH AFRICA
LESOTHO
Durban
Cape Town
C. of Good Hope
Port Elizabeth
Tropic of Capricorn
North West C.
NORTHERN TERRITORY
Cairns
Townsville
VANUATU
Vanua Levu
FIJI
Viti Levu
Suva
New Caledonia (Fr.)
WESTERN AUSTRALIA
Alice Springs
QUEENSLAND
AUSTRALIA
Rockhampton
SOUTH AUSTRALIA
Kalgoorlie
Brisbane
Perth
Fremantle
C. Leeuwin
NEW SOUTH WALES
Darling
Lord Howe I. (Australia)
Norfolk I. (Australia)
Newcastle
Great Australian Bight
Adelaide
Sydney
Canberra
VICTORIA
Melbourne
Tasman Sea
North C.
Auckland
North I.
NEW ZEALAND
Wellington
TASMANIA
Hobart
C. Farewell
Christchurch
South I.
Dunedin
Stewart I.
Bounty Is.
Antipodes Is. (N.Z.)
Auckland I. (N.Z.)
Campbell I. (N.Z.)
Macquarie I. (Australia)
Amsterdam (Fr.)
St. Paul (Fr.)
Pr. Edward Is. (South Africa)
Crozet Is. (Fr.)
Kerguelen (Fr.)
McDonald I. (Australia)
Heard I. (Australia)
SOUTHERN OCEAN
Antarctic Circle
Enderby Land
Wilkes Land
AUSTRALIAN DEPENDENCY
S. Magnetic Pole 1980
Balleny Is.
TERRE ADÉLIE
Ross Sea
from Greenwich
20
40
60
80
100
120
140
160
180

1:20 000 000

100 0 100 200 300 400 500 miles
100 0 200 400 600 800 km

COPYRIGHT GEORGE PHILIP & SON, LTD.

Ob

Ural Mountains

Obshchsyrt

Pechora
Pechora

Kama

Ural

CASPIAN SEA -28

Caucasus
Elbrus 5633

Armenia

Kurdistan

Ararat 5165

Euphrates

Tigris

Volga Uplands

Volga

Volga

Rybinsk Res.

Tsimlyansk Res.

Don

Sea of Azov

Kerch

BLACK SEA 2211

Anatolia

Cyprus 1951

Central Russian Uplands

Kizil Irmak

Mezen

N. Dvina

Onega

L. Onega

Ladoga

Don

Oka

Donets

Crimea

Dnepr (Dnieper)

Ukraine

Bug

Danube

Kamin Peninsula

Kola Peninsula

White Sea

L. Ladoga

Chudskoye

Neva

G. of Finland

G. of Riga

Niemen

Pripyat (Pripet)

Pripyat Marshes

Prut

Dniestr (Dnieper)

North European Plain

Danube

Wallachia

Transylvanian Alps

Mureș

Balkans

Rhodope

Balkan Peninsula

Aegean Sea

Pindus

Morea

Crete

Nordkinn

North Cape

Lapland

Finland

Torne

Enontekiö

Muonio

Ume

Indals

Scandinavia

G. of Bothnia

Gotland

BALTIC SEA

Mälaren

Vänern

Vättern

Wisła (Vistula)

Odra (Oder)

Sudetes

Carpathians

Tatra 2655

Plain of Hungary

Tisza

Drava

Sava

Save

Danube

Dinaric Alps

5121 C. Matapan

Str. of Otranto

ADRIATIC SEA

Ionian Is.

Ionian Sea

Calabria

Str. of Messina

Sicily 3263 Etna

Malta

MEDITERRANEAN SEA

Vesterålen

Lofoten

Glittertind 2469

Skagerrak

Kattegat

Jutland

Elbe

Weser

Harz 1142

Erz Geb.

Bohemian For.

Moravian Hts.

Morava

Belgrade

Iron Gate

Danube

Apennines

Gran Sasso 2914

Vesuvius 1270

Ligurian Sea

Corsica

Str. of Bonifacio

Sardinia

Tyrrhenian Sea

NORWEGIAN SEA

3734

Arctic Circle

FISHER

VIKING

FORTIES

DOGGER Dogger Bank

NORTH SEA

GERMAN BIGHT

Heligoland

Helgoland

Netherlands

Weser

Wesser Wald

Rhine

Taunus

Black For.

Vosges

Ardennes

Eifel

Jura

Alps 4807

Mt. Blanc

Po

Rhône

C. Blanco

FAIR ISLE

Shetland Is.

Orkney Is.

CROMARTY

FORTH

TYNE

HUMBER

THAMES

DOVER

WIGHT

PORTLAND

Thames

Seine

Central Massif 1886 Mt. Dore

G. of Lions

Cévennes

Maritime Alps

South East Iceland

Hvannadalshnúkur 2119

Iceland 1491

Fisher Bank

BAILEY

HEBRIDES

Hebrides

British Isles

Ben Nevis 1343

Great Britain

Irish Sea

IRISH SEA

Ireland

English Channel

Brittany

PLYMOUTH

Loire

Garonne

Gironde

Bay of Biscay

BISCAY 4851

SOLE

FINISTERRE

ROCKALL

Rockall

SHANNON

Valencia I.

C. Clear

FASTNET

Land's End

LUNDY

Cantabrian Mts.

Pyrenees 3404

Old Castile

New Castile

Iberian Peninsula

Douro

Tagus

Duero

Sierra Morena

Guadalquivir

Andalusia

Sa. Nevada

Guadiana

Str. of Gibraltar

C. Trafalgar

C. de la Nao

Picos de Europa

Ebro

Balearic Is.

Plateau of the Shotts

C. St. Vincent

C. Spartel

Er Rif

ATLANTIC OCEAN

ft m
12 000 4000
6000 2000
3000 1000
1200 400
600 200
0 0
 200 600
 2000 6000
 4000 12 000
m ft

Projection : Bonne West from Greenwich 0 East from Greenwich

1:20 000 000

100 0 100 200 300 400 500 miles

100 0 200 400 600 800 km

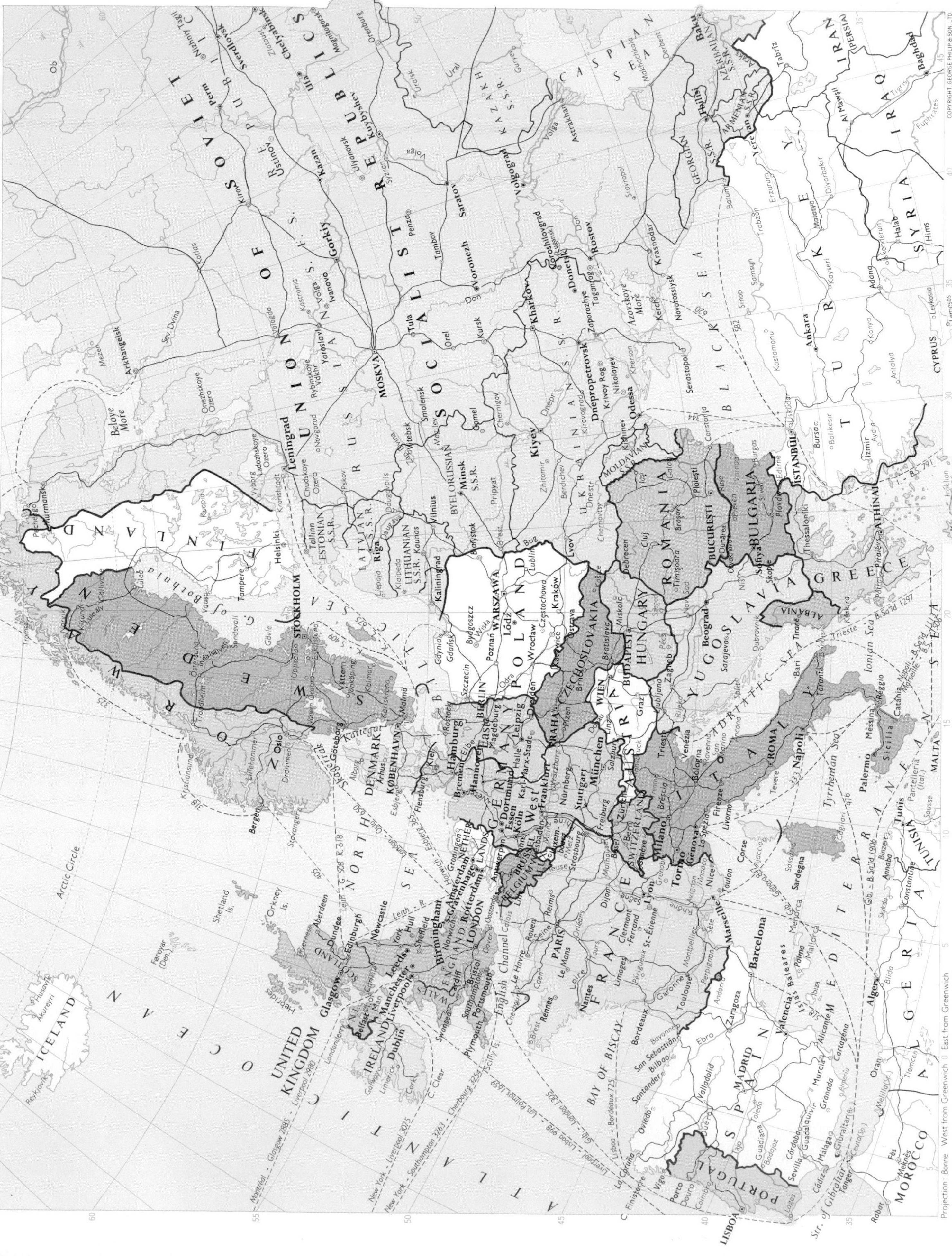

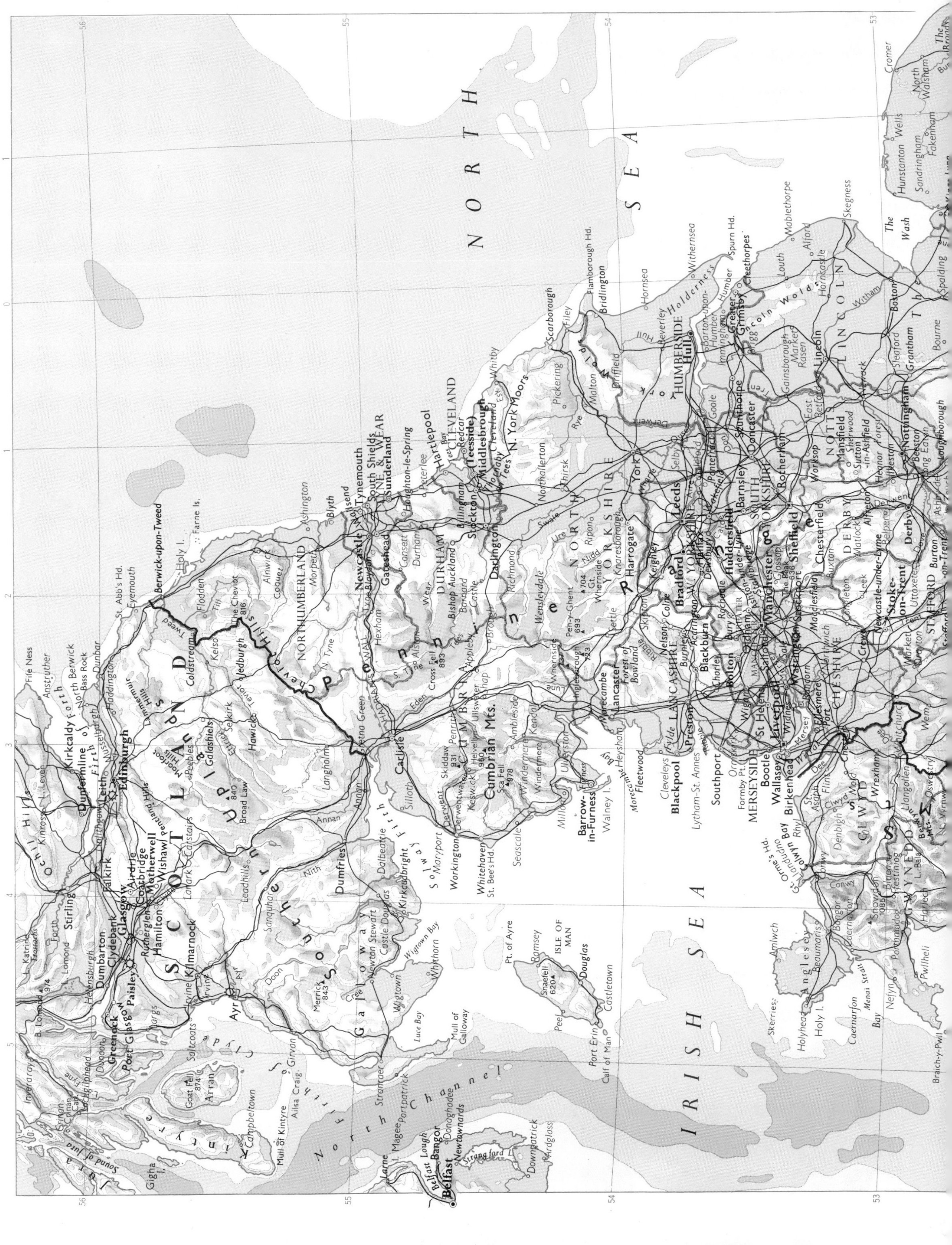
NORTH SEA
IRISH SEA
SCOTLAND
Southern Uplands
Pennines
Cumbrian Mts.
Lincoln Wolds
Holderness
The Wash
North Channel
Firth of Forth
Firth of Clyde
Solway Firth
Morecambe Bay
Edinburgh
Glasgow
Newcastle
Sunderland
Middlesbrough
Leeds
Bradford
Hull
Manchester
Liverpool
Sheffield
Nottingham
Derby
Carlisle
Dumfries
Belfast
Douglas
ISLE OF MAN
NORTHUMBERLAND
DURHAM
CLEVELAND
CUMBRIA
LANCASHIRE
MERSEYSIDE
HUMBERSIDE
CHESHIRE
DERBY
NOTTS
LINCOLN
GWYNEDD
CLWYD
Anglesey
Berwick-upon-Tweed
Scarborough
Whitby
York
Harrogate
Preston
Blackpool
Lancaster
Barrow-in-Furness
Doncaster
Grimsby
Lincoln
Stoke-on-Trent

Projection: Conical with two standard parallels.

1:2 000 000

10 0 10 20 30 40 50 miles

10 0 10 20 30 40 50 60 70 80 km

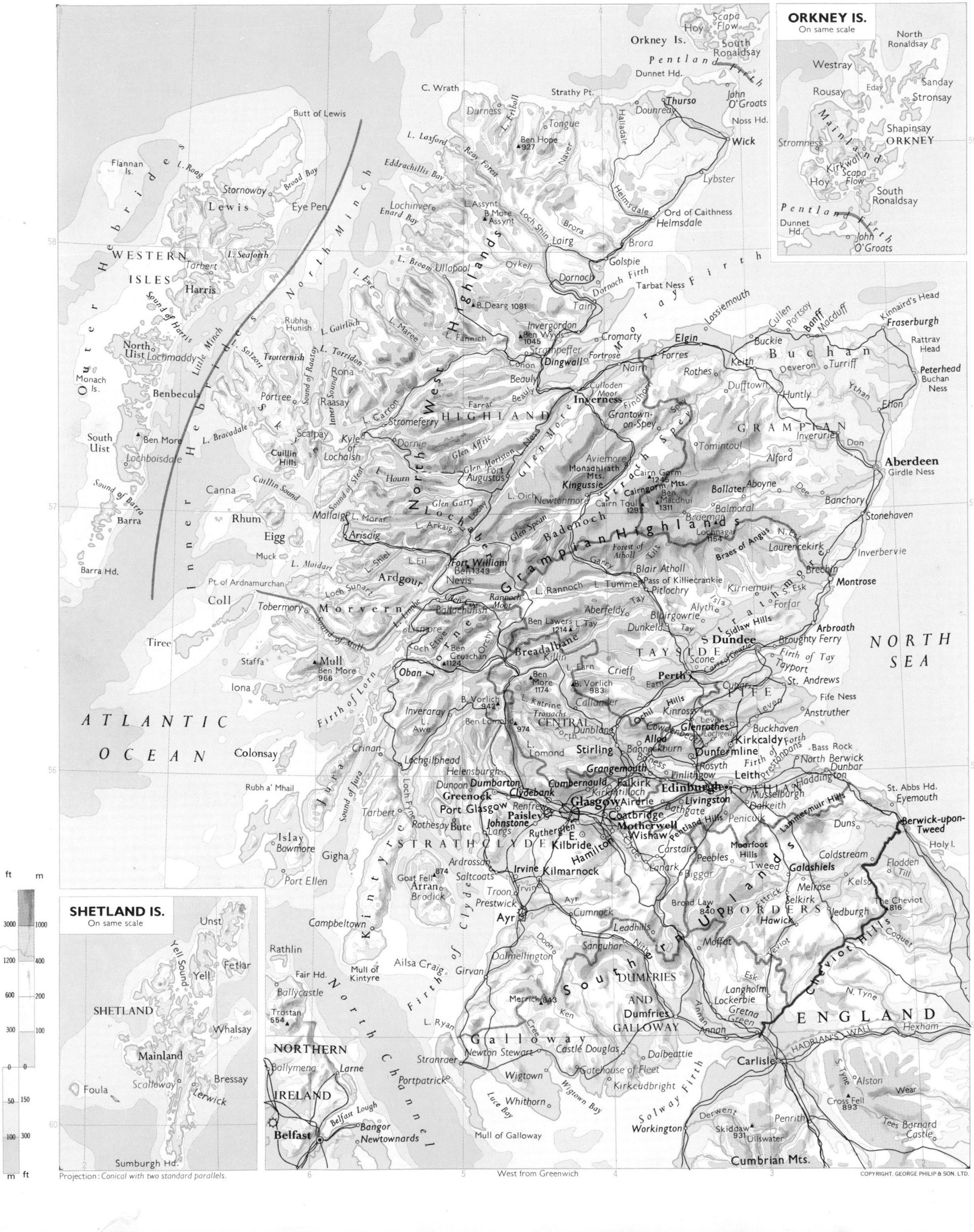

Projection: *Conical with two standard parallels.*

1 : 2 000 000

| 10 | 0 | 10 | 20 | 30 | 40 | 50 miles |

| 10 | 0 | 10 | 20 | 30 | 40 | 50 | 60 | 70 | 80 km |

Towns underlined in Northern Ireland give their
names to the Districts in which they stand

The remaining Districts are:—

1	Fermanagh	5	Castlereagh
2	Moyle	6	Ards
3	Newtownabbey	7	Down
4	North Down	8	Newry & Mourne

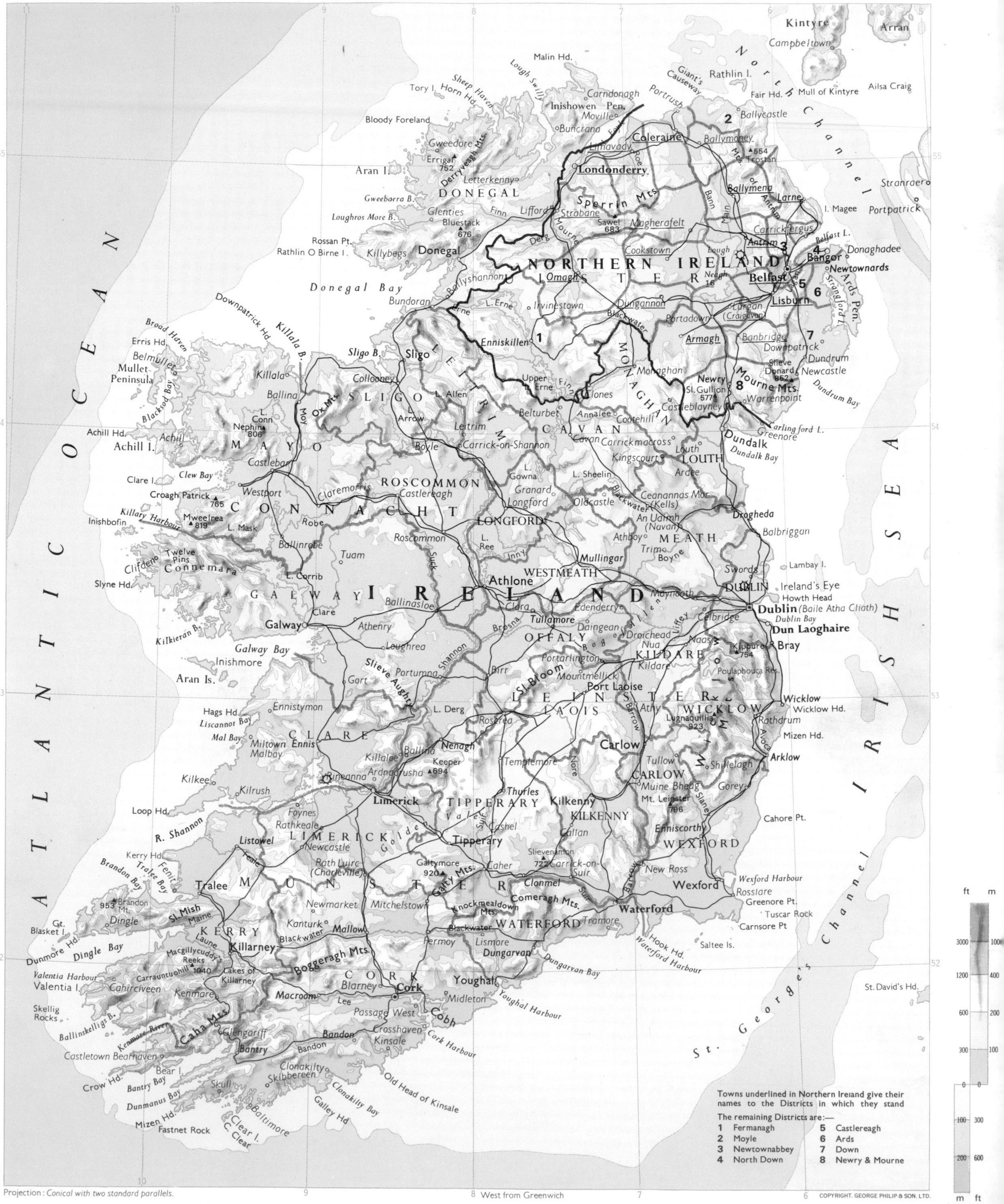

Projection : Conical with two standard parallels.

West from Greenwich

1 : 4 000 000

20 0 20 40 60 miles
20 0 20 40 60 80 km

The DISTRICTS of Northern Ireland have been numbered and can be identified by reference to this table.

1	Londonderry	14	Craigavon
2	Limavady	15	Armagh
3	Coleraine	16	Newry & Mourne
4	Ballymoney	17	Banbridge
5	Moyle	18	Down
6	Larne	19	Lisburn
7	Ballymena	20	Antrim
8	Magherafelt	21	Newtownabbey
9	Cookstown	22	Carrickfergus
10	Strabane	23	North Down
11	Omagh	24	Ards
12	Fermanagh	25	Castlereagh
13	Dungannon	26	Belfast

1 Merseyside
2 Greater Manchester
3 West Yorkshire
4 South Yorkshire
5 West Glamorgan
6 Mid Glamorgan
7 South Glamorgan

ATLANTIC OCEAN

NORTH SEA

IRISH SEA

St. George's Channel

Bristol Channel

ENGLISH CHANNEL

SCOTLAND

HIGHLAND

GRAMPIAN

TAYSIDE

CENTRAL

STRATHCLYDE

FIFE

LOTHIAN

BORDERS

DUMFRIES AND GALLOWAY

NORTHUMBERLAND

TYNE & WEAR

DURHAM

CLEVELAND

CUMBRIA

NORTH YORKSHIRE

LANCASHIRE

HUMBERSIDE

ISLE OF MAN

NORTHERN IRELAND
ULSTER

IRELAND

CONNACHT

DONEGAL

SLIGO

LEITRIM

MAYO

ROSCOMMON

CAVAN

MONAGHAN

LONGFORD

WESTMEATH

MEATH

GALWAY

OFFALY

KILDARE

DUBLIN

LEINSTER

LAOIS

WICKLOW

CLARE

TIPPERARY

KILKENNY

CARLOW

WEXFORD

LIMERICK

MUNSTER

WATERFORD

KERRY

CORK

GWYNEDD

CLWYD

POWYS

DYFED

SHROPSHIRE

CHESHIRE

DERBY

NOTTS

LINCOLN

STAFFORD

WEST MIDLANDS

LEICESTER

WARWICK

NORTHAMPTON

NORFOLK

SUFFOLK

CAMBRIDGE

HEREFORD AND WORCESTER

GLOUCESTER

OXFORD

BUCKS

BEDFORD

HERTFORD

ESSEX

GWENT

AVON

WILTS

BERKS

LONDON

SURREY

KENT

SOMERSET

HANTS

WEST SUSSEX

EAST SUSSEX

DORSET

DEVON

CORNWALL

ISLE OF WIGHT

Orkney Is.
ORKNEY
Shetland Is.
SHETLAND
Mainland

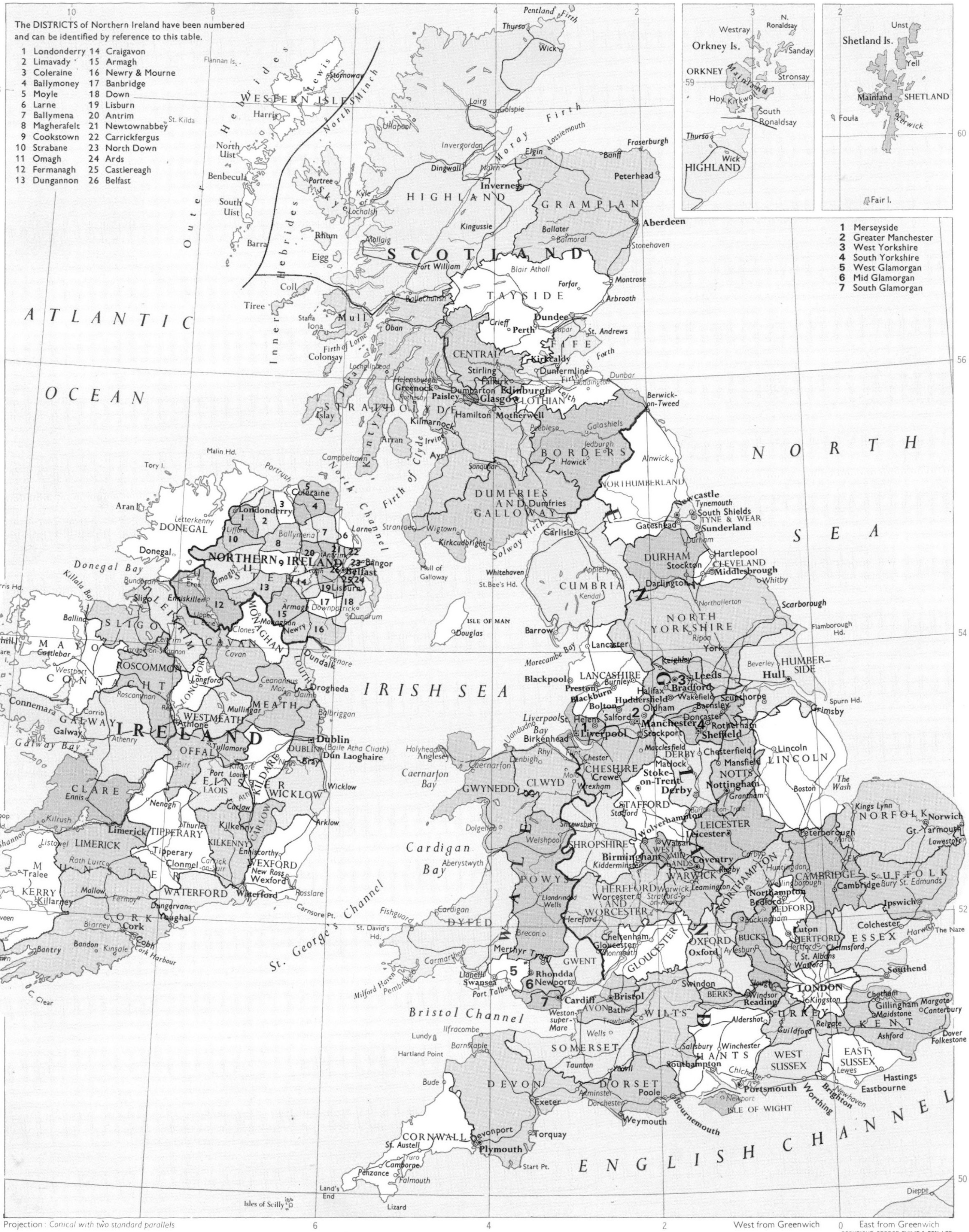

Projection : Conical with two standard parallels

West from Greenwich East from Greenwich
COPYRIGHT. GEORGE PHILIP & SON. LTD.

1:2 500 000

Projection: Conical with two standard parallels

1:5 000 000

50 0 50 100 miles

50 0 50 100 150 km

FRENCH DEPARTMENTS

A.	01 Ain
Ai.	02 Aisne
Al.	03 Allier
A.H.P.	04 Alpes-de-Haute-Provence
H.A.	05 Hautes-Alpes
A.M.	06 Alpes-Maritimes
Ard.	07 Ardèche
Ard.	08 Ardennes
Ari.	09 Ariège
Aub.	10 Aube
Aud.	11 Aude
Av.	12 Aveyron
B.Rh.	13 Bouches-du-Rhône
C.	14 Calvados
Ca.	15 Cantal
Ch.	16 Charente
Ch.M.	17 Charente-Maritime
Che.	18 Cher
Co.	19 Corrèze
—	20 a) Corse; b) Corse du Sud
C.O.	21 Côte-d'Or
C.N.	22 Côtes-du-Nord
Do.	23 Creuse
Do.	24 Dordogne
Do.	25 Doubs
Dr.	26 Drôme
E.	27 Eure
E.L.	28 Eure-et-Loir
F.	29 Finistère
G.	30 Gard
H.G.	31 Haute-Garonne
Ge.	32 Gers
Gi.	33 Gironde
H.	34 Hérault
I.V.	35 Ille-et-Vilaine
I.	36 Indre
I.L.	37 Indre-et-Loire
Is.	38 Isère
J.	39 Jura
La.	40 Landes
L.C.	41 Loir-et-Cher
Lo.	42 Loire
H.L.	43 Haute-Loire
L.A.	44 Loire-Atlantique
Loi.	45 Loiret
Lo.	46 Lot
L.G.	47 Lot-et-Garonne
Loz.	48 Lozère
M.L.	49 Maine-et-Loire
M.	50 Manche
Ma.	51 Marne
H.M.	52 Haute-Marne
May.	53 Mayenne
M.M.	54 Meurthe-et-Moselle
Me.	55 Meuse
Mo.	56 Morbihan
Mo.	57 Moselle
N.	58 Nièvre
No.	59 Nord
O.	60 Oise
Or.	61 Orne
P.C.	62 Pas-de-Calais
P.D.	63 Puy-de-Dôme
P.A.	64 Pyrénées-Atlantiques
H.P.	65 Hautes-Pyrénées
P.O.	66 Pyrénées-Orientales
B.R.	67 Bas-Rhin
H.R.	68 Haut-Rhin
Rh.	69 Rhône
H.S.	70 Haute-Saône
S.L.	71 Saône-et-Loire
Sa.	72 Sarthe
Sa.	73 Savoie
H.Sa.	74 Haute-Savoie
—	75 Paris
S.Me.	76 Seine-Maritime
S.M.	77 Seine-et-Marne
Y.	78 Yvelines
D.S.	79 Deux-Sèvres
So.	80 Somme
T.	81 Tarn
T.G.	82 Tarn-et-Garonne
Va.	83 Var
Ve.	84 Vaucluse
Ve.	85 Vendée
Vi.	86 Vienne
H.V.	87 Haute-Vienne
Vo.	88 Vosges
Y.	89 Yonne
B.	90 Belfort
Es.	91 Essonne
H.Se.	92 Hauts-de-Seine
S.St.D.	93 Seine-St-Denis
V.M.	94 Val-de-Marne
V.O.	95 Val-d'Oise

CORSICA
On same scale

Corse
Haute-Corse
Corse du Sud

COPYRIGHT GEORGE PHILIP & SON LTD.

MEDITERRANEAN SEA

ENGLISH CHANNEL

BAY OF BISCAY

BELGIUM

GERMANY

SWITZERLAND

ITALY

SPAIN

Projection: Conical with two standard parallels

East from Greenwich

West from Greenwich

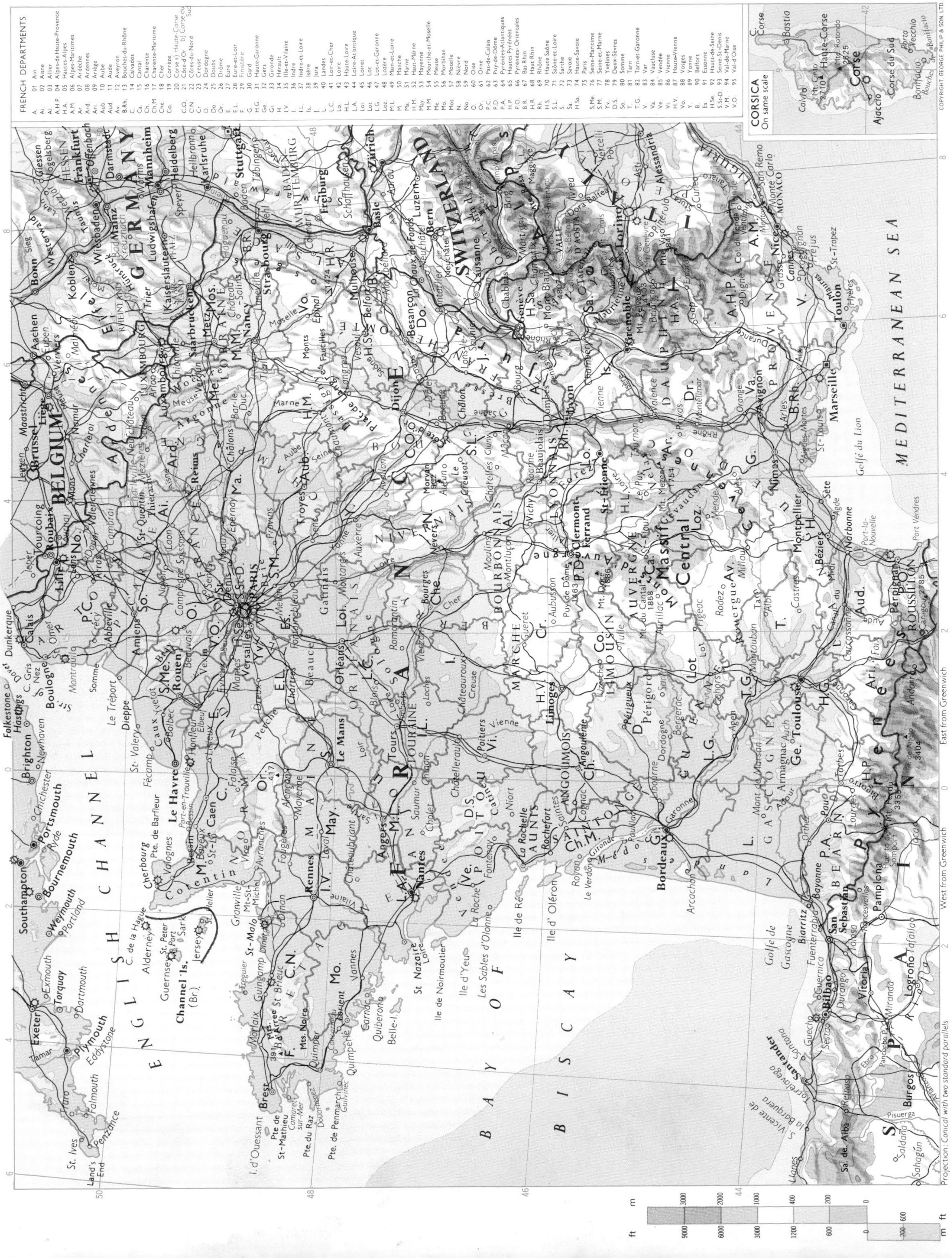

1:5,000,000

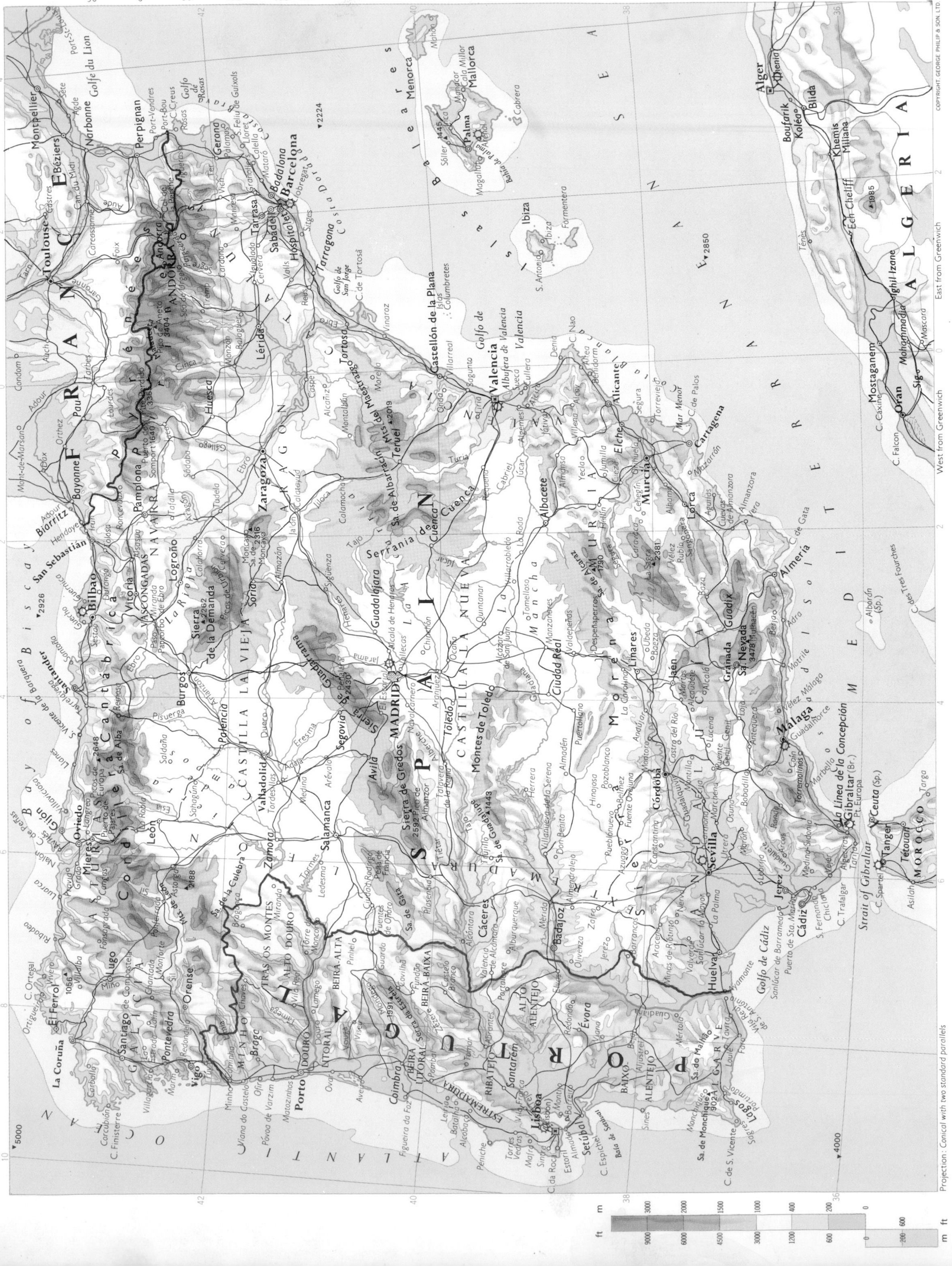
SPAIN
PORTUGAL
FRANCE
ALGERIA
MOROCCO
ATLANTIC OCEAN
MEDITERRANEAN SEA
Bay of Biscay
Islas Baleares
Golfe du Lion
Golfo de Cádiz
Strait of Gibraltar
Madrid
Lisboa (Lisbon)
Barcelona
Valencia
Sevilla
Zaragoza
Bilbao
Málaga
Porto
Coimbra
Granada
Córdoba
Murcia
Alicante
Cartagena
Valladolid
Salamanca
Burgos
León
Oviedo
Gijón
Santander
San Sebastián
Pamplona
Logroño
Vitoria
Huesca
Lérida
Tarragona
Castellón de la Plana
Teruel
Cuenca
Albacete
Ciudad Real
Toledo
Badajoz
Cáceres
Mérida
Huelva
Cádiz
Jerez
Almería
Jaén
Linares
Guadix
Lorca
Elche
La Coruña
El Ferrol
Lugo
Orense
Pontevedra
Vigo
Santiago de Compostela
Braga
Évora
Setúbal
Santarém
Palma
Mallorca
Menorca
Ibiza
Formentera
Alger
Oran
Tanger
Ceuta (Sp.)
Gibraltar (Br.)
Toulouse
Montpellier
Perpignan
Béziers
Narbonne
Bayonne
Biarritz
Pau
ANDORRA
Pyrénées
Cordillera Cantábrica
Sierra de Guadarrama
Sierra de Gredos
Sierra Nevada
Sierra Morena
Montes de Toledo
Serranía de Cuenca
CASTILLA LA VIEJA
CASTILLA LA NUEVA
ARAGÓN
CATALUÑA
NAVARRA
GALICIA
ASTURIAS
EXTREMADURA
ANDALUCÍA
La Mancha
MURCIA
ALGARVE
ALENTEJO
Projection: Conical with two standard parallels
West from Greenwich
East from Greenwich
COPYRIGHT, GEORGE PHILIP & SON, LTD

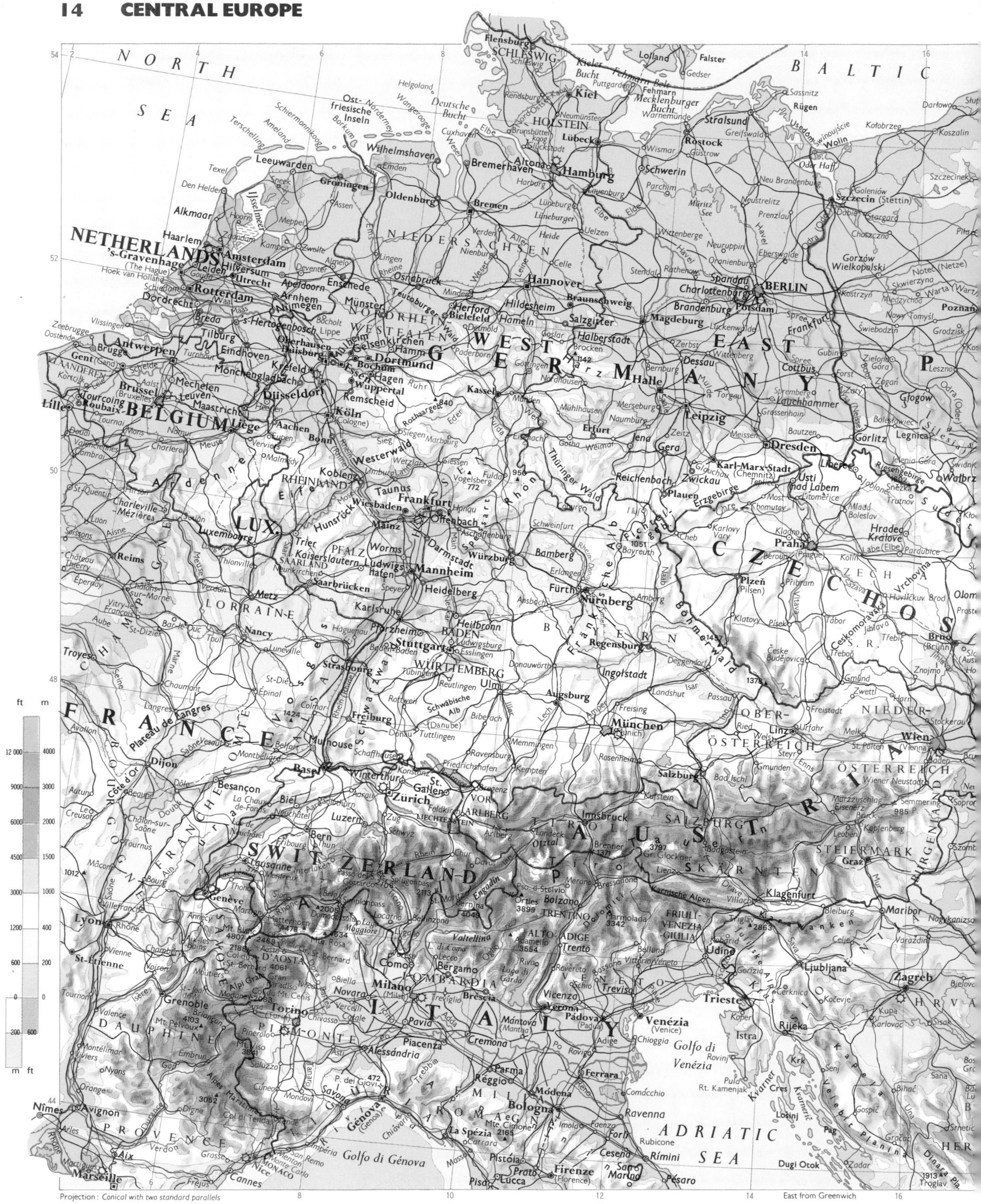
NORTH SEA
BALTIC
NETHERLANDS
BELGIUM
LUX.
WEST GERMANY
EAST GERMANY
CZECHOSLOVAKIA
AUSTRIA
SWITZERLAND
FRANCE
ITALY
ADRIATIC SEA
Golfo di Venézia
Golfo di Génova
Amsterdam
Rotterdam
's-Gravenhage (The Hague)
Utrecht
Antwerpen
Brussel (Bruxelles)
Liège
Luxembourg
Hamburg
Bremen
Hannover
Kiel
Lübeck
Berlin
Leipzig
Dresden
Magdeburg
Halle
Karl-Marx-Stadt (Chemnitz)
Köln (Cologne)
Düsseldorf
Dortmund
Essen
Frankfurt
Stuttgart
München
Nürnberg
Praha (Prague)
Brno
Wien (Vienna)
Linz
Salzburg
Innsbruck
Graz
Klagenfurt
Zürich
Basel
Bern
Genève
Lausanne
Milano
Torino
Genova
Venézia (Venice)
Verona
Bologna
Trieste
Ljubljana
Zagreb
Rijeka
Szczecin (Stettin)
Poznań
Lyon
Marseille
Strasbourg
Dijon
Reims
Lille
Metz
Nancy
Nice
Projection: Conical with two standard parallels
East from Greenwich

15

1:5 000 000

50 0 50 100 miles

50 0 50 100 150 km

DENMARK
København
WEST GERMANY
Berlin
EAST GERMANY
BELGIUM
Brussel
Bonn
LUX.
's Gravenhage
POLAND
Warszawa
U.S.S.R.
Praha
CZECHOSLOVAKIA
Wien
AUSTRIA
Bern
SWITZ.
LIECHT.
HUNGARY
Budapest
ROMANIA
Beograd
București
MONACO
SAN MARINO
Roma
YUGOSLAVIA
BULGARIA
Sofiya
FRANCE
ITALY

Zatoka Gdańska
Wejherowo
Gdynia
Sopot
Gdańsk (Danzig)
Starogard
Kaliningrad (Königsberg)
Pregolya
Chernyakhovsk
Gusev
LITHUANIAN
S.S.R.
Vilnius
R.S.F.S.R.
Braniewo
Elbląg
Malbork
Lyna
Kętrzyn
Gizycko
Olsztyn
▲309
Suwałki
Augustów
Varėna
Alitus
Lida
Grodno
Neman
Mosty
Slonim
Novogrudok
BYELORUSSIAN
Chełmno
Grudziądz
Iława
Ostróda
Mława
Ciechanów
Ostrów Mazowiecka
Brańsk
Hajnówka
238▲
Sokółka
Białystok
Volkovysk
Shchara
S.S.R.
Toruń
Wabrzeżno
Rypin
Lipno
Łomża
Ostrołęka
Bereza
Zduńska Wola
Płock
Pułtusk
Bug
Czeremcha
Włocławek
Wisła (Vistula)
Kutno
Warszawa (Warsaw)
Mińsk Mazowiecki
Siedlce
Biała Podlaska
Brest
Zhabinka
Pripyat
Łęczyca
Łowicz
Pruszków
Żyrardów
Otwock
Łuków
Międzyrzec Podlaska
Skierniewice
Grójec
Dubrovitsa
316▲
Koło
Konin
Łódź
P O L A N D
Pilica
Kozienice
Włodawa
Kovel
Sarny
Palysye
Uzh
Korosten
Turek
Kalisz
Radom
Puławy
Chełm
Lublin
Vladimir Volynskiy
Lutsk
Styr
Goryn
Sluch
Radomyshl
Kiyev
Borispol
Ostrów Wielkopolski
Piotrków Trybunalski
Końskie
Radomsko
Kielce
Ostrowiec Świętokrzyski
Kraśnik
Zamość
Sokal
Dubno
Ostrog
Rovno
Shepetovka
Zhitomir
Fastov
Belaya Tserkov
Częstochowa
Tarnowskie Góry
Jędrzejów
Zawiercie
Pińczów
Sandomierz
Tarnobrzeg
390▲
Kamenka Bugskaya
Radekhov
Brody
Kremenets
Starokonstantinov
Kazatin
Żabrze
Bytom
Gliwice
Sosnowiec
Chorzów
Katowice
Kraków
Dąbrowa
Tarnowska
Wisła (Vistula)
Tarnów
Rzeszów
Przeworsk
Jarosław
Przemyśl
Gorodok
Lvov
471▲
Zolochev
Ternopol
Khmelnitskiy
384▲
Vinnitsa
U. S. S. R.
Zhmerinka
Uman
Bielsko-Biała
Cieszyn
Český Těšín
Nowy Sącz
Jasło
Krosno
Sanok
Sambor
Drogobych
Borislav
Stryi
Turka
Buchach
Chortkov
Zaleshchiki
Kamenets-Podolskiy
Mogilev-Podolskiy
Pervomaisk
U K R A I N I A N
S. S. R.
Ostrava
Frýdek Místek
550
Jablunkovsky Pr.
Západné Beskydy
1725
Tatry
2655
Ružomberok
Nizké Tatry
Východné Beskydy
430
Prešov
Uzhgorod
Ivano-Frankovsk
Nadvornaya
1881▲
Kolomyya
Snyatyn
Khotin
Dnestr
Dnestr
Soroki
Kotovsk
S L O V A K I A
Gottwaldov
Žilina
Váh
Kremnica
Banská Bystrica
Zvolen
Slovenské Rudohorie
Banská Štiavnica
Lučenec
Nitra
Košice
Sátoraljaújhely
Mukachevo
Beregovo
931
Khust
2061▲
Chernovtsy
Starozhinets
Yablonitse
Yedintsy
Beltsy
M O L D A V I A N
Pervomaisk
N. Zámky
Komárno
Hron
Sajó
Miskolc
Tokaj
Tisza
Hernád
Bodrog
Satu Mare
Sighetul
Baia Mare
Pietrosul
2305▲
Vatra-Dornei
Rădăuți
Suceava
Dorohoi
Botoșani
Beltsy
Győr
Tatabánya
Vértes Hg.
Esztergom
Vác
Gyöngyös
Eger
Mezőkövesd
Nyíregyháza
Hajdúböszörmény
Carei
Someș
Dej
Bistrița
2102
Pietrosu
Piatra Neamț
Roman
Iași
429▲
Kishinev
Benderi
Tiraspol
Újpest
BUDAPEST
Cegléd
Szolnok
Karcag
Nagykőrös
Mezőtúr
Debrecen
Oradea
Salonta
Cluj
Turda
Târgu Mureș
Praid
Odorheiul Secuiesc
Bistrița
Bacău
Vaslui
Bîrlad
Székesfehérvár
Kecskemét
Kiskunfélegyháza
H U N G A R Y
Gyula
Mții Bihor
1848▲
Abrud
Aiud
T r a n s i l v a n i a
Miercurea Ciuc
Bretcu
Tecuci
Odessa
Dunaújváros
Dunaföldvár
Kalocsa
Kiskőrös
Kiskunhalas
Szentes
Hódmezővásárhely
Makó
Szeged
Arad
Mureș
Deva
Simeria
Hunedoara
Brad
Alba-Iulia
Media
Sighișoara
Sibiu
Olt
Sfîntu Gheorghe
Brașov
Focșani
Galați
Brăila
467
Tulcea
Sulina
Pécs
Mohács
Baja
Szekszárd
Bátaszék
Subotica
Senta
Kikinda
R O M A N I A
Timișoara
Lugoj
B a n a t
Caransebeș
Carpații Meridionali
Pelea
350
2535▲
Negoiu
2507
Omul
Cîmpina
Cîmpulung
Târgoviște
Ploiești
Rîmnicu Sărat
Buzău
Dunărea (Danube)
Osijek
Novi Sad
Zrenjanin (Petrovgrad)
Petrovaradin
Bečej
Vršac
Bela Crkva
Reșița
2518
2509
Pârîngul Mare
Petroșeni
Porta Orientalis
Târgu Jiu
Rîmnicu Vîlcea
Pitești
Argeș
Dîmbovița
Ialomița
Cernavodă
Constanța
Vinkovci
Brod
Odžak
Brčko
Bijeljina
Zemun
BEOGRAD (Belgrade)
Pančevo
Smederevo
Požarevac
Mehadia
Porțile de Fier
Orșova
Turnu-Severin
V a l a h i a
Jiu
Olt
Slatina
București (Bucharest)
Călărași
Oltenița
Mangalia
B L A C K
S E A
Tuzla
Sava
Valjevo
Kolubara
1346
Kragujevac
Čačak
Bor
Negotin
Craiova
Caracal
Vedea
Turnu Măgurele
Corabia
Danube
Giurgiu
Ruse (Ruschuk)
Zimnica
Silistra
Tolbukhin
G O S L A V I A
Sarajevo
Titova Užice
Timok
Zaječar
Vidin
B U L G A R I A
Sofiya
Mamaia

COPYRIGHT. GEORGE PHILIP & SON, LTD.

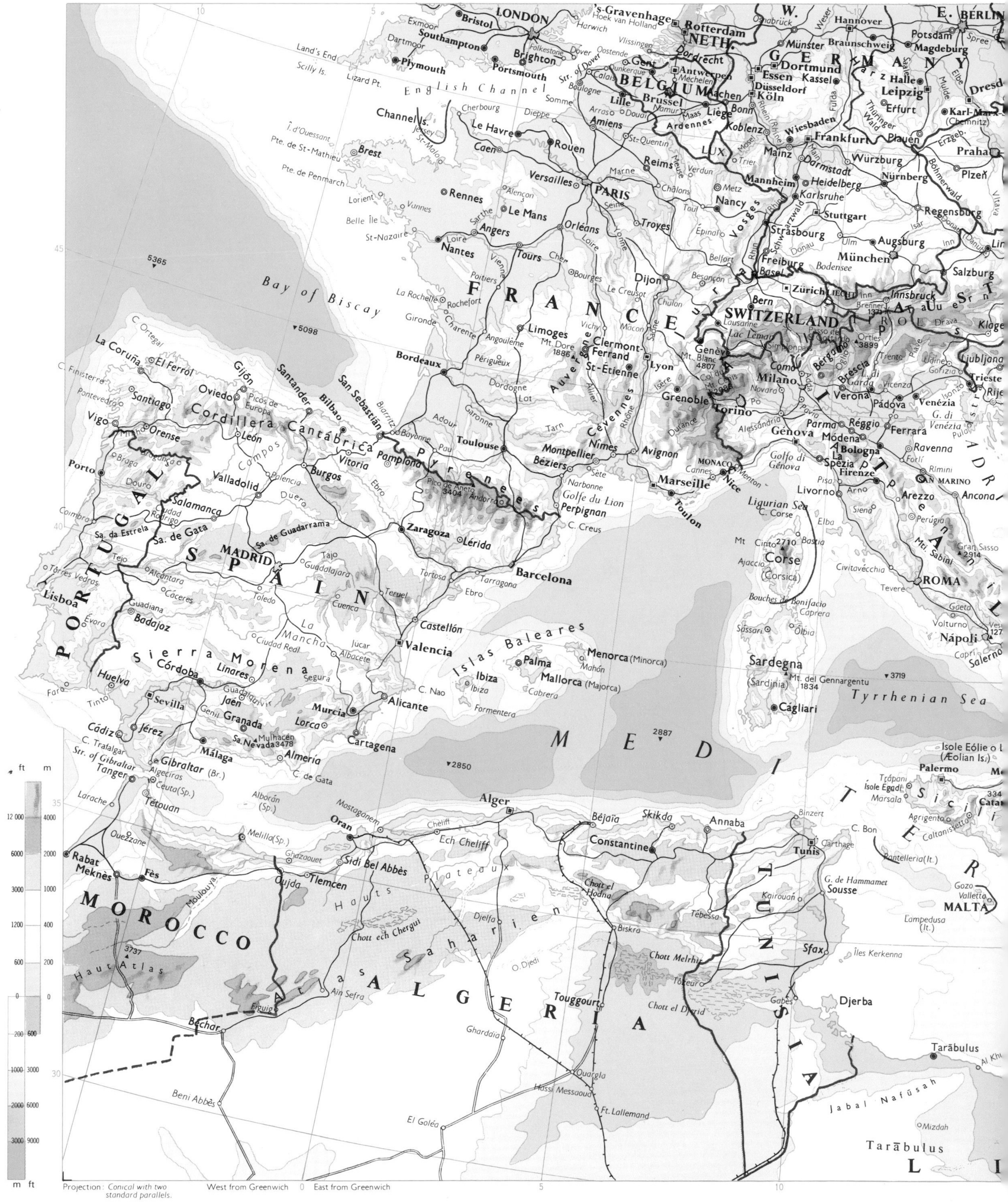

Projection: Conical with two standard parallels.

West from Greenwich 0 East from Greenwich

1:10 000 000

50 0 50 100 150 200 miles
50 0 100 200 300 km

POLAND
Płock
Poznań Wisła (Vistula) Warszawa
Łódź
Brest Pinsk
Radom Polesye Chernigov Konotop Sumy Belgorod Kazanskaya
Lublin Desna Nezhin Poltava Kharkov Volgograd
Legnica Kielce Pripyat Konotop
Wrocław Kraków Tarnów Kiyev Slavyansk Voroshilovgrad Kamensk-Shakhtinskiy
Chorzów Przemyśl Lutsk Styr Goryn Zhitomir Pereyaslav-Khmelnitskiy (Lugansk) Tsimlyansk
CHOSLOVAKIA Lvov Rovno U. Vinnitsa Belaya Tserkov Dnepr (Dnieper) Kremenchug Pavlograd S. R. Shakhty Vdkhr.
Ostrava 550 2655 U. Kirovograd Dnepropetrovsk Gorlovka Makeyevka Novocherkassk
Slavkov Banská Košice Kamenets-Podol'skiy Uman Dneprodzerzhinsk Donetsk Rostov
Bratislava Štiavnica Miskolc Kolomyya Mogilev-Podolskiy Pervomaysk Krivoy Zaporozhye Taganrog Azov
Vah Hron Tokaj Chernovtsy Botosani MOLDAVIAN Balta Voznesensk Rog Zhdanov (Mariupol) Don Manych
Budapest Debrecen Iasi M.S.S.R. Pervomaysk Nikolayev Melitopol Berdyansk Oz. Manych Gudilo
HUNGARY Oradea Pietrosul Beltsy Kishinev Bendery Tiraspol Kherson Perekop Yeisk Tikhoretsk
Kecskemét Körös Cluj 2305 Pietrosu s. s. a Bendery Odessa Belgorod- Karkinitskiy Zaliv Krymskaya Stavropol
Balaton Hódmezővásárhely 2102 Ismail Dnestrovskiy M. Tarkhankut (Crimea) Krasnodar 45
Pécs Szeged Arad ROMANIA Brasov Galati Sulina Yevpatoriya Simferopol 1545 Feodosiya Novorossiysk Armavir Kuban
Zagreb Subotica Timisoara Mures Sibiu (Orasul Stalin) Braila Sevastopol Yalta Kerch
Novi Sad Petrovaradin Negoiu 2535 Carpatii Meridionali Balaklava BLACK SEA Sukhumi
YUGOSLAVIA Sava Beograd 2543 Portile de Fier Pitesti Ploiesti 2211 Batumi
Brod Banja Luka Smederevo Drina Turnu-Severin Craiova Bucuresti Silistra Constanta Potu
BOSNA Sarajevo Morava Dunarea (Danube) Ruse Tolbukhin Ince Burnu Sinop Giresun Tirebolu Trabzon
Durmitor Novi Pazar Vidin Stara Pleven Varna BLACK SEA Samsun Kuzey Anadolu Daglari Rize
2522 Nis Iskur Turnovo Sven Burgas Amasya Kastamonu 2565 Sebin Karahisar Erzincan
Mostar Dubrovnik CRNA GORA Sofiya Planina Maritsa Shipchenski prokhod Inebolu Tokat Sivas
(Ragusa) Kotor Cetinje 2764 Musala Plovdiv BULGARIA Edirne Zonguldak Kastamonu Cankiri Corum Yozgat Firat Keban
Lastovo Skopje 2925 Rhodopi Planina Istanbul Karadeniz Bogazi Eregli Bolu Beypazari Ankara Gurun Malatya
Shkodra Strumica Vardar Serrai Kavalla Tekirdag Marmara Uskudar Iznik Golu Bilecik Sakarya TURKEY Kirsehir Kayseri
Tirana Elbasani Alexandroupolis Enez Denizi Bursa Bandirma Bilecik Sivrihisar Kirsehir Tuz Ercyes Dagi 3770
ALBANIA Bitola Florina Gelibolu (Gallipoli) Canakkale Eskisehir Golu Gokceada Troy Balikesir Kutahya Afyon Karahisar Aksaray Maras
Durresi GREECE Thessaloniki Gokceada Limnos 2033 Canakkale Bogazi Ayvalik Bolvadin Egirdir Konya Niğde Adana Gaziantep
Bari Vlora Oros Athos Enez Lesvos Manisa Biyuk Golu Beysehir Karaman Seyhan Tarsus Osmaniye
Barletta Notia Pindhos Olimbos 2917 Turgutlu Menderes Egirdir Golu Mersin Iskenderun Korfezi Halab
Brindisi Larisa 2033 Izmir Alasehir Isparta Toros Antakya SYRIA
Taranto Kerkira Voriai Sporadhes Volos Khios Samos Aydin Denizli Burdur Toros Daglari Silifke Iskenderun Korfezi Al Ladhiqiyah
Golfo di Taranto Kefallinia Navpaktos Evvoia Ikaria Mugla Elmali Antalya Antalya Korfezi Hama
C. Sta. Maria di Leuca Olympia Athinai Kikladhes Ios 3085 Rodhos Megiste Levkosia (Nicosia) Tarabulus
La Sila 1929 Zakinthos Piraievs Siros Naxos Dhodhekanisos Rodhos 4486 (Kastellorizon) Ammokhostos (Famagusta) Baniyas Dimashq (Damascus)
Reggio Kalamata Navplion Dhodhekanisos CYPRUS Troodos 1951 Larnax Bayrut (Beirut) ash Sheikh 2814
Str. di Messina Spartivento Peloponnisos Sparti Milos Ios Kithira Lemesos LEBANON 3083 Jabal ad Duruz
Ionian Sea 5121 Akra Tainaron Andikithira Khania Idhi Oros 2456 Iraklion Karpathos Sayda Jordan Bosra
4135 AEGEAN SEA Kriti Akko Haifa Amman
Bahr el Miyet -395
Cyrene (Barce) Al Marj 3174 Tel Aviv-Yafo Jerusalem
Banghazi Tobruq Rashid Bahra el Burullus Gaza ISRAEL JORDAN Petra Ma'an
Khalij Surt Barqa Matruh Salum Khalig el Salum El 'Alamein El Iskandariya El Mahalla el Kubra Dumyat Bur Said El 'Arish Buheirat Murrat el-Kubra Gebel Al Aqabah
LIBYA A EGYPT Tanta El Qantara Isma'iliya Suez El Suweis el Tih Es Sina' 2637
EL QAHIRA El Faiyum Beni Suef Nile Khalig es Suweis Khalij al 'Aqabah

------ Division between Greeks
and Turks in Cyprus;
Turks to the North.

ITALY AND THE BALKAN STATES

SWITZERLAND

Lyon
Genève
Thonon
Annecy
Mte Blanc 4807
D'AOSTA
Matterhorn Mte 4478
Mte Rosa 4637
Grenoble
Mt Pelvoux 4103
Briançon
Col du M. Cenis 2083
Embrun
DAUPHINÉ
Nyons
Orange
Avignon
Valence
Montélimar
Vienne
Tournon
Voiron
Moûtiers
St-Jean-de-Maurienne
Col du Galibier 2556
Mont Viso 3841
Cúneo
P. dei Giovi 472
Saluzzo
Mondovì
PIEMONTE
Pinerolo
Torino (Turin)
Chivasso
Ivrea
Biella
Novara
Vercelli
Casale
Asti
Alba
Alessándria
Tortona
Acqui
Savona
Riv. di Ponente
Genova (Genoa)
Chiávari
Riv. di Levante
La Spézia
Carrara

SWITZERLAND
Brenner
Passo di Resia
Merano
Ortles 3899
Bressanone
Brennero 1371
Bolzano
Adamello 3554
TRENTINO ALTO ADIGE
Trento
Rovereto
Lago di Garda
Brescia
Bérgamo
Como
Lecco
LOMBARDIA
Busto Arsizio
Milano (Milan)
Pavia
Lodi
Crema
Piacenza
Cremona
Mántova (Mantua)
Verona
Vicenza
Pádova (Padua)
Venézia (Venice)
Golfo di Venézia
Chióggia
Rovigo
Adige
Ferrara
Comácchio
Ravenna
Réggio
Módena
Bologna
Parma
EMÍLIA ROMAGNA
Imola
Faenza
Forlì
Cesena
Rímini
Rubicone
Pésaro
Fano
San Marino
SAN MARINO
Mte. Cimone
P. di Porretta
Pistóia
Lucca
Prato
Firenze (Florence)
Livorno (Leghorn)
Pisa
Pontedera
Arno
Volterra
TOSCANA
Siena
Arezzo
Cortona
L. Trasimeno
Chiusi
Senigállia
Ancona
Loreto
Úrbino
Fabriano
Macerata
Civitanova
Perúgia
Assisi
Fóligno
Monti Vettore
UMBRIA
Spoleto 2478
Ascoli Piceno
San Benedetto
Téramo
Gran Sasso 2914
Terni
Rieti
MARCHE
Pescara
Chieti
Ortona
Mt. Amaro 2795
Vasto
Térmoli
Sannicandro
Monte Gargano
Monte S. Ángelo
G. di Manfredónia
Manfredónia
Fóggia
Cerignola
Barletta
Trani
Andria
Corato
Bari
Molfetta
Bitonto

Merano
Villach
Klagenfurt
Bleiburg
Maribor
FRIULI VENEZIA GIULIA
Udine
Kobarid (Caporetto)
Gorizia
Trieste
Ljubljana
Sava
Zagreb
HRVATSKA
Rijeka (Fiume)
Pula (Pola)
Rovinj
ISTRA
Krk
Cres
Lošinj
Pag
Dugi Otok
Zadar
Šibenik
Vis
Split
Brač
Hvar
Korčul
Lastovo
Palagruža (Yugoslavia)

ADRIATIC

A L P I

GÉNOVA
Impéria
San Remo
MONACO
Monte Carlo
Menton
Nice
Cannes
Antibes
Grasse
Draguignan
Fréjus
St-Tropez
Toulon
Marseille
Aix
Martigues
Iles d'Hyères
PROVENCE
LIGURIAN SEA

C. Corse
Calvi
Mt. Cinto 2710
Bastia
CORSE (CORSICA) (Fr.)
Ajaccio
Aléria
Sartène
Eto. Vecchio
Bonifacio
Bouches de Bonifacio
Maddalena
Caprera
Asinara
C. Falcone
Golfo dell' Asinara
Golfo Aranci
Ólbia
Terranova
Pta Falcone
Porto Torres
Sássari
Álghero
Bosa
Nuoro
Orosei
Ozieri
2855
Orgosolo
Tirso
Oristano
Ghilarza
Sorgono
Mt Santo
SARDEGNA (SARDINIA)
Mt. Gennargentu 1834
Arbatax
Iérzu
Golfo di Oristano
Terralba
Iglésias
Carbónia
Portoscuso
G. di Pálmas
Carbonara
Cágliari
Golfo di Cágliari
C. Spartivento

Caprária
Piombino
Portoferráio
Elba
Grosseto
Orbetello
Mte. Argentário
Fiora
Civitavécchia
L. di Bolsena
Orvieto
Viterbo
Rieti
L. di Bracciano
ROMA (Rome)
Ostia
Tívoli
Anzio
Latina
Sabáudia
Terracina
Gaeta
Fondi
Gariglianо
Ísole Ponziane
Ischia
Cápri
Torre Annunziata
Nápoli (Naples)
Vesúvio 1277
Nocera
Avellino
Salerno
Sele
CAMPÁGNA
Frosinone
Cassino
Benevento
Caserta
Aversa
Potenza
Matera
Spinazzola
Putignano
BASILICATA
Agri
PUGLIA
Táranto
Golfo di Táranto
Pisciotta
Sinni
2271
3719
Castellabate

MOLISE
S. Severo
Campobasso
LÁZIO

▼3719

TYRRHENIAN SEA

Cágliari
Cosenza 1929
CALÁBRIA
Nicastro
Catanzaro
Crotone
Sambiase
Pizzo
Strómboli
Salina
Ísole Eólie o Lípari
Lípari
Vulcano
C. Peloro
Milazzo
Messina
Str. di Messina
Réggio
Táurianova
Pálmi
Scilla
Gioia
Squillace
C. Spartivento

Ústica (It.)
Trápani
Érice
Castellammare
Palermo
Términi
Cefalù
Patti
Mistretta
Monti Nébrodi
Randazzo
Adrano
Etna 3340
Giarre
Isole Égadi
Favignana
Marsala
Castelvetrano
Segesta
Alcamo
Menfi
Selinunte
Sciacca
Pto. Empédocle
Agrigento
Licata
Caltanissetta
Enna
Piazza Armerina
Caltagirone
Adrano
Paternò
Lentini
Catánia
Augusta
Siracusa (Syracuse)
Favara
Platani
Salso
Gela
Vittória
Ragusa
Ferla
Noto
Mòdica
Íspica
C. Passero
SICILIA

1730

Pantelleria (It.)
AFRICA
C. Bon

MEDIT

Gozo
Comino
Valletta
MALTA

MALTA INSET:
C. S. Dimitri
Gozo (Għawdex)
Comino (Kemmuna)
Victoria (Rabat)
St Pauls Bay
Mosta
Mdina
Rabat
239
Hamrun
Valletta
Sliema
Luqa
Marsaxlokk
Zurrieq
Birzebbuga
MALTA
1:1 000 000
10 miles
5 10 15 km

S.E. EUROPE INSET:
FRANCE
SWITZ.
LIECHT.
AUSTRIA
Wien
Bern
HUNGARY
Budapest
U.S.S.R.
ROMANIA
București
ITALY
SAN MARINO
Venezia
Trieste
Roma
Nápoli
Corse (Fr.)
ADRIATIC SEA
YUGOSLAVIA
Beograd
Sofiya
BULGARIA
ALBANIA
Tiranë
Thessaloníki
GREECE
Athínai
AEGEAN SEA
TURKEY
Sicília
MALTA
Kríti
MEDITERRANEAN SEA
S.E. EUROPE
POLITICAL
1:25 000 000

1:5 000 000
50 0 50 100 miles
50 0 50 100 150 km
ROMANIA
U.S.S.R.
YUGOSLAVIA
BULGARIA
TURKEY
ALBANIA
GREECE
BLACK SEA
IONIAN SEA
MEDITERRANEAN SEA
AEGEAN SEA
Transilvania
Carpatii Meridionali
Carpathians
Banat
Valahia
Dobrogea
Stara Planina
Rhodopi Planina
MAKEDONIJA
MAKEDHONIA
SERBIA
CRNA GORA
THRÁKI
THESSALÍA
STEREÁ ELLÁS
PELOPÓNNISOS
ÍPIROS
Píndhos Óros
KIKLÁDHES
DHODHEKÁNISOS
KRITI
Anadolu
Istranca Dağları
Str. of Otranto
Marmara denizi
Bucureşti (Bucharest)
Beograd (Belgrade)
Sofiya (Sofia)
Tirana
Athínai (Athens)
Piraievs (Piraeus)
İstanbul
Üsküdar
Thessaloníki
Timişoara
Szeged
Arad
Hódmezővásárhely
Makó
Pécs
Mohács
Subotica
Osijek
Novi Sad
Zemun
Pančevo
Sarajevo
Titograd (Podgorica)
Skopje
Niš
Priština
Kragujevac
Kraljevo
Craiova
Ploieşti
Braşov
Sibiu
Galaţi
Brăila
Constanţa
Izmail
Reni
Ruse (Ruschuk)
Pleven
Varna
Burgas
Plovdiv
Edirne
Bitola (Monastir)
Ohrid
Lárisa
Vólos
Pátrai
Kérkira (Corfu)
Brindisi
Lecce
Otranto
C. d'Otranto
Capo Sta. Maria di Leuca
Bursa
Izmir (Smyrna)
Çanakkale
Limnos
Lésvos
Khíos
Sámos
Rodhos
Náxos
Thíra
Kíthira
Irákion
Khaniá
Thásos
Samothráki
Gökçeada
Bozcaada
Évvoia
Voríai Sporádhes
Skíros
Ándros
Tínos
Ikaría
Kárpathos
Kásos
Kefallinía
Zákinthos
Levkás (Sta. Maura)
Dunărea (Danube)
Olt
Mureşul
Drava
Sava
Drina
Morava
Vardar
Struma
Mesta
Maritsa
Arda
Ergene
Tundzha
Prut
Siret
Musala 2925
Olimbos 2917
Durmitor 2522
Korab 2764
Smólikas 2637
Moldoveanu 2535
Athos 2033
Ida 1766
East from Greenwich
18 20 22 24 26 28

ICELAND
on the same scale
as general map
Vatnajökull
Reykjavík
Akureyri
Húsavík
Keflavík
Akranes
Hafnarfjörður
Ísafjörður
Faxaflói
Hekla
NORWEGIAN
SEA
Lofoten
Vesterålen
Tromsø
Narvik
Bodø
Kiruna
Gällivare
Luleå
Umeå
Skellefteå
Oulu
Kemi
Tornio
Haparanda
Hammerfest
Vadsø
Trondheim
Kristiansund
Ålesund
Molde
Namsos
Östersund
Härnösand
Vaasa
Kokkola
Jakobstad
Rovaniemi
Inari
Arctic Circle
OULU
KUOPIO
KESKI-SUOMEN
VAASA
N-TRÖNDELAG
SØR-TRØNDELAG
JÄMTLAND
NORRBOTTEN
VÄSTERBOTTEN
Kvarken

1:5 000 000

20 20 0 20 40 60 80 100 miles
40 20 0 40 80 120 160 km

East from Greenwich

Projection: Conical with two standard parallels

FINLAND

Helsinki (Helsingfors), Lahti, Heinola, Kotka, Lovisa (Lovisa), Hämeenlinna, Tampere, Pori, Rauma, Turku (Åbo), Uusikaupunki, Hangö (Hanko), Porvoo (Borgå)

ESTONIAN S.S.R.

Tallinn, Haapsalu, Pärnu, Viljandi, Valga, Kingisepp, Hiiumaa (Dagö), Saaremaa (Ösel), Paldiski

LATVIAN S.S.R.

Riga, Valmiera, Cēsis, Ventspils, Liepāja, Jelgava, Bauska, Tukums, Kuldīga

Rīgas Jūras Līcis (Gulf of Riga)
Ruhnu
Runö

LITHUANIAN S.S.R.

Kaunas, Vilnius, Klaipėda, Šiauliai, Panevėžys, Telšiai

R.S.F.S.R.

Sovetsk, Chernyakhovsk, Kaliningrad

POLAND

Gdańsk, Gdynia, Zatoka Gdańska, Elbląg, Malbork, Grudziądz, Toruń, Bydgoszcz, Szczecin (Stettin), Grodno, Białystok, Łomża, Ostrołęka, Augustów, Suwałki

SWEDEN

STOCKHOLM, Uppsala, Västerås, Eskilstuna, Södertälje, Nyköping, Norrköping, Linköping, Motala, Örebro, Karlstad, Gävle, Sandviken, Söderhamn, Hudiksvall, Bollnäs, Falun, Borlänge, Mora, Siljan, Ludvika, Hedemora, Avesta, Fagersta, Köping, Kumla, Katrineholm, Nässjö, Jönköping, Värnamo, Växjö, Kalmar, Oskarshamn, Västervik, Nybro, Karlskrona, Karlshamn, Kristianstad, Hässleholm, Halmstad, Varberg, Falkenberg, Göteborg, Borås, Mölndal, Trollhättan, Vänersborg, Lidköping, Skövde, Mariestad, Uddevalla, Strömstad, Ulricehamn, Kungsbacka, Huskvarna, Vetlanda, Ljungby, Helsingborg, Landskrona, Malmö, Trelleborg, Ystad

Lake Vänern, Lake Vättern, Lake Mälaren, Lake Hjälmaren, Lake Siljan

Öland, Gotland, Visby, Gotska Sandön, Fårö

Åland (Ahvenanmaa), Mariehamn (Maarianhamina)

NORWAY

OSLO, Drammen, Kongsberg, Skien, Larvik, Sandefjord, Tønsberg, Moss, Fredrikstad, Sarpsborg, Halden, Hamar, Lillehammer, Gjøvik, Kongsvinger, Arendal, Grimstad, Lillesand, Kristiansand, Mandal, Farsund, Flekkefjord, Egersund (Eigersund), Stavanger, Sandnes, Haugesund, Kopervik, Bergen

OPPLAND, HEDMARK, BUSKERUD, TELEMARK, AUST-AGDER, VEST-AGDER, ROGALAND, HORDALAND, ØSTFOLD

DENMARK

KØBENHAVN (Copenhagen), Helsingør, Roskilde, Køge, Næstved, Slagelse, Korsør, Kalundborg, Holbæk, Odense, Svendborg, Nyborg, Ålborg, Hjørring, Frederikshavn, Randers, Århus, Horsens, Vejle, Fredericia, Kolding, Esbjerg, Varde, Ribe, Viborg, Silkeborg, Herning, Holstebro, Skive, Struer, Thisted

Sjælland, Fyn, Lolland, Falster, Møn, Bornholm, Rønne, Nexø

The Sound, Store Bælt, Lille Bælt, Kattegat, Skagerrak, Limfjorden, Jylland

WEST GERMANY

Hamburg, Lübeck, Kiel, Flensburg, Schleswig, Bremen, Bremerhaven, Oldenburg, Wilhelmshaven, Cuxhaven, Groningen, Emden

EAST GERMANY

Rostock, Schwerin, Wismar, Stralsund, Greifswald, Anklam, Neubrandenburg, Neustrelitz, Prenzlau, Güstrow, Rügen, Usedom

NETHERLANDS

BALTIC SEA

GULF OF FINLAND

SKAGERRAK

m ft
6000 4500 3000 1500 600 0
2000 1500 1000 400 200 0 200-600 ft

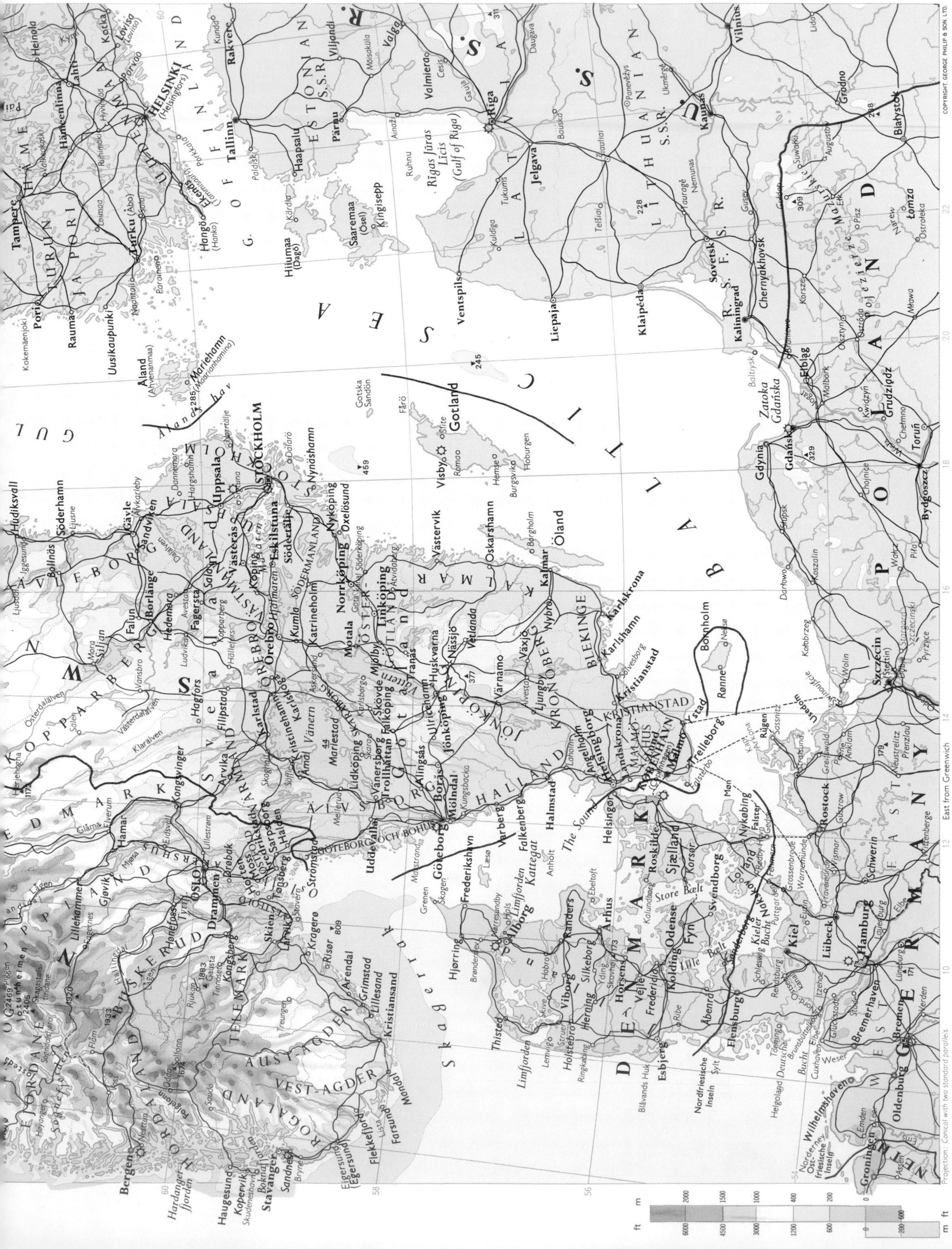

Kolguyev
P-ov. Kanin
Cheshskaya Guba
Timanskiy Kryazh
Bolshezemelskaya Tundra
Malozemelskaya Tundra
Pechorskaya Guba
Pechora
Arctic Circle
Kolskiy Poluostrov
P-ov. Rybachiy
Murmansk
Beloye More (White Sea)
Arkhangelsk (Archangel)
Onezhskaya Guba
Dvinskaya Guba
Kandalakshskiy Zaliv
Ostrov Morzhovets
Mezen
Kotlas
Syktyvkar
Ukhta
Vorkuta
Salekhard
Kirov
Perm
Nizhniy Tagil
SVERDLOVSK
Zlatoust
Chelyabinsk
Ufa
Magnitogorsk
Orenburg
Serov
Berezniki
Izhevsk
KUYBYSHEV
Tolyatti
Syzran
Kazan
Ulyanovsk
Penza
Saransk
Cheboksary
Yoshkar Ola
GORKIY
Dzerzhinsk
Ivanovo
Kostroma
Yaroslavl
Vologda
Cherepovets
Rybinskoye Vdkhr.
Vladimir
Ryazan
MOSKVA (Moscow)
Kalinin
Tula
Kaluga
Lipetsk
Tambov
Orel
Bryansk
Smolensk
Vitebsk
Mogilev
Gomel
Minsk
Vilnius
Kaunas
Riga
Tallinn
Tartu
Pskov
Novgorod
LENINGRAD
Petrozavodsk
Ladozhskoye Ozero
Onezhskoye Ozero
Helsinki
Tampere
Turku
Oulu
Stockholm
Gulf of Bothnia
G. of Finland
FINLAND
LAPPLAND
SWEDEN
NORWAY
KARELIAN A.S.S.R.
ESTONIAN S.S.R.
LATVIAN S.S.R.
LITHUANIAN S.S.R.
BYELORUSSIAN S.S.R. (WHITE RUSSIA)
RUSSIAN SOVIET FEDERATIVE SOCIALIST REPUBLIC
TATAR A.S.S.R.
UDMURT A.S.S.R.
MARI A.S.S.R.
CHUVASH A.S.S.R.
MORDOVIAN A.S.S.R.
BASHKIR A.S.S.R.
U r a l s
Severnyye Uvaly
Valdayskaya Vozvyshennost
Polesye (Pripet Marshes)
Kaliningrad (Königsberg)
Klaipeda (Memel)
Liepaja
Brest
Grodno
Bialystok
WARSZAWA (Warsaw)
POLAND
Lublin
Aland (Ahvenanmaa)
Saaremaa (Ösel)
Hiiumaa (Dagö)

1:10 000 000

100 50 0 50 100 150 200 miles

100 0 100 200 300 km

R.S.F.S.R.
1. Daghestan A.S.S.R.
2. Kabardino–Balkar A.S.S.R.
3. Mari A.S.S.R.
4. Mordovian A.S.S.R.
5. North Ossetian A.S.S.R.
6. Tatar A.S.S.R.
7. Udmurt A.S.S.R.
8. Chuvash A.S.S.R.
9. Checheno–Ingush A.S.S.R.
AZERBAIJAN
10. Nakhichevan A.S.S.R.
GEORGIA
11. Abkhaz A.S.S.R.
12. Adzhar A.S.S.R.

Projection: Conical Orthomorphic with two standard parallels

East from Greenwich

1:20 000 000

100 0 100 200 300 400 500 miles

100 0 200 400 600 800 km

1:50 000 000

250 0 250 500 750 1000 miles

250 0 500 1000 1500 km

COPYRIGHT. GEORGE PHILIP & SON, LTD.

Projection: Bonne

PACIFIC OCEAN

Aleutian Is.
Bering Sea
C. Dezhnev
Bering Str.
Kamchatka Peninsula
Klyuchevsk Vol. 4750
Sea of Okhotsk
Kuril Is.
Sakhalin
Hokkaido
Honshu
Shikoku
Kyushu
Japan
Sea of Japan
Korea Str.
Ryukyu Is.
Formosa
Tropic of Cancer
Bonin Is.
Caroline Is.
Guam
Palau Is.
Philippine Is.
Luzon
Mindanao
Cape Johnson Deep 10 497
Philippine Sea
Halmahera
Moluccas
New Guinea
Arafura Sea
Australia
Banda Sea
Ceram
Timor
Flores
Celebes Sea
Celebes
Sulu Sea
Palawan
Borneo
Kinabalu 4101
Makasar Strait
Java Sea
Bali
East Indies
Sunda Is.
Lesser
Sumatra
South China Sea
Hainan
G. of Tonkin
Si-kiang
Canton
Str. of Malacca
Malay Peninsula
G. of Thailand
Mekong
Menam
Irrawaddy
Salween
Tsangpo
Brahmaputra
Bay of Bengal
Andaman Is.
Nicobar Is.
Ceylon
Polk Strait
Equator
Maldive Is.
Laccadive Is.
Chagos Arch.
Amirantes
Seychelles
Socotra (C. Guardafui)
Ras Asir
G. of Aden
Somali Peninsula
G. of Oman
The Gulf
Arabian Sea
INDIAN OCEAN
C. Comorin
Gulf of Mannar
Western Ghats
Eastern Ghats
Deccan
Godavari
Krishna
Narmada
Godavari
Yamuna
Ganga
Indus
Thar Desert
Sutlej
Sulaiman Range
Hindu Kush
Karakoram Ra.
Pamir
Takla Makan
Tarim Basin
Tarim
Lop Nor
Turfan Basin
Tien Shan
Altai
Belukha 4506
Sayan Mts.
Selenga
Plateau of Mongolia
Koko Nor
Kunlun Shan
Plateau of Tibet
Everest 8848
Himalaya
Ganges
C H I N A
Great Plain of China
Hwang-ho
Yang-tze-kiang
Yellow Sea
East China Sea
Pei Ho
Manchurian Plain
Sungari
Amur
Great Khingan Mts.
Yablonovy Ra.
Stanovoy Ra.
Vitim
Aldan
Lena
Verkhoyansk Range
Indigirka
Kolyma
Gydan Ra. (Kolyma)
New Siberian Is.
Wrangel I.
ARCTIC OCEAN
C. Chelyuskin
Severnaya Zemlya
Taimyr Peninsula
Laptev Sea
Kotuy
Lower Tunguska
Yenisei
Central Siberian Plateau
Angara
Ob
Irtysh
West Siberian Plain
Tobol
L. Balkhash
Ili
Chu
Syr Darya
Amu Darya
Aral Sea
Turanian Plain
Ural
Irtysh
Narodnaya 1894
Ural Mountains
Ob
N. Dvina
Kolguyev
Novaya Zemlya
Kara Sea
Barents Sea
Kola Pen.
White Sea
North Cape
Svalbard
Greenland
Iceland
British Isles
North Sea
Baltic Sea
Scandinavia
Finland
North European Plain
Central Russian Uplands
S t e p p e
Volga
Don
Dnepr
Black Sea
Bosporus
Anatolia
Taurus Mts.
Cyprus
Mediterranean Sea
Adriatic Sea
Rhine
Elbe
Oder
Vistula
Danube
Carpathians
Caucasus
Elbruz 5633
Caspian Sea
Elburz Mts.
Great Salt Desert
Plateau of Iran
Zagros
Helmand
Harirud
Tigris
Euphrates
Mesopotamia
Syrian Desert
Dead Sea
Sinai Pen.
Suez Canal
Red Sea
Nile
Libyan Desert
A r a b i a
Er Rub al Khali
Asir
Lake Victoria

m 6000 4000 2000 1000 400 200 0
ft 18 000 12 000 6000 3000 1200 600 0
m 0 200 2000 4000 6000 8000
ft 0 600 6000 12 000 18 000 24 000

1:50 000 000

250 0 250 500 750 1000 miles
250 0 500 1000 1500 km

COPYRIGHT GEORGE PHILIP & SON, LTD.

A R C T I C O C E A N

P A C I F I C O C E A N

I N D I A N O C E A N

Oceans, Seas and Water bodies:
Bering Sea, Sea of Okhotsk, Sea of Japan, Yellow Sea, East China Sea, South China Sea, Philippine Sea, Celebes Sea, Sulu Sea, Banda Sea, Molucca Sea, Java Sea, Bay of Bengal, Arabian Sea, The Gull, G. of Oman, Caspian Sea, Black Sea, Red Sea, Mediterranean Sea, Baltic Sea, North Sea, Kara Sea, Barents Sea, Laptev Sea, Aral Sea, Ozero Balkhash, Ozero Baykal

Countries and Regions:
U. S. S. R., MONGOLIA, MANCHURIA, INNER MONGOLIA, CHINESE REPUBLIC, CHINA, SINKIANG UIGUR, TIBET, INDIA, PAKISTAN, AFGHANISTAN, IRAN (PERSIA), KASHMIR, NEPAL, BHUTAN, BANGLADESH, BURMA, THAILAND (SIAM), CAMBODIA, VIETNAM, LAOS, MALAYSIA, INDONESIA, PHILIPPINES, JAPAN, KOREA, SRI LANKA (CEYLON), SAUDI ARABIA, IRAQ, SYRIA, TURKEY, CYPRUS, ISRAEL, JORDAN, LEBANON, KUWAIT, BAHRAIN, QATAR, UNITED ARAB EMIRATES, OMAN, YEMEN, SOUTH YEMEN, EGYPT, LIBYA, SUDAN, ETHIOPIA, SOMALI REP., KENYA, TANZANIA, UGANDA, RWANDA, BURUNDI, ZAIRE, ZAMBIA, MALAWI, DJIBOUTI, SEYCHELLES, MALDIVES, BRUNEI, BORNEO, EUROPE, AFRICA, UNITED KINGDOM, ICELAND, AUSTRALIA

Cities and Towns:
London, Paris, Berlin, Roma, Wien, Warszawa, Beograd, Thessaloníki, Athínai, Istanbul, Izmir, Bursa, Ankara, Erzurum, Halab, Dimashq, Bayrūt, Jerusalem, Jidda, Makkah (Mecca), Al Madinah, El Qâhira, El Iskandarîya, Aswân, El Obeid, El Khartûm, Kassala, Port Sudan, Suakin, Addis Abeba, Harer, Juba, Mogadishu, Obbia, Nairobi, Mombasa, Dar es Salaam, Moskva, Leningrad, Murmansk, Arkhangelsk, Odessa, Rostov, Tbilisi, Yerevan, Baku, Astrakhan, Orenburg, Chelyabinsk, Magnitogorsk, Sverdlovsk, Tobolsk, Omsk, Tomsk, Novosibirsk, Barnaul, Semipalatinsk, Krasnoyarsk, Kemerovo, Irkutsk, Chita, Kyakhta, Yakutsk, Okhotsk, Nikolayevsk, Vladivostok, Khabarovsk, Komsomolsk, Petropavlovsk, Kurganskiy, Mys Chukotskiy, Alma Ata, Tashkent, Samarkand, Bukhara, Khiva, Ashkhabad, Mary, Mashhad, Tehrān, Esfahān, Shiraz, Tabriz, Bandar e Bushehr, Zāhedān, Baghdad, Al Basrah, Kuwait, Muscat, Gwadar, Karachi, Quetta, Kandahār, Kabul, Herāt, Peshawar, Lahore, Delhi, Agra, Kanpur, Allahabad, Lucknow, Varanasi, Calcutta, Bombay, Hyderabad, Madras, Pondicherry, Goa, Ahmadabad, Simla, Colombo, Ulaanbaatar (Ulan Bator), Hovd, Wulumuchi (Urumchi), Kashgar, Soche, Aksu, Yarkand, Harbin, Changchun, Shenyang (Mukden), Peiping, Tientsin, Tsingtao, Tsinan, Lu-ta, Sian, Lanchow, Chengtu, Chungking, Kweiyang, Kunming, Nanking, Wuhan, Shanghai, Hangchow, Nanchang, Soochow, Foochow, Canton, Hong Kong, Macau, Hankiang, Changsha, Hainan, Hanoi, Hué, Phnom Penh, Ho Chi Minh, Bangkok, Rangoon, Mandalay, Myitkyina, Lhasa, Dacca, Kuala Lumpur, George Town, Singapore, Jakarta, Manila, Davao, Tokyo, Yokohama, Nagoya, Kyoto, Osaka, Kobe, Sapporo, Hakodate, Pusan, Seoul

Rivers and physical features:
Rhine, Danube, Nile, Tigris, Euphrates, Volga, Dnepr, Ob, Irtysh, Yenisey, Lena, Aldan, Amur, Angara, Ganges, Indus, Brahmaputra, Irrawaddy, Mekong, Yangtze Kiang, Hwang Ho, Narmada, Godavari, Syr Darya, Tarim

Tropic of Cancer
Arctic Circle
Equator
East from Greenwich

Projection: Bonne

ISRAEL AND WEST JORDAN

1:1 000 000

Projection: Conical with two standard parallels

East from Greenwich

1:15 000 000

100 0 100 200 300 400 miles
100 0 100 200 300 400 500 600 km

Major labels

LEBANON
Bayrût
SYRIA
Dimashq (Damascus)
Haifa
ISRAEL
Tel Aviv-Yafo
Jerusalem
Gaza
Amman
JORDAN
IRAQ
Baghdad
Karbalā'
An Nāsiriyah
Al Basrah
KUWAIT
Al Kuwayt (Kuwait)
IRAN (PERSIA)
Esfahan
Yazd
Shiraz
Bandar 'Abbās
THE GULF
BAHRAIN
QATAR
Doha
UNITED ARAB EMIRATES (TRUCIAL STATES)
Abū Zabī (Abu Dhabi)
Gulf of Oman
Masqat (Muscat)

EGYPT
Aswân
RED SEA
SAUDI ARABIA
An Nafūd
Ar Riyād (Riyadh)
Al Madinah
Jiddah
Makkah (Mecca)
Tropic of Cancer
Ar Rab'al Khālī
OMAN
Al Masirah
Socotra (South Yemen)

SUDAN
BAHR EL AHMAR
El Khartûm (Khartoum)
Omdurmân
KASSALA
Bûr Sûdân (Port Sudan)
ERITREA
Asmera (Asmara)
L. Tana
ETHIOPIA
Addis Abeba (Addis Ababa)
YEMEN
Sana
SOUTH YEMEN
Al 'Adan (Aden)
Madinat al Shaab
Gulf of Aden
DJIBOUTI
Djibouti
Hargeisa
SOMALI REP.
Mogadishu

KENYA
L. Turkana
UGANDA
JONGLEI
SHARQ EL ISTIWA'IYA
ZAIRE
INDIAN OCEAN

Projection: Sanson-Flamsteed's Sinusoidal
East from Greenwich
COPYRIGHT. GEORGE PHILIP & SON. LTD

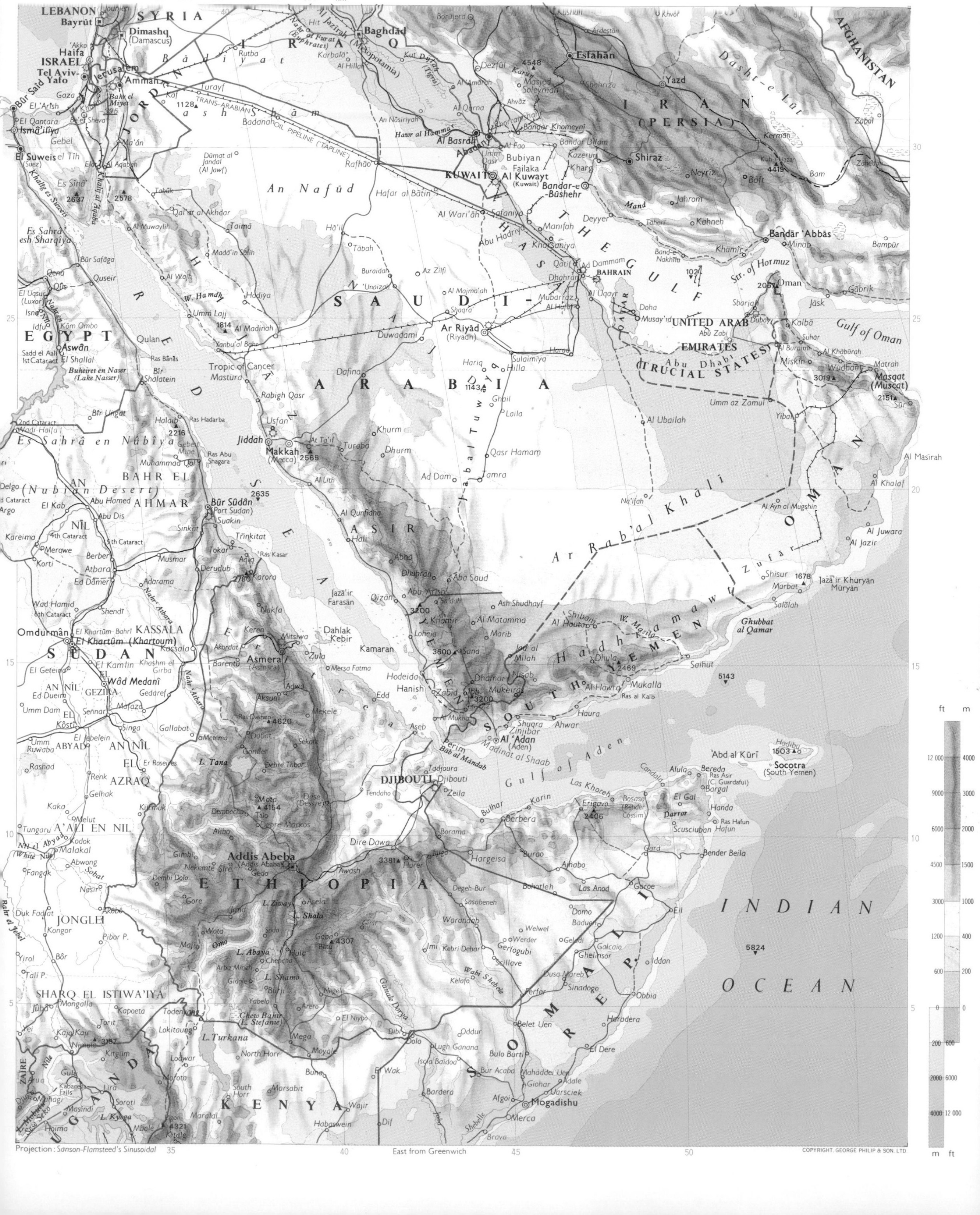

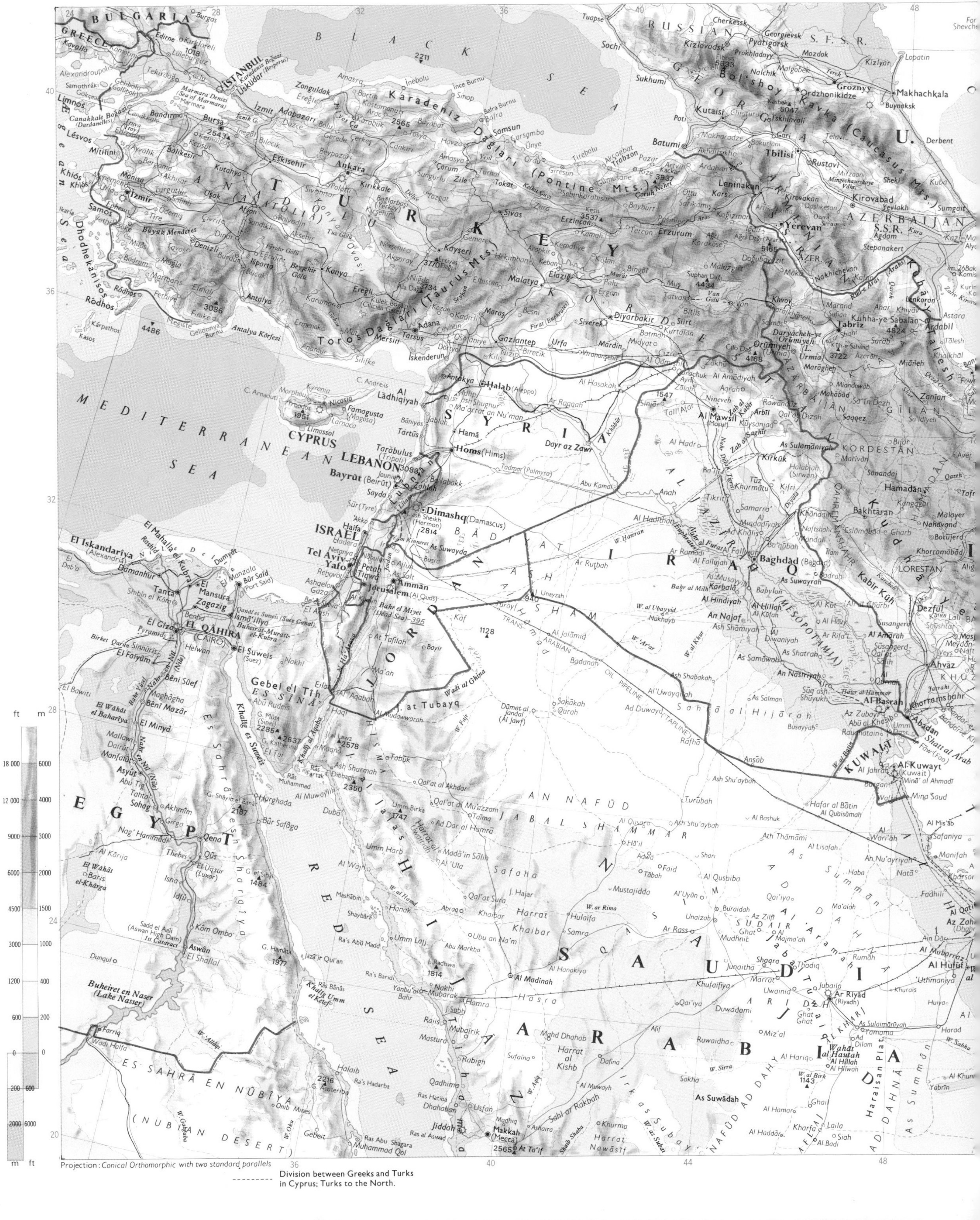

Projection: Conical Orthomorphic with two standard parallels

----- Division between Greeks and Turks in Cyprus; Turks to the North.

1:10 000 000

100 0 100 200 300 miles

100 0 100 200 300 400 500 km

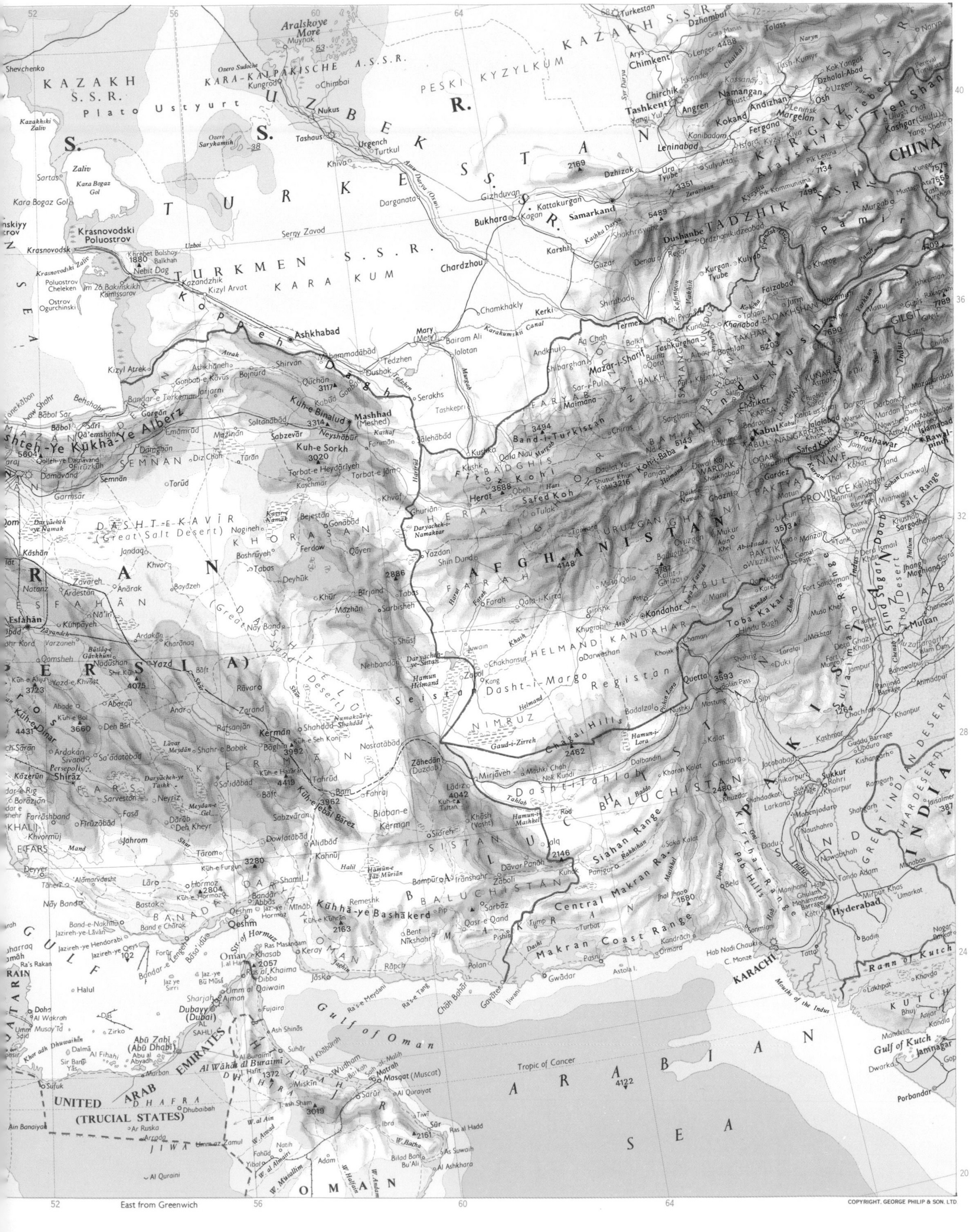

52 East from Greenwich 56 60 64

U.S.S.R.

ARABIAN SEA

Tropic of Cancer

HINDU KUSH
KARAKORAM Mountains
HERAT
BADGHIS
FARYAB
SAMANGAN
BADAKHSHAN
TAKHAR
BAGHLAN
GHOR
URUZGAN
GHAZNI
ZABUL
KANDAHAR
HELMAND
NIMRUZ
FARAH
AFGHANISTAN
Kabul
Peshawar
Rawalpindi
Islamabad
Srinagar
JAMMU AND KASHMIR
NORTH WEST FRONTIER
Khyber Pass
Nanga Parbat
K
PAKISTAN
BALUCHISTAN
Quetta
Kalat
Makran Coast Range
Central Makran Range
Siahan Range
Kirthar Range
Pab Hills
Toba Kakar
Chagai Hills
Gwadar
Karachi
Hyderabad
SIND
Sukkur
Larkana
PUNJAB
Lahore
Amritsar
Sialkot
Gujranwala
Faisalabad
Multan
Bahawalpur
HIMACHAL PRADESH
Simla
Ludhiana
Chandigarh
Ambala
Dehra Dun
Hardwar
Saharanpur
HARYANA
DELHI
Meerut
Moradabad
Bikaner
Great Indian Desert
Thar Desert
RAJASTHAN
Jaipur
Jodhpur
Ajmer
Udaipur
Kota
Jhansi
Gwalior
Agra
Mathura
Aligarh
Rann of Kutch
Gulf of Kutch
GUJARAT
Ahmadabad
Rajkot
Jamnagar
Junagadh
Vadodara (Baroda)
Surat
Bhavnagar
Kathiawar
Diu
Daman
Gulf of Cambay
DADRA & NAGAR HAVELI
BOMBAY
MADHYA PRADESH
Indore
Bhopal
Ujjain
Nagpur
Amravati
Akola
Satpura Range
Ajanta Range
MAHARASHTRA
Nasik
Aurangabad
Pune (Poona)
Sholapur
Kolhapur
Satara
Gulbarga
ANDHRA PRADESH
Hyderabad
Secunderabad
Raichur

Continuation Southwards on same scale

GOA
Dharwar
Hubli
Gadag
Bellary
KARNATAKA
Mangalore
Bangalore
Mysore
Kolar Gold Fields
Western Ghats
Eastern Ghats
Malabar Coast
Coromandel Coast
Madras
Vellore
Pondicherry
Cuddalore
TAMIL NADU
Salem
Erode
Coimbatore
Tiruchchirappalli
Thanjavur
Madurai
Trichur
Calicut (Kozhikode)
Ernakulam
Alleppey
Quilon
Trivandrum
Nagercoil
Cape Comorin
Palk Strait
Palk Bay
Gulf of Mannar
Adam's Bridge
Jaffna
SRI LANKA (CEYLON)
Colombo
Kandy
Trincomalee
Anuradhapura
Moratuwa
Galle
Dondra Head

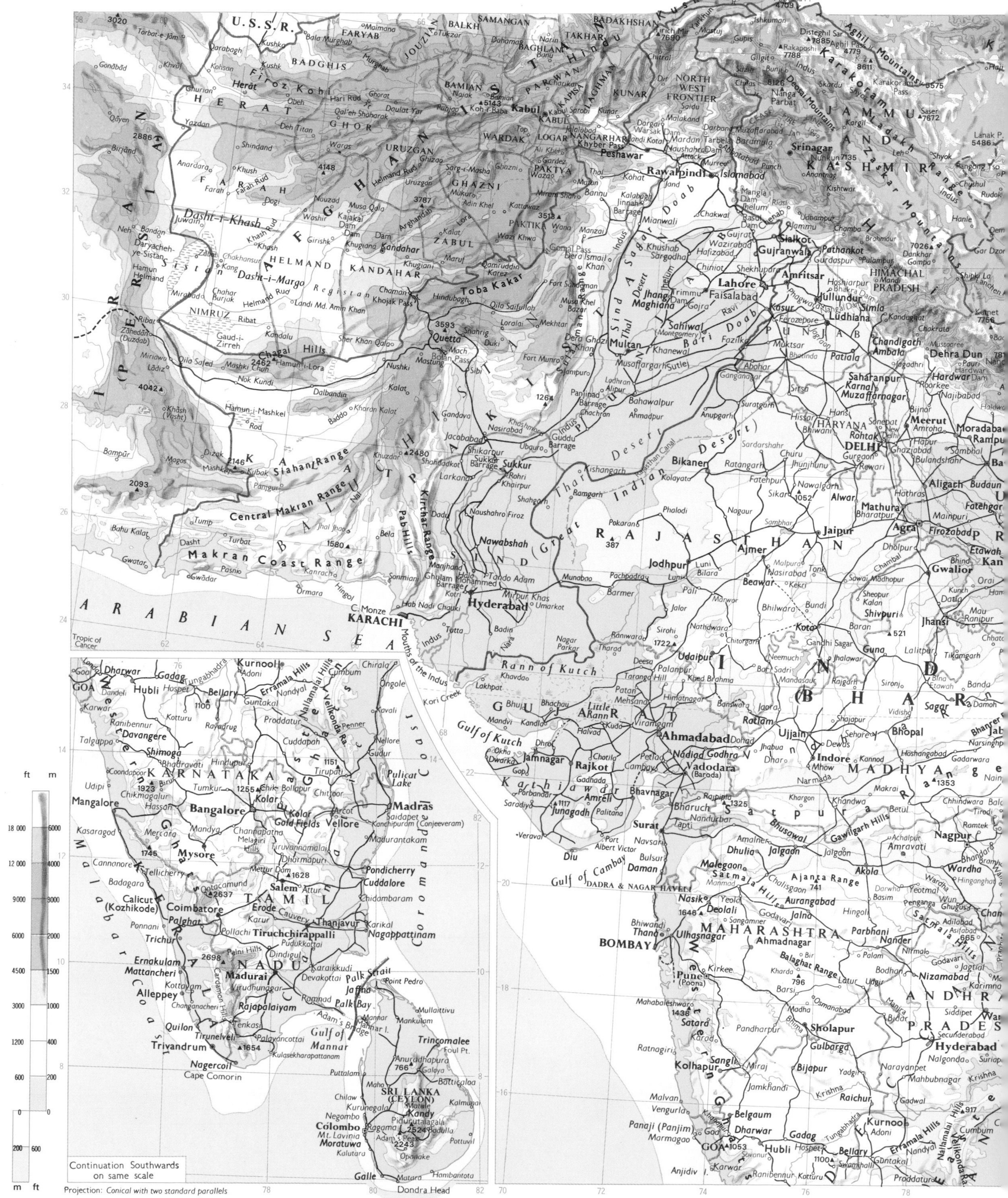

Projection: Conical with two standard parallels

ft m
18 000 6000
12 000 4000
9000 3000
6000 2000
4500 1500
3000 1000
1200 400
600 200
0 0
200 600
m ft

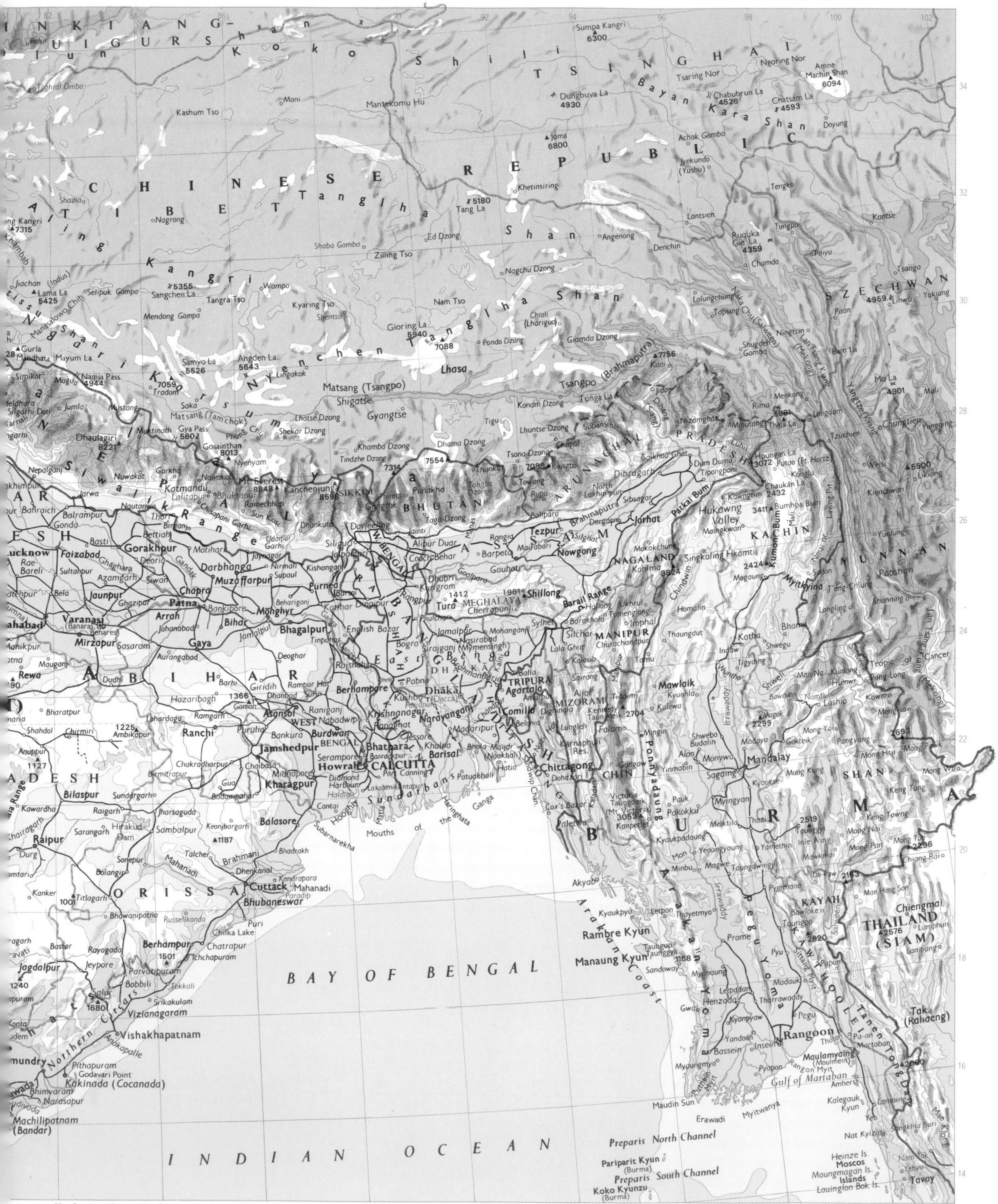
CHINESE REPUBLIC
TSINGHAI
TIBET
Kuln Shan
Tangla Shan
Bayan Kara Shan
Nyenchen Tanglha Shan
SZECHWAN
YUNNAN
Lhasa
Shigatse
Gyangtse
NEPAL
Katmandu
Mt. Everest 8848
Kanchenjunga 8598
SIKKIM
BHUTAN
ARUNACHAL PRADESH
ASSAM
NAGALAND
MANIPUR
MIZORAM
TRIPURA
MEGHALAYA
Shillong
BIHAR
Patna
Varanasi
Lucknow
ORISSA
Cuttack
Bhubaneswar
WEST BENGAL
CALCUTTA
Howrah
BANGLADESH
Dhaka
Chittagong
Barisal
Sundarbans
Mouths of the Ganga
BAY OF BENGAL
INDIAN OCEAN
BURMA
KACHIN
CHIN
SHAN
KAYAH
Mandalay
Rangoon
Moulmein
Gulf of Martaban
Arakan Coast
Pegu Yoma
Arakan Yoma
Rambre Kyun
Manaung Kyun
Preparis North Channel
Preparis South Channel
THAILAND (SIAM)
Chiengmai
Tak (Rahaeng)
Tavoy
Vishakhapatnam
Kakinada (Cocanada)
Machilipatnam (Bandar)
Northern Circars
Tropic of Cancer
East from Greenwich

1:10 000 000

50 0 50 100 150 200 miles
50 0 50 100 150 200 250 300 km

SINKIANG-
UIGUR S.
Koko Shili

T S I N G H A I

CHINESE REPUBLIC

Sumpa Kangri
6300

Ngoring Nor

Tsaring Nor

Amne
Machin Shan
6094

C H I N E S E R E P U B L I C

Dungbuya La
4526

Chabubrun La

Chatsam La
4593

Doyung

Joma
6800

Khetinsiring

Tengko

Kara Shan

Achak Gomba

Jyekundo
(Yushu)

A T I T I B E T Tanglha

5180
Tang La

Shan

Angenong

Denchin

Ruquka
Gie La
4359

Tungo

Kontse

Nagrong

Shaba Gomba

Zilling Tso

Nagchu Dzong

Lolungchung

Topsing Chu (Salwen)

Shugden
Gomba

Ningtsin Jan

Paiyu

Chamdo

Tsanga

S Z E C H W A N

Kangri
7315

Kangri

Kyaring Tso

Shentsa

Nam Tso

Nyenchen Tanglha Shan

Chiali
(Lhariguo)

Giamda Dzong

Pondo Dzong

4959

Lihwa

Yakiang

Lama La
5425

Mendong Gompa

Gioring La
5940

7088

Tsangpo (Brahmaputra)

Tunga La

Nizamghat

5361

Minutang Thala La

Mo La
4901

Longdam

Chungtien

Yunglng

Mayum La

Samyo La
5526

Angden La
5643

Lingakok

Lhasa

Kondm Dzong

Zayul

Rima

Menkong

Tsangpo (Brahmaputra)

7756

Kani

Zuichien

Simikot

Tradom

Saka

Lhotse Dzong

Shekar Dzong

Khamba Dzong

Tsona Dzong

Subansiri

Dihang

Luhi

Hpungan La
3072 Putao
(Ft. Hertz)

Weisi

5500

Dhaulagiri
8221

Muktinath

Phung Chu

Tindzhe Dzong

Dhama Dzong

7554

Chapal

7085

Kangto

Saikhoa Ghat

North
Lakhimpur

Chaukan La
2432

Kiachwan

Kienchwan

Gosainthan
8013

Nyenyam

7314

Punakha

Towong

A R U N A C H A L P R A D E S H

Dum Duma
Tipongpani

Kawngtm

Bumhpa Bum

Y U N N A N

Paoshon

Mt. Everest
8848

Kanchenjunga
8598

S I K K I M

Gangtok

B H U T A N

Tawang

Rupa

Baltpara

Brahmaputra

Sibsagar

Hukawng
Valley

3411

Teng Chung

Katmandu

Lalitpur

Darjeeling

Thimphu

Jainti

Taga Dzong

Rangia

A S S A M

Dibrugarh

Jorhat

Patkai Bum

2424

Mogaung

Myitkyina

Langling

Shunning

Gurkha

Nautanwa

Dhankuta

Alipur Duar

Coch-Behar

Barpeta

Tezpur

Mokokchung

K A C H I N

2299

Gorakhpur

Deoria

Motihari

Siliguri

Jalpaiguri

Dhubri

Goalpara

Gauhati

N A G A L A N D

Kohima
3924

Singkaling Hkamti

Homalin

Bhamo

Lucknow

Faizabad

Ghaghara

Gandak

Darbhanga

Nirmali

Supaul

Purnea

Barson

1412

Katihar Dinajpur

1961

Tura

Shillong

Barail Range

Haflong

Dikhu

Tamenglong

Imphal

Thaungdut

Indaw

Katha

Shwegu

Rae
Bareli

Sultanpur

Azamgarh

Siwan

Chapra

Patna

Bankipore

Monghyr

Bihar

Jamalpur

Bhagalpur

English Bazar

Bogra

MEGHALAYA

Cherrapunji

Mohanganj

Sylhet

Lala Ghat

Silchar

M A N I P U R

Churachandpur

Tamu

Tigyang

Shwebo

Varanasi
(Banaras)

Arrah

Jahanabad

Gaya

Aurangabad

Barhi

Giridih

Dhanbad

Rajshahi

Siraiganj (Mymensingh)

Balla

Sairang

Tiddim

Kennedy Pk.
Taungdeik 2704

Kalewa

Mingin

Shwebo

Mirzapur

Sasaram

B I H A R

Hazaribagh

1366

Gomoh

Raniganj

Nabadwip

Kushtia

Pabna

Dacca
(Dacca)

Narayanganj

TRIPURA

Agartala

Comilla

Belonia

MIZORAM

Dignala

Lungleh

Falam

Kolasib

Yinmabin

Monywa

Sagaing

Mandalay

Mong Kung

Shahdol

Chirmiri

1225
Ambikapur

Purulia

Bankura

Burdwan

Serampore

Bhola Majdi
(Nookhali)

Hatia

C H I T T A G O N G

Chittagong

C H I N

Aijal

Lunglei

Haka

Victoria
(Mt. Victoria)
3053

Kanpetlet

Pakokku

Myingyan

Mogok
2693

Mong Hsu

Mong Yai

1127

Anuppur

Bilaspur

Ranchi

Jamshedpur

Chaibasa

Midnapore

Kharagpur

Gug

Diamond
Harbour

Howrah

CALCUTTA

Barrackpur

Barisal

Patuakhali

Cox's Bazar

Paletwa

B U R M A

Minbu

Magwe

Meiktila

Thazi

2519

Yamethin

Inle Aing

Mawkmai

Mong Pan

Keng Tung

Raipur

Durg

Kawardha

Raigarh

Sundargarh

Sambalpur

Keonjhargarh

Balasore

Bhadrak

Contai

Lakshmikantapur

Port Canning

Sundarbans

Patanghata

Ganga

A r a k a n C o a s t

Akyab

Minbu

Kyaukpadaung

Mon

Yenangyaung

Minbu

2820

Pyu

Chieng Rai
2296

Titlagarh
1001

Sonepur

Bolangir

Mahanadi

Talcher

Dhenkanal

Kendrapara

Paradip

Mouths of the Ganga

Taunggauk
anggya

1168

Sandoway

Prome

T H A I L A N D
(S I A M)
2576

Lamphun

Lampang

Bastar

Jagdalpur

1240

Kanker

1187

O R I S S A

Cuttack

Bhubaneswar

Puri

Chilka Lake

Chatrapur

Rambre Kyun

Manaung Kyun

Myanaung

Henzada

Letpadan

Tharrawaddy

Pegu

Pyu

Mydungmya

Maulamyaing
(Moulmein)

Rayagada

Berhampur
1501

Jeypore

Parvatipuram

Bobbili

Tekkali

Ichchapuram

Srikakulam

B A Y O F B E N G A L

Yandoon

Bassein

Insein

Rangoon

Thaton

Pa-an

Martaban

2689

Vizianagaram

Vishakhapatnam

Kakinada (Cocanada)

Gulf of Martaban

Amherst

Pithapuram

Godavari Point

Bhimavaram

Narasapur

Machilipatnam
(Bandar)

Maudin Sun

Erawadi

Myitwanya

Heinze Is.
Moscos
Islands

Tavoy

I N D I A N O C E A N

Preparis North Channel

Pariparit Kyun
(Burma)

Preparis
South Channel

Koko Kyunzu
(Burma)

Nat Kyizing

Lauinglon Bok Is.

THAILAND
(SIAM)
BURMA
LAOS
VIET-NAM
CAMBODIA
MALAYSIA
PENINSULAR MALAYSIA
INDONESIA
BORNEO
SUMATERA
JAWA
(JAVA)
SARAWAK
SABAH
BRUNEI
KALIMANTAN
SOUTH CHINA SEA
ANDAMAN SEA
INDIAN OCEAN
Gulf of Thailand (Siam)
G. of Martaban
Strait of Malacca
Selat Karimata
Selat Berhala
Greater Sunda Isla
JAVA SEA
Java Trench
Rangoon
Moulmein
Bangkok
Phnom Penh
Vientiane
Hue
Da Nang (Tourane)
PHANH BHO HO CHI MINH (Saigon)
Kuala Lumpur
SINGAPORE
Johor Baharu
George Town
Ipoh
Medan
Padang
Palembang
JAKARTA
Bandung
Semarang
Surabaya
Yogyakarta
Pontianak
Kuching
Banjarmasin
Kota Kinabalu (Jesselton)
Bandar Seri Begawan
Pangkalpinang
Bangka
Belitung (Billiton)
Madura
Bali
Lombok
Nias
Siberut
Simeulue
Enggano
Palawan
Hsisha
Spratly I.
Kepulauan Riau
Kepulauan Lingga
Kepulauan Natuna Selatan
Kepulauan Anambas
Kepulauan Mentawai
NUSA TENGG
ft
m
Projection: Mercator
East from Greenwich

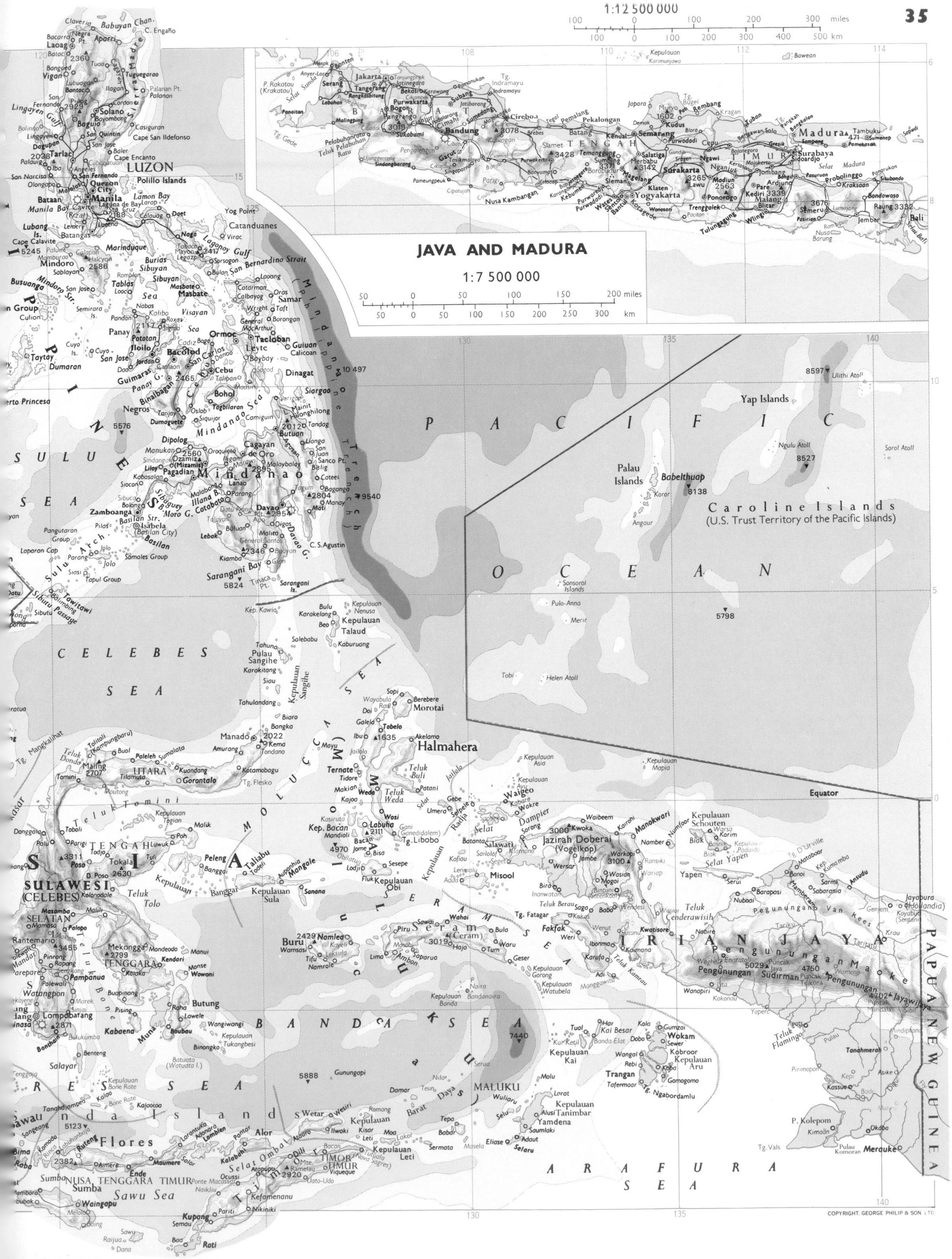
1:12 500 000
miles
km
JAVA AND MADURA
1:7 500 000
miles
km
LUZON
Polillo Islands
Manila
Quezon City
Manila Bay
Bataan
Lamon Bay
Catanduanes
Babuyan Chan.
C. Engaño
Lingayen Gulf
Baguio
Cape San Ildefonso
Mindoro
Mindoro Str.
Marinduque
Sibuyan Sea
Masbate
Samar
Leyte
Panay
Iloilo
Bacolod
Cebu
Negros
Bohol
Dinagat
Siargao
Visayan Sea
San Bernardino Strait
Mindanao Sea
Mindanao
Zamboanga
Davao
Davao G.
Moro G.
Basilan
Sulu Arch.
SULU SEA
Jolo
Tawitawi
Sibutu Passage
Sarangani Bay
Sarangani Is.
Mindanao or Philippine Trench
10 497
9540
PACIFIC OCEAN
Yap Islands
Ulithi Atoll
Ngulu Atoll
Sorol Atoll
Palau Islands
Babelthuap
Koror
Angaur
Caroline Islands
(U.S. Trust Territory of the Pacific Islands)
Sonsorol Islands
Pulo-Anna
Merir
Tobi
Helen Atoll
Equator
CELEBES SEA
Kepulauan Talaud
Pulau Sangihe
Kepulauan Sangihe
Manado
MOLUCCA SEA
Morotai
Halmahera
Ternate
Tidore
Kep. Bacan
Obi
Kepulauan Sula
Taliabu
Mangole
Kepulauan Banggai
Peleng
Teluk Tomini
Teluk Tolo
Teluk Bone
SULAWESI (CELEBES)
UTARA
TENGAH
SELATAN
TENGGARA
Gorontalo
Poso
Kendari
Butung
Muna
Kabaena
Salayar
Buru
Seram (Ceram)
Ambon
Misool
Salawati
Waigeo
Dampier Selat
Sorong
Jazirah Doberai (Vogelkop)
Manokwari
Kepulauan Schouten
Biak
Yapen
Teluk Cenderawasih
IRIAN JAYA
Pegunungan Van Rees
Pegunungan Maoke
Puncak Jaya 5029
Pegunungan Sudirman
Pegunungan Jayawijaya
Jayapura (Hollandia)
PAPUA NEW GUINEA
Fakfak
Kepulauan Kai
Kepulauan Aru
Kepulauan Tanimbar
Yamdena
Trangan
Teluk Flamingo
P. Kolepom
Merauke
Tg. Vals
BANDA SEA
SERAM SEA
FLORES SEA
ARAFURA SEA
TIMOR
Dili
Kupang
Roti
Sawu Sea
Sumba
Flores
Alor
Wetar
Kepulauan Leti
Damar
MALUKU
NUSA TENGGARA TIMUR
Sunda Islands
7440
5888
5798
8138
8527
8597
5824
5576
Jakarta
Bandung
Semarang
Surakarta
Yogyakarta
Surabaya
Madura
Malang
Kediri
Madiun
Cirebon
Pekalongan
Tegal
Bogor
Serang
Bali
Nusa Barung
Bawean
Kepulauan Karimunjawa
P. Rakatau (Krakatau)
Selat Sunda
Selat Madura
BARAT
TENGAH
TIMUR
Slamet 3428
Semeru 3676
Raung 3332
Nusa Kambangan

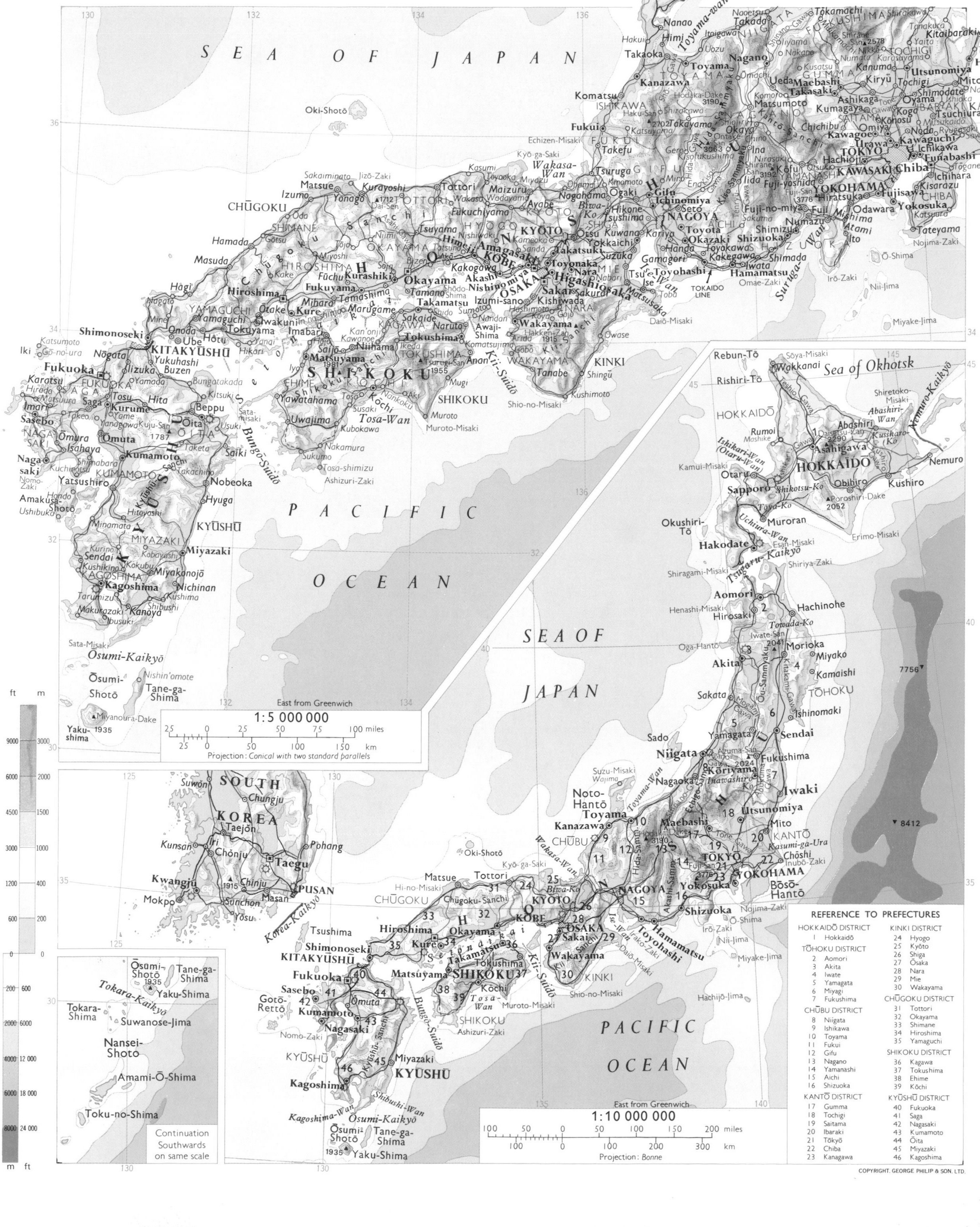

SEA OF JAPAN

Suzu-misaki
Wajima
Suzu
Naoetsu
Takada
Nanao
Itoigawa
Himi
Toyama-wan
Takaoka
Uozu
Kanazawa
Toyama
Komatsu
Nagano
Ueda
Matsumoto
Takasaki
Maebashi
Kiryū
Ashikaga
Tochigi
Utsunomiya
Mito
Kitaibaraki
Hitachi
Nikko 2578
ISHIKAWA
Fukui
Takefu
Echizen-Misaki
FUKUI
Takayama 3063
Ontake 3190
Gifu
Ichinomiya
NAGOYA
Nagoya
Kōfu 3776 Fuji-San
Hachiōji
TŌKYŌ
KAWASAKI Chiba
YOKOHAMA
Fujisawa
Yokosuka
Odawara
Kisarazu
CHIBA
Ichihara
Kamakura

Oki-Shotō
Matsue
Izumo
Yonago
Tottori
Kurayoshi
TOTTORI
Kasumi
Toyooka
Maizuru
Ayabe
Nagahama
Ōgaki
KYŌTO
Ōtsu
Biwa-Ko
Hikone
Kuwana
Yokkaichi
Kariya
Okazaki
Toyota
Shizuoka
Fuji-no-miya
Fuji
Numazu
Atami
Itō
Tateyama
Nojima-Zaki
Ō-Shima
Omae-Zaki
Irō-Zaki
Suruga-Wan
TOKAIDO LINE
Hamamatsu
Iwata
Toyohashi
Gamagōri
Suzuka
AICHI
Tsu
Ise
Toba
Matsusaka
Daiō-Misaki
Miyake-Jima

CHŪGOKU
Hamada
Masuda
Hagi
Matsue
Tottori
Tsuyama
Okayama
Kurashiki
Fukuyama
Mihara
Tamashima
Takamatsu
Marugame
Naruto
Tokushima
Wakayama
NARA
Nara
Sakurai
Matsusaka
Toba
Hiroshima
Fūchū
Okayama
Akashi
Nishinomiya
KŌBE
Amagasaki
OSAKA
Sakai
Kishiwada
Higashi-Ōsaka
Izumi-sano
WAKAYAMA
Tanabe
Shingū
Kushimoto
Shio-no-Misaki
KINKI

Shimonoseki
Ube
Hōfu
Onoda
Tokuyama
KITAKYŪSHŪ
Yukuhashi
Buzen
Nakatsu
Ōita
Beppu
Saiki
Usuki
Bungo-Suidō
Saeki
Nobeoka
Hyūga
KYŪSHŪ

Fukuoka
FUKUOKA
SAGA
Karatsu
Hirado
Imari
Saga
Tosu
Kurume
Yame
Hita
Kumamoto
KUMAMOTO
Yatsushiro
MIYAZAKI
Miyazaki
Miyakonojō
Nichinan
Kanoya
Shibushi
KAGOSHIMA
Kagoshima
Sendai
Ibusuki
Makurazaki
Sata-Misaki

Sasebo
Ōmura
Isahaya
NAGASAKI
Naga-saki
Nomo-Zaki
Amakusa
Ushibuka

Ōsumi-Kaikyō
Ōsumi-Shotō
Tane-ga-Shima
Nishin'omote
Yaku- 1935 shima
Miyanoura-Dake

PACIFIC OCEAN

SEA OF JAPAN

East from Greenwich

1:5 000 000

25 0 25 50 100 miles
25 0 50 100 150 km
Projection: Conical with two standard parallels

Hokkaidō inset

Rebun-Tō
Rishiri-Tō
Wakkanai
Sōya-Misaki
Sea of Okhotsk
Shiretoko-Misaki
Abashiri-Wan
Nemuro-Kaikyō
HOKKAIDŌ
Rumoi
Mashike
Asahigawa
Daisetsu-Zan 2290
Kushiro-Ko
Kamui-Misaki
Ishikari-Wan (Otaru-Wan)
Otaru
Sapporo
Shikotsu-Ko
Tōya-Ko
Obihiro
Poroshiri-Dake 2052
Nemuro
Kushiro
Okushiri-Tō
Muroran
Uchiura-Wan
Esan-Misaki
Hakodate
Shiriya-Zaki
Tsugaru-Kaikyō
Shiragami-Misaki
Aomori
Henashi-Misaki
Hirosaki
Hachinohe
Towada-Ko
Iwate-San 2041
Oga-Hantō
Morioka
Miyako
Akita
Kamaishi
TŌHOKU
Sakata
Ishinomaki
Niigata
Yamagata
Sendai
Sado
Azuma-San
Fukushima
Kōriyama
Inawashiro-Ko 2024
Nagaoka
Iwaki
Noto-Hantō
Toyama
Kanazawa
Maebashi
Utsunomiya
Mito
KANTŌ
Kasumi-ga-Ura
Chōshi
Inubō-Zaki
TŌKYŌ
YOKOHAMA
Yokosuka
Bōsō-Hantō
Shizuoka
Ō-Shima
Nojima-Zaki
Hamamatsu
Toyohashi
NAGOYA
KYŌTO
KŌBE
OSAKA
Sakai
Wakayama
KINKI
Kii-Suidō
Muroto-Misaki
Hachijō-Jima

8412
7756

PACIFIC OCEAN

South Korea inset

SOUTH KOREA
Suwŏn
Chungju
Taejŏn
Chŏnju
Iri
Kunsan
Chinju 1915
Taegu
PUSAN
Masan
Kwangju
Mokpo
Sunchŏn
Yŏsu
Chinju
Korea-Kaikyō
Tsushima

1:10 000 000

East from Greenwich

100 50 0 50 100 200 miles
100 0 100 200 300 km
Projection: Bonne

CHŪGOKU
Matsue
Tottori
Hi-no-Misaki
Chūgoku-Sanchi
Hiroshima
Okayama
Kure
KŌBE
KITAKYŪSHŪ
Shimonoseki
Fukuoka
Takamatsu
Matsuyama
Kōchi
SHIKOKU
Tosa-Wan
Ashizuri-Zaki
Muroto-Misaki
Sasebo
Gotō-Rettō
Ōmuta
Kumamoto
Nagasaki
Miyazaki
KYŪSHŪ
Kagoshima
Kagoshima-Wan
Ōsumi-Shotō
Tane-ga-Shima
Yaku-Shima 1935
Shibushi-Wan

Nansei-Shotō inset

Ōsumi-Shotō
Tokara-Kaikyō
Yaku-Shima 1935
Tane-ga-Shima
Tokara-Shima
Suwanose-Jima
Nansei-Shotō
Amami-Ō-Shima
Toku-no-Shima

Continuation Southwards on same scale

Elevation scale

ft	m
9000	3000
6000	2000
4500	1500
3000	1000
1200	400
600	200
0	0
600	200
6000	2000
12 000	4000
18 000	6000
24 000	8000
m	ft

REFERENCE TO PREFECTURES

HOKKAIDŌ DISTRICT	KINKI DISTRICT
1 Hokkaidō	24 Hyogo
TŌHOKU DISTRICT	25 Kyōto
2 Aomori	26 Shiga
3 Akita	27 Ōsaka
4 Iwate	28 Nara
5 Yamagata	29 Mie
6 Miyagi	30 Wakayama
7 Fukushima	**CHŪGOKU DISTRICT**
CHŪBU DISTRICT	31 Tottori
8 Niigata	32 Okayama
9 Ishikawa	33 Shimane
10 Toyama	34 Hiroshima
11 Fukui	35 Yamaguchi
12 Gifu	**SHIKOKU DISTRICT**
13 Nagano	36 Kagawa
14 Yamanashi	37 Tokushima
15 Aichi	38 Ehime
16 Shizuoka	39 Kōchi
KANTŌ DISTRICT	**KYŪSHŪ DISTRICT**
17 Gumma	40 Fukuoka
18 Tochigi	41 Saga
19 Saitama	42 Nagasaki
20 Ibaraki	43 Kumamoto
21 Tōkyō	44 Ōita
22 Chiba	45 Miyazaki
23 Kanagawa	46 Kagoshima

1:20 000 000

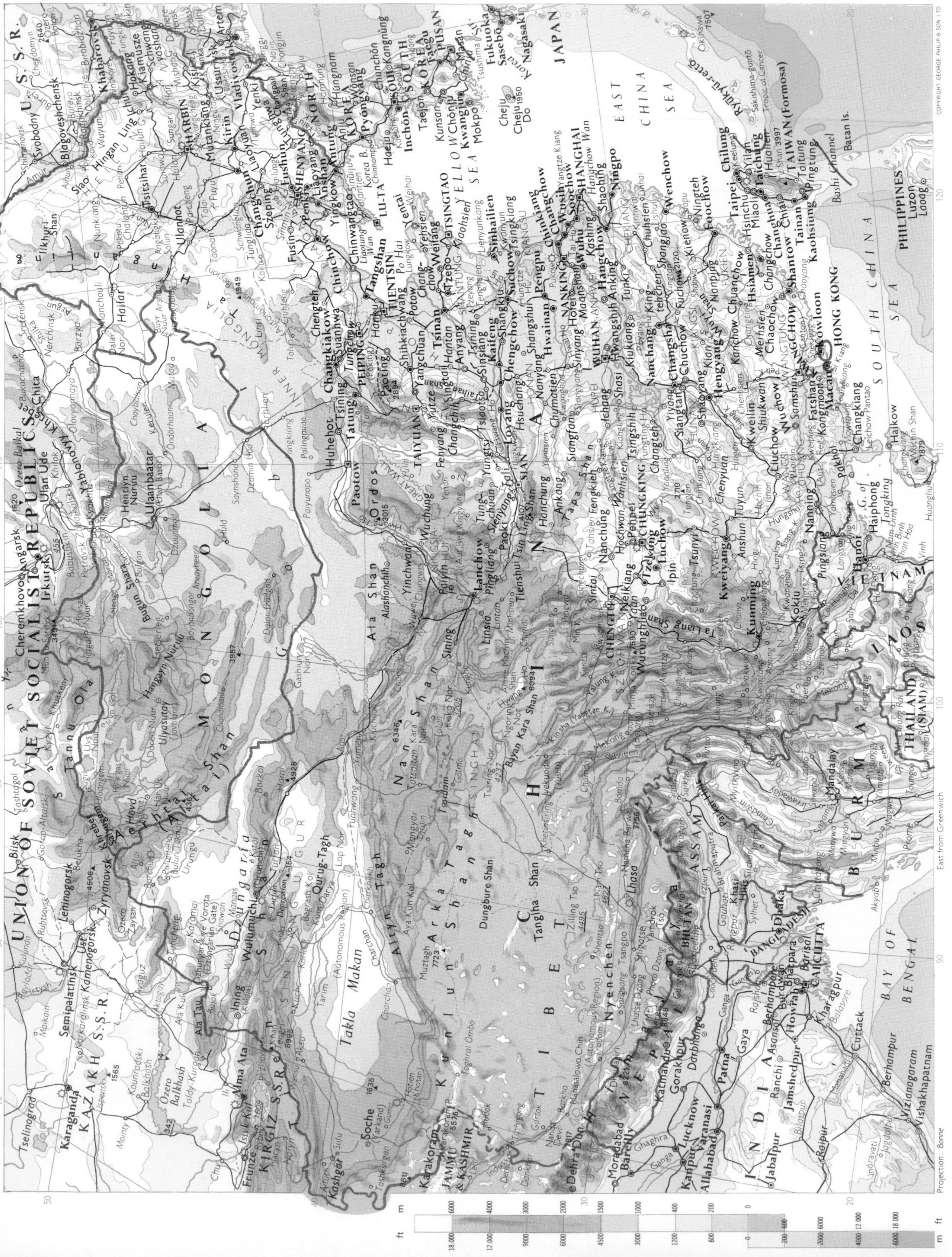
100 0 100 200 300 400 miles
100 0 100 200 300 400 500 600 km
UNION OF SOVIET SOCIALIST REPUBLICS
MONGOLIA
CHINA
TIBET
JAPAN
NORTH KOREA
SOUTH KOREA
EAST CHINA SEA
SOUTH CHINA SEA
YELLOW SEA
BAY OF BENGAL
INDIA
BURMA
THAILAND (SIAM)
LAOS
VIETNAM
PHILIPPINES
TAIWAN (Formosa)
HONG KONG
NEPAL
BHUTAN
ASSAM
BANGLADESH
JAMMU & KASHMIR
PEIPING
SHANGHAI
NANKING
TIENTSIN
CHUNGKING
CHENGTU
WUHAN
CANTON
KAZAKH S.S.R.
KIRGIZ S.S.R.
Takla Makan
Kunlun Shan
Tien Shan
Altai
Projection: Bonne
East from Greenwich
COPYRIGHT GEORGE PHILIP & SON, LTD
m 6000 4000 3000 2000 1500 1000 400 200 0 200 2000 4000 6000
ft 18 000 12 000 9000 6000 4500 3000 1200 600 0 600 6000 12 000 18 000

U. S. S. R.
MONGOLIA
INNER MONGOLIAN AUTONOMOUS REGION
HEILUNGKIANG
KIRIN
LIAONING
HOPEH
NORTH KOREA
SOUTH KOREA
SEA OF JAPAN
YELLOW SEA
Po Hai (Gulf of Chihli)
Korea Bay
Ulaanbaatar (Ulan Bator)
Irkutsk
Ulan Ude
Chita
Khabarovsk
Vladivostok
Harbin
Tsitsihar
Changchun
Kirin
Shenyang (Mukden)
Fushun
Anshan
Lu-ta
Peiping (Peking)
Tientsin
Tangshan
Changkiakow
Paotow
Huhehot
Taiyuan
Tsinan
Tzepo
Yinchwan
Lanchow
Pyŏngyang
Sŏul (Seoul)
Inchŏn
Taegu
Hailar
Ulanhot
Ozero Baykal
THE GREAT WALL

1:10 000 000

50 0 50 100 150 200 250 miles
50 0 50 100 150 200 250 300 350 400 km

P A C I F I C O C E A N

E A S T C H I N A S E A

JAPAN

KITAKYŪSHŪ
Fukuoka
Omuta
Sasebo
Nagasaki
Kagoshima
Kurume
Kumamoto

Cheju Do
(Quelpart)

Nansei-shoto

Tropic of Cancer

R Y U K Y U

TAIWAN
(FORMOSA)

Chilung
(Keelung)
Taipei
Taichung
Hualien
Tainan
Kaohsiung
Pingtung

Penghu
(Pescadores)

PHILIPPINES

Luzon

Batan Is.
Babuyan Is.

S O U T H C H I N A S E A

SHANGHAI

KIANGSU

NANKING
WUHAN
Hankow

CHEKIANG
Hangchow
Ningpo
Wenchow

ANHWEI

HONAN

KIANGSI
Nanchang

FUKIEN
Foochow
(Minhow)

Hsiamen
(Amoy)

HUNAN
Changsha
Hengyang

KWANGTUNG
KWANGCHOW
(Canton)

HONGKONG (Br.)
Kowloon
Macau

SZECHWAN

KWEICHOW

KWANGSI-
CHUANG

Nanning

HAINAN
Haikow

VIETNAM
HANOI
Haiphong

Gulf of Tongking

Tongking (Pratas)

East from Greenwich

Projection: Lambert's Equivalent Azimuthal

ft m
12 000 ———— 4000
9000 ———— 3000
6000 ———— 2000
 1500
3000 ———— 1000
 600
 400
 200
 0

m ft
200 600
2000 6000
4000 12 000
6000 18 000

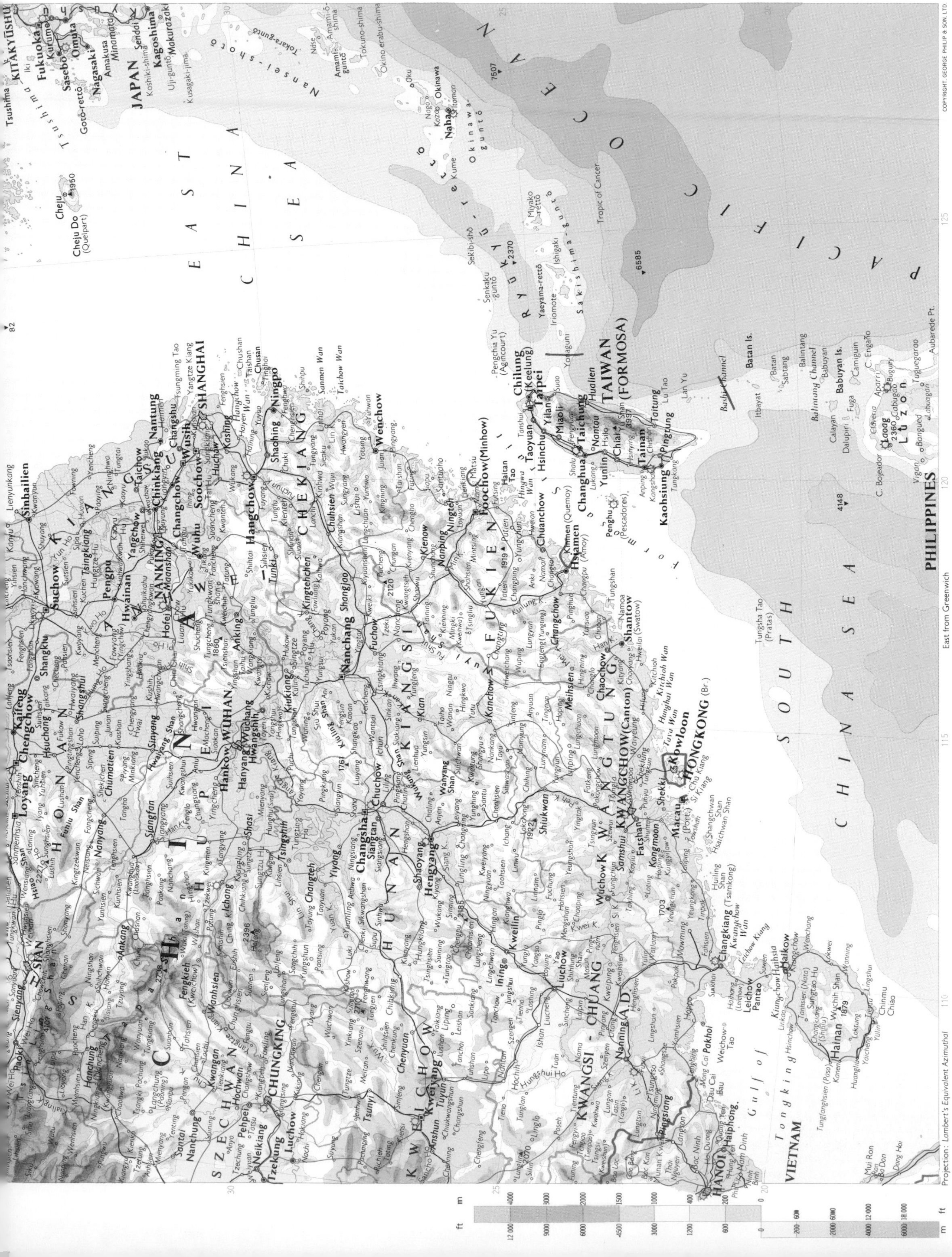

Projection: Bonne

East from Greenwich

Boundaries of the artesian basins

Java Trench ▼6389

TIMOR SEA

Ashmore Reef

Cartier I.

C. Londonderry

Croker

Dundas

Cobourg Pen.

Bathurst I.

Melville I. Str.

Goulburn

Junction B. Elc

Van Diemen Gulf

Crocodile I.

Clarence Str.

P. Darwin

Darwin

Castlereagh B.

Buckingham

Arnh

C. Talbot

Vansittart I.

C. Bougainville

Admiralty G.

Montague Sd.

York. Sd.

Brunswick B.

Koolan & Cockatoo Is.

Collier B.

King Sd.

C. Lévêque

Lacepede Is.

Cambridge G.

Jos. Bonaparte Gulf

Queens Chan.

Pt. Blaze

Anson B.

C. Ford

Batchelor

Rum Jungle

Frances Creek

Pine Creek

Katherine

Arnhem Land

Roper

Mataranka

Wyndham

Kununurra

Victoria

Birdum

Larrimah

Mt. Hann 776 ▲

Gulf Basin

L. Argyle

Victoria River Downs

Daly Waters

Yampi Sound

Mt. Ord 936

Glenroy

Wave Hill

Newcastle Waters

Meda

Derby

Hall's Creek

L. Woods

Barkl

Powell Creek

Renner Springs T.O.

C. Baskerville

Carnot B.

C. Boileau

Broome

Roebuck B.

C. Latouche Treville

C. Bossut

La Grange

Dampier Downs

Fitzroy Crossing

Gordon Downs

Tanami Desert

NORTHE

Rowley Shoals

Eighty Mile Beach

Canning Basin

Gregory Lake

Hordern Hills

The Granites

TERRITO

P. Hedland

Finucane I.

Mount Goldsworthy

De Grey

Nimingarra

Shaw

Great Sandy Desert

Mt. Singleton ▲ 844

Barrow Creek T.O.

Sando

Dampier Archipelago

Hampton Harb.

Dampier

Roebourne

Marble Bar

Nullagine

L. Dora

Mt. Freeling 998

Reynolds Ra.

Hatc

Davenpo Ra.

Monte Bello Is.

Barrow I.

C. Preston

Pilbara

Yule

Throssell Ra.

L. Blanche

L. Mackay

Mt. Ziel 1510

Mt. Liebig 1524

Mt. Laughlen 1169

Macdonnell Ras.

N.W. Cape

Exmouth G.

Deepdale

Onslow

Fortescue

Hamersley Ra.

Wittenoom

Mt. Enid

Mt. Bruce 1227

Ophthalmia Ra.

Mt. Nicholas

Robertson Ra.

L. Disappointment

L. Macdonald

Alice Springs

James Ra.

Hugh

Learmonth

Pt. Cloates

Tom Price 1251

Parraburdoo

Mt. Meharry

Ashburton

Mount Whaleback

Newman

Gibson Desert

Rawlinson Ra.

L. Amadeus

Mt. Olga 1069

Ayers Rock 867

Finke

Palmer

C. Farquhar

Barlee Ra.

Mt. Augustus 1105

WESTERN

Blackstone Ra.

Barrow Ra.

Musgrave Ranges

Mt. Woodroffe 1440

Charlo Water

C. Cuvier

Bernier I.

McLeod

Lyons

Mt. Egerton 994

Peak Hill Ras.

L. Buchanan

L. Carnegie

Barrow Ra.

Everard Ras.

Hamilton

Alberga

Geographe Chan.

North West

Gascoyne

Robinson

Wiluna

L. Wells 661

Oodnadatta

Dorre I.

Naturaliste Chan.

Shark B.

Dirk Hartog

Denham

Wooramel

West Basin

Murchison

Meekatharra

AUSTRALIA

L. Yeo

Great Victoria Desert

L. Maurice

Coober Pedy

S. Passage

Steep Pt.

Sanford

Nannine

Cue

L. Austin

Sandstone

Laverton

L. Rason

SOUTH AUS

Gantheaume B.

Tallering Peak 453

Mt. Magnet

Yalgoo

Leonora

Malcolm

L. Carey

L. Minigwal

Maralinga

Oodlea

Tarcoola

P. Gregory

Houtman

Abrolhos

Mullewa

Northampton

Champion B.

Geraldton

Dongara

L. Monger

L. Barlee

L. Raeside

L. Ballard

Menzies

Kanowna

Premier Downs

Rawlinna

Forrest

Deakin

L. Harris

L. Everard

Jurien B.

Wedge I.

Coastal

Plains

Basin

L. Moore

Bonnie Rock

Kalgoorlie

Coolgardie

Boulder

L. Lefroy

Zanthus

Eucla Basin

Nullarbor Plain

Hampton Tableland

Eyre

Penong

Ceduna

L. Gai

Nuke

Dongara

Bencubbin

Bullfinch

Southern Cross

L. Cowan

Norseman

Eyre

Head of Bight

C. Adieu

Fowlers B.

Nuyts Archipelago

Jurien B.

Northam

Merredin

Kellerberrin

The Johnston Lakes

L. Dundas

Pt. Dover

Pt. Culver

Great Australian Bight

Streaky B.

C. Radstock

Anxious B.

Pe

Midland

Perth

Fremantle

Kwinana

Beverley

Brookton

Narrogin

Newdegate

Ravensthorpe

Hopetoun

Rocky Pt.

Investigator Group

Coffin B. Penin.

Whidbey Is.

Port Linc

Pinjarra

Bunbury

Collie

Geographe B.

C. Naturaliste

Busselton

Katanning

Wagin

Nyabing

Gnowangerup

Doubtful B.

Esperance

Esperance B.

C. le Grand

C. Pasley

C. Arid

Archipelago of the Recherche

Augusta

C. Leeuwin

Flinders B.

Bridgetown

Manjimup

Pemberton

Stirling Ra.

Pt. Hood

Mt. Barker

Albany

C. Knob

King George Sound

C. Catastro

Th

Pt. d'Entrecasteaux

Pt. Nuyts

Denmark

Tor B.

INDIAN OCEAN

ft m

6000 2000

4500 1500

3000 1000

1200 400

600 200

0 0

200 600

2000 6000

4000 12 000

6000 18 000

m ft

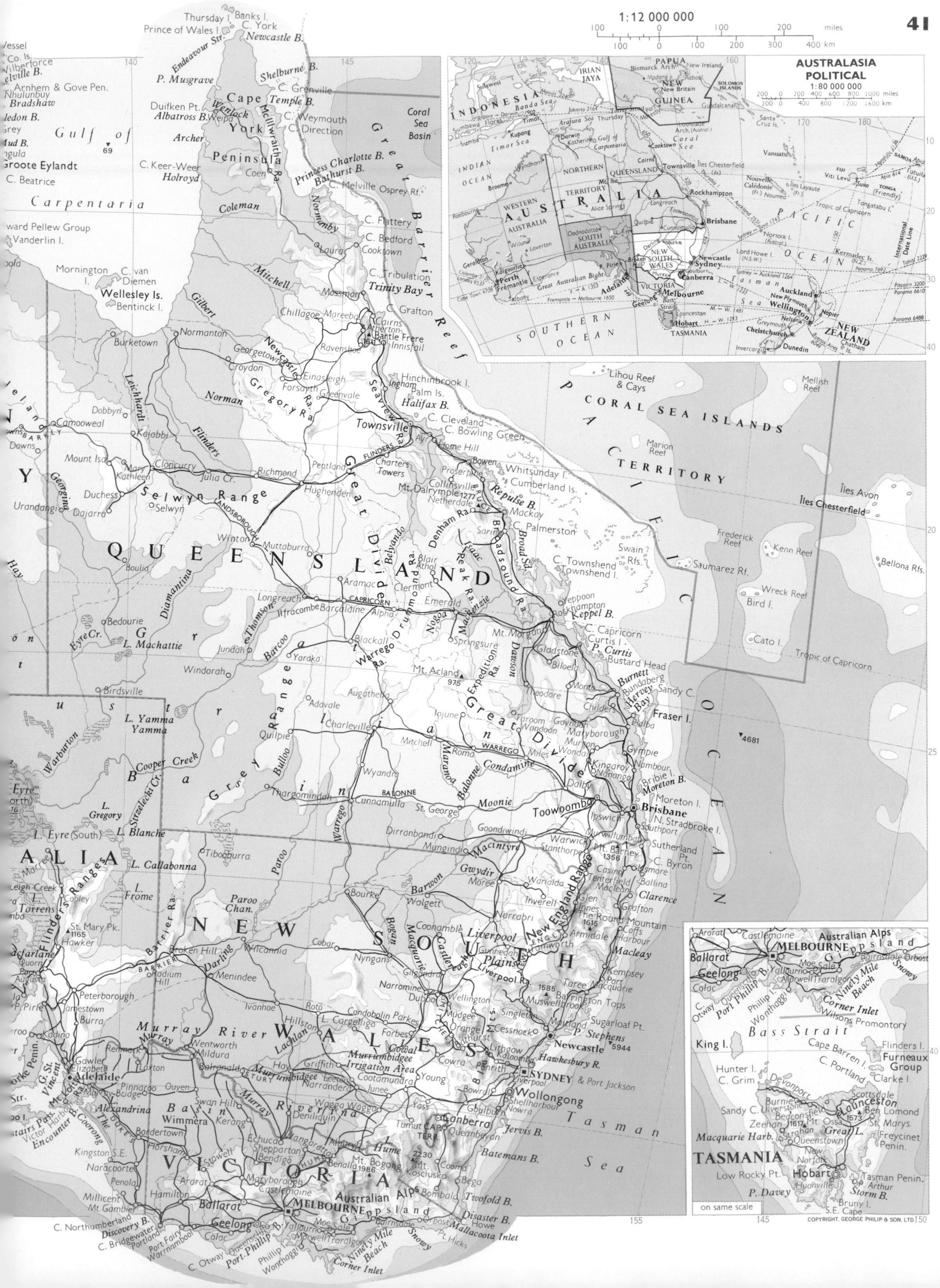
1:12 000 000
miles
km
AUSTRALASIA
POLITICAL
1:80 000 000
INDONESIA
PAPUA NEW GUINEA
IRIAN JAYA
SOLOMON ISLANDS
INDIAN OCEAN
AUSTRALIA
WESTERN AUSTRALIA
NORTHERN TERRITORY
QUEENSLAND
SOUTH AUSTRALIA
NEW SOUTH WALES
VICTORIA
TASMANIA
PACIFIC OCEAN
Tasman Sea
SOUTHERN OCEAN
NEW ZEALAND
Coral Sea
Great Australian Bight
Tropic of Capricorn
International Date Line
Gulf of Carpentaria
Cape York Peninsula
Coral Sea Basin
Great Barrier Reef
CORAL SEA ISLANDS TERRITORY
PACIFIC OCEAN
QUEENSLAND
Great Dividing Range
Great Artesian Basin
Selwyn Range
Gregory Ra.
Grey Range
Cooper Creek
NEW SOUTH WALES
VICTORIA
Murray River Basin
Australian Alps
Thursday I.
Banks I.
Prince of Wales I.
C. York
Newcastle B.
Groote Eylandt
Wellesley Is.
Mornington I.
Cooktown
Cairns
Townsville
Mackay
Rockhampton
Gladstone
Bundaberg
Maryborough
Fraser I.
Gympie
Toowoomba
Brisbane
Mount Isa
Cloncurry
Longreach
Charleville
Birdsville
Tibooburra
Broken Hill
Bourke
Dubbo
Tamworth
Armidale
Newcastle
SYDNEY
Wollongong
Canberra
Wagga Wagga
Albury
Mildura
Adelaide
Bendigo
Ballarat
Geelong
MELBOURNE
Mt. Kosciusko
Bass Strait
King I.
Flinders I.
Furneaux Group
Devonport
Launceston
Hobart
TASMANIA
on same scale
L. Eyre (South)
L. Frome
L. Torrens
Flinders Ranges
Darling
Murray
Murrumbidgee
Lachlan
Barwon
Fitzroy

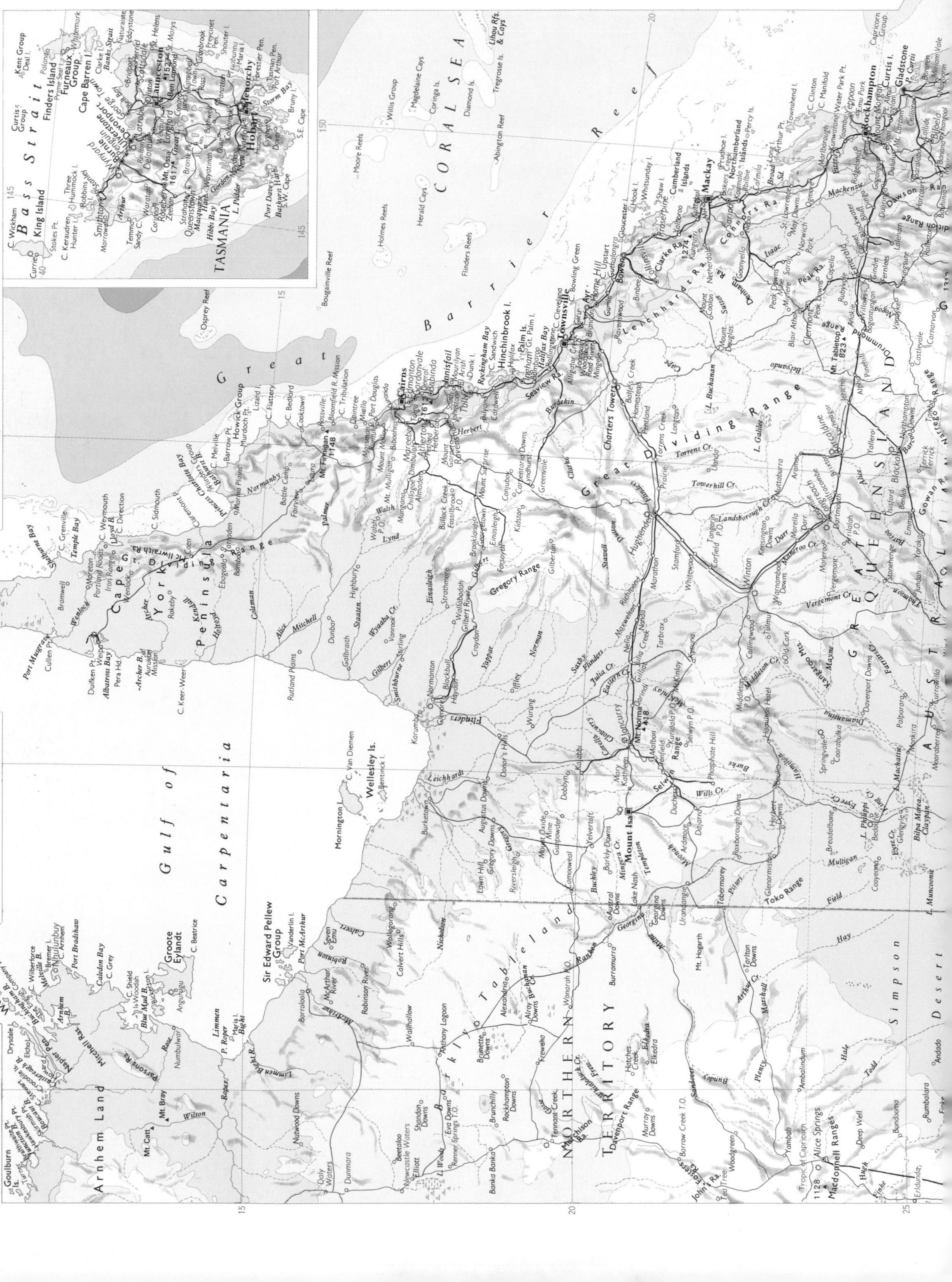
Bass Strait
King Island
Flinders Island
Furneaux Group
Cape Barren I.
Banks Strait
Kent Group
TASMANIA
Launceston
Devonport
Burnie
Hobart
New Norfolk
Storm Bay
Queenstown
Strahan
Macquarie Harb.
Port Davey
S.W. Cape
S.E. Cape
Tasman Pen.
Great Barrier Reef
CORAL SEA
Willis Group
Magdelaine Cays
Coringa Is.
Diamond Is.
Lihou Rfs. & Cays
Tregrosse Is.
Abington Reef
Moore Reefs
Herald Cays
Holmes Reefs
Flinders Reefs
Bougainville Reef
Osprey Reef
Cumberland Islands
Northumberland Islands
Mackay
Proserpine
Bowen
Home Hill
Ayr
Townsville
Palm Is.
Hinchinbrook I.
Rockingham Bay
Ingham
Innisfail
Cairns
Atherton
Mareeba
Cooktown
Lizard I.
Howick Group
Princess Charlotte Bay
C. Melville
Cape York Peninsula
Temple Bay
Shelburne Bay
Thursday I.
Prince of Wales I.
Endeavour Strait
C. York
Weipa
Albatross Bay
Archer R.
Mitchell
Gilbert
Normanton
Karumba
Burketown
Mornington I.
Wellesley Is.
Gulf of Carpentaria
Sir Edward Pellew Group
Groote Eylandt
Arnhem Land
Wessel Is.
Nhulunbuy
Gove Pen.
Blue Mud B.
Limmen Bight
Roper
Borroloola
Barkly Tableland
NORTHERN TERRITORY
Tennant Creek
Davenport Range
Alice Springs
Tropic of Capricorn
Macdonnell Ranges
Simpson Desert
Mount Isa
Cloncurry
Mt. Norma
Selwyn Range
Julia Cr.
Richmond
Hughenden
Charters Towers
Great Dividing Range
Gregory Range
L. Buchanan
L. Galilee
Winton
Longreach
Barcaldine
Blackall
Emerald
Clermont
Rockhampton
Gladstone
Curtis I.
Dawson Ra.
Mt. Tabletop 823
Drummond Range
Leichhardt Ra.
Clarke Ra.
Connors Ra.
Peak Ra.
Isaac
Burdekin
Flinders
Diamantina
Georgina
Burke
Hamilton
Mulligan
Field
Hay
Plenty
Todd
Hale
Finke
Sandover
Toko Range
Kangaroo Hills
QUEENSLAND
SOUTH AUSTRALIA
Daly Waters
Elliott
Newcastle Waters
Wave Hill
Mt. Catt
Mt. Bray
Wilton
Goulburn Is.
Mitchell Ras.
Parsons Ra.
Caledon Bay
Port Bradshaw
L. Muncoonie
L. Philippi
Bilpa Morea Claypan
Mt. Finnigan 1148
Tropic of Capricorn
135
140
145
150
15
20
25

1:8 000 000

50 0 50 100 150 200 miles

50 0 50 100 150 200 250 300 km

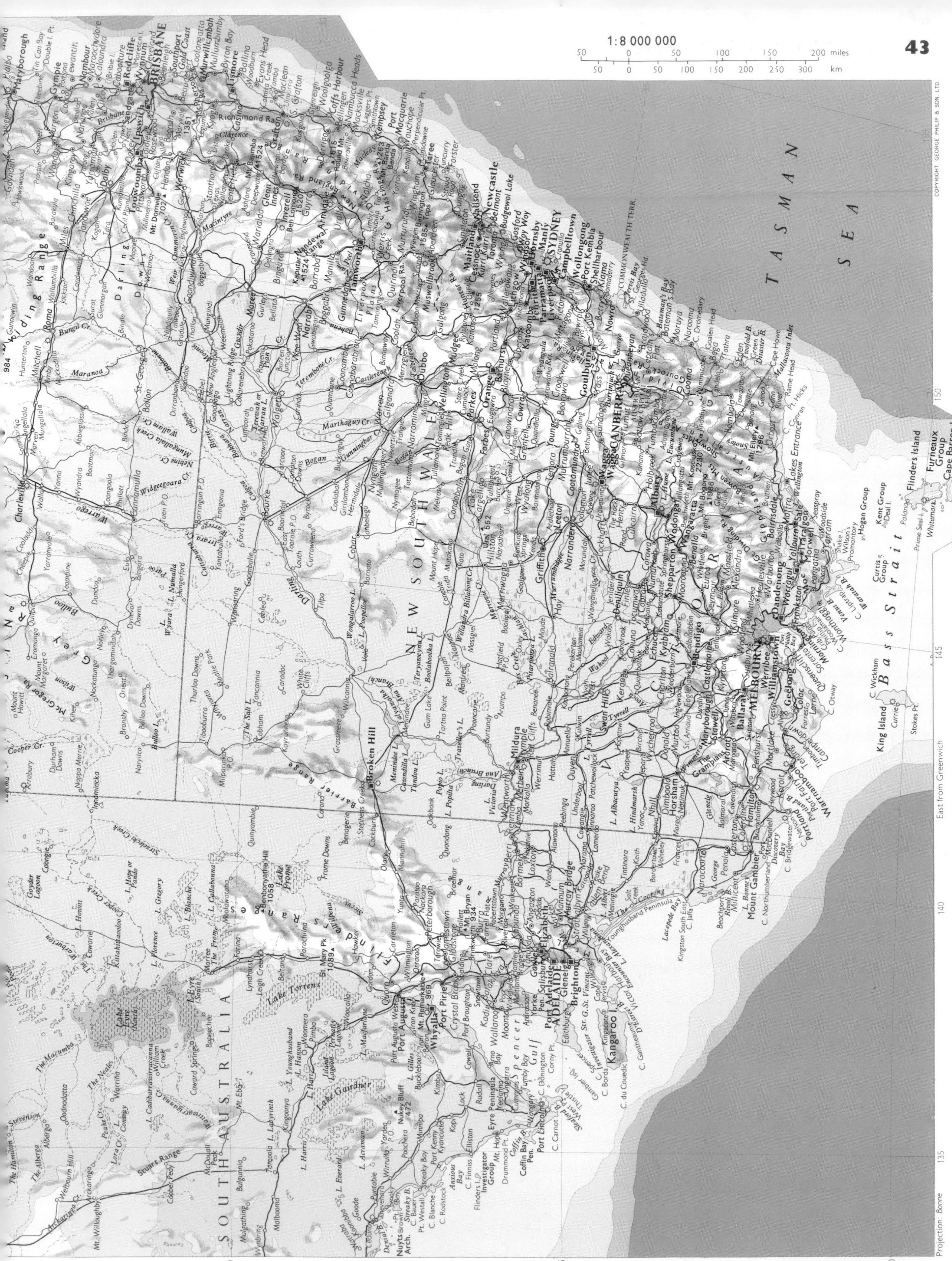

Projection: Bonne

m	1500	1000	400	200	0	200	600	2000	4000	m
ft	4500	3000	1200	600	0	600	6000	6000	12 000	ft

TIMOR SEA
INDIAN OCEAN
INDONESIA
NORTHERN TERRITORY
Tanami Desert
Great Sandy Desert
Joseph Bonaparte Gulf
Bonaparte Archipelago
King Leopold Ranges
Hamersley Range
Durack Range
Timor
Roti
Sawa
Sumba
Sumbawa
Semau
Raidjoea
Danu
Melville I.
Bathurst I.
Darwin
Port Darwin
Katherine
Wyndham
Cockburn
Kununurra
Derby
Broome
Port Hedland
Dampier
Dampier Archipelago
Roebourne
Wittenoom
Tom Price
Mt. Newman
Onslow
Exmouth
Exmouth Gulf
Learmonth
North West C.
Eighty Mile Beach
Roebuck B.
King Sound
Buccaneer Archipelago
Collier B.
Camden Sd.
Admiralty Gulf
Cambridge Gulf
Queens Chan.
Van Diemen Gulf
Cobourg Pen.
Clarence Str.
Dundas Str.
Browse I.
Adele I.
Lacepede Is.
Scott Reef
Seringapatam Reef
Ashmore Reef
Cartier I.
Hibernia Reef
Lynher Reef
Rowley Shoals
Mermaid Reef
Clerke Reef
Imperieuse Reef
Monte Bello Is.
Barrow I.
Tropic of Capricorn
Mt. Ord 1007
Mt. Hann 776
Mt. Bruce 1236
Mt. Greenwood 152
Mt. Singleton 808
Mt. Liebig 1524
Mt. Zeil 1510
Mt. Leisler 901
Fitzroy
Fitzroy Crossing
Halls Creek
Ord
L. Argyle
Victoria
Daly
Drysdale
De Grey
Ashburton
Fortescue
L. Mackay
L. Macdonald
Gregory Lake
Macdonnell Ranges
10
15
20
120
125
130

1:8 000 000

50 0 50 100 150 200 miles
50 0 50 100 150 200 250 300 km

S O U T H E R N O C E A N

S O U T H A U S T R A L I A

Great Australian Bight

Mt. Olga 1151 Ayers Rock 933
Mt. Morris 1387 Mann Ra. 1231
Musgrave Ranges
Mt. Woodroffe 1549
The Officer
Everard Ranges
Downs

Mt. Aloysius 1168
Blackstone Ra.
Cavenagh Ra.
..Ra. 1126
Tomkinson Ra.

Warburton Ra.
Mt. Squires 759
Barrow Ra.
L. Breaden

Mt. Normanhurst
Brassey Ra.
Granite Peak
Errabeedy
L. Buchanan
L. Gillen
L. Carnegie
Ernest Giles Ra. 712
L. Wells
Mt. Eureka
L. Darlot
Bates Ra.
L. Throssell
Cobbs
Rason L.
L. Yeo

Great Victoria Desert

Serpentine Lakes
Narrari Lakes
L. Maurice
Wynbring
L. Dey-Dey
Wilkinson Lakes

L. Minigwal
Jubilee L.
Shell Lakes
Pt. Lillian 502
Saunders Pt. 502
Macintosh Ra.
Baker L.
L. Kutga

Cook
Watson
Fisher
Mardingoo
Loongana
Deakin
Reid
Forrest
Hughes
Nullarbor
Koonalda P.O.
Coorabie
Fowlers B.
Penong
Nurina
Haig
Cocklebiddy Motel
Madura Motel
Mundrabilla Motel
Burnabbie Motel
Eucla Motel
Wilson Bluff
Low Pt.
Red Point Rock
Eyre

Nullarbor Plain
Hampton Tableland

Rawlinna
Naretha
Zanthus
Kitchener
Zanthus

Kalgoorlie 555
Mt. Burges
Coolgardie
Boulder

Widgiemooltha
The Johnston Lakes
L. Lefroy
Kambalda
L. Rebecca
Kanowna
Broad Arrow
Comet Vale
Goongarrie
Menzies
Niagara

L. Yindarlgooda
Higginsville
Norseman
Salmon Gums
L. Cowan

Balladonia
Eastern Group
Mt. Ragged 585
C. Arid
Middle I.
Sandy Bight I.
South East Is.
Archipelago of the Recherche
Montagu B.
C. Pasley
Pt. Malcolm
Israelite B.
Pt. Culver
Pt. Dover

Esperance
Mt. Ridley
L. Gilmore
Peak Charles 658
Grass Patch
Scaddan
Gibson
Salmon Gums
Norseman
L. Dundas
Dundas

Mt. Essendon 906
Carnarvon Ra.
Collier Ra.
Peak Hill
L. Gregory
New Springs
Robinson Ra.
Mt. Fraser 860
Nicholson Ra.
Montague Ra.
Barr Smith Ra.
Maynard Hills
Mt. Pascoe 625
Burlee Mt.
Mt. Marmion
Mt. Redcliffe 576
Pindinni
Depot Springs
Wiluna
L. Way
L. Nabberu
L. Keilko
L. Darlot
Agnew
Sandstone
Yandil
Yundamindera
Murrin Murrin
Leonora
Gwalia
Menzies

Cashmere Downs
Paynes Find
Johnston Ra.
Mt. Elvire
L. Barlee
Copperfield
Ora Banda
Davyhurst
Bullabulling
Woolgangie
Coolgardie

Tallering Peak 453
Dividing Ra.
Mt. Singleton 698
L. Moore
Mount
Beacon
Bonnie Rock
Mukinbudin
Southern Cross
Yellowdine
Koolyanobbing
Merredin

Carnarvon
Kennedy Ra.
Gascoyne
Lyons
Mt. Augustus 1105
Mt. Egerton 994
Thee Rivers
Meekatharra
Cue
Meka
Yalgoo
Mount Magnet
Edah
Paynes Find
Mt. Austin
Murchison

Shark Bay
Hamelin Pool
Dirk Hartog I.
Bernier I.
Dorre I.
C. Ronsard
C. St. Cricq
Denham
Geographe Channel
Houtman Abrolhos
Geraldton
Northampton
Dongara
Mingenew
Three Springs
Mullewa
Murchison

PERTH
Fremantle
Rockingham
Mandurah
Pinjarra
Bunbury
Busselton
Margaret River
Cape Leeuwin
Augusta
Pt. D'Entrecasteaux
Pemberton
Manjimup
Bridgetown
Collie
Harvey
Brunswick Junction
Donnybrook
Nannup
Geographe B.
C. Naturaliste

Albany
Mt. Barker
Stirling Ra. 1108
Denmark
W. C. Howe
Bald Hd.
King George Sound
Frankland
Kojonup
Katanning
Wagin
Narrogin
Pingelly
Brookton
Beverley
Northam
York
Toodyay
Midland
Armadale
Kalamunda
Kwinana

COASTAL PLAINS

Moora
Dandaragan
Gingin
Yanchep
Moore River
Lancelin

Southern Hills

East from Greenwich

Projection: Bonne

115 120 125 130

30 35 25

m ft
3000 1000
1200 400
600 200
0 0
600 2000
6000
12000 4000 m

ft m

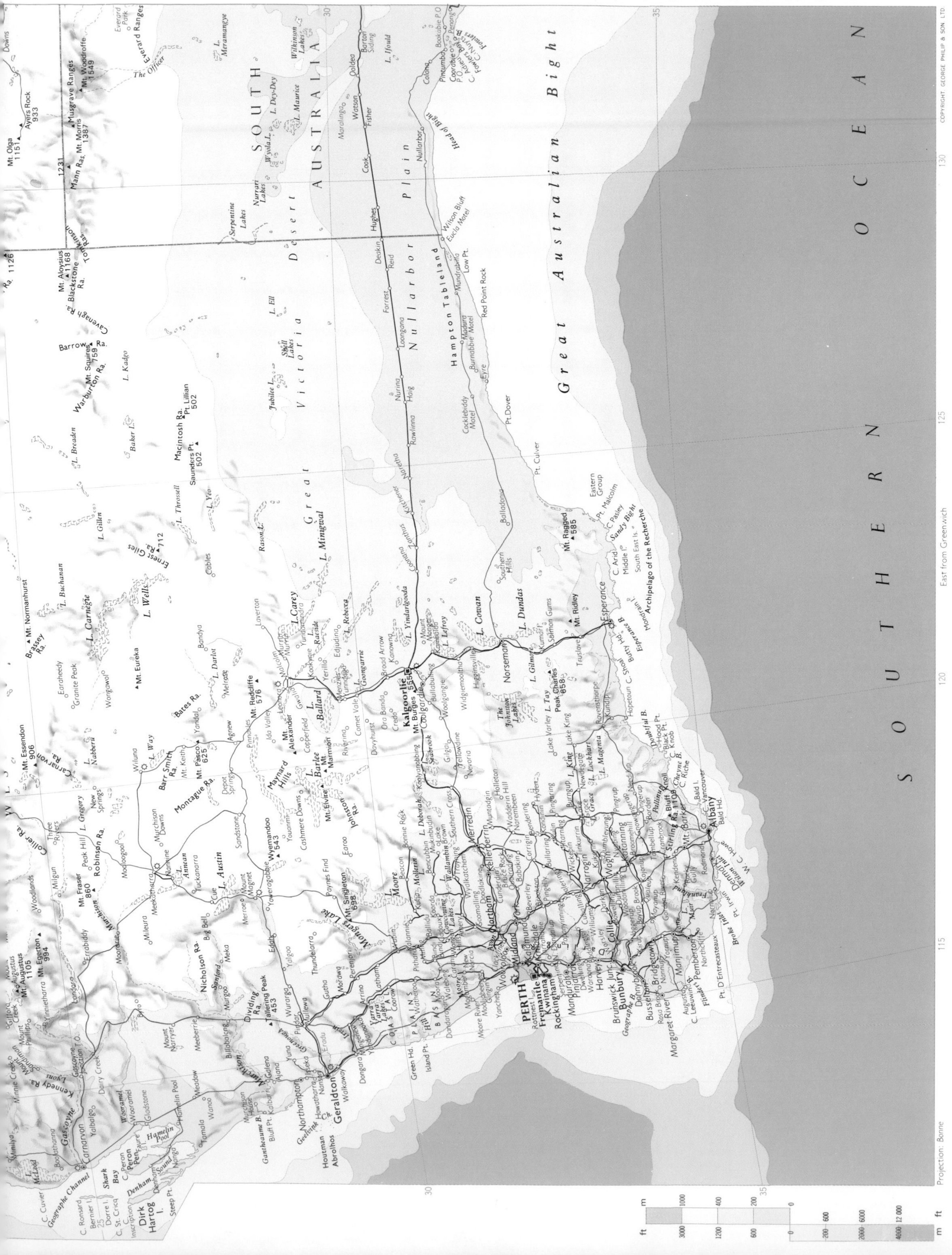

1 : 4 500 000

20 0 20 40 60 80 100 miles
20 0 20 40 60 80 120 160 km

T A S M A N S E A

N E W S O U T H W A L E S

V I C T O R I A

SOUTH AUSTRALIA

SYDNEY
Newcastle
Wollongong
Canberra
AUSTRALIAN CAPITAL TERRITORY
MELBOURNE
Geelong
Ballarat
Bendigo
Broken Hill
Maitland
Cessnock
Parramatta
Liverpool
Fairfield
Penrith
Lithgow
Bathurst
Orange
Mudgee
Dubbo
Parkes
Forbes
Goulburn
Queanbeyan
Wagga Wagga
Albury
Wangaratta
Benalla
Shepparton
Echuca
Mildura
Horsham
Warrnambool
Sale
Traralgon
Morwell
Dandenong
Frankston
Nowra

Projection: Albers' Equal Area with two standard parallels
East from Greenwich
COPYRIGHT GEORGE PHILIP & SON. LTD.

m 6000 4500 3000 1200 600 0 ft
ft 2000 1500 1000 400 200 0 m

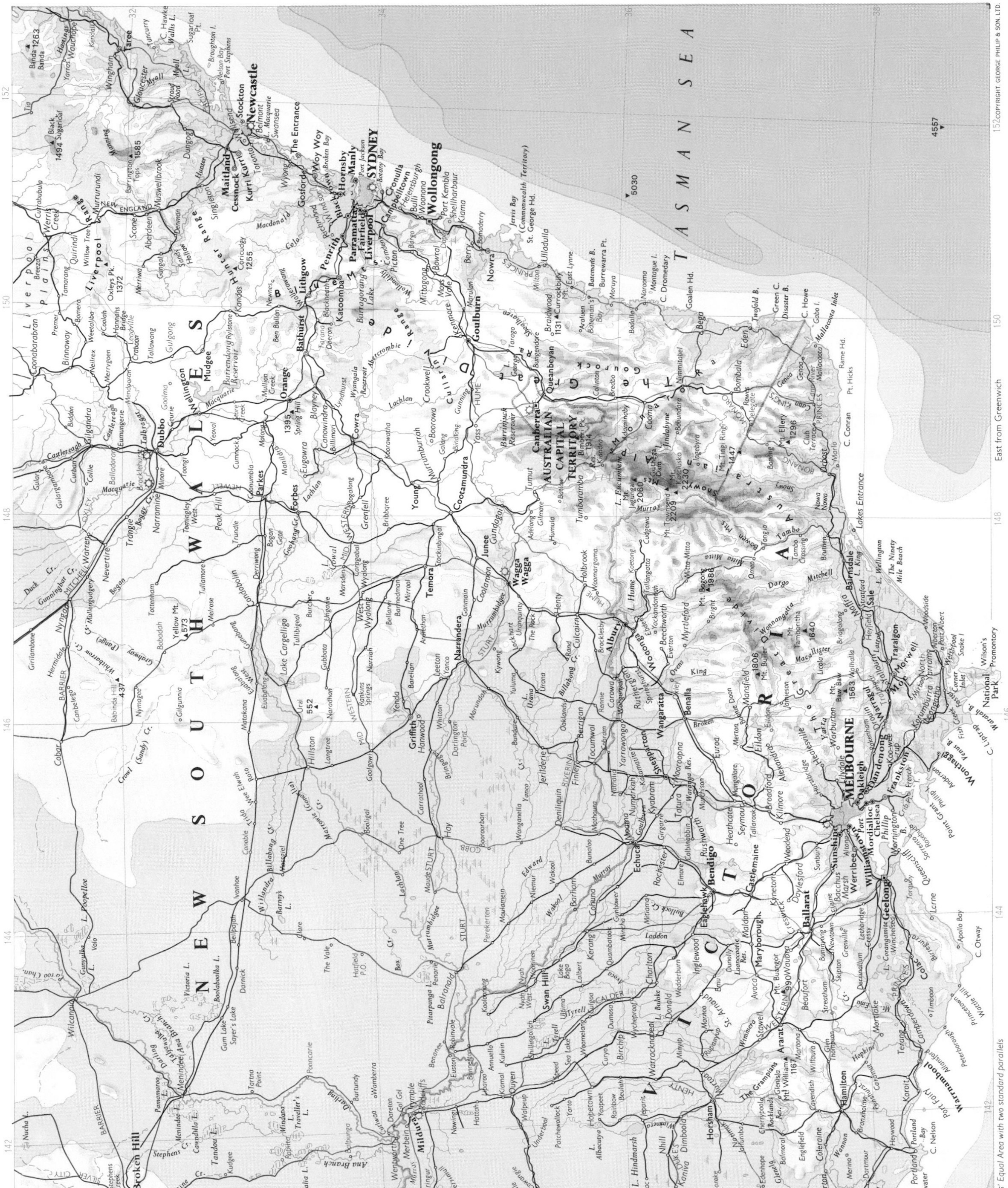

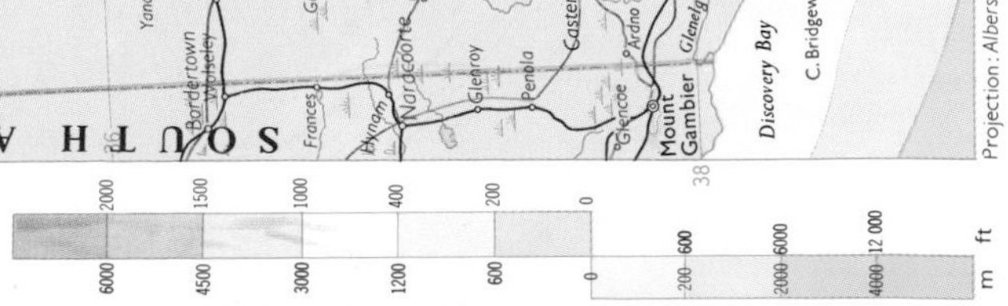

1:6 000 000
20 0 20 40 60 80 100 miles
40 0 40 80 120 160 km

NEW ZEALAND & DEPENDENCIES
1:60 000 000
200 0 200 400 600 800 miles
200 0 400 800 1200 km
New Zealand Territory
Self-governing Territory

SAMOA ISLANDS
1:12 000 000

FIJI AND TONGA ISLANDS
1:12 000 000
50 0 50 100 150 miles
50 0 50 100 150 200 250 km

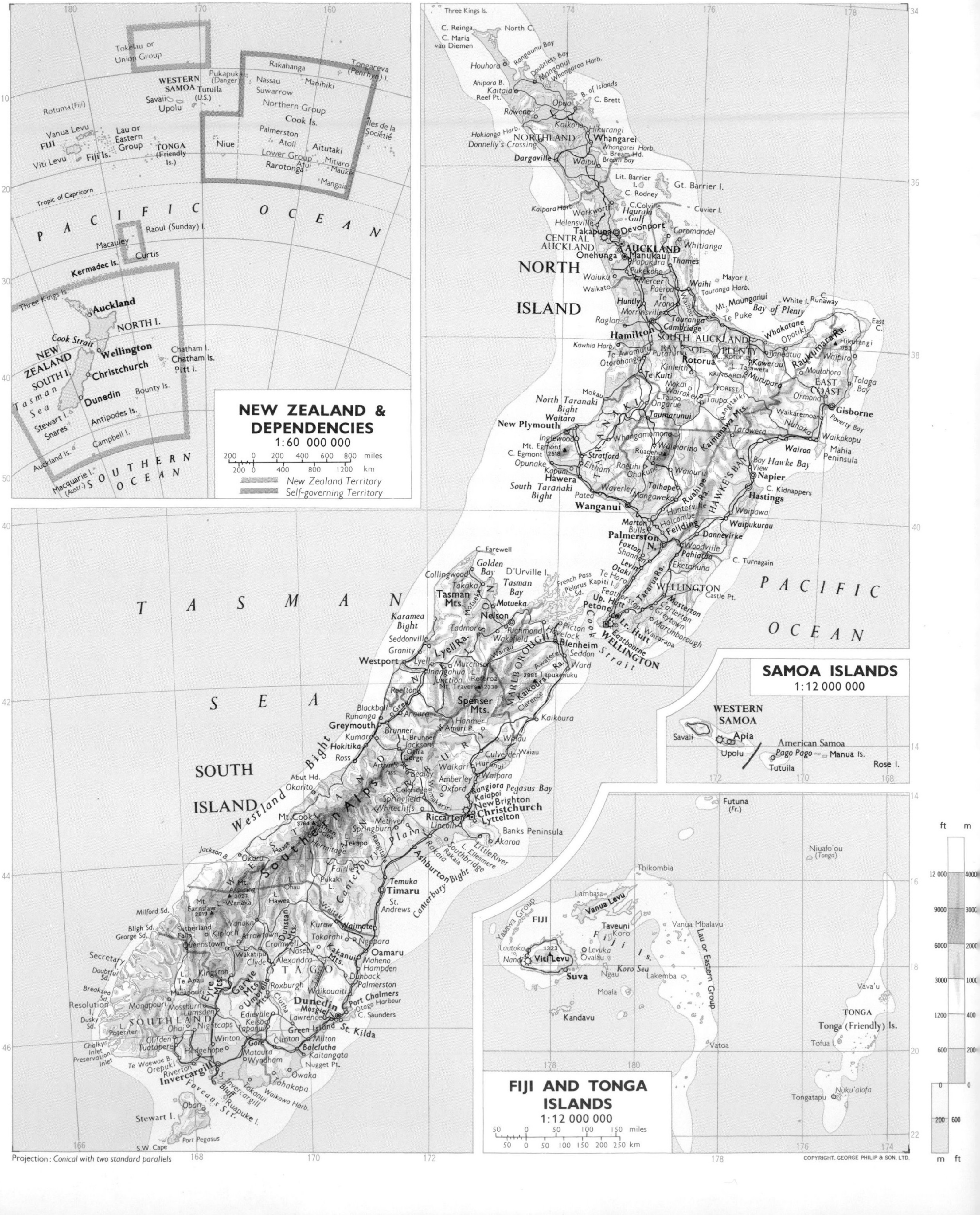

Projection: Conical with two standard parallels

COPYRIGHT. GEORGE PHILIP & SON. LTD.

1:40 000 000
200 0 200 400 600 800 1000 miles
200 0 200 400 600 800 1000 1200 1400 1600 km

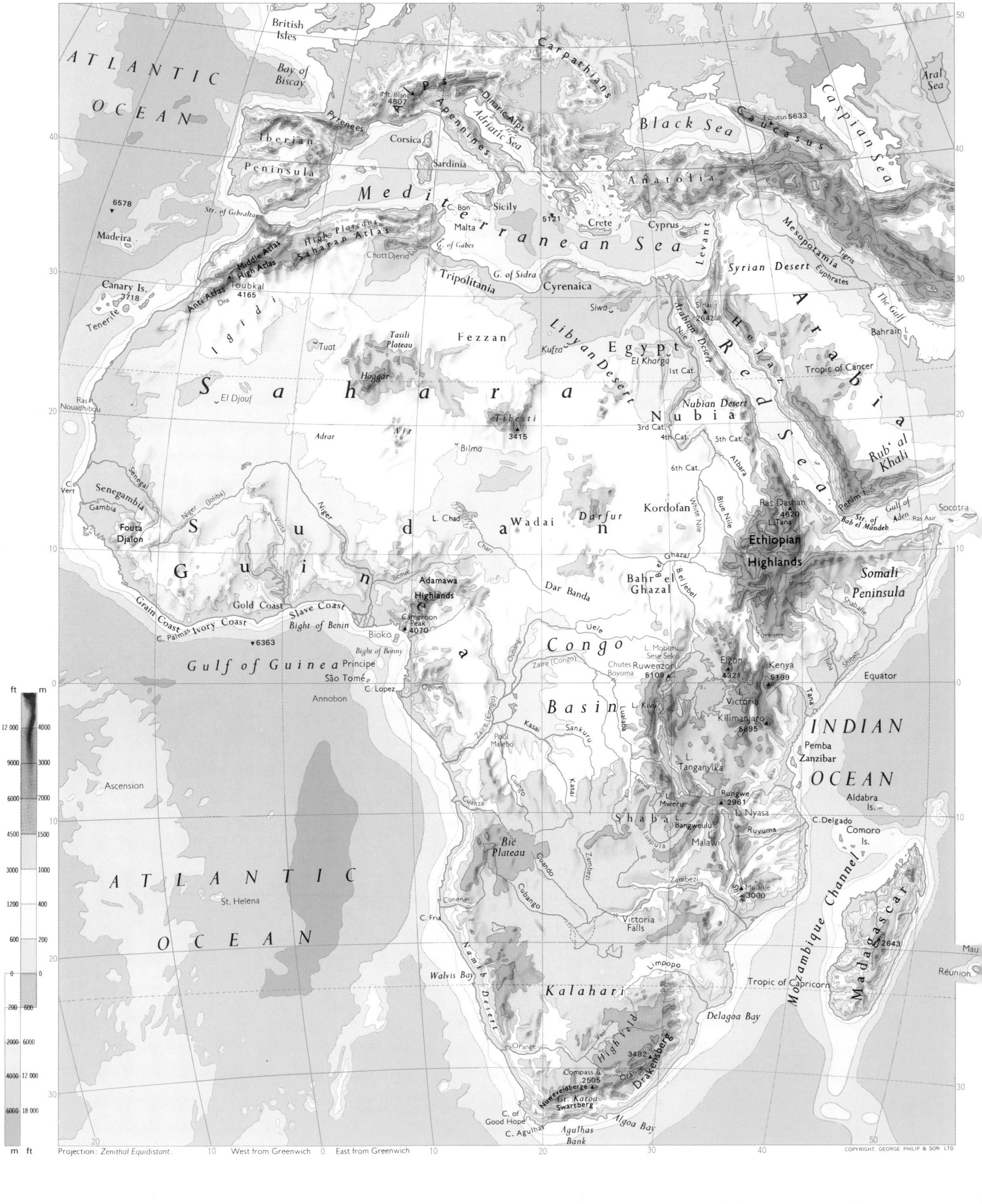

Projection: *Zenithal Equidistant.* 10 West from Greenwich 0 East from Greenwich 10 20 30 40

1:40 000 000

200 0 200 400 600 800 1000 miles

200 0 200 400 600 800 1000 1200 1400 1600 km

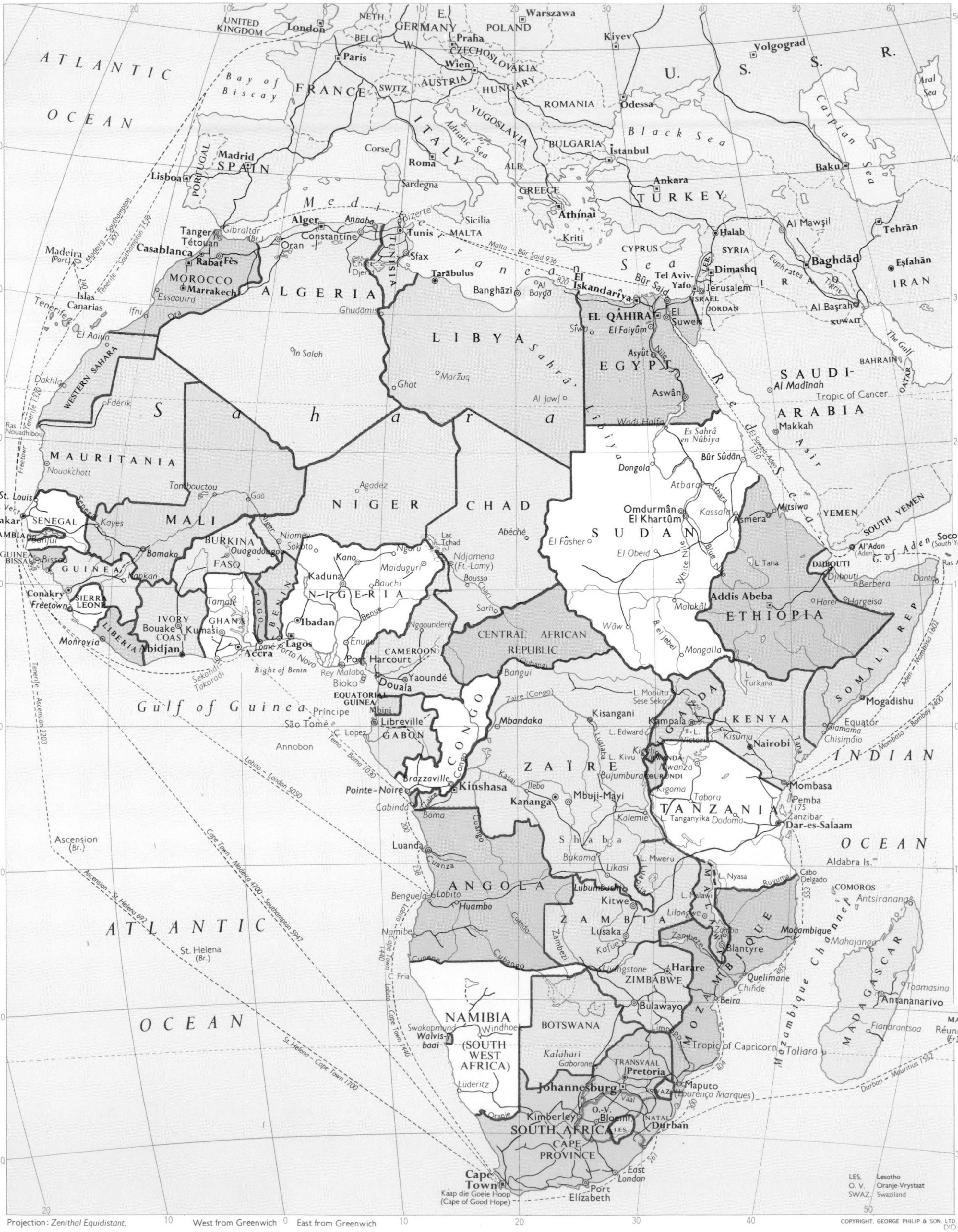

Projection: *Zenithal Equidistant.* West from Greenwich East from Greenwich

1 : 40 000 000

ATLANTIC OCEAN

UNITED KINGDOM London
NETH. E. POLAND Warszawa
GERMANY W.
BELG. Praha CZECHOSLOVAKIA
Paris Wien AUSTRIA HUNGARY Kiyev
FRANCE SWITZ. ROMANIA
Bay of Biscay Volgograd
U. S. S. R.
Aral Sea
Madrid Corse YUGOSLAVIA Odessa
SPAIN PORTUGAL ITALY Roma BULGARIA Black Sea Caspian Sea
Lisboa Sardegna Adriatic Sea GREECE İstanbul Baku
Madeira (Port.) Tanger ALB. Athínai Ankara TURKEY
Tétouan Gibraltar (Br.) Sicilia Kriti Al Mawşil Tehrán
Casablanca Oran Alger Tunis MALTA Halab SYRIA Baghdád Eşfahán
Rabat Fès Constantine Annaba Bizerte Tel Aviv-Yafo Dimashq IRAN
MOROCCO TUNISIA Sfax Malta 936 Bûr Saîd ISRAEL Jerusalem Al Başrah
Marrakech Djerba JORDAN KUWAIT
Islas Canarias Essaouira Banghází El Iskandarîya Al Bayda The Gulf
Tenerife Ifni ALGERIA LIBYA Bûr Saîd EL QÂHIRA EL BAHRAIN
El Aaiún In Salah Ghudámis El Faiyûm El Suweis QATAR
WESTERN SAHARA Ghat Marzuq Siwa SAUDI- Al Madînah
Dakhla S a h a r a Asyût Nile ARABIA Tropic of Cancer
Fdérik Al Jawf EGYPT Aswân Makkah
MAURITANIA Sahrà' Wadi Halfa Es Sahrà Asir
Ras Nouadhibou Tombouctou Libiya en Núbiya
Nouakchott Agadez Dongola Bûr Sûdân YEMEN SOUTH YEMEN
St. Louis NIGER CHAD Atbara Kassala Asmera Mitsiwa Socotra (South Yemen)
Dakar SENEGAL Kayes MALI Gaô Omdurmân S U D A N Al'Adan (Aden) Ras Asir
GAMBIA Banjul Bamako Niamey El Khartûm DJIBOUTI Berbera G. of Aden Dante
GUINEA-BISSAU Bissau BURKINA Sokoto Ndjamena (Ft.-Lamy) El Fasher Mongalla L. Tana Djibouti Hargeisa
GUINEA Kankan Ouagadougou FASO Kano Maiduguri El Obeid Addis Abeba Harer
Conakry SIERRA Kaduna Bauchi Bousso ETHIOPIA SOMALI REP.
Freetown LEONE NIGERIA Benue Sarh Wâw L. Turkana
LIBERIA IVORY COAST Tamale GHANA Ibadan Enugu Ngaoundéré CENTRAL AFRICAN REPUBLIC Bel el Jebel Mogadishu
Monrovia Bouaké Kumasi TOGO BENIN Lagos CAMEROON Bangui Mongalla KENYA Equator Giamama
Abidjan Accra Lomé Porto Novo Port Harcourt Yaoundé Zaïre (Congo) L. Mobutu Sese Seko Kisangani Nairobi Chisimaio
Sekondi-Takoradi Bight of Benin Douala Rey Malaba Bioko CONGO Mbandaka Kampala UGANDA Mombasa INDIAN OCEAN
Gulf of Guinea EQUATORIAL GUINEA Mbini Libreville GABON L. Edward L. Victoria Kisumu
São Tomé Príncipe Brazzaville ZAÏRE L. Kivu Nwanza RWANDA Nairobi
C. Lopez Pointe-Noire Kinshasa Ilebo Bujumbura BURUNDI Kigoma Tabora Dodoma
Annobon Cabinda Kasai Mbuji-Mayi Kananga Kalemie L. Tanganyika TANZANIA Pemba 175 Zanzibar
Ascension (Br.) Boma Congo S h a b a Bukama L. Mweru Dar-es-Salaam
Luanda Cuanza Likasi Aldabra Is.
St. Helena (Br.) Benguela Lobito Lubumbashi L. Nyasa Cabo Delgado COMOROS Antsiranana
ANGOLA Huambo Kitwe L. Malawi Moçambique Antsiranana
Namibe Cuando ZAMBIA Lilongwe MALAWI Mahajanga MAURITIUS Réunion (Fr.)
Lusaka Zambezi Blantyre MADAGASCAR Durban-Mauritius 1592
ATLANTIC OCEAN Cunene Cubango Kafue Livingstone Harare Quelimane Chinde Mozambique Channel
NAMIBIA Swakopmund Windhoek BOTSWANA ZIMBABWE Beira Antananarivo
(SOUTH WEST AFRICA) Walvis-baai Kalahari Bulawayo MOZAMBIQUE Toamasina
Lüderitz Gaborone TRANSVAAL Pretoria Maputo Fianarantsoa Tropic of Capricorn
OCEAN Oranje Johannesburg SWAZ. Toliara
Kimberley O.V. Bloem. Maputo (Lourenço Marques)
SOUTH AFRICA Vaal NATAL Durban
CAPE PROVINCE LES.
Cape Town East London
Kaap die Goeie Hoop Port Elizabeth
(Cape of Good Hope)

LES. Lesotho
O. V. Oranje-Vrystaat
SWAZ. Swaziland

Projection: Zenithal Equidistant. West from Greenwich East from Greenwich COPYRIGHT. GEORGE PHILIP & SON. LTD. DID

NORTH ATLANTIC

OCEAN

SPAIN

Cabo de São Vicente
Cádiz
Málaga
Almería
Str. of Gibraltar
Gibraltar (Br.)
Ceuta (Sp.)
Tanger
Tetouan
Melilla
Larache
Ksar el Kebir
Kenitra
(Port Lyautey)
Salé
Rabat
Casablanca
El Jadida
Berrechid
Settat
Khouribga
Safi
Essaouira
Marrakech
Beni Mellal

MADEIRA
(Port.)
Pto. Santo
Funchal

▼ 6578

MOROCCO

Moyen Atlas
Haut Atlas
Anti Atlas
Agadir
Taroudant
Ifni
Tiznit
Bani

Islas Canarias
(Sp.)
Lanzarote
Fuerteventura
Puerto del Rosario
Arrecife
La Palma
Tenerife
Sta. Cruz
Gomera
Hierro
Gran Canaria
Las Palmas
C. Juby
Tarfaya
(Villa Bens)

Dakhla
Pta. Durnford

WESTERN SAHARA

El Aaiún
Semara
Bu Craa
C. Bojador

Bir Mogrein
Ain Ben Tili
Cheggá
Ferhazza

Foderik
Zouérate
C. Barbas

El Djouf
Taoudenni

MAURITANIA

Nouâdhibou
(Port Etienne)
Ras Nouâdhibou
La Güera
Oujeft
Atâr
Chinguetti
Ouadâne
Rachid
Tidjikja
Tichît
Akreijit
Akjoujt
Boutilimit

Timiris
Nouakchott
Mederdra
Aleg
Moudjéria
Togba
Tâmchekket
Ouâlâta
Néma
Timbedgha
Bassikounou
Nioro du Sahel

St. Louis
C. Vert
Dakar
Thies
Tivaouane
Rufisque
Mbour
Kaolack
Kaffrine
Diourbel
Louga
Dahra
Linguère
Matam
Podor
Dagana
Richard Toll
Bogué
Kaédi
Sélibabi
Yélimané
Kayes
Bakel
Nara
Sokolo

SENEGAL

GAMBIA
Banjul
Bathurst

GUINEA-BISSAU
Bissau
Bafatá
Gabú
Bolama
Arquipélago dos Bijagós
Bolama

GUINEA
Conakry
Dubreka
Kindia
Mamou
Labé
Télimélé
Boké
Fria
Kamsar
Koundara
Gaoual
Touba
Dinguiraye
Siguiri
Kankan
Kouroussa
Dabola
Faranah
Kissidougou
Guéckédou
Macenta
Nzérékoré
Beyla

SIERRA LEONE
Freetown
Waterloo
Bo
Kenema
Makeni
Magburaka
Moyamba
Bonthe
Sherbro I.

LIBERIA
Monrovia
Robertsport
Buchanan
Greenville
River Cess
Harper
Tapeta

ALGERIA

Alger (Algiers)
Tizi-Ouzou
Bejaia
Skikda
Annaba
Constantine
Guelma
Oran
Mostaganem
Sidi-Bel-Abbès
Tlemcen
Saïda
Mecheria
Béchar
El Goléa
Ghardaïa
Ouargla
Hassi Messaoud
Touggourt
El Oued
Biskra
Batna
Sétif
Tiaret
Djelfa
Laghouat
Tindouf
Adrar
Reggane
Timimoun
In Salah
In Belbel
Ouallene
Tamanrasset

Plateau du Tademaït
Plateau du Tademaït
Tanezrouft
Poste Maurice Cortier
(Bidon 5)
Adrar des Iforhas
Tessalit

Ahaggar
Tahat ▲ 3918
Djanet
Illizi

MALI
Tombouctou
Kabara
Goundam
Diré
Gourma-Rharous
Gao
Bourem
Bamba
Kidal
Ansongo
Ménaka
Araouane
Bou Djébéha
Mabrouk
Néma
Niafounké
Hombori
Douentza
Mopti
Djenné
Ségou
Bamako
Koulikoro
Bafoulabé
Kita
Kati
Kangaba
Bougouni
Sikasso
Koutiala
Kolokani
Banamba

NIGER
Agadez
Aïr
(Azbine)
In-Gall
Iférouane
Monts Tamgak
Tahoua
Tanout
Madaoua
Birni Nkonni
Maradi
Zinder
Magaria

BURKINA FASO
Ouagadougou
Bobo-Dioulasso
Koudougou
Kaya
Dori
Djibo
Ouahigouya
Fada N'Gourma
Tenkodogo
Banfora

Niamey
Tillabéri
Téra
Dosso
Gaya
Birnin Kebbi
Sokoto
Gusau
Katsina
Kano
Zaria
Kaduna

NIGERIA
Ilorin
Oshogbo
Ogbomosho
Oyo
Ibadan
Ife
Abeokuta
Lagos
Benin City
Enugu
Onitsha
Warri
Port Harcourt
Aba

IVORY COAST
Bouaké
Daloa
Man
Korhogo
Gagnoa
Dimbokro
Abidjan
Grand Bassam
Sassandra
San-Pédro
Tabou

GHANA
Kumasi
Tamale
Bolgatanga
Wa
Obuasi
Lake Volta
Koforidua
Accra
Tema
Sekondi-Takoradi
Cape Coast

TOGO
Lomé
Atakpamé
Sokodé

BENIN
Cotonou
Porto-Novo
Abomey
Parakou
Natitingou
Kandi

CAMEROON

Bight of Benin

Projection: Sanson Flamsteed's Sinusoidal

West from Greenwich
East from Greenwich

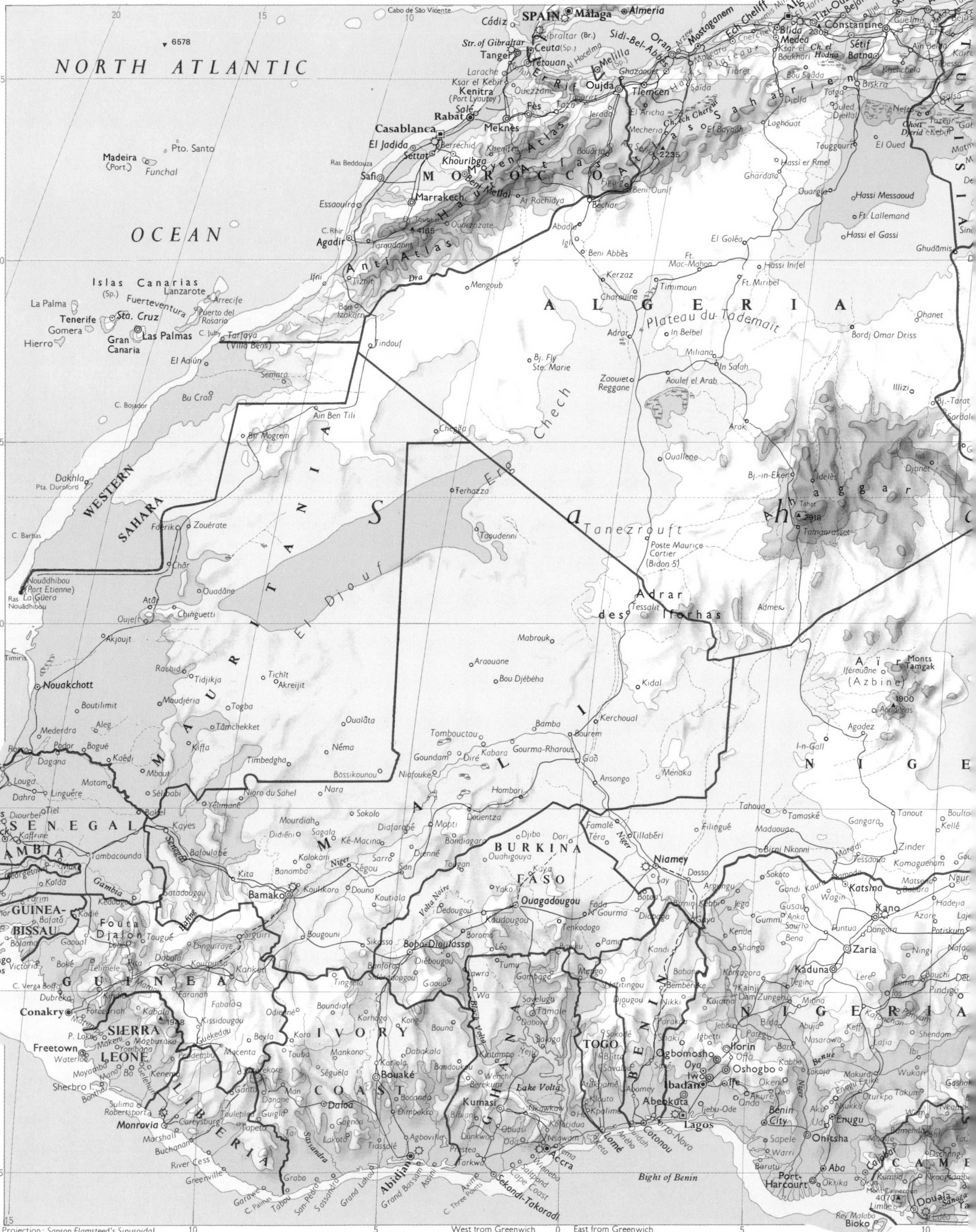

1:15 000 000

100 0 100 200 300 400 miles
100 0 100 200 300 400 500 600 km

MEDITERRANEAN SEA

MALTA
Lampedusa
Pantelleria (It.)
Sicily
Ragusa
C. Passero
Iraklion
Ródhos
Karpathos
Antalya
Antalya Körfezi
TURKEY
İskenderun Körfezi
Antakya
Halab
Al Mawşil (Mosul)
Nahr Dijlah (Tigris)

CYPRUS
Lefkosía
Lárnax
Al Ladhiqiya
Hamā'
SYRIA
Homs
Tarabulus
Mesopotamia
Nahr al Furāt

Tarābulus (Tripoli)
Al Qaşbah
Al Khums
Misrātah
Banghāzi (Benghazi)
Barh
878
LEBANON
Bayrūt
Dimashq (Damascus)
IRAQ
Ar Ruṭbah
Bādiyat

Al 'Uqaylah
Marsa Brega
Ajdābiyah
Ra's Al-Unuf
Zueitina
Khalīj Surt
Surt
Bani Walīd
Gharyān
968
Mizdah
Jādū
Zuwārah

El Iskandarîya (Alexandria)
EL QÂHIRA (Cairo)
EL GIZA
Zagazig
Tanta
El Mahalla el Kubra
Dumyât
El Mansûra
Bûr Said
El Qantara
ISRAEL
Tel Aviv-Yafo
Haifa
Yerusalem (Al Quds)
'Ammân
JORDAN
Bahr el Miyet (Dead Sea)
ash Shām
Al Jawf

El Suweis
El Faiyum
Beni Suef
El Minya
Mallawi
Beni Mazâr
Asyût
Es Sahrâ
Sinâ
Tābūk
An Nafūd
SAUDI
ARABIA
Mada'in Salih
Taymā'

LIBYA
Cyrenaica
Sahrâ'
Fezzan
Tarābulus
1200
Sabhah
Marzūq
Idehan
Marzūq
Awjilah
Al 'Iraq
Siwa
Qâra
Munkhafed el Qattâra (Qattara Depression)
El Jaghbûb
Marâdah
Zillah
Hūn

LIBYAN DESERT
Līb î y a
Egypt
Sahrâ'
El Wâhât el Dâkhla
Mût
El Wâhât el Khârga
El Khârga
Bâris
Girga
Sohâg
Akhmîm
Qena
El Uqsur (Luxor)
Isna
Idfu
Aswân
Sadd el Aali (Aswân High Dam)
Bur Safâga
Quseir
Al Wajh
Umm Lajj
Yanbu' al Bahr
Al Madinah
RED SEA
Ras Bânâs
Tropic of Cancer
Al Kufrah
Al Jawf
Rebiana
3150
Tibesti
Emi Koussi 3415
Ouniango-Kébir
Depression du Mourdi
Borkou
Ennedi
Djourab

CHAD
Ndjamena
Lac Tchad
L. Fitri
Abéché
Am Dam
Biltine
Harazé

SHAMÂL DÂRFÛR
JANUB DÂRFÛR
El Fasher
Nyâlâ
Buram
3088

SUDAN
SHAMÂL KORDOFAN
JANUB KORDOFAN
El Obeid
En Nahud
Omdurmân
El Khartûm (Khartoum)
Wâd Medani
GEZIRA
EL AZRAQ
AN NÎL EL ABYAD
BAHR EL GHAZAL
JONGLEI
Bentiu
Malakâl
Bôr
AN NÎL EL AZRAQ
Singa
Gedaref
KASSALA
Kassala
Asmera
Eritrea
Mitsiwa
RED SEA
Bûr Sûdân (Port Sudan)
Suakin
2635

ETHIOPIA
Addis Abeba (Addis Ababa)
L. Tana
4620
L. Abaya
L. Shama
L. Stefanie

CENTRAL AFRICAN REPUBLIC
Bangui
ZAÏRE (CONGO)
GHARB EL ISTIWA'IYA
SHARQ EL ISTIWA'IYA
Jûba
KENYA
L. Turkana

COPYRIGHT. GEORGE PHILIP & SON, LTD.

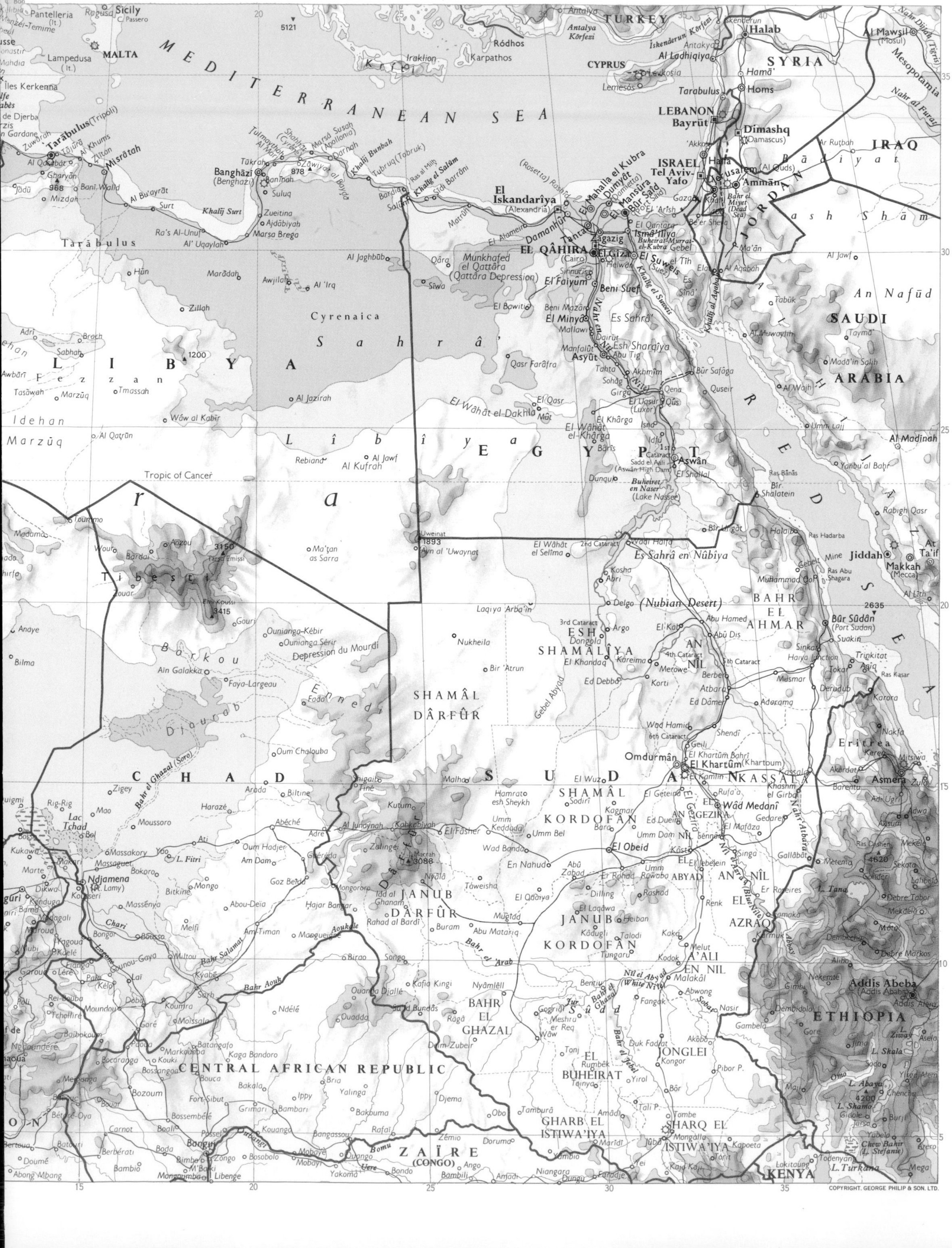

1 : 7 500 000

SUDAN

ETHIOPIA

UGANDA

KENYA

SOMALI REP.

RWANDA

BURUNDI

TANZANIA

ZAIRE

ZAMBIA

MALAWI

MOZAMBIQUE

INDIAN OCEAN

LAKE VICTORIA 1134

Nairobi

Kampala

Dar-es-Salaam

Mombasa and Kilindini

Dodoma

Zanzibar

Pemba I.

Mafia I.

Lake Turkana (Lake Rudolf)

Kilimanjaro 5895

Projection: Modified Polyconic

East from Greenwich

COPYRIGHT. GEORGE PHILIP & SON. LTD.

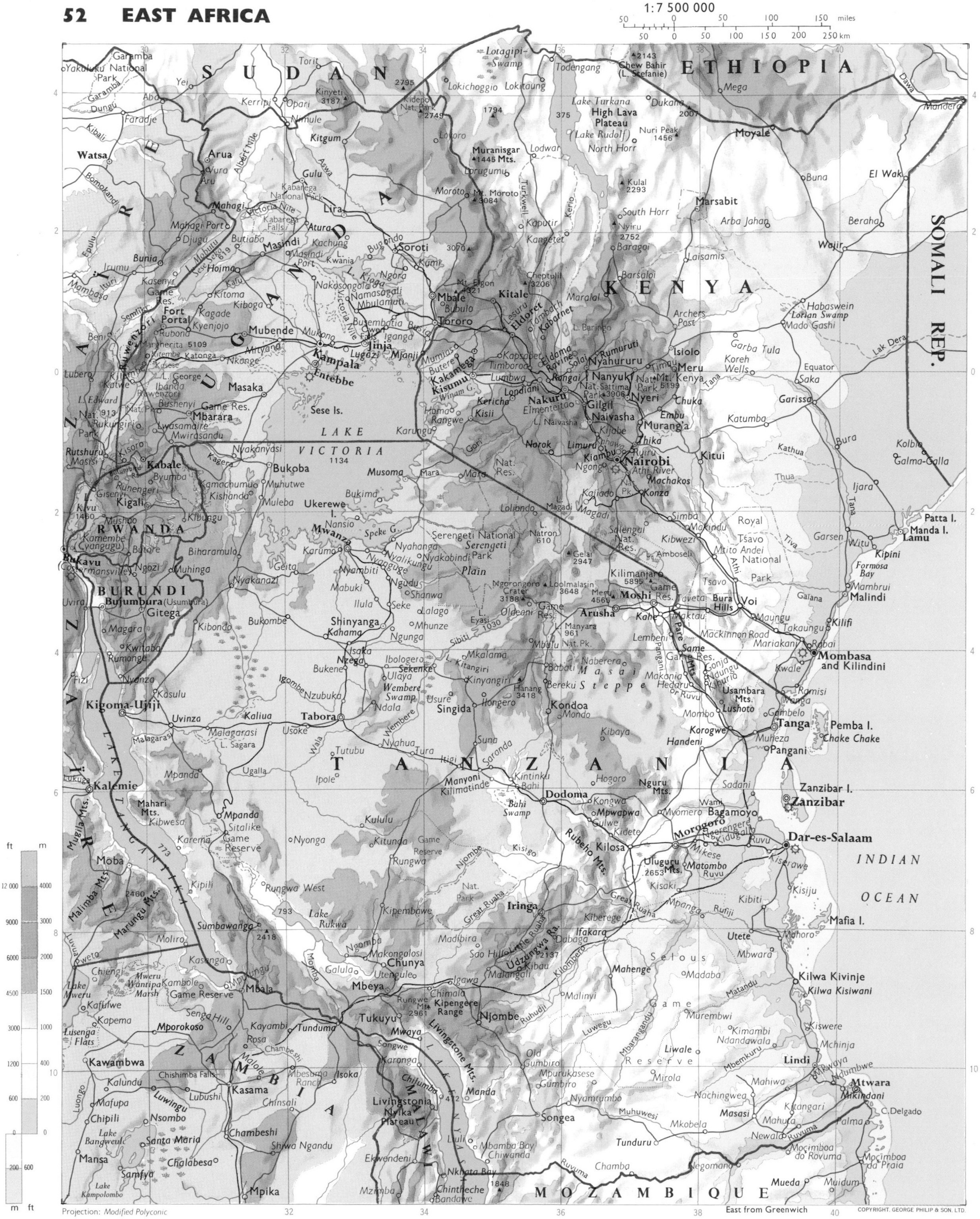

1:8 000 000

50 0 50 100 150 200 miles

50 0 50 100 150 200 250 300 km

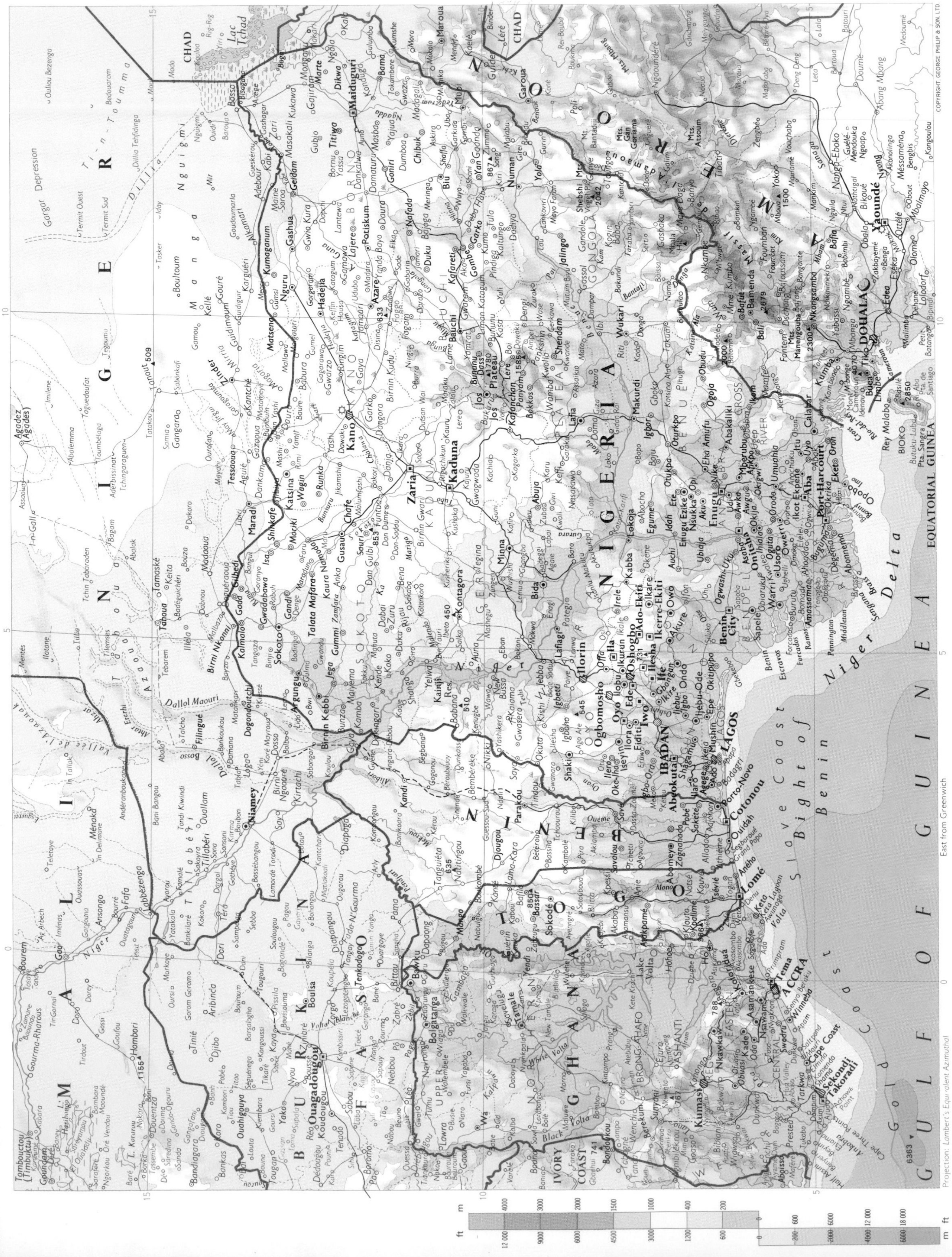

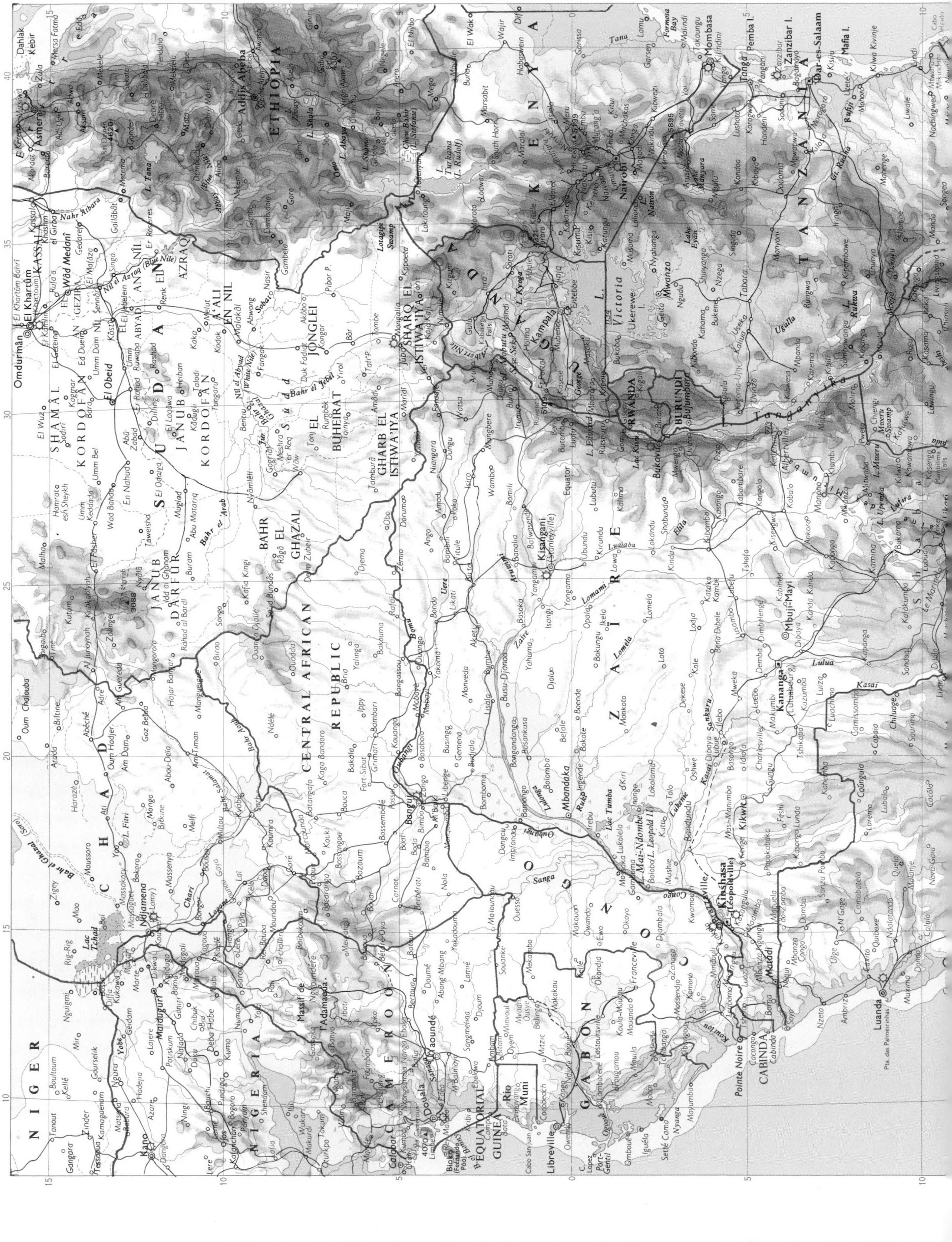
NIGER
NIGERIA
CHAD
SUDAN
ETHIOPIA
KENYA
UGANDA
TANZANIA
RWANDA
BURUNDI
ZAIRE
CENTRAL AFRICAN REPUBLIC
CAMEROON
GABON
CONGO
EQUATORIAL GUINEA
Rio Muni
CABINDA
Addis Abeba
El Khartûm
Omdurmân
Asmera
Nairobi
Mombasa
Dar-es-Salaam
Zanzibar I.
Pemba I.
Mafia I.
Kampala
Kisangani (Stanleyville)
Kinshasa (Léopoldville)
Brazzaville
Luanda
Libreville
Douala
Yaoundé
Bangui
Ndjamena (Fort Lamy)
Kano
Lac Tchad
L. Victoria
L. Tana
L. Turkana (L. Rudolf)
Tanganyika
L. Kyoga
L. Albert
L. Edward
L. Kivu
Kananga
Mbuji-Mayi
Pointe Noire
Port-Gentil
Matadi
Mbandaka
Lac Tumba
Lac Mai-Ndombe (L. Leopold II)
Massif de l'Adamaoua
KASSALA
EL GEZIRA
AN NIL AL AZRAQ
SHAMAL KORDOFAN
JANUB KORDOFAN
JANUB DARFUR
BAHR EL GHAZAL
EL BUHEIRAT
JONGLEI
SHARQ EL ISTIWA'IYA
GHARB EL ISTIWA'IYA
AALI EN NIL

1:15 000 000

100 0 100 200 300 400 miles
100 0 100 200 300 400 500 600 km

MADAGASCAR

On same scale as General Map

COPYRIGHT GEORGE PHILIP & SON LTD.

I N D I A N O C E A N

A T L A N T I C O C E A N

Tropic of Capricorn

East from Greenwich

Projection: Sanson Flamsteed's Sinusoidal 10

Countries and regions

ZIMBABWE

BOTSWANA

Kalahari

NAMIBIA (SOUTH WEST AFRICA)

Namib Desert

Damaraland

Namaland

Bushmanland

SOUTH AFRICA

CAPE PROVINCE

ORANJE-VRYSTAAT (O.F.S.)

TRANSVAAL

NATAL

LESOTHO

SWAZILAND

Caprivi Strip

Okavango Swamps

Etosha Pan

Makarikari Salt Pans

Major cities and places

Harare (Salisbury)

Bulawayo

Lusaka

Gaborone

Windhoek

Johannesburg

Pretoria

Bloemfontein

Kimberley

Durban

Pietermaritzburg

East London

Port Elizabeth

Cape Town (Kaapstad)

Kaap die Goeie Hoop (C. of Good Hope)

Beira

Maputo (Lourenço Marques)

Madagascar

Antananarivo (Tananarive)

Toamasina (Tamatave)

Mahajanga

Toliara

Fianarantsoa

Antsiranana

Nosy Be

Iles Glorieuses (Reunion)

Île Europa (Réunion)

Bassas da India (Reunion)

Mozambique Channel

5283

5349

ft / m elevation scale:
18 000 / 6000
12 000 / 4000
9000 / 3000
6000 / 2000
4500 / 1500
3000 / 1000
1200 / 400
600 / 200
0

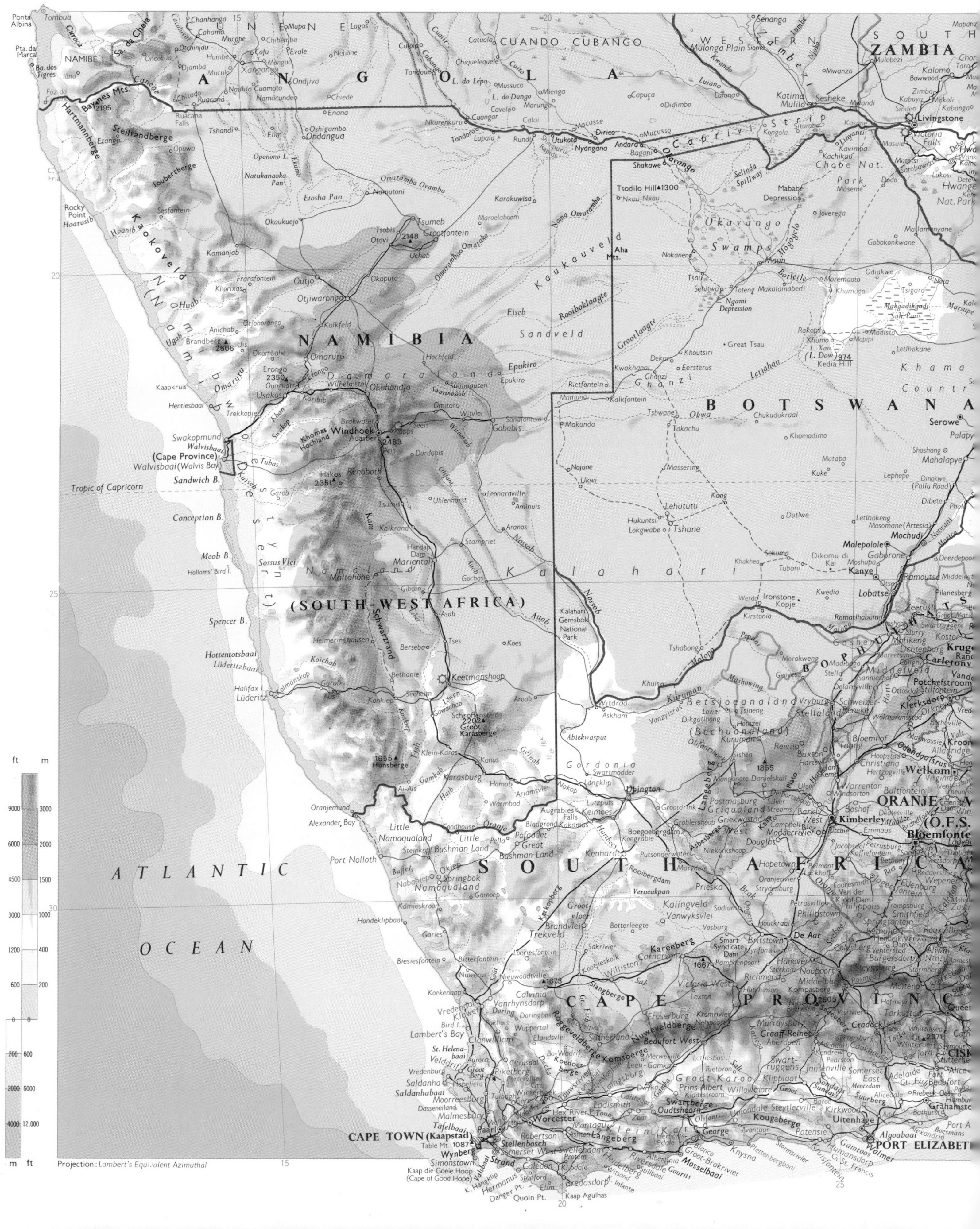
ANGOLA
CUANDO CUBANGO
WESTERN
ZAMBIA
SOUTH
NAMIBIA
(SOUTH-WEST AFRICA)
BOTSWANA
SOUTH AFRICA
CAPE PROVINCE
ORANJE
(O.F.S.)
ATLANTIC
OCEAN
Tropic of Capricorn
Windhoek
Walvisbaai
(Cape Province)
Walvisbaai (Walvis Bay)
Swakopmund
Lüderitz
Keetmanshoop
Kalahari
Okavango Swamps
Caprivi Strip
Kaukauveld
Damaraland
Namaland
Namib Desert
Kaokoveld
Great Namaqualand
Little Namaqualand
Bushman Land
Groot Karoo
Klein Karoo
Kimberley
Bloemfontein
Upington
De Aar
Beaufort West
Graaff-Reinet
Oudtshoorn
George
Mosselbaai
Uitenhage
PORT ELIZABETH
CAPE TOWN (Kaapstad)
Table Mt. 1087
Stellenbosch
Paarl
Worcester
Wynberg
Simonstown
Kaap die Goeie Hoop
(Cape of Good Hope)
Kaap Agulhas
Lobatse
Kanye
Gaborone
Mochudi
Molepolole
Serowe
Mahalapye
Livingstone
Victoria Falls
Maun
Ghanzi
Tsumeb
Grootfontein
Otjiwarongo
Outjo
Okahandja
Gobabis
Rehoboth
Mariental
Port Nolloth
Springbok
Calvinia
Lambert's Bay
Saldanha
Saldanhabaai
Tafelbaai
Hermanus
Knysna
Prieska
Kenhardt
Vryburg
Mafikeng
Klerksdorp
Welkom
Colesberg
Cradock
Grahamstown
Ft. Beaufort
Queenstown
Atlantic Ocean
ft m
9000 3000
6000 2000
4500 1500
3000 1000
1200 400
600 200
0 0
200 600
2000 6000
4000 12,000
m ft
Projection: Lambert's Equivalent Azimuthal
15
20
25
30

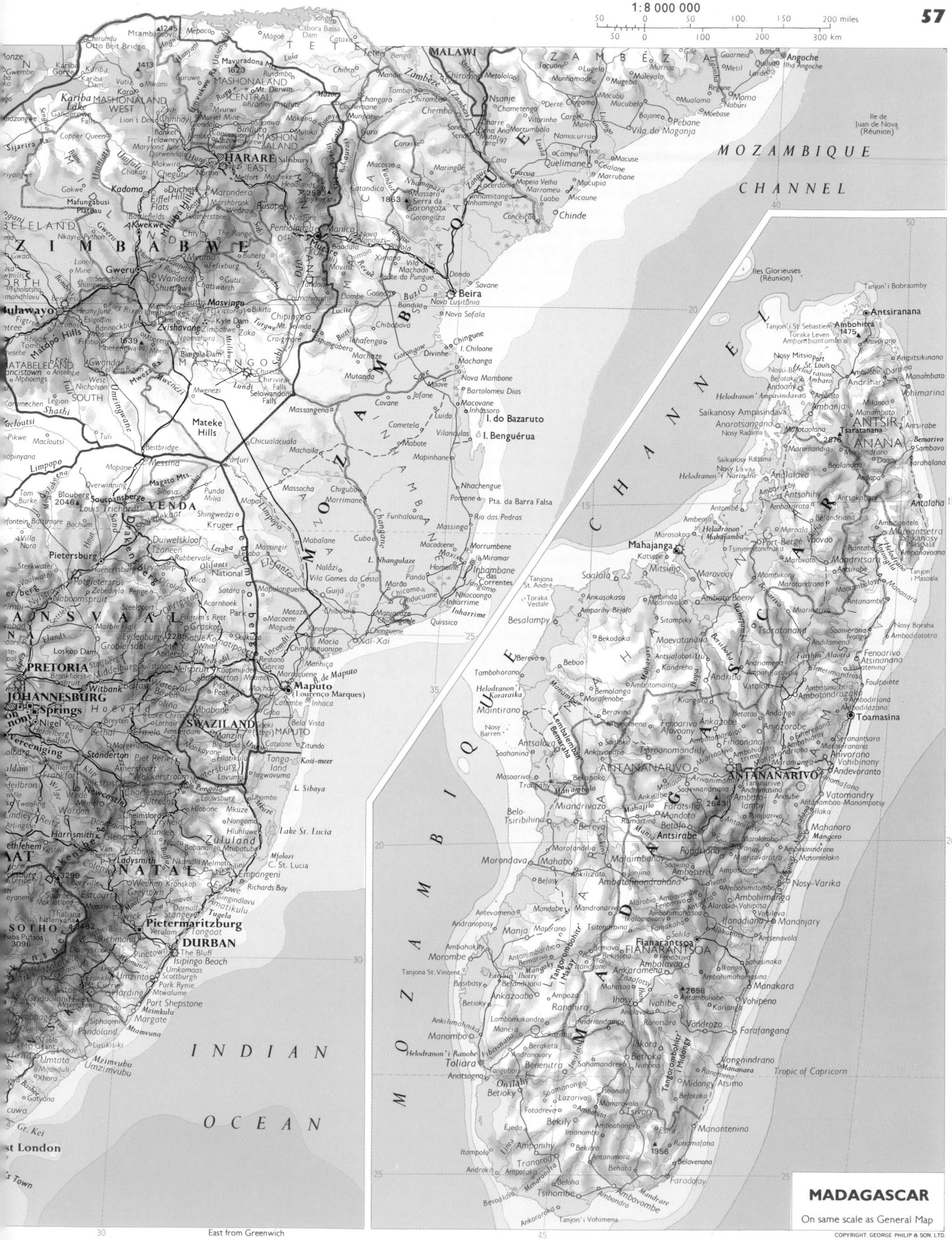
1:8 000 000
50 0 50 100 150 200 miles
50 0 100 200 300 km
MADAGASCAR
On same scale as General Map
MOZAMBIQUE CHANNEL
INDIAN OCEAN
MOZAMBIQUE
ZIMBABWE
MALAWI
ZAMBÉZIA
TETE
MANICA
SOFALA
GAZA
INHAMBANE
MAPUTO
SWAZILAND
NATAL
TRANSVAAL
VENDA
Zululand
MASHONALAND CENTRAL
MASHONALAND WEST
MASHONALAND EAST
MASVINGO
MATABELELAND SOUTH
HARARE (Salisbury)
Bulawayo
Gweru
Masvingo
Kadoma
Kwekwe
Mutare
Beira
Quelimane
Chinde
Angoche
Maputo (Lourenço Marques)
Inhambane
Xai-Xai
Vilanculos
I. do Bazaruto
I. Benguérua
Messina
Beitbridge
Pietersburg
PRETORIA
JOHANNESBURG
Springs
Vereeniging
Standerton
Newcastle
Ladysmith
Pietermaritzburg
DURBAN
Richards Bay
Port Shepstone
Lake St. Lucia
Limpopo
Zambèze
Ile de Juan de Nova (Réunion)
Iles Glorieuses (Réunion)
Antsiranana
Mahajanga
Toamasina
ANTANANARIVO
Antsirabe
Fianarantsoa
FIANARANTSOA
Toliara
Morondava
Maintirano
Manakara
Farafangana
Mananjary
Tropic of Capricorn
Tanjon' i Vohimena
East from Greenwich

ARCTIC OCEAN
Greenland
Iceland
Greenland Sea
Denmark Strait
Davis Strait
Baffin Bay
Baffin Island
Ellesmere I.
Axel Heiberg
Sverdrup Land
Queen Elizabeth Islands
Devon I.
Parry Is.
Melville I.
Victoria I.
Banks I.
Prince of Wales I.
Hudson Bay
James Bay
Hudson Strait
Southampton I.
Foxe Basin
Foxe Channel
Melville Pen.
Boothia Pen.
Gulf of Boothia
Ungava Peninsula
Labrador
Laurentian Plateau
Newfoundland
Gulf of St. Lawrence
Nova Scotia
Bay of Fundy
Beaufort Sea
Mackenzie Mts.
Selkirk Mts.
Rocky Mountains
Great Plains
Great Basin
Sierra Nevada
Cascade Range
Coast Range
Coast Mountains
Alaska Range
Alaska
Brooks Range
Alexander Archipelago
Queen Charlotte Islands
Vancouver I.
Gulf of Alaska
Alaska Pen.
Aleutian Islands
Bering Sea
Bering Strait
Asia
St. Lawrence I.
Nunivak I.
Wrangel I.
Kodiak I.
Mt. McKinley 6194
Mt. St. Elias 5489
Mt. Logan 6050
Great Bear L.
Great Slave L.
Athabasca L.
Lake Winnipeg
L. Superior
L. Michigan
L. Huron
L. Erie
L. Ontario
Appalachian Mts
Allegheny Mts
Blue Ridge 2037
Cumberland Plateau
Ozark Plateau
Colorado Plateau
Llano Estacado
Wasatch Mountains
Great Salt Lake
Mt. Elbert 4399
Blanca Pk. 4364
Mt. Whitney 4418
Death Valley
Mt. Rainier 4392
Mt. Shasta 4317
Mt. Robson 3954
Mendocino Seascarp
Murray Seascarp
PACIFIC
ATLANTIC
Edmonton
Calgary
Regina
Winnipeg
Minneapolis
Chicago
Detroit
Toronto
Hamilton
Ottawa
Montreal
Quebec
New York
Philadelphia
Washington
Atlanta
Memphis
St. Louis
Kansas City
Dallas
Denver
Los Angeles
San Francisco
Portland
Seattle
Vancouver
Halifax
Bermuda
Chesapeake Bay
Mississippi
Missouri
Arkansas
Ohio
Red
Colorado
Columbia
Fraser
Yukon
Mackenzie
Nelson
Churchill
Saskatchewan
Hudson

1:30 000 000

100 0 100 200 300 400 500 600 700 miles

100 0 200 400 600 800 1000 km

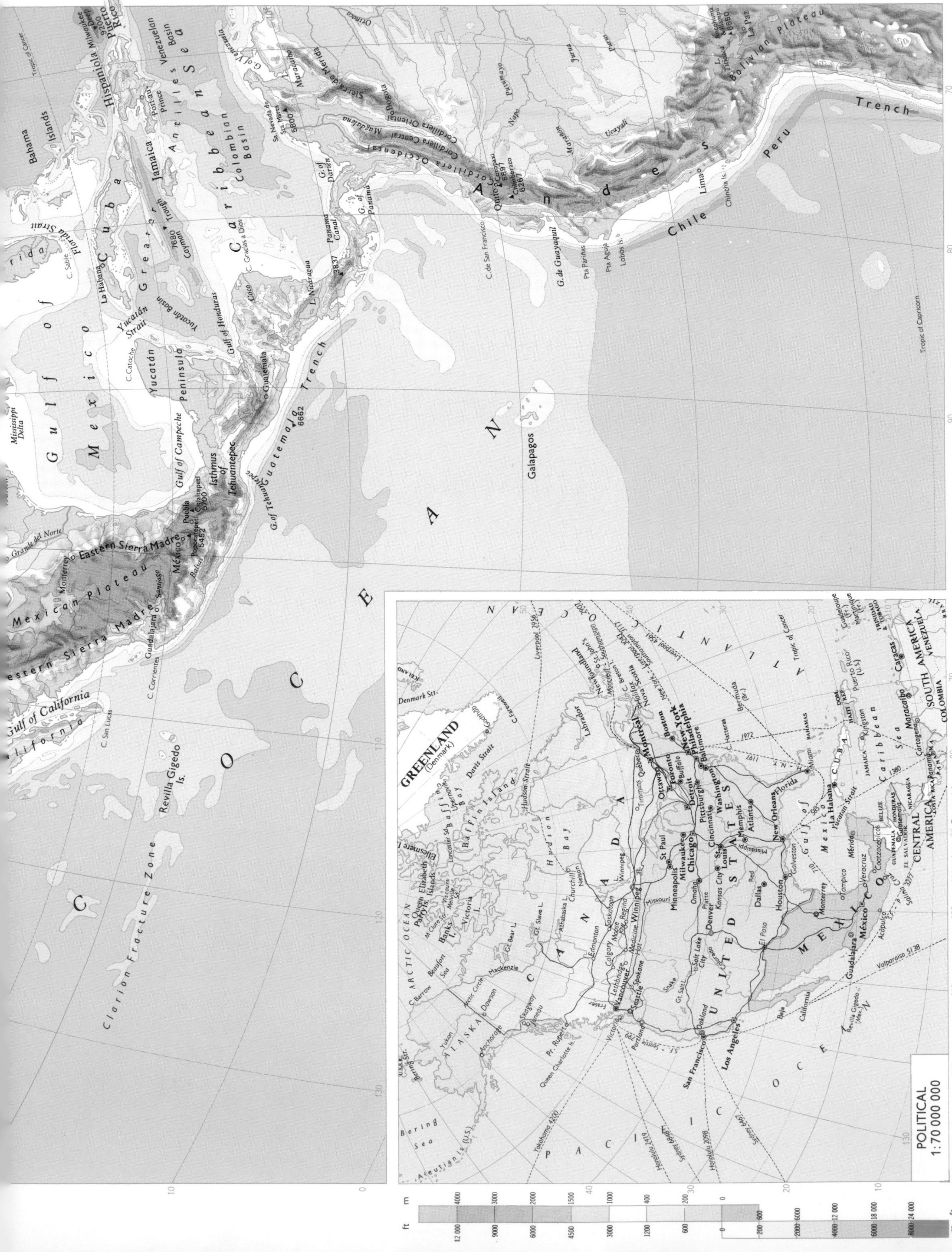

PACIFIC OCEAN
ALASKA
YUKON TERRITORY
NORTHWEST TERRITORIES
INUVIK
KITIKMEOT
KEEWATIN
BRITISH COLUMBIA
ALBERTA
SASKATCHEWAN
MANITOBA
WASHINGTON
MONTANA
NORTH DAKOTA
SOUTH DAKOTA
MINNESOTA
NEBRASKA
WYOMING
UNITED STATES
Victoria Island
Banks Island
Prince Albert Pen.
Prince of Wales Island
Melville Sound
M'Clintock Channel
Amundsen Gulf
Coronation Gulf
Queen Maud Gulf
Great Bear Lake
Great Slave L.
Lake Athabasca
Reindeer Lake
Lake Winnipeg
Mackenzie Mountains
Rocky Mountains
Coast Mountains
Cassiar Mountains
Queen Charlotte Is.
Vancouver I.
Anchorage
Fairbanks
Whitehorse
Dawson
Yellowknife
Edmonton
Calgary
Vancouver
Victoria
Seattle
Tacoma
Spokane
Saskatoon
Regina
Moose Jaw
Prince Albert
Lethbridge
Medicine Hat
Winnipeg
Minneapolis
Omaha
Des Moines
Sioux Falls
Bismarck
Projection: Bonne
ALASKA
1:30 000 000
miles
km
Brooks Range
BERING SEA
GULF OF ALASKA
Aleutian Is.
PACIFIC OCEAN
West from Greenwich
ft
m

1:15 000 000

100 50 0 100 200 300 400 miles

100 0 100 200 300 400 500 600 km

GREENLAND

ATLANTIC

Baffin Bay

Davis Strait

Angmagssalik

2850

Disko

Christianshåb

Holsteinsborg

Godthåb

Frederikshåb

Ivigtut

Julianehåb

Kap Farvel

Devon Island

Lancaster Sound

2136

1890

Bylot I.

Arctic Bay

Pond Inlet

Pond Inlet

Milne Inlet

Scott I.

Clyde

C. Hewett

Home B.

Broughton Island

Padloping Island

C. Dyer
Cape
Dyer

B A F F I N

Fury & Hecla Str.

Igloolik
Island

Hall
Lake

2591

Cumberland
Peninsula

C. Mercy

Cumberland Sd.

Hoare B.

Melville
Peninsula

Prince
Charles
I.

Foxe

Nettilling

Amadjuak
L.

Foxe
Penin.

Foxe
Basin

Frobisher
Bay

Rae Isthmus

Repulse B.

Committee B.

Wager
B.

Southampton
I.

Coral Harbour

Bell
Pen.

Digges Is.

Coats
I.

Mansel
I.

Frobisher Bay

Resolution I.

C. Dorchester

Cape Dorset

Lake
Harbour

Hudson Strait

C. Chidley

V I C T O R I A

Ross Welcome Sd.

Channel

Rae
Isthmus

TIN

Winisk

Severn

Big
Trout L.

HUDSON

Bay

257

Ottawa
Isls.

Sleeper Is.

King
George Is.

King George Is.

Baker's
Dozen
Is.

Belcher
Is.

C. Henrietta
Maria

Pte.
Louis-XIV

D

A

Attawapiskat

Akimiski
I.

James Bay

Charlton

Ft. Albany
(Fort
Albany)

Albany

Moosonee

Olnuvjouk
(Sugluk)

Maricourt
(Wakeham)

Koartac
(Notre Dame
de Koartac)

Akpatok
I.

Arnaud (Bellin)
(Payne Bay)

Ungava Bay

Port Nouveau Québec
(George R.)

Hebron

Nutak

Nain

COAST OF LABRADOR

C. Harrison

Indian Harbour

Hopedale

Rigolet

Cartwright

Smallwood
Reservoir

North West R.

Churchill

Goose
Bay

Battle Harbour

Belle Isle

L. Payne

Ungava
Peninsula

Portland
Promontory

Inoucdjouac
(Port Harrison)

Payne L.

L. Minto

Mélèzes

Larch

Ft Chimo

George

Whale

Kaniapiskau

Feuilles

Kaksok

1676

Scheffervile

Petitsikapau
L.

Lobstick L.

Churchill
Falls

Ashuanipi

N E W F O U N D L A N D

Twillingate

Lewisporte

Gander

Grand
Falls

Notre Dame B.

Trinity B.

Bonavista

Carbonear

Harbour Grace

Conception
B.

Placentia

St. John's

C. Race

Trepassey

Grand Baleine
Poste-de-
la-Baleine
(Great Whale River)

Kanaaupscow

La Grande

Ft. George

L. à l'Eau Claire

Lac Bienville

Kaniapiskau

Chisasibi

Q U E B E C

1128

Gagnon

Mingan

Romaine

Moisie

St-Augustin

Saguenay

Harrington
Harbour

Natashquan

Anticosti

d'Anticosti

Str. of Belle Isle

Port aux Basques

Channel

Ramea

Nouveau Comptoir
(Paint Hills)

Eastmain

Fort Rupert
(Rupert
House)

Rupert R.

Nottaway

L. Albanel

Mistassini

Chibougamau

Péribonca

Bersimis

Rés. de Gouin

L. Albane

Betsiamites

Baie-Comeau

Matane

Rimouski

Pén. de Gaspé

C. de Gaspé

Gulf of
St. Lawrence

Magdalen Is.

Îs. de la Madeleine

Cabot Str.

Cape Breton I.

North
Sydney

ST-PIERRE
et MIQUELON
(Fr.)

Glace Bay

Sydney

Port Hawkesbury

Mulgrave

Sable I.
(Nova Scotia)

6309

Nakina

Longlac

Kenogami

Hearst

Cochrane

Abitibi

Timmins

Kirkland Lake

Haileybury

Cobalt

Rouyn

Noranda

Val d'Or

Senneterre

La Tuque

Shawinigan

Trois-Rivières

Joliette

Sorel

St-Hyacinthe

Chicoutimi

Jonquière

Roberval

Dolbeau

St-Jean

Saguenay

La Malbaie

Rivière-
du-Loup

Edmundston

St-Léonard

Woodstock

Chatham

Newcastle

Bathurst

Campbellton

Matane

Dalhousie

Northumberland Str.

PR. EDWARD I.

Charlottetown

Summerside

NEW
BRUNSWICK

Moncton

Amherst

Springhill

Truro

New Glasgow

Antigonish

NOVA SCOTIA

Stellarton

Windsor

Kentville

Halifax

Dartmouth

Bridgewater

Liverpool

Shelburne

Yarmouth

Sable C.

B. of Fundy

Digby

Saint
John

Fredericton

St. Stephen

MAINE

Bangor

Augusta

Thunder Bay

Michipicoten

Marathon

Schreiber

Heron Bay

Franz

Oba

Wawa

Chapleau

Foleyet

Gogama

Sault Ste. Marie

Sudbury

Copper Cliff

North Bay

Mattawa

Pembroke

Renfrew

Arnprior

Cornwall

Ottawa

Hull

Lachute

MONTREAL

Lachine

Sherbrooke

Drummondville

Granby

St-Jean

Valleyfield

Québec

Lévis

Thetford Mines

VERMONT

NEW
HAMPSHIRE

Montpelier

Concord

Manchester

Portland

Lewiston

L. Champlain

Burlington

Georgian
Bay

Parry
Sound

Owen Sound

Orillia

Barrie

Peterboro

Belleville

Kingston

Watertown

Lake Huron

Collingwood

Midland

TORONTO

Guelph

Kitchener

Stratford

London

Sarnia

Brantford

Hamilton

St. Catharines

Niagara
Falls

Lake Ontario

Oshawa

Rochester

Syracuse

Utica

Albany

NEW
YORK

Binghamton

Elmira

MASS.

Worcester

Boston

Providence

C. Cod

CONN.

New Haven

Bridgeport

Hartford

Waterbury

Springfield

Scranton

Williamsport

Allentown

Reading

Trenton

NEW JERSEY

NEW YORK

Jersey City

Newark

PENNSYLVANIA

Youngstown

Akron

Cleveland

Toledo

Windsor

DETROIT

Sandusky

OHIO

South Bend

INDIANA

Gary

CHICAGO

Evanston

Waukegan

Kenosha

Racine

Milwaukee

Manitowoc

Sheboygan

Appleton

Green Bay

Oshkosh

WISCONSIN

Madison

Janesville

Kalamazoo

Grand Rapids

Muskegon

Saginaw

Flint

Lansing

Cadillac

Cheboygan

Ludington

Lake Michigan

Manistique

Escanaba

Marinette

Menominee

Marquette

Iron Mt.

Ironwood

Keweenaw
Bay

L'Anse

Houghton

Calumet

Lake Superior

Sault Ste. Marie

Mackinaw City

St. Ignace

Michipicoten

Wisconsin R.

Wausau

Antigo

Rhinelander

Missinaibi

Matagami

Harricana

Temagami

Temiscamingue

Rés. de
Cabonga

Maniwaki

Gatineau

St. Lawrence

Matane

Lac St-Jean

Chidley

West from Greenwich

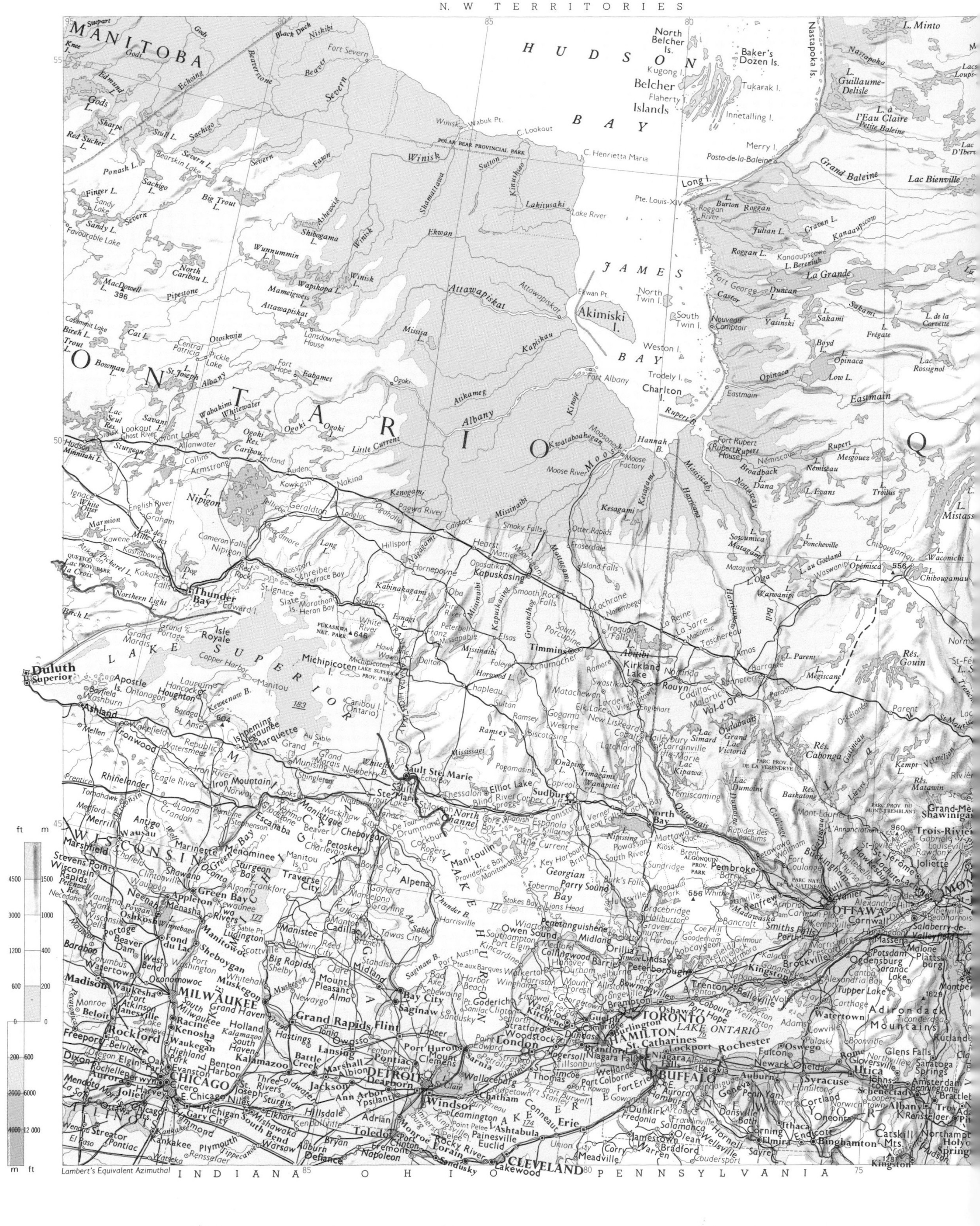
N. W TERRITORIES
HUDSON BAY
JAMES BAY
MANITOBA
ONTARIO
Q
Belcher Islands
North Belcher Is.
Baker's Dozen Is.
Kugong I.
Flaherty I.
Tukarak I.
Innetalling I.
Merry I.
Long I.
Nastapoka Is.
L. Minto
L. Guillaume-Delisle
L. à l'Eau Claire
Lac Bienville
Grand Baleine
Poste-de-la-Baleine
C. Lookout
C. Henrietta Maria
Winisk
Wabuk Pt.
POLAR BEAR PROVINCIAL PARK
Akimiski I.
North Twin I.
South Twin I.
Weston I.
Trodely I.
Charlton I.
Fort Albany
Moosonee
Moose Factory
Hannah B.
Rupert B.
Fort Rupert
Fort George
La Grande
Eastmain
Opinaca
Nouveau Comptoir
Lansdowne House
Central Patricia
Pickle Lake
Fort Severn
Sandy Lake
Big Trout L.
Attawapiskat
Albany
Kenogami
Missinaibi
Nakina
Geraldton
Hearst
Kapuskasing
Cochrane
Timmins
Kirkland Lake
Rouyn
Noranda
Val-d'Or
Amos
Chibougamau
Mistassini
Lac Seul
Sioux Lookout
Hudson
L. Nipigon
Nipigon
Thunder Bay
Isle Royale
LAKE SUPERIOR
Michipicoten I.
Caribou I. (Ontario)
Duluth
Superior
Ashland
Ironwood
Houghton
Marquette
Ishpeming
Negaunee
Sault Ste Marie
Wawa
Chapleau
Elliot Lake
Sudbury
North Bay
Temiscaming
Lac Simard
Rés. Cabonga
Rés. Gouin
Rés. Baskatong
ALGONQUIN PROV. PARK
Pembroke
Renfrew
Hull
OTTAWA
Cornwall
Trois-Rivières
Joliette
St-Jérôme
Shawinigan
Grand-Mère
Mont-Laurier
Manitoulin I.
North Channel
Georgian Bay
Parry Sound
Huntsville
Owen Sound
Barrie
Orillia
Lindsay
Peterborough
Belleville
Kingston
Brockville
Ogdensburg
Massena
Watertown
Adirondack Mountains
Plattsburg
Rutland
Glens Falls
Saratoga Springs
Amsterdam
Schenectady
Troy
Albany
Kingston
Catskill Mts.
Binghamton
Utica
Rome
Syracuse
Oswego
Auburn
Geneva
Rochester
Lockport
Niagara Falls
BUFFALO
St. Catharines
Welland
HAMILTON
TORONTO
LAKE ONTARIO
Brampton
Oshawa
Guelph
Kitchener
Brantford
Woodstock
Stratford
London
St. Thomas
Sarnia
Port Huron
Chatham
Windsor
DETROIT
Dearborn
Ann Arbor
Jackson
Lansing
Flint
Saginaw
Bay City
Midland
Alpena
Cheboygan
Petoskey
Traverse City
Cadillac
Manistee
Ludington
Muskegon
Grand Rapids
Kalamazoo
Battle Creek
Toledo
Monroe
Sandusky
Lorain
CLEVELAND
Lakewood
Euclid
Painesville
Ashtabula
Erie
LAKE ERIE
LAKE HURON
LAKE MICHIGAN
Green Bay
Appleton
Oshkosh
Fond du Lac
Sheboygan
Manitowoc
MILWAUKEE
Racine
Kenosha
Waukegan
Evanston
CHICAGO
Joliet
Gary
Hammond
Elgin
Aurora
Rockford
Madison
Janesville
Beloit
Freeport
Kankakee
South Bend
Elkhart
Fort Wayne
Defiance
WISCONSIN
MICHIGAN
ILLINOIS
NEW YORK
INDIANA
OHIO
PENNSYLVANIA
Jamestown
Olean
Bradford
Corning
Elmira
Ithaca
Meadville
ft
m
4500
1500
3000
1000
1200
400
600
200
0
0
200
600
2000
6000
4000
12 000
m
ft
Lambert's Equivalent Azimuthal

NEWFOUNDLAND
COAST OF LABRADOR
QUEBEC
LABRADOR
South Aulatsivik I.
High I.
Paul I.
Nain
Voiseys B.
Tunungayualok I.
Davis Inlet
Nunaksaluk I.
Hopedale
Kaipokok B.
Aillik
Makkovik
Adlavik Is.
C. Harrison
Holton
Indian Harbour
Groswater B.
Rigolet
Hamilton Inlet
Table B.
Cartwright
Sandwich B.
Island of Ponds
Separation Point
Mealy Mts.
1128
L. Melville
North-West River
Goose
Happy Valley-Goose Bay
Square Islands
Alexis
Paradise
Eagle
Battle Harbour
St. Lewis
Mary's Harbour
Red Bay
Belle I.
Str. of Belle Isle
St. Lunaire-Griquet
St. Anthony
Hare B.
Anse-au-Loup
Forteau
Bradore Bay
Lourdes-de-Blanc-Sablon
St-Augustin
St-Paul
Erlandson L.
Whale
George
Fraser
Fort McKenzie
L. Nachicapau
L. de la Hutte Sauvage
Kogaluk
Mistastin L.
Chakonipau L.
Otelnuk L.
Kaniapiskau
Wheeler
Champdoré
L. Tudor
Whitegull L.
Big Bay
610
Sérigny
L. Wakuach
Sandy
Harp L.
Big
Attikamagen L.
Schefferville
Kanairiktok
Naskaupi
Seal L.
Nipishish L.
L. Neret
Lac Verneuil
Lac Petitsikapau
Lac Clairambault
Lac Delorme
Woods L.
Smallwood Reservoir
Grand L.
Kaniapiskau L.
Menihek Lakes
Lobstick L.
Churchill Falls
Churchill
L. Bermen
Ossokmanuan L.
Winokapau L.
Shabogamo L.
Opiskotish L.
Opiscoteo L.
Atikonak L.
Minipi L.
Little Mecatina
L. Naococane
Labrador City
Wabush
Lac Joseph
Burnt L.
1128
Ashuanipi L.
Petit Lac Manicouagan
Moisie
L. Plétipi
Gagnon
Rés. Manicouagan
Ste-Marguerite
Nipissis
West Matapédia
Magpie L.
Romaine
St-Jean
Natashquan
Aguanus
Nabisipi
Olomane
St-Augustin Saguenay
Outer I.
Port Saunders
Roddickton
Conche
Groais I.
Bell I.
Englee
Great Harbour Deep
White B.
Horse Is.
1048
L. Manitou
Lac Allard
L. Musquaro
I. du Petit-Mécatina
Harrington Harbour
Daniel's Harbour
Étamamu
Péribonca
L. Manouane
Quiardes
Manicouagan
Betsiamites
Clarke City
Sept-Îles
Moisie
Walker L.
Port-Cartier
Sheldrake
Mingan
Havre-St-Pierre
Aguanish
Natashquan
Kegaska
Gethsémani
Dét. de Jacques-Cartier
Pte. Ouest
Port-Menier
Î. d'Anticosti
Jupiter
Heath Pt.
Rivière-Pentecôte
Rés. Pipmuacan
Godbout
Baie-Trinité
Pte. des Monts
Baie-Comeau
Hauterive
Betsiamites
Forestville
Cap-Chat
Ste-Anne-des-Monts
Mont-Louis
Grande-Vallée
Dét. d'Honguedo
Pte. Sud
Petit-Cap
Rivière-au-Renard
C. de Gaspé
Gaspé
Douglastown
Percé
Grande-Rivière
Mt. Jacques-Cartier
1310
PARC PROV. DE LA GASPÉSIE
Mts. Chic-Chocs
Pén. de Gaspé
Chandler
Matane
Mont-Joli
Sayabec
Amqui
Causapscal
Matapédia
Bonaventure
Paspébiac
Miscou I.
Lamèque
Shippegan
Tracadie
GULF OF ST. LAWRENCE
572
Î. Brion
Grande-Entrée
Îs. de la Madeleine (Quebec)
Cap-aux-Meules
Havre-Aubert
St. Paul
C. North
Cabot Strait
St. Lawrence
Rimouski
Bic
Trois-Pistoles
Rivière-du-Loup
Cabano
Alma
Arvida
Chicoutimi
Saguenay
Tadoussac
Grandes-Bergeronnes
Port Alfred
Bagotville
La Malbaie
Baie-St-Paul
PARC PROV. LAURENTIDES
1190
St-Pascal
Edmundston
St. Leonard
819
Grand Falls
Plaster Rock
Ft. Kent
Van Buren
Caribou
Presque Isle
Ashland
Houlton
Eagle L.
Island Falls
Chesuncook L.
1606
Patten
Millinocket
Moosehead L.
Mattawamkeag
Greenville
Lincoln
Dalhousie
Campbellton
Chaleur Bay
Belledune
Atholville
Kedgwick
St. Arthur
Bathurst
Heath Steele
Nepisiguit
Miramichi B.
Newcastle
Chatham
Blackville
NEW BRUNSWICK
Richibucto
Buctouche
Notre Dame
Chipman
Shediac
Moncton
Amherst
Hartland
Woodstock
Fredericton
Fredericton Junc.
Oromocto
Gagetown
McAdam
St. Stephen
St. George
Sussex
Saint John
Bay of Fundy
St. Martins
Calais
Montmagny
Lauzon
Lévis
Québec
Thetford Mines
Plessisville
Beauceville
St-Georges
Lac-Mégantic
Sherbrooke
Coaticook
East Angus
MAINE
Jackman
Guilford
Bingham
Skowhegan
Dover-Foxcroft
Old Town
Brewer
Bangor
Ellsworth
Waterville
Augusta
Belfast
Camden
Rockland
Rumford
Berlin
Bethel
Auburn
Lewiston
Bath
Brunswick
Portland
Sanford
Saco
Biddeford
Rochester
Dover
Portsmouth
Manchester
Nashua
Haverhill
Lawrence
Lowell
Gloucester
C. Ann
Lynn
BOSTON
Brockton
Bar Harbor
Mt. Desert I.
Machias
Jonesport
Eastport
Blacks Hr.
Grand Manan I.
North Pt.
Tignish
Alberton
PRINCE EDWARD ISLAND
Summerside
Kensington
Charlottetown
Borden
Cape Montague
Tormentine
Georgetown
Souris
East Pt.
Northumberland Str.
Sackville
Springhill
Parrsboro
Minas Basin
Truro
New Glasgow
Stellarton
Pictou
Antigonish
Joggins
Stewiacke
Upper Musquodoboit
Kentville
Windsor
Middleton
Annapolis Royal
Bridgetown
Digby
Weymouth
Dartmouth
Halifax
Musquodoboit Hr.
Sheet Hr.
Mahone Bay
Lunenburg
Bridgewater
Liverpool
Port Mouton
Shelburne
Lockeport
Yarmouth
Wedgeport
Clark's Harbour
C. Sable
St. Mary's B.
Freeport
L. Rossignol
NOVA SCOTIA
Chéticamp
Inverness
Pleasant Bay
CAPE BRETON NAT. PARK
532
Ingonish
St. Ann's B.
Sydney Mines
New Waterford
N. Sydney
Glace Bay
Sydney
Cape Breton Island
Louisbourg
Bras d'Or L.
Port Hood
Port Hawkesbury
Murray Hr.
Mulgrave
Sherbrooke
St. Peters
I. Madame
Fourchu
Canso
Chedabucto B.
Sable I. (Nova Scotia)
ATLANTIC OCEAN
Long Range Mts.
GROS MORNE NAT. PARK
Trout River
Deer Lake
Bay of Islands
Corner Brook
814
Port au Port B.
C. St. George
St. George's B.
Stephenville
St. George's
St. David's
South Branch
St. Andrew's
C. Ray
Channel-Port aux Basques
Isle aux Morts
Rose Blanche
Burgeo
Ramea
François
Harbour Breton
Grand Bank
Fortune B.
Burin
Marystown
Miquelon
Langlade
St. Pierre
SAINT-PIERRE ET MIQUELON (Fr.)
Long Range Mts.
Grey Res.
Victoria Res.
Red Indian L.
Buchans
Howley
Badger
Grand Falls
Windsor
Bishop's Falls
Botwood
Springdale
South Brook
Baie Verte
Seal Cove
Sop's Arm
La Scie
C. St. John
Notre Dame B.
Twillingate
Fogo
Fogo I.
Lewisporte
Carmanville
Glenwood
Gander
C. Freels
Wesleyville
Bonavista B.
C. Bonavista
Bonavista
Catalina
Trinity B.
Dark Cove
Glovertown
NEWFOUNDLAND
Port Blandford
381
Clarenville
Salmon Res.
White Bear Res.
Grey
St. Alban's
Belleoram
Terrenceville
Heart's Content
Carbonear
Harbour Grace
Bay de Verde
Conception B.
Wabana
Torbay
St. John's
Mt. Pearl
Bay Bulls
Holyrood
Spaniard's Bay
Placentia
Placentia B.
Argentia
St. Lawrence
St. Bride's
St. Mary's B.
C. St. Mary's
Ferryland
Avalon Peninsula
C. Race
Trepassey
C. Pine
70
65
60
55
50
45

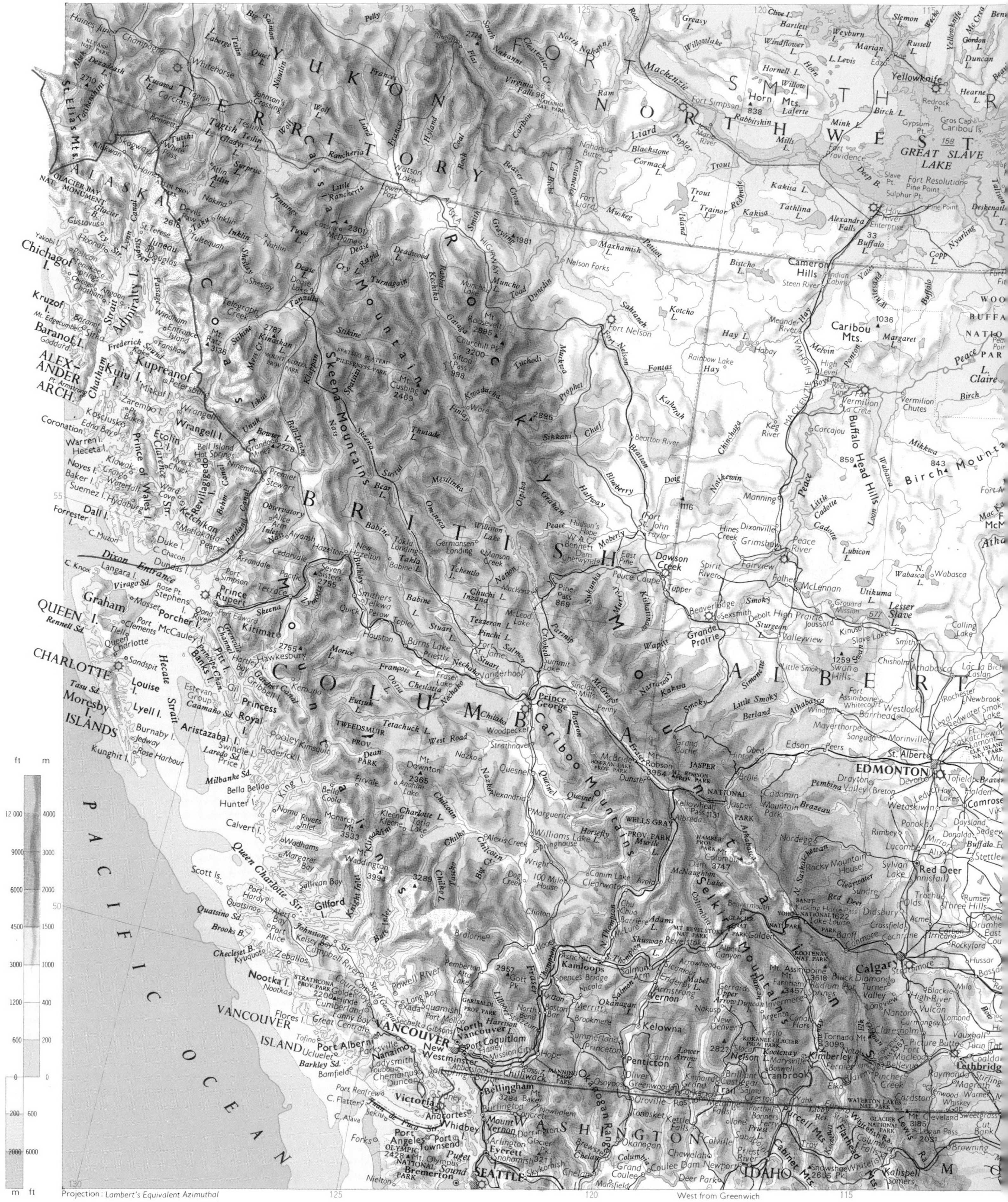
YUKON TERRITORY
NORTHWEST TERRITORIES
BRITISH COLUMBIA
ALBERTA
ALASKA
WASHINGTON
IDAHO
PACIFIC OCEAN
ROCKY MOUNTAINS
COAST MOUNTAINS
Skeena Mountains
Cassiar Mountains
Cariboo Mountains
Monashee Mountains
Selkirk Mountains
Purcell Mts.
Cabinet Mts.
Okanogan Range
Birch Mountains
Buffalo Head Hills
Caribou Mts.
Horn Mts.
Cameron Hills
GREAT SLAVE LAKE
Yellowknife
Fort Simpson
Fort Nelson
Fort St. John
Dawson Creek
Grande Prairie
Peace River
Prince George
Prince Rupert
Kitimat
Kamloops
Kelowna
Penticton
Vernon
Nelson
Cranbrook
Revelstoke
Whitehorse
Juneau
Ketchikan
VANCOUVER
Victoria
Nanaimo
North Vancouver
New Westminster
Bellingham
SEATTLE
EDMONTON
St. Albert
Red Deer
Calgary
Lethbridge
Banff
JASPER NATIONAL PARK
VANCOUVER ISLAND
QUEEN CHARLOTTE ISLANDS
Graham I.
Moresby I.
Dixon Entrance
Hecate Strait
Queen Charlotte Str.
Chichagof I.
Baranof I.
Admiralty I.
Prince of Wales I.
ALEXANDER ARCH.
Mt. Robson 3954
Mt. Waddington 3994
Mt. Columbia 3747
Mt. Assiniboine 3618
Lesser Slave L.
Williston Lake
Projection: Lambert's Equivalent Azimuthal
West from Greenwich
ft
m
12 000
9000
6000
4500
3000
1200
600
0
200
2000
4000
3000
2000
1500
1000
400
200
0
600
6000

1:7 000 000

50 0 100 150 200 miles
50 0 50 100 150 200 250 300 km

HUDSON

BAY

NORTHWEST TERRITORIES

KEEWATIN

DISTRICT OF KEEWATIN REGION

SASKATCHEWAN

MANITOBA

ONTARIO

Lake Athabasca

Wollaston L.

Reindeer L.

Southern Indian L.

Churchill

Lac la Ronge

Flin Flon

The Pas

Cedar Lake

LAKE WINNIPEG

Lake Winnepegosis

Lake Manitoba

Prince Albert

Saskatoon

Yorkton

Dauphin

Selkirk

WINNIPEG

St. Boniface

Transcona

Portage la Prairie

Brandon

Regina

Moose Jaw

Swift Current

Medicine Hat

Cypress Hills

RIDING MOUNTAIN NATIONAL PARK

PRINCE ALBERT NAT. PARK

MEADOW LAKE PROV. PARK

NORTH DAKOTA

MINNESOTA

MONTANA

Minot

Devils Lake

Grand Forks

East Grand Forks

Bemidji

Duluth

Fort Peck Res.

Williston

Lake of the Woods

International Falls

Fort Frances

Kenora

Thief River Falls

COPYRIGHT. GEORGE PHILIP & SON LTD

DID

ft m

12 000 4000

9000 3000

6000 2000

4500 1500

3000 1000

1200 400

600 200

0 0

200 200

2000 6000

m ft

HAWAII
1:10 000 000
20 0 20 40 60 80 miles
20 0 40 80 120 km

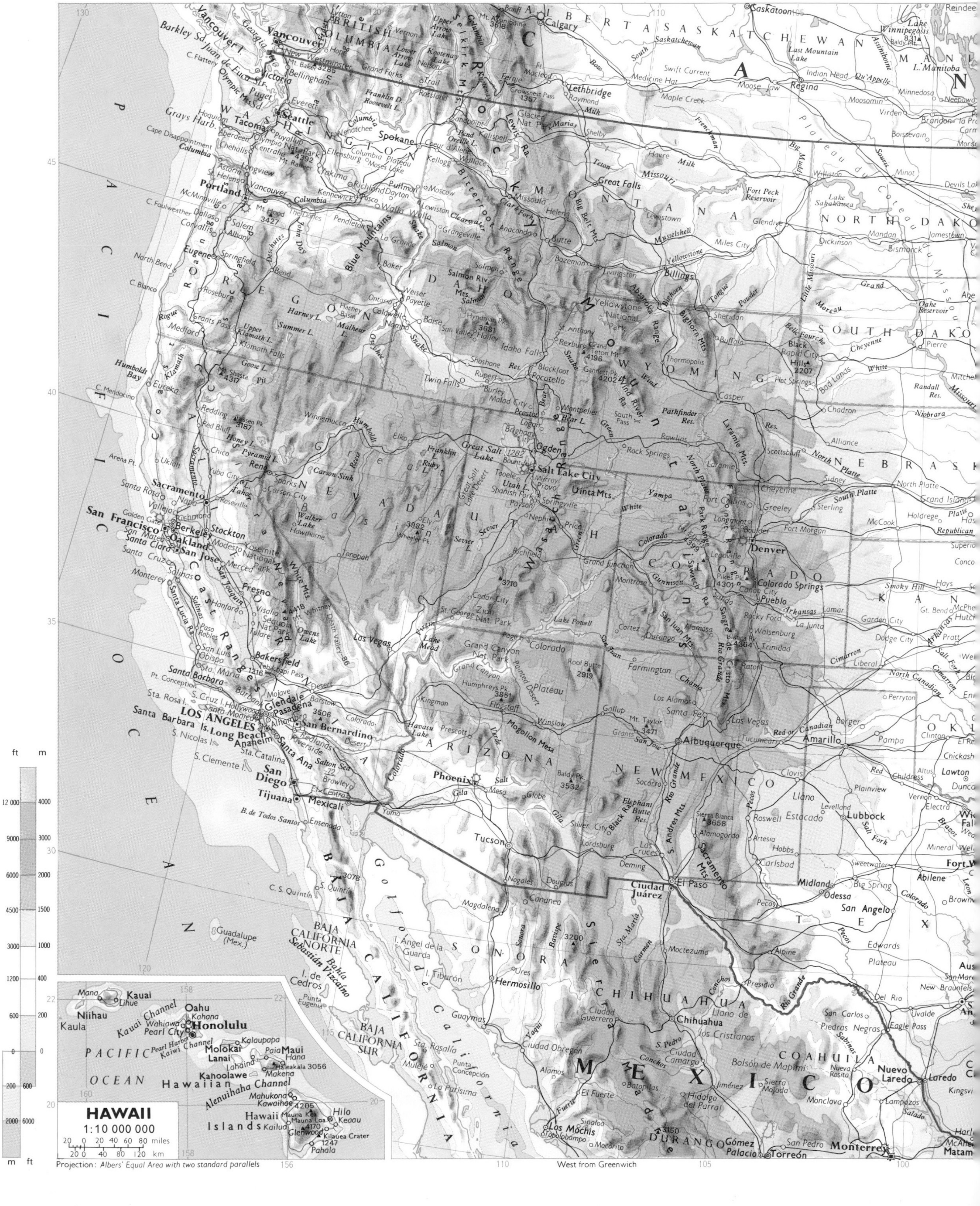

Projection: Albers' Equal Area with two standard parallels

West from Greenwich

1:12 000 000

50 0 50 100 150 200 250 300 miles

50 0 50 100 150 200 250 300 350 400 450 km

CANADA

Lake Winnipeg

MINNESOTA

WISCONSIN

IOWA

ILLINOIS

MISSOURI

ARKANSAS

LOUISIANA

MINNESOTA

Lake Superior

Lake Michigan

Lake Huron

Lake Erie

Lake Ontario

Minneapolis **St. Paul**

Milwaukee **Grand Rapids**

CHICAGO

DETROIT

MONTRÉAL

TORONTO

Buffalo

NEW YORK

PHILADELPHIA

Baltimore

Washington D.C.

MAINE

VERMONT

NEW HAMPSHIRE

Boston

MASS.

CONN.

INDIANA

OHIO

PENNSYLVANIA

NEW JERSEY

WEST VIRGINIA

VIRGINIA

KENTUCKY

Indianapolis

Cincinnati

Columbus

Dayton

Pittsburgh

Cleveland

Richmond

Norfolk

St. Louis

Kansas City

Memphis

Nashville

TENNESSEE

NORTH CAROLINA

SOUTH CAROLINA

Charlotte

Chattanooga

Knoxville

Atlanta

Birmingham

ALABAMA

MISSISSIPPI

GEORGIA

Columbus

Montgomery

Savannah

Jacksonville

Mobile

New Orleans

Shreveport

Jackson

Baton Rouge

Houston

Tampa

St. Petersburg

Miami

West Palm Beach

Orlando

FLORIDA

BAHAMAS

Eleuthera I.

GULF OF MEXICO

ATLANTIC OCEAN

N.W. Providence Channel

N.E. Providence Channel

Gt. Abaco

Grand Bahama I.

Key West

Florida Keys

Andros I.

Long I.

Cat I.

COPYRIGHT. GEORGE PHILIP & SON. LTD.

LAKE SUPERIOR
ONTARIO
QUEBEC
LAKE HURON
LAKE ONTARIO
LAKE ERIE
MICHIGAN
WISCONSIN
ILLINOIS
INDIANA
OHIO
KENTUCKY
WEST VIRGINIA
VIRGINIA
PENNSYLVANIA
NEW YORK
NEW JERSEY
MARYLAND
DELAWARE
VERMONT
NEW HAMPSHIRE
MASS.
CONN.
MONTREAL
OTTAWA
TORONTO
CHICAGO
DETROIT
CLEVELAND
BUFFALO
PITTSBURGH
PHILADELPHIA
BALTIMORE
WASHINGTON D.C.
NEW YORK
BOSTON
CINCINNATI
INDIANAPOLIS
MILWAUKEE
Georgian Bay
Chesapeake Bay

1:6 000 000

50 0 50 100 miles
50 0 50 100 150 km

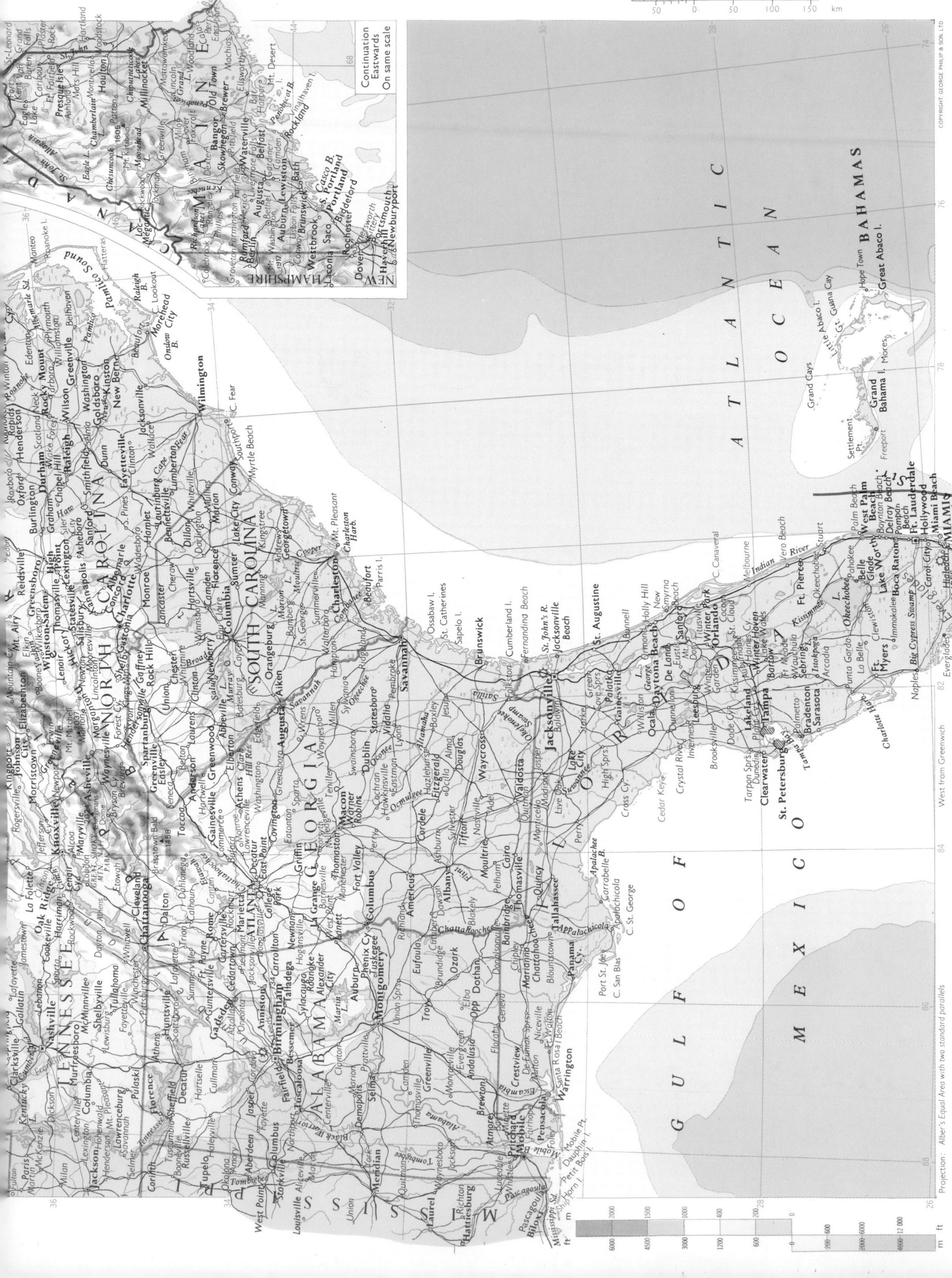

m ft
6000 2000
4500 1500
3000 1000
1200 400
600 200
0 0
200 600
2000 6000
4000 12 000

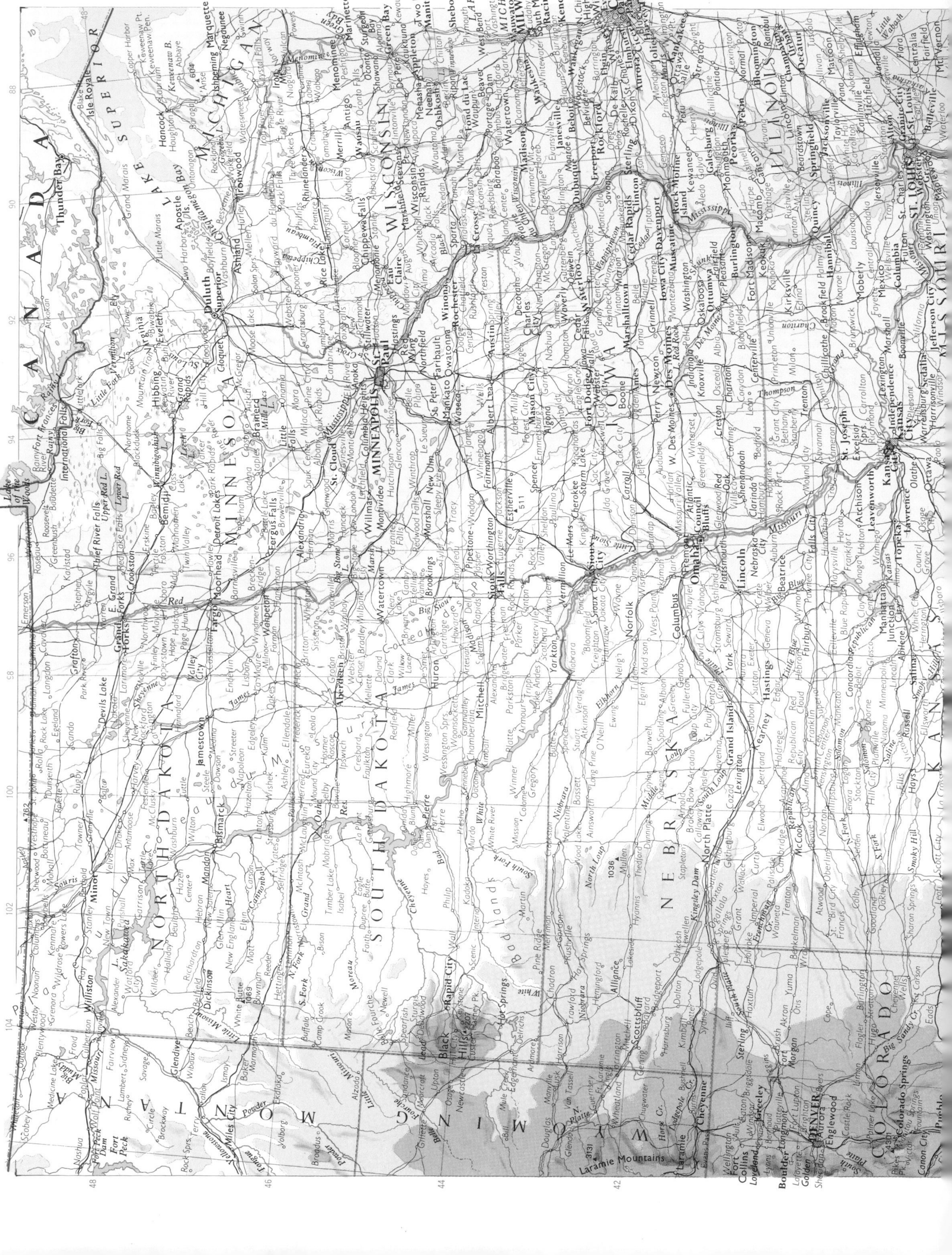
C A N A D A
LAKE SUPERIOR
LAKE MICHIGAN
MICHIGAN
WISCONSIN
MINNESOTA
IOWA
ILLINOIS
MISSOURI
NORTH DAKOTA
SOUTH DAKOTA
NEBRASKA
KANSAS
MONTANA
WYOMING
COLORADO
CHICAGO
MILWAUKEE
MINNEAPOLIS
St. Paul
Duluth
Superior
Des Moines
Omaha
Lincoln
Kansas City
St. Joseph
Topeka
Denver
Cheyenne
Bismarck
Pierre
Fargo
Sioux Falls
Sioux City
Rapid City
Madison
Green Bay
Dubuque
Davenport
Cedar Rapids
Springfield
Peoria
Jefferson City
Thunder Bay
Laramie Mountains
Black Hills
Bad Lands
48
46
44
42
104
102
100
98
96
94
92
90
88

1 : 6 000 000

50 0 50 100 miles
50 0 50 100 150 km

TENNESSEE

MISSISSIPPI

ARKANSAS

LOUISIANA

OKLAHOMA

TEXAS

NEW MEXICO

MEXICO

COAHUILA

CHIHUAHUA

GULF OF MEXICO

Laguna Madre

NEW ORLEANS

Memphis

Little Rock

Shreveport

Dallas

Fort Worth

Houston

San Antonio

Baton Rouge

Corpus Christi

Wichita

Oklahoma City

Tulsa

Amarillo

Lubbock

Nuevo Laredo

Laredo

Rio Grande / Rio Bravo del Norte

Sierra de Cristo Mts.

West from Greenwich

Projection: Albers' Equal Area with two standard parallels

COPYRIGHT GEORGE PHILIP & SON, LTD.

Continuation Southwards on same scale

ft m
12 000
9000
6000
4500
3000
1500
1200
600
400
200
0
m ft

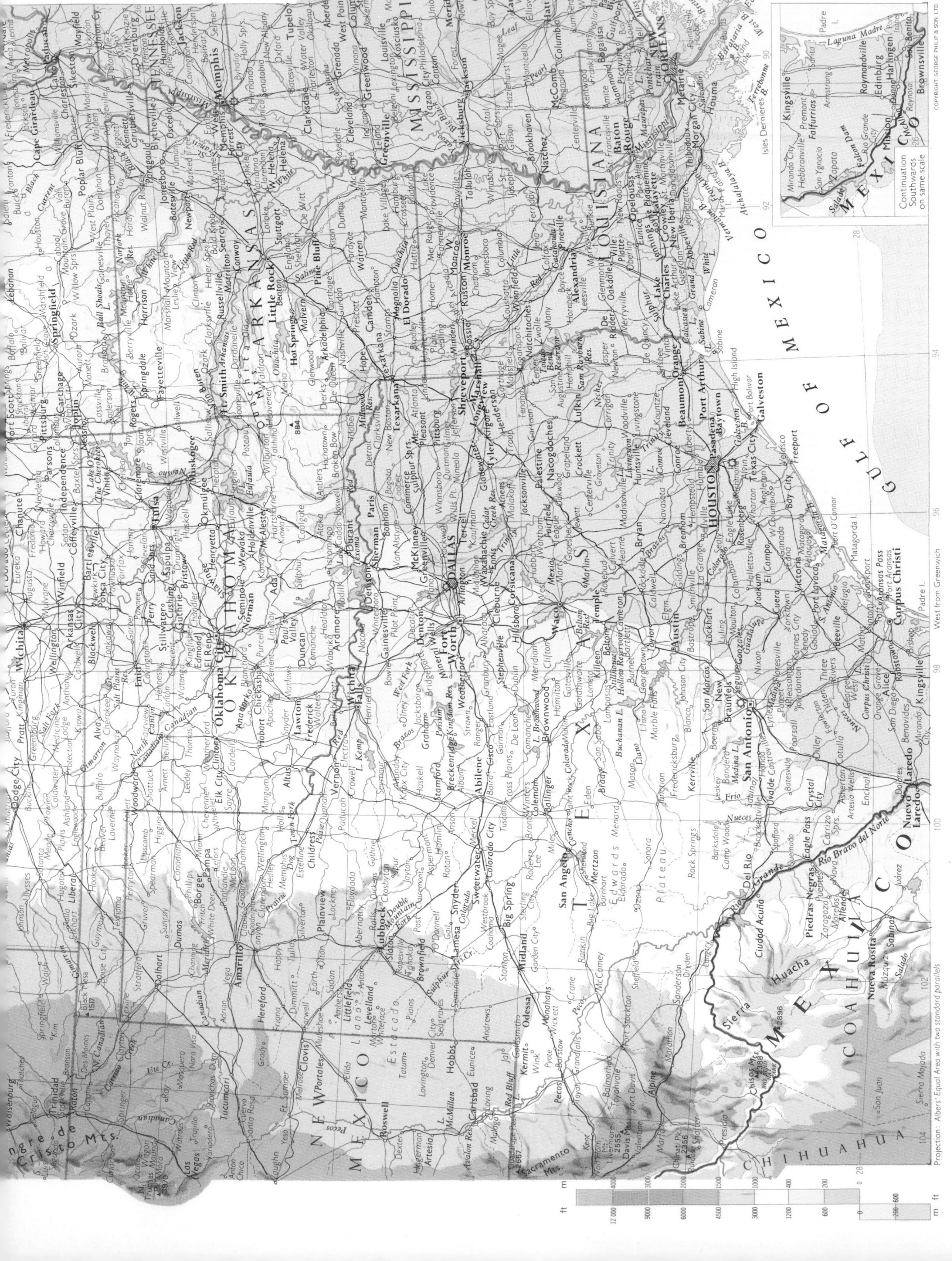

1:6 000 000

50 0 50 100 miles

50 0 50 100 150 km

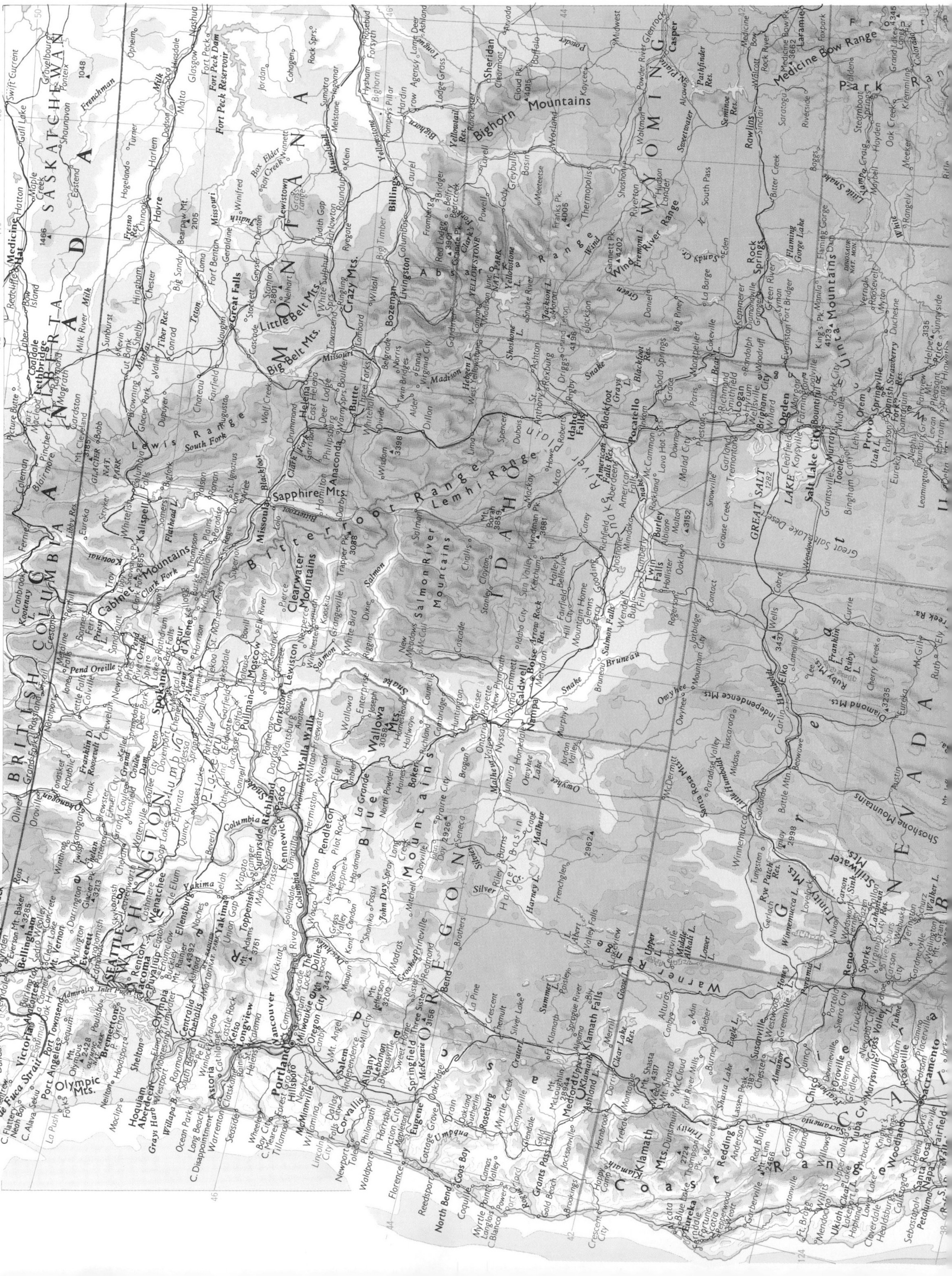

COLORADO
NEW MEXICO
TEXAS
ARIZONA
CHIHUAHUA
SONORA
MEXICO
BAJA CALIFORNIA
Golfo de California
Sangre de Cristo Mts.
San Juan Mts.
Sacramento Mts.
San Andres Mts.
Colorado Plateau
Grand Canyon
Painted Desert
Mojave Desert
Death Valley
Santa Lucia Range
Sierra de Juarez
Albuquerque
Santa Fe
El Paso
Ciudad Juárez
Las Cruces
Phoenix
Tucson
Flagstaff
Las Vegas
LOS ANGELES
San Diego
San Bernardino
Bakersfield
Fresno
Mexicali
Tijuana
Ensenada
Nogales
Hermosillo
Chihuahua
Colorado
Rio Grande
West from Greenwich
ft m
m ft

1:12 000 000

100 0 100 200 miles
100 0 100 200 300 km

COPYRIGHT GEORGE PHILIP & SON LTD.

REFERENCE TO NUMBERS

1 Distrito Federal	5 México
2 Aguascalientes	6 Morelos
3 Guanajuato	7 Querétaro
4 Hidalgo	8 Tlaxcala

PANAMA CANAL
1:1 000 000

0 5 10 miles
0 5 10 15 km

Projection: Bi-polar oblique Conical Orthomorphic

West from Greenwich

G U L F O F M E X I C O

P A C I F I C O C E A N

ATLANTIC OCEAN

UNITED STATES

GULF OF CALIFORNIA

BAJA CALIFORNIA

SIERRA MADRE OCCIDENTAL

SIERRA MADRE ORIENTAL

Bahía de Campeche

GUATEMALA

BELIZE

HONDURAS

EL SALVADOR

PANAMÁ

REPUBLIC OF PANAMA

m ft elevation scale:
4000 3000 2000 1500 1000 600 400 200 0
12000 9000 6000 4500 1200 600 0

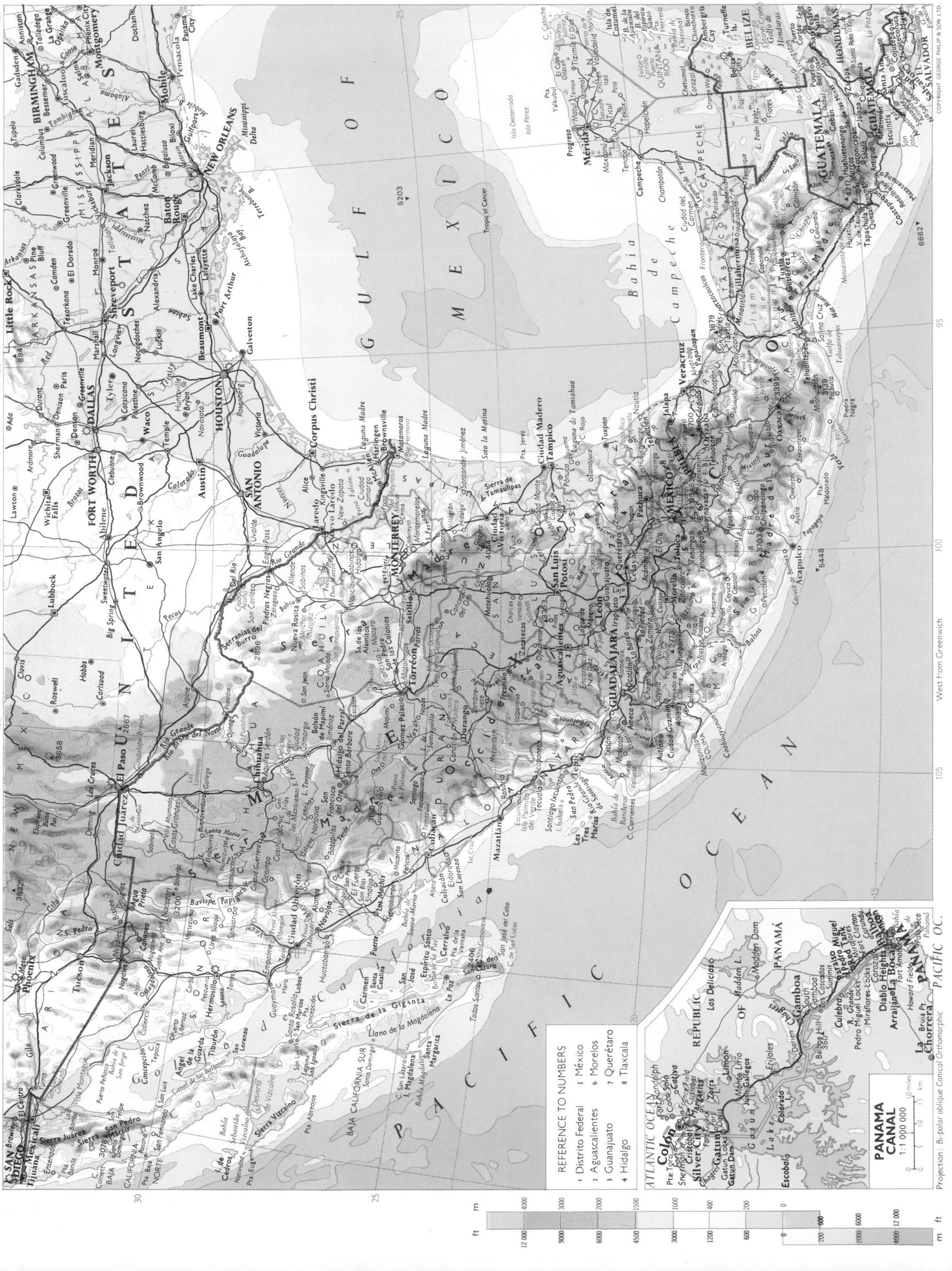

1:12 000 000

100 0 100 200 miles
100 0 100 200 300 km

WINDWARD ISLANDS 1:8 000 000

BARBADOS
Speightstown
Bridgetown
Martinique Passage
Fort-de-France
St-Pierre
MARTINIQUE (Fr.)
Le François
ST. LUCIA
Castries
Soufrière
St. Vincent Passage
Kingstown
ST. VINCENT
Bequia
The Grenadines
Carriacou
Ronde
St. Catherine
GRENADA
St. George's
Pointe Saline

Tobago
Margarita
Grande
TRINIDAD
Port of Spain
Galeota

TRINIDAD & TOBAGO 1:8 000 000

Tobago
Golfo de Paria
Port of Spain
San Fernando
TRINIDAD
Point Fortin

JAMAICA 1:8 000 000

Montego Bay
St. Ann's Bay
Falmouth
Port Maria
Spanish Town
KINGSTON
Mandeville
Morant Town
Morant Point
Portland Point

LEEWARD ISLANDS 1:8 000 000

Anguilla (Br.)
St. Martin (Fr.)
St. Maarten (Neth.)
St. Barthélemy (Fr.)
Barbuda
ANTIGUA & BARBUDA
St. John's
Antigua
Saba (Neth.)
St. Eustatius (Neth.)
ST. KITTS–NEVIS
Basseterre
Charlestown
Montserrat (Br.)
Guadeloupe Passage
Basse Terre
GUADELOUPE (Fr.)
Grande Terre
Marie Galante
Les Saintes
Dominica Passage
Portsmouth
DOMINICA
Roseau
Scotts Head

BERMUDA 1:1 000 000

St. George's
St. David's I.
St. George's I.
Crow Lane
Tucker's Town
Somerset
North Village
Hamilton
Spanish Point
Ireland I.
Somerset I.

ATLANTIC OCEAN

BAHAMAS
Grand Bahama I.
West End
Freeport
Little Abaco
Great Abaco
Nassau
New Providence
Andros I.
Eleuthera I.
Cat I.
San Salvador (Watling I.)
Rum Cay
Long I.
Crooked I.
Acklins I.
Mayaguana I.
GREAT BAHAMA BANK
Great Exuma I.
George Town
Tropic of Cancer
Caicos Islands (Br.)
Turks Islands (Br.)
Great Inagua I.
Little Inagua I.

FLORIDA
Vero Beach
West Palm Beach
Fort Pierce
Fort Lauderdale
MIAMI
Key West
Florida Straits
Fort Myers
Everglades

GULF OF MEXICO

MEXICO
C. Catoche
Canal de Yucatán
Isla de Cozumel
B. de la Ascensión

CUBA
Pinar del Río
La Habana
Marianao
Matanzas
Cárdenas
Colón
Cienfuegos
Santa Clara
Sancti Spíritus
Ciego de Ávila
Camagüey
Victoria
Holguín
Bayamo
Manzanillo
Santiago de Cuba
Sierra Maestra
Guantánamo
Nuevitas
I. de la Juventud
Arch. de los Canarreos
Golfo de Batabanó
Jardines de la Reina

Cayman Islands (Br.)
Grand Cayman 7680

HAITI
Port-au-Prince
Cap-Haïtien
Gonaïves
Jérémie
Les Cayes
Île de la Gonâve
Île de la Tortue

DOMINICAN REP.
Santo Domingo
Santiago
San Pedro
La Romana
Barahona
Puerto Plata
San Juan

HISPANIOLA

PUERTO RICO (U.S.A.)
San Juan
Ponce
Mayagüez
Arecibo
Fajardo
Mona Passage
Isla Mona

Virgin Islands
St. Thomas (U.S.A.)
St. Croix (U.S.A.)
Virgin Gorda (Br.)
Anegada (Br.)
Tortola (Br.)

CARIBBEAN SEA

LESSER ANTILLES

GREATER ANTILLES

NETH. ANTILLES
Aruba
Curaçao
Bonaire
Willemstad

I. de Providencia (Colombia)
I. de San Andrés (Colombia)

HONDURAS
Tegucigalpa
Trujillo
La Ceiba
Golfo de Honduras

NICARAGUA
Managua
León
Chinandega
Granada
Puerto Cabezas
Cayos Miskitos
Laguna de Perlas
Bluefields
C. Gracias a Dios

COSTA RICA
Puerto Limón
Golfo de Nicoya

PANAMA
Colón
PANAMA CANAL
Golfo de Panamá
Archipiélago de San Blas
Arch. de las Perlas

COLOMBIA
BARRANQUILLA
Cartagena
Santa Marta
Magdalena
Golfo de Urabá
Cúcuta
Bucaramanga

VENEZUELA
CARACAS
Maracaibo
Lago de Maracaibo
Maracay
Valencia
Barquisimeto
Puerto Cabello
La Guaira
Ciudad Bolívar
Orinoco
Cumaná
Barcelona
Maturín
Margarita
La Asunción
Porlamar
Los Testigos
Los Hermanos
Los Roques
La Orchila
La Blanquilla
La Tortuga

Tobago
TRINIDAD & TOBAGO
Port of Spain
San Fernando
Golfo de Paria

Port of Spain
GRENADA
BARBADOS
Bridgetown
ST. VINCENT
WINDWARD ISLANDS

PACIFIC OCEAN

West from Greenwich

m ft
6000 18 000
4500 12 000
3000 9000
2000 6000
1200 4500
600 3000
400 2000
200 1200
0 600
0

Projection: Bi-polar oblique Conical Orthomorphic

COPYRIGHT GEORGE PHILIP & SON LTD.

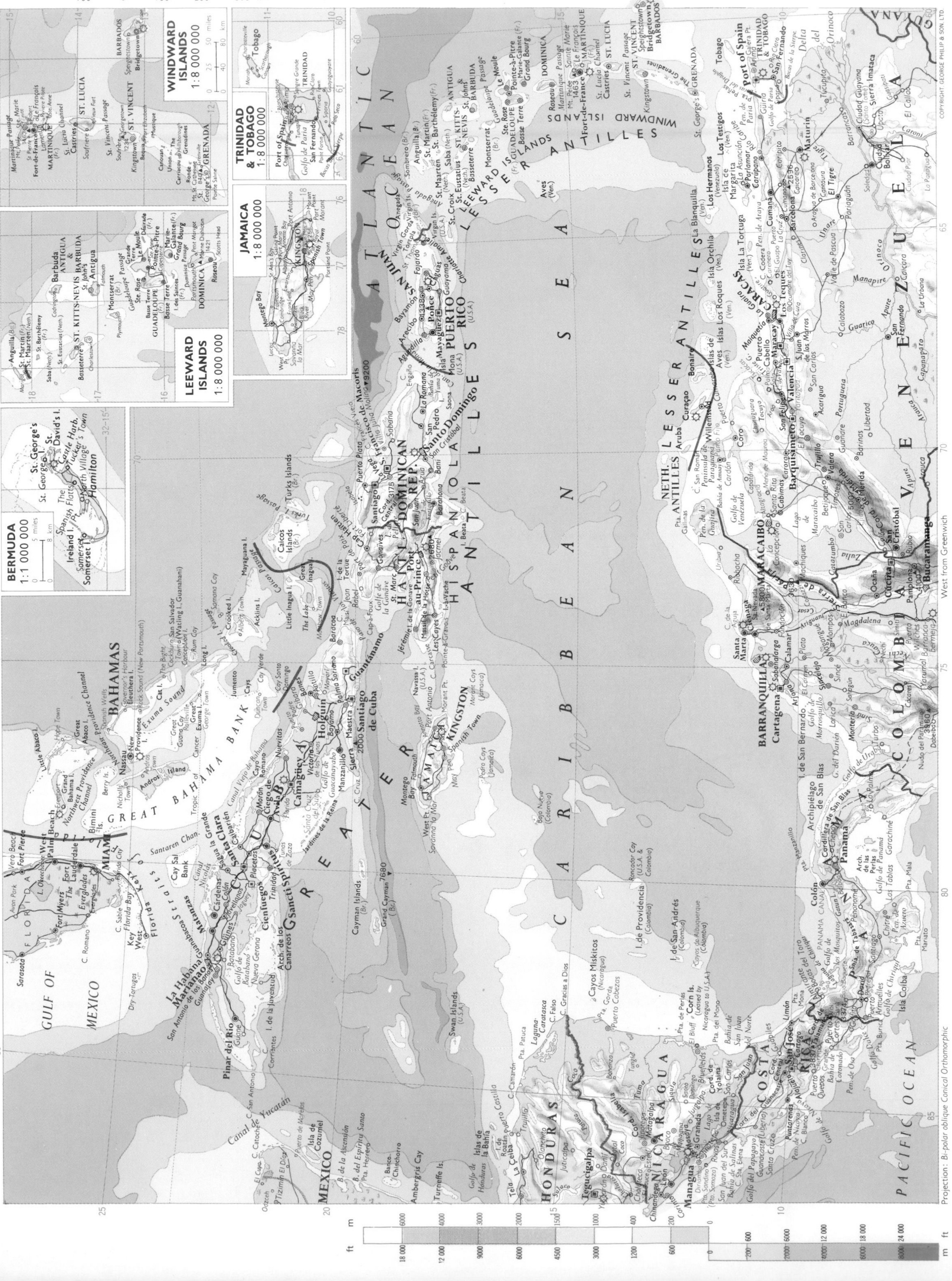

1:30 000 000
100 0 100 200 300 400 500 miles
100 0 200 400 600 800 km

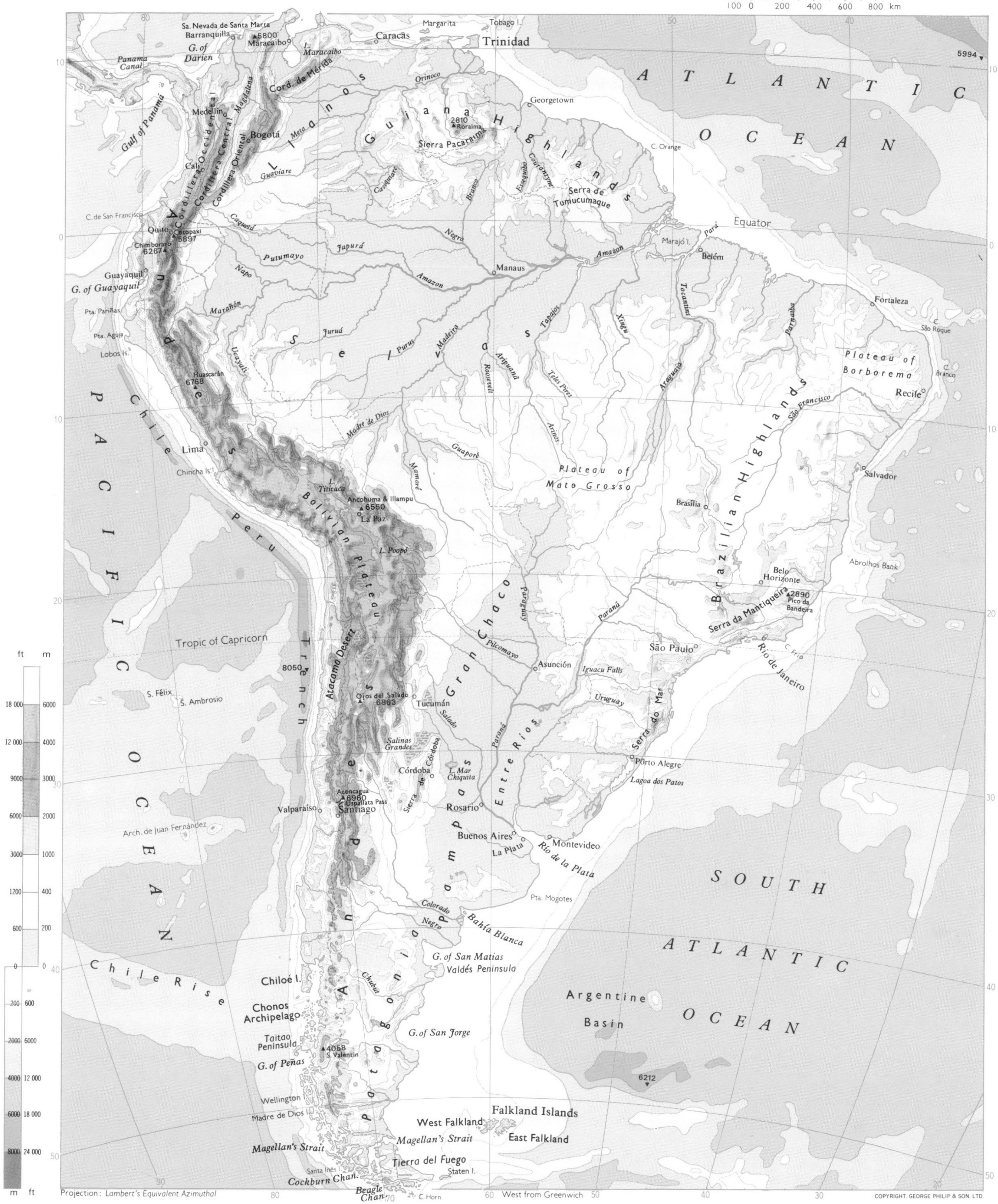

Projection: *Lambert's Equivalent Azimuthal*

1:30 000 000
100 0 100 200 300 400 500 miles
100 0 200 400 600 800 km

NORTH ATLANTIC OCEAN

VENEZUELA

TRINIDAD AND TOBAGO

Barranquilla
Cartagena
Maracaibo
Barquisimeto
Cabimas
Valencia
Caracas
Cumaná
Port of Spain
Trinidad
Isla de Margarita
Tobago
Punta Fijo
Ciénaga
Monteria
Cúcuta
Mérida
San Cristóbal
San Fernando
Orinoco
Ciudad Guayana
Ciudad Bolívar
Maturín
Pto. Ayacucho
Georgetown
New Amsterdam
Paramaribo
Cayenne
C. Orange

COSTA RICA
San José
PANAMA
Panamá
Golfo de Darién
Golfo de Panamá
S.F. 3277
Honolulu 4683

Medellín
Manizales
Pereira
Ibagué
Bogotá
Buenaventura
Cali
COLOMBIA
Popayán
Pasto
Caquetá
Meta
Orinoco
Branco

GUYANA
SURINAM
FRENCH GUIANA
Essequibo

C. de San Francisco
Quito
ECUADOR
Guayaquil
Riobamba
Cuenca
G. de Guayaquil
Pta. de Aguja
Iquitos
Marañón
Napo
Putumayo
Japurá
Tefé
Manaus
Amazonas (Amazon)
Santarem
Ilha de Marajó
Belém (Pará)
Macapá
Equator

Honolulu 4834
Salina Cruz 2010
San Francisco 3990

Chiclayo
Trujillo
Pacalipa
Ucayali
Cruzeiro do Sul
Benjamim Constant
Juruá
Purus
Manicoré
Madeira
Tapajós
Xingu
Araguaia
Tocantins
São Luis
Bacabal
Teresina
Parnaíba
Fortaleza (Ceara)
C. de São Roque
Natal
João Pessoa (Paraiba)
Recife (Pernambuco)
Maceió

Honolulu 5139
Islas de Chincha
Callao
Lima
Huancayo
Ayacucho
Cuzco
PERU
Madre de Dios
Pôrto Velho
Rio Branco
Guajará-Mirim
Guaporé
Mamoré
Beni
B R A Z I L
Cuiabá
Juazeiro do Norte
Aracaju
São Francisco
Salvador (Bahia)

Wellington 5718
Juliaca
Titicaca
Arequipa
Mollendo
Tacna
Arica
Oruro
La Paz
Cochabamba
BOLIVIA
Sucre
Uyuni
Santa Cruz
Corumbá
Brasília
Goiânia
Jataí
Montes Claros
Gov. Valadares
Belo Horizonte
Vitória

Iquique
Tarija
Cueto
Campo Grande
Pedro Juan Caballero
PARAGUAY
Paraguay
Uberaba
Ribeirão Prêto
Pres. Prudente
Bauru
Campinas
Juiz de Fora
Campos

Tropic of Capricorn
Antofagasta
Salta
San Miguel de Tucumán
Asunción
Pilcomayo
Paraná
Londrina
Ponta Grossa
Curitiba
SÃO PAULO
Santos
RIO DE JANEIRO
Niterói

San Francisco 5136
Isla San Félix (Chile)
Isla San Ambrosio (Chile)
Honolulu 5916
Yokohama 9339

Resistencia
Corrientes
Uruguay
Santa Maria
Florianópolis
Pôrto Alegre
Santiago del Estero
Salado
Uruguaiana
Lagoa dos Patos
Pelotas

Coquimbo
ARGENTINA
Córdoba
Santa Fe
Paraná
Rosario
URUGUAY
Mendoza
Valparaíso
Arch de Juan Fernández (Chile)
Santiago
Mercedes
San Rafael
BUENOS AIRES
La Plata
Río de la Plata
Montevideo
Talca
Concepción
Santa Rosa
Tandil
Mar del Plata
Bahía Blanca
Colorado
Río Negro

Wellington 5044, Sydney 6257

SOUTH ATLANTIC OCEAN

Valdivia
Zapala
Viedma
Puerto Montt
Isla de Chiloé
San Carlos de Bariloche
Chubut
Trelew
Península Valdés
Archipiélago de los Chonos
Golfo Comodoro Rivadavia
San Jorge
G. de Penas

PACIFIC OCEAN

I. Wellington
Santa Cruz
Estrecho de Magallanes
Punta Arenas
Strait of Magellan
Isla Grande de Tierra del Fuego
Río Gallegos
West Falkland
FALKLAND ISLANDS (ISLAS MALVINAS) (U.K.)
Stanley
East Falkland
Cabo de Hornos (Cape Horn)

Montevideo — Cape Town 3649
Buenos Aires — Adelaide 8885, Melbourne 9099, Sydney 9564
Punta Arenas — Cape Town 4036
Wellington — Rio de Janeiro 6815

West from Greenwich

Projection: Lambert's Equivalent Azimuthal

Projection: *Sanson-Flamsteed's Sinusoidal*

1:16 000 000

100 100 200 300 400 500 miles
100 0 100 200 300 400 500 600 700 800 km

A T L A N T I C

ATLANTIC

OCEAN

O C E A N

SU-RI-NAM
FR. GUIANA

Paramaribo
Nieuw Amsterdam
Albina
St. Laurent
Cayenne
C. Orange
Oiapoque

AMAPÁ
C. do Norte
Macapá
Estuario do Rio Amazonas
Ilha Caviana
Ilha de Marajó
Ilha Mexiana

Equator

Belém (Pará)
São Luís (Maranhão)

Fernando de Noronha (Braz.)

Santarém
Amazonas
PARÁ
Parnaíba
Fortaleza (Ceará)
Sobral
MARANHÃO
Teresina
CEARÁ
RIO GRANDE DO NORTE
Natal
C. de São Roque

Rocas

PIAUÍ
PARAÍBA
João Pessoa (Paraíba)
Campina Grande
Caruaru
PERNAMBUCO
RECIFE (Pernambuco)

Juàzeiro
Paulo Afonso
Maceió
ALAGOAS
SERGIPE
Aracaju

BAHIA
Feira de Santana
Santo Amaro
Salvador (Bahia)

GOIÁS
Brasília
DIST. FED.
Anápolis
Goiânia

Vitória da Conquista
Ilhéus

Montes Claros
Diamantina
Gov. Valadares
Teófilo Otoni
Nanuque

MATO GROSSO
Planalto do Mato Grosso

MINAS GERAIS
Belo Horizonte
Vitória

MATO GROSSO DO SUL
Campo Grande
Três Lagoas
Araçatuba
Marília
Bauru
SÃO PAULO
Piracicaba
Campinas
Ribeirão Preto
Juiz de Fora
Campos
Petrópolis
Niterói
RIO DE JANEIRO

55 50 45 40 35 30

1:16 000 000

Projection: *Sanson-Flamsteed's Sinusoidal*

60 West from Greenwich 55

INDEX

Introduction

The number in bold type which precedes each name in the index refers to the number of the page where that feature or place will be found.

The geographical co-ordinates which follow the place name are sometimes only approximate but are close enough for the place name to be located.

An open square □ signifies that the name refers to an administrative division of a country while a solid square ■ follows the name of a country.

Rivers have been indexed to their mouth or to their confluence.

The alphabetical order of names composed of two or more words is governed primarily by the first word and then by the second. This is an example of the rule:

West Wyalong
West Yorkshire
Westbrook
Westbury
Western Australia

Names composed of a proper name (Gibraltar) and a description (Strait of) are positioned alphabetically by the proper name. All river names are followed by R. If the same word occurs in the name of a town and a geographical feature, the town name is listed first followed by the name or names of the geographical features.

Names beginning with M', Mc are all indexed as if they were spelled Mac.

If the same place name occurs two or more times in the index and all are in the same country, each is followed by the name of the administrative subdivision in which it is located. The names are placed in the alphabetical order of the subdivisions. For example:

Stour, R., Dorset
Stour, R., Hereford and Worcester
Stour, R., Kent
Stour, R., Suffolk

If the same place name occurs twice or more in the index and the places are in different countries they will be followed by the country names and the latter in alphabetical order.

Sydney, Australia
Sydney, Canada

If there is a mixture of these situations, the primary order is fixed by the alphabetical sequence of the countries and the secondary order by that of the country subdivisions. In the latter case the country names are omitted.

Rochester, U.K.
Rochester, Minn. (U.S.A.) are omitted from
Rochester, N.H. (U.S.A.) the index
Rochester, N.Y. (U.S.A.)

The following is a list of abbreviations used in the index

A.S.S.R. – *Autonomous Soviet Socialist Republic*
Ala. – *Alabama*
Alas. – *Alaska*
Ang. – *Angola*
Arch. – *Archipelago*
Arg. – *Argentina*
Ariz. – *Arizona*
Ark. – *Arkansas*
B. – *Baie, Bahĩa, Bay, Boca, Bucht, Bugt*
B.C. – *British Columbia*
Br. – *British*
C. – *Cabo, Cap, Cape*
C.A.R. – *Central African Republic*
C. Prov. – *Cape Province*
Calif. – *California*
Chan. – *Channel*
Col. – *Colombia*
Colo. – *Colorado*
Conn. – *Connecticut*
Cord. – *Cordillera*
D.C. – *District of Columbia*
Del. – *Delaware*
Dep. – *Dependency*
Des. – *Desert*
Dist. – *District*
Dom. Rep. – *Dominican Republic*
E. – *East*
Eng. – *England*
Fd. – *Fjord*
Fed. – *Federal, Federation*
Fla. – *Florida*
Fr. – *France, French*
G. – *Golfe, Golfo, Gulf, Guba*
Ga. – *Georgia*
Gt. – *Great*
Hants. – *Hampshire*
Hd. – *Head*
Hts. – *Heights*
I.(s) – *Ile, Ilha, Insel, Isla, Island (s)*
Id. – *Idaho*
Ill. – *Illinois*
Ind. – *Indiana*
J. – *Jezero (L.)*
K. – *Kap, Kapp*
Kans. – *Kansas*
Kep. – *Kepulauan (I.)*
Kól. – *Kólpos (B.)*
Ky. – *Kentucky*
L. – *Lac, Lacul, Lago, Lagoa, Lake, Limni, Loch, Lough*
La. – *Louisana*
Ld. – *Land*
Mad. P. – *Madhya Pradesh*
Man. – *Manitoba*
Mass. – *Massachusetts*
Md. – *Maryland*
Me. – *Maine*
Mich. – *Michigan*
Minn. – *Minnesota*
Miss. – *Mississippi*
Mo. – *Missouri*
Mont. – *Montana*
Mt.(s) – *Mont, Monte, Monti, Muntii, Montaña, Mountain (s)*
Mys. – *Mysore*
N. – *North, Northern*
N.B. – *New Brunswick*
N.C. – *North Carolina*
N.D. – *North Dakota*
N.H. – *New Hampshire*
N. Ire. – *Northern Ireland*
N.J. – *New Jersey*
N. Mex. – *New Mexico*
N.S.W. – *New South Wales*
N.Y. – *New York*
N.Z. – *New Zealand*
Nat. Park – *National Park*
Nebr. – *Nebraska*
Neth. – *Netherlands*
Nev. – *Nevada*
Newf. – *Newfoundland*
Nic. – *Nicaragua*
Nig. – *Nigeria*
O.F.S. – *Orange Free State*
Okla. – *Oklahoma*
Ont. – *Ontario*
Oreg. – *Oregon*
Os. – *Ostrov (I.)*
Oz – *Ozero (L.)*
P. – *Pass, Passo, Pasul*
P.N.G. – *Papua New Guinea*
Pa. – *Pennsylvania*
Pak. – *Pakistan*
Pass. – *Passage*
Pen. – *Peninsula*
Pk. – *Peak*
Plat. – *Plateau*
Pol. – *Poluostrov*
Port. – *Portugal, Portuguese*
Prov. – *Province, Provincial*
Pt. – *Point*
Pta. – *Ponta, Punta*
Pte. – *Pointe*
Que. – *Quebec*
Queens. – *Queensland*
R. – *Rio, River*
R.S.F.S.R. – *Russian Soviet Federative Socialist Republic*
Ra.(s) – *Range(s)*
Reg. – *Region*
Rep. – *Republic*
Res. – *Reserve, Reservoir*
S. – *South*
S. Africa – *South Africa*
S.C. – *S. Carolina*
S.D. – *South Dakota*
S. Leone – *Sierra Leone*
S.S.R. – *Soviet Socialist Republic*
Sa. – *Serra, Sierra*
Sask. – *Saskatchewan*
Scot. – *Scotland*
Sd. – *Sound*
Sp. – *Spain, Spanish*
St. – *Saint*
Str. – *Strait, Stretto*
Switz. – *Switzerland*
Tanz. – *Tanzania*
Tas. – *Tasmania*
Tenn. – *Tennessee*
Terr. – *Territory*
Tex. – *Texas*
U.K. – *United Kingdom*
U.S.A. – *United States of America*
U.S.S.R. – *Union of Soviet Socialist Republics*
Ut. P. – *Uttar Pradesh*
Va. – *Virginia*
Vdkhr. – *Vodokhranilishche (Res.)*
Ven. – *Venezuela*
Vic. – *Victoria*
Vt. – *Vermont*
W. – *West*
W. Va. – *West Virginia*
Wis. – *Wisconsin*
Wyo. – *Wyoming*
Yorks. – *Yorkshire*
Yug. – *Yugoslavia*

In the index each placename is followed by its geographical co-ordinates which allow the reader to find the place on the map. These co-ordinates give the latitude and longitude of a particular place.

The latitude (or parallel) is the distance of a point north or south of the Equator measured as an angle with the centre of the earth. The Equator is latitude 0°, the North Pole is 90°N and the South Pole 90°S. On a globe the lines could be drawn as concentric circles parallel to the Equator, decreasing in diameter from the Equator until they become a point at the Poles. On the maps these lines of latitude are usually represented as lines running across the map from East to West in smooth curves. They are numbered on the sides of the map; north of the Equator the numbers increase northwards, to the south they increase southwards. The degree interval between them depends on the scale of the map. On a large scale map (for example, 1:2 000 000) the interval is one degree, but on a small scale (for example 1:50 000 000) it will be ten degrees.

Lines of longitude (or meridians) cut the latitude lines at right angles on the globe and intersect with one another at the Poles. Longitude is measured by the angle at the centre of the earth between it and the meridian of origin which runs through Greenwich (0°). It may be a measurement East or West of this line and from 0° to 180° in each direction. The longitude line of 180° runs North – South through the Pacific Ocean. On a particular map the interval between the lines of longitude is always the same as that between the lines of latitude and normally they are drawn vertically. They are numbered in the top and bottom margins and a note states East or West from Greenwich.

The unit of measurement for latitude and longitude is the degree and it is subdivided into 60 minutes. An index entry states the position of a place in degrees and minutes, a space being left between the degrees and minutes. The latitude is followed by N(orth) or S(outh) and the longitude by E(ast) or W(est).

The diagrams below illustrate how the reader has to estimate the required distance from the nearest line of latitude or longitude. In the case of the first diagram there is one degree, or 60 minutes between the lines and so to find the position of Calais an estimate has to be made, 57 parts of 60 north of the 50 degree latitude line and 50 parts of 60, or 50 minutes east of the one degree longitude line. In the case of the second diagram it is a little more difficult to estimate since there are 10 degrees between the lines. In the example of Anchorage the reader has to estimate 1 degree 10 minutes north of 60° and 9° 50 minutes west of 140°.

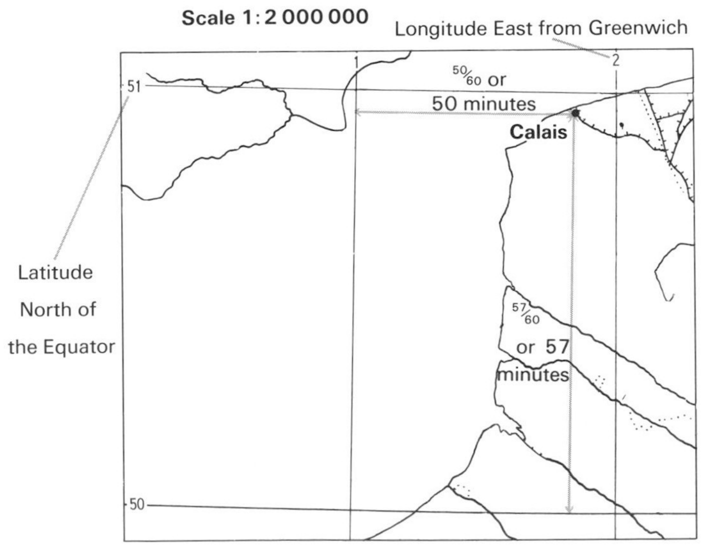

Calais 12 50 57 N 1 50 E
page latitude longitude

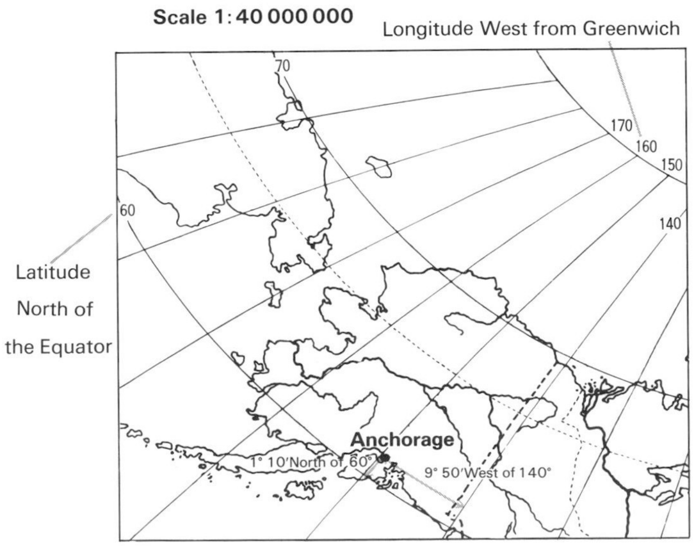

Anchorage 60 61 10 N 149 50 W
page latitude longitude

Aachen Aleksandrovskiy Zavod

A

14 Aachen 50 47N 6 4E
51 A'Âlâ en Nîl □ 8 50N 29 55E
11 Aalsmeer 52 17N 4 43E
11 Aalst 50 56N 4 2E
11 Aalten 51 56N 6 35E
14 Aarau 47 23N 8 4E
14 Aare, R. 47 37N 8 13E
11 Aarschot 50 59N 4 49E
53 Aba 5 10N 7 19E
29 Abā Saud 17 15N 43 55E
30 Abadan 30 22N 48 20E
80 Abai 25 58S 55 54W
53 Abakaliki 6 22N 8 2E
25 Abakan 53 40N 91 10E
31 Abarqu 31 10N 53 20E
28 Abasan 31 19N 34 21E
36 Abashiri 44 0N 144 15E
36 Abashiri-Wan, G. 44 0N 144 30E
24 Abay 49 38N 72 53E
54 Abaya, L. 6 30N 37 50E
24 Abaza 52 39N 90 6E
28 Abba Hillēl 31 42N 34 38E
12 Abbeville, Fr. 50 6N 1 49E
69 Abbeville, U.S.A. 30 0N 92 7W
32 Abbottabad 34 10N 73 15E
51 Abéché 13 50N 20 35E
21 Åbenrå 55 3N 9 25E
53 Abeokuta 7 3N 3 19E
7 Aberayron 52 15N 4 16W
7 Aberdare 51 43N 3 27W
46 Aberdeen, Australia 32 9S 150 56E
56 Aberdeen, S. Africa 32 28S 24 2E
8 Aberdeen, U.K. 57 9N 2 6W
72 Aberdeen, Id. 42 57N 112 50W
69 Aberdeen, Miss. 33 49N 88 13W
70 Aberdeen, S.D. 45 28N 98 29W
72 Aberdeen, Wash. 46 59N 123 50W
7 Aberdovey 52 33N 4 3W
8 Aberfeldy 56 37N 3 50W
7 Abergavenny 51 49N 3 1W
7 Aberystwyth 52 25N 4 6W
29 Abhā 18 0N 42 34E
50 Abidjan 5 26N 3 58W
70 Abilene, Kans. 39 0N 97 16W
71 Abilene, Tex. 32 22N 99 40W
7 Abingdon 51 40N 1 17W
23 Abkhaz A.S.S.R. 43 0N 41 0E
25 Abkit 64 10N 157 10E
53 Abocho 7 35N 6 56E
32 Abohar 30 10N 74 10E
53 Aboisso 5 30N 3 5W
53 Abomey 7 10N 2 5E
54 Abong Mbang 4 0N 13 8E
53 Abonnema 4 41N 6 49W
53 Aboso 5 23N 1 57W
51 Abou Deïa 11 20N 19 20E
8 Aboyne 57 4N 2 48W
30 Abqaiq 26 0N 49 45E
13 Abrantes 39 24N 8 7W
15 Abrud 46 19N 23 5E
18 Abruzzi □ 42 15N 14 0E
72 Absaroka Ra. 44 40N 110 0W
30 Abū al Khasib 30 25N 48 0E
29 Abu Arish 16 53N 42 48E
51 Abu Dis 19 12N 33 38E
28 Abū Ghōsh 31 48N 35 6E
51 Abu Hamed 19 32N 33 13E
51 Abu Tig 27 4N 31 15E
51 Abû Zabad 12 25N 29 10E
31 Abū Zabī 24 28N 54 36E
53 Abuja 9 16N 7 2E
51 Abyad, Gebel, Reg. 17 30N 28 0E
29 Abyssinia ■ = Ethiopia ■ 8 0N 40 0E
74 Acajutla 13 36N 89 50W
74 Acámbaro 20 0N 100 40W
74 Acaponeta 22 30N 105 20W
74 Acapulco 16 51N 99 56W
79 Acará 1 57S 48 11W
74 Acatlan 18 10N 98 3W
74 Acayucan 17 59N 94 58W
53 Accra 5 35N 0 6W
6 Accrington 53 46N 2 22W
34 Aceh □ 4 50N 96 0E
9 Achill 53 56N 9 55W
9 Achill, I. 53 58N 10 5W
25 Achinsk 56 20N 90 20E
75 Acklins I. 22 30N 74 0W
64 Acme 51 33N 113 30W
80 Aconcagua, Mt. 32 39S 70 0W
28 Acre = Akko 32 55N 35 4E
78 Acre □ 9 1S 71 0W
29 Ad Dam 20 33N 44 45E
30 Ad Dammam 26 20N 50 5E
30 Ad Khālis 33 40N 44 55E
53 Ada, Ghana 5 44N 0 40E
71 Ada, U.S.A. 34 50N 96 45W
29 Adale 2 58N 46 27E
53 Adamaoua, Massif de l' 7 20N 12 20E
18 Adamello, Mt. 46 10N 10 34E
68 Adams, N.Y. 43 50N 76 3W
70 Adams, Wis. 43 59N 89 50W
72 Adams, Mt. 46 10N 121 28W
32 Adam's Bridge 9 15N 79 40E
32 Adam's Pk. 6 55N 80 45E
30 Adana 37 0N 35 16E
35 Adaut 8 8S 131 7E
18 Adda, R. 45 8N 9 53E
51 Addis Ababa = Addis Abeba 9 2N 38 42E
51 Addis Abeba 9 2N 38 42E
53 Adebour 13 17N 11 50E
43 Adelaide, Australia 34 52S 138 30E
56 Adelaide, S. Afr. 32 42S 26 20E
60 Adelaide Pen. 67 40N 98 0W
44 Adelaide River 13 15S 131 7E
29 Aden = Al 'Adan 12 50N 45 0E
29 Aden, G. of 13 0N 50 0E
18 Adige, R. 45 10N 12 20E
68 Adirondack Mts. 44 0N 74 15W
53 Adjohon 6 41N 2 32E
44 Admiralty, G. 14 20S 125 55E
72 Admiralty Inlet 48 0N 122 40W
64 Admiralty I. 57 50N 134 30W
3 Admiralty Is. 2 0S 147 0E
53 Ado 6 36N 2 56E
53 Ado-Ekiti 7 38N 5 12E
32 Adoni 15 33N 77 18E
12 Adour, R. 43 32N 1 32W
13 Adra 36 43N 3 3W
18 Adrano 37 40N 14 19E
50 Adrar des Iforas, Mts. 19 40N 1 40E
68 Adrian 41 55N 84 0W
18 Adriatic Sea 43 0N 16 0E
23 Adzhar A.S.S.R. 42 0N 42 0E
19 Ægean Sea 37 0N 25 0E
18 Æolian Is. = Eólie o Lípari, I. 38 30N 14 50E
37 Aerhtai Shan, Mts. 48 0N 90 0E
31 Afghanistan ■ 33 0N 65 0E
29 Afgoi 2 7N 44 59E
53 Afikpo 5 53N 7 54E
1 Africa 5 0N 20 0E
79 Afuá 0 15S 50 10W
28 Afula 32 37N 35 17E
30 Afyon 38 20N 30 15E
53 Agadez 16 58N 7 59E
50 Agadir 30 28N 9 25W
25 Agapa 71 27N 89 15E
33 Agartala 23 50N 91 23E
35 Agats 5 34S 138 5E
50 Agboville 5 55N 4 15W
12 Agde 43 19N 3 28E
53 Agege 6 37N 3 20E
12 Agen 44 12N 0 38E
45 Agnew 28 1S 120 30E
53 Agnibilekrou 7 10N 3 11W
32 Agra 27 17N 77 58E
30 Ağri Daği, Mt. 39 50N 44 15E
18 Agrigento 37 19N 13 33E
19 Agrinion 38 37N 21 27E
79 Agua Clara 20 25S 52 45W
74 Agua Prieta 31 20N 109 32W
78 Aguadas 5 40N 75 38W
75 Aguadilla 18 27N 67 10W
63 Aguanish 50 14N 62 2W
80 Aguas Blancas 24 15S 69 55W
74 Aguascalientes 22 0N 102 12W
74 Aguascalientes □ 22 0N 102 20W
13 Aguilas 37 23N 1 35W
56 Agulhas, K. 34 52S 20 0E
28 Agur 31 42N 34 55E
50 Ahaggar, Reg. 23 0N 6 30E
47 Ahaura 42 20S 171 32E
32 Ahmadabad 23 0N 72 40E
32 Ahmadnagar 19 7N 74 46E
74 Ahuachapán 13 54N 89 52W
30 Ahvāz 31 20N 48 40E
21 Ahvenanmaa = Åland, I. 60 15N 20 0E
29 Ahwar 13 31N 46 42E
31 Aibaq 36 15N 68 5E
36 Aichi □ 35 0N 137 15E
12 Aigues-Mortes 43 35N 4 2E
38 Aihun 49 55N 127 30E
33 Aijal 23 40N 92 44E
69 Aiken 33 44N 81 50W
8 Ailsa Craig, I. 55 15N 5 7W
25 Aim 59 0N 133 55E
79 Aimorés 19 30S 41 4W
12 Ain □ 46 5N 5 20E
50 Aïn Beida 35 50N 7 35E
30 Ain Dār 25 55N 49 10E
29 Ainabo 9 0N 46 25E
50 Aïr 18 0N 8 0E
8 Airdrie 55 53N 3 57W
6 Aire, R. 53 44N 0 44W
12 Aisne, R. 49 26N 2 50E
12 Aisne □ 49 42N 3 40E
37 Aitush 39 54N 75 40E
15 Aiud 46 19N 23 44E
12 Aix-en-Provence 43 32N 5 27E
12 Aix-les-Bains 45 41N 5 53E
12 Ajaccio 41 55N 8 40E
45 Ajana 27 56S 114 35E
32 Ajanta Ra. 20 28N 75 50E
51 Ajdābiyah 30 54N 20 4E
28 'Ajlun 32 18N 35 47E
31 Ajman 25 25N 55 30E
32 Ajmer 26 28N 74 37E
73 Ajo 32 18N 112 54W
53 Ajua 4 50N 1 55W
53 Akaba 8 10N 1 2E
47 Akaroa 43 49S 172 59E
36 Akashi 34 45N 135 0E
21 Akershus □ 60 10N 11 15E
54 Aketi 2 38N 23 47E
19 Akhelóös, R. 38 36N 21 14E
30 Akhisar 38 56N 27 48E
51 Akhmîm 26 31N 31 47E
62 Akimiski I. 52 50N 81 30W
36 Akita 39 45N 140 0E
36 Akita □ 39 40N 140 30E
50 Akjoujt 19 45N 14 15W
28 Akko 32 55N 35 4E
24 Akkol 43 36N 70 45E
60 Aklavik 68 25N 135 0W
36 Akō, Japan 34 45N 134 24E
53 Ako, Nigeria 10 19N 10 48E
32 Akola 20 42N 77 2E
51 Akordat 15 30N 37 40E
53 Akosombo Dam 6 20N 0 5E
61 Akpatok I. 60 30N 68 0W
20 Akranes 64 19N 22 6W
68 Akron 41 7N 81 31W
24 Aksarka 66 31N 67 50E
30 Aksehir 38 18N 31 30E
25 Aksenovo Zilovskoye 53 20N 117 40E
37 Aksu 41 4N 80 5E
51 Aksum 14 5N 38 40E
24 Aktogay 44 25N 76 44E
24 Aktyubinsk 50 10N 57 3E
53 Aku 6 40N 7 18E
53 Akure 7 15N 5 5E
20 Akureyri 65 40N 18 5W
33 Akyab 20 15N 92 45E
29 Al 'Adan 12 50N 45 0E
30 Al Amārah 31 55N 47 15E
30 Al 'Aqabah 29 37N 35 0E
28 Al Barah 31 55N 35 12E
30 Al Basrah 30 30N 47 55E
29 Al Baydā 32 30N 21 40E
31 Al Buraimi 24 15N 55 53E
30 Al Hadithan 34 0N 41 13E
30 Al Hadr 35 35N 42 44E
30 Al Hasa, Reg. 25 40N 50 0E
30 Al Hasakah 36 35N 40 45E
29 Al Hauta 16 5N 48 20E
29 Al Hawra 13 49N 47 37E
30 Al Hillah, Iraq 32 30N 44 25E
30 Al Hillah, Saudi Arabia 23 35N 46 50E
15 Al Hilwah 23 24N 46 48E
30 Al Hindiyah 32 30N 44 10E
50 Al Hoceïma 35 15N 3 58W
30 Al Hufūf 25 25N 49 45E
30 Al Jahrah 29 25N 47 40E
30 Al Jalāmid 31 20N 39 45E
29 Al Jazir 18 30N 56 31N
30 Al Jazirah, Reg. 26 10N 21 20E
30 Al Jubail 27 0N 49 50E
29 Al Juwara 19 0N 57 13E
31 Al Khābūrah 23 57N 57 5E
29 Al Khalaf 20 30N 57 56E
51 Al Khums 32 40N 14 17E
30 Al Kūt 32 30N 46 0E
30 Al Kuwayt 29 20N 48 0E
30 Al Lādhiqiyah 35 30N 35 45E
29 Al Līth 20 9N 40 15E
30 Al Madīnah 24 35N 39 52E
28 Al Mafraq 32 17N 36 14E
31 Al Manamah 26 10N 50 30E
51 Al Marj 32 25N 20 30E
29 Al Masīrah 20 25N 58 50E
29 Al Matamma 16 43N 33 22E
30 Al Mawsil 36 15N 43 5E
28 Al Mazra' 31 18N 35 32E
30 Al Miqdadīyah 34 0N 45 0E
30 Al Mubarraz 25 30N 49 40E
31 Al Muharraq 26 15N 50 40E
29 Al Mukha 13 18N 43 15E
30 Al Qamishli 37 10N 41 10E
30 Al Qatif 26 35N 50 0E
51 Al-Qatrūn 24 56N 15 3E
29 Al Qunfidha 19 3N 41 4E
29 Al Ubailah 21 59N 50 57E
51 Al 'Uqaylah 30 12N 19 10E
31 Al Wakrah 25 10N 51 40E
30 Al Wari 'ah 27 50N 47 30E
38 Ala Shan, Reg. 40 0N 104 0E
69 Alabama, R. 31 8N 87 57W
69 Alabama □ 31 0N 87 0W
79 Alagôa Grande 7 3S 35 35W
79 Alagôas □ 9 0S 36 0W
79 Alagoinhas 12 0S 38 20W
75 Alajuela 10 2N 84 8W
22 Alakurtti 67 0N 30 30E
73 Alameda 35 10N 106 43W
73 Alamogordo 32 59N 106 0W
73 Alamosa 37 30N 106 0W
21 Åland, I. 60 15N 20 0E
21 Ålands hav 60 0N 19 20E
24 Alapayevsk 57 52N 61 42E
38 Alashanchih 38 58N 105 14E
60 Alaska □ 65 0N 150 0W
60 Alaska, G. of 58 0N 145 0W
60 Alaska Pen. 56 0N 160 0W
60 Alaska Ra. 62 50N 151 0W
22 Alatyr 54 45N 46 35E
78 Alausi 2 0S 78 50W
43 Alawoona 34 45S 140 30E
18 Alba 44 41N 8 1E
15 Alba-Iulia 46 4N 23 35E
13 Albacete 39 0N 1 50W
19 Albania ■ 41 0N 20 0E
45 Albany, Australia 35 1S 117 58E
69 Albany, Ga. 31 40N 84 10W
68 Albany, N.Y. 42 40N 73 47W
72 Albany, Oreg. 44 41N 123 0W
62 Albany, R. 52 17N 81 31W
80 Albardón 31 20S 68 30W
13 Albarracin 40 25N 1 26W
13 Albarracin, Sa. de 40 30N 1 30W
69 Albemarle 35 27N 80 15W
13 Alberche, R. 39 58N 4 46W
64 Alberni 49 20N 124 50W
63 Albert 45 51N 64 38W
54 Albert, L. = Mobutu Sese Seko, L. 1 30N 31 0E
70 Albert Lea 43 32N 93 20W
54 Albert Nile, R. 3 36N 32 2E
75 Albert Town 18 17N 77 33W
64 Alberta □ 54 40N 115 0W
56 Albertinia 34 11S 21 34E
46 Alberton 38 35S 146 40E
54 Albertville = Kalemie 5 55S 29 9E
31 Alberz, Reshteh-Ye-Kūkhā-Ye, Mts. 36 0N 52 0E
12 Albi 43 56N 2 9E
79 Albina, 5 37N 54 15W
68 Albion 42 15N 84 45W
13 Alboran, I. 35 57N 3 0W
21 Ålbôrg 57 2N 9 54E
73 Albuquerque 35 5N 106 47W
46 Albury 36 3S 146 56E
13 Alcalá de Henares 40 28N 3 22W
13 Alcalá la Real 37 27N 3 57W
13 Alcaníz 41 2N 0 8W
79 Alcántara, Brazil 2 20S 44 30W
13 Alcántara, Sp. 39 41N 6 57W
13 Alcaraz, Sa. de 38 40N 2 20W
13 Alcaudete 37 35N 4 5W
13 Alcazar de San Juan 39 24N 3 12W
13 Alcira 39 9N 0 30W
13 Alcobaça 39 32N 9 0W
13 Alcoy 38 43N 0 30W
49 Aldabra Is. 9 22S 46 28E
25 Aldan, R. 63 28N 129 35E
7 Aldeburgh 52 9N 1 35E
7 Alderney, I. 49 42N 2 12W
7 Aldershot 51 15N 0 43W
50 Aleg 17 3N 13 55W
80 Alegrete 29 40S 56 0W
24 Aleisk 52 40N 83 0E
23 Aleksandrov Gai 50 15N 48 35E
25 Aleksandrovsk-Sakhalinskiy 50 50N 142 20E
25 Aleksandrovskiy Zavod 50 40N 117 50E

Aleksandrovskoye Anupgarh

24 Aleksandrovskoye 60 35N 77 50E
12 Alençon 48 27N 0 4E
66 Alenuihaha Chan. 20 25N 156 0W
30 Aleppo=Ḩalab 36 10N 37 15E
64 Alert Bay 50 30N 127 35W
12 Alès 44 9N 4 5E
18 Alessandria 44 54N 8 37E
20 Ålesund 62 28N 6 12E
2 Aleutian Is. 52 0N 175 0W
64 Alexander Arch. 57 0N 135 0W
55 Alexander Bay 28 36S 16 33E
69 Alexander City 32 56N 85 57W
2 Alexander I. 69 0S 70 0W
47 Alexandra 45 14S 169 25E
51 Alexandria=El Iskandarîya 31 0N 30 0E
62 Alexandria, Canada 45 19N 74 38W
56 Alexandria, S. Africa 33 38S 26 28E
71 Alexandria, La. 31 20N 92 30W
70 Alexandria, Minn. 45 50N 95 20W
68 Alexandria, Va. 38 47N 77 1W
68 Alexandria Bay 44 20N 75 52W
19 Alexandroúpolis 40 50N 25 24E
8 Alford 53 16N 0 10E
6 Alfreton 53 6N 1 22W
24 Alga 49 46N 57 20E
13 Algarve, Reg. 37 15N 8 10W
13 Algeciras 36 9N 5 28W
13 Algemesí 39 11N 0 27W
50 Alger 36 42N 3 8E
50 Algeria ■ 35 10N 3 0E
18 Alghero 40 34N 8 20E
50 Algiers=Alger 36 42N 3 8E
56 Algoabaai 33 50S 25 45E
62 Algonquin Prov. Park 45 35N 78 35W
13 Alhama de Murcia 37 51N 1 25W
73 Alhambra 34 0N 118 10W
19 Aliákmon, R. 40 30N 22 36E
13 Alicante 38 23N 0 30W
13 Alicante □ 38 30N 0 37W
71 Alice 27 47N 98 1W
64 Alice Arm 55 29N 129 23W
44 Alice Downs 17 45S 127 56E
42 Alice Springs 23 40S 135 50E
55 Alicedale 33 15S 26 4E
32 Aligarh 27 55N 78 10E
30 Aligudarz 33 25N 49 45E
21 Alingsås 57 56N 12 31E
32 Alipur 29 25N 70 55E
33 Alipur Duar 26 30N 89 35E
68 Aliquippa 40 38N 80 18W
56 Aliwal Nord 30 45S 26 45E
13 Aljustrel 37 55N 8 10W
53 Alkamari 13 27N 11 10E
11 Alkmaar 52 37N 4 45E
73 All American Canal 32 45N 115 0W
53 Allada 6 41N 2 9E
33 Allahabad 25 25N 81 58E
65 Allan 51 53N 106 4W
56 Allanridge 27 45S 26 40E
63 Allard Lake 50 40N 63 10W
58 Allegheny Mts. 38 0N 80 0W
68 Allegheny, R. 40 27N 80 0W
74 Allende 28 20N 100 50W
68 Allentown 40 36N 75 30W
32 Alleppey 9 30N 76 28E
14 Aller, R. 52 57N 9 11E
70 Alliance, Nebr. 42 10N 102 50W
68 Alliance, Ohio 40 53N 81 7W
12 Allier, R. 46 58N 3 4E
12 Allier □ 46 25N 3 0E
42 Alligator Creek 19 23S 146 58E
62 Alliston 44 15N 79 55W
8 Alloa 56 7N 3 49W
62 Alma, Canada 48 35N 71 40W
63 Alma, U.S.A. 43 25N 84 40W
24 Alma Ata 43 15N 76 57E
13 Almada 38 40N 9 9W
42 Almaden 17 22S 144 40E
13 Almadén 38 49N 4 52W
13 Almansa 38 51N 1 5W
13 Almanzor, P. de 40 15N 5 18W
13 Almazán 41 30N 2 30W
79 Almeirim, Brazil 1 30S 52 0W
11 Almelo 52 22N 6 42E
13 Almendralejo 38 41N 6 26W
13 Almería 36 52N 2 32W
75 Almirante 9 10N 82 30W
6 Alnwick 55 25N 1 42W
33 Alon 22 12N 95 5E
65 Alonsa 50 50N 99 0W
35 Alor, I. 8 15S 124 30E
34 Alor Setar 6 7N 100 22E
45 Aloysius, Mt. 26 0S 128 38E
68 Alpena 45 6N 83 24W
12 Alpes-Maritimes □ 43 55N 7 10E
12 Alpes-de-Haute-Provence □ 44 8N 6 10E
42 Alpha 24 8S 146 39E
18 Alpi Carniche, Mts. 46 36N 13 0E
71 Alpine 30 35N 103 35W
4 Alps, Mts. 47 0N 8 0E
42 Alroy Downs 19 20S 136 5E
12 Alsace, Reg. 48 15N 7 25E
13 Alsasua 42 54N 2 10W
6 Alston 54 48N 2 26W
20 Alta 69 55N 23 12E
80 Alta Gracia 31 40S 64 30W
64 Alta Lake 50 10N 123 0W
20 Altaelv, R. 69 57N 23 17E
78 Altagracia 10 45N 71 30W
26 Altai, Mts. 48 0N 90 0E
37 Altai, Mts.= Aerhtai Shan, Mts. 48 0N 90 0E
79 Altamira 3 0S 52 10W
38 Altanbulag 50 19N 106 30E
13 Altea 38 38N 0 2W
13 Alto-Alentejo, Reg. 38 50N 7 40W
79 Alto Araguaia 17 15S 53 20W
7 Alton, U.K. 51 8N 0 59W
70 Alton, U.S.A. 38 55N 90 5W
14 Altona 53 32N 9 56E
68 Altoona 40 32N 78 24W
71 Altus 34 30N 99 25W
37 Altyn Tagh, Mts. 39 0N 89 0E
29 Alula 11 50N 50 45E
35 Alusi 7 35S 131 40E
71 Alva 36 50N 98 50W
74 Alvarado 18 40N 95 50W
80 Alvear 29 5S 57 40W
21 Alvesta 56 54N 14 35E
46 Alvie 38 15S 143 30E
21 Älvkarleby 60 34N 17 35E
21 Alvsborgs □ 58 30N 12 30E
20 Älvsbyn 65 39N 20 59E
32 Alwar 27 38N 76 34E
23 Alyat Pristan 39 59N 49 28E
8 Alyth 56 38N 3 15W
51 Am-Timan 11 0N 20 10E
61 Amadjuak 64 0N 72 50W
61 Amadjuak L. 65 0N 71 0W
36 Amagasaki 34 42N 135 20E
36 Amakusa-Shotō, Is. 32 15N 130 10E
21 Åmål 59 2N 12 40E
32 Amalner 21 5N 75 5E
24 Amangeldy 50 10N 65 10E
79 Amapá 2 5N 50 50W
79 Amapá □ 1 40N 52 0W
79 Amarante 6 14S 42 50W
79 Amargosa 13 2S 39 36W
71 Amarillo 35 14N 101 46W
18 Amaro, Mt. 42 5N 14 6E
53 Amassama 5 1N 6 2E
30 Amasya 40 40N 35 50E
57 Amatikulu 29 3S 31 33E
74 Amatitlán 14 29N 90 38W
79 Amazon= Amazonas, R. 2 0S 53 30W
79 Amazonas, R. 2 0S 53 30W
78 Amazonas □ 4 20S 64 0W
32 Ambala 30 23N 76 56E
57 Ambalavao 21 50S 46 56E
57 Ambanja 13 40S 48 27E
25 Ambarchik 69 40N 162 20E
57 Ambaro, H. 13 23S 48 38E
57 Ambato-Boeny 16 28S 46 43E
78 Ambato 1 5S 78 42W
57 Ambatofinandrahana 20 33S 46 48E
57 Ambatolampy 19 20S 47 35E
57 Ambatondrazaka 17 55S 48 28E
19 Ámbelos, Ákra 39 56N 23 55E
14 Amberg 49 25N 11 52E
74 Ambergris Cay 18 0N 88 0W
47 Amberley 43 9S 172 44E
33 Ambikapur 23 15N 83 15E
6 Ambleside 54 26N 2 58W
57 Ambohimanga (du Sud) 20 52S 47 36E
12 Amboise 47 25N 0 59E
35 Ambon 3 35S 128 20E
57 Ambositra 20 31S 47 25E
57 Ambovombe 25 11S 46 5E
73 Amboy 34 33N 115 51W
* **57** Ambre, C. d' 12 40S 49 10E
43 Amby 26 30S 148 11E
24 Amderma 69 45N 61 30E
74 Ameca 20 30N 104 0W
11 Ameland, I. 53 27N 5 45E
25 Amen 68 45N 180 0E
72 American Falls 42 46N 112 56E
47 American Samoa, I. 14 20S 170 0W
69 Americus 32 0N 84 10W
11 Amersfoort, Neth 52 9N 5 23E
57 Amersfoort, S. Afr. 26 59S 29 53E
45 Amery, Australia 31 9S 117 5E
65 Amery, Canada 56 45N 94 0W
70 Ames 42 0N 93 40W
25 Amga, R. 62 38N 134 32E
25 Amgu 45 45N 137 15E
33 Amherst, Burma 16 0N 97 40E
63 Amherst, Canada 45 48N 64 8W
62 Amherstburg 42 6N 83 6W
12 Amiens 49 54N 2 16E
27 Amirantes, Is. 6 0S 53 0E
6 Amlwch 53 24N 4 21W
28 'Ammān 32 0N 35 52E
28 Ammi'ad 32 55N 35 32E
19 Amorgós 36 50 25 57E
62 Amos 48 35N 78 5W
39 Amoy=Hsiamen 24 25N 118 4E
57 Ampanihy 24 40S 44 45E
53 Amper 9 25N 9 40E
63 Amqui 48 28N 67 27W
32 Amroati 20 55N 77 45E
32 Amreli 21 35N 71 17E
32 Amritsar 31 35N 74 57E
32 Amroha 28 53N 78 30E
11 Amsterdam, Neth. 52 23N 4 54E
57 Amsterdam, S. Afr. 26 35S 30 45E
68 Amsterdam, U.S.A. 42 58N 74 10W
3 Amsterdam, I. 37 30S 77 30E
24 Amu Darya, R. 43 40N 59 1E
60 Amukta Pass. 52 25N 172 0W
60 Amundsen G. 70 30N 123 0W
2 Amundsen Sea 72 0S 115 0W
25 Amur, R. 52 56N 141 10E
30 An Najaf 32 3N 44 15E
30 An Nasiriyah 31 0N 46 15E
34 An Nhon 13 53N 109 6E
30 An Nu'ayriyah 27 30N 48 30E
9 An Uaimh 53 39N 6 40W
28 Anabta 32 19N 35 7E
72 Anaconda 46 7N 113 0W
72 Anacortes 48 30N 122 40W
71 Anadarko 35 4N 98 15W
30 Anadolu, Reg. 38 0N 39 0E
25 Anadyr 64 35N 177 20E
25 Anadyr, R. 64 55N 176 5E
64 Anahim Lake 52 28N 125 18W
33 Anakapalle 17 42N 83 6E
42 Anakie 23 32S 147 45E
57 Analalava 14 35S 48 0E
34 Anambas, Kep. 3 20N 106 30E
53 Anambra □ 6 30N 7 30E
36 Anan 33 54N 134 40E
32 Anantnag 33 45N 75 10E
79 Anápolis 16 15S 48 50W
31 Anar 30 55N 55 13E
30 Anatolia, Reg.= Anadolu, Reg. 38 0N 39 0E
80 Añatuya 28 20S 62 50W
60 Anchorage 61 10N 149 50W
78 Ancohuma, Mt. 16 0S 68 50W
18 Ancona 43 37N 13 30E
80 Ancud 42 0S 73 50W
80 Ancud, G. de 42 0S 73 0W
20 Andalsnes 62 35N 7 43E
13 Andalusia 31 51N 86 30W
27 Andaman Is. 12 30N 92 30E
11 Andenne 50 30N 5 5E
72 Anderson, Calif. 40 30N 122 19W
68 Anderson, Ind. 40 5N 85 40W
69 Anderson, S.C. 34 32N 82 40W
60 Anderson, R. 69 43N 128 58W
76 Andes, Mts. 20 0S 68 0W
57 Andevorante 18 57S 49 6E
32 Andhra Pradesh □ 15 0N 80 0E
24 Andizhan 41 10N 72 0E
31 Andkhui 36 52N 65 8E
13 Andorra ■ 42 30N 1 30E
13 Andorra 42 31N 1 32E
7 Andover 51 13N 1 29W
79 Andradina 20 54S 51 23W
60 Andreanof Is. 51 0N 178 0W
18 Ándria 41 13N 16 17E
57 Andriba 17 30S 46 58E
75 Andros, I. 24 30N 78 4W
19 Ándros I. 37 50N 24 50E
75 Andros Town 24 43N 77 47W
13 Andújar 38 3N 4 5W
53 Anécho 6 12N 1 34E
75 Anegada I. 18 45N 64 20W
75 Anegada Pass. 18 15N 63 45W
13 Aneto, Pico de 42 37N 0 40E
80 Angamos, Pta. 23 1S 70 32W
38 Anganki 47 9N 123 48E
25 Angara, R. 58 6N 93 0E
25 Angarsk 52 30N 104 0E
43 Angaston 34 30S 139 8E
20 Ånge 62 31N 15 35E
74 Angel de la Guarda, I. 29 30N 113 30W
35 Angeles 15 9N 120 35E
21 Ängelholm 56 15N 12 58E
73 Angels Camp 38 8N 120 30W
20 Ångermanälven, R. 62 48N 17 56E
12 Angers 47 30N 0 35E
6 Anglesey, I. 53 17N 4 20W
54 Ango 4 10N 26 5E
55 Angoche 16 8S 40 0E
80 Angol 37 48S 72 43W
55 Angola ■ 12 0S 18 0E
12 Angoulême 45 39N 0 10E
12 Angoumois, Reg. 45 30N 0 25E
24 Angren 41 1N 69 45E
75 Anguilla, I. 18 14N 63 5W
42 Angurugu 14 0S 136 25E
8 Angus, Braes of 56 51N 3 0W
39 Anhsien 31 30N 104 35E
39 Anhwei □ 33 15N 116 50E
53 Anie 7 42N 1 8E
57 Anivorzno 18 44S 48 58E
12 Anjou, Reg. 47 20N 0 15W
57 Anjozorobe 18 22S 47 52E
38 Anju 39 36N 125 40E
53 Anka 12 13N 5 58E
39 Ankang 32 38N 109 5E
30 Ankara 40 0N 32 54E
57 Ankaramina 21 57S 46 39E
57 Ankazoaba 22 18S 44 31E
57 Ankazobe 18 20S 47 10E
39 Anking 30 31N 117 2E
68 Ann Arbor 42 17N 83 45W
44 Anna Plains 19 17S 121 37E
50 Annaba 36 50N 7 46E
34 Annam, Reg.= Trung-Phan, Reg. 16 30N 107 30E
8 Annan 54 59N 3 16W
8 Annan, R. 54 59N 3 16W
68 Annapolis 38 59N 76 30W
63 Annapolis Royal 44 44N 65 32W
12 Annecy 45 55N 6 8E
37 Anning 24 58N 102 30E
69 Anniston 33 45N 85 50W
49 Annobón=Pagalu 1 35S 3 35E
70 Anoka 45 10N 93 26W
57 Anorotsangana 13 56S 47 55E
39 Anping 23 0N 120 6E
14 Ansbach 49 17N 10 34E
38 Anshan 41 3N 122 58E
39 Anshun 26 2N 105 57E
37 Ansi 40 21N 96 10E
44 Anson, B. 13 20S 130 6E
53 Ansongo 15 25N 0 35E
62 Ansonville 48 46N 80 43W
8 Anstruther 56 14N 2 40W
35 Ansuda 2 11S 139 22E
38 Anta 46 18N 125 34E
30 Antakya 36 14N 36 10E
57 Antalaha 14 57S 50 20E
30 Antalya 36 52N 30 45E
30 Antalya Körfezi 36 15N 31 30E
57 Antananarivo 18 55S 47 35E
1 Antarctica 90 0S 0 0
2 Antarctic Pen. 67 0S 60 0W
13 Antequera 37 5N 4 33W
73 Anthony 32 1N 106 37W
42 Anthony Lagoon 18 0S 135 30E
63 Anticosti I.d' 49 20N 62 40W
70 Antigo 45 8N 89 5W
63 Antigonish 45 38N 61 58W
74 Antigua 14 34N 90 41W
75 Antigua, I. 17 0N 61 50W
75 Antilla 20 40N 75 50W
73 Antimony 38 7N 112 0W
78 Antioquia 6 40N 75 55W
3 Antipodes Is. 49 45S 178 40E
80 Antofagasta 23 50S 70 30W
* **57** Antongil, B. d' 15 30S 49 50E
57 António Enes= Angoche 16 8S 40 0E
9 Antrim 54 43N 6 13W
9 Antrim □ 54 55N 6 10W
9 Antrim, Mts. of 54 57N 6 10W
57 Antsalova 18 40S 44 37E
57 Antsirabe 19 55S 47 2E
57 Antsohihy 14 50S 47 50E
38 Antung 40 10N 124 18E
11 Antwerp= Antwerpen 51 13N 4 25E
11 Antwerpen 51 13N 4 25E
11 Antwerpen □ 51 15N 4 40E
32 Anupgarh 29 10N 73 10E

* Renamed Bobraomby, T. 'i

* Renamed Antongila, H.

Anuppur Australian Alps, Mts

33 Anuppur 22 58N 81 44 E
32 Anuradhapura 8 22N 80 28 E
11 Anvers= Antwerpen 51 13N 4 25 E
60 Anvik 62 40N 160 12W
38 Anyang 36 7N 114 26 E
35 Anyer-Lor 6 6S 105 56 E
39 Anyi 28 50N 115 31 E
24 Anzhero Sudzhensk 56 10N 83 40 E
18 Ánzio 41 28N 12 37 E
36 Aomori 40 45N 140 45 E
36 Aomori □ 40 45N 140 40 E
18 Aosta 45 43N 7 20 E
51 Aozou 21 49N 17 25 E
53 Apam 5 17N 0 44W
53 Apapa 6 25N 3 25 E
35 Aparri 18 22N 121 38 E
74 Apatzingán 19 0N 102 20W
11 Apeldoorn 52 13N 5 57 E
34 Apenam 8 35S 116 13 E
18 Apennines, Mts.= Appennini, Mts. 41 0N 15 0 E
47 Apia 14 0S 171 55W
74 Apizaco 19 26N 98 9W
51 Apollonia= Marsa Susa 32 52N 21 59 E
70 Apostle Is. 47 0N 90 30W
80 Apóstoles 27 55S 55 45W
78 Apoteri 4 2N 58 32W
58 Appalachian Mts. 38 0N 80 0W
6 Appleby 54 35N 2 29W
68 Appleton 44 17N 88 25W
79 Approuagne 4 20N 52 0W
80 Apucarana 23 55S 51 33W
31 Aq Chah 37 0N 66 5 E
30 'Aqaba 29 31N 35 0 E
30 'Aqaba, Khalîj al 28 15N 33 20 E
51 Aqiq 18 14N 38 12 E
28 Aqraba 32 9N 35 20 E
79 Aquidauana 20 30S 55 50W
29 Ar Rab' al Khālī 21 0N 51 0 E
28 Ar-Ramthā 32 34N 36 0 E
30 Ar Raqqah 35 56N 39 1 E
30 Ar Riyād 24 41N 46 42 E
31 Ar Ruska 23 35N 53 30 E
30 Ar Ruṭbah 33 0N 40 15 E
51 Arab, Bahr el, R. 9 2N 29 28 E
26 Arabia, Reg. 25 0N 45 0 E
48 Arabian Des. 28 0N 32 30 E
26 Arabian Sea 16 0N 65 0 E
79 Aracajú 10 55S 37 4W
78 Aracataca 10 38N 74 9W
79 Aracati 4 30S 37 44W
79 Araçatuba 21 10S 50 30W
13 Aracena 37 53N 6 58W
79 Araçuai 16 52S 42 4W
28 'Arad 31 17N 35 12 E
15 Arad 46 10N 21 20 E
26 Arafura Sea 10 0S 135 0 E
13 Aragón, R. 42 13N 1 44W
13 Aragon, Reg. 41 0N 1 0W
79 Araguacema 8 50S 49 20W
79 Araguaia, R. 5 21S 48 41W
79 Araguari 18 38S 48 11W
30 Arak 34 0N 49 40 E
33 Arakan Coast 19 0N 94 0 E
33 Arakan Yoma, Mts. 20 0N 94 30 E
23 Araks, R. 40 1N 48 28 E
24 Aral Sea= Aralskoye More 44 30N 66 0 E
24 Aralsk 46 50N 61 20 E
24 Aralskoye More 44 30N 60 0 E
9 Aran, I. 55 0N 8 30W
9 Aran Is. 53 5N 9 42W
13 Aranjuez 40 1N 3 40W
71 Aransas P. 28 0N 97 9W
34 Aranyaprathet 13 41N 102 30 E
80 Arapongas 23 29S 51 28W
80 Araranguá 29 0S 49 30W
79 Araraquara 21 50S 48 0W
46 Ararat 37 16S 143 0 E
30 Ararat, Mt.= Ağri Daği, Mt. 39 50N 44 15 E
80 Arauca 7 0N 70 40W
79 Araxá 19 35S 46 55W
78 Araya, Pen. de 10 40N 64 0W
18 Arbatax 39 57N 9 42 E
30 Arbīl 36 15N 44 5 E
8 Arbroath 56 34N 2 35W
12 Arcachon 44 40N 1 10W
70 Arcadia 44 13N 91 29W
72 Arcata 40 55N 124 4W
22 Archangel= Arkhangelsk 64 40N 41 0 E
52 Archers Post 0 35N 37 35 E
65 Arcola 49 40N 102 30W
13 Arcos de los Frontera 36 45N 5 49W
32 Arcot 12 53N 79 20 E
79 Arcoverde 8 25S 37 4W
61 Arctic Bay 73 2N 85 11W
3 Arctic Ocean 78 0N 160 0W
60 Arctic Red River 67 15N 134 0W
19 Arda, R. 41 39N 26 29 E
30 Ardabīl 38 15N 48 18 E
12 Ardèche □ 44 42N 4 16 E
9 Ardee 53 51N 6 32W
11 Ardennes, Reg. 49 30N 5 10 E
12 Ardennes □ 49 35N 4 40 E
31 Ardestan 33 20N 52 25 E
8 Ardgour, Reg. 56 45N 5 25W
46 Ardlethan 34 22S 146 53 E
71 Ardmore, Australia 21 39S 139 11 E
71 Ardmore, U.S.A. 34 10N 97 5W
9 Ardnacrusha 52 43N 8 38W
8 Ardnamurchan Pt. 56 44N 6 14W
8 Ardrossan 55 39N 4 50W
9 Ards □ 54 35N 5 30W
9 Ards Pen. 54 30N 5 25W
75 Arecibo 18 29N 66 42W
79 Areia Branca 5 0S 37 0W
13 Arenal 39 28N 2 47 E
21 Arendal 58 28N 8 46 E
78 Arequipa 16 20S 71 30W
54 Arero 4 41N 38 50 E
13 Arévalo 41 3N 4 43W
18 Arezzo 43 28N 11 50 E
63 Argentia 47 18N 53 58W
76 Argentine Basin, Reg. 44 0S 51 0 E
80 Argentina ■ 35 0S 66 0W
80 Argentino, L. 50 10S 73 0W
15 Arges, R. 44 10N 26 45 E
51 Argo 19 28N 30 30 E
19 Argolikós Kól. 37 20N 22 52 E
12 Argonne, Mts. 49 0N 5 20 E
19 Árgos 37 40N 22 43 E
19 Argostólion 38 12N 20 33 E
73 Arguello, Pt. 34 34N 120 40W
25 Argun, R. 43 22N 45 55 E
53 Argungu 12 40N 4 31 E
44 Argyle, L. 16 20S 128 40 E
21 Århus 56 8N 10 11 E
78 Arica, Chile 18 32S 70 20W
78 Arica, Col. 1 30S 75 30W
45 Arid, C. 34 1S 123 10 E
36 Arida 33 29N 135 44 E
12 Ariège □ 42 56N 1 30 E
75 Arima 10 38N 61 17W
8 Arisaig 56 50N 5 40W
80 Arizona 35 45S 65 25W
73 Arizona □ 34 20N 111 30W
78 Arjona 10 14N 75 22W
25 Arka 60 15N 142 0 E
37 Arka Tagh, Mts. 36 30N 90 0 E
71 Arkadelphia 34 5N 93 0W
8 Arkaig, L. 56 58N 5 10W
71 Arkansas, R. 33 48N 91 4W
71 Arkansas □ 35 0N 92 30W
71 Arkansas City 37 4N 97 3W
22 Arkhangelsk 64 40N 41 0 E
9 Arklow 52 48N 6 10W
12 Arles 43 41N 4 40 E
57 Arlington, S. Afr. 28 1S 27 53 E
71 Arlington, U.S.A. 44 25N 97 4W
11 Arlon 49 42N 5 49 E
45 Armadale 32 12S 116 0 E
9 Armagh 54 22N 6 40W
9 Armagh □ 54 16N 6 35W
12 Armagnac, Reg. 43 44N 0 10 E
23 Armavir 45 2N 41 7 E
78 Armenia 4 35N 75 45W
23 Armenian S.S.R. □ 40 0N 41 10 E
43 Armidale 30 30S 151 40 E
64 Armstrong, B.C. 50 25N 119 10W
62 Armstrong, Ont. 50 20N 89 0W
11 Arnhem 51 58N 5 55 E
42 Arnhem, B. 12 20S 136 10 E
40 Arnhem Land 13 0S 135 0 E
18 Arno, R. 43 31N 10 17 E
62 Arnprior 45 23N 76 25W
43 Arrabury 26 45S 141 0 E
33 Arrah 25 35N 84 32 E
8 Arran, I. 55 34N 5 12W
12 Arras 50 17N 2 46 E
50 Arrecife 28 59N 13 40W
12 Arrée, Mts. d' 48 26N 3 55W
45 Arrino 29 30S 115 40 E
64 Arrowhead 50 40N 117 55W
47 Arrowtown 44 57S 168 50 E
38 Arshan 46 59N 120 0 E
19 Árta 39 8N 21 2 E
61 Artemovsk 48 35N 37 55 E
71 Artesia 32 55N 104 25W
42 Arthur, Pt. 22 7S 150 3 E
80 Artigas 30 20S 56 30W
12 Artois, Reg. 50 20N 2 30 E
30 Artvin 41 14N 41 44 E
35 Aru, Kep. 6 0S 134 30 E
52 Arua 3 1N 30 58 E
79 Aruanã 15 0S 51 10W
75 Aruba, I. 12 30N 70 0W
33 Arunachal Pradesh □ 28 0N 95 0 E
52 Arusha 3 20S 36 40 E
72 Arvada 44 43N 106 6W
38 Arvayheer 46 15N 102 48 E
63 Arvida 48 16N 71 14W
20 Arvidsjaur 65 35N 19 10 E
21 Arvika 59 40N 12 36 E
24 Arys 42 26N 68 48 E
22 Arzamas 55 27N 43 55 E
50 Arzew 35 50N 0 23W
28 As Salt 32 2N 35 43 E
30 As Samawah 31 15N 45 15 E
30 As Sulaimānīyah 24 8N 47 10 E
30 As Sulamānīyah 35 35N 45 29 E
31 As Suwaih 22 10N 59 33 E
30 As Suwayda 32 40N 36 30 E
30 As Suwayrah 32 55N 45 0 E
53 Asaba 6 12N 6 38 E
36 Asahikawa 43 45N 142 30 E
53 Asamankese 5 50N 0 40W
33 Asansol 23 40N 87 1 E
63 Asbestos 45 47N 71 58W
68 Asbury Park 40 15N 74 1W
74 Ascensión, B. de la 19 50N 87 20W
49 Ascension, I. 8 0S 14 15W
14 Aschaffenburg 49 58N 9 8 E
18 Ascoli Piceno 42 51N 13 34 E
29 Aseb 13 0N 42 40 E
73 Ash Fork 35 14N 112 32W
30 Ash Shāmiyah 31 55N 44 35 E
30 Ash Sharma 28 1N 35 18 E
28 Ash Shuna 32 32N 35 34 E
22 Asha 55 10N 33 38 E
53 Ashanti □ 7 30N 2 0W
47 Ashburton 43 53S 171 48 E
44 Ashburton, R. 37 52S 145 5 E
44 Ashburton Downs 23 25S 117 4 E
6 Ashby-de-la-Zouch 52 45N 1 29W
28 Ashdod 31 39N 34 35 E
28 Ashdot Yaaqov 32 39N 35 35 E
69 Asheboro 35 43N 79 46W
69 Asheville 35 39N 82 30W
7 Ashford 51 8N 0 53 E
36 Ashikaga 36 28N 139 29 E
6 Ashington 55 12N 1 35W
24 Ashkhabad 38 0N 57 50 E
68 Ashland, Ky. 38 25N 82 40W
68 Ashland, Ohio 40 52N 82 20W
72 Ashland, Oreg. 42 10N 122 38W
70 Ashland, Wis. 46 40N 90 52W
28 Ashquelon 31 42N 34 55 E
68 Ashtabula 41 52N 80 50W
72 Ashton 44 6N 111 30W
6 Ashton-under-Lyne 53 30N 2 8W
1 Asia 45 0N 75 0 E
50 Asilah 35 29N 6 0W
18 Asinara, G. dell' 41 0N 8 30 E
18 Asinara, I. 41 5N 8 15 E
24 Asino 57 0N 86 0 E
29 Asir, Ras 11 55N 51 0 E
29 Asir, Reg. 18 40N 42 30 E
28 Asira esh Shamaliya 32 16N 35 16 E
21 Askersund 58 58N 14 8 E
31 Asmar 35 10N 71 27 E
51 Asmera 15 19N 38 55 E
47 Aspiring, Mt. 44 23S 168 46W
33 Assam □ 25 45N 92 30 E
11 Asse 50 54N 4 6 E
11 Assen 53 0N 6 35 E
65 Assiniboia 49 40N 106 0W
64 Assiniboine, Mt. 50 52N 115 39W
65 Assiniboine, R. 49 53N 97 8W
79 Assis 22 40S 50 20W
18 Assisi 43 4N 12 36 E
8 Assynt, L. 58 25N 5 10W
23 Astara 38 30N 48 50 E
18 Asti 44 54N 8 11 E
19 Astipálaia, I. 36 32N 26 22 E
13 Astorga 42 29N 6 8W
72 Astoria 46 16N 123 50W
23 Astrakhan 46 25N 48 5 E
13 Asturias, Reg. 43 15N 6 0W
80 Asunción 25 21S 57 30W
51 Aswân 24 4N 32 57 E
51 Aswân High Dam 24 5N 32 54 E
51 Asyût 27 11N 31 4 E
30 At Ta'if 21 5N 40 27 E
80 Atacama Des. 24 0S 69 20W
80 Atacama, Pune de 25 0S 67 30W
80 Atacama, Salar de 24 0S 68 20W
53 Atakpamé 7 31N 1 13 E
36 Atami 35 0N 139 55 E
50 Atar 20 30N 13 5W
25 Atara 63 10N 129 10 E
24 Atasu 48 30N 71 0 E
51 Atbara 17 42N 33 59 E
51 'Atbara, Nahr, R 17 40N 33 56 E
24 Atbasar 51 48N 68 20 E
70 Atchison 39 40N 95 0W
11 Ath 50 38N 3 47 E
64 Athabasca 54 45N 113 20W
65 Athabasca, L. 59 10N 109 30W
65 Athabasca, R. 58 40N 110 50W
9 Athboy 53 37N 6 55W
9 Athenry 53 18N 8 45W
69 Athens, Ala. 34 49N 86 58W
69 Athens, Ga. 33 56N 83 24W
68 Athens, Ohio 39 52N 82 64W
71 Athens, Tex. 32 11N 95 48W
19 Athens=Athínai 37 58N 23 46 E
42 Atherton 17 17S 145 30 E
52 Athi River 1 29S 36 58 E
53 Athiéme 6 37N 1 40 E
19 Athínai 37 58N 23 46 E
9 Athlone 53 26N 7 57W
68 Athol 42 36N 72 14W
8 Atholl, Forest of 56 51N 3 50W
63 Atholville 48 5N 67 5W
19 Athos, Mt. 40 9N 24 22 E
9 Athy 53 0N 7 0W
25 Atka 60 50N 151 48 E
60 Atka I. 52 15N 174 30W
69 Atlanta 33 50N 84 24W
70 Atlantic 41 25N 95 0W
68 Atlantic City 39 25N 74 25W
2 Atlantic Ocean 0 0 30 0W
50 Atlas, Anti, Mts. 30 0N 8 0W
50 Atlas, Moyen, Mts. 37 0N 5 0W
50 Atlas Saharien, Mts. 34 10N 3 30 E
64 Atlin 59 31N 133 41W
28 Atlit 32 42N 34 56 E
69 Atmore 31 2N 87 30W
78 Atocha 21 0S 66 10W
74 Atotonilco 20 20N 98 40W
62 Attawapiskat 53 0N 82 30W
62 Attawapiskat L. 52 20N 88 0W
62 Attawapiskat, R. 52 57N 82 18W
28 Attil 32 23N 35 4 E
68 Attleboro 41 56N 71 18W
32 Attock 33 52N 72 20 E
34 Attopeu 14 56N 106 50 E
60 Attu I. 52 55N 173 0 E
52 Atura 2 5N 32 17 E
70 Atwood 39 52N 101 3W
56 Auasberg 22 45S 17 22 E
12 Aube, R. 48 34N 3 43 E
12 Aube □ 48 15N 4 0 E
69 Auburn, Ala. 32 57N 85 30W
72 Auburn, Calif. 38 50N 121 10W
69 Auburn, Me. 44 6N 70 14W
12 Aubusson 45 57N 2 11 E
12 Auch 43 39N 0 36 E
53 Auchi 7 6N 6 13 E
47 Auckland 36 52S 174 46 E
3 Auckland Is. 51 0S 166 0 E
12 Aude, R. 43 13N 3 14 E
12 Aude □ 44 13N 3 15 E
62 Auden 50 17N 87 54W
43 Augathella 25 48S 146 35 E
14 Augsburg 48 22N 10 54 E
45 Augusta, Australia 34 22S 115 10 E
18 Augusta, Italy 37 14N 15 12 E
69 Augusta, U.S.A. 33 29N 81 59W
69 Augusta 44 20N 69 46W
* 55 Augusto Cardoso 12 44S 34 50 E
15 Augustów 53 51N 23 0 E
45 Augustus, Mt. 24 20S 116 50 E
42 Augustus Downs 18 35S 139 55 E
53 Auna 10 9N 4 42 E
12 Aunis, Reg. 46 0N 0 50W
32 Aurangabad, Maharashtra 19 50N 75 23 E
12 Aurillac 44 55N 2 26 E
70 Aurora, Colo. 39 44N 104 55W
68 Aurora, Ill. 41 42N 88 20W
21 Aust-Agde □ 58 55N 7 40 E
70 Austin, Minn. 43 37N 92 59W
72 Austin, Nev. 39 30N 117 1W
71 Austin, Tex. 30 20N 97 45W
40 Australia ■ 23 0S 135 0 E
46 Australian Alps, Mts. 36 30S 148 8 E

* *Renamed Metangula*

Australian Capital Terr. □ Barat Daja, Kep.

46 Australian Capital Terr. □ . 35 15 s 149 8 E
3 Australian Dependency □ .. 73 0 s 90 0 E
14 Austria ■ .... 47 0 N 14 0 E
74 Autlán .... 19 40 N 104 30 W
12 Autun .... 46 58 N 4 17 E
44 Auvergne .... 15 39 s 130 1 E
12 Auvergne, Mts. ... 45 20 N 2 45 E
12 Auvergne, Reg. ... 45 30 N 3 20 E
12 Auxerre .... 47 48 N 3 32 E
12 Avallon .... 47 30 N 3 53 E
63 Avalon Pen. ...... 47 0 N 53 20 W
79 Aveiro, Brazil ..... 3 10 s 55 5 W
13 Aveiro, Port. ...... 40 37 N 8 38 W
80 Avellaneda .... 34 50 s 58 10 W
18 Avellino .... 40 54 N 14 46 E
18 Aversa .... 40 58 N 14 11 E
78 Aves, Is. de .... 12 0 N 67 40 W
21 Avesta .... 60 9 N 16 10 E
12 Aveyron □ .... 44 22 N 2 45 E
80 Aviá Terai .... 26 45 s 60 50 W
8 Aviemore .... 57 11 N 3 50 W
12 Avignon .... 43 57 N 4 50 E
13 Ávila .... 40 39 N 4 43 W
13 Avilés .... 43 35 N 5 57 W
46 Avoca .... 37 5 s 143 28 E
9 Avoca, R. .... 52 48 N 6 10 W
64 Avola, Canada .... 51 45 N 119 30 W
45 Avon, R., Australia .... 31 40 s 116 7 E
7 Avon, R., Avon ... 51 30 N 2 43 W
7 Avon, R., Dorset .. 50 43 N 1 46 W
7 Avon, R., Gloucester ...... 51 59 N 2 10 W
7 Avon □ .... 51 30 N 2 40 W
7 Avonmouth .... 51 30 N 2 42 W
12 Avranches .... 48 40 N 1 20 W
36 Awaji-Shima, I. ... 34 30 N 134 50 E
31 Awali .... 26 0 N 50 30 E
54 Awash .... 9 1 N 40 10 E
47 Awatere, R. ...... 41 37 s 174 10 E
8 Awe, L. .... 56 15 N 5 15 W
53 Awgu .... 6 4 N 7 24 E
51 Awjilah .... 29 8 N 21 7 E
53 Awka .... 6 12 N 7 5 E
58 Axel Heiberg Ld. .... 80 0 N 90 0 W
53 Axim .... 4 41 N 2 15 W
7 Axminster .... 50 47 N 3 1 W
36 Ayabe .... 35 20 N 135 20 E
80 Ayacucho, Arg. ... 37 5 s 58 20 W
78 Ayacucho, Peru ... 13 0 s 74 0 W
24 Ayaguz .... 48 10 N 80 0 E
13 Ayamonte .... 37 12 N 7 24 W
25 Ayan .... 56 30 N 138 16 E
22 Aykin .... 62 20 N 49 56 E
65 Aylesbury, Canada 50 55 N 105 53 W
7 Aylesbury, U.K. ... 51 48 N 0 49 W
60 Aylmer, L. .... 64 0 N 109 0 W
42 Ayr, Australia .... 19 35 s 147 25 E
8 Ayr, U.K. .... 55 28 N 4 37 W
8 Ayr, R. .... 55 29 N 4 28 W
6 Ayre, Pt. of .... 54 27 N 4 21 W
19 Aytos .... 42 47 N 27 16 E
30 Ayvalik .... 39 20 N 26 46 E
28 Az Zahiriya ...... 31 25 N 34 58 E
30 Az Zahrān .... 26 10 N 50 7 E
28 Az-Zarqā' .... 32 5 N 36 4 E
30 Az Zilfi .... 26 12 N 44 52 E
30 Az Zubayr .... 30 20 N 47 50 E
33 Azamgarh .... 26 35 N 83 13 E
30 Āzārbāijān □ ..... 37 0 N 44 30 E
53 Azare .... 11 55 N 10 10 E
50 Azbine=Aïr ...... 18 0 N 8 0 E
23 Azerbaijan S.S.R. □ .... 40 20 N 48 0 E
28 Azor .... 32 2 N 34 48 E
2 Azores, Is. .... 38 44 N 29 0 W
23 Azov .... 47 3 N 39 25 E
23 Azov Sea= Azovskoye More 46 0 N 36 30 E
23 Azovskoye More .. 46 0 N 36 30 E
24 Azovy .... 64 55 N 64 35 E
73 Aztec .... 36 54 N 108 0 W
75 Azua .... 18 25 N 70 44 W
13 Azuaga .... 38 16 N 5 39 W
75 Azuero, Pen. de ... 7 40 N 80 30 W
80 Azul .... 36 42 s 59 43 W

B

34 Ba Don .... 17 45 N 106 26 E
31 Baba, Koh-i-, Mts. 34 40 N 67 20 E
78 Babahoyo .... 1 40 s 79 30 W
45 Babakin .... 32 11 s 117 52 E
53 Babana .... 10 31 N 5 9 E
52 Babati .... 4 13 s 35 45 E
35 Babelthuap, I. .... 7 30 N 134 36 E
42 Babinda .... 17 27 s 146 0 E
35 Babo .... 2 30 s 133 30 E
31 Bābol .... 36 40 N 52 50 E
31 Babol Sar .... 36 45 N 52 45 E
53 Babura .... 12 51 N 8 59 E
35 Babuyan Chan. ... 18 58 N 122 0 E
39 Babuyan Is. .... 19 0 N 122 0 E
30 Babylon .... 32 40 N 44 30 E
79 Bacabal .... 5 20 s 56 45 W
35 Bacan, I. .... 1 0 s 127 30 E
24 Bachelina .... 57 45 N 67 20 E
60 Back, R. .... 67 15 N 95 15 W
35 Bacolod .... 10 50 N 123 0 E
14 Bad Ischl .... 47 44 13 38 E
32 Badagara .... 11 35 N 75 40 E
53 Badagri .... 6 25 N 2 55 E
13 Badajoz .... 38 50 N 6 59 W
31 Badakhshan □ .... 36 30 N 71 0 E
13 Badalona .... 41 26 N 2 15 E
31 Badalzal .... 29 50 N 65 35 E
30 Badanah .... 30 58 N 41 30 E
34 Badas .... 4 20 N 114 37 E
14 Baden .... 48 1 N 16 13 E
14 Baden-Baden ..... 48 45 N 8 14 E
14 Baden Württemberg □ . 48 40 N 9 0 E
8 Badenoch, Reg. ... 57 0 N 4 0 W
14 Badgastein .... 47 7 N 13 9 E
31 Badghis □ .... 35 0 N 63 0 E
32 Badin .... 24 38 N 68 54 E
13 Baeza .... 37 57 N 3 25 W
53 Bafang .... 5 9 N 10 11 E
61 Baffin B. .... 72 0 N 65 0 W
61 Baffin I. .... 68 0 N 77 0 W
53 Bafia .... 4 40 N 11 10 E
53 Bafilo .... 9 22 N 1 22 E
53 Bafoussam .... 5 2 N 10 25 E
30 Bafra .... 41 34 N 35 54 W
31 Bāft .... 29 15 N 56 38 W
52 Bagamoyo .... 6 28 s 38 55 E
25 Bagdarin .... 54 26 N 113 36 E
30 Baghdād .... 32 20 N 44 30 E
31 Baghīn .... 30 12 N 56 45 E
31 Baghlan .... 36 12 N 69 0 E
31 Baghlan □ .... 36 0 N 68 30 E
63 Bagotville .... 48 22 N 70 54 W
37 Bagrash Kol, L. ... 42 0 N 87 0 E
35 Baguio .... 16 26 N 120 34 E
75 Bahamas ■ .... 24 0 N 74 0 W
32 Bahawalpur .... 29 37 N 71 40 E
* 32 Bahawalpur □ .... 29 5 N 71 3 E
52 Bahi .... 5 58 s 35 21 E
79 Bahia= Salvador .... 13 0 s 38 30 W
75 Bahia, Is. de la .... 16 45 N 86 15 W
79 Bahia □ .... 12 0 N 42 0 E
80 Bahia Blanca ..... 38 35 s 62 13 W
78 Bahia de Caráquez .... 0 40 s 80 27 W
80 Bahia Laura ...... 48 10 s 66 30 W
78 Bahia Negra ...... 20 5 s 58 5 W
51 Bahr el Ghazâl □ . 7 0 N 28 0 E
33 Bahraich .... 27 38 N 81 50 E
31 Bahrain ■ .... 26 0 N 50 35 E
15 Baia Mare .... 47 40 N 23 37 E
79 Baião .... 2 50 s 49 15 W
63 Baie Comeau ..... 49 12 N 68 10 W
63 Baie-St-Paul ...... 47 28 N 70 32 W
30 Ba 'iji .... 35 0 N 43 30 E
9 Baile Atha Cliath=Dublin .. 53 20 N 6 18 W
69 Bainbridge .... 30 53 N 84 34 W
60 Baird Mts. .... 67 10 N 160 15 W
46 Bairnsdale .... 37 48 s 147 36 E
13 Baixo-Alentejo, Reg. .... 38 0 N 8 40 W
15 Baja .... 46 12 N 18 59 E
74 Baja California Norte □ .... 30 0 N 116 0 W
74 Baja California Sur □ .... 26 0 N 112 0 W
43 Bajimba, Mt. ..... 29 17 s 152 6 E
53 Bajoga .... 10 57 N 11 20 E
42 Bajool .... 24 30 s 150 35 E
24 Bakchar .... 57 0 N 82 5 E
72 Baker, Calif. ...... 36 16 N 116 2 W
70 Baker, Mont. ..... 46 22 N 104 12 W
2 Baker I. .... 0 10 N 176 35 E
60 Baker L. .... 64 0 N 97 0 W
72 Baker, Mt. .... 48 50 N 121 49 W
60 Baker Lake .... 64 20 N 96 10 W
62 Baker's Dozen Is. . 57 30 N 79 0 W

* Now part of Punjab

73 Bakersfield .... 35 25 N 119 0 W
30 Bakhtiari □ .... 32 0 N 49 0 E
23 Bakinskikh Komissarov ..... 39 20 N 49 15 E
15 Bakony Forest= Bakony Hegyseg, Reg. .... 47 10 N 17 30 E
53 Bakori .... 11 34 N 7 27 E
23 Baku .... 40 25 N 49 45 E
28 Bal'a .... 32 20 N 35 6 E
6 Bala, L. .... 52 53 N 3 38 W
34 Balabac I. .... 8 0 N 117 0 E
34 Balabac Str. ...... 7 53 N 117 5 E
32 Balaghat .... 21 49 N 80 12 E
32 Balaghat Ra. ...... 18 50 N 76 30 E
13 Balaguer .... 41 50 N 0 50 E
43 Balaklava, Australia .... 34 7 s 138 22 E
23 Balaklava, U.S.S.R. .... 44 30 N 33 30 E
22 Balakovo .... 52 4 N 47 55 E
22 Balashov .... 51 30 N 43 10 E
33 Balasore .... 21 35 N 87 3 E
15 Balaton, L. .... 46 50 N 17 40 E
74 Balboa .... 9 0 N 79 30 W
9 Balbriggan .... 53 35 N 6 10 W
80 Balcarce .... 38 0 s 58 10 W
47 Balclutha .... 46 15 s 169 45 E
45 Bald, Hd. .... 35 6 s 118 1 E
73 Baldy Pk. .... 33 55 N 109 35 W
13 Baleares, Is. .... 39 30 N 3 0 E
13 Balearic Is.= Baleares, Is. .... 39 30 N 3 0 E
42 Balfe's Creek ..... 20 12 s 145 55 E
57 Balfour .... 26 38 s 28 35 E
53 Bali .... 5 54 N 10 0 E
34 Bali, I. .... 8 20 s 115 0 E
30 Balikesir .... 39 35 s 27 58 E
34 Balikpapan .... 1 10 s 116 55 E
39 Balintang Chan. ... 19 50 N 122 0 E
33 Balipara .... 26 50 N 92 45 E
79 Baliza .... 16 0 s 52 20 W
4 Balkan Pen. ...... 42 0 N 22 0 E
4 Balkans, Mts. ..... 42 45 N 25 0 E
31 Balkh □ .... 36 30 N 67 0 E
24 Balkhash .... 46 50 N 74 50 E
24 Balkhash, Oz. ..... 46 0 N 74 50 E
8 Ballachulish ...... 56 40 N 5 10 W
45 Balladonia .... 32 27 s 123 51 E
46 Ballarat .... 37 33 s 143 50 E
45 Ballard, L. .... 29 20 s 120 10 E
8 Ballater .... 57 2 N 3 2 W
45 Ballidu .... 30 35 s 116 45 E
43 Ballina, Australia .... 28 50 s 153 31 E
9 Ballina, Mayo ..... 54 7 N 9 10 W
9 Ballina, Tipperary . 52 49 N 8 27 W
9 Ballinasloe .... 53 20 N 8 12 W
71 Ballinger .... 31 45 N 99 58 W
9 Ballinrobe .... 53 36 N 9 13 W
9 Ballycastle .... 55 12 N 6 15 W
9 Ballymena .... 54 53 N 6 18 W
9 Ballymena □ ...... 54 53 N 6 18 W
9 Ballymoney .... 55 5 N 6 30 W
9 Ballymoney □ ..... 55 5 N 6 30 W
9 Ballyshannon ..... 54 30 N 8 10 W
80 Balmaceda .... 46 0 s 71 50 W
8 Balmoral .... 57 3 N 3 13 W
55 Balovale .... 13 30 s 23 15 E
33 Balrampur .... 27 30 N 82 20 E
46 Balranald .... 34 38 s 143 33 E
74 Balsas, R. .... 17 55 N 102 10 W
23 Balta .... 48 2 N 29 45 E
4 Baltic Sea .... 56 0 N 20 0 E
9 Baltimore, Eire ... 51 29 N 9 22 W
68 Baltimore, U.S.A. . 39 18 N 76 37 W
32 Baluchistan, Reg. .. 27 30 N 65 0 E
31 Bam .... 29 7 N 58 14 E
53 Bama .... 11 33 N 13 33 E
50 Bamako .... 12 34 N 7 55 W
54 Bambari .... 5 40 N 20 35 E
42 Bambaroo .... 18 50 s 146 10 E
14 Bamberg .... 49 54 N 10 53 E
53 Bamenda .... 5 57 N 10 11 E
31 Bamian □ .... 35 0 N 67 0 E
31 Bampur .... 27 15 N 60 21 E
34 Ban Kantang ..... 7 25 N 99 35 E
31 Banadar Daryay Oman □ .... 25 30 N 56 0 E
54 Banalia .... 1 32 N 25 5 E
50 Banamba .... 13 29 N 7 22 W
42 Banana .... 24 32 s 150 12 E
79 Bananal, I. de ..... 11 30 s 50 30 W
33 Banaras=Varanasi 25 22 N 83 8 E
51 Bânâs, Ras .... 23 57 N 35 50 E
15 Banat, Reg. .... 45 30 N 21 30 E
9 Banbridge .... 54 26 N 6 16 W
9 Banbridge □ ...... 54 21 N 6 16 W
7 Banbury .... 52 4 N 1 21 W
8 Banchory .... 57 3 N 2 30 W
62 Bancroft .... 45 3 N 77 51 W
31 Band-e Charak .... 26 45 N 54 20 E
31 Band-e Nakhīlu ... 26 58 N 53 30 E
32 Banda .... 25 30 N 80 26 E
34 Banda Aceh ...... 5 35 N 95 20 E
43 Banda Banda, Mt. . 31 10 s 152 28 E
35 Banda Sea .... 6 0 s 130 0 E
33 Bandar= Machilipatnam .. 16 12 N 81 12 E
31 Bandar Abbas .... 27 15 N 56 15 E
34 Bandar Maharani .. 2 3 N 102 34 E
34 Bandar Seri Begawan .... 4 52 N 115 0 E
31 Bandar-e Bushetir . 28 55 N 50 55 E
31 Bandar-e Lengeh .. 26 35 N 54 58 E
30 Bandar-e Ma'shur . 30 35 N 49 10 E
* 30 Bandar-e-Pahlavi .. 37 30 N 49 30 E
31 Bandar-e Rig ..... 29 30 N 50 45 E
‡ 31 Bandar-e Shāh .... 37 0 N 54 10 E
† 30 Bandar-e Shahpur . 30 30 N 49 5 E
52 Bandawe .... 11 58 s 34 5 E
79 Bandeira, Pico da . 20 26 s 41 47 W
80 Bandera .... 28 55 s 62 20 W
53 Bandiagara .... 14 12 N 3 29 W
30 Bandirma .... 40 20 N 28 0 E
9 Bandon .... 51 44 N 8 45 W
9 Bandon, R. .... 51 40 N 8 35 W
54 Bandundu .... 3 15 s 17 22¼
35 Bandung .... 6 36 s 107 48 E
75 Banes .... 20 58 N 75 43 W
64 Banff, Canada .... 51 20 N 115 40 W
8 Banff, U.K. .... 57 40 N 2 32 W
64 Banff Nat. Park ... 51 38 N 116 22 W
34 Bang Saphan ..... 11 14 N 99 28 E
55 Bangala Dam ..... 21 7 s 31 25 E
32 Bangalore .... 12 59 N 77 40 E
54 Bangassou .... 4 55 N 23 55 E
51 Banghazi .... 32 11 N 20 3 E
35 Bangil .... 7 36 s 112 50 E
34 Bangka, I., Selatan 3 30 s 105 30 E
35 Bangka, I., Utara .. 1 50 N 12 s 5 E
35 Bangkalan .... 7 2 s 112 46 E
34 Bangkok (Krung Thep) .... 13 45 N 100 31 E
33 Bangladesh ■ ..... 24 0 N 90 0 E
6 Bangor, Gwynedd . 53 13 N 4 9 W
9 Bangor, N. Down . 54 40 N 5 40 W
69 Bangor, Me. ...... 44 48 N 68 42 W
35 Bangued .... 17 40 N 120 37 E
54 Bangui .... 4 23 N 18 35 E
54 Bangweulu, L. .... 11 0 s 30 0 E
75 Bani .... 18 16 N 70 22 W
28 Bani Na'im .... 31 31 N 35 10 E
51 Baninah .... 32 0 N 20 12 E
18 Banja Luka .... 44 49 N 17 26 E
35 Banjar .... 7 24 s 108 30 E
34 Banjarmasin ...... 3 20 s 114 35 E
35 Banjarnegara ..... 7 24 s 109 42 E
50 Banjul .... 13 28 N 16 40 W
42 Banka Banka ..... 18 50 s 134 0 E
33 Bankipore .... 25 35 N 85 10 E
58 Banks I. .... 73 30 N 120 0 W
47 Banks, Pen. .... 43 45 s 173 15 E
33 Bankura .... 23 11 N 87 18 E
9 Bann, R. .... 55 2 N 6 35 W
73 Banning .... 48 44 N 91 56 W
32 Bannu .... 33 0 N 70 18 s
8 Bannockburn ..... 56 5 N 3 55 W
15 Banská Bystrica ... 48 46 N 19 14 E
32 Banswara .... 23 32 N 74 24 E
35 Banten .... 6 5 s 106 8 E
9 Bantry .... 51 40 N 9 28 W
9 Bantry, B. .... 51 35 N 9 50 W
35 Bantul .... 7 55 s 110 19 E
33 Bapatla .... 15 55 N 80 30 E
28 Baqa el Gharbiya . 32 25 N 35 2 E
19 Bar .... 42 8 N 19 8 E
35 Barabai .... 2 32 s 115 34 E
24 Barabinsk .... 55 20 N 78 20 E
70 Baraboo .... 43 28 N 89 46 W
75 Baracoa .... 20 20 N 74 30 W
75 Barahona .... 18 13 N 71 7 W
33 Barail Ra. .... 25 15 N 93 20 E
36 Barak □ .... 38 20 N 140 0 E
33 Barakhola .... 25 0 N 92 45 E
32 Baramula .... 34 15 N 74 20 E
32 Baran .... 25 9 N 76 40 E
64 Baranof .... 57 0 N 135 10 W
64 Baranof I. .... 57 0 N 135 10 W
22 Baranovichi ...... 53 10 N 26 0 E
35 Barat□, Java ..... 7 0 s 107 0 E
34 Barat□, Kalimantan ..... 0 0 s 111 0 E
34 Barat□, Sumatera . 1 0 s 101 0 E
35 Barat Daja, Kep. .... 7 30 s 128 0 E

* Renamed Bandar Anzalī
† Renamed Bandar Khomeynī
‡ Renamed Bandar-e Torkeman

79 Barbacena 21 15s 43 56w
78 Barbacoas 1 45N 78 0w
75 Barbados ■ 13 0N 59 30w
57 Barberton, S. Africa 25 42s 31 2E
68 Barberton, U.S.A. 41 0N 81 40w
75 Barbuda, I. 17 30N 61 40w
42 Barcaldine 22 33s 145 13E
51 Barce=Al Marj 32 25N 20 40E
13 Barcelona, Sp. 41 21N 2 10E
78 Barcelona, Ven. 10 10N 64 40w
78 Barcelos 1 0s 63 0w
51 Bardaî 21 25N 17 0E
29 Bardera 2 20N 42 0s
51 Bardiyah 31 45N 25 0E
6 Bardsey I. 52 46N 4 47w
32 Bareilly 28 22N 79 27E
4 Barents Sea 73 0N 39 0E
12 Barfleur, Pte. de 49 42N 1 17w
29 Bargal 11 25N 51 0E
42 Bargara 24 50s 152 25E
25 Barguzin 53 37N 109 37E
18 Bari 41 6N 16 52E
32 Bari Doab, Reg. 30 20N 73 0E
32 Bari Sadri 24 25N 74 29E
78 Barinas 8 36N 70 15w
60 Baring, C. 70 0N 116 30w
51 Bârîs 24 42N 30 31E
33 Barisal 22 30N 90 20E
34 Barisan, Bukit, Mts. 3 30s 102 15E
34 Barito, R. 4 0s 114 50E
31 Barkah 24 30N 58 0E
37 Barkha 31 0N 81 45E
56 Barkly East 30 58s 27 33E
42 Barkly Tableland 19 50s 138 40E
56 Barkly West 28 38s 24 11E
12 Bar-le-Duc 48 47N 5 10E
45 Barlee, L. 29 15s 119 30E
18 Barletta 41 20N 16 17E
46 Barmedman 34 9s 147 21E
32 Barmer 25 45N 71 20E
43 Barmera 34 15s 140 28E
6 Barmouth 52 44N 4 3w
6 Barnard Castle 54 33N 1 55w
24 Barnaul 53 20N 83 40E
70 Barnesville 33 6N 84 9w
7 Barnet 51 37N 0 15w
11 Barneveld 52 7N 5 36E
6 Barnsley 53 33N 1 29w
7 Barnstaple 51 5N 4 3w
32 Baroda= Vadodara 22 20N 73 10E
33 Barpeta 26 20N 91 10E
51 Barqa 27 0N 20 0E
78 Barquisimeto 9 58N 69 13w
79 Barra 11 5s 43 10w
8 Barra, I. 57 0N 7 30w
79 Barra de Corda 5 30s 45 10w
79 Barra do Piraí 22 30s 43 50w
43 Barraba 30 21s 150 35E
78 Barranca 10 45s 77 50w
78 Barrancabermeja 7 0N 73 50w
78 Barrancas 8 55N 62 5w
13 Barrancos 38 10N 6 58w
80 Barranqueras 27 30s 59 0w
78 Barranquilla 11 0N 74 50w
79 Barras 1 45s 73 13w
62 Barraute 47 30N 76 50w
68 Barre 44 15N 73 30w
79 Barreiras 12 8s 45 0w
79 Barreirinhas 2 30s 42 50w
13 Barreiro 38 40N 9 6w
79 Barreiros 8 49s 35 12w
79 Barretos 20 30s 48 35w
64 Barrhead 54 10N 114 30w
62 Barrie 44 25N 79 45w
6 Barrow, U.K. 54 8N 3 15w
60 Barrow, U.S.A. 71 16N 156 50w
44 Barrow, I. 20 45s 115 20E
9 Barrow, R. 52 46N 7 0w
42 Barrow Creek 21 30s 133 55E
7 Barry 51 23N 3 19w
62 Barry's Bay 45 30N 77 40w
52 Barsaloi 1 20N 36 52E
32 Barsi 18 10N 75 50E
73 Barstow 34 58N 117 2w
78 Bartica 6 25N 58 40w
71 Bartlesville 36 50N 95 58w
45 Barton Siding 30 31s 132 39E
6 Barton-upon-Humber 53 41N 0 27w
69 Bartow 27 53N 81 49w
38 Baruun Urt 46 46N 113 15E
12 Bas Rhin □ 48 40N 7 30E
14 Basel 47 35N 7 35E
22 Bashkir A.S.S.R. □ 54 0N 57 0E
35 Basilan, I. 6 35N 122 0E
35 Basilan City= Isabela 6 37N 122 0E
35 Basilan Str. 13 10s 122 0E
7 Basildon 51 34N 0 29E
18 Basilicata □ 40 30N 16 0E
32 Basim 20 4N 77 4E
7 Basingstoke 51 15N 1 5w
62 Baskatong Res. 46 46N 75 50w
14 Basle=Basel 47 35N 7 35E
54 Basoka 1 16N 23 40E
13 Basque □ 42 50N 2 45w
30 Basra=Al Basrah 30 30N 47 55E
8 Bass Rock 56 5N 2 40w
42 Bass, Str. 39 15s 146 30E
18 Bassano del Grappa 45 45N 11 45E
53 Bassar 9 19N 0 57E
55 Bassas da India, I. 22 0s 39 0E
75 Basse Terre 16 0N 61 40w
33 Bassein, Burma 16 45N 94 30E
75 Basseterre 17 17N 62 43w
70 Bassett 42 37N 99 30w
12 Bassigny, Reg. 48 0N 5 10E
31 Bastak 27 15N 54 25E
33 Basti 26 52N 82 55E
12 Bastia 42 40N 9 30E
11 Bastogne 50 1N 5 43E
57 Basutoland■= Lesotho ■ 29 40s 28 0E
28 Bat Yam 32 2N 34 44E
54 Bata 1 57N 9 50E
35 Bataan, Pen. 14 38N 120 30E
75 Barabanó, G. de 22 30N 82 30w
25 Batagoy 67 38N 134 38E
13 Batalha 39 40N 8 50w
25 Batamay 63 30N 129 15E
39 Batan Is. 20 25N 121 59E
35 Batang 6 55s 109 40E
35 Batangas 13 35N 121 10E
15 Bataszék 46 12N 18 44E
68 Batavia 43 0N 78 10w
44 Batchelor 13 4s 131 1E
71 Batesville 35 48N 91 40w
7 Bath, U.K. 51 22N 2 22w
68 Bath, N.Y. 42 20N 77 17w
8 Bathgate 55 54N 3 38w
50 Bathurst=Banjul 13 28N 16 40w
46 Bathurst, Australia 33 25s 149 31E
63 Bathurst, Canada 47 37N 65 43w
60 Bathurst, C. 70 30N 128 30w
44 Bathurst, I., Australia 11 30s 130 10E
58 Bathurst I., Canada 76 30N 130 10w
60 Bathurst Inlet 67 15N 108 30w
63 Bathurst Mines 47 30N 65 47w
31 Batinah, Reg. 24 0N 57 0E
50 Batna 35 34N 6 15E
71 Baton Rouge 30 30N 91 5w
54 Batouri 4 30N 14 25E
34 Battambang 13 7N 103 12E
32 Batticaloa 7 43N 81 45E
28 Battir 31 44N 35 8E
7 Battle 50 55N 0 30E
65 Battle, R. 52 45N 108 15w
68 Battle Creek 42 20N 85 10w
63 Battle Harbour 52 13N 55 42w
72 Battle Mountain 40 45N 117 0w
65 Battleford 52 45N 108 15w
34 Batu, Kep. 0 30s 98 25E
34 Batu Pahat= Bandar Penggaram 1 50N 102 56E
23 Batumi 41 30N 41 30E
34 Baturadja 4 11s 104 15E
79 Baturité 4 28s 38 45w
35 Baubau 5 25s 123 50E
53 Bauchi 10 22N 9 48E
53 Bauchi □ 10 25N 10 0E
42 Bauhinia Downs 24 35s 149 18E
79 Bauru 22 10s 49 0w
79 Baus 18 22s 52 47½
14 Bautzen 51 11N 14 25w
14 Bavaria□= Bayern □ 49 7N 11 30E
33 Bawdwin 23 5N 97 50E
34 Bawean, I. 5 46s 112 35E
53 Bawku 11 3N 0 19w
33 Bawlake 19 11N 97 21E
68 Bay City, Mich. 43 35N 83 51w
71 Bay City, Tex. 28 59N 95 55w
68 Bay Shore 40 44N 73 15w
47 Bay View 39 25w 176 50E
75 Bayamón 18 24N 66 10w
38 Bayan 47 20N 107 55E
37 Bayan Kara Shan, Mts. 34 0N 98 0E
38 Bayan-Uul 49 6N 112 12E
24 Bayanaul 50 45N 75 45E
38 Bayantsogt 47 58N 105 1E
14 Bayern □ 49 7N 11 30E
12 Bayeux 49 17N 0 42w
25 Baykal, Oz. 53 0N 108 0E
25 Baykal, L.= Baykal, Oz. 53 0N 108 0s
25 Baykir 61 50N 95 50E
24 Baykonur 47 48N 65 50E
56 Baynes Mts. 22 40s 12 50E
12 Bayonne 43 30N 1 28E
14 Bayreuth 49 56N 11 35E
30 Bayrūt 33 53N 35 31E
28 Bayt Aula 31 37N 35 2E
28 Bayt Jālā 31 43N 35 11E
28 Bayt Lahm 31 43N 35 12E
28 Bayt Sāhūr 31 42N 35 13E
28 Baytin 31 56N 35 14E
71 Baytown 29 42N 94 57w
13 Baza 37 30N 2 47w
57 Bazaruto, I. do 21 40s 35 28E
65 Beach 46 57N 104 0w
7 Beachy Hd. 50 44N 0 16E
45 Beacon, Australia 30 20s 117 55E
68 Beacon, U.S.A. 41 32N 73 58w
80 Beagle 55 0s 68 30w
47 Bealey 43 2s 171 36E
62 Beardmore 49 36N 87 59w
70 Beardstown 40 0N 90 25w
12 Béarn, Reg 43 28N 0 36w
70 Beatrice 40 20N 96 40w
12 Beauce, Reg. 48 10N 2 0E
63 Beauceville 46 13N 70 46w
43 Beaudesert 27 59s 153 0E
34 Beaufort, Malaysia 5 30N 115 40E
46 Beaufort, Australia 37 25s 143 25E
69 Beaufort, U.S.A. 34 45N 76 40w
58 Beaufort Sea 70 30N 146 0w
56 Beaufort West 32 18s 22 36E
62 Beauharnois 45 20N 73 20w
12 Beaujolais, Reg. 46 0N 4 25E
8 Beauly 57 29N 4 27w
6 Beaumaris 53 16N 4 7w
71 Beaumont 30 5N 94 8w
12 Beaune 47 2N 4 50E
65 Beausejour 50 5N 96 35E
12 Beauvais 49 25N 2 8E
65 Beauval 55 9N 107 35w
60 Beaver, U.S.A. 66 40N 147 50w
70 Beaver Dam 43 28N 88 50w
68 Beaver Falls 40 44N 80 20w
32 Beawar 26 3N 74 18E
7 Beccles 52 27N 1 33E
50 Béchar 31 38N 2 18E
56 Bechuanaland■= Botswana ■ 23 0s 24 0E
56 Bechuanaland, Reg.= Betsjoeanaland, Reg. 26 30s 22 30E
68 Beckley 37 50N 81 8w
62 Bedford, Canada 45 10N 73 0w
56 Bedford, S. Africa 32 40s 26 10E
7 Bedford, U.K. 52 8N 0 29w
68 Bedford, Ohio 41 23N 81 32w
68 Bedford, Ind. 38 50N 86 30w
7 Bedford □ 52 4N 0 28w
64 Bednesti 53 50N 123 10w
42 Bedourie 24 30s 139 30E
43 Beenleigh 27 43s 153 10E
28 Be'er Sheva 31 15N 34 48E
28 Be'erotayim 32 19N 34 59E
6 Beeston 52 55N 1 11w
71 Beeville 28 27N 97 44w
46 Bega 36 41s 149 51E
53 Begoro 6 23N 0 23w
30 Behbehan 30 30N 50 15E
31 Behshahr 36 45N 53 35E
11 Beilen 52 52N 6 27E
57 Beira 19 50s 34 52E
13 Beira-Alta, Reg. 41 0N 7 20w
13 Beira-Baixa, Reg. 40 0N 7 30w
13 Beira Litoral, Reg. 40 0N 8 30w
30 Beirut=Bayrut 33 53N 35 31E
28 Beit Hanun 31 32N 34 32E
28 Beit'Ur et Tahta 31 54N 35 5E
57 Beitbridge 22 12s 30 0E
28 Beituniya 31 54N 35 10E
13 Beja, Port. 38 2N 7 53w
50 Béja, Tunisia 36 10N 9 0E
50 Béjaïa 36 42N 5 2E
15 Békéscsaba 46 40N 21 10E
57 Bekily 24 13s 45 19E
53 Bekwai 6 25N 1 37w
33 Bela, India 25 50N 82 0E
32 Bela, Pak. 26 12N 66 20E
79 Bela Vista 17 0s 49 0w
34 Belawan 3 33N 98 32E
23 Belaya Tserkov 49 45N 30 10E
62 Belcher Is. 56 20N 79 20w
22 Belebey 54 72N 54 7E
79 Belém 1 20s 48 30w
80 Belén 27 40s 67 5w
73 Belen 34 40N 106 50w
29 Belet Uen 4 30N 45 5E
57 Belfast, S. Afr. 25 42s 30 2E
9 Belfast, U.K. 54 35N 5 56w
69 Belfast, U.S.A. 44 30N 69 0w
9 Belfast, L. 54 40N 5 50w
9 Belfast □ 54 35N 5 56w
12 Belfort 47 38N 6 50E
12 Belfort, Terr. de □ 47 38N 6 52E
32 Belgaum 15 55N 74 35E
11 Belgium ■ 51 30N 5 0E
9 Belgooly 51 44N 8 30w
23 Belgorod 50 35N 36 35E
23 Belgorod-Dnestrovskiy 46 11N 30 23E
19 Belgrade= Beograd 44 50N 20 37E
34 Belitung, Pulau, I. 3 10s 107 50E
74 Belize ■ 17 0N 88 30w
74 Belize City 17 25N 88 0w
80 Bell Ville 32 40s 62 40w
64 Bella Coola 52 25N 126 40w
80 Bella Vista 28 33s 59 0w
68 Bellaire 40 1N 80 46w
32 Bellary 15 10N 76 56E
43 Bellata 29 53s 149 46E
12 Belle I. 47 20N 3 10w
63 Belle I, Str. of 51 30N 56 30w
70 Belle Fourche 44 43N 103 52w
69 Belle Glade 26 43N 80 38w
68 Bellefontaine 40 20N 83 45E
62 Belleville, Canada 44 15N 77 37w
70 Belleville, U.S.A. 38 30N 90 0w
64 Bellevue 46 35N 84 10w
61 Bellin 60 0N 70 0w
43 Bellingen 30 25s 152 50E
72 Bellingham 48 45N 122 27w
2 Bellingshausen Sea 66 0s 80 0w
14 Bellinzona 46 11N 9 1E
68 Bellows Falls 43 10N 72 30w
18 Belluno 46 8N 12 6E
13 Bélmez 38 17N 5 17w
46 Belmont 33 4s 151 42E
79 Belmonte 16 0s 39 0w
74 Belmopan 17 18N 88 30w
9 Belmullet 54 13N 9 58w
79 Belo Horizonte 19 55s 43 56w
25 Belogorsk 51 0N 128 20E
70 Beloit 42 35N 89 0w
22 Belomorsk 64 35N 34 30E
22 Beloretsk 53 58N 58 24E
57 Belo-Tsiribihina 19 40s 44 30E
24 Belovo 54 30N 86 0E
22 Beloye, Oz. 60 10N 37 35E
22 Beloye More 66 0N 38 0E
22 Belozersk 60 0N 37 30E
23 Belsty 47 48N 28 0E
43 Beltana 30 48s 138 25E
79 Belterra 2 45s 55 0w
71 Belton 31 4N 97 30w
9 Belturbet 54 6N 7 28w
70 Belvidere 42 15N 88 55w
24 Belyy Os. 73 30N 71 0E
24 Belyy Yar 58 26N 84 30E
70 Bemidji 47 30N 94 50w
8 Ben Cruachan, Mt. 56 26N 5 8w
51 Ben Gardane 33 11N 11 11E
8 Ben Hope, Mt. 58 24N 4 36w
8 Ben Lawers, Mt. 56 33N 4 13w
43 Ben Lomond, Mt., Australia 30 1s 151 43E
8 Ben Lomond, Mt., U.K. 56 12N 4 39w
8 Ben Macdhui, Mt. 57 4N 3 40w
8 Ben More, Mt. 56 26N 6 2w
8 Ben More Assynt, Mt. 58 7N 4 51w
8 Ben Nevis, Mt. 56 48N 5 0w
8 Ben Wyvis, Mt. 57 40N 4 35w
53 Bena 11 20N 5 50E
54 Bena Dibele 4 4s 22 50E
46 Benalla 36 30s 146 0E
33 Benares=Varanasi 25 22N 83 8E
8 Benbecula, I. 57 26N 7 20w
43 Benbonyathe Hill 30 25s 139 11E
45 Bencubbin 30 48s 117 52E

72 Bend 44 2N 121 15W
53 Bendel □ 6 0N 5 40E
29 Bender Beila 9 30N 50 48E
45 Bendering 32 23S 118 18E
23 Bendery 46 50N 29 50E
46 Bendigo 36 40S 144 15E
28 Bene Beraq 32 5N 34 50E
57 Benenitra 23 27S 45 5E
18 Benevento 41 7N 14 45E
26 Bengal, B. of 15 0N 90 0E
51 Benghazi= Banghazı 32 11N 20 3E
34 Bengkalis 1 30N 102 10E
34 Bengkulu 3 50S 102 12E
34 Bengkulu □ 3 50S 102 10E
65 Bengough 49 25N 105 10W
55 Benguela 12 37S 13 25E
54 Beni 32 11S 148 43E
51 Beni Mazar 28 32N 30 44E
50 Beni Mellal 32 21N 6 21W
51 Benî Suêf 29 5N 31 6E
13 Benidorm 38 33N 0 9W
53 Benin ■ 8 0N 2 0E
53 Benin, B. of 5 0N 3 0E
53 Benin City 6 20N 5 31E
78 Benjamin Constant 4 40S 70 15W
42 Benlidi 24 35S 144 50E
69 Bennettsville 34 38N 79 39W
68 Bennington 42 52N 73 12W
57 Benoni 26 11S 28 18E
73 Benson 31 59N 110 19W
35 Benteng 6 10S 120 30E
71 Benton, Ark. 34 30N 92 35W
70 Benton, Ill. 38 0N 88 55W
68 Benton Harbor 42 10N 86 28W
53 Benue, R. 7 47N 6 45E
53 Benue □ 7 20N 8 20E
19 Beograd 44 50N 20 37E
36 Beppu 33 15N 131 30E
28 Ber Dagan 32 1N 34 49E
19 Berati 40 43N 19 59E
51 Berber 18 0N 34 0E
29 Berbera 10 30N 45 2E
54 Berbérati 4 15N 15 40E
23 Berdicher 49 57N 28 30E
24 Berdsk 54 47N 83 2E
23 Berdyansk 46 45N 36 50E
29 Bereda 11 45N 51 0E
53 Berekum 7 29N 2 34W
65 Berens River 52 25N 97 0W
57 Berevo 19 44S 44 58E
22 Berezniki 59 24N 56 46E
24 Berezovo 64 0N 65 0E
18 Bérgamo 45 42N 9 40E
11 Bergen, Neth. 52 40N 4 42E
21 Bergen, Norway 60 23N 5 27E
11 Bergen-op-Zoom 51 30N 4 18E
12 Bergerac 44 51N 0 30E
11 Bergum 53 13N 5 59E
33 Berhampore 24 2N 88 27E
33 Berhampur 19 15N 84 54E
60 Bering Sea 59 0N 175 0W
60 Bering Str. 66 0N 170 0W
11 Beringen 51 3N 5 14E
25 Beringovskiy 63 3N 179 19E
13 Berja 36 50N 2 56W
72 Berkeley 38 0N 122 20W
2 Berkner I. 79 30S 50 0W
7 Berkshire □ 51 30N 1 20W
14 Berlin, Germany 52 32N 13 24E
68 Berlin, U.S.A. 44 29N 71 10W
80 Bermejo, R. 26 51S 58 23W
2 Bermuda, I. 32 45N 65 0W
14 Bern 46 57N 7 28E
73 Bernalilo 35 17N 106 37W
80 Bernardo de Irigoyen 26 15S 53 40W
14 Bernburg 51 48N 11 44E
45 Bernier, I. 24 50S 113 12E
14 Bernina, Piz 46 20N 9 54E
14 Beroun 49 57N 14 5E
46 Berowra 33 35S 151 12E
50 Berrechid 33 18N 7 36W
43 Berri 34 14S 140 35E
46 Berrigan 35 38S 145 49E
12 Berry, Reg. 47 0N 2 0E
54 Bertoua 4 30N 13 45E
68 Berwick 41 4N 76 17W
6 Berwick on Tweed 55 47N 2 0W
6 Berwyn Mts. 52 54N 3 26W
57 Besalampy 16 43S 44 29E
12 Besançon 47 9N 6 0E
23 Beskids, Mts.= Vychodné Beskydy 49 30N 22 0E
69 Bessemer 46 27N 90 0W
12 Bessin, Reg. 49 21N 1 0W
28 Bet Ha 'Emeq 32 58N 35 8E
28 Bet Ha Shitta 32 31N 35 27E
28 Bet Ha'tmeq 32 58N 35 8E
28 Bet Oren 32 43N 34 59E
28 Bet Qeshet 32 41N 35 21E
28 Be't She'an 32 30N 35 30E
28 Bet Shemesh 31 45N 35 0E
28 Bet Yosef 32 34N 35 33E
57 Betafo 19 50S 46 51E
54 Bétaré-Oya 5 40N 14 5E
57 Bethal 26 27S 29 28E
55 Bethanien 26 31S 17 8E
28 Bethany= Eizariya 31 47N 35 15E
28 Bethlehem, Jordan= Bayt Lahm 31 43N 35 12E
57 Bethlehem, S. Africa 28 14S 28 18E
68 Bethlehem, U.S.A. 40 39N 75 24W
56 Bethulie 30 30S 25 29E
57 Betioky 23 48S 44 20E
42 Betoota 25 40S 140 42E
57 Betroka 23 16S 46 6E
56 Betsjoeanaland, Reg. 26 30S 22 30E
33 Bettiah 26 48N 84 33E
32 Betul 21 48N 77 59E
36 Betung 2 0S 103 10E
46 Beulah, Australia 35 58S 142 29E
65 Beulah, Canada 50 16N 101 2W
45 Beverley, Australia 32 9S 116 56E
6 Beverley, U.K. 53 52N 0 26W
64 Beverly 53 36N 113 21W
73 Beverly Hills 34 4N 118 29W
11 Beverwijk 52 28N 4 38E
50 Beyla 8 30N 8 38W
7 Bexhill 50 51N 0 29E
24 Beyneu 45 10N 55 3E
30 Beypazari 40 10N 31 48E
30 Beyşehir Gólú, L. 37 40N 31 45E
28 Bezet 33 4N 35 8E
22 Bezhitsa 53 19N 34 17E
12 Béziers 43 20N 3 12E
32 Bhachau 23 10N 70 15W
33 Bhadgaon 27 42N 85 27E
33 Bhadrakh 21 10N 86 30E
33 Bhagalpur 25 10N 87 0E
33 Bhamo 24 15N 97 15E
32 Bhandara 21 5N 79 42E
32 Bhanrer Ra. 23 40N 79 45E
32 Bharatpur 27 15N 77 30E
32 Bharuch 21 47N 73 0E
32 Bhatinda 30 15N 74 57E
33 Bhatpara 22 50N 88 25E
32 Bhavnagar 21 45N 72 10E
32 Bhilwara 25 25N 74 38E
32 Bhima, R. 17 20N 76 30E
33 Bhimavaram 16 30N 81 30E
32 Bhind 26 30N 78 46E
32 Bhiwandi 19 15N 73 0E
32 Bhiwani 28 50N 76 9E
32 Bhopal 23 20N 77 53E
33 Bhubaneswar 20 15N 85 50E
32 Bhusaval 21 1N 75 56E
33 Bhutan ■ 27 25N 89 50E
48 Biafra, B. of= Bonny, B. of 4 0N 8 0E
15 Biała Podłaska 52 4N 23 6E
15 Białystok 53 10N 23 10E
12 Biarritz 43 29N 1 33W
14 Biberach 48 5N 9 49E
53 Bibiani 6 30N 2 8W
63 Bic 48 20N 68 41W
53 Bida 9 3N 5 58E
7 Bicester 51 53N 1 9W
32 Bidar 17 55N 77 35E
69 Biddeford 43 30N 70 28E
7 Bideford 51 1N 4 13W
* 55 Bié 12 22S 16 55E
55 Bié Plat. 12 0S 16 0E
72 Bieber 41 4N 121 6W
14 Biel 47 8N 7 14E
15 Bielé Karpaty, Mts. 49 5N 18 0E
14 Bielefeld 52 2N 8 31E
18 Biella 45 33N 8 3E
15 Bielsko-Biała 49 50N 19 8E
34 Biên Hoa 10 57N 106 49E
62 Big Beaver House 52 59N 89 50W
71 Big Bend Nat. Park 29 15N 103 15W
60 Big Delta 64 15N 145 0W
68 Big Rapids 43 42N 85 27W
65 Big River 53 50N 107 0W
60 Big Salmon 61 50N 136 0W
71 Big Spring 32 10N 101 25W
69 Big Stone Gap 36 52N 82 45W
62 Big Trout L. 53 40N 90 0W
65 Biggar, Canada 52 10N 108 0W
8 Biggar, U.K. 55 38N 3 31W
44 Bigge, I. 14 35S 125 10E
43 Biggenden 25 31S 152 4E
72 Bighorn Mts. 44 30N 107 20W
12 Bigorre, Reg. 43 5N 0 2E
72 Bigtimber 45 33N 110 0W
18 Bihác 44 49N 15 57E
33 Bihar 25 5N 85 40E
33 Bihar □ 25 0N 86 0E
52 Biharamulo 2 25S 31 25E
50 Bijagos, Arquipélago dos 11 15N 16 10W
32 Bijapur 26 2N 77 36E
32 Bijnor 29 27N 78 11E
32 Bikaner 28 2N 73 18E
25 Bikin 46 50N 134 20E
32 Bilara 26 14N 73 53E
33 Bilaspur 22 2N 82 15E
13 Bilbao 43 16N 2 56W
30 Bilecik 40 5N 30 5E
25 Bilibino 68 3N 166 20E
25 Bilir 65 40N 131 20E
45 Billabalong 27 25S 115 49E
44 Billiluna 19 37S 127 41E
6 Billingham 54 36N 1 18W
72 Billings 45 43N 108 29W
51 Bilma 18 50N 13 30E
42 Biloela 24 34S 150 31E
71 Biloxi 30 30N 89 0W
51 Biltine 14 40N 20 50E
42 Bilyana 18 5S 145 50E
35 Bima 8 22S 118 49E
32 Bina-Etawah 24 13N 78 14E
35 Binalbagan 10 12N 122 50E
34 Binatang 2 10N 111 40E
42 Binbee 20 19S 147 56E
11 Binche 50 26N 4 10E
45 Bindi Bindi 30 37S 116 22E
57 Bindura 17 18S 31 18E
43 Bingara, N.S.W. 29 40S 150 40E
43 Bingara, Queens. 28 10S 144 37E
72 Bingham Canyon 40 31N 112 10W
68 Binghamton 42 9N 75 54W
34 Binh Son 15 20N 104 40E
34 Binjai 3 50N 98 30E
28 Binyamina 32 32N 34 56E
50 Binzerte 37 15N 9 50E
51 Bir Atrun 18 15N 26 40E
28 Bir Nabala 31 52N 35 12E
51 Bîr Shalatein 23 5N 35 25E
28 Bir Zeit 31 59N 35 11E
65 Birch Hills 53 10N 105 10W
46 Birchip 35 52S 143 0E
41 Bird, I. 22 20S 155 20E
42 Birdsville 25 51S 139 20E
44 Birdum 15 50S 133 0E
34 Bireuen 5 14N 96 39E
31 Bırjand 32 57N 59 10E
6 Birkenhead 53 24N 3 1W
15 Bîrlad 46 15N 27 38E
7 Birmingham, U.K. 52 30N 1 55W
69 Birmingham, U.S.A. 33 31N 86 50W
53 Birni Ngaouré 13 5N 2 51E
53 Birni Nkonni 13 55N 5 15E
53 Birnin Gwari 11 0N 6 45E
53 Birnin-Kebbi 12 32N 4 12E
53 Birnin Kuku 11 30N 9 29E
25 Birobidzhan 48 50N 132 50E
9 Birr 53 7N 7 55W
65 Birtle 50 30N 101 5W
73 Bisbee 31 30N 110 0W
12 Biscay, B. of 45 0N 2 0W
73 Bishop 37 20N 118 26W
6 Bishop Auckland 54 40N 1 40W
63 Bishop's Falls 49 2N 55 24W
7 Bishop's Stortford 51 52 0 11E
50 Biskra 34 50N 5 52E
70 Bismarck 46 49N 100 49W
41 Bismark Arch. 3 30S 148 30E
20 Bispfors 63 2N 16 40E
50 Bissau 11 45N 15 45W
65 Bissett 46 14N 78 4W
15 Bistrita 47 9N 24 35E
15 Bistrita, R. 46 30N 26 57E
19 Bitola 41 5N 21 21E
55 Bitterfontein 31 0S 18 32E
72 Bitterroot Ra. 46 0N 114 20W
53 Bittou 11 17N 0 18W
53 Biu 10 40N 12 3E
36 Biwa-Ko, L. 35 15N 135 45E
24 Biysk 52 40N 85 0E
36 Bizen 34 44N 134 9E
50 Bizerte=Binzerte 37 15N 9 50E
18 Bjelovar 45 56N 16 49E
14 Black Forest= Schwarzwald 48 0N 8 0E
70 Black Hills, Mts 44 0N 103 50W
7 Black Mts. 51 52N 3 50W
4 Black Sea 43 30N 35 0E
53 Black Volta, R. 8 41N 1 33W
42 Blackall 24 26S 145 27E
42 Blackbull 18 0S 141 7E
6 Blackburn 53 44N 2 30W
72 Blackfoot 43 13N 112 12W
46 Blackheath 33 39S 150 17E
6 Blackpool 53 48N 3 3W
63 Blacks Harbour 45 3N 66 49W
63 Blackville 47 5N 65 58W
42 Blackwater 23 35S 149 0E
9 Blackwater, R., Cork 51 51N 7 50W
9 Blackwater, R., Dungannon 54 31N 6 34W
9 Blackwater, R., Meath 53 39N 6 43W
71 Blackwell 36 55N 97 20W
6 Blaenau Ffestiniog 53 0N 3 57W
23 Blagodarnoye 45 7N 43 37E
25 Blagoveshchensk 50 20N 127 30E
65 Blaine Lake 52 51N 106 52W
42 Blair Atholl, Australia 22 42S 147 31E
8 Blair Atholl, U.K. 56 46N 3 50W
8 Blairgowrie 56 36N 3 20W
64 Blairmore 49 40N 114 25W
50 Blanc, C.= Ras Nouadhibou 37 15N 9 56E
12 Blanc, Mt. 45 50N 6 52E
80 Blanca, B. 39 10S 61 30W
73 Blanca Pk. 37 35N 105 29W
56 Blanco 33 57S 22 24E
7 Blandford 50 52N 2 10W
73 Blanding 37 35N 109 30W
55 Blantyre 15 45S 35 0E
9 Blarney 51 57N 8 35W
21 Blåvands Huk 55 33N 8 5E
6 Blaydon 54 56N 1 47W
46 Blayney 33 32S 149 14E
14 Bleiburg 46 35N 14 49E
21 Blekinge □ 56 15N 15 15E
47 Blenheim 41 38S 174 5E
7 Bletchley 51 59N 0 54W
50 Blida 36 30N 2 49E
62 Blind River 46 15N 83 0W
35 Blitar 8 5S 112 11E
53 Blitta 8 23N 1 6E
68 Block I. 41 13N 71 35W
56 Bloemfontein 29 6S 26 14E
56 Bloemhof 27 38S 25 32E
12 Blois 47 35N 1 20E
70 Bloomington, Ill. 40 25N 89 0W
68 Bloomington, Ind. 39 10N 86 30W
68 Bloomsburg 41 0N 76 30W
68 Blue Island 41 40N 87 41W
42 Blue Mud, B. 13 30S 136 0E
68 Blue Mts. 45 15N 119 0W
51 Blue Nile, R.= Nîl el Azraq, R. 10 30N 35 0E
58 Blue Ridge, Mts 36 30N 80 15W
68 Bluefield 37 18N 81 14W
75 Bluefields 12 0N 83 50W
42 Bluff, Australia 23 40S 149 0E
47 Bluff, N.Z. 46 36S 168 21E
45 Bluff Knoll, Mt. 34 23S 118 20E
68 Bluffton 40 43N 85 9W
80 Blumenau 27 0S 49 0W
6 Blyth 55 8N 1 32W
73 Blythe 33 40N 114 33W
71 Blytheville 35 56N 89 55W
50 Bo 7 55N 11 50W
78 Boa Vista 2 48N 60 30W
75 Boaco 12 29N 85 35W
54 Boali 4 48N 18 7E
13 Bobadilla 36 58N 5 10W
33 Bobbili 18 35N 83 30E
62 Bobcaygeon 44 33N 78 35W
50 Bobo-Dioulasso 11 8N 4 13W
22 Bobruysk 53 10N 29 15E
79 Bocaiuva 17 7S 43 49W
75 Bocas del Toro 9 15N 82 20W
14 Bocholt 51 50N 6 35E
14 Bochum 51 28N 7 12E
54 Boda 4 19N 17 26E
25 Bodaybo 57 50N 114 0E
45 Boddington 32 50S 116 30E
20 Boden 65 50N 21 42E
14 Bodensee, L. 47 35N 9 25E
32 Bodhan 18 40N 77 55E
53 Bodinga 12 58N 5 10E
7 Bodmin 50 28N 4 44W

* Renamed Kuito

7 Bodmin Moor, Reg. 50 33N 4 36W
20 Bodø 67 17N 14 27E
15 Bodrog, R. 48 15N 21 35E
71 Bogalusa 30 50N 89 55W
46 Bogan Gate 33 6S 147 44E
42 Bogantungan 23 41S 147 17E
55 Bogenfels 27 25S 15 25E
43 Boggabri 30 45S 150 0E
7 Bognor Regis 50 47N 0 40W
35 Bogor 6 36S 106 48E
25 Bogorodskoye 52 22N 140 30E
78 Bogota 4 34N 74 0W
24 Bogotal 56 15N 89 50E
33 Bogra 24 26N 89 22E
25 Boguchany 58 40N 97 30E
14 Bohemia □ 49 50N 14 0E
14 Bohemian Forest= Böhmerwald 49 30N 12 40E
14 Böhmerwald, Mts. 49 30N 12 40E
35 Bohol, I. 9 58N 124 20E
29 Bohotleh 8 20N 46 25E
53 Boi 9 34N 9 27E
63 Boiestown 46 27N 66 26W
72 Boise 43 43N 116 9W
65 Boissevain 49 15N 100 0W
35 Bojonegoro 7 9S 111 52E
53 Boju 7 22N 7 55E
50 Boké 10 56N 14 17W
53 Bokkos 9 19N 9 1E
21 Bokna, Fd. 59 12N 5 30E
54 Bokote 0 12S 21 8E
34 Bokpyin 11 18N 98 42E
31 Bol, Kuh-e 30 40N 52 45E
50 Bolama 11 30N 15 30W
32 Bolan Pass 29 50N 67 20E
33 Bolangir 20 42N 83 20E
12 Bolbec 49 30N 0 30E
53 Bolgatanga 10 44N 0 53W
78 Bolívar, Arg. 36 2S 60 53W
72 Bolívar, Col. 2 0N 77 0W
78 Bolivia ■ 17 6S 64 0W
76 Bolivian Plat. 19 0S 69 0W
21 Bollnäs 61 22N 16 28E
18 Bologna 44 30N 11 20E
22 Bologoye 57 55N 34 0E
18 Bolsena, L. di 42 35N 11 55E
25 Bolshevik, Os. 78 30N 102 0E
23 Bolshoi Kavkaz 42 50N 44 0E
24 Bolshoy Atlym 62 25N 66 50E
25 Bolshoy Shantar,Os. 55 0N 137 42E
6 Bolton 53 35N 2 26W
18 Bolzano 46 30N 11 20E
79 Bom Despacho 19 46S 45 15W
79 Bom Jesus da Lapa 13 10S 43 30W
54 Boma 5 50S 13 4E
46 Bomaderry 34 52S 150 37E
53 Bomadi 5 9N 6 0E
46 Bombala 36 56S 149 15E
32 Bombay 18 55N 72 50E
54 Bomboma 2 25N 18 55E
37 Bomda 29 59N 96 25E
51 Bon, C. 37 1N 11 2E
75 Bonaire, I. 12 10N 68 15W
44 Bonaparte Arch. 15 0S 124 30E
63 Bonaventure 48 5N 63 32W
63 Bonavista 48 40N 53 5W
63 Bonavista B. 48 58N 53 25W
50 Bondoukoro 9 51N 4 25W
53 Bondoukou 8 2N 2 47W
35 Bondowoso 7 56S 113 49E
35 Bone, Teluk, G. 4 10S 120 50E
8 Bo'ness 56 0N 3 38W
51 Bongor 10 35N 15 20E
71 Bonham 33 30N 96 10W
12 Bonifacio 41 24N 9 10E
18 Bonifacio, Bouches de 41 23N 9 10E
14 Bonn 50 43N 7 6E
72 Bonners Ferry 48 38N 116 21W
45 Bonnie Rock 30 29S 118 22E
53 Bonny, R. 4 20N 7 10E
48 Bonny, B. of 4 0N 8 0E
65 Bonnyville 54 20N 110 45W
34 Bontang 0 10N 117 30E
35 Bonthain 5 34S 119 56E
11 Boom 51 6N 4 20E
43 Boonah 28 0S 152 35E
70 Boone 42 5N 93 46W
68 Boonville, Ind 38 3N 87 13W
70 Boonville, Mo. 38 57N 92 45W
68 Boonville, N.Y. 43 31N 75 20W
61 Boothia, G. of 70 0N 90 0W
60 Boothia Pen. 70 30N 95 0W
6 Bootle 53 28N 3 1W
54 Booué 0 5S 11 55E
43 Bopeechee 29 35S 137 30E
21 Borås 57 42N 13 1E
78 Borba 4 12S 59 34W
12 Bordeaux 44 50N 0 36W
45 Borden, Australia 34 3S 118 12E
63 Borden, Canada 46 18N 63 47W
8 Borders □ 55 30N 3 0W
46 Bordertown 36 14S 140 58E
11 Borger, Neth. 52 54N 7 33E
71 Borger, U.S.A. 35 40N 101 20W
21 Borgholm 56 54N 16 48E
23 Borisoglebsk 51 27N 42 5E
22 Borisov 54 17N 28 28E
78 Borja 4 20S 77 40W
51 Borkou 18 15N 18 50E
21 Borlänge 60 28N 14 33E
34 Borneo, I. 1 0N 115 0E
21 Bornholm, I. 55 8N 14 55E
53 Borno □ 12 0N 12 0E
53 Bornu Yassu 12 14N 12 25E
25 Borogontsy 62 42N 131 8E
53 Boromo 11 45N 2 58W
22 Borovichi 58 25N 35 55E
42 Borroloola 16 4S 136 17E
22 Borsod-Abaüj-Zemplén □ 48 20N 21 0E
30 Borujerd 33 55N 48 50E
25 Borzya 50 24N 116 31E
18 Bosa 40 17N 8 32E
18 Bosanska Gradiška 45 9N 17 15E
29 Bosaso 11 13N 49 8E
7 Boscastle 50 42N 4 42W
56 Boshof 28 31S 25 13E
19 Bosna, R. 45 4N 18 29E
18 Bosna i Hercegovina □ 44 0N 18 0E
30 Bosporus, Str.= Karadeniz Boğazi 41 10N 29 5E
54 Bossangoa 6 35N 17 30E
71 Bossier City 32 28N 93 38W
53 Bosso 13 30N 13 15E
6 Boston, U.K. 52 59N 0 2W
68 Boston, U.S.A. 42 20N 71 0W
46 Botany B. 34 2S 151 6E
56 Bothaville 27 23S 26 34E
20 Bothnia, G. 63 0N 21 0E
42 Bothwell 42 37N 81 54W
56 Botletle, R. 20 10S 24 10E
15 Botoşani 47 42N 26 41E
56 Botswana ■ 23 0S 24 0E
79 Botucatu 22 55S 48 30W
63 Botwood 49 6N 55 23W
50 Bou Saâda 35 11N 4 9E
50 Bouaké 7 40N 5 2W
54 Bouar 6 0N 15 40E
50 Bouârfa 32 32N 1 58E
12 Bouches-du-Rhône 43 37N 5 2E
44 Bougainville, C. 13 57S 126 4E
50 Bougouni 11 30N 7 20W
53 Boukombé 10 11N 1 6E
70 Boulder 40 3N 105 10W
73 Boulder City 36 0N 114 58W
42 Boulia 22 52S 139 51E
12 Boulogne-sur-Mer 50 42N 1 36E
53 Boulsa 12 39N 0 34W
53 Bouna 9 10N 3 0N
72 Bountiful 40 57N 111 58W
12 Bourbonnais, Reg. 46 28N 3 0E
53 Bourem 17 0N 0 24W
12 Bourg en Bresse 46 13N 5 12E
12 Bourges 47 5N 2 22E
12 Bourgogne, Reg. 47 0N 4 30E
43 Bourke 30 8S 145 55E
62 Bourlamaque 48 5N 77 56W
7 Bournemouth 50 43N 1 53W
3 Bouvet, I. 55 0S 3 30E
64 Bow Island 49 50N 111 23W
45 Bowelling 33 25S 116 30E
42 Bowen 20 0S 148 16E
73 Bowie 32 15N 109 30W
6 Bowland Forest 54 0N 2 30W
68 Bowling Green, Ky. 37 0N 86 25W
68 Bowling Green, Ohio 41 22N 83 40W
42 Bowling Green, C. 19 19S 147 25E
70 Bowman 46 12N 103 21W
62 Bowmanville 43 55N 78 40W
8 Bowmore 55 45N 6 18W
64 Bowness 50 55N 114 25W
46 Bowser 36 19S 146 23E
65 Bowsman 52 15N 101 12W
11 Boxtel 51 36N 5 9E
9 Boyle 53 58N 8 19W
9 Boyne, R. 53 40N 6 34W
48 Boyoma, Chutes 0 12N 25 25E
45 Boyup Brook 33 47S 116 40E
72 Bozeman 45 40N 111 0W
54 Bozoum 6 25N 16 35E
11 Brabant □ 49 15N 5 20E
18 Brac, I. 43 20N 16 40E
62 Bracebridge 45 5N 79 20W
20 Bräcke 62 42N 15 32E
15 Brad 46 10N 22 50E
69 Bradenton 27 25N 82 35W
6 Bradford, U.K. 53 47N 1 45W
68 Bradford, U.S.A. 41 58N 78 41W
63 Bradore Bay 51 27N 57 18W
71 Brady 31 8N 99 25W
8 Braemar 57 2N 3 20W
13 Braga 41 35N 8 32W
79 Bragança, Brazil 1 0S 47 2W
13 Bragança, Port. 41 48N 6 50W
33 Brahmanbaria 23 50N 91 15E
33 Brahmani, R. 21 0N 85 15E
33 Brahmaputra, R. 26 30N 93 30E
6 Braich-y-Pwll, Pt. 52 47N 4 46W
15 Brăila 45 19N 27 59E
70 Brainerd 46 20N 94 10W
7 Braintree 51 53N 0 34E
56 Brak, R. 29 35S 22 55E
64 Bralorne 50 50N 123 15W
62 Brampton 43 42N 79 46W
78 Branco, R. 1 30N 61 15W
14 Brandenburg 52 24N 12 33E
65 Brandon 49 50N 100 0W
56 Brandvlei 30 25S 20 30E
15 Braniewo 54 25N 19 50E
15 Brańsk 52 45N 22 51E
62 Brantford 43 15N 80 15W
46 Branxholme 37 52S 141 49E
79 Brasília 15 55S 47 40W
79 Brasilia Legal 3 45S 55 40W
15 Braşov 45 7N 25 39E
11 Brasschaat 51 19N 4 27E
14 Bratislava 48 10N 17 7E
25 Bratsk 56 10N 101 3E
68 Brattleboro 42 53N 72 37W
14 Braunschweig 52 17N 10 28E
7 Braunton 51 6N 4 9W
29 Brava 1 20N 44 8E
73 Brawley 32 58N 115 30W
9 Bray 53 12N 6 6W
12 Bray, Reg. 49 40N 1 40E
77 Brazil ■ 10 0S 50 0W
68 Brazil 39 30N 87 8W
76 Brazilian Highlands, Mts. 18 0S 46 30W
71 Brazol, R. 30 30N 96 20W
54 Brazzaville 4 9S 15 12E
42 Breadalbane 23 48S 139 33E
8 Breadalbane, Reg. 56 30N 4 15W
47 Bream, B. 35 56S 174 35E
47 Bream Head 35 51S 174 36E
35 Brebes 6 52S 109 3E
8 Brechin 56 44N 2 40W
71 Breckenridge 32 48N 98 55W
7 Breckland, Reg. 52 30N 0 40E
7 Brecon 51 57N 3 23W
7 Brecon Beacons, Mts. 51 53N 3 27W
11 Breda 51 35N 4 45E
56 Bredasdorp 34 33S 20 2E
46 Bredbo 35 38S 149 10E
14 Bregenz 47 30N 9 45E
20 Breidafjördur 65 20N 23 0W
79 Brejo 3 41S 42 50W
14 Bremen 53 4N 8 47E
14 Bremerhaven 53 34N 8 35E
72 Bremerton 47 30N 122 48W
71 Brenham 30 5N 96 27W
14 Brenner P. 47 0N 11 30E
62 Brent, Canada 46 0N 78 30W
7 Brent, U.K. 51 33N 0 18W
7 Brentwood 51 37N 0 19W
18 Bréscia 45 33N 10 13E
14 Breslau=Wrocław 51 5N 17 5E
18 Bressanone 46 43N 11 40E
8 Bressay, I. 60 10N 1 5W
12 Bresse, Reg. 46 20N 5 10E
12 Brest, Fr. 48 24N 4 31W
22 Brest, U.S.S.R. 52 10N 23 40E
12 Bretagne, Reg. 48 0N 3 0W
15 Bretçu 46 7N 26 18E
47 Brett, C. 35 10S 174 20E
79 Breves 1 38S 50 25W
43 Brewarrina 30 0S 146 51E
69 Brewer 44 43N 68 50W
69 Brewton 31 9N 87 2W
57 Breyten 26 16S 30 0E
54 Bria 6 30N 21 58E
12 Briançon 44 54N 6 39E
* 57 Brickaville 18 49S 49 4E
7 Bridgend 51 30N 3 35W
68 Bridgeport 41 12N 73 12W
68 Bridgeton 39 29N 75 10W
45 Bridgetown, Australia 33 58S 116 7E
75 Bridgetown, Barbados 13 0N 59 30W
63 Bridgetown, Can. 44 55N 65 12W
46 Bridgewater, Australia 36 36S 143 59E
63 Bridgewater, Can. 44 25N 64 31W
7 Bridgnorth 52 33N 2 25W
7 Bridgwater 51 7N 3 0W
6 Bridlington 54 4N 0 10W
7 Bridport 50 43N 2 45W
12 Brie, Reg. 48 35N 3 10E
14 Brig 46 18N 7 59E
6 Brigg 53 33N 0 30W
72 Brigham City 41 30N 112 1W
43 Brighton, Australia 35 1S 138 30E
62 Brighton, Canada 44 3N 77 44W
7 Brighton, U.K. 50 50N 0 9W
19 Bríndisi 40 39N 17 55E
43 Brisbane 27 25S 152 54E
7 Bristol, U.K. 51 26N 2 35W
68 Bristol, U.S.A. 41 44N 72 37W
60 Bristol B. 58 0N 159 0W
7 Bristol Chan. 51 18N 3 30W
71 Bristow 35 5N 96 28W
2 British Antarctic Terr. 66 0S 45 0W
64 British Columbia □ 55 0N 125 15W
74 British Honduras■= Belize ■ 17 0N 88 30W
10 British Is. 55 0N 4 0W
57 Brits 25 37S 27 48E
56 Britstown 30 37S 23 30E
62 Britt 45 46N 80 35W
12 Brittany, Reg.= Bretagne, Reg. 48 0N 3 0W
70 Britton 45 50N 97 47W
42 Brixton 23 32S 144 52E
14 Brno 49 10N 16 35E
45 Broad Arrow 30 23S 121 15E
8 Broad Law, Mt. 55 30N 3 22W
46 Broadford 37 14S 145 4E
6 Broads, The 52 30N 1 15E
65 Brock 51 27N 108 42W
14 Brocken, Mt. 51 48N 10 40E
68 Brockton 42 8N 71 2W
62 Brockville 44 37N 75 38W
19 Brod 41 35N 21 17E
61 Brodeur Pen. 72 0N 88 0W
8 Brodick 55 34N 5 9W
70 Broken Bow 41 25N 99 35W
46 Broken Hill 31 58S 141 29E
7 Bromley 51 20N 0 5E
21 Brönderslev 57 17N 9 55E
53 Brong-Ahafo □ 7 50N 2 0W
57 Bronkhorstspruit 25 46S 28 45E
42 Bronte Pk. 42 8S 146 30E
70 Brookfield 39 50N 92 50W
71 Brookhaven 31 40N 90 25W
70 Brookings 44 19N 96 48W
60 Brooks Ra. 68 40N 147 0W
45 Brookton 32 22N 116 57E
68 Brookville 41 10N 79 6W
8 Broom, L. 57 55N 5 15W
44 Broome 18 0S 122 15W
45 Broomehill 33 40S 117 36E
8 Brora 58 0N 3 50W
9 Brosna, R. 53 8N 8 0W
61 Broughton I. 67 35N 63 50W
8 Broughty Ferry 56 29N 2 50W
7 Brown Willy, Mt. 50 35N 4 34W
71 Brownfield 33 10N 102 15W
72 Browning 48 35N 113 10W
65 Brownlee 50 43N 105 59N
71 Brownsville 25 54N 97 30W
71 Brownwood 31 45N 99 0W
44 Bruce, Mt. 22 31S 118 6E
62 Bruce Mines 46 20N 83 45W
45 Bruce Rock 31 51S 118 2E
14 Bruck 47 24N 15 16E
7 Brue, R. 51 10N 2 50W
11 Brugge 51 13N 3 13E
64 Brule 53 15N 117 38W
79 Brumado 14 13S 41 40W
34 Brunei ■ 4 52N 115 0E
42 Brunette Downs 18 38S 135 57E
14 Brünn=Brno 49 10N 16 35E
47 Brunner 42 27S 171 20E
65 Bruno 52 20N 105 30W
11 Brunssum 50 57N 5 59E
69 Brunswick, Ga. 31 10N 81 30W
69 Brunswick, Me. 43 53N 69 50W
80 Brunswick, Pen. 53 30S 71 30W
45 Brunswick Junction 33 15S 115 50E
80 Brusque 27 5S 49 0W

* *Renamed Vohibinany*

11 Brussel 50 51N 4 21 E
46 Bruthen 37 43S 147 48 E
11 Bruxelles= Brussel 50 51N 4 21 E
68 Bryan, Ohio 41 30N 84 30W
71 Bryan, Tex. 30 40N 96 27W
22 Bryansk 53 13N 34 25 E
21 Bryne 58 45N 5 36 E
15 Brzeg 50 52N 17 30 E
30 Bucak 37 28N 30 36 E
78 Bucaramanga 7 0N 73 0W
8 Buchan, Reg. 57 32N 2 8W
8 Buchan Ness, Pt. 57 29N 1 48W
65 Buchanan, Canada 51 40N 102 45W
50 Buchanan, Liberia 5 57N 10 2W
63 Buchans 49 0N 57 2W
15 Bucharest = Bucureşti 44 27N 26 10 E
73 Buckeye 33 28N 112 40W
68 Buckhannon 39 2N 80 10W
8 Buckie 57 40N 2 58W
7 Buckingham, U.K. 52 0N 0 59W
62 Buckingham, U.S.A. 45 37N 75 24W
7 Buckinghamshire □ 51 50N 0 55W
63 Buctouche 46 30N 64 45W
15 Bucureşti 44 27N 26 10 E
68 Bucyrus 40 48N 83 0W
33 Budalin 22 20N 95 10 E
15 Budapest 47 29N 19 5 E
32 Budaun 28 5N 79 10 E
7 Bude 50 49N 4 33W
53 Buea 4 10N 9 9 E
78 Buenaventura 29 15S 69 40W
80 Buenos Aires 34 30S 58 20W
80 Buenos Aires, L. 46 35S 72 30W
65 Buffalo, Canada 50 49N 110 42W
68 Buffalo, U.S.A. 42 55N 78 50W
65 Buffalo Narrows 55 52N 108 28W
15 Bug, R. 51 20N 23 40 E
78 Buga 4 0N 77 0W
52 Bugondo 1 33N 33 10 E
22 Bugulma 54 38N 52 40 E
53 Buguma 4 42N 6 55 E
38 Bugun Shara, Mts. 48 30N 102 0 E
22 Buturuslan 53 39N 52 26 E
22 Bui 58 23N 41 27 E
7 Builth Wells 52 10N 3 26W
52 Bujumbura 3 16S 29 18 E
25 Bukachacha 52 55N 116 50 E
52 Bukavu 2 20S 28 52 E
52 Bukene 4 15S 32 48 E
24 Bukhara 39 50N 64 10 E
34 Bukit Mertajam 5 22N 100 28 E
34 Bukittinggi 0 20S 100 20 E
52 Bukoba 1 20S 31 49 E
52 Bukombe 3 31S 32 3 E
53 Bukuru 9 42N 8 48 E
37 Bulak 45 2N 82 5 E
57 Bulawayo 20 7S 28 32 E
19 Bulgaria ■ 42 35N 25 30 E
29 Bulhar 10 25N 44 30 E
45 Bullabulling 31 0S 120 55 E
44 Bullara 22 30S 114 2 E
45 Bullaring 32 28S 117 40 E
42 Bullock Creek 17 40S 144 30 E
47 Bulls 40 10S 175 24 E
29 Bulo Burti 3 50N 45 33 E
32 Bulsar 20 40N 72 58 E
56 Bultfontein 28 18S 26 10 E
25 Bulun 70 37N 127 30 E
32 Bulundshahr 28 30N 77 45 E
54 Bumba 2 13N 22 30 E
53 Bumbum 14 0N 8 10 E
33 Bumhpa Bum, Mt. 26 40N 97 20 E
45 Bunbury 33 20S 115 35 E
9 Buncrana 55 8N 7 28W
43 Bundaberg 24 54S 152 22 E
32 Bundi 25 30N 75 35 E
42 Bundooma 24 54S 134 16 E
52 Bunia 1 35N 30 20 E
53 Bununu Dass 10 6N 9 25 E
53 Bununu Kasa 9 51N 9 32 E
53 Bunza 12 8N 4 0 E
52 Bura 1 6S 39 57 E
52 Bura Hills 3 20S 38 20 E
33 Burdwan 23 16N 87 54 E
6 Bure, R. 52 38N 1 38 E
19 Burgas 42 33N 27 29 E
14 Burgenland □ 47 20N 16 20 E
63 Burgeo 47 36N 57 34W
56 Burgersdorp 31 0S 26 20 E
13 Burgos 42 21N 3 41W
21 Burgsvik 57 3N 18 19 E
35 Burias, I. 13 5N 122 55 E
75 Burica, Pta 8 3N 82 51W
28 Burin 32 11N 35 15 E
34 Buriram 15 0N 103 0 E
42 Burketown 17 45S 139 33 E
62 Burks Falls 45 37N 79 10W
72 Burley 42 37N 113 55W
62 Burlington, Canada 43 25N 79 45W
70 Burlington, Colo. 39 21N 102 18W
70 Burlington, Iowa 40 50N 91 5W
70 Burlington, Kans. 38 15N 95 47W
69 Burlington, N.C. 36 7N 79 27W
68 Burlington, N.J. 40 5N 74 50W
68 Burlington, Vt. 44 27N 73 14W
72 Burlington, Wash. 48 29N 122 19W
24 Burlyu-Tyube 46 30N 79 10 E
33 Burma ■ 21 0N 96 30 E
45 Burngup 33 0S 118 35 E
42 Burnie 41 4S 145 56 E
6 Burnley 53 47N 2 15W
72 Burns 43 40N 119 4W
64 Burns Lake 54 20N 125 45W
65 Burntwood, L. 55 35N 99 40W
28 Burqa 32 18N 35 11 E
43 Burra 33 40S 138 55 E
46 Burrendong Res. 32 45S 149 10 E
80 Burruyacú 26 30S 64 45W
7 Burry Port 51 41N 4 17W
30 Bursa 40 15N 29 5 E
6 Burton-on-Trent 52 48N 1 39W
35 Buru, I. 3 30S 1263 . E
52 Burundi ■ 3 15S 30 0 E
34 Burung 0 21N 108 25 E
53 Burutu 5 20N 5 29 E
6 Bury 53 36N 2 19W
7 Bury St. Edmunds 52 15N 0 42 E
25 Buryat A.S.S.R. □ 53 0N 110 0 E
52 Busembatia 0 45N 33 32 E
52 Bushenyi 0 32S 30 11 E
52 Busia 0 25N 34 6 E
21 Buskerud □ 60 20N 9 0 E
45 Busselton 33 42S 115 15 E
11 Bussum 52 16N 5 10 E
18 Busto Arsizio 45 38N 8 50 E
54 Busu-Djanoa 1 50N 21 5 E
35 Busuanga, I. 12 10N 120 0 E
54 Buta 2 50N 24 53 E
52 Butare 2 31S 29 52 E
8 Bute, I. 55 48N 5 2W
54 Butembo 0 9N 29 18 E
52 Butere 0 14N 34 51 E
52 Butiaba 1 50N 31 20 E
68 Butler 40 52N 79 52W
8 Butt of Lewis, Pt. 58 30N 6 20W
72 Butte, Mont. 46 0N 112 31W
70 Butte, Neb. 42 56N 98 54W
34 Butterworth 5 24N 100 23 E
33 Butuan 8 52N 125 36 E
35 Butung, I. 5 0S 122 45 E
23 Buturlinovka 50 50N 40 35 E
56 Buxton, S. Afr. 27 38S 24 42 E
6 Buxton, U.K. 53 16N 1 54W
25 Buyaga 59 50N 127 0 E
38 Buyr Nuur, L. 47 50N 117 35 E
15 Buzău 45 10N 26 50 E
15 Buzău, R. 45 10N 27 20 E
36 Buzen 33 35N 131 5 E
22 Buzuluk 52 48N 52 12 E
68 Buzzards Bay 41 45N 70 38W
15 Bydgoszcz 53 10N 18 0 E
22 Byelorussian S.S.R. □ 53 30N 27 0 E
73 Bylas 33 11N 110 9W
61 Bylot I. 73 0N 78 0W
2 Byrd Ld. 79 30S 125 0W
43 Byrock 30 40S 146 27 E
43 Byron Bay 28 30S 153 30 E
20 Byske 64 59N 21 17 E
25 Byrranga, Gory 75 0N 100 0 E
15 Bytom 50 25N 19 0 E
52 Byumba 1 35S 30 4 E

C

63 Cabana 8 25S 78 5W
35 Cabanatuan 15 30N 121 5 E
79 Cabedelo 7 0S 34 50W
78 Cabimas 10 30N 71 25W
54 Cabinda 5 40S 12 11 E
72 Cabinet Mts. 48 8N 115 46W
80 Cabo Blanco 47 56S 65 47W
79 Cabo Frio 22 51S 42 3W
62 Cabonga Rés. 47 35N 76 40W
43 Caboolture 27 5S 152 47 E
55 Cabora Bassa Dam 15 30S 32 40 E
74 Caborca 30 40N 112 10W
63 Cabot Str. 47 15N 59 40W
13 Cabrera, I. 39 6N 2 59 E
65 Cabri 50 35N 108 25W
13 Cabriel, R. 39 14N 1 3W
78 Cabruta 7 50N 66 10W
19 Čačak 43 54N 20 20 E
13 Cáceres 39 26N 6 23W
62 Cache Bay 46 26N 80 0W
62 Cache Lake 49 55N 74 35W
80 Cachinal 24 59S 69 35W
79 Cachoeira 12 30S 39 0W
79 Cachoeiro de Itapemirim 20 51S 41 7W
80 Cachoeira do Sul 30 3S 52 53W
55 Caconda 13 48S 15 8 E
62 Cadillac, Canada 49 45N 108 0W
68 Cadillac, U.S.A. 44 16N 85 25W
35 Cadiz, Philippines 11 30N 123 15 E
13 Cádiz, Sp. 36 30N 6 20W
13 Cádiz, G. de 36 35N 6 20W
64 Cadomin 52 59N 117 28½W
45 Cadoux 30 47S 117 8 E
12 Caen 49 10N 0 22W
6 Caernarfon 53 8N 4 17W
6 Caernarfon B. 53 4N 4 40W
7 Caerphilly 51 34N 3 13W
28 Caesarea=Qesari 32 30N 34 53 E
79 Caetité 13 50S 42 50W
35 Cagayan de Oro 8 30N 124 40 E
18 Cágliari 39 15N 9 6 E
18 Cágliari, G. di 39 8N 9 10 E
75 Caguas 18 14N 66 4W
9 Caher 52 23N 7 56W
9 Cahirciveen 51 57N 10 13W
9 Cahore Pt. 52 34N 6 11W
12 Cahors 44 27N 1 27 E
75 Caibarién 22 30N 79 30W
78 Caicara 7 50N 66 10W
79 Caicó 6 20S 37 0W
75 Caicos Is. 21 40N 71 40W
8 Cairn Gorm, Mt. 57 7N 3 40W
8 Cairngorm Mts. 57 6N 3 42W
42 Cairns 16 55S 145 51 E
51 Cairo, Egypt= El Qâhira 30 1N 31 14 E
69 Cairo, Ga. 30 52N 84 12W
71 Cairo, Mo. 37 0N 89 10W
78 Cajamarca 7 5S 78 28W
79 Cajazeiras 7 0S 38 30W
13 Cala Millor 39 34N 3 18 E
53 Calabar 4 57N 8 20 E
78 Calaboza 9 0N 67 20W
18 Calabria □ 39 4N 16 30 E
80 Calafate 50 25S 72 25W
13 Calahorra 42 18N 1 59W
12 Calais 50 57N 1 56 E
78 Calama 22 30S 68 55W
78 Calamar 10 15N 74 55W
35 Calamian Group, Is. 11 50N 119 55 E
13 Calamocha 40 50N 1 17W
15 Călăraşi 44 14N 27 23 E
13 Calatayud 41 20N 1 40W
35 Calauag 13 55N 122 15 E
33 Calcutta 22 36N 88 24 E
6 Calder R. 53 44N 1 21W
80 Caldera 27 5S 70 55W
72 Caldwell 43 45N 116 42W
56 Caledon 34 14S 19 26 E
56 Caledon, R. 30 31S 26 5 E
13 Calella 41 37N 2 40 E
6 Calf of Man, I. 54 4N 4 48W
64 Calgary 51 0N 114 10W
78 Cali 3 25N 76 35W
32 Calicut 11 15N 75 43 E
73 Caliente 37 43N 114 34W
73 California □ 37 25N 120 0W
74 California, G. de 27 0N 111 0W
74 California, Baja, Reg. 30 0N 115 0W
80 Calingasta 31 15S 69 30W
73 Calipatria 33 8N 115 30W
56 Calitzdorp 33 30S 21 41 E
9 Callan 52 33N 7 25W
78 Callao 12 0S 77 0W
43 Callide 24 23S 150 33 E
42 Calliope 24 0S 151 16 E
57 Calo 31 37S 27 33 E
43 Caloundra 26 45S 153 10 E
18 Calatagirone 37 13N 14 30 E
18 Caltanissetta 37 30N 14 3 E
12 Calvados □ 49 5N 0 15W
12 Calvi 42 34N 8 45 E
56 Calvinia 31 28S 19 45 E
7 Cam, R. 52 21N 0 15 E
75 Camagüey 21 20N 78 0W
80 Camarones 44 50S 66 0W
32 Cambay 22 23N 72 33 E
32 Cambay, G. of 20 45N 72 30 E
34 Cambodia ■ 12 15N 105 0 E
7 Camborne 50 13N 5 18W
12 Cambrai 50 11N 3 14 E
7 Cambrian Mts. 52 10N 3 52W
62 Cambridge, Canada 43 23N 80 19W
47 Cambridge, N.Z. 37 54S 175 29 E
7 Cambridge, U.K. 52 13N 0 8 E
68 Cambridge, Mass. 42 20N 71 8W
68 Cambridge, Ohio 40 1N 81 22W
7 Cambridge □ 52 21N 0 5 E
60 Cambridge B. 69 10N 105 0W
44 Cambridge, G. 14 45S 128 0 E
46 Camden, Australia 34 5S 150 38 E
69 Camden, Ala. 31 59N 87 15W
71 Camden, Ark. 33 30N 92 50W
69 Camden, S.C. 34 17N 80 34W
71 Cameron 30 53N 97 0W
51 Cameroon ■ 3 30N 12 30 E
53 Cameroun, Mt. 4 45N 8 55 E
79 Cametá 2 0S 49 30W
13 Caminha 41 50N 8 50W
43 Camira Creek 29 15S 153 10 E
79 Camocim 2 55S 40 50W
42 Camooweal 19 56S 138 7 E
79 Camopi 3 45N 52 50W
18 Campania □ 40 50N 14 45 E
80 Campana, I. 48 20S 75 10W
3 Campbell I. 52 30S 169 0 E
64 Campbell River 50 1N 125 15W
42 Campbell Town 41 52S 147 30 E
46 Campbelltown, Australia 34 5S 150 48 E
63 Campbellton, N.B. 47 57N 66 43W
64 Campbellton, Alta. 53 32N 113 15W
8 Campbeltown 55 25N 5 36W
74 Campeche 19 50N 90 32W
74 Campeche □ 19 50N 90 32W
74 Campeche, B. de 19 30N 93 0W
46 Camperdown 38 4S 143 12 E
79 Campino Grande 7 20S 35 47W
79 Campinas 22 50S 47 0W
79 Campo Formoso 10 30S 40 20W
80 Campo Gallo 26 35S 62 50W
79 Campo Grande 20 25S 54 40W
79 Campo Maior, Brazil 4 50S 42 12W
78 Campalegre 2 48N 75 20W
18 Campobasso 41 34N 14 40 E
79 Campos 21 50S 41 20W
79 Campos Belos 13 10S 46 45W
64 Camrose 53 0N 112 50W
34 Can Tho 10 2N 105 46 E
60 Canada ■ 60 0N 100 0W
80 Cañada de Gómez 32 55S 61 30W
71 Canadian, R. 35 27N 95 3W
74 Canal Zone 9 10N 79 48W
74 Cananea 31 0N 110 20W
50 Canarias, Is. 29 30N 17 0W
75 Canarreos, Arch. de los 21 35N 81 40W
50 Canary Is.= Canarias, Is. 29 30N 17 0W
69 Canaveral, C. 28 28N 80 31W
79 Canavieiras 15 45S 39 0W
46 Canberra 35 15S 149 8 E
19 Candia=Iráklion 35 20N 25 12 E
60 Candle 65 55N 161 56W
80 Canelones 34 32S 56 10W
80 Cañete 37 50S 73 10W
55 Cangamba 13 40S 19 54W
13 Cangas de Narcea 43 10N 6 32W
79 Canguaretama 6 20S 35 5W
80 Canguçu 31 22S 52 43W
34 Canipaan 8 33N 117 15 E
64 Canmore 51 7N 115 18W
46 Cann River 37 35S 149 6 E
8 Canna, I. 57 3N 6 33W
30 Cannakale 40 5N 27 20 E
30 Cannakale Boğazi= Dardenelles, Str. 40 10N 27 20 E
32 Cannanore 11 53N 75 27 E
12 Cannes 43 32N 7 0 E
6 Cannock 52 42N 2 2W
70 Canon City 39 30N 105 20W
65 Canora 51 40N 102 30W
63 Canso 45 20N 61 0W
13 Cantabrian Mts.= Cantábrica, Cord. 43 0N 5 10W
13 Cantábrica, Cord. 43 0N 5 10W
12 Cantal □ 45 4N 2 45 E
47 Canterbury □ 43 45S 117 19 E
42 Canterbury, Australia 33 55S 151 7 E
7 Canterbury, U.K. 51 17N 1 5 E
47 Canterbury Bight 44 16S 171 55 E

47 Canterbury Plain .. 43 55S 171 22E
39 Canton, China= Kwangchow 23 10N 133 10E
70 Canton, Mo. 40 10N 91 33W
68 Canton, N.Y. 44 32N 75 3W
68 Canton, Ohio 40 47N 81 22W
2 Canton I. 36 12N 98 40W
73 Canutillo 31 55N 106 36W
72 Canyon 44 43N 110 36W
73 Canyonlands Nat. Park 38 25N 109 30W
63 Cap Breton, I. 46 0N 61 0W
63 Cap Chat 49 6N 66 40W
75 Cap Haïtien 19 40N 72 20W
42 Cape Barren, I. ... 40 25S 184 15E
53 Cape Coast 5 5N 1 15W
61 Cape Dorset 64 30N 77 0W
61 Cape Dyer 66 30N 61 0W
71 Cape Girardeau ... 37 20N 89 30W
56 Cape Province □ .. 32 0S 23 0E
56 Cape Town 33 55S 18 22E
2 Cape Verde Is.■ .. 17 10N 25 20W
42 Cape York Pen. ... 13 30S 142 30E
79 Capela 10 15S 37 0W
42 Capella 23 2S 148 1E
18 Capraia, I. 43 2N 9 50E
62 Capreol 46 40N 80 50W
18 Caprera, I. 41 12N 9 28E
18 Capri, I. 40 34N 14 15E
56 Caprivi Strip, Reg. 18 0S 23 0E
78 Caquetá, R. 3 8S 64 46W
15 Caracal 44 8N 24 22E
78 Caracas 10 30N 66 50W
79 Caracol 9 15S 64 20W
46 Caragabal 33 54S 147 50E
79 Carangola 20 50S 42 5W
45 Carani 30 57S 116 28E
15 Caransebeş 45 28N 22 18E
75 Caratasca, L. 15 30N 83 40W
79 Caratinga 19 50S 42 10W
79 Caraúbas 5 50S 37 25W
13 Caravaca 38 8N 1 52W
79 Caravelas 17 50S 39 20W
13 Carballo 43 13N 8 41W
65 Carberry 49 50N 99 25W
18 Carbonara, C. 39 8N 9 30E
72 Carbondale, Colo. . 39 30N 107 10W
71 Carbondale, Ill. ... 37 45N 89 10W
68 Carbondale, Pa. ... 41 37N 75 30W
63 Carbonear 47 42N 53 13W
12 Carcassonne 43 13N 2 20E
64 Carcross 60 20N 134 40W
44 Cardabia 23 2S 113 55E
32 Cardamon Hills ... 9 30N 77 15E
75 Cárdenas, Cuba ... 23 0N 81 30W
74 Cárdenas, Mexico . 22 0N 99 41W
7 Cardiff 51 28N 3 11W
7 Cardigan 52 6N 4 41W
7 Cardigan Bay 52 30N 4 30W
65 Cardross 49 50N 105 40W
64 Cardston 49 15N 113 20W
42 Cardwell 18 14S 146 2E
15 Carei 47 40N 22 29E
45 Carey, L. 29 0S 122 15E
3 Cargados Garajos, Is. 17 0S 59 0E
80 Carhué 37 10S 62 50W
75 Caribbean Sea 15 0N 75 0W
64 Cariboo Mts. 53 0N 121 0W
79 Carinhanha 14 15S 44 0W
14 Carinthia□= Kärnten 46 52N 13 30E
78 Caripito 10 2N 63 0W
62 Carleton Place 45 8N 76 11W
56 Carletonville 26 23S 27 22E
72 Carlin 40 50N 116 5W
9 Carlingford L. 54 0N 6 5W
70 Carlinville 39 20N 89 55W
6 Carlisle, U.K. 54 54N 2 55W
68 Carlisle, U.S.A. ... 40 12N 77 10W
9 Carlow 52 50N 6 58W
9 Carlow □ 52 43N 6 50W
71 Carlsbad 32 20N 104 7W
14 Carlsruhe= Karlsruhe 49 3N 8 23E
60 Carmacks 62 0N 136 0W
65 Carman 49 30N 98 0W
7 Carmarthen 51 52N 4 20W
28 Carmel, Mt. 32 45N 35 3E
80 Carmelo 34 0S 58 10W
78 Carmen, Col. 9 43N 75 6W
80 Carmen de Patagones 40 50S 63 0W
42 Carmila 21 53S 149 5E
13 Carmona 37 28N 5 42W
12 Carnac 47 13N 3 10W
45 Carnarvon, Australia 24 51S 113 42E
56 Carnarvon, S. Africa 30 56S 22 8E
32 Carnatic, Reg. 12 0N 79 0E
9 Carndonagh 55 15N 7 16W
45 Carnegie, L. 26 5S 122 30E
9 Carnsore Pt. 52 10N 6 20W
79 Carolina, Brazil ... 7 10S 47 30W
57 Carolina, S. Afr. .. 26 5S 30 6E
35 Caroline Is. 8 0N 150 0E
65 Caron 50 30N 105 50W
4 Carpathians, Mts. . 46 20N 26 0E
15 Carpatii Meridionali, Mts. 45 30N 25 0E
42 Carpentaria, G. of . 14 0S 139 0E
42 Carpentaria Downs 18 44S 144 20E
18 Carrara 44 5N 10 7E
9 Carrick-on-Shannon 53 57N 8 7W
9 Carrick-on-Suir ... 52 22N 7 30W
9 Carrickfergus 54 43N 5 50W
9 Carrickfergus □ ... 54 43N 5 50W
9 Carrickmacross 54 0N 6 43W
43 Carrieton 32 27S 138 27E
80 Carrizal Bajo 28 5S 71 20W
73 Carrizozo 33 40N 105 57W
70 Carroll 42 2N 94 55W
69 Carrollton 33 36N 85 5W
65 Carrot River 53 50N 101 17W
72 Carson City 39 12N 119 52W
72 Carson Sink 39 50N 118 40W
8 Carstairs 55 42N 3 41W
78 Cartagena, Col. ... 10 25N 75 33W
13 Cartagena, Sp. 37 38N 0 59W
78 Cartago, Col. 4 45N 75 55W
75 Cartago, Costa Rica 9 50N 84 0W
69 Cartersville 34 11N 84 48W
47 Carterton 41 2S 175 31E
71 Carthage, Mo. 37 10N 94 20W
68 Carthage, N.Y. 43 59N 75 37W
63 Cartwright 53 41N 56 58W
79 Caruaru 8 15S 35 55W
78 Carúpano 10 45N 63 15W
71 Caruthersville 36 10N 89 40W
73 Casa Grande 32 53N 111 51W
79 Casa Nova 9 10S 41 5W
50 Casablanca 33 43N 7 24W
18 Casale Monferrato 45 8N 8 28E
74 Casas Grandes 30 22N 108 0W
72 Cascade Ra. 44 0N 122 10W
18 Caserta 41 5N 14 20E
9 Cashel 52 31N 7 53W
80 Casilda 33 10S 61 10W
43 Casino 28 52S 153 3E
78 Casiquiare, R. 2 1N 67 7W
13 Caspe 41 14N 0 1W
80 Casper 42 52N 106 27W
4 Caspian Sea 42 30N 51 0E
14 Cassel=Kassel 51 19N 9 32E
64 Cassiar Mts. 39 30N 130 30W
55 Cassinga 15 5S 16 23E
18 Castellammare del Golfo 38 2N 12 53E
18 Castellammare di Stábia 40 47N 14 29E
13 Castellón de la Plana 39 58N 0 3W
13 Castelo Branco 39 50N 7 31W
18 Castelvetrano 37 40N 12 46E
46 Casterton 37 30S 141 30E
13 Castilla la Nueva, Reg. 39 45N 3 20W
13 Castilla la Vieja, Reg. 41 55N 4 0W
8 Castle Douglas 54 57N 3 57W
75 Castle Harbour ... 32 17N 64 44W
72 Castle Rock 46 20N 122 58W
9 Castlebar 53 52N 9 17W
9 Castleblayney 54 7N 6 44W
6 Castleford 53 43N 1 21W
64 Castlegar 49 20N 117 40W
46 Castlemaine 37 2S 144 12E
9 Castlereagh 53 47N 8 30W
9 Castlereagh □ 53 47N 8 30W
6 Castletown 54 4N 4 40W
9 Castletown Bearhaven 51 40N 9 54W
42 Castlevale 24 30S 146 48E
64 Castor 52 15N 111 50W
12 Castres 43 37N 2 13E
75 Castries 14 0N 60 50W
80 Castro, Brazil 24 45S 50 0W
80 Castro, Chile 42 30S 73 50W
79 Castro Alves 12 46S 39 33W
13 Castro del Rio 37 41N 4 29W
75 Cat I. 24 30N 75 30W
79 Catalão 18 5S 47 52W
80 Catalina 25 13S 69 43W
13 Cataluña, Reg. 41 40N 1 15E
80 Catamarca 28 30S 65 50W
18 Catánia 37 31N 15 4E
18 Catanzaro 38 54N 16 38E
35 Catarman 12 28N 124 1E
56 Cathcart 32 18S 27 10E
12 Catine, Reg. 46 30N 0 15W
41 Cato, I. 23 15S 155 32E
74 Catoche, C. 21 40N 87 0W
80 Catriló 36 23S 63 24W
78 Catrimani 0 27N 61 41W
68 Catskill 42 14N 73 52W
68 Catskill Mts. 42 15N 74 15W
23 Caucasus Mts.= Bolshoi Kavkaz . 42 50N 44 0E
79 Caucia 3 40S 38 55W
80 Cauquenes 36 0S 72 30W
63 Causapscal 48 19N 67 12W
32 Cauvery, R. 11 10N 79 51E
12 Caux, Reg. 49 38N 0 35E
9 Cavan □ 53 58N 7 10W
9 Cavan 54 0N 7 22W
46 Cavendish 37 31S 142 2E
79 Caviana, I. 0 15N 50 0W
35 Cavite 14 20N 120 55E
79 Caxias 5 0S 43 27W
80 Caxias do Sul 29 10S 51 10W
54 Caxito 8 30S 13 30E
78 Cayambe 0 3N 78 22W
79 Cayenne 5 0N 52 18W
75 Cayman Is. 19 40N 79 50W
* 74 Cayo 17 10N 89 0W
55 Cazombo 12 0S 22 48E
9 Ceanannas Mor ... 53 42N 6 53W
79 Ceara □ 5 0S 40 0W
79 Ceará=Fortaleza .. 3 35S 38 35W
80 Cebollar 29 10S 66 35W
35 Cebu 10 30N 124 0E
35 Cebu, I. 10 23N 123 58E
73 Cedar City 37 41N 113 3W
71 Cedar Creek Res. . 32 15N 96 0W
70 Cedar Falls 42 39N 92 29W
65 Cedar L. 53 30N 100 30W
70 Cedar Rapids 42 0N 91 38W
69 Cedartown 34 1N 85 15W
64 Cedarvale 55 1N 128 22W
72 Cedarville 41 37N 120 13W
79 Cedro 6 34S 39 3W
74 Cedros, I. de 28 10N 115 20W
43 Ceduna 32 7S 133 46E
18 Cefalù 38 3N 14 1E
15 Cegléd 47 11N 19 47E
74 Celaya 20 31N 100 37W
9 Celbridge 53 20N 6 33W
35 Celebes, I.= Sulawesi, I. 2 0S 120 0E
35 Celebes Sea 3 0N 123 0E
18 Celje 46 16N 15 18E
14 Celle 52 37N 10 4E
70 Centerville 31 15N 95 56W
73 Central 32 46N 108 9W
53 Central □, Ghana . 5 40N 1 20W
8 Central □, U.K. ... 56 12N 4 25W
54 Central Africa ■ .. 7 0N 20 0E
32 Central Makan Ra. 26 30N 64 15E
4 Central Russian Uplands 54 0N 36 0E
26 Central Siberian Plat. 65 0N 105 0E
70 Centralia, Ill. 38 32N 89 5W
72 Centralia, Wash. .. 46 46N 122 59W
19 Cephalonia, I.= Kefallinía, I. 38 28N 20 30E
35 Ceram, I.= Seram, I. 3 10S 129 0E
80 Ceres, Arg. 29 55S 61 55W
56 Ceres, S. Africa ... 33 21S 19 18E
18 Cerignola 41 17N 15 53E
30 Çerkeş 40 40N 32 58E
15 Cernavodă 44 22N 28 3E
74 Cerralvo, I. 24 20N 109 45E
74 Cerritos 22 20N 100 20W
13 Cervera 41 40N 1 16E
18 Cesena 44 9N 12 14E
14 Česke Budějovice . 48 55N 14 25E
14 Ceskomoravská Vrchovina 49 20N 15 30E
15 Český Těšín 49 45N 18 39E
46 Cessnock 33 0S 151 15E
19 Cetinje 42 23N 18 59E
50 Ceuta 35 52N 5 26W
12 Cevennes, Mts. 44 10N 3 50E
30 Ceyhan 37 4N 35 47E
32 Ceylon= Sri Lanka ■ 7 30N 80 50E
12 Chablais, Reg. 46 20N 6 45E
32 Chachran 28 55N 70 28E
80 Chaco Austral, Reg. 27 30S 61 40W
78 Chaco Boreal, Reg. 22 30S 60 10W
80 Chaco Central, Reg. 24 0S 61 0W
51 Chad ■ 12 30N 17 15E
51 Chad, L. 13 30N 14 30W
70 Chadron 42 50N 103 0W
53 Chafe 11 56N 6 55E
31 Chagai Hills 29 30N 63 0E
3 Chagos Arch. 6 0S 72 0E
31 Chah Bahar 25 20N 60 40E
52 Chake Chake 5 15S 39 45E
31 Chakhansur 31 10N 62 0E
* 31 Chakhansur □ 30 25N 62 0E
33 Chakradharpur 22 45N 85 40E
32 Chakwal 32 50N 72 45E
39 Chaling 26 55N 113 30E
32 Chalisgaon 20 30N 75 10E
78 Challapata 19 0S 66 50W
12 Chalon-sur-Saône . 46 48N 4 50E
12 Châlons-sur-Marne 48 58N 4 20E
32 Chaman 30 55N 66 22E
32 Chamba, India 32 35N 76 10E
52 Chamba, Tanz. 11 35S 36 58E
68 Chambersburg 39 53N 77 41W
12 Chambéry 45 34N 5 55E
55 Chambeshi 10 58S 31 5E
63 Chambord 48 25N 72 6W
37 Chamdo 31 21N 97 2E
80 Chamical 30 22S 66 19W
12 Chamonix 45 55N 6 51E
12 Champagne, Reg. . 49 0N 4 40E
70 Champaign 40 8N 88 14W
68 Champlain, L. 44 30N 73 20W
74 Champotón 19 20N 90 50W
80 Chañaral 26 15S 70 50W
39 Chanchiang= Chankiang 21 7N 110 21E
32 Chanda 19 57N 79 25E
60 Chandalar 67 30N 148 30W
71 Chandeleur Sd. ... 29 58N 88 40W
32 Chandigarh 30 44N 76 47E
63 Chandler, Canada . 48 18N 64 46W
73 Chandler, U.S.A. .. 33 20N 111 56W
33 Chandpur 29 8N 78 19E
57 Changane, R. 24 45S 33 37E
38 Changchih 36 7N 113 0E
39 Changchow, Fukien 24 32N 117 44E
39 Changchow, Kiangsu 31 45N 120 0E
38 Changchow, Shantung 36 55N 118 3E
38 Changchun 43 58N 125 9E
39 Changhua 24 2N 120 30E
38 Changkiakow 40 52N 114 45E
39 Changkiang 21 7N 110 21E
38 Changli 39 40N 119 19E
38 Changpai 41 26N 128 0E
38 Changpai Shan, Mts. 42 0N 128 0E
39 Changping, Fukien 25 30N 117 33E
38 Changping, Peiping 40 15N 116 15E
39 Changpu 24 2N 117 31E
39 Changsha 28 5N 113 1E
39 Changshu 31 33N 120 45E
39 Changtai 24 34N 117 50E
39 Changteh 29 12N 111 43E
39 Changting 25 46N 116 30E
38 Changwu 42 21N 122 45E
37 Changyeh 39 0N 100 59E
32 Channaptna 12 40N 77 15E
7 Channel Is. 49 30N 2 40W
13 Chantada 42 37N 7 46W
34 Chanthaburi 12 38N 102 12E
71 Chanute 37 45N 95 25W
37 Chanyi 25 56N 104 1E
34 Chao Phraya, R. .. 13 32N 100 36E
39 Chaoan 23 45N 117 11E
39 Chaochow 23 45N 116 32E
39 Chaohwa 32 16N 105 41E
37 Chaotung 27 30N 103 40E
38 Chaoyang 41 46N 120 16E
74 Chapata, L. 20 10N 103 20W
24 Chapayevo 50 25N 51 10E
22 Chapayevsk 53 0N 49 40E
69 Chapel Hill 35 53N 79 3W
62 Chapleau 47 45N 83 30W
33 Chapra 25 48N 84 50E
80 Charadai 27 40S 59 55W
78 Charagua 19 45S 63 10W
78 Charambira, Pta. .. 4 20N 77 30W
78 Charaña 17 30S 69 35W
37 Charchan 38 4N 85 16E
37 Charchan, R. 39 0N 86 0E
7 Chard, U.K. 50 52N 2 59W
65 Chard, U.S.A. 55 55N 111 10W
24 Chardara 41 16N 67 59E
24 Chardzhou 39 0N 63 20E

* Renamed San Ignacio

* Renamed Nīmrūz

12 Charente □ 45 50N 0 36W
12 Charente-Maritime □ 45 50N 0 35W
51 Chari, R. 12 58N 14 31E
31 Charikar 35 0N 69 10E
37 Charkhlikh 39 16N 88 17E
11 Charleroi 50 24N 4 27E
68 Charles, C. 37 10N 75 52W
70 Charles City 43 2N 92 41W
71 Charleston, Mass. 34 2N 90 3W
69 Charleston, S.C. 32 47N 79 56W
68 Charleston, W.Va. 38 24N 81 36W
75 Charlestown, Nevis 17 8N 62 37W
57 Charlestown, S. Afr. 27 30S 29 55E
43 Charleville, Australia 26 24S 146 15E
9 Charleville, Eire= Rath Luire 52 21N 8 40W
43 Charleville 26 24S 146 15E
12 Charleville-Mézières 49 44N 4 40E
69 Charlotte 35 16N 80 46W
75 Charlotte Amalie 18 22N 64 56W
14 Charlottenburg 52 31N 13 16E
68 Charlottesville 38 1N 78 30W
63 Charlottetown 46 19N 63 3W
46 Charlton 36 16S 143 24E
70 Charlton 40 59N 93 20W
62 Charlton I. 52 0N 79 20W
63 Charny 46 43N 71 15W
12 Charolles 46 27N 4 16E
42 Charters Towers 20 5S 146 13E
12 Chartres 48 29N 1 30E
80 Chascomús 35 30S 58 0W
60 Chatanika 65 7N 147 31W
12 Château Salins 48 49N 6 30E
12 Châteaubriant 47 43N 1 23W
12 Châteauroux 46 50N 1 40E
12 Châtellerault 46 50N 0 30E
7 Chatham, U.K. 51 22N 0 32E
63 Chatham, N.B. 47 2N 65 28W
62 Chatham, Ont. 42 23N 82 15W
68 Chatham, Alas. 57 30N 135 0W
2 Chatham Is. 44 0S 176 40W
64 Chatham Str. 57 0N 134 40W
33 Chatrapur 19 21N 85 0E
69 Chattahoochee 30 43N 84 51W
69 Chattanooga 35 2N 85 17W
12 Chaumont 48 7N 5 8E
79 Chaves, Brazil 0 15S 49 55W
13 Chaves, Port. 41 45N 7 32W
14 Cheb 50 9N 12 20E
22 Cheboksary 56 8N 47 30E
68 Cheboygan 45 38N 84 29W
38 Chefoo=Yentai 37 30N 121 21E
25 Chegdomyn 51 7N 132 52E
72 Chehallis 46 44N 122 59W
39 Cheju 33 28N 126 30E
39 Cheju Do, I. 33 29N 126 34E
39 Chekiang □ 29 30N 120 0E
80 Chelforó 39 0S 66 40W
24 Chelkar 47 40N 59 32E
24 Chelkar Tengiz Solonchak 48 0N 62 30E
15 Chełm 51 8N 23 30E
15 Chełmno 53 20N 18 30E
7 Chelmsford 51 44N 0 29E
15 Chełmza 53 10N 18 39E
46 Chelsea 38 5S 145 8E
7 Cheltenham 51 55N 2 5W
24 Chelyabinsk 55 10N 61 35E
64 Chemainus 48 54N 123 41W
57 Chemba 17 11S 34 53E
22 Chemikovsk 54 58N 56 0W
14 Chemnitz= Karl Marx Stadt 50 50N 12 55E
72 Chemult 43 14N 121 54W
32 Chenab, R. 29 23N 71 2E
39 Chengchou= Chengchow 34 47N 113 46E
39 Chengchow 34 47N 113 46E
37 Chengkiang 24 58N 102 59E
38 Chengteh 41 0N 117 55E
38 Chengting 38 8N 114 37E
37 Chengtu 30 45N 104 0E
38 Chengyang 36 20N 120 16E
39 Chenhsien 25 45N 112 37E
39 Chenning 25 57N 105 51E
38 Chentung 46 2N 123 1E
39 Chenyuan 27 0N 108 20E
75 Chepo 9 10N 79 6W
7 Chepstow 51 39N 2 41W
70 Chequamegon B. 46 40N 90 30W
12 Cher, R. 47 21N 0 29E
12 Cher □ 47 10N 2 30E
12 Cherbourg 49 39N 1 40W
50 Cherchell 36 35N 21 63E
22 Cherdyn 60 20N 56 20E
25 Cheremkhovo 53 32N 102 40E
24 Cherepanovo 54 15N 83 30E
22 Cherepovets 59 5N 37 55E
23 Cherkassy 49 30N 32 0E
22 Chernigov 51 28N 31 20E
23 Chernovtsy 48 0N 26 0E
25 Chernoye 70 30N 89 10E
70 Cherokee 42 40N 95 30W
22 Cheropovets 59 5N 37 55E
80 Cherquenco 38 35S 72 0W
33 Cherrapunji 25 17N 91 47E
25 Cherskogo Khrebet 65 0N 143 0E
7 Cherwell, R. 51 44N 1 15W
68 Chesapeake B. 38 0N 76 12W
6 Cheshire □ 53 14N 2 30W
6 Chester, U.K. 53 12N 2 53W
68 Chester, Pa. 39 54N 75 20W
69 Chester, S.C. 34 44N 81 13W
6 Chesterfield 53 14N 1 26W
60 Chesterfield Inlet 63 30N 91 0W
41 Chesterfield Is. 19 52S 158 15E
74 Chetumal 18 30N 88 20W
74 Chetumal, B. de 18 40N 88 10W
6 Cheviot, The, Mt. 55 28N 2 8W
6 Cheviot Hills 55 20N 2 30W
54 Chew Bahir, L. 4 40N 30 50E
72 Chewelah 48 25N 117 56W
70 Cheyenne 41 9N 104 49W
70 Cheyenne, R. 44 40N 101 15W
32 Chhindwara 22 2N 78 59E
34 Chi, R. 15 13N 104 45E
39 Chiai 23 29N 120 25E
55 Chianje 15 35S 13 40E
74 Chiapas □ 17 0N 92 45W
18 Chiávari 44 20N 9 20E
18 Chiavenna 46 18N 9 23E
36 Chiba 35 30N 140 7E
36 Chiba □ 35 30N 140 20E
55 Chibemba 15 48S 14 8E
62 Chibougamau 49 56N 74 24W
53 Chibuk 10 52N 12 50E
68 Chicago 41 45N 87 40W
68 Chicago Heights 41 29N 87 37W
64 Chichagof I. 58 0N 136 0W
7 Chichester 50 50N 0 47W
74 Chichén Itzá 20 40N 88 34W
36 Chichibu 36 5N 139 10E
38 Chichirin 50 35N 123 45E
71 Chickasha 35 0N 98 0W
13 Chiclana de la Frontera 36 26N 6 9W
78 Chiclayo 6 42S 79 50W
72 Chico 39 45N 121 54W
80 Chico, R. 43 50S 66 25W
68 Chicopee 42 6N 72 37W
63 Chicoutimi 48 28N 71 5W
61 Chidley, C. 60 30N 64 15W
54 Chiengi 8 38S 29 10E
37 Chiengmai 18 55N 98 55E
18 Chieti 42 22N 14 10E
78 Chiguana 21 0S 67 50W
38 Chihfeng 42 10N 118 56E
39 Chihing 25 2N 113 45E
39 Chihkiang 27 21N 109 45E
38 Chihli, G. of= Po Hai, G. 38 30N 119 0E
39 Chihsien 35 29N 114 1E
74 Chihuahua 28 40N 106 3W
74 Chihuahua □ 28 40N 106 3W
24 Chiilí 44 10N 66 55E
32 Chilas 35 25N 74 5E
43 Childers 25 15S 152 17E
71 Childress 34 30N 100 50W
77 Chile ■ 35 0S 71 15W
80 Chilecito 29 0S 67 40W
78 Chilete 7 10S 78 50W
55 Chililabombwe 12 18S 27 43E
38 Chilin=Kirin 43 58N 126 31E
33 Chilka L. 19 40N 85 25E
80 Chillán 36 40S 72 10W
70 Chillicothe, Mo. 39 45N 93 30W
68 Chillicothe, Ohio. 39 53N 82 58W
64 Chilliwack 49 10N 122 0W
80 Chiloé, I. de 42 50S 73 45W
74 Chilpancingo 17 30N 99 40W
46 Chiltern 36 10S 146 36E
7 Chiltern Hills 51 44N 0 42W
52 Chilumba 10 28N 34 12E
39 Chilung 25 3N 121 45E
55 Chilwa, L. 15 15S 35 40E
37 Chimai 34 0N 101 39E
52 Chimala 8 55S 34 4E
78 Chimborazo, Mt. 1 20S 78 55W
78 Chimbote 9 0S 78 35W
24 Chimkent 42 40N 69 25E
33 Chin □ 22 0N 93 0E
37 China ■ 35 0N 100 0E
38 Chinan=Tsinan 34 50N 105 40E
75 Chinandega 12 30N 87 0W
78 Chincha Alta 13 20S 76 0W
43 Chinchilla 26 45S 150 38E
38 Chinchow 41 10N 121 2E
57 Chinde 18 45S 36 30E
33 Chindwin, R. 21 26N 95 15E
39 Ching Ho, R. 34 20N 109 0E
55 Chingola 12 31S 27 53E
55 Chingole 13 4S 34 17E
38 Ch'ingtao= Tsingtao 36 0N 120 25E
38 Chinhae 35 9N 128 58E
32 Chiniot 31 45N 73 0E
38 Chinju 35 12N 128 2E
39 Chinkiang 32 2N 119 29E
73 Chino Valley 34 54N 112 28W
12 Chinon 47 10N 0 15E
65 Chinook, Canada 51 28N 110 59W
72 Chinook, U.S.A. 48 35N 109 19W
52 Chintheche 11 50S 34 5E
38 Chinwangtao 40 0N 119 31E
18 Chióggia 45 13N 12 15E
19 Chios, I.= Khíos, I. 38 20N 26 0E
64 Chip Lake 53 35N 115 35W
55 Chipata 13 38S 32 28E
* 57 Chipinga 20 13S 32 36E
7 Chippenham 51 27N 2 7W
70 Chippewa, R. 44 25N 92 10W
70 Chippewa Falls 44 56N 91 24W
74 Chiquimula 14 51N 89 37W
78 Chiquinquira 5 37N 73 50W
32 Chirala 15 50N 80 20E
24 Chirchik 81 58N 69 15E
60 Chirikof I. 55 50N 155 35W
75 Chiriquí, G. de 8 0N 82 10W
75 Chiriquí, L. de 9 10N 82 0W
75 Chiriqui, Mt. 8 55N 82 35W
57 Chiromo 16 30S 35 7E
55 Chisamba 14 55S 28 20E
25 Chita 52 0N 113 25E
55 Chitembo 13 30S 16 50E
32 Chitorgarh 24 52N 74 43E
75 Chitré 7 59N 80 27W
33 Chittagong 22 19N 91 55E
33 Chittagong □ 24 5N 91 25E
32 Chittoor 13 15N 79 5E
18 Chiusi 43 1N 11 58E
18 Chivasso 45 10N 7 52E
80 Chivilcoy 35 0S 60 0W
52 Chiwanda 11 22S 34 54E
56 Chobe Nat. Park 18 25S 24 15E
80 Choele Choel 39 11S 65 40W
15 Choinice 53 42N 17 40E
12 Cholet 47 4N 0 52W
75 Choluteca 13 20N 87 14W
55 Choma 16 48S 26 59E
14 Chomutov 50 28N 13 23E
34 Chon Buri 13 21N 101 1E
38 Chonan 36 56N 127 3E
78 Chone 0 40S 80 0W
38 Chongjin 41 51N 129 58E
38 Chŏngju, N. Korea 39 41N 125 13E
38 Chŏngju, S. Korea 36 39N 127 27E
38 Chŏnju 35 50N 127 4E
80 Chonos, Arch. de los 45 0S 75 0W
6 Chorley 53 39N 2 39W
15 Chorzow 50 18N 19 0E
80 Chos-Malal 37 20S 70 15W
36 Chóshi 35 45N 140 45E
14 Choszczno 53 7N 15 25E
72 Choteau 47 50N 112 10W
32 Chotila 22 25N 71 11E
38 Choybalsan 48 3N 114 28E
47 Christchurch, N.Z. 43 33S 172 47W
7 Christchurch, U.K. 50 44N 1 47W
56 Christiana 27 52S 25 8E
44 Christmas Creek 18 29S 125 23E
3 Christmas I. Indian Oc. 10 0S 105 40E
† 2 Christmas I. Pacific Oc. 1 58N 157 27W
24 Chu 43 36N 73 42E
39 Chu Kiang, R. 24 50N 113 37E
39 Chuanchow 24 57N 118 31E
39 Chuanhsien 25 50N 111 12E
36 Chūbu □ 36 45N 137 0E
80 Chubut, R. 43 20S 65 5W
38 Chucheng 36 0N 119 16E
39 Chuchow 27 56N 113 3E
22 Chudskoye, Oz. 58 13N 27 30E
60 Chugiak 61 25N 149 30W
36 Chūgoku □ 35 0N 133 0E
36 Chūgoku-Sanchi, Mts. 35 0N 133 0E
39 Chuhsien 30 51N 107 1E

† Renamed Kiritimati
* Renamed Chipinge

52 Chuka 0 23S 37 38E
34 Chukai 4 13N 103 25E
25 Chukotskiy Khrebet 68 0N 175 0E
25 Chukotskoye More 68 0N 175 0W
73 Chula Vista 33 44N 117 8W
39 Chumatien 33 0N 114 4E
80 Chumbicha 29 0S 66 10W
25 Chumikan 54 40N 135 10E
34 Chumphon 10 35N 99 14E
38 Chunchŏn 37 58N 127 44E
39 Ch'ungch'ing= Chungking 29 30N 106 30E
39 Chunghsien 30 17N 108 4E
39 Chungking 29 30N 106 30E
37 Chungtien 28 0N 99 30E
38 Chungwei 37 35N 105 10E
52 Chunya 8 30S 33 27E
14 Chur 46 52N 9 32E
65 Churchill 58 45N 94 5W
65 Churchill, R., Man. 58 47N 94 12W
63 Churchill, R., Newf. 53 30N 60 10W
64 Churchill Pk. 58 10N 125 10W
32 Churu 28 20N 75 0E
39 Chusan, I. 30 0N 122 20E
22 Chuvash A.S.S.R. □ 53 30N 48 0E
22 Chuvovoy 58 15N 57 40E
35 Cianjur 6 81S 107 7E
35 Cibatu 7 8S 107 59E
68 Cicero 41 48N 87 48W
15 Ciechanów □ 53 0N 20 0E
75 Ciego de Avila 21 50N 78 50W
78 Ciénaga 11 0N 74 10W
75 Cienfuegos 22 10N 80 30W
15 Cieszyn 49 45N 18 35E
13 Cieza 38 17N 1 23W
35 Cilacap 7 43S 109 0E
71 Cimarron, R. 36 10N 96 17W
35 Cimahi 6 53S 107 33E
15 Cîmpina 45 10N 25 45E
15 Cîmpulung 45 17N 25 3E
13 Cinca, R. 41 26N 0 21E
68 Cincinnati 39 10N 84 26W
12 Cinto, Mt. 42 24N 8 54E
60 Circle 47 26N 105 35W
68 Circleville, Ohio 39 35N 82 57W
73 Circleville, Utah 38 12N 112 24W
35 Cirebon 6 45S 108 32E
7 Cirencester 51 43N 1 59W
71 Cisco 32 25N 99 0W
74 Citlaltepetl, Mt. 19 0N 97 20W
56 Citrusdal 32 35S 19 0E
74 Ciudad Acuña 29 20N 101 10W
78 Ciudad Bolívar 8 5N 63 30W
74 Ciudad Camargo 27 41N 105 10W
74 Ciudad de Valles 22 0N 98 30W
74 Ciudad del Carmen 18 20N 97 50W
78 Ciudad Guayana 8 20N 62 35W
74 Ciudad Guzmán 19 40N 103 30W
74 Ciudad Juárez 31 40N 106 28W
74 Ciudad Madero 22 19N 97 50W
74 Ciudad Mante 22 50N 99 0W
74 Ciudad Obregón 27 28N 109 59W
78 Ciudad Piar 7 27N 63 19W
13 Ciudad Real 38 59N 3 55W
13 Ciudad Rodrigo 40 35N 6 32W
74 Ciudad Victoria 23 41N 99 9W
18 Civitanova Marche 43 18N 13 41E
18 Civitavécchia 42 6N 11 46E
30 Çivril 38 20N 29 55E
45 Clackline 31 40S 116 32E
7 Clacton 51 47N 1 10E
56 Clanwilliam 32 11S 18 52E
9 Clara 53 20N 7 38W
43 Clare 33 20S 143 50E
9 Clare □ 52 52N 8 55W
9 Clare, R. 53 20N 9 3W
68 Claremont 43 23N 72 20W
71 Claremore 36 20N 95 20W
9 Claremorris 53 45N 9 0W
80 Clarence, I. 54 0S 72 0W
44 Clarence, Str. 12 0S 131 0E
47 Clarence, R. 42 10S 173 56E
71 Clarendon 34 41N 91 20W
63 Clarenville 48 10N 54 1W
64 Claresholm 50 0N 113 45W
70 Clarinda 40 45N 95 0W
72 Clark Fork, R. 48 9N 116 15W
73 Clarkdale 34 53N 112 3W
63 Clarke City 50 12N 66 38W
63 Clarkes Harbour 43 25N 65 38W
68 Clarksburg 39 18N 80 21W
71 Clarksdale 34 12N 90 33W
72 Clarkston 46 28N 117 2W

69 Clarksville 36 32N 87 20W
68 Clayton 44 14N 76 5W
9 Clear, I. 51 26N 9 30W
68 Clearfield 41 0N 78 27W
64 Clearwater, Canada 51 38N 120 2W
69 Clearwater, U.S.A. 27 58N 82 45W
* 62 Clearwater L. 56 10N 75 0W
71 Cleburne 32 18N 97 25W
7 Clee Hills 55 25N 2 35W
6 Cleethorpes 53 33N 0 2W
42 Clermont, Australia 22 46S 147 38E
12 Clermont-Ferrand 45 46N 3 4E
7 Clevedon 51 27N 2 51W
43 Cleveland, Australia 27 31S 153 3E
71 Cleveland, Miss. 33 34N 90 43W
68 Cleveland, Ohio 41 28N 81 43W
69 Cleveland, Tenn. 35 9N 84 52W
71 Cleveland, Tex. 30 18N 95 0W
6 Cleveland □ 54 30N 1 12W
72 Cleveland, Mt. 48 56N 113 51W
6 Cleveleys 53 53N 3 3W
9 Clew B. 53 54N 9 50W
9 Clifden, Eire 53 30N 10 2W
47 Clifden, N.Z. 46 1S 167 42E
73 Clifton 33 8N 109 23W
68 Clifton Forge 37 49N 79 51W
69 Clingmans Dome, Mt. 35 35N 83 30W
64 Clinton, B.C. 51 0N 121 40W
62 Clinton, Ont. 43 38N 81 33W
47 Clinton, N.Z. 46 12S 169 23E
70 Clinton, Ark. 35 37N 92 30W
69 Clinton, Ill. 40 8N 89 0W
70 Clinton, Iowa 41 50N 90 18W
68 Clinton, Mass. 42 26N 71 40W
70 Clinton, Mo. 38 20N 93 40W
71 Clinton, N.C. 35 5N 78 15W
60 Clinton Colden L. 64 0N 107 0W
2 Clipperton I. 10 18N 109 13W
57 Clocolan 28 55S 27 34E
9 Clonakilty 51 37N 8 53W
42 Cloncurry 20 40S 140 28E
75 Clones 54 10N 7 13W
9 Clonmel 52 22N 7 42W
70 Cloquet 46 40N 92 30W
71 Clovis, Calif. 36 54N 119 45W
73 Clovis, N.Mex 34 20N 103 10W
15 Cluj 46 47N 23 38E
47 Clutha, R. 46 20S 169 49E
6 Clwyd □ 53 0N 3 15W
6 Clwyd, R. 53 20N 3 30W
61 Clyde, Canada 70 30N 68 30W
47 Clyde, N.Z. 45 12S 169 20E
8 Clyde, R. 55 56N 4 29W
8 Clyde, Firth of 55 42N 5 0W
8 Clydebank 55 54N 4 25W
73 Coachella 33 44N 116 13W
63 Coachman's Cove 50 6N 56 20W
74 Coahuila □ 27 0N 112 30W
64 Coaldale, Canada 49 45N 112 35W
73 Coalinga 36 10N 120 21W
6 Coalville 52 43N 1 21W
64 Coast Mts. 52 0N 126 0W
72 Coast Ra. 40 0N 124 0W
45 Coastal Plains Basin 30 10S 115 30E
8 Coatbridge 55 52N 4 2W
74 Coatepeque 14 46N 91 55W
63 Coaticook 45 10N 71 46W
61 Coats I. 62 30N 82 0W
74 Coatzalcoalcos 18 7N 94 35W
80 Coazapá 26 0S 56 35W
62 Cobalt 47 25N 79 42W
74 Coban 15 30N 90 21W
46 Cobar 31 27S 145 48E
9 Cobh 51 50N 8 18W
43 Cobham 30 10S 142 0E
62 Cobourg 44 0N 78 20W
14 Coburg 50 15N 10 58E
33 Cocanada = Kakinada 16 55N 82 20E
78 Cochabamba 17 15S 66 20W
34 Cochin-China, Reg. = Nam-Phan, Reg. 10 30N 106 0E
64 Cochrane, Alta. 51 20N 114 30W
62 Cochrane, Ont. 49 0N 81 0W
80 Cochrane, L. 47 10S 72 0W
46 Cockburn, Australia 32 5S 141 2E
80 Cockburn, Canada 54 30S 72 0W
75 Coco, R. 15 0N 83 8W
3 Cocos Is. 12 12S 96 54E
58 Cod, C. 42 8N 70 10W
78 Codajás 3 40S 62 0W
79 Codó 4 30S 43 55W
75 Codrington 17 43N 61 49W
72 Cody 44 35N 109 0W
42 Coen 13 52S 143 12E
72 Coeur d'Alene 47 45N 116 51W
71 Coffeyville 37 0N 95 40W
43 Coffs Harbour 30 16S 153 5E
12 Cognac 45 41N 0 20W
68 Cohoes 42 47N 73 42W
46 Cohuna 35 45S 144 15E
75 Coiba, I. 7 30N 81 40W
80 Coig, R. 51 0S 69 10W
80 Coihaique 45 35S 72 8W
32 Coimbatore 11 2N 76 59E
13 Coimbra 40 15N 8 27W
13 Coín 36 40N 4 48W
78 Cojimies 0 20N 80 0W
74 Cojutepeque 13 41N 88 54W
46 Colac 38 10S 143 30E
70 Colby 39 27N 101 2W
7 Colchester 51 54N 0 55E
65 Cold Lake 54 27N 110 10W
8 Coldstream 55 39N 2 14W
62 Coldwell 48 45N 86 30W
68 Colebrook 44 54N 71 29W
71 Coleman 31 52N 99 30W
57 Colenso 28 44S 29 50E
46 Coleraine, Australia 37 36S 141 40E
9 Coleraine, U.K. 55 8N 6 40W
9 Coleraine □ 55 8N 6 40W
56 Colesburg 30 45S 25 5E
80 Colhué Huapí, L. 45 30S 69 0W
56 Coligny 26 17S 26 18E
74 Colima 19 10N 103 50W
74 Colima □ 19 10N 103 40W
79 Colinas 6 0S 44 10W
46 Colinton 35 50S 149 10E
8 Coll, I. 56 40N 6 35W
69 College Park 33 42N 84 27W
45 Collie 33 25S 116 30E
44 Collier, B. 16 0S 124 0E
42 Collingwood, Australia 22 20S 142 31E
62 Collingwood, Canada 44 30N 80 20W
47 Collingwood, N.Z. 40 42S 172 40E
42 Collinsville 20 30S 147 56E
9 Collooney 54 11N 8 28W
12 Colmar 48 5N 7 20E
6 Colne 53 51N 2 11W
46 Colo, R. 33 20S 150 40E
14 Cologne = Köln 50 56N 9 58E
78 Colombia ■ 3 45N 73 0W
79 Colombia 3 24N 79 49W
32 Colombo 6 56N 79 58E
74 Colón 9 20N 80 0W
45 Colona 31 38S 132 5E
80 Colonia del Sacramento 34 25S 57 50W
80 Colonia 25 de Mayo 38 0S 67 32W
8 Colonsay, I. 56 4N 6 12W
73 Colorado □ 37 40N 106 0W
80 Colorado, R., Arg. 39 50S 62 8W
73 Colorado, R. Mex.–U.S.A. 31 45N 114 40W
71 Colorado, R., U.S.A. 28 36N 95 58W
73 Colorado Aqueduct 34 0N 115 20W
71 Colorado City 32 25N 100 50W
73 Colorado Plat. 36 40N 110 30W
70 Colorado Springs 38 55N 104 50W
71 Columbia, La. 32 7N 92 5W
70 Columbia, Mo. 38 58N 92 20W
69 Columbia, S.C. 34 0N 81 0W
69 Columbia, Tenn. 35 40N 87 0W
68 Columbia, District of □ 38 55N 77 0W
64 Columbia, Mt. 52 20N 117 30W
72 Columbia, R. 45 49N 120 0W
72 Columbia Falls 48 25N 114 16W
70 Columbia Heights 45 5N 93 10W
72 Columbia Plat. 47 30N 118 30W
69 Columbus, Ga. 32 30N 84 58W
68 Columbus, Ind. 39 14N 85 55W
69 Columbus, Miss. 33 30N 88 26W
70 Columbus, N.D. 48 52N 102 48W
68 Columbus, Ohio 39 57N 83 1W
47 Colville, C. 36 29S 175 21E
60 Colville, R. 70 25N 150 30W
6 Colwyn Bay 53 17N 3 44W
18 Comácchio 44 41N 12 10E
80 Comallo 41 0S 70 5W
42 Comet 23 36S 148 38E
33 Comilla 23 22N 91 18E
18 Comino, I. 36 0N 14 22E
74 Comitán 16 18N 92 9W
61 Committee B. 68 0N 87 0W
71 Commerce 33 15N 95 50W
18 Como 45 48N 9 5E
18 Como, L. di 46 5N 9 17E
80 Comodoro Rivadavia 45 50S 67 40W
32 Comorin, C. 8 3N 77 40E
48 Comoro Is. 12 10S 44 15E
64 Comox 49 42N 125 0W
12 Compiègne 49 24N 2 50E
50 Conakry 9 29N 13 49W
42 Conard Junction 41 48S 143 70E
12 Concarneau 47 52N 3 56W
79 Conceição do Araguaia 8 0S 49 2W
79 Conceiçao do Barra 18 50S 39 50W
80 Concepción, Chile 36 50S 73 0W
80 Concepción, Paraguay 23 30S 57 20W
80 Concepción, Canal. 50 50S 75 0W
73 Concepcion, Pt. 34 30N 120 34W
74 Concepción del Oro 24 40N 101 30W
80 Concepción del Uruguay 32 35S 58 20W
69 Concord, N.C. 35 28N 80 35W
68 Concord, N.H. 43 5N 71 30W
80 Concordia, Arg. 31 20S 58 2W
70 Concordia, U.S.A. 39 35N 97 40W
43 Condamine 26 55S 150 3E
46 Condobolin 33 4S 147 6E
6 Congleton 53 10N 2 12W
54 Congo ■ 1 0S 16 0E
54 Congo (Kinshasa)■ = Zaïre ■ 3 0S 22 0E
54 Congo, R. = Zaïre, R. 6 4S 12 24E
48 Congo Basin 1 0S 23 0E
73 Congress 34 11N 112 56W
62 Coniston 46 32N 80 51W
32 Conjeeveram = Kanchipuram 12 52N 79 45E
42 Conjuboy 18 35S 144 45E
9 Connacht □ 53 23N 8 40W
68 Conneaut 41 55N 80 32W
68 Connecticut □ 41 40N 72 40W
68 Connecticut, R. 41 17N 72 21W
9 Connemara 53 29N 9 45W
68 Connersville 39 40N 85 10W
65 Conquest 53 35N 107 0W
71 Conroe 30 15N 95 28W
79 Conselheiro 20 40S 43 8W
6 Consett 54 51N 1 49W
65 Consort 52 1N 110 46W
14 Constance, L. = Bodensee 47 35N 9 25E
15 Constanța 44 14N 28 38E
50 Constantine 36 25N 6 42E
80 Constitución 35 20S 72 30W
71 Conway, Ark. 35 5N 92 30W
68 Conway, N.H. 43 58N 71 8W
69 Conway, S.C. 33 49N 79 2W
6 Conwy 53 17N 3 50W
6 Conwy R. 53 17N 3 50W
33 Cooch Behar 26 22N 89 29E
45 Cook 30 42S 130 48E
80 Cook, B. 55 10S 70 0W
60 Cook Inlet 59 0N 151 0W
2 Cook Is. 22 0S 157 0W
47 Cook, Mt. 43 36S 170 9E
47 Cook, Str. 41 15S 174 29E
69 Cookeville 36 12N 85 30W
56 Cookhouse 32 44S 25 47E
42 Cooktown 15 30S 145 16E
9 Cookstown □ 54 40N 6 43W
43 Coolabah 31 0S 146 15E
43 Coolangatta 28 11S 153 29E
45 Coolgardie 30 55S 121 8E
73 Coolidge 33 1N 111 35W
73 Coolidge Dam 33 10N 110 30W
46 Cooma 36 12S 149 8E
46 Coonabarabran 31 14S 149 18E
46 Coonamble 30 56S 148 27E
45 Coonana 31 0S 123 0E
43 Coongoola 27 43S 145 47E
69 Cooper. 39 57N 75 7W
43 Cooper Creek, R., L. 28 0S 139 0E
43 Coorong, The 35 50S 139 20E
45 Coorow 29 50S 115 59E
43 Cooroy 26 22S 152 54E
72 Coos Bay 43 26N 124 7W
46 Cootamundra 34 36S 148 1E
9 Cootehill 54 5N 7 5W
21 Copenhagen = København 55 41N 12 34E
80 Copiapó 27 15S 70 20E
60 Copper Center 62 10N 145 25W
62 Copper Cliff 46 30N 81 4W
64 Copper Mountain 49 20N 120 30W
60 Coppermine 68 0N 116 0W
6 Coquet, R. 55 22N 1 37W
54 Coquilhatville = Mbandaka 0 1N 18 18E
80 Coquimbo 30 0S 71 20W
15 Corabia 43 48N 24 30E
78 Coracora 15 5S 73 45W
61 Coral Harbour 64 0N 83 0W
62 Coral Rapids 50 20N 81 40W
41 Coral Sea 15 0S 150 0E
68 Corbin 37 0N 84 3W
7 Corby 52 29N 0 41W
73 Corcoran 36 6N 119 35W
13 Corcubión 42 56N 9 12W
69 Cordele 31 55N 83 49W
80 Córdoba, Arg. 31 20S 64 10W
74 Córdoba, Mexico 26 20N 103 20W
13 Córdoba, Sp. 37 50N 4 50W
80 Córdoba, Sa. de 31 10S 64 25W
35 Cordon 16 42N 121 32E
60 Cordova 60 36N 145 45W
42 Corfield 21 40S 143 21E
19 Corfu, I. = Kérkira, I. 39 38N 19 50E
18 Corigliano Cálabro 39 36N 16 31E
69 Corinth 34 54N 88 30W
75 Corinto, Nic. 12 30N 87 10W
79 Corinto, Brazil 18 20S 44 30W
9 Cork 51 54N 8 30W
9 Cork □ 51 54N 8 30W
30 Çorlu 41 11N 27 49E
65 Cormorant 54 5N 100 45W
75 Corn Is. 12 0N 83 0W
63 Corner Brook 49 0N 58 0W
72 Corning, Calif. 39 56N 122 9W
68 Corning, N.Y. 42 10N 77 3W
62 Cornwall 45 5N 74 45W
7 Cornwall □ 50 26N 4 40W
78 Coro 11 30N 69 45W
79 Coroatá 4 20S 44 0W
78 Corocoro 17 15S 69 19W
47 Coromandel 36 45S 175 31E
32 Coromandel Coast Reg. 12 30N 81 0E
73 Corona 33 49N 117 36W
73 Coronado 32 45N 117 9W
75 Coronado, B. de 9 0N 83 40W
60 Coronation G. 68 0N 114 0W
80 Coronel 37 0S 73 10W
80 Coronel Dorrego 38 40S 61 10W
80 Coronel Pringles 38 0S 61 30W
80 Coronel Suárez 37 30S 62 0W
71 Corpus Christi 27 50N 97 28W
57 Correntes, C. das 24 11S 35 34E
12 Corrèze □ 45 20N 1 50E
9 Corrib, L. 53 25N 9 10W
80 Corrientes 27 30S 58 45W
75 Corrientes, C., Cuba 21 43N 84 30N
78 Corrientes, C., Col. 5 30N 77 34W
45 Corrigin 32 18S 117 45E
68 Corry 41 55N 79 39W
12 Corse, C. 43 1N 9 25E
12 Corse, I. 42 0N 9 0E
12 Corse du Sud □ 41 40N 9 0E
12 Corsica, I. = Corse, I. 42 0N 9 0E
71 Corsicana 32 5N 96 30W
73 Cortez 37 24N 108 35W
68 Cortland 42 35N 76 11W
18 Cortona 43 16N 12 0E
30 Çorum 40 30N 35 5E
78 Corumbá 19 0S 57 30W
13 Corunna = La Coruña 43 20N 8 25W
72 Corvallis 44 36N 123 15W
74 Cosamalopan 18 23N 95 50W
18 Cosenza 39 17N 16 14E
68 Coshocton 40 17N 81 51W
80 Costa, Cord. de la 30 0S 71 0W
13 Costa Blanca, Reg. 38 25N 0 10W
13 Costa Brava, Reg. 41 30N 3 0E
13 Costa del Sol, Reg. 36 30N 4 30W
13 Costa Dorada, Reg. 40 45N 1 15E
75 Costa Rica ■ 10 0N 84 0W
35 Cotabato 7 8N 124 13E
12 Côte d'Or □ 47 30N 4 50E
12 Côte d'Or, Reg. 47 10N 4 50E
12 Cotentin, Reg. 49 30N 1 30W
12 Côtes-du-Nord □ 48 28N 2 50W
53 Cotonou 6 20N 2 25E

* *French nameform*

 Eau Claire, L. à l'

78 Cotopaxi, Mt. 0 30s 78 30w
7 Cotswold Hills 51 42n 2 10w
72 Cottage Grove 43 48n 123 2w
14 Cottbus .... 51 44n 14 20 e
73 Cottonwood 34 48n 112 1w
72 Coulee City 47 44n 119 12w
60 Council, Alas. 64 55n 163 45w
72 Council, Id. 44 45n 116 30w
70 Council Bluffs 41 20n 95 50w
64 Courtenay 49 45n 125 0w
7 Coventry 52 25n 1 32w
13 Covilhã 40 17n 7 31w
69 Covington, Ga. 33 36n 83 50w
68 Covington, Ky. 39 5n 84 30w
65 Cowan 52 5n 100 45w
45 Cowan, L. .... 31 45s 121 45 e
46 Cowangie .... 35 12s 141 26 e
62 Cowansville 45 14n 72 46w
8 Cowdenbeath 56 7n 3 20w
43 Cowell .... 33 38s 136 40 e
7 Cowes 50 45n 1 18w
46 Cowra .... 33 49s 148 42 e
79 Coxim 18 30s 54 55w
33 Cox's Bazar ...... 21 25n 92 3 e
74 Cozumel, I. de 20 30n 86 40w
15 Cracow=
Kraków .... 50 4n 19 57 e
56 Cradock .... 32 8s 25 36 e
72 Craig 40 32n 107 44w
9 Craigavon □ 54 27n 6 26w
15 Craiova .... 44 21n 23 48 e
* 54 Crampel .... 7 8n 19 8 e
65 Cranberry Portage . 54 36n 101 22w
42 Cranbrook,
Tas. .... 42 0s 148 5 e
45 Cranbrook,
W. Australia .... 34 20s 117 35 e
64 Cranbrook
Canada 49 30n 115 55w
79 Crateús 5 10s 40 50w
79 Crato, Brazil 7 10s 39 25w
68 Crawfordsville 40 2n 86 51w
7 Crawley 51 7n 0 10w
12 Crécy .... 48 50n 2 53 e
65 Cree L. 57 30n 107 0w
18 Cremona .... 45 8n 10 2 e
18 Cres, I. .... 44 58n 14 25 e
72 Crescent City 41 45n 124 12w
62 Cressman 47 40n 72 55w
64 Creston, Canada .. 49 10n 116 40w
70 Creston, U.S.A. ... 41 0n 94 20w
69 Crestview 30 45n 86 35w
4 Crete, I. .... 35 10n 25 0 e
13 Creus, C. .... 42 20n 3 19 e
12 Creuse □ .... 46 0n 2 0 e
12 Creuse, R. .... 47 0n 0 34 e
6 Crewe 53 6n 2 28w
80 Criciúma 28 40s 49 23w
8 Crieff 56 22n 3 50w
23 Crimea=
Krymskaya, Reg. 45 0n 34 0 e
8 Crinan 56 4n 5 30w
74 Cristóbal 9 10n 80 0w
15 Crişul Alb, R. ..... 46 42n 21 17 e
15 Crişul Negru, R. .. 46 42n 21 16 e
19 Crna, R. .... 41 35n 21 59 e
19 Crna Gora □ ..... 42 40n 19 20 e
19 Crna Gora, Mts. .. 42 20n 21 30 e
71 Crockett 31 20n 95 30w
44 Croker, I. .... 11 12s 132 32 e
8 Cromarty 57 40n 4 2w
6 Cromer .... 52 56n 1 18 e
47 Cromwell .... 45 3s 169 14 e
46 Cronulla .... 34 3s 151 8 e
75 Crooked I. 22 50n 74 10w
70 Crookston 47 50n 96 40w
6 Cross Fell, Mt. 54 44n 2 29w
53 Cross River □ .... 6 20n 8 20 e
9 Crosshaven 51 48n 8 19w
18 Crotone .... 39 5n 17 6 e
72 Crow Agency 45 40n 107 30w
9 Crow Hd. 51 34n 10 9w
71 Crowley 30 15n 92 20w
64 Crowsnest P. 49 40n 114 40w
42 Croydon,
Australia ...... 18 15s 142 14 e
7 Croydon, U.K. 51 18n 0 5w
3 Crozet Is. .... 46 27s 52 0 e
80 Cruz Alta 28 40s 53 32w
80 Cruz del Eje 30 45s 64 50w
79 Cruzeiro 22 50s 45 0w
78 Cruzeiro do Sul ... 7 35s 72 35w
43 Crystal Brook .... 33 21s 138 13 e
71 Crystal City 38 15n 90 23w
15 Csongrád .... 46 43n 20 12 e
55 Cuamba .... 14 45s 36 22 e
55 Cuando, R. .... 14 0s 19 30 e
75 Cuba ■ 22 0n 79 0w

* Renamed Kaga Bandoro

45 Cuballing .... 32 50s 117 15 e
56 Cubango, R. ...... 18 50s 22 25 e
78 Cucui 1 10n 66 50w
78 Cúcuta 7 54n 72 31w
32 Cuddalore .... 11 46n 79 45 e
32 Cuddapah .... 14 30n 78 47 e
45 Cue .... 27 20s 117 55 e
78 Cuenca, Ecuador .. 2 50s 79 9w
13 Cuenca, Sa. de 39 55n 1 50w
74 Cuernavaca 18 50n 99 20w
71 Cuero 29 5n 97 17w
13 Cuevas de
Almanzora 37 18n 1 58w
79 Cuiabá 15 30s 56 0w
8 Cuillin Hills 57 14n 6 15w
56 Cuito, R. .... 18 1s 20 48 e
74 Cuitzeo, L. 19 55n 101 5w
46 Culcairn .... 35 41s 147 3 e
13 Culebra, Sa. de la . 41 55n 6 20w
74 Culiacán 24 50n 107 40w
8 Cullen 57 45n 2 50w
44 Cullen, Pt. .... 11 50s 141 47 e
13 Cullera 39 9n 0 17w
8 Culloden Moor 57 29n 4 7w
47 Culverden .... 42 47s 172 49 e
78 Cumaná 10 30n 64 5w
64 Cumberland,
Canada 49 40n 125 0w
68 Cumberland,
U.S.A. 39 40n 78 43w
61 Cumberland Pen. .. 67 0n 65 0w
58 Cumberland Plat. .. 36 0n 84 30w
61 Cumberland Sd. ... 65 30n 66 0w
6 Cumbria □ 54 44n 2 55w
6 Cumbrian, Mts. ... 54 30n 3 0w
32 Cumbum .... 15 40n 79 10 e
45 Cunderdin .... 31 39s 117 15 e
56 Cunene, R. .... 17 20s 11 50 e
18 Cúneo .... 44 23n 7 32 e
43 Cunnamulla ...... 28 4s 145 41 e
65 Cupar, Canada 51 0n 104 10w
8 Cupar, U.K. 56 20n 3 0w
78 Cupica, G. de 6 25n 77 30w
75 Curaçao 12 10n 69 0w
78 Curiapo 8 33n 61 5w
80 Curicó 34 55s 71 20w
80 Curitiba 25 20s 49 10w
79 Currais Novos 6 13s 36 30w
79 Curralinho 1 35s 49 30w
43 Currawilla .... 25 10s 141 20 e
72 Currie 40 16n 114 45w
42 Curtis, I. .... 23 40s 151 15 e
79 Curuçá 0 35s 47 50w
79 Cururupu 1 50s 44 50w
80 Curuzú Cuatiá 29 50s 58 5w
79 Curvelo 18 45s 44 27w
46 Curya .... 35 53s 142 54 e
71 Cushing 31 43n 94 50w
70 Custer 43 45n 103 38w
72 Cut Bank 48 40n 112 15w
33 Cuttack .... 20 25n 85 57 e
45 Cuvier, C. .... 23 14s 113 22 e
14 Cuxhaven .... 53 52n 8 42 e
68 Cuyahoga Falls 41 8n 81 30w
78 Cuzco, Mt. 20 0s 66 50w
78 Cuzco 13 32s 72 0w
19 Cyclades, Is.=
Kikládhes, Is. ... 37 20n 24 30 e
42 Cygnet .... 43 8s 147 1 e
30 Cyprus ■ .... 35 0n 33 0 e
51 Cyrenaica=Barqa
Reg. .... 27 0n 20 0 e
51 Cyrene=Shahhat .. 32 39n 21 18 e
14 Czechoslovakia ■ . 49 0n 17 0 e
15 Częstochowa ...... 50 49n 19 7 e

D

37 Da, R. .... 16 0n 107 0 e
34 Da Lat .... 12 3n 108 32 e
34 Da Nang .... 16 10n 108 7 e
53 Dabai .... 11 25n 5 15 e
50 Dabakala 8 15n 4 20w
14 Dąbie .... 53 27n 14 45 e
50 Dabola 10 50n 11 5w
* 33 Dacca .... 23 43n 90 26 e
* 33 Dacca □ .... 24 0n 90 0 e
78 Dadanawa 3 0n 59 30w
53 Dadiya .... 9 35n 11 24 e
32 Dadu .... 26 45n 67 45 e
23 Dagesta
A.S.S.R. □ ..... 42 30n 47 0 e
35 Dagupan .... 16 3n 120 33 e

* Renamed Dhākā

50 Dahomey ■=
Benin ■ .... 8 0n 2 0 e
9 Daingean 53 18n 7 15w
38 Dairen=Talien .... 39 0n 121 31 e
51 Dairût .... 27 34n 30 43 e
45 Dairy Creek ..... 25 12s 115 48 e
36 Daisetsu-Zan, Mt. . 43 30n 142 57 e
42 Dajarra .... 21 42s 139 30 e
50 Dakar 14 34n 17 29w
50 Dakhla 23 50n 15 53w
23 Dakhovskaya ..... 44 13n 40 13 e
53 Dakingari .... 11 37n 4 1 e
38 Dalai Nor, L. ..... 49 0n 117 50 e
21 Dalälven, R. ...... 60 38n 17 27 e
38 Dalandzadgad .... 43 35n 104 30 e
21 Dalarö .... 59 8n 18 24 e
32 Dalbandin .... 28 53n 64 25 e
8 Dalbeattie 54 56n 3 49w
43 Dalby .... 27 11s 151 16 e
71 Dalhart 36 4n 102 31w
63 Dalhousie 48 0n 66 26w
28 Daliyat el Karmel . 32 41n 35 3 e
8 Dalkeith 55 54n 3 4w
71 Dallas 32 47n 96 48w
31 Dalma, I. .... 24 30n 52 20 e
18 Dalmacija, Reg. ... 43 0n 17 0 e
18 Dalmatia, Reg.=
Dalmacija, Reg. . 43 0n 17 0 e
8 Dalmellington 55 20n 4 25w
25 Dalnerechensk .... 45 50n 133 40 e
50 Daloa 6 53n 6 27w
62 Dalton, Canada ... 60 10n 137 0n
69 Dalton, Neb. 41 27n 103 0w
44 Daly, R. .... 13 20s 130 19 e
42 Daly Waters ..... 16 15s 133 22 e
32 Daman .... 20 25n 72 57 e
32 Daman, Dadra &
Nagar Haveli □ . 20 25n 72 58 e
51 Damanhûr .... 31 2n 30 28 e
56 Damaraland, Reg. . 22 33s 17 6 e
30 Damascus=
Dimashq .... 33 30n 36 18 e
53 Damataru .... 11 45n 11 55 e
31 Damāvand .... 35 45n 52 10 e
31 Damāvand,
Qolleh-ye, Mt. .. 35 56n 52 8 e
15 Dâmboviţa, R. .... 44 40n 26 0 e
31 Dāmghan .... 36 10n 54 17 e
51 Damietta=
Dumyât .... 31 24n 31 48 e
28 Damiya .... 32 6n 35 34 e
32 Damoh .... 23 50n 79 28 e
44 Dampier .... 20 39s 116 45 e
35 Dampier, Selat .... 0 40s 130 40 e
28 Dan .... 33 13n 35 39 e
53 Dan Dume .... 11 28n 7 8 e
53 Dan Gulbi .... 11 40n 6 15 e
53 Dan Yashi .... 12 0n 8 5 e
50 Danané 7 16n 8 9w
68 Danbury 41 23n 73 29w
46 Dandenong ...... 37 52s 145 12 e
53 Dangora .... 11 25n 8 7 e
63 Daniel's Harbour . 50 13n 57 35w
22 Danilov .... 58 16n 40 13 e
53 Danja .... 11 29n 7 30 e
53 Dankama .... 13 20n 7 44 e
32 Dankhar Gompa .. 32 9n 78 10 e
21 Dannemora .... 60 11n 16 49 e
47 Dannevirke ...... 40 12s 176 8 e
57 Dannhauser ...... 28 0s 30 3 e
68 Dansville 42 32n 77 41w
15 Danube,
R. (Donau)
=Dunărea, R. .. 45 20n 29 40 e
68 Danville, Ill. 40 10n 87 45w
68 Danville, Ky. 37 40n 84 45w
69 Danville, Va. 36 40n 79 20w
15 Danzig=
Gdánsk .... 54 22n 18 40 e
53 Dapango .... 10 52n 0 12 e
46 Dapto .... 34 30s 150 47 e
28 Dar'a .... 32 37n 36 6 e
52 Dar-es-Salaam .... 6 50s 39 12 e
31 Dārāb .... 28 50n 54 30 e
53 Darazo .... 11 1n 10 24 e
32 Darband .... 34 30n 72 50 e
33 Darbhanga ...... 26 15n 86 3 e
64 D'Arcy 50 35n 122 30w
30 Dardanelles=
Cannakale
Boğazi, Str. ..... 40 0n 26 20 e
51 Dârfûr □ .... 15 35n 25 0 e
51 Dârfûr, Reg. ...... 12 35n 25 0 e
32 Dargai .... 34 25n 71 45 e
24 Dargan Ata ...... 40 40n 62 20 e
47 Dargaville .... 35 57s 173 52 e
38 Darhan .... 49 27n 105 57 e
78 Darién, G. del 9 0n 77 0w

14 Darmstadt .... 49 51n 8 40 e
57 Darnall .... 29 23s 31 18 e
60 Darnley, B. 69 30n 124 30w
42 Darr .... 24 34s 144 52 e
7 Dart, R. 50 34n 3 56w
46 Dartmoor .... 37 56s 141 19 e
7 Dartmoor, Reg. ... 50 36n 4 0w
42 Dartmouth,
Australia ...... 23 30s 144 40 e
63 Dartmouth
Canada 44 40n 63 30w
7 Dartmouth, U.K. .. 50 21n 3 35w
33 Darjeeling .... 27 3n 88 18 e
63 Dark Cove 49 54n 54 5w
45 Darkan .... 33 19s 116 37 e
46 Darling, R. .... 34 4s 141 54 e
43 Darling Downs .... 27 30s 150 30 e
45 Darling Ra. .... 32 0s 116 30 e
6 Darlington 54 33n 1 33w
14 Darłowo .... 54 26n 16 23 e
24 Darvaza .... 40 12n 58 24 e
44 Darwin .... 12 20s 130 50 e
44 Darwin River ..... 12 49s 130 58 e
* 30 Daryācheh-ye
Reza'iyeh, L. ... 37 30n 45 30 e
31 Das .... 35 5n 75 4 e
51 Dashen, Ras, Mt. .. 13 10n 38 26 e
38 Dashinchilen ..... 47 50n 103 60 e
32 Dasht, R. .... 25 10n 61 40 e
31 Dasht-e Kavir,
Des. .... 34 30n 55 0 e
31 Dasht-e Lút,
Des. .... 31 30n 58 0 e
32 Datia .... 25 39n 78 27 e
22 Daugavpils ...... 55 53n 26 32 e
31 Daulat Yar ...... 34 33n 65 46 e
65 Dauphin 51 15n 100 5w
12 Dauphiné, Reg. ... 45 15n 5 25 e
53 Daura .... 13 2n 8 21 e
32 Davangere .... 14 25n 75 50 e
35 Davao .... 7 0n 125 40 e
35 Davao G. .... 6 30n 125 48 e
70 Davenport,
Iowa 41 30n 90 40w
72 Davenport,
Wash. 47 40n 118 5w
7 Daventry 52 16n 1 10w
75 David 8 30n 82 30w
60 Davis, Alas. 51 52n 176 39w
72 Davis, Calif. 38 39n 121 45w
63 Davis Inlet 55 50n 60 45w
2 Davis Str. 68 0n 58 0w
14 Davos .... 46 48n 9 50 e
60 Dawson 64 4n 139 25w
64 Dawson Creek 55 46n 120 14w
80 Dawson, I. 53 50s 70 50w
28 Dayr al-Ghusūn ... 32 21n 35 5 e
30 Dayr az Zawr .... 35 20n 40 9 e
28 Dayral Balah .... 31 25n 34 21 e
68 Dayton, Ohio 39 45n 84 10w
72 Dayton, Wash. 46 20n 118 0w
69 Daytona Beach ... 29 14n 81 0w
45 D'Entrecasteaux,
Pt. .... 34 50s 116 0 e
56 De Aar .... 30 39s 24 0 e
44 De Grey .... 20 30s 120 0 e
44 De Grey, R. ...... 20 12s 119 11 e
70 De Kalb 41 55n 88 45w
69 De Land 29 1n 81 19w
71 De Ridder 30 48n 93 15w
70 De Soto 38 8n 90 34w
28 Dead Sea=
Miyet, Bahr el .. 31 30n 35 30 e
70 Deadwood 44 25n 103 43w
45 Deakin .... 30 46s 129 0 e
7 Deal .... 51 13n 1 25 e
7 Dean, Forest of ... 51 50n 2 35w
80 Deán Funes 30 20s 64 20w
60 Dease Arm, B. 66 45n 120 6w
64 Dease Lake 58 40n 130 5w
73 Death Valley 36 0n 116 40w
73 Death Valley
Nat. Mon. 36 30n 117 0w
73 Death Valley
Junction 36 15n 116 30w
53 Deba Habe ...... 10 14n 11 20 e
51 Debre Markos .... 10 20n 37 40 e
51 Debre Tabor ..... 11 50n 38 5 e
15 Debrecen .... 47 33n 21 42 e
69 Decatur, Ala. 34 35n 87 0w
69 Decatur, Ga. 33 47n 84 17w
70 Decatur, Ill. 39 50n 89 0w
68 Decatur, Ind. 40 52n 85 28w
26 Deccan, Reg. ..... 18 0n 77 0 e
70 Decorah 43 20n 91 50w
53 Dédougou 12 30n 3 35w
8 Dee, R., Scot. 57 4n 3 7w
6 Dee, R., Wales 53 15n 3 7w

* Renamed Orūmīyeh, L.

42 Deep Well 24 25 S 134 5 E
43 Deepwater 29 25 S 151 51 E
63 Deer Lake 49 11 N 57 27 W
72 Deer Lodge 46 25 N 112 40 W
32 Deesa 24 18 N 72 10 E
68 Defiance 41 20 N 84 20 W
28 Deganya 32 43 N 35 34 E
29 Degeh Bur 8 14 N 43 35 E
53 Degema 4 50 N 6 48 E
14 Deggendorf 48 49 N 12 59 E
31 Deh Bīd 30 39 N 53 11 E
32 Dehra Dun 30 20 N 78 4 E
28 Deir Dibwan 31 55 N 35 15 E
15 Dej 47 10 N 23 52 E
73 Del Norte 37 47 N 106 27 W
71 Del Rio 29 15 N 100 50 W
48 Delagoa B. 25 50 S 32 45 E
73 Delano 35 48 N 119 13 W
56 Delareyville 26 41 S 25 26 E
68 Delaware 40 20 N 83 0 W
68 Delaware □ 39 0 N 75 40 W
68 Delaware, R. 41 50 N 75 15 W
11 Delft 52 1 N 4 22 E
11 Delfzijl 53 20 N 6 55 E
52 Delgado, C. 10 45 S 40 40 E
51 Delgo 20 6 N 30 40 E
32 Delhi 28 38 N 77 17 E
74 Delicias 28 10 N 105 30 W
79 Delmiro Gonveia 9 24 S 38 6 W
25 Delong, Os. 76 30 N 153 0 E
42 Deloraine 41 30 S 146 40 E
68 Delphos 40 51 N 84 17 W
69 Delray Beach 26 27 N 80 4 W
73 Delta 38 44 N 108 5 W
43 Delungra 29 40 S 150 45 E
13 Demanda, Sa. de 42 15 N 3 0 W
73 Deming 48 49 N 122 13 W
64 Demmit 55 26 N 119 54 W
69 Demopolis 32 31 N 87 50 W
34 Dempo, Mt. 4 2 S 103 9 E
11 Den Helder 52 54 N 4 45 E
24 Denau 38 16 N 67 54 E
6 Denbigh 53 11 N 3 25 W
34 Dendang 3 5 S 107 54 E
11 Dendermonde 51 2 N 4 7 E
53 Denge 12 52 N 5 21 E
53 Dengi 9 25 N 9 55 E
45 Denham 25 55 S 113 32 E
65 Denholm 52 40 N 108 0 W
13 Denia 38 49 N 0 8 E
46 Deniliquin 35 32 S 144 58 E
71 Denison 33 45 N 96 33 W
30 Denizli 37 46 N 29 6 E
45 Denmark 34 57 S 117 21 E
21 Denmark ■ 56 0 N 10 0 E
2 Denmark Str. 67 0 N 25 0 W
34 Denpasar 8 39 S 115 13 E
71 Denton 33 13 N 97 8 W
70 Denver 39 43 N 105 1 W
33 Deoghar 24 30 N 86 59 E
32 Deolali 19 56 N 73 50 E
32 Deosai Mts. 35 10 N 75 20 E
45 Depot Springs 27 55 S 120 3 E
25 Deputatskiy 69 18 N 139 54 E
32 Dera Ghazi Khan 30 3 N 70 38 E
32 Dera Ismail Khan 31 50 N 70 50 E
† 32 Dera Ismail Khan □ 31 50 N 70 54 E
23 Derbent 42 3 N 48 18 E
44 Derby, Australia 17 18 S 123 38 E
6 Derby, U.K. 52 55 N 1 29 W
6 Derby □ 52 55 N 1 29 W
9 Derg, L. 53 0 N 8 20 W
* 51 Derna 32 40 N 22 35 E
46 Derrinallum 37 57 S 143 13 E
46 Derriwong 33 6 S 147 21 E
9 Derry= Londonderry 55 0 N 7 20 W
9 Derryveagh Mts. 55 0 N 8 40 W
51 Derudub 17 31 N 36 7 E
6 Derwent R. Cumbria 54 42 N 3 22 W
6 Derwent, R. Derby 53 26 N 1 44 W
6 Derwent, R. Yorks 54 13 N 0 35 W
6 Derwentwater, L. 53 34 N 3 9 W
70 Des Moines 41 35 N 93 37 W
70 Des Moines, R. 41 15 N 93 0 W
80 Deseado, R. 40 0 S 69 0 W
73 Desert Center 33 45 N 115 27 W
22 Desna, R. 52 0 N 33 15 E
80 Desolación, I. 53 0 S 74 10 W
14 Dessau 51 50 N 12 14 E
14 Detmold 51 56 N 8 52 E
68 Detroit 42 20 N 83 3 W
70 Detroit Lakes 46 49 N 95 57 W
11 Deurne, Belgium 51 13 N 4 28 E
11 Deurne, Neth. 51 28 N 5 47 E

* Darnah
† Now part of North West Frontier

14 Deutsche, B. 54 30 N 7 30 E
12 Deux-Sèvres □ 46 30 N 0 20 W
15 Deva 45 53 N 22 55 E
11 Deventer 52 15 N 6 10 E
8 Deveron, R. 57 22 N 3 0 W
70 Devils Lake 48 7 N 98 59 W
7 Devizes 51 22 N 1 59 W
64 Devon 53 22 N 113 44 W
7 Devon □ 50 45 N 3 50 W
58 Devon I. 75 0 N 87 0 W
42 Devonport, Australia 41 11 S 146 21 E
47 Devonport, N.Z. 36 49 S 174 48 E
7 Devonport, U.K. 50 22 N 4 10 W
32 Dewas 22 57 N 76 4 E
6 Dewsbury 53 42 N 1 37 W
31 Deyhūk 33 17 N 57 30 E
31 Deyyer 27 50 N 51 55 E
30 Dezfūl 32 23 N 48 24 E
† 30 Dezh Shāhpūr 35 31 N 46 10 E
30 Dhahaban 21 58 N 39 3 E
30 Dhahran= Az Zahrān 26 10 N 50 7 E
29 Dhamar 14 46 N 44 23 E
33 Dhamtari 20 42 N 81 33 E
33 Dhanbad 23 47 N 86 26 E
32 Dhar 22 36 N 75 18 E
32 Dharmapuri 12 8 N 78 10 E
32 Dharwar 15 28 N 75 1 E
33 Dhaulagiri, Mt. 28 42 N 83 31 E
33 Dhenkanal 20 45 N 85 35 E
19 Dhidhimotikhon 41 21 N 26 30 E
19 Dhodhekánisos, Is. 36 35 N 27 10 E
32 Dholpur 26 42 N 77 54 E
32 Dhrol 22 34 N 70 25 E
33 Dhubri 26 1 N 89 59 E
29 Dhula 15 5 N 48 5 E
32 Dhulia 20 54 N 74 47 E
56 Diamante 32 5 S 60 35 W
79 Diamantina 18 5 S 43 40 W
42 Diamantina, R. 26 45 S 139 10 E
79 Diamantino 14 25 S 56 27 W
33 Diamond Harbour 22 11 N 88 14 E
53 Diapangou 12 5 N 0 10 E
54 Dibaya Lubue 4 12 S 19 54 E
31 Dibba 25 45 N 56 16 E
29 Dibi 4 12 N 41 58 E
33 Dibrugarh 27 29 N 94 55 E
70 Dickinson 46 53 N 102 47 W
64 Didsbury 51 40 N 114 8 W
65 Diefenbaker L. 51 0 N 106 55 W
3 Diego Garcia, I. 7 20 S 72 25 E
80 Diego Ramirez, Is. 56 30 S 68 44 W
* 57 Diégo-Suarez 12 16 S 49 17 E
* 57 Diégo-Suarez □ 14 0 S 49 0 E
12 Dieppe 49 56 N 1 5 E
11 Differdange 49 32 N 5 32 E
63 Digby 44 41 N 65 50 W
33 Dighinala 23 15 N 92 5 E
12 Digne 44 6 N 6 14 E
33 Dihang, R. 27 30 N 96 30 E
30 Dijlah, Nahr 30 90 N 47 50 E
12 Dijon 47 19 N 5 1 E
24 Dikson 73 30 N 80 35 E
53 Dikwa 12 2 N 13 56 E
35 Dili 8 33 S 125 35 E
72 Dillon, Mont. 45 13 N 112 38 W
69 Dillon, S.C. 34 25 N 79 22 W
30 Dimashq 33 30 N 36 18 E
50 Dimbokro 6 39 N 4 42 W
46 Dimboola 36 27 S 142 2 E
19 Dimitrovgrad, Bulgaria 42 3 N 25 36 E
22 Dimitrovgrad, U.S.S.R. 54 25 N 49 33 E
35 Dinagat, I. 10 10 N 125 35 E
33 Dinajpur 35 38 N 88 38 E
12 Dinan 48 27 N 2 2 W
11 Dinant 50 16 N 4 55 E
30 Dinar 38 4 N 30 10 E
31 Dinar, Kuh-e, Mt. 30 48 N 51 40 E
18 Dinara Planina, Mts. 43 50 N 16 35 E
12 Dinard 48 38 N 2 4 W
4 Dinaric Alps, Mts. 43 50 N 16 35 W
32 Dindigul 10 21 N 77 58 E
9 Dingle 52 8 N 10 15 W
9 Dingle, B. 52 5 N 10 15 W
42 Dingo 23 39 S 149 20 E
50 Dinguiraye 11 18 N 10 43 W
8 Dingwall 57 35 N 4 29 W
72 Dinosaur Nat. Mon. 40 32 N 108 58 W
73 Dinuba 36 32 N 119 23 W
50 Diourbel 14 40 N 16 15 W

* Renamed Antsiranana
† Renamed Marīvān

35 Dipolog 8 36 N 123 20 E
29 Dire Dawa 9 37 N 41 52 E
75 Diriamba 11 53 N 86 15 W
56 Dirico 17 50 S 20 42 E
45 Dirk Hartog, I. 25 48 S 113 0 E
43 Dirranbandi 28 35 S 148 14 E
72 Disappointment.C. 46 18 N 124 3 W
44 Disappointment, L. 23 30 S 122 50 E
60 Discovery 63 0 N 115 0 W
46 Discovery, B. 38 12 S 141 7 E
53 Disina 11 35 N 9 50 E
2 Disko, I. 69 50 N 53 30 W
7 Diss 52 23 N 1 6 E
32 Disteghil Sar, Mt. 36 22 N 75 12 E
79 Districto Federal □ 15 45 S 47 45 W
74 Distrito Federal □ 19 15 N 99 10 W
32 Diu 20 43 N 70 69 E
23 Divnoye 45 55 N 43 27 E
70 Dixon 41 50 N 89 29 W
64 Dixon Entrance 54 25 N 132 30 W
30 Diyarbakir 37 55 N 40 14 E
35 Djajapura= Jayapura 2 28 S 140 38 E
35 Djakarta= Jakarta 6 9 S 106 49 E
54 Djambala 2 33 S 14 45 E
34 Djangeru 2 20 S 116 29 E
35 Djawa, I.= Java, I. 7 0 S 110 0 E
50 Djelfa 34 30 N 3 20 E
54 Djema 6 3 N 25 19 E
51 Djerba, I. de 33 56 N 11 0 E
50 Djerid, Chott el, Reg. 35 50 N 8 30 E
29 Djibouti 11 36 N 43 9 E
29 Djibouti ■ 11 30 N 42 15 E
* 50 Djidjelli 36 52 N 5 50 E
34 Djirlagne 11 44 N 108 15 E
54 Djolu 0 37 N 22 21 E
53 Djougou 9 42 N 1 40 E
51 Djourab, Erg du 16 40 N 18 50 E
54 Djugu 1 55 N 30 30 E
20 Djúpivogur 64 40 N 14 10 W
23 Dnepr, R. 46 30 N 32 18 E
23 Dneprodzerzhinsk 48 30 N 34 37 E
23 Dnepropetrovsk 48 30 N 35 0 E
23 Dnestr, R. 46 18 N 30 17 E
23 Dnieper, R.= Dnepr, R. 46 30 N 32 18 E
23 Dniester, R.= Dnestr, R. 46 18 N 30 17 E
51 Doba 8 39 N 16 51 E
35 Doberai, Jazirah 1 25 S 133 0 E
80 Doblas 37 5 S 64 0 W
35 Dobo 5 46 S 134 13 E
15 Dobruja, Reg. 44 30 N 28 30 E
19 Dodecanese Is.= Dhodhekánisos, Is. 36 35 N 27 10 E
71 Dodge City 37 45 N 100 1 W
52 Dodoma 6 11 S 35 45 E
65 Dodsland 51 48 N 108 49 W
11 Doetinchem 51 58 N 6 17 E
64 Dog Creek 51 35 N 122 18 W
53 Dogondoutchi 13 38 N 4 2 E
31 Doha 25 15 N 51 36 E
32 Dohad 22 50 N 74 15 E
33 Dohazari 22 10 N 92 5 E
63 Dolbeau 48 53 N 72 14 W
12 Dôle 47 6 N 5 30 E
6 Dolgellau 52 44 N 3 53 W
† 54 Dolisie 4 12 S 12 41 E
29 Dolo, Somali Rep. 4 13 N 42 8 E
18 Dolomiti, Mts. 46 25 N 11 50 E
80 Dolores, Arg. 36 19 S 57 40 W
80 Dolores, Uruguay 33 33 S 58 13 W
80 Dolphin, C. 51 15 S 58 58 W
60 Dolphin & Union Str. 69 5 N 114 45 W
53 Doma 8 25 N 8 18 E
24 Dombarovskiy 50 46 N 59 39 E
21 Dombås 62 5 N 9 8 E
12 Dombes, Reg. 46 0 N 5 3 E
75 Dominica, I. 15 30 N 61 20 W
75 Dominica Pass 15 10 N 61 20 W
75 Dominican Rep. ■ 19 0 N 70 40 W
18 Domodossola 46 7 N 8 17 E
6 Don, R., Eng. 53 39 N 0 59 W
8 Don, R., Scot. 57 10 N 2 4 W
23 Don, R., U.S.S.R. 47 4 N 39 18 E
9 Donaghadee 54 39 N 5 33 W
64 Donalda 52 35 N 112 34 W
14 Donau, R.= Dunárea, R. 45 20 N 29 40 E
14 Donauwörth 48 43 N 10 46 E
6 Doncaster 53 32 N 1 7 W
32 Dondra Hd. 5 55 N 80 35 E

* Jijel
† Renamed Loubomo

9 Donegal 54 39 N 8 7 W
9 Donegal □ 54 50 N 0 8 W
9 Donegal, B. 54 30 N 8 30 W
23 Donetsk 48 0 N 37 48 E
34 Dong Hoi 17 18 N 106 36 E
45 Dongara 29 15 S 114 56 E
51 Dongola 19 9 N 30 22 E
63 Donnacona 46 40 N 71 47 W
47 Donnelly's Crossing 35 43 S 173 33 E
57 Donnybrook 33 35 S 115 48 E
42 Donor's Hills 18 42 S 140 33 E
45 Doodlakine 31 35 S 117 28 E
8 Doon, R. 55 26 N 4 38 W
28 Dor 32 37 N 34 55 E
18 Dora Báltea, R. 45 11 N 8 5 E
7 Dorchester 50 43 N 2 26 W
61 Dorchester, C. 65 29 N 77 30 W
12 Dordogne □ 45 10 N 0 45 E
12 Dordogne, R. 45 2 N 0 35 W
11 Dordrecht, Neth. 51 49 N 107 45 W
56 Dordrecht, S. Afr. 31 20 S 27 3 E
12 Dore, Mt. 45 32 N 2 50 E
65 Dore Lake 54 56 N 107 45 W
53 Dori 14 3 N 0 2 W
62 Dorion 45 23 N 74 3 W
8 Dornie 57 17 N 5 30 W
8 Dornoch 57 52 N 4 2 W
8 Dornoch Firth 57 52 N 4 2 W
37 Döröö Nuur, L. 47 40 N 93 30 E
45 Dorre, I. 25 9 S 113 7 E
43 Dorrigo 30 21 S 152 43 E
7 Dorset □ 50 47 N 2 20 W
14 Dortmund 51 31 N 7 28 E
80 Dos Bahias, C. 44 55 S 65 32 W
31 Doshi 35 37 N 68 41 E
53 Dosso 13 3 N 3 12 E
64 Dot 50 12 N 121 25 W
69 Dothan 31 13 N 85 24 W
12 Douai 50 22 N 3 4 E
53 Douala 4 3 N 9 42 E
12 Douarnenez 48 6 N 4 20 W
12 Doubs □ 47 10 N 6 25 E
47 Doubtless, B. 34 55 S 173 27 E
62 Doucet 48 15 N 76 35 W
53 Douentza 14 58 N 2 48 W
56 Douglas, S. Afr. 29 4 S 23 46 E
6 Douglas, U.K. 54 9 N 4 25 W
73 Douglas, Ariz 31 21 N 109 33 W
69 Douglas, Ga. 31 31 N 82 51 W
70 Douglas, Wyo. 42 45 N 105 24 W
8 Dounreay 58 40 N 3 28 W
79 Dourada, Sa. 13 10 S 48 45 W
13 Douro, R. 41 8 N 8 40 W
13 Douro Litoral, Reg. 41 5 N 8 20 W
6 Dove, R. 54 20 N 0 55 W
42 Dover, Australia 43 19 S 147 1 E
7 Dover, U.K. 51 8 N 1 19 E
68 Dover, Del. 39 10 N 75 32 W
68 Dover, N.H. 43 12 N 70 56 W
68 Dover, Ohio 40 32 N 81 30 W
12 Dover, Str. of 51 0 N 1 30 E
7 Dovey, R. 52 32 N 4 0 W
20 Dovrefjell, Mts. 62 6 N 9 25 E
68 Dowagiac 41 59 N 86 6 W
31 Dowlātābad 28 18 N 56 40 E
9 Down □ 54 24 N 5 55 W
7 Downham Market 52 36 N 0 23 E
9 Downpatrick 54 20 N 5 43 W
12 Draguignan 43 32 N 6 28 E
2 Drake Pass. 58 0 S 70 0 W
57 Drakensberg, Mts. 27 0 S 30 0 E
19 Dráma 41 9 N 24 8 E
21 Drammen 59 44 N 10 15 E
19 Drava, R. 45 33 N 18 55 E
64 Drayton Valley 53 13 N 114 59 W
11 Drenthe □ 52 45 N 6 30 E
14 Dresden 51 3 N 13 44 E
12 Dreux 48 44 N 1 22 E
6 Driffield 54 0 N 0 27 W
19 Drina, R. 44 53 N 19 21 E
19 Drini, R. 41 17 N 20 2 E
21 Drøbak 59 39 N 10 48 E
9 Drogheda 53 43 N 6 21 W
23 Drogobych 49 20 N 23 30 E
7 Droitwich 52 16 N 2 9 W
12 Drôme □ 44 35 N 5 10 E
46 Dromedary, C. 36 17 S 150 10 E
42 Dronfield 53 19 S 1 27 W
3 Dronning Maud Ld. 75 0 S 10 0 E
46 Drouin 38 8 S 145 51 E
64 Drumheller 51 28 N 112 42 W
62 Drummondville 45 53 N 72 30 W
25 Druzhina 68 11 N 14 S 19 E
65 Dryden 49 47 N 92 50 W
44 Drysdale, R. 13 59 S 126 51 E
53 Dschang 5 27 N 10 4 E

68 Du Bois 41 7N 78 46W
70 Du Quoin 38 0N 89 10W
42 Duaringa 23 42S 149 42E
30 Dubā 27 10N 35 40E
60 Dubawnt L. 63 0N 102 0W
31 Dubayy 25 18N 55 18E
46 Dubbo 32 15S 148 36E
9 Dublin, Eire 53 20N 6 15W
69 Dublin, U.S.A. 32 32N 82 54W
9 Dublin □ 53 20N 6 15W
72 Dubois 44 10N 112 14W
23 Dubovka 49 5N 44 50E
50 Dubreka 9 48N 13 31W
19 Dubrovnik 42 38N 18 7E
25 Dubrovskoye 47 28N 42 40E
70 Dubuque 42 30N 90 41W
72 Duchesne 40 10N 110 24W
42 Duchess 21 22S 139 52E
2 Ducie I. 24 47S 124 50W
65 Duck Lake 52 47N 106 13W
65 Duck Mt. Prov. Park 51 36N 100 55W
25 Dudinka 69 25N 86 15E
7 Dudley 52 30N 2 5W
13 Duero, R. 41 37N 4 25W
8 Dufftown 57 26N 3 9W
18 Dugi Otok, I. 44 0N 15 0E
14 Duisburg 51 27N 6 42E
57 Duiwelskloof 23 42S 30 10E
31 Dukhan 25 25N 50 50E
12 Duku 10 43N 10 43E
75 Dulce, G. 8 40N 83 20W
57 Dullstroom 25 24S 30 7E
42 Dululu 23 48S 150 15E
70 Duluth 46 48N 92 10W
33 Dum Duma 27 40N 95 40E
34 Dumai 1 35N 101 20E
71 Dumas 35 50N 101 58W
8 Dumbarton 55 58N 4 35W
45 Dumbleyung 33 17S 117 42E
8 Dumfries 55 4N 3 37W
8 Dumfries-Galloway □ 55 12N 3 30W
46 Dumosa 35 52S 143 6E
51 Dumyât 31 25N 31 48E
9 Dun Laoghaire 53 17N 6 9W
9 Dun Leary= Dun Laoghaire 53 17N 6 9W
15 Dunaföldvár 46 50N 18 57E
15 Dunárea, R. 45 20N 29 40E
15 Dunaújváros 47 0N 18 57E
47 Dunback 42 23S 170 36E
8 Dunbar 56 0N 2 32W
65 Dunblane, Canada 51 11N 106 52W
8 Dunblane, U.K. 56 10N 3 58W
64 Duncan, Canada 48 45N 123 40W
71 Duncan, U.S.A. 34 25N 98 0W
75 Duncan Town 22 20N 75 80W
9 Dundalk, U.K. 53 55N 6 45W
62 Dundas 43 17N 79 59W
45 Dundas, L. 32 35S 121 50E
44 Dundas, Str. 11 15S 131 35E
57 Dundee, S. Africa 28 11S 30 15E
8 Dundee, U.K. 56 29N 3 0W
9 Dundrum 54 17N 5 50W
9 Dundrum, B. 54 12N 5 40W
47 Dunedin 45 50S 170 33E
8 Dunfermline 56 5N 3 28W
9 Dungannon 54 30N 6 47W
9 Dungannon □ 54 30N 6 47W
9 Dungarvan 52 6N 7 40W
37 Dunbure Shan, Mts. 35 0N 90 0E
7 Dungeness, Pt. 50 54N 0 59E
54 Dungu 3 42N 28 32E
46 Dunkeld, Australia 37 40S 142 22E
8 Dunkeld, U.K. 56 34N 3 36W
12 Dunkerque 51 2N 2 20E
7 Dunkery Beacon 51 15N 3 37W
68 Dunkirk 42 30N 79 18W
53 Dunkwa, Ghana 6 0N 1 47W
53 Dunkwa, Ghana 5 30N 1 0W
42 Dunmara 16 42S 133 25E
68 Dunmore 41 27N 75 38W
9 Dunmore Hd. 53 37N 8 44W
69 Dunn 35 18N 78 36W
8 Dunnet Hd. 58 38N 3 22W
8 Dunoon 55 57N 4 56W
8 Duns 55 47N 2 20W
72 Dunsmuir 41 0N 122 10W
7 Dunstable 51 53N 0 31W
47 D'Urville, I. 40 50S 173 55E
28 Dūrā 31 30N 35 2E
44 Durack, R. 15 33S 127 52E
12 Durance, R. 43 55N 4 44E
74 Durango, Mexico 24 3N 104 39W
13 Durango, Sp. 43 13N 2 40W
73 Durango, U.S.A. 37 10N 107 50W
74 Durango □ 25 0N 105 0W
45 Duranillin 33 30S 116 45E
71 Durant 34 0N 96 25W
80 Durazno 33 25S 56 38W
57 Durban 29 49S 31 1E
33 Durg 21 15N 81 22E
62 Durham, Canada 44 10N 80 48W
6 Durham, U.K. 54 47N 1 34W
69 Durham, U.S.A. 36 0N 78 55W
6 Durham □ 54 42N 1 45W
19 Durrësi 41 19N 19 28E
24 Dushak 37 20N 60 10E
24 Dushanbe 38 40N 68 50E
47 Dusky, Sd. 45 47S 166 29E
14 Düsseldorf 51 15N 6 46E
60 Dutch Harbor 53 54N 166 35W
30 Duzce 40 50N 31 10E
22 Drinskaya Guba 65 0N 39 45E
32 Dwarka 22 18N 69 8E
45 Dwellingup 32 38S 115 58E
71 Dyersburg 36 2N 89 20W
7 Dyfed □ 52 0N 4 30W
22 Dzerzhinsk 56 15N 43 15E
24 Dzhalal Abad 41 0N 73 0E
25 Dzhalinda 53 50N 124 0E
24 Dzhambul 43 10N 71 0E
23 Dzhankoi 45 40N 34 30E
25 Dzhardzhan 68 43N 124 2E
25 Dzhelinde 70 0N 114 20E
24 Dzhezkazgan 47 10N 67 40E
24 Dzhizak 40 20N 68 0E
25 Dzhugdzur Khrebet, Ra. 57 30N 138 0E
37 Dzungaria, Reg. 44 10N 88 0E
37 Dzungarian Gate= Dzungarskiye Vorota 45 25N 82 25E
37 Dzungarskiye Vorota 45 25N 82 25E
38 Dzuunbulag 46 58N 115 30E
38 Dzuunmod 47 45N 106 58E

E

60 Eagle 64 44N 141 29W
71 Eagle Pass 28 45N 100 35W
46 Eaglehawk 36 43S 144 16E
7 Ealing 51 30N 0 19W
73 Earlimart 35 57N 119 14W
8 Earn, L. 56 23N 4 14W
47 Earnslaw, Mt. 44 32S 168 27E
69 Easley 34 52N 82 35W
47 East, C. 37 42S 178 35E
63 East Angus 45 30N 71 40W
33 East Bengal, Reg. 23 0N 90 0E
60 East C. 65 50N 168 0W
68 East Chicago 41 40N 87 30W
26 East China Sea 30 0N 126 0E
68 East Cleveland 41 32N 81 35W
80 East Falkland 51 30S 58 30W
14 East Germany ■ 52 0N 12 30E
70 East Grand Forks 47 55N 97 5W
26 East Indies, Is. 0 0 120 0E
8 East Kilbride 55 48N 4 12W
68 East Lansing 42 44N 84 37W
68 East Liverpool 40 39N 80 35W
57 East London 33 0S 27 55E
62 East Main 52 20N 78 30W
68 East Orange 40 45N 74 15W
64 East Pine 55 48N 120 5W
69 East Point 33 40N 84 28W
6 East Retford 53 19N 0 55W
70 East St. Lovis 38 36N 90 10W
25 East Siberian Sea 73 0N 160 0E
7 East Sussex □ 50 55N 0 20E
47 Eastbourne, N.Z. 41 19S 174 55E
7 Eastbourne, U.K. 50 46N 0 18E
65 Eastend 49 32N 108 50W
2 Easter Is. 27 0S 109 0W
32 Eastern Ghats, Mts. 15 0N 80 0E
53 Eastern □, Ghana 6 20N 1 0W
* 34 Eastern Malaysia □ 3 0N 112 30E
7 Eastleigh 50 58N 1 21W
62 Eastmain, R. 52 20N 78 30W
68 Easton 40 41N 75 15W
63 Eastport 44 57N 67 0W
62 Eastview 45 27N 75 40W
65 Eatonia 51 20N 109 25W
70 Eau Claire 44 46N 91 30W

* *Now part of Malaysia*

7 Ebbw Vale 51 47N 3 12W
46 Ebden 36 10S 147 1E
21 Ebeltoft 56 12N 10 41E
14 Eberswalde 52 49N 13 50E
18 Eboli 40 39N 15 2E
13 Ebro, R. 40 43N 0 54E
46 Echuca 36 3S 144 46E
13 Ecija 37 30N 5 10W
78 Ecuador ■ 2 0S 78 0W
51 Ed Dâmer 17 27N 34 0E
51 Ed Debba 18 0N 30 51E
51 Ed Dueim 10 10N 28 20E
45 Edah 28 16S 117 10E
11 Edam 52 31N 5 3E
8 Eday, I. 59 11N 2 47W
7 Eddystone Rock 50 11N 4 16W
11 Ede, Neth. 52 4N 5 40E
53 Ede, Nigeria 7 45N 4 29E
53 Edea 3 51N 10 9E
6 Eden, R. 54 57N 3 1W
56 Edenburg 29 43S 25 58E
9 Edenderry 53 21N 7 3W
57 Edenville 27 37S 27 34E
14 Eder, R. 51 13N 9 27E
7 Edge Hill 52 7N 1 28W
70 Edgeley 46 27N 98 41W
70 Edgemont 43 15N 103 53W
19 Edhessa 40 48N 22 5E
47 Edievale 45 49S 169 22E
71 Edinburg 26 22N 98 10W
8 Edinburgh 55 57N 3 12W
30 Edirne 41 40N 26 45E
44 Edith River 14 12S 132 2E
71 Edmond 35 37N 97 30W
42 Edmonton, Australia 17 2S 145 45E
64 Edmonton, Canada 53 30N 113 30W
63 Edmundston 47 23N 68 20W
30 Edremit 39 40N 27 0E
64 Edson 53 40N 116 28W
54 Edward, L.=Idi Amin Dada, L. 0 25S 29 40E
71 Edwards Plat. 30 30N 101 5W
11 Eekloo 51 11N 3 33E
57 Eersterus 25 45S 28 20E
68 Effingham 39 8N 88 30W
18 Égadi, Is. 37 55N 12 10E
62 Eganville 45 32N 77 5W
15 Eger 47 53N 20 27E
21 Egersund= Eigersund 58 2N 6 1E
44 Eginbah 20 53S 119 47E
47 Egmont, Mt. 39 17S 174 5E
53 Egume 7 30N 7 14E
25 Egvekind 66 19N 179 10W
51 Egypt ■ 28 0N 31 0E
53 Eha Amufu 6 30N 7 40E
36 Ehime □ 33 30N 132 40E
43 Eidsvold 25 25S 151 12E
21 Eidsvoll 60 19N 11 14E
14 Eifel, Mts. 50 10N 6 45E
57 Eiffel Flats 18 20S 30 0E
21 Eigersund 58 2N 6 1E
8 Eigg, I. 56 54N 6 10W
44 Eighty Mile Beach 19 30S 120 40E
8 Eil, L. 56 50N 5 15E
46 Eildon, L. 37 10S 146 0E
42 Einasleigh 18 32S 144 5E
11 Eindhoven 51 26N 5 30E
9 Eire ■= Irish Rep. ■ 53 0N 8 0W
14 Eisenerz 47 32N 15 54E
28 Eizariya 31 47N 35 15E
53 Ejura 7 25N 1 25E
21 Ekenäs 59 58N 23 26E
53 Eket 4 38N 7 56W
47 Eketahuna 40 38S 175 43E
24 Ekibastuz 51 40N 75 22E
25 Ekimchan 53 0N 133 0W
50 El Aaiun 27 0N 12 0W
51 El Alamein 30 48N 28 58E
50 El Aricha 34 13N 1 16W
28 El Ariha 31 52N 35 27E
42 El Arish 17 49S 146 1E
51 El'Arîsh 31 8N 33 50E
* 50 El Asnam 36 10N 1 20E
51 El Bawiti 28 25N 28 45E
50 El Bayadh 33 40N 1 1E
73 El Cajon 32 49N 117 0W
71 El Campo 29 10N 96 20W
73 El Centro 32 50N 115 40W
80 El Cuy 39 55S 68 25W
29 El Dere 3 50N 47 8E
78 El Diviso 1 22N 78 14W
50 El Djouf 20 0N 11 30E
71 El Dorado, Ark. 33 10N 92 40W
71 El Dorado, Kans. 37 55N 96 56W

* *Renamed Ech Cheliff*

78 El Dorado, Venezuela 6 55N 61 30W
13 El Escorial 40 35N 4 7W
51 El Faiyûm 29 19N 30 50E
51 El Fâsher 13 33N 25 26E
13 El Ferrol 43 29N 3 14W
51 El Geneina 13 27N 22 45E
51 El Geteina 14 50N 32 27E
51 El Gezira 14 0N 33 0E
51 El Gîza 30 0N 31 10E
50 El Goléa 30 30N 2 50E
50 El Harrach 36 45N 3 5E
51 El Iskandarîya 31 0N 30 0E
51 El Istwâ'ya □ 5 0N 32 0E
50 El Jadida 33 16N 9 31W
51 El Jebelein 12 30N 32 45E
50 El Kef 36 12N 8 47E
51 El Khandaq 18 30N 30 30E
51 El Khârga 25 30N 30 33E
51 El Khartûm 15 31N 32 35E
51 El Khartum Bahrî 15 40N 32 31E
51 El Mafâza 13 38N 34 30E
51 El Mahalla el Kubra 31 0N 31 0E
51 El Mansura 31 0N 31 19E
51 El Minyâ 28 7N 30 33E
54 El Niybo 4 32N 39 59E
51 El Obeid 13 8N 30 18E
74 El Oro 3 30S 79 50W
50 El Oued 33 20N 6 58E
73 El Paso 31 50N 106 30W
74 El Progreso 15 26N 87 51W
51 El Qâhira 30 1N 31 14E
51 El Qantara 30 51N 32 20E
51 El Qasr 25 44N 28 42E
51 El Qubba 11 10N 27 5E
71 El Reno 35 30N 98 0W
51 El Suweis 29 58N 32 31E
78 El Tigre 8 55N 64 15W
78 El Tocuyo 9 47N 69 48W
80 El Turbio 51 30S 72 40W
51 El Uqsur 25 41N 32 38E
78 El Vigia 8 38N 71 39W
51 El Wâhat el-Dakhla 26 0N 27 50E
51 El Wâhât el Khârga 24 0N 23 0E
52 El Wak 2 49N 40 56E
46 Elaine 37 44S 144 2E
28 Elat 5 40S 133 5E
30 Elazig 38 37N 39 22E
18 Elba, I. 42 48N 10 15E
18 Elbasani 41 9N 20 9E
14 Elbe, R. 53 50N 9 0E
73 Elbert, Mt. 39 12N 106 30W
69 Elberton 34 7N 82 51W
12 Elbeuf 49 17N 1 2E
15 Elbląg 54 10N 19 25E
23 Elbrus, Mt. 43 30N 42 30E
26 Elburz Mts.= Alberz, Reshteh-Ye-Kakha-Ye 36 0N 52 0E
13 Elche de la Sierra 38 27N 2 3W
52 Eldama 0 3N 35 43E
14 Elde, R. 53 17N 12 40E
65 Eldorado 59 35N 108 30W
52 Eldoret 0 30N 35 25E
57 Elefantes, R. 24 10S 32 40E
53 Elele 5 5N 6 50E
73 Elephant Butte Res. 33 45N 107 30W
75 Eleuthera I. 25 0N 76 20W
8 Elgin, U.K. 57 39N 3 20W
68 Elgin, Ill. 42 0N 88 20W
72 Elgin, Ore. 45 37N 118 0W
70 Elgin, Tex. 30 21N 97 22W
52 Elgon, Mt. 1 10N 34 30E
35 Eliase 8 10S 130 55E
55 Elisabethville= Lubumbashi 11 32S 27 38E
23 Elista 46 16N 44 14E
43 Elizabeth, Australia 34 45S 138 39E
68 Elizabeth, U.S.A. 40 37N 74 12W
69 Elizabeth City 36 18N 76 16W
69 Elizabethton 36 20N 82 13W
68 Elizabethtown 37 40N 85 54W
71 Elk City 35 25N 99 25W
62 Elk Lake 47 40N 80 25W
65 Elk Point 54 10N 110 55W
68 Elkhart 41 42N 85 55W
65 Elkhorn 50 0N 101 11W
19 Elkhovo 42 10N 26 40E
68 Elkins 38 53N 79 53W
64 Elko, Canada 49 20N 115 10W
72 Elko, U.S.A. 40 40N 115 50W

Ellen Mt. Felipe Carillo Puerto

73 Ellen Mt. 38 4N 110 56W
44 Ellendale,
Australia 17 56S 124 48E
70 Ellendale, U.S.A. 46 3N 98 30W
72 Ellensburg 47 0N 120 30W
58 Ellesmere I. 79 30N 80 0W
6 Ellesmere Port 53 17N 2 55W
3 Ellice Is=
Tuvalu ■ 8 0S 176 0E
57 Elliot 31 22S 27 48E
62 Elliot Lake 46 35N 82 35W
42 Elliott 41 5S 145 38E
43 Elliston 33 39S 134 55E
8 Ellon 57 21N 2 5W
33 Ellore=Eluru 16 48N 81 8E
70 Ellsworth 38 47N 98 15W
2 Ellsworth Ld. 75 30S 80 0W
68 Ellwood City 40 52N 80 19W
72 Elma 47 0N 123 30E
30 Elmali 36 44N 29 56E
52 Elmenteita 0 32S 36 14E
68 Elmhurst 41 52N 87 58W
53 Elmina 5 5N 1 21W
68 Elmira 42 8N 76 49W
46 Elmore 36 30S 144 37E
65 Elrose 51 20N 108 0W
73 Elsinore 33 40N 117 15W
47 Eltham 39 26S 174 19E
33 Eluru 16 48N 81 8E
13 Elvas 38 50N 7 17W
21 Elverum 60 55N 11 34E
68 Elwood 40 20N 85 50W
7 Ely, U.K. 52 24N 0 16E
70 Ely, U.S.A. 47 54N 91 52W
28 Elyashiv 32 23N 34 55E
68 Elyria 41 22N 82 8W
24 Emba 48 50N 58 8E
80 Embarcación 23 10S 64 0W
52 Embu 0 32S 37 38E
14 Emden 53 22N 7 12E
42 Emerald 23 30S 148 11E
65 Emerson 49 0N 97 10W
18 Emilia Romagna □ 44 33N 10 40E
11 Emmen 52 48N 6 57E
72 Emmett 24 45S 144 30W
74 Empalme 28 1N 110 49W
57 Empangeni 28 50S 31 52E
80 Empédrado 28 0S 58 46W
70 Emporia, Kans. 38 25N 96 16W
69 Emporia, Va. 36 41N 77 32W
68 Emporium 41 30N 78 17W
14 Ems, R. 51 9N 9 26E
28 'En Kerem 31 47N 35 6E
51 En Nahud 12 45N 28 25E
28 'En Yahav 30 37N 35 11E
36 Ena 35 25N 137 25E
80 Encarnación 27 15S 56 0W
74 Encarnación de
Diaz 21 30N 102 20W
53 Enchi 5 53N 2 48W
78 Encontrados 9 3N 72 14W
35 Ende 8 45S 121 30E
42 Endeavour, Str. 10 45S 142 0E
64 Enderby 50 35N 119 10W
44 Enderby, I. 20 35S 116 30E
3 Enderby Ld. 66 0S 53 0E
68 Endicott 42 6N 76 2W
7 Enfield 51 38N 0 4W
75 Engaño, C.,
Dom. Rep. 18 30N 68 20W
35 Engaño, C.,
Philippines 18 35N 122 23E
57 Engcobo 31 39S 28 1E
22 Engels 51 28N 46 6E
34 Enggano 5 20S 102 40E
10 England ■ 53 0N 2 0W
63 Englee 50 45N 56 5W
62 Englehart 47 49N 79 52W
70 Englewood 39 39N 104 59W
65 English, R. 50 12N 95 0W
33 English Bazar 24 58N 88 21E
4 English Chan. 50 0N 2 30W
71 Enid 36 26N 97 52W
* 57 Enkeldoorn 19 2S 30 52E
11 Enkhuizen 52 42N 5 17E
18 Enna 37 34N 14 15E
51 Ennedi 17 15N 22 0E
9 Ennis, Eire 52 51N 8 59W
71 Ennis, U.S.A. 32 15N 96 40W
9 Enniscorthy 52 30N 6 35W
9 Enniskillen 54 20N 7 40W
9 Ennistymon 52 56N 9 18W
20 Enontekio 68 23N 23 38E
11 Enschede 52 13N 6 53E
52 Entebbe 0 4N 32 28E
72 Enterprise 45 25N 117 17W
† 55 Entre Rios 14 57S 37 20E
80 Entre Rios, Reg. 30 0S 58 30W

53 Enugu 6 30N 7 30E
53 Enugu Ezike 7 0N 7 29E
18 Eólie o
Lípari, I. 38 30N 14 50E
11 Epe, Neth. 52 21N 5 59E
53 Epe, Nigeria 6 36N 3 59E
12 Épernay 49 3N 3 56E
72 Ephraim 39 30N 111 37W
12 Épinal 48 19N 6 27E
7 Epping 51 42N 0 8E
54 Equatorial
Guinea ■ 2 0N 8 0E
51 Er Rahad 12 45N 30 32E
50 Er Rif 35 1N 4 1W
51 Er Roseires 11 55N 34 30E
45 Eradu 28 40S 115 2E
25 Ercha 69 45N 147 20E
38 Erdene 44 30N 111 10E
38 Erdenedalay 46 3N 105 1E
80 Erechim 27 35S 52 15W
30 Ereğli 41 15N 31 30E
14 Erfurt 50 58N 11 2E
30 Ergani 38 26N 39 49E
23 Ergeni
Vozvyshennost 47 0N 44 0E
38 Erhlien 43 42N 112 2E
8 Eriboll, L. 58 28N 4 41W
68 Erie 42 10N 80 7W
68 Erie, L. 42 30N 82 0W
29 Erigavo 10 35N 47 35E
65 Eriksdale 50 52N 98 5W
19 Erímanthos, Mt. 37 57N 21 50E
64 Erith 53 25N 116 46W
51 Eritrea □ 14 0N 41 0E
14 Erlangen 49 35N 11 0E
42 Erldunda 25 14S 133 12E
11 Ermelo, Neth. 52 35N 5 35E
57 Ermelo, S. Afr. 26 31S 29 59E
32 Ernakulam 9 59N 76 19E
9 Erne, L. 54 14N 7 30W
9 Erne, R. 54 30N 8 16W
32 Erode 11 24N 77 45E
32 Erramala Hills 15 30N 78 15E
53 Eruwa 7 33N 3 26E
14 Erzgebirge Mts. 50 25N 13 0E
30 Erzurum 39 57N 41 15E
51 Es Sider 30 50N 18 21E
21 Esbjerg 55 29N 8 29E
68 Escanaba 45 44N 87 5W
11 Esch 49 32N 6 0E
73 Escondido 33 9N 117 4W
74 Escuintla 14 20N 90 48W
31 Esfahan 32 40N 51 38E
31 Esfahan □ 33 0N 53 0E
51 Esh Shimâliya □ 20 0N 31 0E
57 Eshowe 28 50S 31 30E
28 Eshta'ol 31 47N 35 0E
6 Esk, R., Eng. 54 29N 0 37W
8 Esk, R., Scot. 54 58N 3 2W
21 Eskilstuna 59 22N 16 32E
65 Eskimo Point 61 10N 94 15W
30 Eskisehir 39 50N 30 35E
13 Esla, R. 41 29N 6 3W
78 Esmeraldas 1 0N 79 40W
62 Espanola 46 15N 81 46W
24 Espe 44 0N 74 5E
45 Esperance 33 51S 121 53E
45 Esperance, B. 33 48S 121 55E
80 Esperanza 31 29S 61 3W
13 Espichel, C. 38 22N 9 16W
78 Espinal 4 9N 74 53W
79 Espinhaço, Sa. do 17 30S 43 30W
74 Espíritu Santo,
B. del 19 15N 79 40W
79 Espírito Santo □ 19 30S 40 30W
80 Esquel 42 40S 71 20W
50 Essaouira 31 32N 9 42W
11 Essen, Belgium 51 28N 4 28E
14 Essen,
W. Germany 51 28N 6 59E
7 Essex □ 51 48N 0 30E
14 Esslingen 48 43N 9 19E
12 Essonne □ 48 30N 2 20E
80 Estados,
I. de los 54 40S 64 30W
79 Estância, Brazil 11 15S 37 30W
73 Estancia, U.S.A. 34 50N 106 1W
57 Estcourt 28 58S 29 53E
75 Estelí 13 9N 86 22W
65 Esterhazy 50 37N 102 5W
65 Estevan 49 10N 103 0W
70 Estheville 43 25N 94 50W
22 Estonian S.S.R. □ 48 30N 25 30E
13 Estoril 38 42N 9 23W
13 Estrêla, Sa. da 40 10N 7 45W
13 Estremadura, Reg. 39 0N 9 0W
79 Estrondo, Sa. de 7 20S 48 0W
15 Esztergom 47 47N 18 44E

32 Etawah 26 48N 79 6E
44 Ethel Creek 22 55S 120 11E
65 Ethelbert 51 32N 100 25W
29 Ethiopia ■ 8 0N 40 0E
48 Ethiopian
Highlands, Mts. 10 0N 37 0E
8 Etive, L. 56 30N 5 12W
18 Etna, Mt. 37 45N 15 0E
56 Etoshapan 18 40S 16 30E
8 Ettrick, R. 55 31N 2 55W
74 Etzatlán 20 48N 104 5W
68 Euclid 41 32N 81 31W
46 Eucumbene, L. 36 2S 148 40E
69 Eufaula 31 55N 85 11W
72 Eugene 44 0N 123 8W
71 Eunice 30 35N 92 28W
11 Eupen 50 37N 6 3E
30 Euphrates, R.=
Furat, Nahr al 33 30N 43 0E
12 Eure □ 49 6N 1 0E
72 Eureka, Calif. 40 50N 124 0W
72 Eureka, Nev. 39 32N 116 2W
72 Eureka, Utah 40 0N 112 0W
12 Eure-et-Loir □ 48 22N 1 30E
46 Euroa 36 44S 145 35E
55 Europa, Île 22 20S 40 22E
13 Europa, Picos de 43 10N 5 0W
13 Europa, Pta. de 36 3N 5 21W
5 Europe 50 0N 20 0E
11 Europoort 51 57N 4 10E
43 Evans Head 29 7S 153 27E
68 Evanston, Ill. 42 0N 87 40W
72 Evanston, Wyo. 41 10N 111 0W
68 Evansville 38 0N 87 35W
70 Eveleth 47 35N 92 40W
28 Even Yehuda 32 16N 34 53E
33 Everest, Mt. 28 5N 86 58E
72 Everett 48 0N 122 10W
69 Everglades
Nat. Park 25 50N 80 40W
7 Evesham 52 6N 1 57W
13 Evora 38 33N 7 57W
12 Évreux 49 0N 1 8E
28 Evron 32 59N 35 6E
19 Evvoia □ 38 40N 23 40E
8 Ewe, L. 57 49N 5 38W
70 Excellsior Springs 39 20N 94 10W
7 Exe, R. 50 37N 3 25W
7 Exeter 50 43N 3 31W
7 Exmoor, Reg. 51 10N 3 55W
44 Exmouth,
Australia 22 6S 114 0E
7 Exmouth, U.K. 50 37N 3 24W
44 Exmouth, G. 22 15S 114 15E
13 Extremadura, Reg. 39 30N 6 5W
75 Exuma Sd. 24 30N 76 20W
52 Eyasi, L. 3 30S 35 0E
8 Eye Pen. 58 20N 0 51E
8 Eyemouth 55 53N 2 5W
43 Eyre, L. 28 30S 136 45E
43 Eyre, Pen. 33 30S 137 17E

F

73 Fabens 31 30N 106 8W
18 Fabriano 43 20N 12 52E
78 Facatativa 4 49N 74 22W
53 Fada N'Gourma 12 10N 0 30E
18 Faenza 44 17N 11 53E
53 Fafa 15 22N 0 48E
53 Fagam 11 1N 10 1E
15 Fagaraş 45 48N 24 58E
21 Fagernes 61 0N 9 16E
21 Fagersta 61 1N 15 46E
80 Fagnano, L. 54 30S 68 0W
31 Fahraj 29 0N 59 0E
39 Fahsien 21 19N 110 33E
31 Fahud 22 18N 56 28E
68 Fair Haven 43 36N 76 16W
73 Fairbank 31 44N 110 12W
60 Fairbanks 64 59N 147 40W
70 Fairbury 40 5N 97 5W
46 Fairfield,
Australia 37 45S 175 17E
69 Fairfield, Ala. 33 30N 87 0W
72 Fairfield, Calif. 38 14N 122 1W
70 Fairfield, Ill. 38 20N 88 20W
70 Fairfield, Iowa 41 0N 91 58W
71 Fairfield, Tex. 31 40N 96 0W
47 Fairlie 44 5S 170 49E
70 Fairmont, Minn. 43 37N 94 30W
68 Fairmont, W. Va. 39 29N 80 10W
68 Fairport 43 8N 77 29W

42 Fairview,
Australia 15 31S 144 17E
64 Fairview, Canada 56 5N 118 25W
60 Fairweather, Mt. 58 55N 137 45W
31 Faizabad,
Afghanistan 37 7N 70 33E
33 Faizabad, India 26 45N 82 10E
75 Fajardo 18 20N 65 39W
6 Fakenham 52 50N 0 51E
35 Fakfak 3 0S 132 15E
38 Faku 42 31N 123 26E
12 Falaise 48 54N 0 12W
33 Falam 23 0N 93 45E
18 Falcone, C. 41 0N 8 10E
71 Falfurrias 27 8N 98 8E
21 Falkenberg 56 54N 12 30E
8 Falkirk 56 0N 3 47W
80 Falkland, Sd. 52 0S 60 0W
80 Falkland Is. □ 51 30S 59 0W
2 Falkland Is.
Dependencies □ 57 0S 40 0N
21 Falköping 58 12N 13 33E
68 Fall River 41 45N 71 5W
72 Fallon 39 31N 118 51W
70 Falls City 40 0N 95 40W
75 Falmouth, Jamaica 18 30N 77 40W
7 Falmouth, U.K. 50 9N 5 5W
75 Falso, C. 17 45N 71 40W
21 Falster, I. 54 48N 11 58E
21 Falsterbo 55 23N 12 50E
21 Falun 60 37N 15 37E
30 Famagusta 35 8N 33 55E
57 Fandriana 20 14S 47 21E
39 Fangcheng 31 2N 118 13E
2 Fanning I. 3 51N 159 22W
18 Fano 43 50N 13 0E
64 Fanshaw 57 11N 133 30W
52 Faradje 3 50N 29 45E
57 Farafangana 22 49S 47 50E
50 Faranah 10 2N 10 45W
31 Farar 32 30N 62 17E
31 Farar □ 32 25N 62 10E
29 Farasān, Jazā'ir, I. 16 45N 41 55E
57 Faratsiho 19 24S 46 57E
7 Fareham 50 52N 1 11W
61 Farewell, C.,
Greenland=
Farvel, K. 66 0N 44 0W
47 Farewell, C., N.Z. 40 29S 172 43E
70 Fargo 47 0N 97 0W
70 Faribault 44 15N 93 19W
33 Faridpur 23 36N 89 53E
43 Farina 30 3S 138 15E
73 Farmington, N. Mex. 36 45N 108 28W
72 Farmington, Utah 41 0N 111 58W
7 Farnborough 51 17N 0 46W
6 Farne Is. 55 38N 1 37W
79 Faro, Brazil 2 0S 56 45W
13 Faro, Port. 37 2N 7 55W
4 Faroe Is. 62 0N 7 0W
45 Farquhar, C. 23 38S 113 36E
31 Farrāshband 28 57N 52 5E
68 Farrell 41 13N 80 29W
43 Farrell Flat 33 48S 138 48E
31 Fars □ 29 30N 55 0E
21 Farsund 58 5N 6 55E
53 Faru 12 48N 6 12E
61 Farvel, K. 60 0N 44 0W
31 Faryab □ 36 0N 65 0E
9 Fastnet Rock 51 22N 9 27W
32 Fatehgarh 27 25N 79 35E
32 Fatehpur,
Rajasthan 28 0N 75 4E
33 Fatehpur, Ut.P. 27 8N 81 7E
39 Fatshan 23 0N 113 4E
70 Faulkton 45 4N 99 8W
45 Faure, I. 25 52S 113 50E
55 Fauresmith 29 44S 25 17E
20 Fauske 67 17N 15 25E
18 Favara 37 19N 13 39E
18 Favignana, I. 37 56N 12 18E
20 Faxaflói, B. 64 29N 23 0W
71 Fayetteville, Ark. 36 0N 94 5W
69 Fayetteville, N.C. 35 0N 78 58W
32 Fazilka 30 27N 74 2E
50 Fdérik 22 40N 12 45E
9 Feale, R. 52 26N 9 28W
69 Fear, C. 33 45N 78 0W
47 Featherston 41 6S 175 20E
12 Fécamp 49 45N 0 22E
14 Fehmarn, I. 54 26N 11 10E
14 Fehmarn Bælt 54 35N 11 20E
47 Feilding 40 13S 175 35E
79 Feira de
Santana 12 15S 38 57W
14 Feldkirch 47 15N 9 37E
74 Felipe
Carillo Puerto 19 38N 88 3W

* Renamed Chivhu
† Renamed Malema

7 Felixstowe 51 58N 1 22W
20 Femund, L. 62 5N 11 55E
38 Fen Ho, R. 35 36N 110 42E
* 57 Fénérive 17 22S 49 25E
39 Fencheng 28 2N 115 46E
38 Fengcheng, Heilungkiang 45 41N 128 54E
38 Fengcheng, Liaoning 40 28N 124 4E
39 Fenghsien 33 56N 106 41E
39 Fengkieh 31 0N 109 33E
38 Fengtai 39 57N 116 21E
39 Fengyuan 24 10N 120 45E
57 Fenoarivo 18 26S 46 34E
6 Fens, Reg. 52 45N 0 2E
38 Fenyang 37 19N 111 46E
23 Feodosiya 45 2N 35 28E
24 Fergana 40 23N 71 46E
62 Fergus 43 43N 80 24W
70 Fergus Falls 46 25N 96 0W
62 Ferland 50 19N 88 27W
9 Fermanagh □ 54 21N 7 40W
9 Fermoy 52 4N 8 18W
2 Fernando de Noronha, Is. 4 0S 33 10W
† 53 Fernando Póo, I.= Macias Nguema Biyoga 3 30N 8 4E
64 Fernie 49 30N 115 5W
42 Fernlees 23 51S 148 7E
32 Ferozepore 30 55N 74 40E
18 Ferrara 44 50N 11 36E
50 Fès 34 0N 5 0½W
8 Fetlar, I. 60 36N 0 52W
51 Fezzan 27 0N 15 0E
57 Fianarantsoa 21 26S 47 5E
57 Fianarantsoa □ 21 30S 47 0E
14 Fichtelgebirge, Mts. 50 10N 12 0E
57 Ficksburg 28 51S 27 53E
53 Fiditi 7 45N 3 53E
15 Fier, Portile de 44 42N 22 30E
8 Fife □ 56 13N 3 2W
12 Figeac 44 37N 2 2E
57 Figtree 20 22S 28 20E
13 Figueira da Foz 40 7N 8 54W
13 Figueras 42 18N 2 58E
50 Figuig 32 5N 1 11W
57 Fihaonana 18 36S 47 12E
47 Fiji ■ 17 20S 179 0E
6 Filey 54 13N 0 10W
19 Filiatrá 37 9N 21 35E
53 Filingué 14 21N 3 19E
21 Filipstad 59 43N 14 9E
73 Fillmore 34 23N 118 58W
8 Findhorn 57 30N 3 45W
68 Findlay 41 0N 83 41W
12 Finistère □ 48 20N 4 20W
13 Finisterre, C. 42 50N 9 19W
42 Finke 25 34S 134 35E
20 Finland ■ 70 0N 27 0E
22 Finland, G. of 60 0N 26 0¼E
46 Finley 35 38S 145 35E
64 Finnegan 51 7N 112 5W
42 Finnigan, Mt. 15 49S 145 17E
43 Finniss, C. 33 38S 134 51E
20 Finnmark □ 69 30N 25 0E
18 Firenze 43 47N 11 15E
32 Firozabad 27 10N 78 25E
31 Fīrūzābād 28 52N 52 35E
31 Fīrūzkūh 35 50N 52 40E
45 Fisher 30 30S 131 0E
7 Fishguard 51 59N 4 59W
68 Fitchburg 42 35N 71 47W
80 Fitz Roy 47 10S 67 0W
69 Fitzgerald 31 45N 83 10W
42 Fitzroy, R., Queens. 23 32S 150 52E
44 Fitzroy, R., W. Australia 17 31S 138 35E
44 Fitzroy Crossing 18 9S 125 38E
54 Fizi 4 17S 28 55E
73 Flagstaff 35 10N 111 40W
21 Flåm 60 52N 7 14E
6 Flamborough Hd. 54 8N 0 4W
72 Flaming Gorge L. 41 15N 109 30W
11 Flanders= Flandres, Plaines des 51 10N 3 15E
11 Flandre Occidentale □ 51 0N 3 0E
11 Flandre Orientale □ 51 0N 4 0E
11 Flandres, Plaines des 51 10N 3 15E
8 Flannan Is. 58 9N 7 52W
72 Flathead L. 47 50N 114 0W
42 Flattery, C., Australia 14 58S 145 21E
72 Flattery, C., U.S.A. 48 21N 124 31W
6 Fleetwood 53 55N 3 1W
21 Flekkefjord 58 18N 6 39E
14 Flensburg 54 46N 9 28E
7 Fletton 52 34N 0 13W
65 Flin Flon 54 46N 101 53W
45 Flinders, B. 34 19S 114 9E
42 Flinders, I. 40 0S 148 0E
43 Flinders, Ras. 31 30S 138 30E
6 Flint, U.K. 53 15N 3 7W
68 Flint, U.S.A. 43 0N 83 40W
1 Flint I. 11 26S 151 48W
6 Flodden 55 37N 2 8W
70 Flora 38 40N 88 30W
18 Florence, Italy= Firenze 43 47N 11 15E
69 Florence, Ala. 34 50N 87 50W
73 Florence, Ariz. 33 0N 111 25W
72 Florence, Oreg. 44 0N 124 3W
69 Florence, S.C. 34 5N 79 50W
78 Florencia 1 36N 75 36W
74 Flores 16 50N 89 40W
35 Flores, I. 8 35S 121 0¼E
35 Flores Sea 6 30S 124 0E
79 Floriano 6 50S 43 0W
80 Florianópolis 27 30S 48 30W
80 Florida 34 7S 56 10W
69 Florida □ 28 30N 82 0W
59 Florida Str. 25 0N 80 0W
19 Flórina 40 48N 21 26E
21 Florø 61 35N 5 1E
11 Flushing= Vlissingen 51 26N 3 34E
41 Fly, R. 7 50S 141 20E
65 Foam Lake 51 40N 103 15W
15 Focşani 45 41N 27 15E
18 Fóggia 41 28N 15 31E
53 Foggo 11 21N 9 57E
63 Fogo 49 43N 54 17W
12 Foix, Reg. 43 0N 1 30E
62 Foleyet 48 15N 82 25W
18 Foligno 42 58N 12 40E
7 Folkestone 51 5N 1 11E
65 Fond du Lac, Canada 59 20N 107 10W
70 Fond-du-Lac, U.S.A. 43 46N 88 26W
18 Fondi 41 21N 13 25E
13 Fonsagrada 43 8N 7 4W
74 Fonseca, G. de 13 10N 87 40W
12 Fontainebleau 48 24N 2 40E
78 Fonte Boa 2 25S 66 0W
53 Fontem 5 32N 9 52E
12 Fontenay-le-Comte 46 28N 0 48W
39 Foochow 26 5N 119 18E
46 Forbes 33 22S 148 0E
64 Forest Lawn 51 4N 114 0W
64 Forestburg 52 35N 112 1W
63 Forestville 48 48N 69 20W
12 Forez, Mts. du 45 40N 3 50E
8 Forfar 56 40N 2 53W
18 Forlí 44 14N 12 2E
6 Formby Pt. 53 33N 3 7W
13 Formentera, I. 38 40N 1 30E
79 Formiga 20 27S 45 25W
80 Formosa, Arg. 26 15S 58 10W
79 Formosa, Brazil 15 32S 47 20W
39 Formosa= Taiwan ■ 24 0N 121 0E
79 Formosa, Sa. 12 0S 55 0W
39 Formosa Str. 24 40N 124 0E
8 Forres 57 37N 3 38W
45 Forrest 38 22S 143 40E
71 Forrest City 35 1N 90 47W
42 Forsayth 18 33S 143 34E
14 Forst 51 43N 15 37E
72 Forsyth 46 14N 106 37W
62 Fort Albany 52 15N 81 35W
51 Fort-Archambault =Sarh 9 5N 18 23E
64 Fort Assinboine 54 20N 114 45W
8 Fort Augustus 57 9N 4 40W
56 Fort Beaufort 32 46S 26 40E
72 Fort Benton 47 50N 110 40W
72 Fort Bragg 39 28N 123 50W
72 Fort Bridger 41 22N 110 20W
61 Fort Chimo 58 9N 68 12W
65 Fort Chipewyan 58 46N 111 9W
70 Fort Collins 40 30N 105 4W
62 Fort Coulonge 45 50N 76 45W
* 57 Fort-Dauphin 25 2S 47 0E
70 Fort Dodge 42 29N 94 10W
65 Fort Frances 48 35N 93 25W
60 Fort Franklin 65 30N 123 45W
62 Fort George 53 40N 79 0W
† 62 Fort George, R. 53 50N 77 0W
60 Fort Good Hope 66 14N 128 40W
64 Fort Graham 56 38N 124 35W
73 Fort Hancock 31 19N 105 56W
62 Fort Hope 51 30N 88 10W
63 Fort Kent 47 12N 68 30W
51 Fort-Lamy= Ndjamena 12 4N 15 8E
70 Fort Laramie 42 15W 104 30W
69 Fort Lauderdale 26 10N 80 5W
64 Fort Liard 60 20N 123 30W
64 Fort Mackay 57 12N 111 41W
63 Fort McKenzie 56 50N 69 0W
64 Fort Macleod 49 45N 113 30W
50 Fort MacMahon 29 51N 1 45E
60 Fort McPherson 67 30N 134 55W
70 Fort Madison 40 39N 91 20W
50 Fort Mirabel 29 31N 2 55E
70 Fort Morgan 40 10N 103 50W
32 Fort Munro 30 0N 69 55E
69 Fort Myers 26 30N 82 0W
64 Fort Nelson 58 50N 122 30W
60 Fort Norman 64 57N 125 30W
69 Fort Payne 34 25N 85 44W
72 Fort Peck 47 1N 105 30W
72 Fort Peck Res. 47 40N 107 0W
69 Fort Pierce 27 29N 80 19W
52 Fort Portal 0 40N 30 20E
64 Fort Providence 61 20N 117 30W
65 Fort Qu'Appelle 50 45N 103 50W
64 Fort Resolution 61 10N 114 40W
54 Fort-Rousset 0 29S 15 55E
62 Fort Rupert 51 30N 78 40W
64 Fort St. James 54 30N 124 10W
64 Fort St. John 56 15N 120 50W
32 Fort Sandeman 31 20N 69 25E
64 Fort Saskatchewan 53 40N 113 15W
71 Fort Scott 38 0N 94 40W
60 Fort Selkirk 62 43N 137 22W
62 Fort Severn 56 0N 87 40W
64 Fort Simpson 61 45N 121 30W
24 Fort Shevchenko 44 30N 50 10E
71 Fort Smith 35 25N 94 25W
71 Fort Stockton 30 48N 103 2W
71 Fort Sumner 34 24N 104 8W
69 Fort Valley 32 33N 83 52W
64 Fort Vermilion 58 30N 115 57W
* 57 Fort Victoria 20 8S 30 55E
68 Fort Wayne 41 5N 85 10W
62 Fort William, Canada= Thunder Bay 48 20N 89 10W
8 Fort William, U.K. 56 48N 5 8W
71 Fort Worth 32 45N 97 25W
60 Fort Yukon 66 35N 145 12W
79 Fortaleza 3 35S 38 35W
75 Fort-de-France 14 36N 61 5W
44 Fortescue, R. 21 20S 116 5E
8 Forth, Firth of 56 5N 2 55W
8 Fortrose 57 35N 4 10W
72 Fortuna 48 38N 124 8W
60 Forty Mile 64 20N 140 30W
68 Fostoria 41 8N 83 25W
12 Fougères 48 21N 1 14W
8 Foula, I. 60 10N 2 5W
7 Foulness, I. 51 26N 0 55E
53 Foumban 5 45N 10 50E
44 Fourcroy, C. 11 45S 130 2E
57 Fouriesburg 28 38S 28 14E
50 Fouta Djalon, Mts. 11 20N 12 10W
47 Foveaux, Str. 46 42S 168 10E
7 Fowey 50 20N 4 39W
45 Fowlers, B. 31 59S 132 34E
39 Fowning 33 30N 119 40E
65 Fox Valley 50 30N 109 25W
61 Foxe Basin 68 30N 77 0W
61 Foxe Chan. 66 0N 80 0W
61 Foxe Pen. 65 0N 76 0W
47 Foxton 40 29S 175 18E
9 Foyle, L. 55 6N 7 18W
9 Foynes 52 37N 9 6W
80 Foz do Iguaçu 25 30S 54 30W
79 Franca 20 25S 47 30W
19 Francavilla Fontana 40 32N 17 35E
12 France ■ 47 0N 3 0E
54 Franceville 1 38S 13 35E
12 Franche Comté, Reg. 46 30N 5 50E
63 Francis Harbour 52 34N 55 44W
57 Francistown 21 11S 27 32E
63 François 47 34N 56 44W
14 Franconia 50 0N 9 0E
57 Frankfort, S. Afr. 27 16S 28 30E
68 Frankfort, Ind. 40 20N 86 33W
68 Frankfort, Ky. 38 12N 85 44W
14 Frankfurt am Main 50 7N 8 40E
14 Frankfurt an der Oder 52 50N 14 31E
14 Fränkishe Alb. 49 20N 11 30E
70 Franklin, Nebr. 40 9N 98 55W
68 Franklin, N.H. 43 28N 71 39W
68 Franklin, Pa. 41 22N 79 45W
69 Franklin, Tenn. 35 54N 86 53W
68 Franklin, W. Va. 38 38N 79 21W
* 60 Franklin, Reg. 71 0N 99 0W
72 Franklin D. Roosevelt L. 48 30N 118 16W
60 Franklin Mts. 66 0N 125 0W
60 Franklin Str. 72 0N 96 0W
46 Frankston 38 8S 145 8E
24 Frantsa Iosifa, Zemlya, Is. 76 0N 62 0E
62 Franz 48 25N 85 30W
43 Fraser, I. 25 15S 153 10E
64 Fraser, R. 49 9N 123 12W
64 Fraser Lake 54 0N 124 50W
56 Fraserburg 31 55S 21 30E
8 Fraserburgh 47 41N 2 0½W
80 Fray Bentos 33 10S 58 15W
44 Frazier Downs 18 48S 121 42E
21 Fredericia 55 34N 9 45E
68 Frederick, Md. 39 25N 77 23W
71 Frederick, Okla. 34 22N 99 0W
68 Fredericksburg 38 16N 77 29W
63 Fredericton 45 57N 66 40W
21 Frederikshavn 57 28N 10 31E
68 Fredonia 42 26N 79 20W
21 Fredrikstad 59 13N 10 57E
75 Freeport, Bahamas 26 30N 78 35W
70 Freeport, Ill. 42 18N 89 40W
68 Freeport, N.Y. 40 39N 73 35W
71 Freeport, Tex. 28 55N 95 22W
50 Freetown 8 30N 13 10W
14 Freiburg 48 0N 7 50E
80 Freire 39 0S 72 50W
14 Freising 48 24N 11 27E
14 Freistadt 48 30N 14 30E
12 Fréjus 43 25N 6 44E
45 Fremantle 32 1S 115 47E
70 Fremont, Nebr. 41 30N 96 30W
68 Fremont, Ohio 41 20N 83 5W
46 French, I. 38 20S 145 22E
79 French Guiana ■ 4 0N 53 0W
29 French Terr. of the Afars & Issas■= Djibouti ■ 11 30N 42 15E
79 Fresco, R. 6 39S 51 59W
74 Fresnillo 23 10N 103 0W
73 Fresno 36 47N 119 50W
42 Frewena 19 50S 135 50E
80 Frías 28 40S 65 5W
14 Fribourg 46 49N 7 9E
14 Friedrichshafen 47 39N 9 29E
47 Friendly Is.= Tonga Is. 20 0S 173 0W
11 Friesian Is.= Waddeniladen 53 30N 5 30E
11 Friesland □ 53 5N 5 50E
55 Frio, C. 18 0S 12 0E
18 Friuli Venezia Giulia □ 46 0N 13 0E
61 Frobisher B. 63 0N 67 0W
7 Frome 51 16N 2 17W
68 Front Royal 38 55N 78 10W
74 Frontera 18 30N 92 40W
18 Frosinone 41 38N 13 20E
68 Frostburg 39 43N 78 57W
24 Frunze 42 54N 74 36E
79 Frutal 20 0S 49 0W
15 Frýdek Místek 49 40N 18 20E
38 Fuchin 47 10N 132 0E
39 Fuchou=Foochow 26 5N 119 18E
39 Fuchow 27 50N 116 14E
36 Fuchu 34 34N 133 14E
39 Fuchun Kiang, R. 30 10N 120 9E
13 Fuente Ovejuna 38 15N 5 25W
13 Fuentes de Oñoro 40 33N 6 52W
50 Fuerteventura, I. 28 30N 14 0W
31 Fujaira 25 7N 56 18E
36 Fuji 35 9N 138 39E
36 Fuji-san, Mt. 35 22N 138 44E
36 Fuji-no-miya 35 20N 138 40E
36 Fujisawa 35 22N 139 29E
39 Fukien □ 26 0N 117 30E
36 Fukuchiyama 35 25N 135 9E
36 Fukui 36 0N 136 10E
36 Fukui □ 36 0N 136 12E
36 Fukuoka 33 30N 130 30E
36 Fukuoka □ 33 30N 131 0E
36 Fukushima 37 30N 140 15E
36 Fukushima □ 37 30N 140 15E
36 Fukuyama 34 35N 133 20E
14 Fulda 50 32N 9 41E
73 Fullerton 33 52N 117 58W
70 Fulton, Mo. 38 50N 91 55W
68 Fulton, N.Y. 43 20N 76 22W

Renamed Fenoarivo Atsinanana
† *Renamed Bioko*

* *Renamed Faradofay*
† *French nameform La Grande, R.*

* *Renamed Masvingo*

* *Renamed Kitikmeot*

36 Funabashi 35 45N 140 0E
3 Funafuti, I. 8 30S 179 0E
50 Funchal 32 45N 16 55W
78 Fundación 10 31N 74 11W
13 Fundão 40 8N 7 30W
63 Fundy, B. of 45 0N 66 0W
53 Funtua 11 31N 7 17E
30 Furat, Nahr al, R. 33 30N 43 0E
6 Furness 54 14N 3 8W
14 Fürth 49 29N 11 0E
61 Fury & Hecla Str. 69 40N 81 0W
78 Fusagasugá 4 21N 74 22W
38 Fushan 37 30N 121 5E
38 Fushun 42 0N 123 59E
38 Fusin 42 12N 121 33E
39 Futing 27 15N 120 10E
39 Futsing 25 46N 119 29E
39 Fuyang 30 5N 119 56E
38 Fuyu 45 10N 124 50E
21 Fyen, I.=Fyn, I. 55 20N 10 30E
6 Fylde, R. 53 47N 2 56W
21 Fyn, I. 55 20N 10 30E
8 Fyne, L. 56 0N 5 20W

G

53 Gaanda 10 10N 12 27E
50 Gabès 33 53N 10 2E
51 Gabès, G. de 34 0N 10 30E
54 Gabon ■ 0 10S 10 0E
56 Gaborone 24 37S 25 57E
19 Gabrovo 42 52N 25 27E
31 Gach-Sarán 30 15N 50 45E
53 Gada 13 38N 5 36E
32 Gadag 15 30N 75 45E
32 Gadarwara 22 50N 78 50E
32 Gadhada 22 0N 71 35E
69 Gadsden, Ala. 34 1N 86 0W
73 Gadsden, Ariz. 32 35N 114 47W
32 Gadwal 16 10N 77 50E
18 Gaeta 41 12N 13 35E
69 Gaffney 35 10N 81 31W
50 Gafsa 34 24N 8 51E
63 Gagetown 45 46N 66 29W
50 Gagnoa 6 4N 5 55W
63 Gagnon 51 50N 68 5W
69 Gainesville, Fla. 29 38N 82 20W
69 Gainesville, Ga. 34 17N 83 47W
71 Gainesville, Tex. 33 40N 97 10W
6 Gainsborough 53 23N 0 46W
43 Gairdner, L. 32 0S 136 0E
8 Gairloch, L. 57 43N 5 45W
53 Gajiram 12 29N 13 9E
55 Galangue 13 48S 16 3E
2 Galápagos, Is. 0 0N 89 0W
8 Galashiels 55 37N 2 50W
15 Galaţi 45 27N 28 2E
19 Galatina 40 10N 18 10E
69 Galax 36 42N 80 57W
21 Galdhøpiggen, Mt. 61 45N 8 40E
45 Galena 27 50S 114 41E
70 Galesburg 40 57N 90 23W
22 Galich 58 23N 42 18E
13 Galicia, Reg. 42 43N 8 0W
28 Galilee= Hagalil, Reg. 32 53N 35 18E
28 Galilee, Sea of= Kinneret, Yam 32 49N 35 36E
69 Gallatin 36 24N 86 27W
32 Galle 6 5N 80 10E
13 Gállego, R. 41 39N 0 51W
80 Gallegos, R. 51 35S 69 0W
78 Gallinas, Pta. 12 28N 71 40W
19 Gallipoli 40 8N 18 0E
68 Gallipolis 38 50N 82 10W
20 Gällivare 67 7N 20 32E
8 Galloway, Reg. 55 0N 4 25W
8 Galloway, Mull of 54 38N 4 50W
73 Gallup 35 30N 108 54W
62 Galt= Cambridge 43 23N 80 19W
9 Galty Mts. 52 20N 8 10W
71 Galveston 29 15N 94 48W
71 Galveston B. 29 30N 94 50W
80 Gálvez 32 0S 61 20W
9 Galway 53 16N 9 4W
9 Galway, B. 53 10N 9 20W
9 Galway □ 53 16N 9 3W
36 Gamagori 34 50N 137 14E
53 Gamawa 12 10N 10 31E
53 Gambaga 10 30N 0 28W
50 Gambia ■ 13 20N 15 45W
50 Gambia, R. 13 28N 16 34W
44 Gambier, C. 11 56S 130 57E
74 Gamboa 9 8N 79 42W
73 Gamerco 35 33N 108 56W
56 Gamtoos, R. 33 58S 25 1E
28 Gan Shamu'el 32 28N 34 56E
28 Gan Yavne 31 48N 34 42E
62 Gananoque 44 20N 76 10W
11 Gand=Gent 51 2N 3 37E
33 Gandak, R. 25 32N 85 5E
63 Gander 49 1N 54 33W
53 Gandi 12 55N 5 49E
33 Ganga, R. 23 22N 90 32E
32 Ganganagar 29 56N 73 56E
33 Gangaw 22 5N 94 15E
33 Ganges, R.= Ganga, R. 23 22N 90 32E
33 Gangtok 27 20N 88 40E
53 Gao 18 0N 1 0E
53 Gaoua 10 20N 3 8W
50 Gaoual 11 45N 13 25W
12 Gap 44 33N 6 5E
79 Garanhuns 8 50S 36 30W
72 Garberville 40 11N 123 50W
57 Garcia 25 32S 32 13E
12 Gard □ 44 2N 4 10E
18 Garda, L. di 45 40N 10 40E
71 Garden City 38 0N 100 45W
31 Gardez 33 31N 68 59E
72 Gardiner 45 3N 110 53W
68 Gardner 42 35N 72 0W
29 Gardo 9 18N 49 20E
72 Garfield 47 3N 117 8W
18 Gargano, Mte. 41 43N 15 40E
52 Garissa 0 25S 39 40E
53 Garkida 10 27N 12 36E
53 Garko 11 45N 8 53E
72 Garland 41 47N 112 10W
24 Garm 39 0N 70 20E
31 Garmsar 35 20N 52 25E
29 Garoe 8 35N 48 40E
12 Garonne, R. 45 2N 0 36W
53 Garoua 9 19N 13 21E
72 Garrison 46 37N 112 56W
‡70 Garrison Res. 47 30N 102 0W
60 Garry, L. 65 40N 100 0W
62 Garson 50 5N 96 50W
37 Gartok 31 59N 80 30E
35 Garut 7 14S 107 53E
47 Garvie, Mts. 45 27S 169 59E
68 Gary 41 35N 87 20W
78 Garzón 2 10N 75 40W
17 Gascogne, Reg. 43 45N 0 20E
12 Gascogne, G. de 44 0N 2 0W
12 Gascony, Reg.= Gascogne, Reg. 43 45N 0 20E
45 Gascoyne, R. 24 52S 113 37E
45 Gascoyne Junction 25 3S 115 12E
50 Gashaka 7 20N 11 29E
53 Gashua 12 54N 11 0E
63 Gaspé 48 52N 64 30W
63 Gaspé, C. de 48 48N 64 7W
*63 Gaspé Pass. 49 10N 64 0W
63 Gaspé Pén. de 48 45N 65 40W
63 Gaspésie, Parc Prov. de la 49 0N 66 45W
69 Gastonia 35 17N 81 10W
80 Gastre 42 10S 69 15W
13 Gata, C. de 36 41N 2 13W
13 Gata, Sa. de 40 20N 6 20W
8 Gatehouse of Fleet 54 53N 4 10W
6 Gateshead 54 57N 1 37W
57 Gaths 26 2S 30 32E
62 Gatineau, Parc Prov. de la 45 30N 75 52W
†57 Gatooma 18 21S 29 55E
74 Gatun 9 16N 79 55W
74 Gatun L. 9 7N 79 56W
33 Gauhati 26 5N 91 55E
20 Gaula, R. 63 21N 10 14E
31 Gavater 25 10N 61 23E
21 Gavle 60 41N 17 13E
21 Gävleborgs □ 61 20N 16 15E
32 Gawilgarh Hills 21 15N 76 45E
43 Gawler 34 30S 138 42E
33 Gaya, India 24 47N 85 4E
53 Gaya, Nigeria 11 57N 9 0E
43 Gayndah 25 35S 151 39E
28 Gaza 31 30N 34 28E
57 Gaza □ 23 0S 33 0E
28 Gaza Strip 31 29N 34 25E
53 Gazaoua 13 32N 7 55E
30 Gaziantep 37 6N 37 23E
53 Gboko 7 17N 9 4E
53 Gbongan 7 28N 4 20E
57 Gcuwa 32 20S 28 11E
15 Gdańsk 54 22N 18 40E
15 Gdańska, Zatoka 54 30N 19 15E
15 Gdynia 54 35N 18 33E
51 Gebeit Mine 21 3N 36 29E
51 Gedaref 14 2N 35 28E
28 Gedera 31 49N 34 46E
21 Gedser 54 35N 11 55E
46 Geelong 38 2S 144 20E
45 Geelvink, Chan. 28 30S 114 10E
11 Geeraadsbergen 50 45N 3 53E
53 Geidam 12 57N 11 57E
51 Geili 16 1N 32 37E
52 Geita 2 48S 32 12E
18 Gela 37 3N 14 15E
11 Gelderland □ 52 5N 6 10E
11 Geldrop 51 25N 5 32E
11 Geleen 50 57N 5 49E
30 Gelibolu 40 28N 26 43E
14 Gelsenkirchen 51 30N 7 5E
34 Gemas 2 37N 102 36E
11 Gembloux 50 34N 4 43E
54 Gemena 3 20N 19 40E
80 General Acha 37 20S 64 38W
80 General Alvear 36 0S 60 0W
80 General Belgrano 36 0S 58 30W
80 General Guido 36 40S 57 40W
80 General Juan Madariaga 37 0S 57 0W
80 General Paz 27 45S 57 36W
80 General Pico 35 45S 63 50W
80 General Pinedo 27 15S 61 30W
80 General Roca 30 0S 67 40W
80 General Villegas 35 0S 63 0W
14 Geneva, Switz.= Genève 46 12N 6 9E
68 Geneva, U.S.A. 42 53N 77 0W
14 Geneva, L.= Léman, L. 46 26N 6 30E
14 Genève 46 12N 6 9E
13 Genil, R. 37 42N 5 19W
12 Genissiat 46 1N 5 48E
11 Genk 50 58N 5 32E
18 Genoa=Genova 44 24N 8 56E
18 Genova 44 24N 8 56E
18 Génova, G. di 44 0N 9 0E
11 Gent 51 2N 3 37E
45 Geographe, B. 33 30S 115 15E
45 Geographe, Chan. 24 30S 113 0E
56 George 33 58S 22 29E
68 George, L. 43 30N 73 30W
61 George R.=Port Nouveau-Quebec 58 30N 65 50W
42 George Town Australia 41 5S 148 55E
34 George Town, W. Malaysia 5 25N 100 19E
42 Georgetown, Australia 18 17S 143 33E
62 Georgetown, Ont. 43 40N 80 0W
63 Georgetown, P.E.I. 46 13N 62 24W
50 Georgetown, Gambia 13 30N 14 47W
78 Georgetown, Guyana 6 50N 58 12W
69 Georgetown, U.S.A. 33 22N 79 15W
69 Georgia □ 32 0N 82 0W
64 Georgia Str. 49 20N 124 0W
62 Georgian B. 45 15N 81 0W
23 Georgian S.S.R. □ 41 0N 45 0E
23 Georgiu-Dezh 51 3N 39 20E
23 Georgiyevsk 44 12N 43 28E
14 Gera 50 53N 12 5E
45 Geraldton, Australia 28 48S 114 32E
62 Geraldton, Canada 49 44N 86 59W
60 Gerdine, Mt. 61 32N 152 50W
30 Gerede 40 45N 32 10E
29 Gerlogubi 6 53N 45 3E
64 Germansen Landing 55 43N 124 40W
57 Germiston 26 15S 28 5E
36 Gero 35 48N 137 14E
13 Gerona 41 58N 2 46E
12 Gers □ 43 35N 0 38E
12 Gevaudan, Reg. 44 40N 3 40E
72 Geyser 47 17N 110 30W
20 Geysir 64 19N 20 18W
28 Gezer 31 52N 34 55E
33 Ghaghara, R. 25 45N 84 40E
53 Ghana ■ 6 0N 1 0W
50 Ghardaïa 32 31N 3 37E
30 Ghat 24 59N 10 19E
51 Ghazal, Bahr el, R. 9 31N 30 25E
50 Ghazaouet 35 8N 1 50W
32 Ghaziabad 28 42N 77 35E
33 Ghazipur 25 38N 83 35E
31 Ghazni 33 30N 68 17E
31 Ghazni □ 33 0N 68 0E
11 Ghent=Gent 51 2N 3 37E
31 Ghor □ 34 0N 64 20E
62 Ghost River 51 25N 83 20W
50 Ghudames 30 11N 9 29E
32 Ghugus 19 55N 79 15E
32 Ghulam Mohammed Barr. 25 30N 67 0E
31 Ghurian 34 17N 61 25E
14 Giant Mts.= Krkonose 50 50N 16 10E
9 Giant's Causeway 55 15N 6 30W
18 Giarre 37 44N 15 10E
75 Gibara 21 0N 76 20W
55 Gibeon 25 7S 17 45E
13 Gibraltar ■ 36 7N 5 22W
13 Gibraltar, Str. of 35 55N 5 40W
44 Gibson, Des. 24 0S 126 0E
14 Giessen 50 34N 8 40E
36 Gifu 35 30N 136 45E
36 Gifu □ 36 0N 137 0E
74 Giganta, Sa. de la 25 30N 111 30W
8 Gigha, I. 55 42N 5 45W
13 Gijón 43 32N 5 42W
73 Gila, R. 32 43N 114 33W
73 Gila Bend 32 57N 112 43W
30 Gilan □ 37 0N 49 0E
53 Gilbedi 13 40N 5 45E
*3 Gilbert Is. 1 0N 176 0E
65 Gilbert Plains 51 9N 100 28W
42 Gilbert River 18 9S 142 50E
45 Gilgai 31 15S 119 56E
46 Gilgandra 31 42S 148 39E
52 Gilgil 0 30S 36 20E
32 Gilgit 35 50N 74 15E
65 Gillam 56 20N 94 40W
42 Gilliat 20 40S 141 28E
7 Gillingham 51 23N 0 34E
62 Gilmour 44 48N 77 37W
73 Gilroy 37 10N 121 37W
42 Gindie 23 45S 148 10E
45 Gingin 31 22S 115 37E
28 Ginnosar 32 51N 35 32E
35 Giong, Teluk, B. 4 50N 118 20E
78 Girardot 4 18N 74 48W
8 Girdle Ness 57 9N 2 2W
30 Giresun 40 45N 38 30E
51 Girga 26 17N 31 55E
33 Giridih 24 10N 86 21E
31 Girishk 31 47N 64 24E
12 Gironde, R. 45 30N 1 0W
12 Gironde □ 44 45N 0 30W
8 Girvan 55 15N 4 50W
47 Gisborne 38 39S 178 5E
52 Gisenyi 1 41S 29 30E
52 Gitega 3 26S 29 56E
15 Giurgiu 43 52N 25 57E
28 Giv'at Olga 32 28N 34 53E
28 Giv'atayim 32 4N 34 49E
51 Giza=El Gîza 30 0N 31 10E
31 Gizhiga 62 0N 150 27E
25 Gizhiginskaya Guba 61 0N 158 0E
15 Gîzycko 54 2N 21 48E
60 Gjoa Haven 68 20N 96 0W
21 Gjøvik 60 47N 10 43E
63 Glace Bay 46 11N 59 58W
64 Glacier B. Nat. Monument 58 45N 136 30W
72 Glacier Nat. Park 48 40N 114 0W
71 Gladewater 32 30N 94 58W
42 Gladstone, Queens. 23 52S 151 16E
43 Gladstone, S. Australia 33 17S 138 22E
65 Gladstone, Canada 50 20N 99 0W
21 Glåma, R. 59 12N 10 57E
8 Glasgow, U.K. 55 52N 4 14W
68 Glasgow, U.S.A. 37 2N 85 55W
7 Glastonbury 51 9N 2 42W
14 Glauchau 50 50N 12 33E
22 Glazov 58 0N 52 30E
64 Gleichen 50 50N 113 0W
8 Glen Affric 57 15N 5 0W
73 Glen Canyon Dam 37 0N 111 25W
73 Glen Canyon Nat. Recreation Area 37 30N 111 0W
8 Glen Coe 56 40N 5 0W
8 Glen Garry 57 3N 5 7W
8 Glen More 57 12N 4 30E
46 Glen Thompson 37 38S 142 35E
46 Glenalbyn 36 30S 143 48E
47 Glenbrook 33 46S 150 37E
57 Glencoe 28 11S 30 11E
57 Glendale 17 22S 31 5E
73 Glendale, Ariz. 33 40N 112 8W
73 Glendale, Calif. 34 7N 118 18W
72 Glendale, Oreg. 42 44N 123 29W

* *French nameform Honguedo, Dét. d'*
† *Renamed Kadoma*
‡ *Renamed Sakakawea, Lake*

* *Renamed Kiribati*

Glendive Guadalajara, Mexico

70 Glendive 47 7N 104 40W
43 Glenelg 34 58S 138 30E
46 Glenelg, R. 38 3S 141 9E
9 Glengariff 51 45N 9 33W
42 Glengyle 24 48S 139 37E
43 Glenn Innes 29 44S 151 44E
46 Glennies Creek 32 30S 151 8E
42 Glenorchy 36 55S 142 41E
42 Glenore 17 50S 141 12E
42 Glenormiston 22 55S 138 50E
72 Glenrock 42 53N 105 55W
8 Glenrothes 56 12N 3 11W
68 Glens Falls 43 20N 73 40W
9 Glenties 54 48N 8 18W
64 Glenwood, Canada 49 21N 113 24W
70 Glenwood, U.S.A. 45 38N 95 21W
72 Glenwood Springs 39 39N 107 15W
15 Gliwice 50 22N 18 41E
73 Globe 33 25N 110 53W
14 Głogów 51 37N 16 5E
57 Glorieuses, Is. 11 30S 47 20E
6 Glossop 53 27N 1 56W
46 Gloucester, Australia 32 0S 151 59E
7 Gloucester, U.K. 51 52N 2 15W
7 Gloucestershire □ 51 44N 2 10W
68 Gloversville 43 5N 74 18W
14 Glückstadt 53 46N 9 28E
14 Gmünd 48 45N 15 0E
14 Gmunden 47 55N 13 48E
15 Gniezno 52 30N 17 35E
45 Gnowangerup 33 58S 117 59E
34 Gô Công 10 12N 107 0E
32 Goa 15 33N 73 59E
32 Goa □ 15 33N 73 59E
53 Goaso 6 48N 2 30W
8 Goat Fell, Mt. 55 37N 5 11W
54 Goba 7 1N 39 59E
56 Gobabis 22 16S 19 0E
38 Gobi, Des. 44 0N 111 0E
33 Godavari, R. 16 37N 82 18E
33 Godavari Pt. 17 0N 82 20E
63 Godbout 49 20N 67 38W
62 Goderich 43 45N 81 41W
75 Golfito 8 41N 83 5W
32 Godhra 22 49N 73 40E
65 Gods L. 54 40N 94 10W
2 Godthåb 64 10N 51 46W
56 Goei Hoop, K.die =Good Hope, C. of 34 24S 18 30E
11 Goeree 51 50N 4 0E
11 Goes 51 30N 3 55E
62 Gogama 47 35N 81 35W
42 Gogango 23 40S 150 2E
51 Gogriâl 8 30N 28 0E
79 Goiânia 16 35S 49 20W
79 Goias □ 12 10S 48 0W
36 Gojo 34 21N 135 42E
32 Gojra 31 10N 72 40E
33 Gokteik 22 26N 97 0E
53 Gold Coast 4 0N 1 40W
64 Golden, Canada 51 20N 117 0W
70 Golden, U.S.A. 39 42N 105 30W
47 Golden B. 40 40S 172 50E
65 Goldfields 37 45N 117 13W
69 Goldsboro 35 24N 77 59W
44 Goldsworthy 20 21S 119 30E
14 Goleniów 53 35N 14 50E
75 Golfito 8 41N 83 5W
18 Golfo Aranci 41 0N 9 38E
8 Golspie 57 58N 3 58W
54 Goma 1 37S 29 10E
53 Gombe 10 19N 11 2E
22 Gomel 52 28N 31 0E
50 Gomera, I. 28 10N 17 5W
74 Gómez Palacio 25 40N 104 40W
31 Gonābād 34 15N 58 45E
75 Gonaïves 19 20N 72 50W
33 Gonda 27 9N 81 58E
51 Gonder 12 23N 37 30E
32 Gondia 21 30N 80 10E
28 Gonen 33 7N 35 39E
53 Gongola, R. 9 30N 12 10E
53 Goniri 11 30N 12 15E
52 Gonja 4 15S 38 0E
71 Gonzales 29 30N 97 30W
56 Good Hope, C. of 34 24S 18 30E
6 Goole 53 42N 0 52W
46 Goolgowi 33 58S 154 39E
45 Goomalling 31 19S 116 49E
43 Goondiwindi 28 30S 150 21E
11 Goor 52 13N 6 33E
63 Goose Bay 53 15N 60 20W
32 Gop 22 5N 69 50E
33 Gorakhpur 26 47N 83 32E
75 Gorda, Pta. 14 10N 83 10W
70 Gordon 42 49N 102 6W
45 Gordon River 34 10S 117 15E
56 Gordonia, Reg. 28 13S 21 10E
42 Gordonvale 17 5S 145 50E
43 Gore, Australia 28 17S 151 29E
54 Gore, Ethiopia 8 12N 35 32E
47 Gore, N.Z. 46 5S 168 58E
9 Gorey 52 41N 6 18W
78 Gorgona, I. 3 0N 78 10W
23 Goris 39 31N 46 23E
18 Gorízia 45 56N 13 37E
22 Gorki=Gorkiy 56 20N 44 0E
22 Gorkiy 56 20N 44 0E
22 Gorkovskoye Vdkhr 57 2N 43 4E
14 Görlitz 51 10N 14 59E
23 Gorlovka 48 25N 37 58E
19 Gorna Oryakhovitsa 43 7N 25 40E
24 Gorno Filinskoye 60 5N 70 0E
22 Gornyatski 67 49N 64 20E
35 Gorontalo 0 35N 123 13E
53 Goronyo 13 29N 5 39E
9 Gort 53 4N 8 50W
22 Goryn, R. 52 8N 27 17E
14 Gorzów Wielkopolski 52 43N 15 15E
46 Gosford 33 23S 151 18E
68 Goshen 41 36N 85 46W
14 Goslar 51 55N 10 23E
18 Gospič 44 35N 15 23E
7 Gosport 50 48N 1 8W
21 Göta kanal 58 45N 14 15E
21 Göteborg 57 43N 11 59E
21 Göteborgs och Bohus □ 58 30N 11 30E
14 Gotha 50 56N 10 42E
21 Gothenburg= Göteborg 57 43N 11 59E
21 Gotland, I. 57 30N 18 30E
21 Götland, Reg. 58 0N 14 0E
36 Gōtsu 35 0N 132 14E
14 Göttingen 51 31N 9 55E
15 Gottwaldov 49 14N 17 40E
11 Gouda 52 1N 4 42E
2 Gough, I. 40 10S 9 45W
62 Gouin Rés. 48 35N 74 40W
46 Goulburn 32 22S 149 31E
53 Goundam 16 25N 3 45W
51 Gounou-Gaya 9 38N 15 31E
75 Governor's Harbour 25 10N 76 14W
7 Gower, Pen. 51 35N 5 10W
80 Goya 29 10S 59 10W
18 Gozo, I. 36 0N 14 13E
56 Graaff-Reinet 32 13S 24 32E
18 Gračac 44 18N 15 57E
75 Gracias a Dios, C. 15 0N 83 20W
13 Grado 45 40N 13 20E
43 Grafton, Australia 29 35S 152 0E
70 Grafton, U.S.A. 48 30N 97 25W
62 Graham, Canada 49 20N 90 30W
69 Graham, N.C. 36 5N 79 22W
71 Graham, Tex. 33 7N 98 38W
64 Graham I. 53 40N 132 30W
2 Graham Ld. 65 0S 64 0W
65 Grahamdale 51 30N 98 34W
56 Grahamstown 33 19S 26 31E
48 Grain Coast, Reg. 4 20N 10 0W
79 Grajaú 5 50S 46 30W
8 Grampian □ 57 20N 2 45W
8 Grampian Highlands, Mts. 56 50N 4 0W
50 Gran Canaria, I. 27 55N 15 35W
80 Gran Chaco, Reg. 25 0S 61 0W
18 Gran Paradiso, Mt. 49 33N 7 17E
18 Gran Sasso d'Italia, Mts. 42 25N 13 30E
75 Granada, Nic. 11 58N 86 0W
13 Granada, Sp. 37 10N 3 35W
9 Granard 53 47N 7 30W
62 Granby 45 25N 72 45W
75 Grand Bahama I. 26 40N 78 30W
63 Grand Bank 47 6N 55 48W
50 Grand Bassam 5 10N 3 49W
75 Grand Bourg 15 53N 61 19W
73 Grand Canyon 36 10N 112 45W
73 Grand Canyon Nat. Park 36 15N 112 20W
75 Grand Cayman, I. 19 20N 81 20W
72 Grand Coulee Dam 48 0N 118 50W
63 Grand Falls 47 2N 67 46W
64 Grand Forks, Canada 49 0N 118 30W
70 Grand Forks, U.S.A. 48 0N 97 3W
68 Grand Haven 43 3N 86 13W
70 Grand Island 40 59N 98 25W
73 Grand Junction 39 0N 108 30W
50 Grand Lahou 5 10N 5 0W
70 Grand Marais 47 45N 90 25W
62 Grand' Mère 46 36N 72 40W
65 Grand Rapids, Canada 53 12N 99 19W
68 Grand Rapids, Mich. 42 57N 85 40W
70 Grand Rapids, Minn. 47 19N 93 29W
14 Grand St-Bernard, Col. du 45 53N 7 11E
72 Grand Teton, Mt. 43 45N 110 57W
80 Grande, B. 50 30S 68 20W
66 Grande, R. 25 57N 97 9W
63 Grand Baie 48 19N 70 52W
63 Grande-Entrée 47 30N 61 40W
64 Grande Prairie 55 15N 118 50W
63 Grande Rivière 48 26N 64 30W
8 Grangemouth 56 1N 3 43W
72 Grangeville 45 57N 116 4W
70 Granite City 38 45N 90 3W
47 Granity 41 39S 171 51E
79 Granja 3 17S 40 50W
13 Granollers 41 39N 2 18E
6 Grantham 52 55N 0 39W
8 Grantown-on-Spey 57 19N 3 36W
73 Grants 35 14N 107 57W
72 Grants Pass 42 30N 123 22W
72 Grantsville 40 35N 112 32W
12 Granville, France 48 50N 1 35W
68 Granville, U.S.A. 43 24N 73 16W
57 Graskop 24 56S 30 49W
72 Grass Valley 39 18N 121 0W
12 Grasse 43 38N 6 56E
65 Gravelbourg 49 50N 105 35W
62 Gravenhurst 44 52N 79 20W
43 Gravesend, Australia 29 35S 150 20E
7 Gravesend, U.K. 51 25N 0 22E
7 Grays 51 28N 0 23E
65 Grayson 50 45N 102 40W
14 Graz 47 4N 15 27E
75 Great Abaco I. 26 15N 77 10W
42 Great Australian Basin 24 30S 143 0E
45 Great Australian Bight 33 30S 130 0E
75 Great Bahama Bank 23 15N 78 0W
47 Great Barrier I. 37 12S 175 25E
42 Great Barrier Reef 19 0S 149 0E
72 Great Basin 40 0N 116 30W
60 Great Bear L. 65 0N 120 0W
70 Great Bend 38 25N 98 55W
51 Great Bitter Lake 30 15N 32 40E
9 Great Blasket, I. 52 5N 10 30W
56 Great Bushman Land 29 20S 19 0E
46 Great Divide, Mts. 23 0S 146 0E
42 Great Dividing Range 25 0S 147 0E
75 Great Exuma I. 23 30N 75 50W
72 Great Falls 47 27N 111 12W
57 Great Fish, R. 33 30S 27 8E
75 Great Inagua I. 21 0N 73 20W
32 Great Indian Des. 28 0N 72 0E
34 Great L.= Tonlé Sap 13 0N 104 0E
56 Great Namaqualand= Groot Namaqualand 26 0S 18 0E
6 Great Orme's Hd. 53 20N 3 52W
6 Great Ouse, R. 52 47N 0 22E
58 Great Plains 42 0N 100 0W
52 Great Ruaha, R. 7 56S 37 52E
72 Great Salt L. 41 0N 112 30W
72 Great Salt Lake Des. 40 20N 113 50W
44 Great Sandy Des. 21 0S 124 0E
64 Great Slave L. 61 30N 114 20W
69 Great Smoky Mt. Nat. Park 35 39N 83 30W
45 Great Victoria Des. 29 30S 126 30E
* 62 Great Whale, R. 55 20N 77 45E
62 Great Whale River=Poste de la Baleine 55 20N 77 40E
6 Great Whernside, Mt. 54 9N 1 59W
6 Great Yarmouth 52 40N 1 45E
75 Greater Antilles 20 0N 74 0W
6 Greater Manchester □ 53 35N 2 15W
34 Greater Sunda Is. 4 30S 113 0E
13 Gredos, Sa. de 40 20N 5 0W
19 Greece ■ 40 0N 23 0E
70 Greeley 40 30N 104 40W
68 Green Bay 44 30N 88 0W
68 Green B. 45 0N 87 30W
47 Green Island 45 54S 170 27E
73 Green River, Utah 39 0N 110 10W
72 Green River, Wyo. 41 32N 109 28W
68 Greencastle 39 40N 86 48W
69 Greeneville 31 50N 86 38W
68 Greenfield, Ind. 39 47N 85 51W
68 Greenfield, Mass. 42 38N 72 38W
2 Greenland ■ 66 0N 45 0W
8 Greenock 55 57N 4 45W
9 Greenore 54 2N 6 8W
45 Greenough, R. 28 51S 114 38E
69 Greensboro 36 7N 79 46W
68 Greensburg, Ind. 39 20N 85 30W
68 Greensburg, Pa. 40 18N 79 31W
50 Greenville, Liberia 5 7N 9 6W
68 Greenville, Mich. 43 12N 85 14W
71 Greenville, Miss. 33 25N 91 0W
69 Greenville, N.C. 35 37N 77 26W
68 Greenville, Pa. 41 23N 80 22W
69 Greenville, S.C. 34 54N 82 24W
71 Greenville, Tex. 33 5N 96 5W
7 Greenwich, U.K. 51 28N 0 0
71 Greenwood, Miss. 33 30N 90 4W
69 Greenwood, S.C. 34 13N 82 13W
42 Gregory Downs 18 35S 138 45E
44 Gregory L. 20 10S 127 30E
14 Greifswalder Bodden 54 12N 13 35E
22 Gremikha 67 50N 39 40E
71 Grenada 33 45N 89 50W
75 Grenada, I. 12 10N 61 40W
46 Grenfell 33 52S 148 8E
21 Grenen, C. 57 46N 10 34E
12 Grenoble 45 12N 5 42E
35 Gresik 9 13S 112 38E
71 Gretna 30 0N 90 2W
8 Gretna Green 55 0N 3 3W
11 Grevenmacher 49 41N 6 26E
47 Grey, R. 42 27S 171 12E
63 Grey Res. 48 20N 56 30W
72 Greybull 44 30N 108 3W
47 Greymouth 42 29S 171 13E
47 Greytown, N.Z. 41 5S 175 29E
57 Greytown, S. Africa 29 1S 30 36E
72 Gridley 39 27N 121 47W
56 Griekwastad 28 49S 23 15E
69 Griffin 33 15N 84 16W
46 Griffith 34 14S 145 46E
65 Griffith Mine 50 47N 93 25W
6 Grimsby 53 35N 0 5W
20 Grimsey, I. 66 33N 18 0W
64 Grimshaw 56 10N 117 40W
21 Grimstad 58 22N 8 35E
70 Grinnell 41 45N 92 50W
57 Griqualand East, Reg. 30 30S 29 0E
56 Griqualand West, Reg. 28 40S 23 30E
12 Gris Nez, C. 50 50N 1 35E
57 Groblersdal 25 15S 29 25E
22 Grodno 53 42N 23 52E
14 Grodzisk Mâzowiecki 52 7N 20 37E
20 Grong 64 25N 12 8E
11 Groningen 53 15N 6 35E
11 Groningen □ 53 16N 6 40E
56 Groot-Brakrivier 34 2S 22 18E
56 Groot Karasberge, Mts. 27 10S 18 45E
56 Groot Karoo, Reg. 32 35S 23 0E
57 Groot Kei, R. 32 41S 28 22E
55 Groot Namakwaland= Namaland, Reg. 26 0S 18 0E
56 Groot Winterberg, Mt. 32 45S 26 50E
42 Groote Eylandt, I. 14 0S 136 50E
56 Grootfontein 19 31S 18 6E
14 Gross Glockner, Mt. 47 5N 12 40E
18 Grosseto 42 45N 11 7E
68 Groveton 44 34N 71 30W
23 Groznyy 43 20N 45 45E
15 Grudziądz 53 30N 18 47E
22 Gryazi 52 30N 39 58E
33 Gua 22 13N 85 20E
80 Guachípas 25 40S 65 30W
75 Guacanayabo, G. de 20 40N 77 20W
74 Guadalajara, Mexico 20 40N 103 20W

* *French nameform Grande Baleine, R.*

Guadalajara, Sp. Hautes-Pyrénées □

13 Guadalajara, Sp. 40 37N 3 12W
40 Guadalcanal 10 0S 160 0E
13 Guadalete, R. 36 35N 6 13W
13 Guadalquivir, R. 36 47N 6 22W
73 Guadalupe 34 59N 120 33W
13 Guadalupe, Sa. de 39 26N 5 25W
71 Guadalupe Pk. 31 50N 105 30W
13 Guadarrama, Sa. de 41 0N 4 0W
75 Guadeloupe, I. 16 20N 61 40W
75 Guadeloupe Pass. 16 50N 68 15W
13 Guadiana, R. 37 14N 7 22W
13 Guadix 37 18N 3 11W
80 Guafo, B. del 43 35S 74 0W
80 Guaíra 24 5S 54 10W
80 Guaitecas, Is. 44 0S 74 30W
78 Guajira, Pen. de la 12 0N 72 0W
80 Gualeguay 33 10S 59 20W
80 Gualeguaychú 33 3S 58 31W
3 Guam, I. 13 27N 144 45E
75 Guanabacoa 23 8N 82 18W
79 Guanabara □ 23 0S 43 25W
75 Guanacaste 10 40N 85 30W
75 Guanajay 22 56N 82 42W
74 Guanajuato 21 0N 101 20W
74 Guanajuato □ 20 40N 101 20W
78 Guanare 8 42N 69 12W
80 Guandacol 29 30S 68 40W
75 Guantánamo 20 10N 75 20W
78 Guaporé, R. 29 10S 51 54W
78 Guaqui 16 41S 68 54W
80 Guarapuava 25 20S 51 30W
13 Guarda 40 32N 7 20W
29 Guardafui, C.= Asir, Ras 11 55N 51 0E
78 Guasaualito 7 15N 70 44W
78 Guasipati 7 28N 61 54W
74 Guatemala 14 38N 90 31W
74 Guatemala ■ 15 40N 90 30W
78 Guaviare, R. 4 3N 67 44W
79 Guaxupé 21 10S 47 5W
75 Guayama 17 59N 66 7W
78 Guayaquil 2 15S 79 52W
78 Guayaquil, G. de 3 10S 81 0W
14 Gubin 51 58N 14 45E
53 Gubio 12 30N 12 42E
38 Guchin-Us 45 28N 102 10E
21 Gudbrandsdalen 62 0N 9 14E
33 Gudivada 16 30N 81 15E
32 Gudur 14 12N 79 55E
13 Guecho 43 21N 2 59W
50 Guéckédou 8 40N 10 5W
50 Guelma 36 25N 7 29E
62 Guelph 43 35N 80 20W
80 Güemes 24 50S 65 0W
12 Guéret 46 11N 1 51E
53 Guérin Kouka 9 40N 0 40E
13 Guernica 43 19N 2 40W
7 Guernsey, I. 49 30N 2 35W
74 Guerrero □ 17 30N 100 0W
76 Guiana Highlands, Mts. 5 0N 60 0W
55 Guibes 26 41S 16 49E
53 Guider 9 55N 13 59E
7 Guildford 51 14N 0 34W
12 Guilvinec 47 48N 4 17W
79 Guimarães 2 9S 44 35W
35 Guimaras, I. 10 35N 122 37E
48 Guinea, Reg. 9 0N 3 0E
50 Guinea ■ 10 20N 10 0W
48 Guinea, G. of 3 0N 2 30E
50 Guinea-Bissau ■ 12 0N 15 0W
75 Güines 22 50N 82 0W
12 Guingamp 48 34N 3 10W
78 Guiria 10 32N 62 1iW
35 Guiuan 11 2N 125 44E
32 Gujarat □ 23 20N 71 0E
32 Gujranwala 32 10N 74 12E
32 Gujrat 32 40N 74 2E
32 Gulbarga 17 20N 76 50E
71 Gulfport 30 28N 89 3W
65 Gull Lake 50 10N 108 55W
24 Gulshad 46 45N 74 25E
52 Gulu 2 48N 32 17E
52 Gulwe 6 30S 36 25E
46 Gum Lake 32 42S 143 9E
37 Guma 37 37N 78 18E
52 Gumbiro 10 1S 35 20E
42 Gumla 23 2N 84 32E
36 Gumma □ 36 30N 138 20E
53 Gummi 12 4N 5 9E
32 Guna 24 40N 77 19E
46 Gundagai 35 3S 148 6E
43 Gunnedah 30 59S 150 15E
46 Gunning 34 47S 149 14E
73 Gunnison, Colo. 38 32N 106 56W
72 Gunnison, Utah 39 11N 111 48W
32 Guntakal 15 11N 77 27E
69 Guntersville 34 18N 86 16W
33 Guntur 16 23N 80 30E
34 Gunungsitoli 1 15N 97 30E
65 Gunworth 51 20N 108 10W
* 30 Gürchān 34 55N 49 25E
32 Gurdaspur 32 5N 75 25E
32 Gurgaon 28 33N 77 10E
43 Gurley 29 45S 149 48E
79 Gurupá 1 20S 51 45W
24 Guryer 47 5N 52 0E
53 Gusau 12 18N 6 31E
14 Güstrow 53 47N 12 12E
45 Gutha 28 58S 115 55E
71 Guthrie 35 55N 97 30W
78 Guyana ■ 5 0N 59 0W
12 Guyenne, Reg. 44 30N 0 40E
43 Guyra 30 15S 151 40E
33 Gwa 17 30N 94 40E
53 Gwadabawa 13 20N 5 15E
32 Gwādar 25 10N 62 18E
53 Gwagwada 10 15N 7 15E
45 Gwalia 28 55S 121 20E
32 Gwalior 26 12N 78 10E
57 Gwanda 20 55S 29 0E
53 Gwandy 12 30N 4 41E
53 Gwaram 11 15N 9 51E
53 Gwarzo 12 20N 8 55E
53 Gwasero 9 30N 3 30E
9 Gweedore 55 4N 8 15W
† 57 Gwelo 19 27S 29 49E
7 Gwent □ 51 45N 3 0W
53 Gwio Kura 12 40N 11 2E
6 Gwynedd □ 53 0N 4 0W
53 Gwoza 11 12N 13 40E
24 Gydanskiy Pol. 70 0N 78 0E
43 Gympie 26 11S 152 38E
15 Gyöngyös 47 48N 20 15E
15 Györ 47 41N 17 40E
65 Gypsumville 51 45N 98 40W
15 Gyula 46 38N 21 17E

H

37 Ha Dong 20 58N 105 46E
11 Haarlem 52 23N 4 39E
47 Haast, R. 43 50S 169 2E
32 Hab Nadi Chauki 25 0N 66 50E
52 Habaswein 1 1N 39 29E
36 Hachinohe 40 30N 141 29E
36 Hachiōji 33 3N 139 55E
64 Hackett 52 9N 112 28E
28 Hadar Ramatayim 32 8N 34 45E
31 Hadd, Ras al 22 35N 59 50E
8 Haddington 55 57N 2 48W
53 Hadejia 12 30N 9 59E
28 Hadera 32 27N 34 55E
29 Hadhramawt, Reg. 15 30N 49 30E
6 Hadrian's Wall 55 0N 2 30E
38 Haeju 38 12N 125 41E
38 Haerhpin=Harbin 45 46N 126 51E
30 Hafar al Bātin 28 25N 46 50E
32 Hafizabad 32 5N 73 40E
33 Haflong 25 10N 93 5E
20 Hafnarfjördur 64 3N 21 55W
28 Hagalil, Reg. 32 53N 35 18E
14 Hagen 51 21N 7 29E
68 Hagerstown 39 39N 77 46W
21 Hagfors 60 3N 13 45E
20 Hagi, Iceland 65 28N 23 25W
36 Hagi, Japan 34 30N 131 30E
12 Hague, C. de la 49 43N 1 57W
11 Hague, The= s'Gravenhage 52 7N 4 17E
12 Haguenau 48 49N 7 47E
28 Haifa 32 46N 35 0E
45 Haig 30 55S 126 10E
39 Haikow 20 0N 110 20E
38 Hailar 49 12N 119 37E
38 Hailar, R. 49 35N 117 55E
72 Hailey 43 30N 114 15W
62 Haileybury 47 30N 79 38W
38 Hailun 47 24N 127 0E
38 Hailung 42 46N 125 57E
39 Haimen 31 48N 121 8E
39 Hainan, I. 19 0N 110 0E
11 Hainaut □ 50 30N 4 0E
64 Haines Junction 60 45N 137 30W
39 Haining 30 16N 120 47E
37 Haiphong 20 55N 105 42E
39 Haitan Tao, I. 25 30N 119 45E
75 Haiti ■ 19 0N 72 30W
39 Haiyen 30 28N 120 57E
15 Hajdúböszörmény 47 40N 21 30E
15 Hajnówka 52 45N 23 36E
31 Hajr, Reg. 24 0N 56 34E
36 Hakodate 41 45N 140 44E
56 Hakos, Mt. 23 25S 16 25E
36 Haku-San, Mt. 36 9N 136 46E
36 Hakui 36 53N 136 47E
32 Hala 25 49N 68 25E
30 Ḥalab 36 10N 37 15E
51 Halaib 22 5N 36 30E
14 Halberstadt 51 53N 11 2E
47 Halcombe 40 8S 175 30E
21 Halden 59 7N 11 30E
33 Haldia 22 4N 88 4E
32 Haldwani 29 25N 79 30E
66 Haleakala, Mt. 20 42N 156 15W
53 Half Assini 5 1N 2 50W
28 Halhul 31 35N 35 7E
29 Hali 18 40N 41 15E
62 Haliburton 45 3N 78 30W
63 Halifax, Canada 44 38N 63 35W
6 Halifax, U.K. 53 43N 1 51W
61 Hall Lake 68 30N 81 0W
21 Hallands □ 57 0N 12 37E
11 Halle, Belgium 50 44N 4 13W
14 Halle, E. Germany 51 29N 12 0E
21 Hällefors 59 46N 14 30E
43 Hallett 33 25S 138 55E
21 Hallingdal 60 40N 8 45E
20 Hällnäs 64 18N 19 40E
44 Halls Creek 18 20S 128 0E
35 Halmahera, I. 0 40N 128 0E
21 Halmstad 56 37N 12 56E
51 Halq el Oued 36 53N 10 10E
21 Hals 56 59N 10 20E
32 Halvad 23 3N 71 12E
30 Hamā 35 5N 36 40E
36 Hamada 34 50N 132 10E
30 Hamadān 34 52N 48 32E
30 Hamadān □ 35 0N 48 40E
36 Hamamatsu 34 45N 137 45E
21 Hamar 60 48N 11 7E
14 Hamburg 53 32N 9 59E
21 Häme □ 61 30N 24 30E
21 Hämeenlinna 61 3N 24 26E
45 Hamelin Pool 26 22S 114 20E
14 Hameln 52 7N 9 24E
44 Hamersley Ra. 22 0S 117 45E
38 Hamhung 40 0N 127 30E
37 Hami 42 54N 93 28E
46 Hamilton, Australia 37 37S 142 0E
75 Hamilton, Bermuda 32 15N 64 45W
62 Hamilton, Canada 43 20N 79 50W
47 Hamilton, N.Z. 37 47S 175 19E
8 Hamilton, U.K. 55 47N 4 2W
72 Hamilton, Mont. 46 20N 114 6W
68 Hamilton, N.Y. 42 49N 75 31W
68 Hamilton, Ohio 39 20N 84 35W
42 Hamilton Hotel 22 45S 140 40E
65 Hamiota 50 11N 100 38W
69 Hamlet 34 56N 79 40W
14 Hamm 51 40N 7 58E
20 Hammerfest 70 33N 23 50E
68 Hammond, Ind. 41 40N 87 30W
71 Hammond, La. 30 30N 90 28W
47 Hampden 45 18S 170 50E
7 Hampshire □ 51 3N 1 20W
68 Hampton 37 4N 76 8W
30 Hamra 24 2N 38 55E
39 Han Kiang, R. 30 32N 114 22E
19 Han Pijesak 44 3N 18 59E
14 Hanau 50 8N 8 56E
39 Hanchung 33 10N 107 2E
70 Hancock 47 10N 88 35W
29 Handa, Japan 34 53N 137 0E
36 Handa, Somalia 10 37N 51 2E
52 Handeni 5 25S 38 2E
28 Hanegev, Reg. 30 50N 35 0E
64 Haney 49 12N 122 40W
73 Hanford 36 25N 119 45W
39 Hangchou= Hangchow 30 12N 120 1E
39 Hangchow 30 12N 120 1E
39 Hangchow Wan, G. 30 30N 121 30E
21 Hangö 59 59N 22 57E
38 Hanh 51 32N 100 35E
28 Hanita 33 5N 35 10E
39 Hankow 30 32N 114 20E
38 Hanku 39 16N 117 50E
47 Hanmer 42 32S 172 50E
64 Hanna 51 40N 112 0W
70 Hannibal 39 42N 91 22W
14 Hannover 52 23N 9 43E
37 Hanoi 21 5N 150 40E
62 Hanover, Canada 44 9N 81 2W
14 Hanover, Germany= Hannover 52 33N 9 43E
56 Hanover, S. Afr. 31 4S 24 29E
68 Hanover, N.H. 43 43N 72 17W
68 Hanover, Pa. 39 46N 76 59W
80 Hanover, I. 50 58S 74 40W
32 Hansi 29 10N 75 57E
38 Hantan 36 42N 114 30E
39 Hanyang 30 30N 114 19E
20 Haparanda 65 52N 24 8E
63 Happy Valley 155 53N 60 10W
32 Hapur 28 45N 77 45E
38 Har-Ayrag 45 50N 109 30E
37 Har Us Nuur, L. 48 0N 92 0E
28 Har Yehuda, Reg. 31 40N 35 0E
30 Harad 24 15N 49 0E
29 Haradera 4 33N 47 38E
38 Harbin 45 46N 126 51E
63 Harbour Breton 47 29N 55 50W
63 Harbour Deep 50 25N 56 30W
63 Harbour Grace 47 40N 53 22W
14 Harburg 53 27N 9 58E
21 Hardanger Fd. 60 15N 6 0E
56 Hardap Dam 24 28S 17 48E
11 Harderwijk 52 21N 5 36E
57 Harding 30 22S 29 55E
32 Hardoi 27 26N 80 15E
32 Hardwar 29 58N 78 16E
80 Hardy, Pen. 55 30S 68 20W
29 Harer 9 20N 42 8E
29 Hargeisa 9 30N 44 2E
21 Hargshamn 60 12N 18 30E
6 Harlech 52 52N 4 7W
72 Harlem 48 29N 108 39W
11 Harlingen, Neth. 53 11N 5 25E
71 Harlingen, U.S.A. 26 30N 97 50W
7 Harlow 51 47N 0 9E
72 Harlowton 46 30N 109 54W
72 Harney L. 43 0N 119 0W
72 Harney Basin 43 30N 119 0W
70 Harney Pk. 43 52N 103 33W
20 Härnösand 62 38N 18 5E
69 Harriman 36 0N 84 35W
63 Harrington Harbour 50 31N 59 30W
8 Harris, I. 57 50N 6 55W
68 Harrisburg, Ill. 37 42N 88 30W
68 Harrisburg, Pa. 40 18N 76 52W
57 Harrismith 28 15S 29 8E
71 Harrison, Ohio 36 10N 93 4W
60 Harrison B. 70 25N 151 0W
68 Harrisonburg 38 28N 78 52W
70 Harrisonville 38 45N 93 45W
62 Harriston 43 57N 80 53W
6 Harrogate 53 59N 1 32W
7 Harrow 51 35N 0 15W
68 Hartford 41 47N 72 41W
63 Hartland 46 20N 67 32W
7 Hartland Pt. 51 2N 4 32W
6 Hartlepool 54 42N 1 11W
* 57 Hartley 18 10S 30 7E
64 Hartley Bay 46 4N 80 45W
56 Hartmannberge 18 0S 12 30E
65 Hartney 49 30N 100 35W
69 Hartsville 34 23N 80 2W
45 Harvey, Australia 33 4S 115 48E
68 Harvey, U.S.A. 41 40N 87 40W
7 Harwich 51 56N 1 18E
32 Haryana □ 29 0N 76 10E
14 Harz, Mts. 51 40N 10 40E
7 Haslemere 51 5N 0 41W
32 Hassan 13 0N 76 5E
11 Hasselt 50 56N 5 21E
50 Hassi Messaoud 31 15N 6 35E
50 Hassi R'Mel 32 35N 3 24E
47 Hastings, N.Z. 39 39S 176 52E
7 Hastings, U.K. 50 51N 0 36E
68 Hastings, Mich. 42 40N 85 20E
70 Hastings, Neb. 40 34N 98 22W
73 Hatch 32 45N 107 8W
37 Hatgal 50 40N 100 0E
32 Hathras 27 36N 78 6E
33 Hatia 22 30N 91 15E
69 Hatteras, C. 35 10N 75 30W
71 Hattiesburg 31 20N 89 20W
15 Hatvan 47 40N 19 45E
21 Haugesund 59 23N 5 13E
29 Haura 13 50N 47 35E
47 Hauraki, G. 36 35S 175 5E
12 Haut-Rhin □ 48 0N 7 15E
12 Haute-Corse □ 42 30N 9 20E
12 Haute-Garonne □ 43 28N 1 30E
12 Haute-Loire 45 5N 3 50E
12 Haute-Marne □ 48 10N 5 20E
63 Hauterive 49 10N 68 25W
12 Haute-Saône □ 47 45N 6 10E
12 Haute-Savoie □ 46 0N 6 20E
12 Haute-Vienne □ 45 50N 1 10E
12 Hautes-Alpes □ 44 40N 6 30E
12 Hautes-Pyrénées □ 43 0N 0 10E

* Renamed Tafresh
† Renamed Gweru

* Renamed Chegutu

12 Hauts-de-Seine □ 48 52N 2 15E
75 Havana=
La Habana 23 0N 82 41W
7 Havant 50 51N 0 59W
14 Havel, R. 52 53N 11 58E
62 Havelock 44 26N 77 53W
47 Havelock North 39 42S 176 53E
7 Haverfordwest 51 48N 4 59W
68 Haverhill 42 50N 71 2W
7 Havering 51 33N 0 20E
14 Havlíckuv Brod 49 36N 15 33E
72 Havre 48 40N 109 34W
63 Havre St-Pierre 50 18N 63 33W
30 Havza 41 0N 35 35E
66 Hawaii □ 20 0N 155 0W
66 Hawaii, I. 20 0N 155 0W
47 Hawea, L. 44 28S 169 19E
47 Hawera 39 35S 174 19E
8 Hawick 55 25N 2 48W
62 Hawk Junction 48 5N 84 35W
47 Hawke, B. 39 25S 177 20E
43 Hawker 31 59S 138 22E
47 Hawke's Bay □ 39 45S 176 35E
63 Hawke's Harbour 53 2N 55 50W
63 Hawkesbury,
Nova Scotia 45 40N 61 10W
62 Hawkesbury, Ont. 45 35N 74 40W
72 Hawthorne 38 37N 118 47W
46 Hay, Australia 34 30S 144 51E
7 Hay, U.K. 52 4N 3 9W
64 Hay River 60 50N 115 50W
73 Hayden 40 30N 107 22W
42 Haydon 18 0S 141 30E
60 Hayes, Mt. 63 37N 146 43W
65 Hayes, R. 57 3N 92 9W
7 Hayling I. 50 40N 1 0W
70 Hays 38 55N 99 25W
7 Haywards Heath 51 0N 0 5W
31 Hazarān,
Kūh-e, Mt. 29 35N 57 20E
68 Hazard 37 18N 83 10W
33 Hazaribagh 23 58N 85 26E
64 Hazelton 55 20N 127 42W
68 Hazleton 40 58N 76 0W
28 Hazor 33 2N 35 2E
31 Hazrat Imam 37 15N 68 50E
57 Headlands 18 15S 32 2E
72 Healdsburg 38 33N 122 51W
6 Heanor 53 1N 1 20W
3 Heard I. 53 0S 74 0E
62 Hearst 49 40N 83 41W
63 Heart's Content 47 54N 53 27W
63 Heath Steele 48 30N 66 20W
43 Hebel 28 59S 147 48E
63 Hebertville 47 0N 71 30W
8 Hebrides, Inner, Is. 57 20N 6 40W
8 Hebrides, Outer, Is. 57 50N 7 25W
61 Hebron, Canada 58 10N 62 50W
28 Hebron, Jordan 31 32N 35 6E
64 Hecate Str. 53 10N 130 30W
52 Hedaru 4 30S 37 54E
20 Hede 62 22N 13 43E
21 Hedemora 60 18N 15 48E
21 Hedmark □ 61 45N 11 0E
11 Heemstede 52 19N 4 37E
11 Heerde 52 24N 6 2E
11 Heerenveen 52 57N 5 55E
11 Heerlen 50 55N 6 0E
56 Heidelberg,
C. Prov. 34 6S 20 59E
57 Heidelberg, Trans. 26 30S 28 23E
14 Heidelberg,
W. Germ. 49 23N 8 41E
57 Heilbron 27 16S 27 59E
14 Heilbronn 49 8N 9 13E
38 Heilungkiang □ 47 30N 129 0E
21 Heinola 61 13N 26 10E
65 Heinsburg 53 50N 110 30W
33 Heinze Is. 14 25N 97 45E
20 Hekla, Mt. 63 56N 19 35W
71 Helena, Ark. 34 30N 90 35W
72 Helena, Mont. 46 40N 112 0W
8 Helensburgh 56 0N 4 44W
47 Helensville 36 41S 174 29E
28 Helez 31 36N 34 39E
14 Heligoland, I. 54 10N 7 51E
* 55 Hell-Ville 13 25S 48 16E
11 Hellendoorn 52 24N 6 27E
13 Hellín 38 31N 1 40W
31 Helmand, Hamun 31 0N 61 0E
31 Helmand □ 31 0N 64 0E
31 Helmand, R. 31 12N 61 34E
11 Helmond 51 29N 5 41E
8 Helmsdale 58 7N 3 40W
21 Helsingborg 56 3N 12 42E
21 Helsingfors=
Helsinki 60 15N 25 3E
21 Helsingør 56 2N 12 35E
21 Helsinki 60 15N 25 3E
7 Helston 50 7N 5 17W
6 Helvellyn, Mt. 54 31N 3 1W
51 Helwân 29 50N 31 20E
7 Hemel
Hempstead 51 45N 0 28W
68 Hempstead 40 42N 73 37W
21 Hemse 57 15N 18 20E
13 Henares, R. 40 24N 3 30W
13 Hendaye 43 23N 1 47W
68 Henderson, Ky. 37 50N 87 38W
69 Henderson, N.C. 36 18N 78 23W
71 Henderson, Tex. 32 5N 94 49W
69 Hendersonville 35 21N 82 28W
43 Hendon 28 5S 151 50E
56 Hendrik Verwoerd
Dam 30 38S 25 30E
11 Hengelo 52 15N 6 48E
39 Hengyang 26 57N 112 28E
62 Henrietta Maria, C. 55 10N 82 30W
54 Henrique de
Carvalho 9 39S 20 24E
71 Henryetta 35 2N 96 0W
46 Henty 35 30N 147 0E
33 Henzada 17 38N 95 35E
72 Heppner 45 27N 119 34W
31 Herat 34 20N 62 7E
31 Herat □ 34 20N 62 7E
12 Hérault □ 43 34N 3 15E
65 Herbert 50 30N 107 10W
42 Herbert Downs 23 0S 139 11E
19 Hercegnovi 42 30N 18 33E
19 Hercegovina □ 43 20N 18 0E
7 Hereford, U.K. 52 4N 2 42W
71 Hereford, U.S.A. 34 50N 102 28W
7 Hereford and
Worcester □ 52 14N 1 42W
11 Herentals 51 12N 4 51E
14 Herford 52 7N 8 40E
56 Hermanus 34 27S 19 12E
46 Hermidale 31 30S 146 42E
72 Hermiston 45 50N 119 16W
47 Hermitage 43 44S 170 5E
80 Hermite, I. 55 50S 68 0W
30 Hermon, Mt.=
Sheikh, Jabal ash 33 20N 26 0E
74 Hermosillo 29 10N 111 0W
15 Hernad R. 47 56N 21 8E
7 Herne Bay 51 22N 1 8E
21 Herning 56 8N 9 0E
62 Heron Bay 48 40N 85 25W
* 30 Herowabad 37 37N 48 32E
13 Herrera del
Duque 39 10N 5 3W
71 Herrin 37 50N 89 0W
11 Herstal 50 40N 5 38E
7 Hertford 51 47N 0 4W
7 Hertford □ 51 51N 0 5W
28 Herzliyya 32 10N 34 50E
14 Hessen □ 50 57N 9 20E
61 Hewett, C. 70 30N 68 0W
6 Hexham 54 58N 2 7W
6 Heysham 54 5N 2 53W
46 Heywood 38 8S 141 37E
70 Hibbing 47 30N 93 0W
69 Hickory 35 46N 81 17W
36 Hida Sammyaku,
Mts. 36 0N 137 10E
74 Hidalgo □ 20 30N 99 10W
74 Hidalgo del Parral 26 10N 104 50W
50 Hierro, I. 27 57N 17 56W
39 Hifung 22 59N 115 17E
36 Higashiōsaka 34 39N 135 35E
45 Higginsville 31 42S 121 38E
52 High Lava Plat. 3 40N 36 45E
69 High Point 35 57N 79 58W
64 High Prairie 55 30N 116 30W
64 High River 50 30N 113 50W
7 High Wycombe 51 37N 0 45W
48 High Veld 26 30S 30 0E
8 Highland □ 57 30N 4 50W
68 Highland Park, Ill. 42 10N 87 50W
68 Highland Park,
Mich. 42 25N 83 6W
30 Hijāz, Reg. 26 0N 37 30E
36 Hikari 33 58N 131 56E
36 Hikone 35 15N 136 10E
47 Hikurangi 37 54S 178 5E
14 Hildersheim 52 9N 9 55E
11 Hillegom 52 18N 4 35E
7 Hillingdon 51 33N 0 29W
70 Hillsboro, Kan. 38 28N 97 10W
72 Hillsboro, Oreg. 45 31N 123 0W
71 Hillsboro, Tex. 32 0N 97 10W
62 Hillsport 49 27N 85 34W
46 Hillston 33 30S 145 31E
66 Hilo 19 44N 155 5W
11 Hilversum 52 14N 5 10E
32 Himachal
Pradesh □ 31 30N 77 0E
26 Himalaya, Mts. 29 0N 84 0E
32 Himatnagar 23 36N 72 58E
36 Himeji 34 50N 134 40E
36 Himi 36 50N 137 0E
30 Hims=Homs 34 40N 36 45E
42 Hinchinbrook, I. 18 20S 146 15E
7 Hinckley 52 33N 1 21W
46 Hindmarsh, L. 35 50S 141 55E
32 Hindubagh 30 56N 67 57E
31 Hindukush, Mts. 36 0N 71 0E
32 Hindupur 13 49N 77 32E
64 Hines Creek 56 20N 118 40W
39 Hingan 25 39N 110 43E
38 Hingcheng 40 21N 120 10E
72 Hingham 48 40N 110 29W
37 Hingi 25 4N 105 2E
39 Hingning 24 2N 115 55E
32 Hingoli 19 41N 77 15E
39 Hingwa Wan, G. 25 0N 120 0E
20 Hinnoy, I. 68 40N 16 28E
64 Hinton, Canada 53 26N 117 28W
68 Hinton, U.S.A. 37 40N 80 51W
33 Hirakud Dam 21 32N 83 45E
36 Hiratsuka 35 40N 139 36E
36 Hirosaki 40 35N 140 25E
36 Hiroshima 34 30N 132 30E
36 Hiroshima □ 34 30N 133 0E
75 Hispaniola, I. 19 0N 71 0W
32 Hissar 29 12N 75 45E
36 Hita 33 42N 130 52E
36 Hitachi 36 40N 140 35E
7 Hitchin 51 57N 0 16W
36 Hitoyoshi 32 13N 130 45E
20 Hitra, I. 63 30N 8 45E
21 Hjälmaren, L. 59 18N 15 40E
21 Hjørring 57 29N 9 59E
53 Ho 6 37N 0 27E
64 Hoadley 52 45N 114 30W
34 Hoai Nhon 14 28N 103 37E
42 Hobart, Australia 42 50S 147 21E
71 Hobart, U.S.A. 35 0N 99 5W
71 Hobbs 32 40N 103 3W
11 Hoboken 51 11N 4 21E
21 Hobro 56 39N 9 46E
39 Hichih 24 43N 107 43E
39 Hochwan 30 0N 106 15E
36 Hodaka-Dake, Mt. 36 20N 137 30E
29 Hodeida 14 50N 43 0E
65 Hodgson 51 20N 97 40W
15 Hódmezóvásárhely 46 28N 20 22E
50 Hodna, Chott el 35 30N 5 0E
14 Hodonin 48 50N 17 0E
11 Hoek van Holland 52 0N 4 7E
57 Hoëveld 26 30S 30 0E
39 Hofei 31 45N 116 36E
36 Hōfu 34 0N 130 30E
50 Hoggar=
Ahaggar, Mts. 23 0N 6 30E
38 Hohpi 35 59N 114 13E
52 Hoima 1 26N 31 21E
38 Hokang 47 36N 130 28E
38 Hokien 38 30N 116 2E
47 Hokitika 42 42S 171 0E
36 Hokkaidō □ 43 30N 143 0E
36 Hokkaidō, I. 43 30N 143 0E
37 Hokow 22 39N 103 57E
38 Holan Shan 38 40N 105 50E
46 Holbrook,
Australia 35 42S 147 18E
73 Holbrook, U.S.A. 35 0N 110 0W
71 Holdenville 35 5N 96 25W
6 Holderness, Pen. 53 45N 0 5W
75 Holguín 20 50N 76 20W
55 Hollams Bird I. 24 40S 14 30E
11 Holland ■=
Netherlands ■ 52 0N 5 30E
68 Holland 42 47N 86 0W
35 Hollandia=
Jayapura 2 28N 140 38E
73 Hollywood, Calif. 34 0N 118 10W
68 Hollywood, Fla. 26 0N 80 9W
60 Holman Island 70 43N 117 43W
20 Holmsund 63 41N 20 20E
28 Holon 32 2N 34 47E
21 Holstebro 56 22N 8 33E
60 Holy Cross 62 12N 159 47W
6 Holy, I., Eng. 55 42N 1 48W
6 Holy, I., Wales 53 17N 4 37W
6 Holyhead 53 18N 4 38W
68 Holyoke 42 14N 72 37W
33 Homalin 24 55N 95 0E
53 Hombori 15 20N 1 38E
42 Home Hill 19 43S 147 25E
72 Homedale 43 42N 116 59W
60 Homer 59 40N 151 35W
42 Homestead 20 20S 145 40E
30 Homs 34 40N 36 45E
39 Honan □ 33 50N 113 15E
78 Honda 5 12N 74 45W
53 Hohoe 7 8N 0 32E
55 Hondeklipbaai 30 19S 17 17E
74 Hondo, R. 19 26N 99 13W
75 Honduras ■ 14 40N 86 30W
74 Honduras, G. de 16 50N 87 0W
21 Hønefoss 60 10N 10 12E
12 Honfleur 49 25N 0 10E
37 Hongha, R. 22 0N 104 0E
39 Hong Kong ■ 22 11N 114 14E
7 Honiton 50 48N 3 11W
66 Honolulu 21 19N 157 52W
36 Honshū, I. 36 0N 138 0E
45 Hood, Pt. 34 23S 119 34E
11 Hoogeveen 52 44N 6 30E
11 Hoogezand 53 11N 6 45E
33 Hooghly, R. 21 56N 88 4E
9 Hook Hd. 52 8N 6 57W
64 Hoonah 58 15N 135 30W
68 Hoopeston 40 30N 87 40W
11 Hoorn 52 38N 5 4E
73 Hoover Dam 36 0N 114 45W
64 Hope, Canada 49 25N 121 25E
71 Hope, U.S.A. 33 40N 93 30W
60 Hope, Pt. 68 20N 166 40W
75 Hope Town 26 30N 76 30W
56 Hopefield 33 3S 18 22E
38 Hopei □ 39 25N 116 45E
56 Hopetown 29 34S 24 3E
46 Hopetoun, Vic. 35 48S 142 25E
45 Hopetoun,
W. Australia 33 54S 120 6E
68 Hopkinsville 36 52N 87 26W
39 Hoppo 21 32N 109 6E
72 Hoquiam 47 0N 123 55W
21 Hordaland □ 60 25N 6 45E
31 Hormoz 27 35N 55 0E
31 Hormoz, Jazireh-ye 27 4N 56 28E
31 Hormoz, Kūh-e 27 40N 55 30E
31 Hormuz, Str. of 26 30N 56 30E
14 Horn 48 39N 15 40E
80 Horn, C.=
Hornos, C. de 55 50S 67 30W
6 Horncastle 53 13N 0 8W
68 Hornell 42 23N 77 41W
62 Hornepayne 49 14N 84 48W
80 Hornos, C. de 55 50S 67 30W
46 Hornsby 33 42S 151 2E
6 Hornsea 53 55N 0 10W
80 Horqueta 23 15S 56 55W
21 Horsens 55 52N 9 51E
46 Horsham,
Australia 36 44S 142 13E
7 Horsham, U.K. 51 4N 0 20W
21 Horten 59 25N 10 32E
32 Hoshangabad 22 45N 77 44E
32 Hoshiarpur 31 30N 75 58E
32 Hospet 15 15N 76 20E
13 Hospitalet de
Llobregat 41 21N 2 6E
80 Hoste, I. 55 0S 69 0W
60 Hot Springs, Alas. 64 55N 150 10W
71 Hot Springs, Ark. 34 30N 93 0W
70 Hot Springs, S.D. 43 25N 103 30W
37 Hotien 37 6N 79 59E
20 Hoting 64 8N 16 15E
6 Houghton-le-
Spring 54 51N 1 28W
47 Houhora 34 49S 173 9E
69 Houlton 46 5N 68 0W
71 Houma 29 35N 90 50W
8 Hourne, L. 57 7N 5 35W
71 Houston 29 50N 5 20W
7 Hove 50 50N 0 10W
38 Hövsgöl Nuur, L. 51 0N 100 30E
43 Howard 25 16S 152 32E
45 Howatharra 28 29S 114 33E
46 Howe, C. 37 30S 150 0E
57 Howick 29 28S 30 14E
33 Howrah 22 37N 88 27E
9 Howth Hd. 53 21N 6 0W
8 Hoy, I. 58 50N 3 15W
21 Høyanger 61 25N 6 50E
14 Hradec Králové 50 15N 15 50E
15 Hron, R. 47 49N 18 45E
18 Hrvatska □ 45 20N 16 0E
33 Hsenwi 23 22N 97 55E
39 Hsiamen 24 28N 118 7E
39 Hsian=Sian 34 2N 109 0E
39 Hsiao Shan 34 0N 111 30E
39 Hsinchow 19 37N 109 17E
39 Hsinchu 24 55N 121 0E
39 Hsuchang 34 2N 114 0E
39 Hsüchou=Suchow 34 10N 117 20E
78 Huacho 11 10S 77 35W
39 Hualien 24 0N 121 30E

* Renamed Andoany

* Renamed Khalkhāl

78 Huancane 15 10s 69 50w
78 Huancavelica 12 50s 7s 5w
78 Huancayo 12 5s 75 0w
39 Huangliu 18 30n 108 46e
78 Huánuco 9 55s 76 15w
78 Huaraz 9 30s 77 32w
78 Huascarán, Mt. 9 0s 77 30w
80 Huasco 28 24s 71 15w
74 Huatabampo 26 50n 109 50w
32 Hubli 15 22n 75 15e
39 Huchow 30 57n 120 1e
74 Huchuetenango 15 25n 91 30w
6 Huddersfield 53 38n 1 49w
21 Hudiksvall 61 43n 17 10e
68 Hudson 42 15n 73 46w
68 Hudson, R. 40 42n 74 2w
61 Hudson B. 60 0n 86 0w
68 Hudson Falls 43 18n 73 34w
64 Hudson Hope 56 0n 121 54w
61 Hudson Str. 62 0n 70 0w
34 Hué 16 30n 107 35e
13 Huelva 37 18n 6 57w
13 Huesca 42 8n 0 25w
42 Hughenden 20 52s 144 10e
45 Hughes, Australia 30 40s 129 30e
60 Hughes, U.S.A. 66 3n 154 16w
38 Huhehot 40 52n 111 36e
78 Huila, Mt. 3 0n 76 0w
39 Huiling Shan, I. 21 35n 111 57e
80 Huinca Renancó 34 51s 64 22w
74 Huixtla 15 9n 92 28w
33 Hukawng Valley 26 30n 96 30e
39 Hukow 29 38n 116 25e
38 Hulan 46 0n 126 44e
28 Hūlda 31 50n 34 51e
38 Hulin 45 45n 133 0e
62 Hull, Canada 45 20n 75 40w
6 Hull, U.K. 53 45n 0 20w
6 Hull, R. 53 44n 0 19w
38 Huma 51 44n 126 42e
38 Huma, R. 51 40n 126 44e
80 Humahuaca 23 10s 65 25w
78 Humaitá 7 35s 62 40w
56 Humansdorp 34 2s 24 46e
6 Humber, R. 53 32n 0 8e
6 Humberside □ 53 45n 0 20w
65 Humboldt, Canada 52 15n 105 9w
71 Humboldt, U.S.A. 35 50n 88 55w
72 Humboldt, R. 40 2n 118 31w
51 Hūn 29 2n 16 0e
20 Hunaflói, B. 65 50n 21 0w
39 Hunan □ 27 30n 111 30e
38 Hunchun 42 49n 130 31e
15 Hunedoara 45 40n 22 50e
39 Hung Ho, R. 33 0n 117 0e
15 Hungary ■ 47 20n 19 20e
39 Hunghai Wan, G. 20 30n 115 0e
39 Hungshui Ho, R. 23 70n 110 30e
39 Hunghu 29 49n 113 30e
39 Hungkiang 27 0n 109 49e
38 Hungnam 39 59n 127 40e
39 Hungtze Hu, L. 33 20n 118 35e
56 Hunsberge 27 45s 17 12e
14 Hunsruck, Mts. 50 0n 7 30e
6 Hunstanton 52 57n 0 30e
46 Hunter, R. 32 50s 151 40e
47 Hunterville 39 56s 175 35e
62 Huntingdon, Canada 45 10n 74 10w
7 Huntingdon, U.K. 52 20n 0 11w
68 Huntingdon, U.S.A. 40 28n 78 1w
68 Huntington, Ind. 40 52n 85 30w
68 Huntington, W. Va. 38 20n 82 30w
73 Huntington Beach 34 40n 118 0w
73 Huntington Park 33 58n 118 15w
47 Huntly, N.Z. 37 34s 175 11e
8 Huntly, U.K. 57 27n 2 48w
62 Huntsville, Canada 45 20n 79 14w
69 Huntsville, Ala. 34 45n 86 35w
71 Huntsville, Tex. 30 50n 95 35w
42 Huonville 43 0s 147 5e
39 Hupei □ 31 5n 113 5e
70 Huron 44 30n 98 20w
68 Huron, L. 45 0n 83 0w
73 Hurricane 37 10n 113 12w
47 Hurunui, R. 42 54s 173 18e
20 Húsavik 66 3n 17 13w
21 Huskvarna 57 47n 14 15e
28 Hussein Bridge 31 53n 35 33e
38 Hutag 49 25n 102 34e
71 Hutchinson 38 3n 97 59w
28 Huwarā 32 9n 35 15e
11 Huy 50 31n 5 15e
18 Hvar, I. 43 11n 16 28e
20 Hvítá, R., Iceland 63 50n 21 0w
20 Hvítá, R., Iceland 64 40n 22 0w
39 Hwainan 32 44n 117 1e
38 Hwang Ho, R. 37 32n 118 19e
39 Hwangshih 30 27n 115 0e
39 Hweian 25 2n 118 56e
37 Hweitseh 26 32n 103 6e
38 Hwo Shan, Mts. 37 0n 112 30e
38 Hwohsien 36 30n 111 42e
68 Hyannis 42 3n 101 45w
37 Hyargas Nuur, L. 49 0n 92 30e
64 Hydaburg 55 15n 132 45w
45 Hyden 32 24s 118 46e
32 Hyderabad, India 17 10n 78 29e
32 Hyderabad, Pak. 25 23n 68 36e
* 32 Hyderabad □ 25 3n 68 24e
12 Hyères 43 8n 6 9e
12 Hyères, Îs. d' 43 0n 6 28e
72 Hyndman Pk. 44 4n 114 0w
36 Hyōgo □ 35 15n 135 0e
72 Hyrum 41 35n 111 56w
7 Hythe 51 4n 1 5e
21 Hyvinkää 60 38n 25 0e

I

57 Iakora 23 6s 46 40e
15 Ialomiţa, R. 44 42n 27 51e
15 Iaşi 47 10n 27 40e
78 Iaurête 0 30n 69 5w
50 Ibadan 7 22n 3 58e
78 Ibagué 4 27n 73 14w
19 Ibar, R. 43 43n 20 45e
78 Ibarra 0 21n 78 7w
29 Ibb 14 1n 44 10e
4 Iberian Pen. 40 0n 5 0w
62 Iberville 5 19n 73 17w
80 Ibicuy 33 55s 59 10w
13 Ibiza 38 54n 1 26e
13 Ibiza, I. 39 0n 1 30e
35 Ibonma 3 22s 133 31e
36 Ibusuki 31 16n 130 39e
78 Icá 14 0s 75 30w
78 Içana 0 21n 67 19w
35 Iceland ■ 65 0n 19 0w
25 Icha 55 30n 156 0e
39 Ichang 30 48n 111 29e
33 Ichchapuram 19 10n 84 40e
36 Ichihara 35 35n 140 6e
36 Ichinomiya 35 20n 136 50e
38 Ichun 47 42n 129 8e
53 Idah 6 10n 6 40e
72 Idaho □ 44 10n 114 0w
72 Idaho Falls 43 30n 112 10w
72 Idaho Springs 39 49n 105 30w
51 Idd el Ghanam 11 30n 24 25e
51 Idehan Marzúq 24 50n 13 51e
51 Idfû 25 0n 32 49e
34 Idi 4 55n 97 45e
† 52 Idi Amin Dada, L. 0 25s 29 40e
30 Idlip 35 55n 36 38e
28 Idna 31 34n 34 58e
57 Idutywa 32 8s 28 18e
11 Ieper 50 51n 2 53e
52 Ifakara 8 10s 36 35e
57 Ifanadiana 21 29s 47 39e
53 Ife 7 30n 4 31e
53 Ifon 6 58n 5 40e
79 Igarapava 20 3s 47 47w
79 Igarapé Açu 1 4s 47 33w
25 Igarka 67 30n 87 20e
52 Igawa 8 45s 34 23e
53 Igbetti 8 44n 4 8e
53 Igbo-Ora 7 10n 3 15e
53 Igboho 8 40n 3 50e
53 Igbor 7 30n 8 32e
21 Iggesund 61 39n 17 10e
18 Iglésias 39 19n 8 27e
61 Igloolik Island 69 20n 81 30w
65 Ignace 49 30n 91 40w
80 Iguaçu, R. 25 30s 53 10w
80 Iguaçu Falls 25 40s 54 33w
74 Iguala 18 20n 99 40w
13 Igualada 41 37n 1 37e
80 Iguape 24 43s 47 33w
79 Iguatu 6 20s 39 18w
53 Ihiala 5 40n 6 55e
57 Ihosy 22 24s 46 8e
38 Ihsien 41 45n 121 3e
36 Iida 35 35n 138 0e
20 Iisalmi 63 32n 27 10e
36 Iizuka 33 38n 130 42e
53 Ijebu-Igbo 6 56n 4 1e
53 Ijebu-Ode 6 47n 3 52e
11 Ijmuiden 52 28n 4 35e
11 Ijsel, R. 52 30n 6 0e
11 Ijsselmeer, L. 52 45n 5 20e

* *Now part of Sind*
† *Renamed Edward, L.*

19 Ikaría, I. 37 35n 26 10e
36 Ikeda 34 1n 133 48e
27 Ikeja 6 28n 3 45e
53 Ikerre-Ekiti 7 25n 5 19e
36 Iki, I. 33 45n 129 42e
53 Ikire 7 10n 4 15e
53 Ikom 6 0n 8 42e
53 Ikot Ekpene 5 12n 7 40e
53 Ikurun 7 55n 4 41e
53 Ila 8 0n 4 51e
35 Ilagan 17 9n 121 53e
38 Ilan 46 14n 129 33e
25 Ilanskiy 56 14n 96 3e
53 Ilaro 6 53n 3 3e
42 Ilbilbie 21 45s 149 20e
12 Île de France, Reg. 49 0n 2 20e
54 Ilebo 4 17s 20 47e
53 Ilero 8 0n 3 20e
53 Ilesha 8 57n 3 28e
42 Ilfracombe, Australia 23 30s 144 30e
7 Ilfracombe, U.K. 51 13n 4 8w
80 Ilha Grande, B. da. 23 10s 44 30w
79 Ilhéus 15 0s 39 10w
60 Iliamna L. 59 30n 155 0w
60 Iliamna, Mt. 60 5n 153 9w
24 Ilich 41 0n 68 10e
68 Ilion 43 0n 75 3w
24 Iliysk=Kapchagai 44 10n 77 20e
6 Ilkeston 52 59n 1 19w
38 Ilkhuri Shan, Mts. 51 30n 124 0e
80 Illapel 32 0s 71 10w
12 Ille-et-Vilaine □ 48 10 1 30w
78 Illimani, Mt. 16 30s 67 50w
70 Illinois, R. 38 58n 90 27w
70 Illinois □ 40 15n 89 30w
50 Illizi 26 31n 8 32e
22 Ilmen, Oz. 5 15n 31 10e
78 Ilo 17 40s 71 20w
53 Ilobu 7 45n 4 25e
35 Iloilo 10 45n 122 33e
52 Ilongero 4 45s 34 55e
53 Ilora 7 45n 3 50e
53 Ilorin 8 30n 4 35e
35 Ilwaki 7 55s 126 30e
36 Imabari 34 4n 133 0e
25 Iman 45 50n 133 40e
22 Imandra, Oz. 67 45n 33 0e
36 Imari 33 15n 129 52e
6 Immingham 53 37n 0 12w
53 Imo □ 4 15n 7 30e
18 Imola 44 20n 11 42e
79 Imperatriz 5 30s 47 29w
18 Impéria 43 52n 8 0e
65 Imperial, Canada 51 21n 105 28w
73 Imperial, U.S.A. 32 52n 115 34w
73 Imperial Dam 32 50n 114 30w
54 Impfondo 1 40n 18 0e
33 Imphal 24 15n 94 0e
28 Imwas 31 51n 34 59e
50 In Salah 27 10n 2 32e
47 Inangahua Junction 41 52s 171 59e
20 Inari 68 54n 27 5e
20 Inari, L. 69 0n 28 0e
13 Inca 39 43n 2 54e
38 Inchŏn 37 32n 126 45e
33 Indaw 24 15n 96 5e
71 Independence, Kans. 37 10n 95 50w
70 Independence, Mo. 39 3n 94 25w
72 Independence, Oreg. 44 53n 123 6w
32 India ■ 23 0n 77 30e
64 Indian Cabin 59 50n 117 12w
65 Indian Head 50 30n 103 35w
1 Indian Ocean 5 0s 75 0e
68 Indiana 40 38n 79 9w
68 Indiana □ 40 0n 86 0w
68 Indianapolis 39 42n 86 10w
70 Indianola 41 20n 93 38w
22 Indiga 67 50n 48 50e
34 Indonesia ■ 5 0s 115 0e
32 Indore 22 42n 75 53e
35 Indramaju 6 21s 108 20e
32 Indravati, R. 18 43n 80 17e
12 Indre □ 46 45n 1 30e
12 Indre-et-Loire □ 47 12n 0 40e
32 Indus, R. 24 20n 67 47e
30 Inebolu 41 55n 33 40e
30 Inegöl 40 5n 29 31e
62 Ingersoll 43 4n 80 55w
42 Ingham 18 43s 146 10e
6 Ingleborough, Mt. 54 11n 2 23w
43 Inglewood, N.S.W. 28 25s 151 8e
46 Inglewood, Vic. 36 29s 143 53e
47 Inglewood, N.Z. 39 9s 174 14e
73 Inglewood 33 58n 118 27w
14 Ingolstadt 48 45n 11 26w
23 Ingulec 47 42n 33 4e
57 Inhambane 23 54s 35 30e
57 Inhambane □ 22 30s 34 20e
55 Inharrime 24 30s 35 0e
39 Ining, Kwangsi-Chuang 25 8n 109 57e
37 Ining Sinkiang-Uigur 43 57n 81 20e
9 Inishmore, I. 53 8n 9 45w
9 Inishowen, Pen. 55 14n 7 15w
36 Inland Sea=Setonaikai 34 10n 133 10e
14 Inn, R. 48 35n 13 28e
38 Inner Mongolian Autonomous Rep. □ 44 50n 117 40e
42 Innisfail, Australia 17 33s 146 5e
64 Innisfail, Canada 52 0n 114 0w
14 Innsbruck 47 16n 11 23e
15 Inowrocław 52 50n 18 20e
45 Inscription, C. 25 29s 112 59e
33 Insein 16 46n 96 18e
22 Inta 66 2n 60 8e
14 Interlaken 46 41n 7 50e
70 International Falls 48 30n 93 25w
80 Intiyaco 28 50s 60 0w
80 Inútil, B. 53 30s 70 15w
60 Inuvik 68 25n 133 30w
8 Inveraray 56 13n 5 5w
8 Inverbervie 56 50n 2 17w
47 Invercargill 46 24s 168 24e
43 Inverell 29 48s 151 36e
8 Invergordon 57 41n 4 10w
64 Invermere 50 51n 116 9w
63 Inverness, Canada 46 15n 61 19w
8 Inverness, U.K. 57 29n 4 12w
8 Inverurie 57 15n 2 21w
44 Inverway 17 50s 129 38e
43 Investigator, Str. 35 30s 137 0e
57 Inyangani, Mt. 18 20s 32 20e
73 Inyokern 35 37n 117 54w
22 Inza 53 55n 46 25e
19 Ioánnina 39 42n 20 55e
71 Iola 38 0n 95 20w
8 Iona, I. 56 20n 6 25w
68 Ionia 42 59n 85 7w
19 Ionian Is.=Iónioi Nísoi 38 40n 20 8e
19 Ionian Sea 37 30n 17 30e
19 Iónioi Nísoi, Is. 38 40n 20 8e
19 Íos, I. 36 41n 25 20e
70 Iowa □ 42 18n 93 30w
70 Iowa City 41 40n 91 35w
70 Iowa Falls 42 30n 93 15w
79 Ipameri 17 44s 48 9w
78 Ipiales 1 0n 77 45w
37 Ipin 28 58n 104 45e
19 Ipiros □ 39 30n 20 30e
34 Ipoh 4 36n 101 4e
43 Ipswich, Australia 27 38s 152 37e
7 Ipswich, U.K. 52 4n 1 9e
79 Ipu 4 23s 40 44w
78 Iquique 20 19s 70 5w
78 Iquitos 3 45s 73 10w
79 Iracoubo 53 .n 53 10w
19 Iráklion 35 20n 25 12e
31 Iran ■ 33 0n 53 0e
26 Iran, Plat. of 32 0n 57 0e
31 Iranshahr 27 75n 60 40e
74 Irapuato 20 40n 101 40w
30 Iraq ■ 33 0n 44 0e
28 Irbid 32 35n 35 48e
75 Ireland, I., Bermuda 32 19n 64 50w
9 Ireland, I., Europe 53 0n 8 0w
53 Irele 7 40n 5 40e
25 Iret 60 10n 154 5e
38 Iri 35 59n 127 0e
35 Irian Jaya □ 5 0s 140 0e
51 Iriba 15 7n 22 15e
52 Iringa 7 48s 33 43e
79 Iriri, R. 3 52s 52 37w
9 Irish Republic ■ 53 0n 8 0e
10 Irish Sea 54 0n 145 12e
25 Irkineyeva 58 30n 96 49e
25 Irkutsk 52 10n 104 20e
70 Iron Mountain 45 49n 88 4w
7 Ironbridge 52 38n 2 29w
68 Ironton 38 35n 82 40w
70 Ironwood 46 30n 90 10w
62 Iroquois Falls 48 40n 80 40w
33 Irrawaddy, R. 15 50n 95 6e
38 Irshih 47 8n 119 57e

24 Irtysh, R. 61 4N 68 52E
54 Irumu 1 32N 29 53E
13 Irún 43 20N 1 52W
8 Irvine 55 37N 4 40W
9 Irvinestown 54 28N 7 38W
45 Irwin, Pt. 35 4S 116 56E
46 Irymple 34 14S 142 8E
53 Isa 13 14N 6 24E
20 Ísafjördur 66 5N 23 9W
36 Isahaya 32 50N 130 3E
52 Isaka 3 56S 32 59E
54 Isangi 0 52N 24 10E
14 Isar, R. 48 49N 12 58E
18 Ischia, I. 40 45N 13 51E
29 Iscia Baidoa 3 40N 43 0E
36 Ise 34 29N 136 42E
36 Ise-Wan, G. 34 45N 136 45E
12 Isère, R. 44 59N 4 51E
12 Isère □ 45 10N 5 50E
53 Iseyin 8 0N 3 36E
31 Isfahan=Esfahan 32 40N 51 38E
39 Ishan 24 30N 108 41E
36 Ishikari-Wan 43 20N 141 20E
36 Ishikawa □ 36 30N 136 30E
24 Ishim, R. 57 45N 71 10E
36 Ishinomaki 38 32N 141 20E
32 Ishkuman 36 40N 73 50E
70 Ishpeming 46 30N 87 40W
52 Isiolo 0 24N 37 33E
57 Isipingo Beach 29 59S 30 57E
54 Isiro 2 53N 27 58E
42 Isisford 24 15S 144 21E
30 Iskenderun 36 32N 36 10E
8 Isla, R. 56 30N 3 25W
32 Islamabad 33 40N 73 0E
45 Island, Pt. 30 20S 115 2E
65 Island L. 53 40N 94 30W
62 Island Falls 49 35N 81 20W
68 Island Pond 44 50N 71 50W
63 Islands, B. of 49 11N 58 15W
80 Islas Malvinas= Falkland Is. 51 30S 59 0W
8 Islay, I. 55 46N 6 10W
6 Isle of Man □ 54 15N 4 30W
7 Isle of Wight □ 36 54N 76 43W
51 Ismâ'ilîya 30 37N 32 18E
51 Isna 25 17N 32 30E
52 Isoka 10 4S 32 42E
30 Isparta 37 47N 30 30E
18 Ispica 36 47N 14 53E
28 Israel ■ 32 0N 34 50E
45 Isseka 28 22S 114 35E
24 Issyk Kul, L. 42 30N 77 30E
30 Istanbul 41 0N 29 0E
18 Istra, Pen. 45 10N 14 0E
79 Itabira 19 29S 43 23W
79 Itabuna 14 48E 39 16W
79 Itacaré 14 18S 39 0W
79 Itaeté 13 0S 41 5W
79 Itaituba 4 10S 55 50W
80 Itajaí 27 0S 48 45W
18 Italy ■ 42 0N 13 0E
79 Itapecuru-Mirim 3 20S 44 15W
79 Itaperaba 12 32S 40 18W
79 Itaperuna 21 10S 42 0W
78 Itaquatiana 2 58S 58 30W
80 Itaqúi 29 0S 56 30W
68 Ithaca 42 25N 76 30W
19 Itháki, I. 38 25N 20 40E
52 Itigi 5 42S 34 29E
36 Ito 34 58N 139 5E
80 Itu, Brazil 23 10S 47 15W
53 Itu, Nigeria 5 10N 7 58E
79 Ituiutaba 19 0S 49 25W
38 Ituliho 50 40N 121 30E
79 Itumbiara 18 20S 49 10W
65 Ituna 51 10N 103 30W
80 Iturbe 23 0S 65 25W
20 Ivalo 68 38N 27 35E
46 Ivanhoe 32 56S 144 20E
23 Ivano-Frankovsk 49 0N 24 40E
22 Ivanovo 57 0N 40 55E
13 Iviza, I.=Ibiza, I. 39 0N 1 30E
57 Ivohibe 22 29S 46 52E
50 Ivory Coast ■ 7 30N 5 0E
18 Ivrea 45 30N 7 52E
61 Ivugivik 62 18N 77 50W
36 Iwaki 37 3N 140 55E
36 Iwakuni 34 15N 132 8E
36 Iwata 34 49N 137 59E
36 Iwate □ 39 30N 141 30E
53 Iwo 7 39N 4 9E
74 Ixtepec 16 40N 95 10W
74 Ixtlán 21 5N 104 28W
74 Izamal 20 56N 89 1W
11 Izegem 50 55N 3 12E
*22 Izhevsk 56 50N 53 0E
30 Izmir 38 25N 27 8E

* Renamed Ustinov

30 Izmit 40 45N 29 50E
28 Izra 32 51N 36 15E
36 Izumi-sano 34 40N 135 43E
36 Izumo 35 20N 132 55E

J

28 Jaba 32 20N 35 13E
28 Jabalīya 31 32N 34 27E
32 Jabalpur 23 9N 79 58E
30 Jablah 35 20N 36 0E
14 Jablonec 50 43N 15 10E
13 Jaca 42 35N 0 33W
80 Jacareí 23 20S 46 0W
80 Jacarèzinho 23 5S 50 0W
43 Jackson, Australia 26 40S 149 30E
68 Jackson, Ky. 37 35N 83 22W
68 Jackson, Mich. 42 18N 84 25W
71 Jackson, Minn. 43 35N 95 30W
69 Jackson, Tenn. 35 40N 88 50W
64 Jackson Bay 50 32N 125 57W
47 Jacksons 42 46N 171 32E
69 Jacksonville, Fla. 30 15N 81 38W
70 Jacksonville, Ill. 39 42N 90 15W
71 Jacksonville, Ill. 39 42N 90 15W
69 Jacksonville, N.C. 34 50N 77 29W
71 Jacksonville, Tex. 31 58N 95 12W
69 Jacksonville Beach 30 19N 81 26W
75 Jacmel 18 20N 72 40W
32 Jacobabad 28 20N 68 29E
79 Jacobina 11 11S 40 30W
28 Jacob's Well 32 13N 35 13E
63 Jacques Cartier, Mt. 48 57N 66 0W
63 Jacques Cartier, Dét. de 49 50N 62 30W
13 Jaén 37 44N 3 43W
28 Jaffa=Tel Aviv-Yafo 32 4N 34 48E
32 Jaffna 9 45N 80 2E
33 Jagdalpur 19 3N 82 6E
56 Jagersfontein 29 44S 25 27E
51 Jaghbub 29 42N 24 38E
32 Jagraon 30 50N 75 25E
32 Jagtial 18 50N 79 0E
80 Jaguarão 32 30S 53 30W
80 Jaguariaíva 24 10S 49 50W
75 Jaguey 22 35N 81 7W
46 Jagungal, Mt. 36 12S 148 28W
31 Jahrom 28 30N 53 31E
32 Jaipur 26 54N 72 52E
35 Jakarta 6 9S 106 49E
20 Jakobstad 63 40N 22 43E
31 Jalalabad 34 30N 70 29E
74 Jalapa, Guatemala 14 45N 89 59W
74 Jalapa, Mexico 19 30N 96 50W
32 Jalgaon 21 0N 75 42E
53 Jalingo 8 55N 11 25E
74 Jalisco □ 20 0N 104 0W
32 Jalna 19 48N 75 57E
32 Jalor 25 20N 72 41E
33 Jalpaiguri 26 32N 88 46E
53 Jamaari 11 44N 9 53E
75 Jamaica ■ 18 10N 77 30W
33 Jamalpur, Bangladesh 24 52N 90 2E
33 Jamalpur, India 25 18N 86 28E
53 Jamari 11 2N 11 0E
34 Jambi 1 38S 103 30E
34 Jambi □ 1 30S 103 30E
62 James B. 53 30N 80 30W
70 James, R. 44 50N 98 0W
43 Jamestown, Australia 33 10S 138 32E
56 Jamestown, S.Afr. 31 6S 26 45E
70 Jamestown, N.D. 47 0N 98 30W
68 Jamestown, N.Y. 42 5N 79 18W
32 Jamkhandi 16 30N 75 15E
32 Jammu 32 46N 75 57E
32 Jammu and Kashmir □ 34 25N 77 0W
32 Jamnagar 22 30N 70 0E
33 Jamshedpur 22 44N 86 20E
20 Jämtlands □ 62 40N 13 50E
2 Jan Mayen, I. 71 0N 11 0W
32 Jand 33 30N 72 0E
43 Jandowae 26 45S 151 7E
70 Janesville 42 39N 89 1W
56 Jansenville 32 57S 24 39E
79 Januária 15 25S 44 25W
32 Jaora 23 40N 75 10E
36 Japan ■ 36 0N 136 0E

35 Japara 6 30S 110 40E
78 Japurá, R. 3 8S 64 46W
73 Jarales 34 44N 106 51W
13 Jarama, R. 40 2N 3 39W
80 Jaramillo 47 10S 67 7W
75 Jardines de la Reina, Is. 20 50N 78 50W
38 Jargalant 47 2N 115 1E
15 Jarosław 50 2N 22 42E
2 Jarvis I. 0 15S 159 55W
33 Jarwa 27 45N 82 30E
31 Jāsk 25 38N 57 45E
15 Jasło 49 45N 21 30E
80 Jason Is. 51 0S 61 0W
64 Jasper, Canada 52 55N 118 0W
69 Jasper, U.S.A. 30 31N 82 58W
64 Jasper Nat. Park 52 53N 118 3W
64 Jasper Place 53 33N 113 25W
15 Jászberény 47 30N 19 55E
79 Jataí 17 50S 51 45W
35 Jatibarang 6 28S 108 18E
35 Jatinegara 6 13S 106 52E
13 Játiva 39 0N 0 32W
79 Jatobal 4 35S 49 33W
28 Jatt 32 24N 35 2E
79 Jaú 22 10S 48 30W
33 Jaunpur 25 46N 82 44E
35 Java, I. 7 0S 110 0E
34 Java Sea 4 35S 107 15E
34 Java Trench 10 0S 110 0E
35 Jaya, Puncak, Mt. 4 0S 137 20E
35 Jayapura 2 28S 140 38E
35 Jayawijaya, Pengunungan 4 50S 139 0E
65 Jaydot 49 15N 110 15W
60 Jean Marie River 62 0N 121 0W
31 Jebāl Barez, Kūh-e 29 0N 58 0E
50 Jebba, Morocco 35 11N 4 43W
53 Jebba, Nigeria 9 9N 4 48E
51 Jebel, Bahr el, R. 9 40N 30 30E
8 Jedburgh 55 28N 2 33W
15 Jędrzejów 50 35N 20 15E
72 Jefferson, Mt. 38 51N 117 0W
70 Jefferson City 36 8N 83 30W
68 Jeffersonville 38 20N 85 42W
53 Jega 12 15N 4 23E
14 Jelenia Góra 50 50N 15 45E
22 Jelgava 56 41N 22 49E
35 Jember 8 11S 113 41E
11 Jemeppe 50 37N 5 30E
14 Jena 50 56N 11 33E
28 Jenīn 32 28N 35 18E
68 Jenkins 37 13N 82 41W
71 Jennings 30 10N 92 45W
79 Jequié 13 51S 40 5W
79 Jequtinhonha 16 30S 41 0W
50 Jerada 34 40N 2 10W
34 Jerantut 3 56N 102 22E
75 Jérémie 18 40N 74 10W
74 Jerez de Gacia Salinas 22 39N 103 0W
13 Jerez de la Frontera 36 41N 6 7W
42 Jericho, Australia 23 38S 146 6E
28 Jericho, Jordan= El Ariha 31 52N 35 27E
46 Jerilderie 35 20S 145 41E
73 Jerome 34 50N 112 0W
7 Jersey, I. 49 15N 2 10W
68 Jersey City 40 41N 74 8W
68 Jersey Shore 41 17N 77 18W
70 Jerseyville 39 5N 90 20W
28 Jerusalem 31 47N 35 10E
46 Jervis Bay 35 8S 150 46E
34 Jesselton=Kota Kinabalu 6 0N 116 12E
33 Jessore 23 10N 89 10E
33 Jeypore 18 50N 82 38E
32 Jhal Jhao 26 20N 65 35E
32 Jhang Maghiana 31 15N 72 15E
33 Jhansi 25 30N 78 36E
33 Jharsuguda 21 51N 84 1E
32 Jhelum 33 0N 73 45E
32 Jhelum, R. 31 12N 72 8E
32 Jhunjhunu 28 10N 75 20E
30 Jiddah 21 29N 39 16E
28 Jifna 31 58N 35 13E
39 Jihchao 35 18N 119 28E
14 Jihlava 49 28N 15 35E
14 Jihlava, R. 48 55N 16 37E
29 Jijiga 9 20N 42 50E
13 Jiloca, R. 41 21N 1 39W
51 Jima 7 40N 36 55E
74 Jiménez 27 10N 105 0W
52 Jinja 0 25N 33 12E
32 Jinnah Barrage 32 58N 71 33E

38 Jinné 51 32N 121 25E
75 Jinotega 13 6N 85 59W
75 Jinotepe 11 50N 86 10W
70 Jipijapa 1 0S 80 40W
30 Jisr ash Shughur 35 49N 36 18E
45 Jitarning 32 48S 117 57E
15 Jiu, R. 43 47N 23 48E
80 Joaçaba 27 5S 51 31W
57 João Belo 25 7S 33 32E
79 João Pessoa 7 10S 34 52W
80 Joaquin Villa González 25 10S 64 0W
32 Jodhpur 26 23N 73 2E
63 Joggins 45 42N 64 27W
57 Johannesburg 26 10S 28 8E
8 John O'Groats 58 39N 3 3W
68 Johnson City, N.Y. 42 9N 67 0W
69 Johnson City, Tenn. 36 18N 82 21W
64 Johnson's Crossing 60 33N 133 27W
68 Johnstown 43 1N 74 20W
34 Johor Baharu 1 45N 103 47E
80 Joinvile 26 15S 48 55E
20 Jokkmokk 66 35N 19 50E
68 Joliet 41 30N 88 0W
62 Joliette 46 3N 73 24W
35 Jolo, I. 6 0N 121 0E
35 Jombang 7 32S 112 12E
62 Jones, C. 54 33N 79 35W
71 Jonesboro 35 50N 90 45W
21 Jönköping 57 45N 14 10E
21 Jönköpings □ 57 30N 14 30E
71 Joplin 37 0N 94 25W
30 Jordan ■ 31 0N 36 0E
28 Jordan, R. 31 46N 35 33E
33 Jorhat 26 45N 94 20E
20 Jörn 65 5N 20 12E
53 Jos 9 53N 8 51E
53 Jos Plat. 9 45N 8 45E
80 José Batlle y Ordóñez 33 20S 55 10W
80 José de San Martín 44 4S 70 26W
44 Joseph Bonaparte, G. 14 0S 29 0E
21 Jotunheimen, Mts. 61 30N 9 0E
30 Jounieh 33 59N 35 30E
31 Jouzjan □ 22 40N 81 10W
64 Juan de Fuca Str. 48 15N 124 0W
2 Juan Fernández, Arch. de 33 50S 80 0W
80 Juárez 37 40S 59 43W
79 Juàzeiro 9 30S 40 30W
79 Juazeiro do Norte 7 10S 39 18W
51 Jûbâ 4 57N 31 35E
30 Jubaila 24 55N 46 25E
50 Juby, C. 28 0N 12 59W
13 Júcar, R. 39 40N 2 18W
74 Juchitán 16 27N 95 5W
28 Judaea=Har Yehuda, Reg. 31 35N 34 57E
79 Juiz de Fora 21 43S 43 19W
78 Juli 16 10S 69 25W
42 Julia Creek 20 40S 141 55E
78 Juliaca 15 25S 70 10W
78 Julianatop, Mt. 3 40N 56 30W
2 Julianehåb 60 43N 46 0W
32 Jullundur 31 20N 75 40E
75 Jumento Cays 23 40N 75 40E
11 Jumet 50 27N 4 25E
13 Jumilla 38 28N 1 19W
33 Jumna, R.= Yamuna, R. 25 25N 81 50E
32 Junagadh 21 30N 70 30E
70 Junction City, Kans. 39 4N 96 55W
72 Junction City, Oreg. 44 20N 123 12W
42 Jundah 24 46S 143 2E
80 Jundiaí 23 10S 47 0W
64 Juneau 58 26N 134 30W
46 Junee 34 49S 147 32W
80 Junín 34 33S 60 57W
80 Junin de los Andes 39 45S 71 0W
80 Juquiá 24 19S 47 38W
8 Jura, I. 56 0N 5 50W
12 Jura, Mts. 46 45N 6 30E
12 Jura □ 46 47N 5 45E
78 Jurado 7 7N 77 46W
31 Jurm 36 50N 70 45E
78 Juruá, R. 2 37S 65 44W
79 Juruti 2 9S 56 4W
80 Justo Daract 33 52S 65 12W
75 Juticalpa 14 40N 85 50W
21 Jutland= Jylland, Reg. 56 25N 9 30E
19 Južna Morava, R. 43 35N 21 20E

Jyekundo Keeling Is. = Cocos Is.

37 Jyekundo 33 0N 96 50 E
21 Jylland, Reg. 56 25N 9 30 E
20 Jyväskylä 62 12N 25 47 E

K

32 K2, Mt. 36 0N 77 0 E
55 Kaap Plato 28 30S 24 0 E
56 Kaapstad= Cape Town 33 55S 18 22 E
35 Kabaena, I. 5 15S 122 0 E
52 Kabale 9 38N 11 37W
54 Kabalo 6 0S 27 0 E
54 Kabambare 4 41S 27 39 E
54 Kabarega Falls 2 15S 31 38 E
52 Kabarnet 0 35N 35 50 E
53 Kabba 7 57N 6 3 E
54 Kabinda 6 23S 24 38 E
54 Kabongo 7 22S 25 33 E
42 Kabra 23 25S 150 25 E
31 Kabul 34 28N 69 18 E
31 Kabul □ 34 0N 68 30 E
55 Kabwe 14 30S 28 29 E
33 Kachin □ 26 0N 97 0 E
24 Kachiry 53 10N 75 50 E
52 Kachung 1 48N 32 50 E
34 Kadan Kyun 12 30N 98 20 E
53 Kade 6 7N 0 56W
43 Kadina 34 0S 137 43 E
* 23 Kadiyerka 48 35N 38 30 E
53 Kaduna 10 30N 7 21 E
53 Kaduna □ 11 0N 7 30 E
53 Kaelé 10 15N 14 15 E
32 Kaerh 31 45N 80 22 E
50 Kaesŏng 37 58N 126 35 E
53 Kafanchan 9 40N 8 20 E
52 Kafulwe 9 0S 29 1 E
51 Kafia Kingi 9 20N 24 25 E
19 Kafirévs, Ákra 38 9N 24 8 E
28 Kafr Kanna 32 45N 35 20 E
28 Kafr Ra'i 32 23N 35 9 E
55 Kafue, R. 15 56S 28 55 E
52 Kafulwe 9 0S 29 1 E
24 Kagan 39 43N 64 33 E
36 Kagawa □ 34 15N 134 0 E
36 Kagoshima 31 36N 130 40 E
36 Kagoshima □ 30 0N 130 0 E
52 Kahama 4 8S 32 30 E
52 Kahe 3 30S 37 25 E
35 Kai, Kep 5 55S 132 45 E
47 Kaiapoi 42 24S 172 40 E
39 Kaifeng 34 50N 114 27 E
47 Kaikohe 35 25S 173 49 E
47 Kaikoura 42 25S 173 43 E
66 Kailua 21 24N 157 44W
53 Kainji Res. 10 1N 4 40 E
47 Kaipara, Harbour 36 25S 174 14 E
38 Kaiping 40 28N 122 10 E
50 Kairouan 35 45N 10 5 E
14 Kaiserslautern 49 30N 7 43 E
47 Kaitaia 35 8S 173 17 E
47 Kaitangata 46 17S 169 51 E
38 Kaiyuan 42 33N 124 4 E
20 Kajaani 64 17N 27 46 E
52 Kajiado 1 53S 36 48 E
52 Kakamega 0 20N 34 46 E
36 Kake 34 6N 132 19 E
36 Kakegawa 34 45N 138 1 E
23 Kakhovka 46 46N 34 28 E
33 Kakinada= Cocanada 16 50N 82 11 E
36 Kakogawa 34 46N 134 51 E
53 Kala 12 2N 14 40 E
32 Kalabagh 33 0N 71 28 E
35 Kalabahi 8 13S 124 31 E
19 Kalabáka 39 42N 21 39 E
53 Kalach 50 22N 41 0 E
33 Kaladan, R. 20 9N 92 57 E
56 Kalahari, Des. 24 0S 22 0 E
55 Kalakan 55 15N 116 45 E
19 Kalamata 37 3N 22 10 E
68 Kalamazoo 42 20N 85 35W
45 Kalamunda 32 0S 116 0 E
30 Kalan 39 7N 39 32 E
45 Kalannie 30 22S 117 5 E
32 Kalat 29 8N 66 31 E
31 Kalat-i-Ghilzai 32 15N 66 58 E
52 Kalemie 5 55S 29 9 E
33 Kalewa 22 41N 95 32 E
45 Kalgoorlie 30 40S 121 22 E
19 Kaliakra, Nos. 43 21N 28 30 E
35 Kalibo 11 43N 122 22 E

* Renamed Stakhanov

34 Kalimantan □ 0 0 115 0 E
19 Kálimnos, I. 37 0N 27 0 E
22 Kalinin 56 55N 35 55 E
22 Kaliningrad 54 44N 20 32 E
72 Kalispell 48 10N 114 22 E
15 Kalisz 53 17N 15 55 E
52 Kaliua 5 5S 31 48 E
28 Kallia 31 46N 35 30 E
53 Kalmalo 13 40N 5 20 E
21 Kalmar 56 40N 16 20 E
21 Kalmar □ 57 25N 16 15 E
23 Kalmyk A.S.S.R. □ 46 5N 46 1 E
24 Kalmykovo 49 0N 51 35 E
15 Kalocsa 46 32N 19 0 E
56 Kalomo 17 0S 26 30 E
60 Kaltag 64 20N 158 44W
56 Kaltungo 9 48N 11 19 E
22 Kaluga 54 35N 36 10 E
21 Kalundborg 55 41N 11 5 E
22 Kama, R. 55 45N 52 0 E
52 Kamachumu 1 37S 31 37 E
36 Kamaishi 39 20N 142 0 E
29 Kamaran, I. 15 28N 42 35 E
52 Kamba 11 50N 3 45 E
45 Kambalda 31 10S 121 37 E
22 Kambarka 56 17N 54 12 E
25 Kamchatka Pol. 57 0N 160 0 E
52 Kamembe 2 29S 28 54 E
24 Kamen 53 50N 81 30 E
23 Kamenets Podolskiy 48 40N 26 30 E
22 Kamenka 65 58N 44 0 E
23 Kamensk Shakhtinskiy 48 23N 40 20 E
24 Kamensk Uralskiy 56 28N 61 54 E
25 Kamenskoye 62 45N 165 30 E
36 Kameoka 35 0N 135 35 E
54 Kamina 8 45S 25 0 E
64 Kamloops 50 40N 120 20W
52 Kampala 0 20N 32 30 E
11 Kampen 52 33N 5 53 E
34 Kampot 10 36N 104 10 E
34 Kampuchea■= Cambodia ■ 12 15N 105 0 E
65 Kamsack 51 35N 101 50W
22 Kamskoye Vdkhr. 58 0N 56 0 E
23 Kamyshin 50 10N 45 30 E
39 Kan Kiang, R. 29 45N 116 10 E
73 Kanab 27 3N 112 29W
54 Kananga 5 55S 22 18 E
22 Kanash 55 48N 47 32 E
36 Kanazawa 36 30N 136 38 E
34 Kanchanaburi 14 8N 99 31 E
33 Kanchenjunga, Mt. 27 50N 88 10 E
32 Kanchipuram 12 52N 79 45 E
39 Kanchow 25 51N 114 59 E
38 Kanchwan 36 29N 109 24 E
24 Kandagach 49 20N 57 15 E
31 Kandahar 31 32N 65 30 E
31 Kandahar □ 31 0N 65 0 E
22 Kandalaksha 67 9N 32 30 E
22 Kandalakshskiy Zaliv 66 0N 35 0 E
34 Kandangan 2 50S 115 20 E
47 Kandavu, I. 19 0S 178 15 E
53 Kandi, Benin 11 7N 2 55 E
32 Kandi, India 23 58N 88 5 E
32 Kandy 7 42N 80 37 E
68 Kane 41 39N 78 53W
58 Kane Basin 79 0N 70 0W
34 Kangar 6 27N 100 12 E
43 Kangaroo, I. 35 45S 137 0 E
30 Kangāvar 34 40N 48 0 E
38 Kangnŭng 37 45N 128 54 E
39 Kangshan 22 43N 120 14 E
37 Kangsu □ 38 0N 101 40 E
33 Kangto, Mt. 27 50N 92 35 E
22 Kanin, Pol. 68 0N 45 0 E
46 Kaniva 36 22S 141 18 E
68 Kankakee 41 6N 87 50W
68 Kankakee, R. 41 23N 88 16W
50 Kankan 10 30N 9 15W
69 Kannapolis 35 32N 80 37W
53 Kano 12 2N 8 30 E
53 Kano □ 12 0N 8 30 E
36 Kanoya 31 23N 130 51 E
33 Kanpetlet 21 10N 93 59 E
32 Kanpur 26 35N 80 20 E
32 Kanrach 25 35N 65 20 E
70 Kansas, R. 39 7N 94 36W
70 Kansas □ 38 40N 98 0W
70 Kansas City, Kans. 39 0N 94 40W
70 Kansas City, Mo. 39 3N 94 30W
25 Kansk 56 20N 96 37 E
53 Kantché 13 31N 8 30 E
36 Kantō □ 36 0N 120 0 E
37 Kantse 31 30N 100 29 E
9 Kanturk 52 10N 8 55W
36 Kanuma 36 44N 139 42 E
56 Kanye 25 0S 25 28 E
39 Kanyu 34 53N 119 9 E
39 Kaohsiung 22 35N 120 16 E
56 Kaokoveld 19 0S 13 0 E
50 Kaolack 14 5N 16 8W
38 Kaomi 36 25N 119 45 E
38 Kaoping 35 48N 112 55 E
39 Kaoyu Hu, L. 32 50N 119 25 E
18 Kapela, Ra. 45 0N 15 15 E
14 Kapfenberg 47 26N 15 18 E
55 Kapiri Mposha 13 59S 28 43 E
31 Kapisa □ 34 45N 69 30 E
56 Kapps 22 32S 17 18 E
52 Kapsabet 0 14N 35 5 E
34 Kapuas, R. 0 25S 109 24 E
43 Kapunda 34 20S 138 56 E
62 Kapuskasing 49 25N 82 30W
43 Kaputar, Mt. 30 15S 130 10 E
52 Kaputir 2 5N 35 28 E
24 Kara 69 10N 65 25 E
24 Kara Bogaz Gol, Zaliv 41 0N 53 30 E
24 Kara Kalpak A.S.S.R. □ 43 0N 59 0 E
24 Kara Sea 75 0N 70 0 E
30 Karabük 41 12N 32 37 E
24 Karabutak 49 59N 60 14 E
* 32 Karachi □ 25 30N 67 0 E
32 Karad 17 54N 74 10 E
30 Karadeniz Boğazi 41 10N 29 5 E
30 Karadeniz Dağlari, Mts. 41 30N 35 0 E
24 Karaganda 49 50N 73 0 E
24 Karagayly 49 26N 76 0 E
32 Karaikkudi 10 0N 78 45 E
31 Karaj 35 4N 51 0 E
24 Karakas 48 20N 83 30 E
38 Karakorum, Mts. 35 20N 76 0 E
32 Karakoram P. 35 33N 77 46 E
30 Karaköse 39 44N 43 3 E
25 Karalon 57 5N 115 50 E
34 Karambu 3 53S 116 6 E
56 Karasburg 28 0S 18 44 E
24 Karasino 66 50N 86 50 E
20 Karasjok 69 27N 25 30 E
24 Karasuk 53 44N 78 2 E
24 Karatau 43 10N 70 28 E
24 Karatau Ra. 44 0N 69 0 E
36 Karatsu 33 30N 130 0 E
18 Karawanken, Mts. 46 30N 14 40 E
24 Karazhal 48 2N 70 49 E
30 Karbalā 32 47N 44 3 E
15 Karcag 47 19N 21 1 E
56 Kareeberge 30 50S 22 0 E
22 Karelian A.S.S.R. □ 65 30N 32 30 E
24 Kargasok 59 3N 80 53 E
24 Kargat 55 10N 80 15 E
32 Kargil 34 32N 76 12 E
22 Kargopol 61 30N 38 58 E
57 Kariba L. 16 40S 28 25 E
32 Karikal 10 59N 79 50 E
51 Karima 18 30N 21 40 E
34 Karimata, Selat, Str. 2 0S 108 20 E
32 Karimnagar 18 26N 79 10 E
36 Kariya 34 58N 137 1 E
24 Karkaralinsk 49 30N 75 10 E
23 Karkinitskiy Zaliv 45 36N 32 35 E
28 Karkur 32 29N 34 57 E
14 Karl-Marx-Stadt 50 50N 12 55 E
18 Karlovac 45 31N 15 36 E
14 Karlovy Vary 50 13N 12 51 E
21 Karlsborg 58 33N 14 33 E
21 Karlshamn 56 10N 14 51 E
21 Karlskoga 59 22N 14 33 E
21 Karlskrona 56 10N 15 35 E
14 Karlsruhe 49 3N 8 23 E
21 Karlstad 59 23N 13 30 E
60 Karluk 57 30N 155 0W
32 Karnal 29 42N 77 2 E
33 Karnaphuli Res. 22 40N 92 20 E
32 Karnataka □ 13 15N 77 0 E
14 Karnische Alpen, Mts. 46 36N 13 0 E
14 Kärnten □ 46 52N 13 30 E
54 Karonga 9 57S 33 55 E
43 Karoonda 35 1S 139 59 E
19 Kárpathos, I. 35 37N 27 10 E
22 Karpogory 63 59N 44 27 E
30 Kars 40 40N 43 5 E
24 Karsakpay 47 55N 66 40 E

* Now part of Baluchistan

24 Karshi 38 53N 65 48 E
24 Kartaly 53 3N 60 40 E
52 Karumo 2 25S 32 50 E
52 Karungu 0 50S 34 10 E
32 Karur 10 59N 78 2 E
32 Karwar 14 44N 74 5 E
54 Kasai, R. 3 2S 16 57 E
52 Kasama 10 16S 31 9 E
54 Kasangulu 4 15S 15 15 E
32 Kasaragod 12 30N 74 58 E
52 Kasenyi 1 24N 30 26 E
52 Kasese 0 13N 30 3 E
31 Kāshān 34 5N 51 30 E
37 Kashgar 39 46N 75 52 E
39 Kashing 30 45N 120 41 E
27 Kashmir □ 34 0N 78 0 E
22 Kasimov 54 55N 41 20 E
64 Kaslo 49 55N 117 0W
54 Kasongo 4 30S 26 33 E
19 Kásos, I. 35 20N 26 55 E
51 Kassala 15 23N 36 26 E
51 Kassalâ □ 15 20N 36 26 E
14 Kassel 51 19N 9 32 E
35 Kassue 6 58S 139 21 E
30 Kastamonu 41 25N 33 43 E
52 Kasulu 4 37S 30 5 E
32 Kasur 31 5N 74 25 E
25 Kata 58 46N 102 40 E
54 Katako Kombe 3 25S 24 20 E
49 Katanga, Reg.= Shaba, Reg. 8 30S 25 0 E
45 Katanning 33 40S 117 33 E
33 Katha 24 10N 96 30 E
44 Katherine 14 27S 132 20 E
32 Kathiawar, Reg. 22 0N 71 0 E
34 Katiet 2 21S 99 14 E
33 Katihar 25 34N 87 36 E
56 Katima Mulilo 17 28S 24 13 E
60 Katmai Mt. 58 20N 154 59W
33 Katmandu 27 45N 85 12 E
55 Katombora 18 0S 25 30 E
54 Katompi 6 2S 26 23 E
46 Katoomba 33 41S 150 19 E
15 Katowice 50 17N 19 5 E
8 Katrine, L. 56 15N 4 30 E
21 Katrineholm 59 9N 16 12 E
53 Katsina 7 10N 9 20 E
* 31 Kattawaz Urgan □ 32 10N 68 20 E
21 Kattegat, Str. 57 0N 11 20 E
11 Katwijk-aan-Zee 52 12N 4 22 E
66 Kauai, I. 19 30N 155 30W
56 Kaukauveld 20 0S 20 15 E
20 Kaukonen 67 42N 24 58 E
22 Kaunas 54 54N 23 54 E
53 Kaura Namoda 12 37N 6 33 E
20 Kautokeino 69 0N 23 4 E
25 Kavacha 60 16N 169 51 E
19 Kaválla 40 57N 24 28 E
79 Kaw 4 30N 52 15W
36 Kawagoe 35 55N 139 29 E
36 Kawaguchi 35 52N 138 45 E
66 Kawaihae 20 5N 155 50W
52 Kawambwa 9 48S 29 3 E
36 Kawanoe 34 1N 133 34 E
36 Kawasaki 35 35N 138 42 E
62 Kawene 48 45N 91 15W
47 Kawerau 38 7S 176 42 E
47 Kawhia Harbour 38 4S 174 49 E
33 Kawnro 22 48N 99 8 E
34 Kawthaung 10 5N 98 36 E
33 Kawthoolei □ 18 0N 97 30 E
53 Kaya 13 25N 1 10W
33 Kayah □ 19 15N 97 15 E
52 Kayambi 9 28S 31 59 E
73 Kayenta 36 46N 110 15 E
50 Kayes 14 25N 11 30W
43 Kayrunnera 30 40S 142 30 E
30 Kayseri 38 45N 35 30 E
34 Kayuagung 3 28S 104 46 E
25 Kazachye 70 52N 135 58 E
24 Kazakh S.S.R. □ 50 0N 58 0 E
22 Kazan 55 48N 49 3 E
19 Kazanlŭk 42 38N 25 35 E
23 Kazbek, Mt. 42 30N 44 30 E
31 Kāzerūn 29 38N 51 40 E
24 Kazym, R. 63 54N 65 50 E
19 Kéa, I. 37 30N 24 22 E
70 Kearney 40 45N 99 3W
20 Kebnekaise, Mt. 67 48N 18 30 E
29 Kebri Dehar 6 45N 44 17W
35 Kebumen 7 42S 109 40 E
15 Kecskemet 46 57N 19 35 E
63 Kedgwick 47 40N 67 20W
35 Kediri 7 51S 112 1 E
3 Keeling Is.= Cocos Is. 12 12S 96 54 E

* Renamed Paktīkā

Keelung = Chilung Kishangarh

39 Keelung=Chilung 25 3N 121 45 E
68 Keene 42 57N 72 17W
56 Keetmanshoop 26 35S 18 8 E
65 Keewatin 47 23N 93 0W
60 Keewatin, Reg. 63 20N 94 40W
19 Kefallinía, I. 38 28N 20 30 E
35 Kefamenanu 9 28S 124 38 E
28 Kefar Gil'adi 33 14N 35 35 E
28 Kefar Sava 32 11N 34 54 E
28 Kefar Szold 33 11N 35 34 E
28 Kefar Tavor 32 42N 35 24 E
28 Kefar Vitkin 32 22N 34 53 E
28 Kefar Yona 32 20N 34 54 E
28 Kefar Zetim 32 49N 35 27 E
53 Keffi 8 55N 7 43 E
20 Keflavik 64 2N 22 35W
6 Keighley 53 52N 1 54W
56 Keimoes 28 41S 21 0 E
53 Keita 14 46N 5 46 E
43 Keith, Australia 36 0S 140 20 E
8 Keith, U.K. 57 33N 2 58W
60 Keith Arm, B. 65 30N 122 0W
25 Kël 69 30N 124 10 E
34 Kelang 3 2N 101 26 E
51 Kelibia 36 50N 11 3 E
45 Kellerberrin 31 36S 117 38 E
72 Kellogg 47 30N 116 5W
9 Kells=Ceanannas
Mor 53 42N 6 53W
64 Kelowna 49 50N 119 25W
64 Kelsey Bay 50 25N 126 0W
47 Kelso, N.Z. 45 54S 169 15 E
8 Kelso, U.K. 55 36N 2 27W
72 Kelso, U.S.A. 46 10N 122 57W
34 Keluang 2 3N 103 18 E
65 Kelvington 52 20N 103 30W
22 Kem 65 0N 34 38 E
22 Kem, R. 64 57N 34 41 E
24 Kemerovo 55 20N 85 50 E
20 Kemi 65 47N 24 32 E
20 Kemijärvi 66 43N 27 22 E
20 Kemijoki, R. 65 47N 24 30 E
72 Kemmerer 41 52N 110 30W
43 Kempsey 31 1S 152 50 E
14 Kempten 47 42N 10 18 E
62 Kemptville 45 0N 75 38W
8 Ken, R. 54 50N 4 4W
35 Kendal, Indonesia 6 56S 110 14 E
6 Kendal, U.K. 54 19N 2 44W
35 Kendari 3 50S 122 30 E
53 Kende 11 30N 4 12 E
45 Kendenup 34 30S 117 38 E
60 Kendi 60 30N 151 0W
33 Kendrapara 20 35N 86 30 E
50 Kenema 7 50N 11 14W
33 Keng Tawng 20 45N 98 18 E
33 Keng Tung 21 0N 99 30 E
38 Kenho 50 43N 121 30 E
50 Kenitra 34 15N 6 40W
9 Kenmare 51 52N 9 35W
69 Kennedy, C.=
Canaveral, C. 28 28N 80 31W
7 Kennet, R. 51 28N 0 57W
71 Kennett 36 7N 90 0W
72 Kennewick 46 11N 119 2W
60 Keno Hill 63 57N 135 25W
65 Kenora 49 50N 94 35W
68 Kenosha 42 33N 87 48W
63 Kensington 46 25N 63 34W
68 Kent 41 8N 81 20W
7 Kent □ 51 12N 0 40 E
60 Kent Pen. 68 30N 107 0W
24 Kentau 43 32N 68 36 E
68 Kenton 40 40N 83 35W
68 Kentucky, R. 38 41N 85 11W
68 Kentucky □ 37 20N 85 0W
63 Kentville 45 6N 64 29W
52 Kenya ■ 2 20N 38 0 E
54 Kenya, Mt. 0 10S 37 18 E
70 Keokuk 40 25N 91 30W
19 Kephallinia, I.=
Kefallinia, I. 38 28N 20 30 E
32 Kerala □ 11 0N 76 15 E
46 Kerang 35 40S 143 55 E
31 Keray 26 15N 57 30 E
23 Kerch 45 20N 36 20 E
28 Kerem Maharal 32 39N 34 59 E
3 Kerguelan, I. 48 15S 69 10 E
52 Kericho 0 22S 35 15 E
34 Kerinci, Mt. 2 5S 101 0 E
51 Kerkenna, Is. 34 48N 11 1 E
24 Kerki 37 10N 65 0 E
19 Kérkira 39 38N 19 50 E
19 Kérkira, I. 39 35N 19 45 E
11 Kerkrade 50 53N 6 4 E
2 Kermadec Is. 31 8S 175 16W
31 Kermān 30 15N 57 1 E
31 Kermān □ 30 0N 57 0 E
* **30** Kermānshāh 34 23N 47 0 E
* **30** Kermānshāh □ 34 0N 46 30 E
71 Kermit 31 56N 103 3W
52 Kerripi 3 55N 31 52 E
65 Kerrobert 52 0N 109 11W
71 Kerrville 30 1N 99 8W
9 Kerry □ 52 7N 9 35W
9 Kerry Hd. 52 26N 9 56W
38 Kerulen, R. 48 48N 117 0 E
50 Kerzaz 29 29N 1 25W
20 Keski-Suomen □ 63 0N 25 0 E
57 Kestell 28 17S 28 42 E
6 Keswick 54 35N 3 9W
53 Keta 5 49N 1 0 E
53 Keta Lagoon 5 50N 1 0 E
34 Ketapang 1 55S 110 0 E
64 Ketchikan 55 25N 131 40W
53 Kete Krachi 7 55N 0 1W
15 Kętrzyn 54 7N 21 22 E
7 Kettering 52 24N 0 44W
72 Kettle Falls 48 41N 118 2W
70 Kewanee 41 18N 90 0W
70 Keweenaw B. 47 0N 88 0W
70 Keweenaw Pt. 47 26N 87 40W
67 Key West 24 40N 82 15W
68 Keyser 39 26N 79 0W
25 Kezhma 59 15N 100 57 E
24 Khabarovo 69 30N 60 30 E
25 Khaborovsk 48 20N 135 0 E
33 Khairagarh 21 27N 81 2 E
32 Khairpur 27 32N 68 49 E
31 Khalij-e Fars 28 20N 51 45 E
19 Khalkís 38 27N 23 42 E
22 Khalmer Yu 67 58N 65 1 E
22 Khalturin 58 40N 48 50 E
56 Khamas Country 21 45S 26 30 E
29 Khamir 16 10N 43 45 E
37 Khan Tengri,
Mt. 42 25N 80 10 E
28 Khān Yūnis 31 21N 34 18 E
31 Khanabad 36 45N 69 5 E
30 Khānaqin 34 23N 45 25 E
32 Khandwa 21 49N 76 22 E
25 Khandyga 62 30N 134 50 E
32 Khanewal 30 20N 71 55 E
19 Khaniá 35 30N 24 4 E
19 Khaníon, Kól. 35 33N 23 55 E
25 Khanka, Oz. 45 0N 132 30 E
24 Khanty-
Mansiysk 61 0N 69 0 E
25 Khapcheranga 49 40N 112 0 E
33 Kharagpur 22 20N 87 25 E
30 Kharfa 22 0N 46 35 E
23 Kharkov 49 58N 36 20 E
22 Kharovsk 59 56N 40 13 E
30 Kharsaniya 27 10N 49 10 E
51 Khartoum=El
Khartûm 15 31N 32 35 E
31 Khasab 26 14N 56 15 E
31 Khāsh 28 15N 61 5 E
51 Khashm el Girba 14 59N 35 58 E
32 Khashmor 28 30N 69 31 E
19 Khaskovo 41 56N 25 30 E
25 Khatanga 72 0N 102 20 E
51 Khatanga, R. 73 30N 109 0 E
30 Khavari □ 37 20N 46 0 E
32 Khed Brahma 24 2N 73 3 E
50 Khemis Miliana 36 11N 2 14 E
50 Khenchela 35 28N 7 11 E
50 Khenifra 32 58N 5 46W
23 Kherson 46 35N 32 35 E
37 Khetinsiring 32 54N 92 50 E
25 Khilok 51 30N 110 45 E
19 Khíos 38 27N 26 9 E
19 Khíos, I. 38 20N 26 0 E
24 Khiva 41 30N 60 18 E
23 Khmelnitisky 49 23N 27 0 E
32 Khojak P. 30 55N 66 30 E
22 Kholm 57 10N 31 15 E
25 Kholmsk 35 5N 139 48 E
34 Khong, R. 14 7N 105 51 E
34 Khonh Hung 9 37N 105 50 E
25 Khonu 66 30N 143 25 E
22 Khoper, R. 52 0N 43 20 E
31 Khorasan □ 34 0N 58 0 E
34 Khorat=Nakhon
Ratchasima 14 59N 102 12 E
24 Khorog 37 30N 71 36 E
30 Khorramābād 33 30N 48 25 E
30 Khorramshahr 30 29N 48 15 E
50 Khouribga 32 58N 6 50W
31 Khugiani 31 28N 66 14 E
33 Khulna 22 45N 89 34 E
33 Khulna □ 22 45N 89 35 E
32 Khushab 32 20N 72 20 E
30 Khuzestan □ 31 0N 50 0 E
31 Khvor 33 45N 55 0 E
31 Khvormūj 28 40N 51 30 E

* *Renamed Bakhtāran*

30 Khvoy 38 35N 45 0 E
31 Khyber P. 34 10N 71 8 E
39 Kialing
Kiang, R. 30 2N 106 18 E
46 Kiama 34 40S 150 50 E
46 Kiamal 34 58S 142 18 E
52 Kiambu 1 8S 36 50 E
38 Kiamusze 46 45N 130 30 E
39 Kian 27 1N 114 58 E
39 Kiangling 30 28N 113 16 E
39 Kiangsi □ 27 45N 115 0 E
39 Kiangsu □ 33 0N 119 50 E
39 Kiangyin 31 51N 120 0 E
38 Kiaohsien 36 20N 120 0 E
52 Kibau 8 35S 35 18 E
52 Kiberege 7 55S 36 53 E
52 Kibiti 7 40S 38 54 E
52 Kibombo 3 57S 25 53 E
52 Kibwezi 2 27S 37 57 E
25 Kichiga 59 50N 163 5 E
64 Kicking Horse P. 51 27N 116 25W
7 Kidderminster 52 24N 2 13W
52 Kidete 6 25S 37 17 E
52 Kidugallo 6 49S 38 15 E
14 Kiel 54 16N 10 8 E
14 Kieler B. 54 30N 10 30 E
39 Kienko 31 50N 105 30 E
39 Kienow 27 0N 118 16 E
37 Kienshui 23 57N 102 45 E
39 Kiensi 26 58N 106 0 E
39 Kienteh 29 30N 119 28 E
39 Kienyang 27 30N 118 0 E
23 Kiev=Kiyev 50 30N 30 28 E
50 Kiffa 16 50N 11 15W
52 Kigali 1 5S 30 4 E
52 Kigoma-Ujiji 5 30S 30 0 E
52 Kihurio 4 32S 38 5 E
36 Kii-Suido,
Chan. 33 0N 134 50 E
52 Kijabe 0 56S 36 33 E
39 Kikiang 28 58N 106 44 E
19 Kikinda 45 50N 20 30 E
19 Kikládhes, Is. 37 20N 24 30 E
19 Kikládhes □ 37 20N 24 30 E
43 Kilcoy 26 59S 152 30 E
9 Kildare 53 10N 6 50W
9 Kildare □ 53 10N 6 50W
52 Kilembe 0 15N 30 3 E
71 Kilgore 32 22N 94 40W
52 Kilifi 3 40S 39 48 E
52 Kilimanjaro, Mt. 3 7S 37 20 E
52 Kilimatinde 5 55S 34 58 E
52 Kilindini 4 4S 39 40 E
30 Kilis 36 50N 37 10 E
9 Kilkee 52 41N 9 40W
9 Kilkenny 52 40N 7 17W
9 Kilkenny □ 52 35N 7 15W
9 Killala 54 13N 9 12W
9 Killaloe 52 48N 8 28W
65 Killarney, Canada 49 10N 99 40W
9 Killarney, Eire 52 2N 9 30W
9 Killary Harbour 53 38N 9 52W
8 Killiecrankie,
P. of 56 44N 3 46W
8 Killin 56 27N 4 20W
9 Killybegs 54 38N 8 26W
46 Kilmany 38 8S 146 55 E
8 Kilmarnock 55 36N 4 30W
46 Kilmore 37 25S 144 53 E
52 Kilosa 6 48S 37 0 E
9 Kilrush 52 39N 9 30W
52 Kilwa Kisiwani 8 58S 39 32 E
52 Kilwa Kivinje 8 45S 39 25 E
43 Kimba 33 8S 136 23 E
70 Kimball 41 17N 103 20W
65 Kimberley, Canada 49 40N 116 10W
56 Kimberley,
S. Africa 28 43S 24 46 E
44 Kimberley Downs 17 24S 124 22 E
72 Kimberly 42 33N 114 25W
38 Kimchaek 40 41N 129 12 E
38 Kimchon 36 11N 128 4 E
22 Kimry 56 55N 37 15 E
34 Kinabalu, Mt. 6 0N 116 0 E
65 Kincaid 49 40N 107 0W
62 Kincardine 44 10N 81 40W
65 Kindersley 51 30N 109 10W
50 Kindia 10 0N 12 52W
54 Kindu 2 55S 25 50 E
22 Kineshma 57 30N 42 5 E
42 King, I. 39 50S 144 0 E
42 King, Mt. 25 10S 147 31 E
44 King Edward, R. 14 14S 126 35 E
80 King George B. 51 30S 60 30W
61 King George Is. 53 40N 80 30W
44 King Leopold,
Ras. 17 20S 124 20 E
44 King Sd. 16 50S 123 20 E
60 King William I. 69 0N 98 0W
56 King William's
Town 32 51S 27 22 E
43 Kingaroy 26 32S 151 51 E
37 Kingku 23 49N 100 30 E
73 Kingman 35 12N 114 2W
43 Kingoonya 30 54N 135 18 E
38 Kingpeng 43 30N 117 25 E
73 Kings Canyon
Nat. Park 37 0N 118 45W
6 Kings Lynn 52 45N 0 25 E
7 Kingsbridge 50 14N 3 46W
9 Kingscourt 53 55N 6 48W
62 Kingston, Canada 44 20N 76 30W
75 Kingston, Jamaica 18 0N 76 50W
47 Kingston, N.Z. 45 20S 168 43 E
68 Kingston, N.Y. 41 55N 74 0W
68 Kingston, Pa. 41 19N 75 58W
43 Kingston South
East 36 52S 139 51 E
75 Kingstown 13 10N 61 10W
62 Kingsville,
Canada 42 3N 82 45W
71 Kingsville, U.S.A. 27 30N 97 53W
38 Kingtai 37 4N 103 59 E
39 Kingtehchen 29 8N 117 21 E
39 Kingtzekwan 33 25N 111 10 E
8 Kingussie 47 5N 4 2W
38 Kinhsien 36 6N 107 49 E
39 Kinhwa 29 5N 119 32 E
65 Kinistino 52 59N 105 0W
54 Kinkala 4 18S 14 49 E
36 Kinki □ 33 30N 136 0 E
47 Kinleith 38 20S 175 56 E
47 Kinloch 44 51S 168 20 E
39 Kinmen, I. 24 25N 118 24 E
28 Kinneret 32 44N 35 34 E
28 Kinneret,
Yam, L. 32 49N 35 36 E
8 Kinross 56 13N 3 25W
9 Kinsale 51 42N 8 31W
9 Kinsale, Old Hd. 51 37N 8 32W
37 Kinsha, R. 32 30N 98 0 E
54 Kinshasa 4 20S 15 15 E
39 Kinsiang 35 4N 116 25 E
69 Kinston 35 18N 77 35W
52 Kintiku 6 0S 35 20 E
8 Kintyre, Pen. 55 30N 5 35W
52 Kinyangiri 4 35S 24 37 E
52 Kioga, L. 1 35N 33 0 E
39 Kioshan 32 50N 114 0 E
19 Kiparissía 37 15N 21 40 E
19 Kiparissiakós
Kól. 37 25N 21 25 E
62 Kipawa Reserve
Prov. Park 47 0N 78 30W
52 Kipembawe 7 38S 33 23 E
52 Kipengere Ra. 9 12S 34 15 E
52 Kipili 7 28S 30 32 E
52 Kipini 2 30S 40 32 E
25 Kirensk 57 50N 107 55 E
24 Kirgiz S.S.R. □ 42 0N 75 0 E
30 Kirikkale 39 51N 33 32 E
22 Kirillov 59 51N 38 14 E
38 Kirin 43 58N 126 31 E
38 Kirin □ 43 45N 125 20 E
8 Kirkcaldy 56 7N 3 10W
8 Kirkcudbright 54 50N 4 3W
32 Kirkee 18 34N 73 56 E
20 Kirkenes 69 40N 30 5 E
8 Kirkintilloch 55 57N 4 10W
62 Kirkland Lake 48 15N 80 0W
70 Kirksville 40 8N 92 35W
30 Kirkūk 35 30N 44 21 E
8 Kirkwall 58 59N 2 59W
56 Kirkwood 33 22S 25 15 E
22 Kirov 58 35N 49 40 E
23 Kirovabad 40 45N 46 10 E
23 Kirovakan 41 0N 44 0 E
23 Kirovograd 48 35N 32 20 E
22 Kirovsk 67 48N 33 50 E
25 Kirovskiy 45 51N 48 11 E
8 Kirriemuir 56 41N 3 0W
22 Kirsanov 52 35N 42 40 E
32 Kirthar Ra. 27 0N 67 0 E
20 Kiruna 67 50N 20 20 E
45 Kirup 33 40S 115 50 E
36 Kiryū 36 25N 139 20 E
52 Kisaki 7 27S 37 40 E
54 Kisangani 0 35N 25 15 E
34 Kisaran 2 47N 99 29 E
36 Kisaratzu 35 25N 139 59 E
24 Kiselevsk 54 5N 86 6 E
54 Kisengwa 6 0S 25 50 E
52 Kiserawe 6 53S 39 0 E
52 Kishanda 1 42S 31 34 E
33 Kishanganj 26 3N 88 14 E
32 Kishangarh 27 50N 70 30 E

53 Kishi 9 1N 3 45 E
23 Kishinev 47 0N 28 50 E
36 Kishiwada 34 28N 135 22 E
28 Kishon 32 33N 35 12 E
32 Kishtwar 33 20N 75 48 E
38 Kisi 45 21N 131 0 E
52 Kisii 0 40S 34 45 E
52 Kisiju 7 23S 39 19 E
60 Kiska I. 52 0N 177 30 E
15 Kiskörös 46 37N 19 20 E
15 Kiskunfélegyháza 46 42N 19 53 E
15 Kiskunhalas 46 28N 19 37 E
23 Kislovodsk 43 50N 42 45 E
36 Kiso-Gawa, R. 35 2N 136 45 E
52 Kisoro 1 17S 29 48 E
50 Kissidougou 9 5N 10 0W
33 Kistna, R.= Krishna, R. 15 43N 80 55 E
52 Kisumu 0 3S 34 45 E
37 Kitai 44 0N 89 27 E
36 Kitaibaraki 36 50N 140 45 E
36 Kitakyūshū 33 50N 130 50 E
52 Kitale 1 0N 35 12 E
52 Kitangari 10 40S 39 20 E
45 Kitchener, Australia 30 55S 124 8 E
62 Kitchener, Canada 43 30N 80 30W
54 Kitega 3 30S 29 58 E
52 Kitgum 3 17N 32 52 E
19 Kíthira 36 9N 23 0 E
19 Kíthira, I. 36 10N 23 0 E
19 Kíthnos, I. 37 26N 24 27 E
64 Kitimat 53 55N 129 0W
52 Kitoma 1 5N 30 55 E
36 Kitsuki 33 35N 131 37 E
68 Kittanning 40 49N 79 30W
52 Kitui 1 17S 38 0 E
55 Kitwe 12 54S 28 7 E
39 Kityang 23 30N 116 29 E
39 Kiukiang 29 37N 116 2 E
39 Kiuling Shan, Mts. 28 40N 115 0 E
39 Kiungchow 19 57N 110 17 E
39 Kiungchow-Haihsia, Str. 20 40N 110 0 E
52 Kivu, L. 1 48S 29 0 E
39 Kiyang 26 36N 111 42 E
23 Kiyev 50 30N 30 28 E
23 Kiyevskoye, Vdkhr. 51 0N 30 0 E
22 Kizel 59 3N 57 40 E
23 Kizlyar 43 51N 46 40 E
24 Kizyl-Arvat 38 58N 56 15 E
24 Kizyl Kiva 40 20N 72 35 E
14 Kladno 50 10N 14 7 E
14 Klagenfurt 46 38N 14 20 E
22 Klaipeda 55 43N 21 10 E
72 Klamath Falls 42 20N 121 50W
21 Klarälven, R. 59 23N 13 32 E
35 Klaten 7 43S 110 36 E
14 Klatovy 49 23N 13 18 E
64 Klawak 55 35N 133 0W
56 Klawer 31 44S 18 36 E
64 Kleena Kleene 52 0N 124 50W
56 Klein Karoo 33 45S 21 30 E
56 Klerksdorp 26 51S 26 38 E
56 Klipplaat 33 0S 24 22 E
14 Kłodzko 50 28N 16 38 E
60 Klondike 64 0N 139 40W
53 Klouto 6 57N 0 44 E
60 Kluane, L. 61 25N 138 50W
6 Knaresborough 54 1N 1 29W
7 Knighton 52 21N 3 2W
11 Knokke 51 20N 3 17 E
70 Knoxville, Iowa 41 20N 93 5W
69 Knoxville, Tenn. 35 58N 83 57W
56 Knysna 34 2S 23 2 E
61 Koartac 61 5N 69 36W
35 Koba 6 37S 134 37 E
18 Kobarid 46 15N 13 30 E
36 Kobe 34 45N 135 10 E
21 København 55 41N 12 34 E
14 Koblenz 50 21N 7 36 E
19 Kočani 41 55N 22 25 E
18 Kočevje 45 39N 14 50 E
36 Kōchi 33 30N 133 35 E
36 Kōchi □ 33 40N 133 30 E
60 Kodiak 57 48N 152 23W
60 Kodiak I. 57 30N 152 45 E
51 Kodok 9 53N 32 7 E
56 Koffiefontein 29 22S 24 58 E
53 Koforidua 6 3N 0 17W
36 Kōfu 35 40N 138 30 E
53 Kogin Baba 7 55N 11 35 E
32 Kohat 33 40N 71 29 E
33 Kohima 25 35N 94 10 E
45 Kojonup 33 48S 117 10W
24 Kokand 40 30N 70 57 E
64 Kokanee Glacier Prov. Park 49 47N 117 10W
24 Kokchetav 53 20N 69 10 E
28 Kokhav Mikha'el 31 37N 34 40 E
37 Kokiu 23 22N 103 6 E
20 Kokkola 63 50N 23 8 E
53 Koko 11 28N 4 29 E
37 Koko Nor, L. 37 0N 100 0 E
68 Kokomo 40 30N 86 6W
61 Koksoak, R. 58 30N 68 10W
57 Kokstad 30 32S 29 29 E
25 Kokuora 61 30N 145 0 E
22 Kola 68 45N 33 8 E
38 Kolan 38 43N 111 32 E
32 Kolar 13 12N 78 15 E
32 Kolar Gold Fields 12 58N 78 16 E
19 Kolarovgrad 43 27N 26 42 E
32 Kolayat 27 51N 72 59 E
21 Kolding 55 30N 9 29 E
35 Kolepom, I. 8 0S 138 30 E
22 Kolguyev 69 20N 48 30 E
32 Kolhapur 16 43N 74 15 E
14 Kolín 50 2N 15 9 E
14 Köln 50 56N 9 58 E
15 Koło 52 14N 18 40 E
14 Kołobrzeg 54 10N 15 35 E
22 Kolomna 55 8N 38 45 E
23 Kolomyya 48 31N 25 2 E
33 Kolosib 24 15N 92 45 E
24 Kolpashevo 58 20N 83 5 E
22 Kolskiy Pol. 67 30N 38 0 E
22 Kolskiy Zaliv 69 23N 34 0 E
54 Kolwezi 10 40S 25 25 E
25 Kolyma, R. 64 40N 153 0 E
3 Komandorskiye Is. 55 0N 167 0 E
15 Komárno 47 49N 18 5 E
57 Komatipoort 25 25S 31 57 E
36 Komatsu 36 25N 136 30 E
53 Komenda 5 4N 1 28W
57 Komga 32 37S 27 56 E
22 Komi A.S.S.R.□ 64 0N 55 0 E
36 Komoro 36 19N 138 26 E
19 Komotiri 41 9N 25 26 E
34 Kompong Bang 12 24N 104 40 E
34 Kompong Cham 11 54N 105 30 E
34 Kompong Som 10 38N 103 30 E
56 Komsberge 32 40S 20 45 E
25 Komsomolets, Os. 80 30N 95 0 E
25 Komsomolsk 50 30N 137 0 E
25 Kondakovo 69 20N 151 30 E
45 Kondinin 32 34S 118 8 E
52 Kondoa 4 0S 36 0 E
53 Konduga 11 35N 13 26 E
50 Koudougou 12 10N 2 20W
25 Kondratyevo 57 30N 98 30 E
34 Kong, Koh 11 20N 103 0 E
38 Kongju 36 30N 127 0 E
33 Konglu 27 13N 97 57 E
39 Kongmoon 22 35N 113 1 E
54 Kongolo 5 22S 27 0 E
21 Kongsberg 59 39N 9 39 E
22 Königsberg= Kaliningrad 54 42N 20 32 E
21 Kongsvinger 60 12N 12 2 E
52 Kongwa 6 11S 36 26 E
3 Kønig Haakon VII Sea 66 0S 35 0 E
15 Konin 52 12N 18 15 E
19 Konjic 43 42N 17 58 E
53 Konongo 6 40N 1 15W
22 Konosha 61 0N 40 5 E
23 Konotop 51 12N 33 7 E
15 Końskie 51 15N 20 23 E
14 Konstanz 47 39N 9 10 E
53 Kontagora 10 23N 5 27 E
30 Konya 37 52N 32 35 E
52 Konza 1 45S 37 0 E
45 Kookynie 29 17S 121 22 E
44 Kooline 22 57S 116 20 E
45 Koolyanobbing 30 48S 119 46 E
43 Koonibba 31 58S 133 27 E
45 Koorda 30 48S 117 35 E
64 Kootenay Nat. Park 51 0N 116 0W
46 Koo-wee-rup 38 13S 145 28 E
19 Kopaonik Planina, Mts. 43 10N 21 0 E
21 Kopervik 59 17N 5 17 E
24 Kopeysk 55 7N 61 37 E
21 Köping 59 31N 16 3 E
21 Kopparberg 59 53N 14 59 E
21 Kopparbergs □ 61 20N 14 15 E
19 Korça 40 37N 20 50 E
18 Korčula, I. 42 57N 17 0 E
30 Kordestān □ 36 0N 47 0 E
51 Kordofân □ 13 0N 29 0 E
38 Korea B. 39 0N 124 0 E
50 Korhogo 9 29N 5 28 E
19 Korinthiakós Kól. 38 16N 22 30 E
19 Kórinthos 37 26N 22 55 E
36 Kōriyama 37 24N 140 23 E
37 Korla 41 45N 86 4 E
53 Koro 14 1N 2 58W
47 Koro Sea 17 30S 179 45W
52 Korogwe 5 5S 38 25 E
46 Koroit 38 18S 142 24 E
15 Körös, R. 46 30N 142 42 E
25 Korsakov 46 30N 142 42 E
21 Korsør 55 20N 11 9 E
11 Kortrijk 50 50N 3 17 E
46 Korumburra 38 26S 145 50 E
25 Koryakskiy Khrebet, Mts. 61 0N 171 0 E
19 Kos, I. 36 50N 27 15 E
14 Kościan 52 5N 16 40 E
71 Kosciusko 33 3N 89 34W
64 Kosciusko I. 56 0N 133 40W
46 Kosciusko, Mt. 36 27S 148 16 E
15 Košice 48 42N 21 15 E
22 Koslan 63 28N 48 52 E
19 Kosovska-Mitrovica 42 54N 20 52 E
56 Koster 25 52S 26 54 E
51 Kôstî 13 8N 32 43 E
22 Kostroma 57 50N 41 58 E
14 Kostrzyn 52 24N 17 14 E
14 Koszalin 54 12N 16 8 E
32 Kota 25 14N 75 49 E
34 Kota Baharu 6 7N 102 14 E
34 Kota Kinabalu 6 0N 116 12 E
34 Kota Tinggi 1 44N 103 53 E
34 Kotabaru 3 20S 116 20 E
34 Kotabumi 4 49S 104 46 E
34 Kotawaringin 2 28S 111 27 E
22 Kotelnich 58 20N 48 10 E
21 Kotka 60 28N 26 55 E
22 Kotlas 61 15N 47 0 E
60 Kotlik 63 2N 163 33W
19 Kotor 42 25N 18 47 E
33 Kottagudem 17 30N 80 40 E
32 Kottayam 9 35N 76 33 E
32 Kotturu 14 45N 76 13 E
60 Kotzebue 66 53N 162 39W
53 Koudougou 12 10N 2 20W
56 Kougaberge 33 40S 23 55 E
54 Koula-Moutou 1 15S 12 25 E
42 Koumala 21 38S 149 15 E
24 Kounradskiy 47 20N 75 0 E
79 Kourou 5 9N 52 39W
50 Kouroussa 10 45N 9 45W
53 Kouvé 6 30N 1 30 E
22 Kovdor 67 34N 30 22 E
22 Kovel 51 10N 25 0 E
22 Kovrov 56 25N 41 25 E
39 Kowloon 22 20N 114 15 E
39 Koyiu 23 2N 112 28 E
60 Koyukuk, R. 64 56N 157 30W
19 Kozáni □ 40 20N 21 45 E
32 Kozhikode= Calicut 11 15N 75 43 E
22 Kozhva 65 10N 57 0 E
50 Kpandu 7 2N 0 18 E
53 Kpessi 7 50N 1 25 E
34 Kra, Isthmus of= Kra, Kho Khot 10 15N 99 30 E
34 Kra, Kho Khot 10 15N 99 30 E
15 Kracków 50 4N 19 57 E
21 Kragerø 58 56N 9 30 E
19 Kragujevac 44 2N 20 56 E
35 Krakatau, I.= Rakatau, P. 6 10S 105 20 E
35 Kraksaan 7 43S 113 23 E
19 Kraljevo 43 44N 20 41 E
23 Kramatorsk 48 50N 37 30 E
20 Kramfors 62 55N 17 48 E
18 Kras, Reg 45 30N 14 0 E
22 Krasavino 60 58N 46 26 E
25 Kraskino 42 45N 130 58 E
15 Krasnik 50 55N 22 5 E
23 Krasnodar 45 5N 38 50 E
22 Krasnokamsk 58 0N 56 0 E
24 Krasnoselkupsk 65 20N 82 10 E
24 Krasnoturinsk 59 39N 60 1 E
22 Krasnoufimsk 56 30N 57 37 E
24 Krasnouralsk 58 0N 60 0 E
24 Krasnovodsk 40 0N 52 52 E
22 Krasnovishersk 60 23N 56 59 E
25 Krasnoyarsk 56 8N 93 0 E
23 Krasnyy Yar 46 43N 48 23 E
34 Kratie 12 32N 106 10 E
14 Krefeld 51 20N 6 22 E
23 Kremenchug 49 5N 33 25 E
23 Kremenchugskoye, Vdkhr. 49 20N 32 30 E
15 Kremnica 48 45N 18 50 E
33 Krishna, R. 15 43N 80 55 E
33 Krishnanagar 23 24N 88 33 E
21 Kristiansand 58 5N 7 50 E
21 Kristianstad 56 5N 14 7 E
21 Kristianstads □ 56 0N 14 0 E
20 Kristiansund 63 10N 7 45 E
21 Kristinehamn 59 18N 14 13 E
20 Kristinestad 62 18N 21 25 E
19 Kriti, I. 35 15N 25 0 E
19 Kriti □ 35 15N 25 0 E
23 Krivoy Rog 47 51N 33 20 E
18 Krk, I. 45 5N 14 56 E
14 Krkonose, Mts. 50 50N 16 10 E
57 Krokodil, R. 25 26S 32 0 E
21 Kronobergs □ 56 45N 14 30 E
22 Kronshtadt 60 5N 29 35 E
56 Kroonstad 27 43S 27 19 E
25 Kropotkin 58 50N 115 10 E
15 Krosno 49 35N 21 56 E
15 Krotoszyn 51 42N 17 23 E
57 Krugersdorp 26 5S 27 46 E
56 Kruisfontein 34 0S 24 43 E
34 Krung Thep 13 45N 100 35 E
9 Kruševac 43 35N 21 28 E
23 Krymskaya 44 57N 37 50 E
50 Ksar El Boukhari 35 5N 2 52 E
50 Ksar-el-Kebir 35 0N 6 0W
34 Kuala 2 46N 105 47 E
34 Kuala Dungun 4 46N 103 25 E
34 Kuala Kerai 5 32N 102 12 E
34 Kuala Kubu Baharu 3 35N 101 38 E
34 Kuala Lipis 4 22N 102 5 E
34 Kuala Lumpur 3 9N 101 41 E
34 Kuala Selangor 3 20N 101 15 E
34 Kuala Terengganu 5 20N 103 8 E
34 Kualakapuas 2 55S 114 20 E
34 Kualakurun 1 10S 113 50 E
34 Kualapembuang 3 14S 112 38 E
34 Kualasimpang 4 16N 98 4 E
34 Kuantan 3 49N 103 20 E
23 Kuba 41 21N 48 22 E
32 Kubak 27 10N 63 10 E
23 Kuban, R. 45 20N 37 30 E
36 Kubokawa 33 12N 133 8 E
37 Kucha 41 50N 82 30 E
34 Kuching 1 33N 110 25 E
36 Kuchinotsu 32 36N 130 11 E
32 Kuda 23 10N 71 18 E
34 Kudat 7 0N 116 42 E
35 Kudus 6 48N 110 51 E
39 Kueiyang= Kweiyang 25 30N 106 35 E
51 Kufra, El Wâhât et 24 17N 23 15 E
14 Kufstein 47 35N 12 11 E
31 Kūhpāyeh 32 44N 52 20 E
53 Kukawa 12 58N 13 27 E
45 Kukerin 33 13S 118 0 E
42 Kulgera 25 50S 133 18 E
45 Kulin 32 40S 118 2 E
45 Kulja 30 35S 117 31 E
24 Kulsary 46 59N 54 1 E
52 Kululu 9 28N 33 1 E
24 Kulunda 52 45N 79 15 E
24 Kulyab 37 55N 69 50 E
37 Kum Darya, R. 41 0N 89 0 E
24 Kum Tekei 43 10N 79 30 E
53 Kumaganum 13 8N 10 38 E
34 Kumai 2 52S 111 45 E
36 Kumamoto 32 45N 130 45 E
36 Kumamoto □ 32 30N 130 40 E
47 Kumara 42 37S 171 12 E
45 Kumari 32 45S 121 30 E
53 Kumasi 6 41N 1 38 E
53 Kumba 4 36N 9 24 E
43 Kumbarilla 27 15S 150 55 E
53 Kumbo 6 15N 10 36 E
36 Kumagaya 36 9N 139 22 E
22 Kumertau 52 46N 55 47 E
52 Kumi 1 30N 33 58 E
21 Kumla 59 8N 15 10 E
53 Kumo 10 1N 11 12 E
33 Kumon Bum, Mts. 26 0N 97 15 E
31 Kunar □ 35 15N 71 0 E
45 Kundip 33 42S 120 10 E
31 Kunduz 36 50N 68 50 E
31 Kunduz □ 36 50N 68 50 E
56 Kunene, R. 17 20S 11 50 E
38 Kungchuling 43 31N 124 58 E
37 Kungho 36 28N 100 45 E
24 Kungrad 43 6N 58 54 E
33 Kungram 25 45N 89 35 E
21 Kungsbacka 57 30N 12 7 E
39 Kunhsien 32 30N 111 17 E
35 Kuningan 6 59S 108 29 E

33 Kunlong 23 20N 98 50 E
26 Kunlun Shan, Mts. 36 0N 82 0 E
37 Kunming 25 11N 102 37 E
38 Kunsan 35 59N 126 35 E
44 Kununurra 15 40s 128 39 E
42 Kunwarara 22 25s 150 7 E
20 Kuopio 62 53N 27 35 E
20 Kuopio □ 63 25N 27 10 E
18 Kupa, R. 45 28N 16 24 E
35 Kupang 10 19s 123 39 E
64 Kupreanof I. 56 50N 133 30w
23 Kura, R. 39 24N 49 24 E
36 Kurashiki 34 40N 133 50 E
36 Kurayoshi 35 26N 133 50 E
36 Kure 34 14N 132 32 E
24 Kurgaldzhino 50 35N 70 20 E
24 Kurgan 55 30N 65 0 E
25 Kurilskiye Os. 45 0N 150 0 E
36 Kurino 31 57N 130 43 E
32 Kurnool 15 45N 78 0 E
47 Kurow 44 4s 170 29 E
46 Kurri Kurri 32 50s 151 28 E
22 Kursk 51 42N 36 11 E
36 Kurume 33 15N 130 30 E
32 Kurunegala 7 30N 80 18 E
25 Kurya 61 15N 108 10 E
38 Kushan 39 58N 123 30 E
36 Kushikino 31 44N 130 16 E
36 Kushima 31 29N 131 14 E
36 Kushimoto 33 28N 135 47 E
36 Kushiro 43 0N 144 30 E
31 Kushk 34 55N 62 30 E
24 Kushka 35 20N 62 18 E
33 Kushtia 23 55N 89 5 E
60 Kuskokwim, R. 60 17N 162 27w
60 Kuskokwim B. 59 45N 162 25w
24 Kustanay 53 20N 63 45 E
34 Kut, Ko 11 40N 102 35 E
30 Kutahya 39 25N 29 59 E
23 Kutaisi 42 19N 42 40 E
34 Kutaraja=Banda Aceh 5 35N 95 20 E
32 Kutch, G. of 22 50N 69 15 E
32 Kutch, Rann of, Reg. 24 0N 70 0N
15 Kutno 52 15N 19 23 E
42 Kuttabul 21 5s 148 48 E
51 Kutum 14 20N 24 10 E
30 Kuwait ■ 29 30N 47 30 E
36 Kuwana 35 0N 136 43 E
38 Kuyang 41 8N 110 1 E
22 Kuybyshev, Kuyb. Obl. 53 12N 50 9 E
22 Kuybyshev, Tatar A.S.S.R. 54 57N 49 5 E
24 Kuybyshev, Novosibirsk Obl. 55 27N 78 19 E
22 Kuybyshevskoye Vdkhr. 55 2N 49 30 E
25 Kuyumba 61 10N 97 10 E
22 Kuyto, Oz. 64 40N 31 0 E
22 Kuznetsk 53 12N 46 40 E
22 Kuzomen 66 22N 36 50 E
18 Kvarner, G. 44 50N 14 10 E
18 Kvarneric 44 43N 14 37 E
57 Kwabhaca 30 51s 29 0 E
79 Kwakoegron 5 25N 55 25w
52 Kwale 4 15s 39 31 E
56 Kwando, R. 16 48s 22 45 E
39 Kwangan 30 35N 106 40 E
39 Kwangchou= Kwangchow 23 10N 113 10 E
39 Kwangchow 23 10N 113 10 E
39 Kwangchow Wan, G. 21 0N 111 0 E
38 Kwangju 35 10N 126 45 E
37 Kwangnan 24 10N 105 0 E
39 Kwangsi-Chuang Aut.Dist. □ 23 30N 108 55 E
39 Kwangtseh 27 30N 117 25 E
39 Kwangtung □ 23 35N 114 0 E
39 Kwangyuan 32 30N 105 49 E
37 Kwanhsien 30 59N 103 40 E
37 Kwantung 25 12N 101 37 E
53 Kwara □ 8 30N 5 0 E
35 Kwatisore 3 7s 139 59 E
39 Kwei Kiang, R. 23 30N 110 30 E
39 Kweichih 30 40N 117 30 E
39 Kweichow= Fengkieh 31 0N 109 33 E
39 Kweichow □ 26 40N 107 0 E
39 Kweihsien 22 59N 109 44 E
39 Kweiki 28 10N 117 8 E
39 Kweilin 25 16N 110 15 E
39 Kweiping 23 12N 110 0 E
39 Kweiting 26 0N 113 35 E
39 Kweiyang 25 30N 106 35 E
15 Kwidzyń 54 5N 18 58 E
60 Kwiguk Island 62 45N 164 28w
45 Kwinana 32 15s 115 47 E
39 Kwo Ho, R. 33 20N 116 50 E
35 Kwoka, Mt. 0 31s 132 27 E
53 Kwolla 8 55N 9 18 E
25 Kyakhta 50 30N 106 25 E
43 Kyancutta 33 8s 135 34 E
33 Kyaukpadaung 20 52N 95 8 E
33 Kyaukpyu 19 28N 93 30 E
33 Kyaukse 21 36N 96 10 E
52 Kyenjojo 0 40N 30 37 E
55 Kyle Dam 20 14s 31 0 E
42 Kynuna 21 35s 141 55 E
54 Kyoga, L. 1 35N 33 0 E
43 Kyogle 28 40s 153 0 E
38 Kyongju 35 59N 129 26 E
33 Kyonpyaw 17 12N 95 10 E
36 Kyōto 35 0N 135 45 E
36 Kyōto □ 35 15N 135 30 E
30 Kyrínia 35 20N 33 19 E
25 Kystatyam 67 15N 123 0 E
25 Kytal Ktakh 65 30N 123 40 E
33 Kyunhla 23 25N 95 15 E
36 Kyūshū, I. 32 30N 131 0 E
36 Kyūshū □ 32 30N 131 0 E
19 Kyustendil 42 25N 22 41 E
25 Kyusyur 70 30N 127 0 E
25 Kyzyl 51 50N 94 30 E
24 Kzyl Orda 44 50N 65 10 E

L

13 La Alcarria, Reg. 40 31N 2 45w
78 La Asunción 11 2N 63 53w
80 La Banda 27 45s 64 10w
74 La Barca 20 20N 102 40w
78 La Blanquilla, I. 11 51N 64 37w
74 La Boca 9 0N 79 30 E
80 La Calera 32 50s 71 10w
80 La Carlota 33 30s 63 20w
13 La Carolina 38 17N 3 38w
75 La Ceiba, Honduras 15 40N 86 50w
78 La Ceiba, Ven. 9 30N 71 0w
14 La Chaux-de-Fonds 47 7N 6 50 E
80 La Cocha 27 50s 65 40w
13 La Coruña 43 20N 8 25w
70 La Crosse 43 48N 91 13w
78 La Dorada 5 30N 74 40w
13 La Estrada 42 43N 8 27w
68 La Fayette 40 22N 86 52w
69 La Folette 36 23N 84 9w
72 La Grande 45 15N 118 0w
69 La Grange 33 4N 85 0w
78 La Guaira 10 36N 66 56w
75 La Habana 23 0N 82 41w
75 La Mabana 23 8N 82 22w
71 La Junta 38 0N 103 30w
13 La Linea de la Concepción 36 15N 5 23w
65 La Loche 56 29N 109 27w
11 La Louvière 50 27N 4 10 E
63 La Malbaie 47 40N 70 10w
13 La Mancha, Reg. 39 10N 2 54w
60 La Martre, L. 63 0N 118 0w
73 La Mesa 32 48N 117 5w
78 La Orchila, I. 12 30N 67 0w
78 La Oroya 11 32s 75 54w
13 La Palma 37 21N 6 38w
75 La Palma 8 15N 78 0w
50 La Palma, I. 28 40N 17 52w
78 La Paragua 6 50N 63 20w
80 La Paz, Arg. 30 50s 59 45w
78 La Paz, Bolivia 16 20s 68 10w
74 La Paz, Mexico 24 10N 110 20w
78 La Pedrera 1 18s 69 43w
36 La Perouse, Str. 45 40N 142 0 E
74 La Piedad 20 20N 102 1w
72 La Pine 40 53N 80 45w
80 La Plata 35 0s 57 55w
68 La Porte 41 40N 86 40w
62 La Reine 48 50N 79 30w
80 La Rioja 29 20s 67 0w
13 La Rioja, Reg. 42 20N 2 20w
13 La Robla 42 50N 5 41w
12 La Roche-sur-Yon 46 40N 1 25w
12 La Rochelle 46 10N 1 9w
13 La Roda 39 13N 2 15w
75 La Romana 18 27N 68 57w
70 La Salle 41 20N 89 5w
62 La Sarre 48 45N 79 15w
80 La Serena 29 55s 71 10w
18 La Spézia 44 8N 9 50 E
78 La Tagua 0 3N 74 40w
78 La Tortuga, I. 10 56N 65 20w
62 La Tuque 47 30N 72 50w
80 La Unión, Chile 40 10s 73 0w
74 La Union, Salvador 13 20N 87 50w
78 La Urbana 7 8N 66 56w
75 La Vega 19 20N 70 30w
78 La Vela 11 30N 69 30w
62 La Verendrye, Parc Prov. de la 47 15N 77 10w
78 La Victoria 10 14N 67 20w
21 Laaland= Lolland, I. 54 45N 11 30 E
53 Labbézenga 14 57N 0 42 E
50 Labé 11 24N 12 16w
34 Labis 2 22N 103 2 E
80 Laboulaye 34 10s 63 30w
58 Labrador, Reg. 53 20N 61 0w
63 Labrador City 52 42N 67 0w
35 Labuha 0 30s 127 30 E
35 Labuhan 6 26s 105 50 E
64 Lac la Biche 54 45N 111 50w
65 Lac Seul 50 28N 92 0w
27 Laccadive Is. 10 0N 72 30 E
62 Lachine 45 30N 73 40w
46 Lachlan, R. 34 21s 143 57 E
62 Lachute 45 39N 74 21w
68 Lackawanna 42 49N 78 50w
64 Lacombe 52 30N 113 50w
68 Laconia 43 32N 71 30w
32 Ladakh Ra. 34 0N 78 0 E
56 Ladismith 33 28s 21 15 E
31 Lādiz 28 55N 61 15 E
22 Ladozhskoye, Oz. 61 15N 30 30 E
3 Ladrone Is. 17 0N 145 0 E
56 Lady Grey 30 43s 27 13 E
56 Ladybrand 29 9s 27 29 E
64 Ladysmith, Canada 49 0N 124 0w
57 Ladysmith, S. Africa 28 32s 29 46 E
21 Laesø, I. 57 15N 10 53 E
71 Lafayette 30 18N 92 0w
53 Lafia 8 30N 8 34 E
53 Lafiagi 8 52N 5 20 E
62 Laforest 47 4N 81 12w
21 Lågen, R. 61 8N 10 25 E
31 Laghman □ 34 20N 70 0 E
50 Laghouat 33 50N 2 59 E
35 Lagonoy G. 13 50N 123 50 E
53 Lagos, Nigeria 6 25N 3 27 E
13 Lagos, Port. 37 5N 8 41w
53 Lagos □ 6 25N 3 35 E
74 Lagos de Moreno 21 21N 101 55w
44 Lagrange 14 13s 125 46 E
80 Laguna 28 30s 48 50 E
73 Laguna Beach 33 31N 117 52w
78 Lagunas 21 0s 69 45w
38 Laha 48 9N 124 30 E
35 Lahad Datu 5 0N 118 30 E
66 Lahaina 20 52N 156 41w
34 Lahat 3 45s 103 30 E
30 Lahijan 37 12N 50 1 E
14 Lahn, R. 50 18N 7 37 E
21 Laholm 56 30N 13 2 E
32 Lahore 31 32N 74 22 E
* 32 Lahore □ 31 55N 74 5 E
37 Lai Chau 22 5N 103 3 E
38 Laichow Wan, G. 37 30N 119 30 E
43 Laidley 27 39s 152 20 E
30 Laila 22 10N 46 40 E
56 Laingsburg 33 9s 20 52 E
39 Laipin 23 42N 109 16 E
8 Lairg 58 1N 4 24w
34 Lais 3 35s 102 0 E
56 Laisamis 1 38N 37 50 E
38 Laiyang 36 58N 120 41 E
80 Lajes 27 48s 50 20w
71 Lake Charles 31 10N 93 10w
69 Lake City, Fla. 30 10N 82 40w
69 Lake City, S.C. 33 51N 79 44w
45 Lake Grace 33 7s 118 28 E
61 Lake Harbour 62 30N 69 50w
73 Lake Havasu City 34 25N 114 20w
45 Lake King 33 5s 119 45 E
73 Lake Mead Nat. Rec. Area 36 20N 114 30w
42 Lake Nash 20 57s 138 0 E
62 Lake Superior Prov. Park 47 45N 85 0w
62 Lake Traverse 45 56N 78 4w
69 Lake Worth 26 36N 80 3w

* Now part of Punjab

62 Lakefield 44 25N 78 16w
69 Lakeland 28 0N 82 0w
72 Lakeport 39 1N 122 56w
46 Lakes Entrance 37 50s 148 0 E
72 Lakeview 34 12N 109 59w
68 Lakewood 41 28N 81 50w
33 Lakhimpur 27 14N 94 7 E
19 Lakonikós Kól. 36 40N 22 40 E
20 Lakselv 70 2N 24 56 E
33 Lala Ghat 24 30N 92 40 E
13 Lalín 42 40N 8 5w
38 Lalin 45 14N 126 52 E
32 Lalitpur 24 42N 78 28 E
53 Lama-Kara 9 30N 1 15 E
33 Lamaing 15 25N 97 53 E
54 Lambaréné 0 20s 10 12 E
50 Lame 10 27N 9 12 E
13 Lamego 41 5N 7 52w
43 Lameroo 35 19s 140 33 E
71 Lamesa 32 45N 101 57w
19 Lamía 38 55N 22 41 E
* 35 Lamitan 6 40N 122 10 E
8 Lammermuir Hills 55 50N 24 0w
35 Lamon B. 14 30N 122 20 E
18 Lampedusa, I. 35 36N 12 40 E
7 Lampeter 52 6N 4 6w
65 Lampman 49 25N 102 50w
34 Lampung □ 5 30s 105 0 E
52 Lamu 2 10s 40 55 E
8 Lanark 55 40N 3 48w
6 Lancashire □ 53 40N 2 30w
63 Lancaster, Canada 45 17N 66 10w
6 Lancaster, U.K. 54 3N 2 48w
73 Lancaster, Calif. 34 47N 118 8w
68 Lancaster, Ky. 37 40N 84 40w
68 Lancaster, N.H. 44 29N 71 34w
69 Lancaster, S.C. 34 45N 80 47w
61 Lancaster Sd. 74 0N 84 0w
39 Lanchi 29 11N 119 30 E
38 Lanchou= Lanchow 36 4N 103 44 E
38 Lanchow 36 4N 103 44 E
18 Lanciano 42 15N 14 22 E
14 Landeck 47 9N 10 34 E
72 Lander 42 50N 108 49w
12 Landes □ 43 57N 0 48w
12 Landes, Reg. 44 0N 1 5w
32 Landi Kotal 34 7N 71 6 E
10 Land's End 50 4N 5 42w
14 Landshut 48 31N 12 10 E
21 Landskrona 56 53N 12 50 E
69 Lanett 33 0N 85 15w
39 Langchung 31 31N 105 58 E
56 Langeberg 33 55s 21 20 E
38 Langfeng 48 4N 121 10 E
8 Langholm 55 9N 2 59w
34 Langkawi, Pulau 6 25N 99 45 E
63 Langlade, I. 46 50N 56 20w
13 Langreo 43 13N 5 42w
12 Langres 47 52N 5 20 E
12 Langres, Plat. de 47 45N 5 20 E
34 Langsa 4 30N 97 57 E
37 Langson 21 52N 106 42 E
12 Languedoc, Reg. 43 58N 3 22 E
62 Lansdowne House 52 5N 88 0w
63 L'Anse au Loup 51 32N 56 50w
68 Lansing 42 47N 84 32w
50 Lanzarote, I. 29 0N 13 40w
37 Lao Cai 22 30N 103 57 E
35 Laoag 18 7N 120 34 E
35 Laoang 12 32N 125 8 E
9 Laois □ 53 0N 7 20w
12 Laon 49 33N 3 35 E
34 Laos ■ 17 45N 105 0 E
68 Lapeer 43 3N 83 20w
20 Lappi □ 64 33N 25 10 E
20 Lappland, Reg. 68 7N 24 0 E
25 Laptev Sea 76 0N 125 0 E
18 L'Aquila 42 21N 13 24 E
31 Lār 27 40N 54 14 E
50 Larache 35 10N 6 5w
70 Laramie 41 15N 105 29w
62 Larder Lake 48 5N 79 40w
71 Laredo 27 34N 99 29w
† 51 Largeau 17 58N 19 6 E
8 Largs 55 48N 4 51w
19 Lárisa 39 38N 22 28 E
32 Larkana 27 32N 68 2 E
30 Lárnax 35 0N 33 35 E
9 Larne 54 52N 5 50w
9 Larne □ 54 55N 5 55w
44 Larrimah 15 35s 133 12 E
21 Larvik 59 4N 10 0 E
24 Laryak 61 15N 80 0 E
29 Las Anod 8 26N 47 19 E
73 Las Cruces 32 25N 106 50w
80 Las Flores 36 0s 59 0w

* Renamed Isabela
† Renamed Faya-Largeau

Las Heras Liverpool, Australia

80 Las Heras 32 51s 68 49w
29 Las Khoreh 11 4n 48 20e
80 Las Lajas 38 30s 70 25w
80 Las Lomitas 24 35s 60 50w
50 Las Palmas 28 10n 15 28w
80 Las Plumas 43 40s 67 15w
80 Las Rosas 32 30s 61 40w
80 Las Varillas 32 0s 62 50w
73 Las Vegas, Nev. 36 10n 115 5w
71 Las Vegas, N. Mex. 35 35n 105 10w
65 Lashburn 53 10n 109 40w
33 Lashio 22 56n 97 45e
72 Lassen Pk. 40 20n 121 0w
78 Latacunga 0 50s 78 35w
30 Latakia= Al Ladhiqiya 35 30n 35 45e
62 Latchford 47 20n 79 50w
45 Latham 29 44s 116 20e
18 Latina 41 26n 12 53e
60 Latouche 60 0n 147 55w
42 Latrobe, Australia 41 14s 146 30e
28 Latrun 31 50n 34 58e
32 Latur 18 25n 76 40e
22 Latvian S.S.R. □ 57 0n 25 0e
47 Lau Is. 17 0s 178 30w
14 Lauchhammer 51 35n 13 40e
42 Launceston, Australia 41 24s 147 8e
7 Launceston, U.K. 50 38n 4 21w
42 Laura 33 10s 138 18e
71 Laurel, Miss. 31 50n 89 0w
72 Laurel, Mont. 45 46n 108 49w
8 Laurencekirk 56 50n 2 30w
69 Laurens 34 32n 82 2w
58 Laurentian Plat. 51 30n 65 0w
63 Laurentides, Parc Prov. des 47 50n 71 50w
69 Lauringburg 34 50n 79 25w
14 Lausanne 46 32n 6 38e
63 Lauzon 46 48n 71 4w
45 Laverton 28 44s 122 29e
28 Lavi 32 47n 35 25e
25 Lavrentiya 65 35n 171 0w
53 Lawra 10 39n 2 51w
47 Lawrence, N.Z. 45 55s 169 41e
68 Lawrence, U.S.A. 42 40n 71 9w
70 Lawrence 39 0n 95 10w
69 Lawrenceburg 35 12n 87 19w
71 Lawton 34 33n 98 25w
35 Lawu, Mt. 7 40s 111 13e
79 Layras 21 20s 45 0w
2 Laysan I. 25 30n 167 0w
18 Lazio □ 42 10n 12 30e
12 Le Creusot 46 50n 4 24e
75 Le François 14 38n 60 57w
12 Le Havre 49 30n 0 5e
80 Le Maire, Estrecho de 54 50s 65 0w
12 Le Mans 48 0n 0 10e
54 Le Marinel 10 25s 25 17e
70 Le Mars 43 0n 96 0w
75 Le Moule 16 20n 61 22w
12 Le Puy 45 3n 3 52e
12 Le Tréport 50 3n 1 20e
12 Le Verdon 45 32n 1 5w
7 Lea, R. 51 30n 0 1e
70 Lead 44 20n 103 40w
65 Leader 50 50n 109 30w
8 Leadhills 55 25n 3 47w
73 Leadville 39 17n 106 23w
55 Lealui 15 10s 23 2e
62 Leamington, Canada 42 10n 82 30w
7 Leamington, U.K. 52 18n 1 32w
44 Learmonth 22 40s 114 10e
65 Leask 53 5n 106 45w
70 Leavenworth 39 25n 95 0w
68 Lebanon, Ind. 40 3n 86 55w
71 Lebanon, Mo. 37 40n 92 40w
68 Lebanon, N.H. 43 38n 72 15w
72 Lebanon, Ore. 44 31n 122 57w
68 Lebanon, Pa. 40 20n 76 28w
69 Lebanon, Tenn. 36 15n 86 20w
30 Lebanon ■ 34 0n 36 0e
57 Lebombo-berg 24 30s 32 0e
13 Lebrija 36 53n 6 5w
80 Lebu 37 40s 73 47w
19 Lecce 40 20n 18 10e
18 Lecco 45 50n 9 27e
15 Łęczyca 52 5n 19 45e
7 Ledbury 52 3n 2 25w
13 Ledesma 41 6n 5 59w
64 Leduc 53 20n 113 30w
9 Lee, R. 51 51n 9 2w
6 Leeds 53 48n 1 34w
6 Leek 53 7n 2 2w
69 Leesburg 28 47n 81 52w
56 Leeu-Gamka 32 43s 21 59e
11 Leeuwarden 53 15n 5 48e
45 Leeuwin, C. 34 20s 115 9e
75 Leeward Is. 16 30n 63 30w
35 Legazpi 13 10n 123 46e
18 Leghorn = Livorno 43 32n 10 18e
14 Legnica 51 12n 16 10e
32 Leh 34 15n 77 35e
7 Leicester 52 39n 1 9w
7 Leicester □ 52 40n 1 10w
39 Leichow Pantao, Pen. 20 40n 110 10e
11 Leiden 52 9n 4 30e
43 Leigh Creek 30 28s 138 24e
14 Leine, R. 48 54n 10 1e
9 Leinster □ 53 0n 7 10w
39 Lienyünchiangshih= Sinhailien 34 31n 119 0e
14 Leipzig 51 20n 12 23e
13 Leiria 39 46n 8 53w
8 Leith 55 59n 3 10w
7 Leith Hill 51 10n 0 23w
9 Leitrim 54 0n 8 5w
9 Leitrim □ 54 8n 8 0w
39 Leiyang 26 24n 112 51e
71 Leland 33 25n 90 52w
80 Leleque 42 15s 71 0w
14 Léman, L. 46 26n 6 30e
52 Lembeni 3 48s 37 33e
35 Lemery 13 58n 120 56e
30 Lemesós 34 42n 33 1e
19 Lemnos, I.= Límnos, I. 39 50n 25 5e
21 Lemvig 56 33n 8 20e
25 Lena 72 25n 126 40e
25 Lena, R. 66 30n 126 3e
24 Leninabad 40 17n 69 37e
23 Leninakan 41 0n 42 50e
22 Leningrad 59 55n 30 20e
24 Leninogorsk 50 20n 83 30e
23 Leninsk 48 40n 45 15e
24 Leninsk Kuznetskiy 55 10n 86 10e
25 Leninskoye 47 56n 132 38e
23 Lenkoran 39 45n 48 50e
69 Lenoir 35 55n 81 36w
69 Lenoir City 35 40n 84 20w
12 Lens 50 26n 2 50e
25 Lensk 60 48n 114 55e
18 Lentini 37 18n 15 0e
53 Leo 11 3n 2 2w
14 Leoben 47 22n 15 5e
7 Leominster, U.K. 52 15n 2 43w
68 Leominster, U.S.A. 42 30n 71 44w
74 León, Mexico 21 7n 101 30w
75 León, Nic. 12 20n 86 51w
13 León, Sp. 42 38n 5 34w
13 León, Reg. 41 30n 6 0w
13 Léon, Mt. de 42 30n 6 18w
46 Leongatha 38 30s 145 58e
45 Leonora 28 49s 121 19e
54 Léopold II, L.= Mai-Ndombe, L. 2 0s 18 0e
54 Léopoldville= Kinshasa 4 20s 15 15e
65 Leoville 53 39n 107 33w
22 Lepel 54 50n 28 40e
25 Lepikha 64 45n 125 55e
53 Lere 9 39n 14 13e
13 Lérida 41 37n 0 39e
8 Lerwick 60 10n 1 10w
75 Les Cayes 18 15n 73 46w
12 Les Sables-d'Olonne 46 30n 1 45w
74 Les Tres Marías, Is. 12 20n 106 30w
19 Lesbos, I.= Lésvos, I. 39 0n 26 20e
19 Leskovac 43 0n 21 58e
57 Leslie 26 16s 28 55e
57 Lesotho ■ 29 40s 28 0e
25 Lesozarodsk 45 30n 133 20e
75 Lesser Antilles, Is. 12 30n 61 0w
35 Lesser Sunda Is. 7 30s 117 0e
52 Lesuru 1 0n 35 15e
19 Lésvos, I. 39 0n 26 20e
14 Leszno 51 50n 16 30e
7 Letchworth 51 58n 0 13w
64 Lethbridge 49 45n 112 45w
78 Lethem 3 20n 59 50w
35 Leti, Kep. 8 10s 128 0e
56 Letiahau, R. 21 16s 24 0e
78 Leticia 4 0s 70 0w
55 Letlhakane 24 0s 24 59e
33 Letpadan 17 45n 96 0e
33 Letpan 19 28n 93 52e
34 Letsôk-au-Kyun 11 37n 98 15e
9 Letterkenny 54 57n 7 42w
34 Leuser, Mt. 4 0n 96 51e
11 Leuven 50 52 4 42e
20 Levanger 63 45n 11 19e
71 Levelland 33 38n 102 17w
8 Leven 56 12n 3 0w
8 Leven, L. 56 12n 3 22w
44 Leveque, C. 16 20s 123 0e
47 Levin 40 37s 175 18e
63 Levis 46 48n 71 9w
19 Lévka, Mt. 35 18n 24 3e
19 Levkás, I. 38 40n 20 43e
30 Levkôsia 35 10n 33 25e
7 Lewes 50 53n 0 2e
8 Lewis, I. 58 10n 6 40w
72 Lewis Ra. 20 3s 128 50e
63 Lewisporte 49 15n 55 3w
72 Lewiston, Id. 45 58n 117 0w
69 Lewiston, Me. 44 6n 70 13w
72 Lewistown, Mont. 47 0n 109 25w
68 Lewistown, Pa. 40 37n 77 33w
68 Lexington, Ky. 38 6n 84 30w
70 Lexington, Mo. 39 7n 93 55w
70 Lexington, Neb. 40 48n 99 45w
69 Lexington, N.C. 35 50n 80 13w
35 Leyte, I. 11 0n 125 0e
37 Lhasa 29 39n 91 6e
37 Lhatse Dzong 29 10n 87 45e
34 Lhokseumawe 5 20n 97 10e
39 Li Kiang, R. 18 25n 98 45e
38 Liangsiang 39 44n 116 8e
38 Liaoning □ 41 15n 122 0e
38 Liaotung, Pen. 40 0n 122 22e
38 Liaotung Wan, G. 40 30n 121 30e
38 Liaoyang 41 17n 123 11e
38 Liaoyuan 42 55n 125 10e
60 Liard, R. 61 52n 121 18w
71 Liberal 37 4n 101 0w
14 Liberec 50 47n 15 7e
50 Liberia ■ 6 30n 9 30w
68 Liberty 41 48n 74 45w
51 Lîbîya, Sahrâ', Des. 27 35n 25 0e
12 Libourne 44 55n 0 14w
54 Libreville 0 25n 9 26e
51 Libya ■ 28 30n 17 30e
80 Licantén 34 55s 72 0w
18 Licata 37 6n 13 55e
6 Lichfield 52 40n 1 50w
55 Lichinga 13 13s 35 11e
56 Lichtenburg 26 8s 26 8e
21 Lidkoping 58 31n 13 14e
44 Liebenwalde 52 51n 13 23e
14 Liechtenstein ■ 47 8n 9 35e
11 Liège 50 38n 5 35e
11 Liège □ 50 32n 5 35e
14 Lienz 46 50n 12 46e
22 Liepaja 56 30n 21 0e
11 Lier 51 7n 4 34e
9 Liffey, R. 53 21n 6 16w
9 Lifford 54 50n 7 30w
18 Ligùria □ 44 30n 9 0e
18 Ligurian Sea 43 15n 8 30e
41 Lihou Reef and Cays 17 25s 151 40e
66 Lihue 21 59n 152 24w
54 Likasi 10 55s 26 48e
37 Likiang 26 50n 100 15e
54 Likati 3 20n 24 0e
39 Liling 27 47n 113 30e
12 Lille 50 38n 3 3e
21 Lille Bælt 55 30n 9 45e
21 Lillehammer 61 8n 10 30e
21 Lillesand 58 15n 8 23e
21 Lillestrøm 59 58n 11 5e
57 Lilliput 22 30s 29 55e
64 Lillooet 50 42n 121 56w
55 Lilongwe 14 0s 33 48e
78 Lima, Peru 12 0s 77 0w
72 Lima, Mont. 44 41n 112 38w
68 Lima, Ohio 40 42n 84 5w
53 Liman Katagum 10 5n 9 42e
9 Limavady □ 55 0n 6 55½
9 Limavady 55 3n 6 58w
80 Limay, R. 39 0s 68 0w
80 Limay Mahuida 37 10s 66 45w
14 Limburg 50 22n 8 4e
11 Limburg □ 51 20n 5 55e
79 Limeira 22 35s 47 28w
9 Limerick 52 40n 8 38w
9 Limerick □ 52 30n 8 50w
21 Limfjorden 56 55n 9 0e
19 Límnos, I. 39 50n 25 5e
79 Limoeiro do Norte 5 5s 38 0w
79 Limoera 7 52s 35 27w
12 Limoges 45 50n 1 15e
75 Limón 10 0n 83 2w
12 Limousin, Reg. 46 0n 1 0e
57 Limpopo, R. 25 15s 33 30e
52 Limuru 1 2s 36 35e
80 Linares, Chile 35 50s 71 40w
74 Linares, Mexico 24 50n 99 40w
13 Linares, Sp. 38 10n 3 40w
38 Lincheng 37 26n 114 34e
6 Lincoln □ 53 14n 0 32w
80 Lincoln, Arg. 34 55s 61 30w
47 Lincoln, N.Z. 43 38s 172 30e
6 Lincoln, U.K. 53 14n 0 32w
70 Lincoln, Ill. 40 10n 89 20w
70 Lincoln, Neb. 40 50n 96 42w
6 Lincoln Wolds 53 20n 0 5w
52 Lindi 9 58s 39 38e
62 Lindsay, Canada 44 22n 78 43w
73 Lindsay, U.S.A. 36 14n 119 6w
57 Lindley 27 52s 27 56e
38 Linfen 36 5n 111 32e
35 Lingayen 16 1n 120 14e
35 Lingayen G. 16 10n 120 15e
14 Lingen 52 32n 7 21e
34 Lingga, Kep. 0 10e 104 30e
39 Lingling 26 13n 111 37e
39 Linglo 24 20n 105 25e
39 Lingshui 18 27n 110 0e
50 Linguéré 15 25n 15 5w
39 Linhai 28 51n 121 7e
38 Linho 40 50n 107 30e
39 Lini 35 5n 118 20e
39 Linkao 19 56n 109 42e
38 Linkiang 46 2n 133 56e
21 Linköping 58 28n 15 36e
38 Linkow 45 16n 130 18e
8 Linlithgow 55 58n 3 38w
8 Linnhe, L. 56 36n 5 25w
39 Linping 24 25n 114 32e
79 Lins 21 40s 49 44w
38 Linsi 43 30n 118 5e
37 Linsia 35 50n 103 0e
37 Lintan 34 59n 103 49e
68 Linton 39 0n 87 10w
38 Lintsing 36 50n 115 45w
43 Linville 26 50s 152 11e
14 Linz 48 18n 14 18e
12 Lion, G. du 43 0n 4 0e
18 Lípari, I. 38 26n 14 58e
18 Lipari Is. 38 40n 15 0e
22 Lipetsk 52 45n 39 35e
39 Liping 26 16n 109 8e
15 Lipno 52 49n 19 15e
14 Lippe, R. 51 39n 6 38e
46 Liptrap, C. 38 50s 145 55e
52 Lira 2 17n 32 57e
13 Liria 39 37n 0 35w
54 Lisala 2 12n 21 38e
13 Lisboa 38 42n 9 10w
13 Lisboa □ 39 0n 9 12w
13 Lisbon = Lisboa 39 0n 9 12w
9 Lisburn 54 30n 6 9w
9 Lisburn □ 54 30n 6 5w
60 Lisburne, C. 68 50n 166 0w
39 Lishui 28 20n 119 48w
12 Lisieux 49 10n 0 12e
43 Lismore, Australia 28 44s 153 21e
9 Lismore, Eire 52 8n 7 58w
62 Listowel, Canada 44 4n 80 58w
9 Listowel, Eire 52 27n 9 30w
70 Litchfield 39 10n 89 40w
46 Lithgow 33 25s 150 8e
22 Lithuanian S.S.R. □ 55 30n 24 0e
14 Litoměřice 50 33n 14 10e
75 Little Abaco I. 26 50n 77 30w
47 Little Barrier, I. 36 12s 175 8e
56 Little Bushman Land 29 10s 18 10e
62 Little Current 45 55n 82 0w
73 Little Colorado, R. 36 11n 111 48w
70 Little Falls, Minn. 45 58n 94 19w
68 Little Falls, N.Y. 43 3n 74 50w
75 Little Inagua I. 21 40n 73 50w
62 Little Longlac 49 42n 86 58w
56 Little Namaqualand 29 0s 17 10e
7 Little Ouse, R. 52 30n 0 22e
32 Little Rann 23 25n 71 25e
47 Little River 43 45s 172 49e
71 Little Rock 34 41n 92 10w
71 Littlefield 33 57n 102 17w
7 Littlehampton 50 48n 0 32w
39 Liuan 31 45n 116 30e
39 Liucheng 24 39n 109 14e
39 Liuchow 24 10n 109 10e
55 Liuwa Plain 14 20s 22 30e
71 Livermore, Mt. 30 45n 104 8w
46 Liverpool, Australia 33 55s 150 52e

Liverpool, Canada — Mackenzie, R.

63 Liverpool, Canada 44 5N 64 41W
6 Liverpool, U.K. 53 25N 3 0W
74 Livingston, Guatemala 15 50N 88 50W
72 Livingston, U.S.A. 45 40N 110 40W
56 Livingstone 17 46S 25 52E
52 Livingstone Mts. 9 40S 34 20E
52 Livingstonia 10 38S 34 5E
22 Livny 52 30N 37 30E
18 Livorno 43 32N 10 18E
52 Liwale 9 48S 37 58E
7 Lizard Pt. 49 57N 5 11W
18 Ljubljana 46 4N 14 33E
20 Ljungan, R. 62 19N 17 23E
21 Ljungby 56 49N 13 55E
21 Ljusdal 61 46N 16 3E
21 Ljusnan, R. 61 12N 17 8E
7 Llandeilo 50 54N 4 0W
7 Llandovery 51 59N 3 49W
7 Llandrindod Wells 52 15N 3 23W
6 Llandudno 53 19N 3 51W
7 Llanelli 51 41N 4 11W
13 Llanes 43 25N 4 50W
6 Llangollen 52 58N 3 10W
7 Llanidloes 52 28N 3 31W
58 Llano Estacado, Reg. 34 0N 103 0W
76 Llanos, Reg. 3 25N 71 35W
80 Llanquihue, L. 41 10S 72 50W
13 Lloret de Mar 41 41N 2 53E
65 Lloydminster 53 20N 110 0W
80 Llullaillaco, Mt. 24 30S 68 30W
55 Lobatse 25 12S 25 40E
80 Lobería 38 10S 58 40W
55 Lobito 12 18S 13 35E
14 Locarno 46 10N 8 47E
8 Lochaber, Reg. 56 55N 5 0W
8 Lochalsh, Kyle of 57 17N 5 43W
8 Lochboisdale 57 10N 7 20W
8 Lochgilphead 56 2N 5 37W
8 Lochmaddy 57 36N 7 10W
8 Lochnagar, Mt. 56 57N 3 14W
8 Lochy, L. 56 58N 4 55W
43 Lock 33 34S 135 46E
63 Lockeport 43 47N 65 4W
8 Lockerbie 55 7N 3 21W
71 Lockhart 29 55N 97 40W
28 Lod 31 57N 34 54E
72 Lodi 38 12N 121 16W
54 Lodja 3 30S 23 23E
52 Lodwar 3 10N 35 40E
15 Łódź 51 45N 19 27E
20 Lofoten, Is. 68 10N 13 0E
68 Logan, Ohio 39 35N 82 22W
72 Logan, Utah 41 45N 111 50W
68 Logan, W. Va. 37 51N 81 59W
60 Logan, Mt. 60 40N 140 0W
68 Logansport 31 58N 93 58W
31 Logar □ 33 50N 69 0E
13 Logrono 42 28N 2 32W
29 Loheia 15 45N 42 40E
39 Loho 33 33N 114 5E
21 Loimaa 60 50N 23 5E
12 Loir, R. 47 33N 0 32W
12 Loir-et-Cher □ 47 40N 1 20E
12 Loire □ 45 40N 4 5E
12 Loire, R. 47 16N 2 11W
12 Loire-Atlantique □ 47 25N 1 40W
12 Loiret □ 47 58N 2 10E
78 Loja, Ecuador 3 59S 79 16W
13 Loja, Sp. 37 10N 4 10W
11 Lokeren 51 6N 3 59E
52 Lokitaung 4 12N 35 48E
20 Lokka, L. 68 0N 27 50E
20 Løkken 57 22N 9 41E
53 Lokoja 7 47N 6 45E
54 Lokolama 2 35S 19 50E
39 Lokwei 19 12N 110 30E
21 Lolland, L. 54 45N 11 30E
19 Lom 43 48N 23 20E
54 Lomami, R. 0 46N 24 16E
18 Lombardia □ 45 35N 9 45E
35 Lomblen, I. 8 30S 116 20E
34 Lombok, I. 8 35S 116 20E
53 Lomé 6 9N 1 20E
54 Lomela 2 5S 23 52E
54 Lomela, R. 0 14S 20 42E
64 Lomond 50 24N 112 36W
8 Lomond, L. 56 8N 4 38W
73 Lompoc 34 41N 120 32W
15 Łomza 53 10N 22 2E
80 Loncoche 39 20S 72 50W
52 Londiani 0 10S 35 33E
62 London, Canada 43 0N 81 15W
7 London, U.K. 51 30N 0 5W
7 London □ 51 30N 0 5W
9 Londonderry 55 0N 7 20W
9 Londonderry □ 55 0N 7 20W
44 Londonderry, C. 13 45S 126 55E
80 Londonderry, I. 55 0S 71 0W
80 Londrina 23 0S 51 10W
73 Lone Pine 36 35N 118 2W
73 Long Beach 33 46N 118 12W
6 Long Eaton 52 54N 1 16W
75 Long I., Bahamas 23 20N 75 10W
62 Long I., Canada 44 23N 66 19W
68 Long I., U.S.A. 40 50N 73 20W
63 Long Range Mts. 48 0N 58 30W
34 Long Xuyen 10 19N 105 28E
9 Longford 53 43N 7 50W
9 Longford □ 53 42N 7 45W
34 Longiram 0 5S 115 45E
70 Longmont 40 10N 105 4W
42 Longreach 23 28S 144 14E
71 Longview, Tex. 32 30N 94 45W
72 Longview, Wash. 46 9N 122 58W
12 Lons-le-Saunier 46 40N 5 31E
20 Lønsdal 66 46N 15 26E
7 Looe 50 21N 4 26W
65 Loomis 49 15N 108 45W
65 Loon Lake 44 50N 77 15W
45 Loongana 30 52S 127 5E
9 Loop Hd. 52 34N 9 55W
37 Lop Nor, L. 40 30N 90 30E
54 Lopez, C. 0 47S 8 40E
68 Lorain 41 20N 82 5W
32 Loralai 30 29N 68 30E
13 Lorca 37 41N 1 42W
3 Lord Howe I. 31 33S 159 6E
73 Lordsburg 32 15N 108 45W
30 Lorestan □ 33 0N 48 30E
79 Loreto, Brazil 7 5S 45 30W
18 Loreto, Italy 43 26N 13 36E
12 Lorient 47 45N 3 23N
8 Lorn, Firth of 56 20N 5 40W
8 Lorne, Reg. 56 26N 5 10W
12 Lorraine, Reg. 49 0N 6 0E
62 Lorrainville 47 21N 79 23W
52 Lorugumu 2 50N 35 15E
73 Los Alamos 35 57N 106 17W
80 Los Andes 32 50S 70 40W
80 Los Angeles, Chile 37 28S 72 23W
73 Los Angeles, U.S.A. 34 0N 118 10W
73 Los Angeles Aqueduct 35 0N 118 20W
73 Los Banos 37 8N 120 56W
80 Los Blancos 23 45S 62 30W
78 Los Hermanos, Is. 11 45N 64 25W
80 Los Lagos 39 51S 72 50W
74 Los Mochis 25 45N 109 5W
78 Los Roques, Is. 11 50N 66 45W
78 Los Testigos, Is. 11 23N 63 6W
80 Los Vilos 32 0S 71 30W
25 Loshkalakh 62 45N 147 20E
18 Losinj 44 35N 14 28E
8 Lossiemouth 57 43N 3 17W
12 Lot □ 44 39N 1 40E
12 Lot, R. 44 18N 0 20E
12 Lot-et-Garonne □ 44 22N 0 30E
80 Lota 37 5S 73 10W
52 Lotagipi Swamp 4 55N 35 0E
8 Lothian □ 55 55N 3 35W
54 Loto 28 50S 22 28E
6 Loughborough 52 46N 1 11W
9 Loughrea 53 11N 8 33W
57 Louis Trichardt 23 0S 25 55E
63 Louisbourg 45 55N 60 0W
62 Louiseville 46 20N 73 0W
3 Louisiade Arch. 11 10S 153 0E
71 Louisiana □ 30 50N 92 0W
68 Louisville, Ky. 38 15N 85 45W
71 Louisville, Miss. 33 7N 89 3W
13 Loulé 37 9N 8 0W
70 Loup City 41 19N 98 57E
12 Lourdes 43 6N 0 3W
57 Lourenço Marques= Maputo 25 58S 32 32E
43 Louth, Australia 30 30S 145 8E
9 Louth, Eire 53 47N 6 33W
6 Louth, U.K. 53 23N 0 0
9 Louth □ 53 55N 6 30W
65 Love 53 29N 104 9W
70 Loveland 40 27N 105 4W
72 Lovelock 40 17N 118 25W
21 Lovisa 60 28N 26 12E
68 Lowell 42 38N 71 19W
47 Lower Hutt 41 10S 174 55E
7 Lowestoft 52 29N 1 44E
15 Łowicz 52 6N 19 55E
68 Lowville 43 48N 75 30W
43 Loxton 34 28S 140 31E
39 Loyang 34 41N 112 28E
39 Loyung 24 25N 109 25E
12 Lozère □ 44 35N 3 30E
38 Lu-ta 39 0N 121 31E
54 Lualaba, R. 0 26N 25 20E
54 Luanda 8 58S 13 9E
37 Luang Prabang 19 45N 102 10E
55 Luangwa, R. 15 40N 30 25E
55 Luanshya 13 3S 28 28E
13 Luarca 43 32N 6 32W
35 Lubang Is. 13 50N 120 12E
28 Lubban 32 9N 35 14E
71 Lubbock 33 40N 102 0W
14 Lübeck 53 52N 10 41E
54 Lubefu 4 47S 24 27E
15 Lublin 51 12N 22 38E
30 Lubnān, Mts. 34 0N 36 0E
34 Lubuklinggau 3 15S 102 55E
34 Lubuksikaping 0 10N 100 15E
55 Lubumbashi 11 32S 27 28E
52 Lubushi 10 32S 30 30E
54 Lubutu 0 45S 26 30E
60 Lucania, Mt. 60 48N 141 25W
18 Lucca 43 50N 10 30E
8 Luce B. 54 45N 4 48W
35 Lucena, Philippines 13 56N 121 37E
13 Lucena, Sp. 37 27N 4 31W
15 Lučenec 48 18N 19 42E
14 Lucerne=Luzern 43 3N 8 13E
39 Luchow 29 2N 105 10E
14 Luckenwalde 52 5N 13 11E
33 Lucknow 26 50N 81 0E
56 Lüderitz 26 41S 15 8E
32 Ludhiana 30 57N 75 56E
68 Ludington 43 58N 86 27W
7 Ludlow 52 23N 2 42W
21 Ludvika 60 8N 15 14E
14 Ludwigsburg 48 53N 9 11E
14 Ludwigshafen 49 27N 8 27E
71 Lufkin 31 25N 94 40W
22 Luga 58 40N 29 55E
14 Lugano 46 0N 8 57E
23 Lugansk= Voroshilovgrad 48 35N 39 29E
52 Lugazi 0 32N 30 42E
29 Lugh Ganana 3 48N 42 40E
13 Lugo 43 2N 7 35W
15 Lugoj 45 42N 21 57E
24 Lugovoy 43 0N 72 20E
79 Luis Correia 3 0S 41 35W
80 Luján 34 45S 59 5W
39 Lukang 24 0N 120 19E
15 Łuków 51 56N 22 23E
55 Lukulu 14 35S 23 25E
20 Luleå 65 35N 22 10E
54 Lulonga, R. 0 43N 18 23E
54 Lulua, R. 5 2S 21 7E
54 Luluabourg= Kananga 5 55S 22 18E
69 Lumberton 34 37N 78 59W
52 Lumbwa 0 12S 35 28E
47 Lumsden 45 44S 168 27E
38 Lun 47 55N 105 1E
21 Lund 55 41N 13 12E
55 Lundazi 12 20S 33 7E
7 Lundy, I. 51 10N 4 41W
6 Lune, R. 54 2N 2 50W
14 Lüneburg 53 15N 10 23E
14 Lüneburger Heide, Reg. 53 0N 10 0E
63 Lunenburg 44 22N 64 18W
12 Lunéville 48 36N 6 30E
38 Lunghwa 41 15N 117 51E
38 Lungkiang 47 22N 123 4E
38 Lungkow 37 40N 120 25E
33 Lungleh 22 55N 92 45E
38 Lungsi 35 0N 104 35E
32 Luni 26 0N 73 6E
32 Luni, R. 24 40N 71 15E
54 Luofu 0 1S 29 15E
18 Luqa 35 35N 14 28E
9 Lurgan 54 28N 6 20W
55 Lusaka 15 28S 28 16E
52 Lushoto 4 47S 38 20E
38 Lushun 38 48N 121 16E
* 55 Luso 11 47S 19 52E
38 Lü-ta 39 0N 122 0E
7 Luton 51 53N 0 24W
34 Lutong 4 30N 114 0E
22 Lutsk 50 50N 25 15E
52 Luwingu 10 15S 30 4E
11 Luxembourg 49 37N 6 9E
11 Luxembourg ■ 50 0N 6 0E
11 Luxembourg □ 49 58N 5 30E
51 Luxor=El Uqsur 25 41N 32 38E
22 Luza 60 39N 47 10E
14 Luzern 47 3N 8 18E
79 Luziania 16 20S 48 0W
35 Luzon, I. 16 0N 121 0E
23 Lvov 49 40N 24 0E
38 Lwanhsien 39 45N 118 45E
52 Lwasamaire 0 53S 30 7E
25 Lyakhovskiye Os. 73 40N 141 0E
* 32 Lyallpur 31 30N 73 5E
8 Lybster 58 18N 3 16W
20 Lycksele 64 38N 18 40E
28 Lydda=Lod 31 57N 34 54E
57 Lydenburg 25 10S 30 29E
47 Lyell 41 48S 172 4E
47 Lyell, Ra. 41 38S 172 20E
7 Lyme Regis 50 44N 2 57W
7 Lymington 50 46N 1 32W
68 Lynchburg 37 23N 79 10W
46 Lyndhurst, N.S.W. 33 41N 149 2E
42 Lyndhurst, Queens. 18 56S 144 30E
68 Lyndonville 44 32N 72 1W
68 Lynn 42 28N 70 57W
65 Lynn Lake 56 51N 101 3W
7 Lynton 51 14N 3 50W
12 Lyon 45 46N 4 50E
12 Lyonnais, Reg. 45 45N 4 15E
12 Lyons=Lyon 45 46N 4 50E
12 Lyons, G. of= Lion, G. du 43 0N 4 0E
45 Lyons, R. 25 2N 115 9W
22 Lysra 57 7N 57 47E
6 Lytham St. Annes 53 45N 2 58W
47 Lyttelton 43 35S 172 44E

M

28 Ma'ad 32 37N 35 36E
39 Maanshan 31 40N 118 30E
11 Maas, R. 51 49N 5 1E
11 Maastricht 50 50N 5 40E
6 Mablethorpe 53 21N 0 14E
52 Mabuki 2 57S 33 12E
79 Macaé 20 20S 41 55W
71 McAllen 26 12N 98 15W
71 McAlester 34 57N 95 40W
79 Macapá 0 5N 51 10W
42 McArthur, R. 15 54S 136 40E
79 Macau 5 0S 36 40W
39 Macau ■ 22 16N 113 35E
64 McBride 53 20N 120 10W
72 McCammon 42 41N 112 11W
6 Macclesfield 53 16N 2 9W
65 McClintock 57 45N 94 15W
60 M'Clintock Chan. 71 0N 103 0W
71 McComb 31 20N 90 30W
70 McCook 40 15N 100 35W
3 McDonald I. 54 0S 73 0E
44 Macdonnell, Ras. 23 40S 133 0E
60 Macdougall, L. 66 20N 98 30W
8 Macduff 57 40N 2 30W
62 Mace 48 55N 80 0W
19 Macedonia □, Greece= Makedhonia □ 40 39N 22 0E
19 Macedonia □, Y.-slav.= Makedonija □ 41 53N 21 40E
79 Maceió 9 40S 35 41W
50 Macenta 8 35N 9 20W
18 Macerata 43 19N 13 28E
72 McGill 35 27N 114 50W
9 Macgillycuddy's Reeks, Mts. 52 2N 9 45W
32 Mach 29 50N 67 20E
52 Machakos 1 30S 37 15E
78 Machala 3 10S 79 50W
25 Machevna 61 20N 172 20E
33 Machilipatnam 16 11N 81 8E
78 Machiques 10 4N 72 34W
7 Machynlleth 52 36N 3 51W
† 53 Macias Nguema Biyoga, I. 3 30N 8 40E
43 Macintyre, R. 28 38S 150 47E
42 Mackay, Australia 21 36S 148 39E
72 Mackay, U.S.A. 43 58N 113 37W
44 Mackay, L. 22 40S 128 35E
68 McKeesport 40 29N 79 50W
‡ 60 Mackenzie, Reg. 61 30N 144 30W
64 Mackenzie 55 20N 123 5W
42 Mackenzie, R. 23 30S 150 0E
60 Mackenzie, R. 69 15N 134 8W

* Renamed Luena

* Renamed Faisalabad
† Renamed Bioko
‡ Renamed Fort Smith

78 Mackenzie City ... 6 0N 58 10W
60 Mackenzie Mts. ... 64 0N 130 0W
42 McKinlay ... 21 16S 141 17E
60 McKinley, Mt. ... 63 10N 151 0W
71 McKinney ... 33 10N 96 40W
52 Mackinnon Road .. 3 40S 39 0E
65 Macklin ... 52 20N 109 56W
43 Macksville ... 30 40S 152 56E
43 Maclean ... 29 26S 153 16E
57 Maclear ... 31 2S 28 23E
43 Macleay, R. ... 30 52S 153 1E
64 McLennan ... 55 42N 116 50W
45 McLeod, L. ... 24 9S 113 47E
64 McLure ... 50 55N 120 20W
58 M'Clure Str. ... 74 40N 117 30W
72 McMinnville, Oreg. ... 45 16N 123 11W
69 McMinnville, Tenn. ... 35 43N 85 45W
65 McMurray ... 56 45N 111 27W
73 McNary ... 34 4N 109 53W
70 Macomb ... 40 25N 90 40W
12 Mâcon ... 46 19N 4 50E
69 Macon ... 32 50N 83 37W
70 McPherson ... 38 25N 97 40W
3 Macquarie Is. ... 54 36S 158 55S
46 Macquarie, R. ... 30 7S 147 24E
9 Macroom ... 51 54N 8 57W
30 Madā'in Sālih ... 26 51N 37 58E
53 Madagali ... 10 56N 13 33E
53 Madagascar ■ ... 20 0S 47 0E
51 Madama ... 22 0N 14 0E
3 Madang ... 5 0S 145 46E
53 Madaoua ... 14 5N 6 27E
53 Madara ... 11 45N 10 35E
33 Madaripur ... 23 2N 90 15E
33 Madauk ... 17 56N 96 52E
33 Madaya ... 22 20N 96 10E
74 Madden L. ... 9 20N 79 37W
50 Madeira, I. ... 32 50N 17 0W
78 Madeira, R. ... 3 22S 58 45W
73 Madera ... 37 0N 120 1W
32 Madhya Pradesh □ 21 50N 81 0E
29 Madinat al Shaab ... 12 50N 45 0E
54 Madingou ... 4 10S 13 33E
68 Madison, Ind. ... 38 42N 85 20W
70 Madison, S.D. ... 44 0N 97 8W
70 Madison, Wis. ... 43 5N 89 25W
68 Madisonville ... 37 42N 86 30W
35 Madiun ... 7 38S 111 32E
52 Mado Gashi ... 0 47N 39 12E
32 Madras, India ... 13 8N 80 19E
72 Madras, U.S.A. ... 44 40N 121 10W
74 Madre, Laguna ... 25 0N 97 30W
78 Madre de Dios, R. 10 59S 66 8W
80 Madre de Dios, I. ... 50 20S 75 10W
74 Madre del Sur, Sa. ... 17 30N 100 0W
74 Madre Occidental, Sa. ... 27 0N 107 0W
74 Madre Oriental, Sa. ... 25 0N 100 0W
13 Madrid ... 40 25N 3 45W
35 Madura, I. ... 7 0N 113 20E
35 Madura, Selat ... 7 30S 113 20E
45 Madura Motel ... 31 55S 127 0E
32 Madurai ... 9 55N 78 10E
32 Madurantakam ... 12 30N 79 50E
34 Mae Sot ... 16 43N 98 34E
36 Maebashi ... 36 23N 139 4E
7 Maesteg ... 51 36N 3 40W
75 Maestra, Sa. ... 20 15N 77 0W
13 Maestrazgo, Mts. de ... 40 30N 0 25W
57 Maevatanàna ... 16 56S 46 49E
65 Mafeking, Canada . 52 40N 101 10W
† **56** Mafeking, S.Africa 25 50S 25 38E
52 Mafia I. ... 7 45S 39 50E
80 Mafra, Brazil ... 26 7S 49 49W
13 Mafra, Port. ... 38 56N 9 20W
52 Mafupa ... 10 30S 29 7E
25 Magadan ... 59 30N 151 0E
52 Magadi ... 1 54S 36 19E
80 Magallanes, Estrecho de, Str. 52 30S 75 0W
78 Magangue ... 9 14N 74 45W
* **63** Magdalen Is. ... 47 30N 61 40W
80 Magdalena, Arg. ... 35 4S 57 32W
74 Magdalena, Mexico ... 30 50N 112 0W
73 Magdalena, U.S.A. 34 10N 107 20W
80 Magdalena, I., Chile ... 44 42S 73 10W
74 Magdalena, I., Mexico ... 24 40N 112 15W
14 Magdeburg ... 52 8N 11 36E

* French nameform Madeleine, Is. de la
† Renamed Mafikeng

28 Magdi'el ... 32 10N 34 54E
9 Magee, I. ... 54 48N 5 44W
35 Magelang ... 7 29S 110 13E
80 Magellan's Str.= Magallanes, Estrecho de ... 52 30S 75 0W
18 Maggiore, L. ... 46 0N 8 35E
28 Maghar ... 32 54N 35 24E
9 Magherafelt ... 54 45N 6 36W
9 Magherafelt □ ... 54 45N 6 36W
24 Magnitogorsk ... 53 20N 59 0E
71 Magnolia ... 33 18N 93 12W
63 Magog ... 45 18N 72 9W
64 Magrath ... 49 25N 112 50W
79 Maguarinho, C. ... 0 15S 48 30W
33 Magwe ... 20 10N 95 0E
30 Mahābād ... 36 50N 45 45E
57 Mahabo ... 20 23S 44 40E
29 Mahaddei Uen ... 3 0N 45 32E
52 Mahagi ... 2 20N 31 0E
52 Mahagi Port ... 2 3N 31 17E
56 Mahalapye ... 23 1S 26 51E
31 Mahallāt ... 33 55N 50 30E
33 Mahanadi, R. ... 20 0N 86 25E
57 Mahanoro ... 19 59S 48 48E
32 Maharashtra □ ... 19 30N 75 30E
32 Mahbubnagar ... 16 45N 77 59E
51 Mahdia ... 35 28N 11 0E
52 Mahenge ... 8 45S 36 35E
47 Maheno ... 45 10S 170 50E
47 Mahia Pen. ... 39 9S 177 55E
13 Mahón ... 39 50N 4 18E
63 Mahone Bay ... 44 27N 64 23W
52 Mahuta ... 11 32N 4 58E
54 Mai-Ndombe, L. .. 2 0S 18 0E
7 Maidenhead ... 51 31N 0 42W
65 Maidstone, Canada ... 53 5N 109 20W
7 Maidstone, U.K. .. 51 16N 0 31E
53 Maiduguri ... 12 0N 13 20E
33 Maijdi ... 22 48N 91 10E
33 Maikala Ra. ... 22 0N 81 0E
9 Main, R. ... 54 43N 6 18W
14 Main, R. ... 50 0N 8 18E
69 Maine □ ... 45 20N 69 0W
12 Maine, Reg. ... 48 0N 0 0E
12 Maine-et-Loire □ . 47 31N 0 30W
33 Maingkwan ... 26 15N 96 45E
8 Mainland, I., Orkney ... 59 0N 3 10W
8 Mainland, I., Shetland ... 60 15N 1 22W
32 Mainpuri ... 27 18N 79 4E
57 Maintirano ... 18 3S 44 5E
14 Mainz ... 50 0N 8 17E
80 Maipú ... 37 0S 58 0W
78 Maiquetía ... 10 36N 66 57W
33 Mairabari ... 26 30N 92 30E
75 Maisí, C. ... 20 10N 74 10W
46 Maitland ... 32 44S 151 36E
57 Maiyema ... 12 5N 4 25E
36 Maizuru ... 35 25N 135 22E
35 Majalengka ... 6 55S 108 14E
28 Majd el Kurum ... 32 56N 35 15E
35 Majene ... 3 27S 118 57E
13 Majorca, I.= Mallorca, I. ... 39 30N 3 0E
* **57** Majunga ... 17 0S 47 0E
* **57** Majunga □ ... 16 30S 46 30E
52 Makania ... 4 21S 37 49E
25 Makarovo ... 57 40N 107 45E
35 Makasar, Selat, Str. ... 1 0S 118 20E
24 Makat ... 47 39N 53 19E
19 Makedhona □ ... 40 39N 22 0E
19 Makedonija □ ... 41 53N 21 40E
50 Makeni ... 8 55N 12 5W
23 Makeyevka ... 48 0N 38 0E
56 Makgadikgadi Salt Pans ... 20 40S 25 45E
23 Makhachkala ... 43 0N 47 15E
52 Makindu ... 2 17S 37 49E
24 Makinsk ... 52 37N 70 26E
30 Makkah ... 21 30N 39 54E
63 Makkovik ... 55 0N 59 10W
25 Maklakovo ... 58 16N 92 29E
15 Makó ... 46 14N 20 33E
54 Makokou ... 0 40N 12 50E
52 Makongolosi ... 8 23S 33 10E
32 Makran Coast Ra. . 25 40N 4 0E
52 Maktau ... 3 25S 38 2E
30 Māku ... 39 15N 44 31E
36 Makurazaki ... 31 15N 130 20E
53 Makurdi ... 7 45N 8 32E
23 Mal Usen, R. ... 48 50N 49 39E
32 Malabar Coast, Reg. ... 11 0N 75 0E
34 Malacca=Melaka .. 2 15N 102 15E

* Renamed Mahajanga

34 Malacca, Str. of ... 3 0N 101 0E
72 Malad City ... 41 10N 112 20W
13 Maladetta, Mt. ... 42 40N 0 30E
13 Málaga ... 36 43N 4 23W
52 Malagarasi ... 5 5S 30 50E
55 Malagasy Rep.= Madagascar ■ .. 19 0S 46 0E
57 Malaimbandy ... 20 20S 45 36E
51 Malakâl ... 9 33N 31 50E
32 Malakand ... 34 40N 71 55E
25 Malamyzh ... 50 0N 136 50E
35 Malang ... 7 59S 112 35E
52 Malangali ... 8 33S 34 57E
† **54** Malange ... 9 30S 16 17E
21 Mälaren, L. ... 59 30N 17 10E
80 Malargüe ... 35 40S 69 30W
62 Malartic ... 48 9N 78 9W
30 Malatya ... 38 25N 38 20E
55 Malawi ■ ... 13 0S 34 0E
55 Malawi, L. ... 12 30S 34 30E
* **34** Malaya □ ... 4 0N 102 0E
30 Malayer ... 28 22N 56 38E
34 Malaysia ■ ... 5 0N 110 0E
42 Malbon ... 21 5S 140 17E
15 Malbork ... 54 3N 19 10E
45 Malcolm ... 28 51S 121 25E
2 Malden I. ... 4 3S 154 59W
27 Maldive Is. ... 2 0N 73 0W
80 Maldonado ... 35 0S 55 0W
19 Malea, Ákra ... 36 58N 23 7E
32 Malegaon ... 20 30N 74 30E
51 Malha ... 15 8N 26 12E
13 Malhão, Sa. do ... 37 20N 8 0W
50 Mali ■ ... 15 0N 10 0W
52 Malimba Mts. ... 7 30S 29 30E
9 Malin Hd. ... 55 18N 7 16W
52 Malindi ... 3 12S 40 5E
35 Malingping ... 6 45S 106 2E
34 Maliwun ... 10 14N 98 37E
46 Mallacoota, Inlet .. 34 40S 149 40E
8 Mallaig ... 57 0N 5 50W
51 Mallawi ... 27 44N 30 44E
13 Mallorca, I. ... 39 30N 3 0E
9 Mallow ... 52 8N 8 39W
20 Malmberget ... 67 11N 20 40E
11 Malmédy ... 50 26N 6 2E
56 Malmesbury ... 33 28S 18 41E
21 Malmö ... 55 36N 12 59E
21 Malmöhus □ ... 55 45N 13 30E
35 Malolos ... 14 50N 21 2E
68 Malone ... 44 50N 74 19W
72 Malta ... 48 20N 107 55W
18 Malta ■ ... 35 50N 14 30E
6 Malton ... 54 9N 0 48W
35 Maluku, Is. ... 3 0S 128 0E
53 Malumfashi ... 11 48N 7 39E
32 Malvan ... 16 2N 73 30E
7 Malvern, U.K. ... 52 7N 2 19W
71 Malvern, U.S.A. ... 34 22N 92 50W
7 Malvern Hills ... 52 0N 2 19W
80 Malvinas, Is.= Falkland Is. □ .. 51 30S 59 0W
79 Mamanguape ... 6 50S 35 4W
35 Mamasa ... 2 55S 119 20E
52 Mambrui ... 3 5S 40 5E
53 Mamfe ... 5 50N 9 15E
73 Mammoth ... 32 46N 110 43W
39 Mamoi ... 26 0N 119 25E
78 Mamoré, R. ... 10 23S 65 53W
50 Mamou ... 10 15N 12 0W
34 Mampawah ... 0 30N 109 5E
50 Man ... 7 30N 7 40W
6 Man, I. of ... 54 15N 4 30W
33 Man Na ... 23 27N 97 19E
79 Mana ... 5 45N 53 55W
78 Manacapuru ... 3 10S 60 50W
13 Manacor ... 39 32N 3 12E
35 Manado ... 1 40N 124 45E
75 Managua ... 12 0N 86 20W
75 Managua, L. de ... 12 20N 86 30W
57 Manakara ... 22 8S 48 1E
57 Mananjary ... 21 13S 48 20E
57 Manantenina ... 24 17S 47 19E
78 Manaos=Manaus .. 3 0S 60 0W
47 Manapouri, L. ... 45 32S 167 32E
37 Manass ... 44 20N 86 21E
33 Manaung Kyun, I. . 18 45N 93 40E
78 Manaus ... 3 0S 60 0W
12 Manche □ ... 49 10N 1 20W
6 Manchester, U.K. . 53 30N 2 15W
68 Manchester, U.S.A. 42 58N 71 29W
38 Manchouli ... 49 46N 117 24E
27 Manchuria, Reg. .. 44 0N 126 0E
52 Manda ... 10 30S 34 40E
21 Mandal ... 58 2N 7 25E
35 Mandala, Puncak, Mt. ... 4 30S 141 0E
33 Mandalay ... 22 0N 96 10E

* Renamed Peninsular Malaysia
† Renamed Malanje

38 Mandalgovi ... 45 40N 106 22E
30 Mandali ... 33 52N 45 28E
70 Mandan ... 46 50N 101 0W
35 Mandar, Teluk, G. 3 35S 119 4E
32 Mandasaur ... 24 4N 75 4E
55 Mandimba ... 14 22S 35 33E
57 Mandoto ... 19 34S 46 17E
57 Mandritsara ... 15 50S 48 49E
45 Mandurah ... 32 32S 115 43E
32 Mandya ... 12 30N 77 0E
53 Manengouba, Mts. . 5 15N 9 15E
51 Manfalût ... 27 20N 30 52E
18 Manfredónia, G. di 41 30N 16 10E
32 Mangalore ... 12 55N 74 47E
47 Mangaweka ... 39 48S 175 47E
34 Manggar ... 2 50S 108 10E
32 Mangla Dam ... 33 32N 73 50E
35 Mangole, I. ... 1 50S 125 55E
47 Mangonui ... 35 1S 173 32E
80 Mangueira, L. ... 33 0S 52 50W
37 Mangyai ... 38 6N 91 37E
24 Mangyshlak Pol. .. 43 40N 52 30E
70 Manhattan ... 39 10N 96 40W
79 Manhuaçu ... 20 15S 42 2W
57 Manica et Sofala □ ... 19 10S 33 45E
57 Manicaland □ ... 19 0S 32 30E
78 Manicoré ... 6 0S 61 10W
63 Manicouagan, Rés. . 51 25N 68 15W
2 Manihiki, I. ... 11 0S 161 0W
33 Manikpur ... 25 5N 81 5E
35 Manila ... 14 40N 121 3E
35 Manila B. ... 14 0N 120 0E
46 Manildra ... 33 11S 148 41E
43 Manilla ... 30 45S 150 43E
33 Manipur □ ... 24 30N 94 0E
30 Manisa ... 38 38N 27 30E
68 Manistee ... 44 15N 86 20W
68 Manistique ... 45 59N 86 18W
65 Manitoba □ ... 55 30N 97 0W
65 Manitoba, L. ... 50 40N 98 30W
70 Manitou Springs ... 38 52N 104 55W
62 Manitoulin I. ... 45 40N 82 30W
68 Manitowoc ... 44 8N 87 40W
78 Manizales ... 5 5N 75 32W
57 Manja ... 21 26S 44 20E
57 Manjakandriana ... 18 55S 47 47E
32 Manjhand ... 25 50N 68 10E
30 Manjil ... 36 46N 49 30E
45 Manjimup ... 34 15S 116 6E
32 Manjra, R. ... 18 49N 77 52E
70 Mankato, Kans. ... 39 49N 98 11W
70 Mankato, Minn. ... 44 8N 93 59W
50 Mankono ... 8 10N 6 10W
32 Mankulam ... 9 7N 80 26E
46 Manly ... 33 48S 151 14E
32 Manmad ... 20 18N 74 28E
43 Mannahill ... 32 26S 139 59E
32 Mannar, G. of ... 8 30N 79 0E
32 Mannar, I. ... 9 4N 79 45E
14 Mannheim ... 49 28N 8 29E
64 Manning ... 56 53N 117 39W
43 Mannum ... 34 57S 139 12E
35 Manokwari ... 0 54N 134 0E
57 Manombo ... 22 57S 43 28E
54 Manono ... 7 18S 27 25E
54 Mansa, Zambia ... 11 13S 28 55E
61 Mansel I. ... 62 0N 80 0W
46 Mansfield, Australia ... 37 0S 146 0E
6 Mansfield, U.K. ... 53 8N 1 12W
68 Mansfield, U.S.A. . 40 45N 82 30W
51 Mansura= El Mansura ... 31 0N 31 19E
78 Manta ... 1 0S 80 40W
73 Manteca ... 37 50N 121 12W
12 Mantes-la-Jolie ... 49 0N 1 41E
72 Manti ... 39 23N 111 32W
79 Mantiqueira, Sa. da ... 22 0S 44 0W
18 Mántova ... 45 10N 10 47E
18 Mantua =Mantova 45 9N 10 48E
35 Manukan ... 8 14N 123 3E
47 Manukau ... 37 2S 174 54E
23 Manych-Gudilo, Oz. ... 46 24N 42 38E
52 Manyoni ... 5 45S 34 55E
32 Manzai ... 32 20N 70 15E
13 Manzanares ... 39 0N 3 22W
75 Manzanillo, Cuba . 20 20N 77 10W
74 Manzanillo, Mexico 19 0N 104 20W
75 Manzanillo, Pta. ... 9 30N 79 40W
57 Manzini ... 26 30S 31 25E
51 Mao ... 14 4N 15 19E
65 Maple Creek ... 49 55N 109 27W
70 Maplewood ... 38 33N 90 18W
57 Maputo ... 25 58S 32 32E
57 Maputo, B. de ... 26 0S 32 50E

57 Maputo □ 26 30S 32 40E
30 Maqnā 28 25N 34 50E
80 Maquinchao 41 15S 68 50W
80 Mar Sa. do 25 30S 49 0W
80 Mar Chiquita, L. 30 40S 62 50W
80 Mar del Plata 38 0S 57 30W
52 Mara 1 30S 34 32E
79 Marabá 5 20S 49 5W
78 Maracaibo 10 40N 71 37W
78 Maracaibo, L. de 9 40N 71 30W
78 Maracay 10 15N 67 36W
51 Maradah 29 4N 19 4E
53 Maradi 13 35N 8 10E
30 Maragheh 37 30N 46 12E
79 Marajó, I. de 1 0S 49 30W
52 Maralal 1 0N 36 58E
56 Maramba = Livingstone 17 50N 25 50E
30 Marand 38 30N 45 45E
† 57 Marandellas 18 5S 31 42E
79 Maranguape 3 55S 38 50W
79 Maranhão=São Luís 2 39S 44 15W
79 Maranhão □ 5 0S 46 0W
78 Marañón, R. 4 50S 75 35W
30 Maraş 37 37N 36 53E
19 Marathón 38 11N 23 58E
42 Marathon 20 51S 143 32E
29 Marbat 17 0N 54 45E
44 Marble Bar 21 9S 119 44E
7 March 57 33N 0 5E
18 Marche □ 43 22N 13 10E
12 Marche, Reg. 46 5N 2 10E
11 Marche-en-Famenne 50 14N 5 19E
13 Marchena 37 18N 5 23W
32 Mardan 34 12N 72 2E
30 Mardin 37 20N 40 36E
8 Maree, L. 57 40N 5 30W
42 Mareeba 16 59S 145 28E
64 Margaret Bay 51 20N 127 20W
44 Margaret River 18 0S 126 30E
78 Margarita, Is. de 11 0N 64 0W
57 Margate, S. Afr. 30 50S 30 20E
7 Margate, U.K. 51 23N 1 24E
52 Margherita, Mt. 0 22N 29 51E
22 Mari A.S.S.R. □ 56 30N 48 0E
47 Maria van Diemen, C. 34 29S 172 40E
52 Mariakani 3 50S 39 27E
3 Mariana Is. 17 0N 145 0E
75 Marianao 23 8N 82 24W
69 Marianna 30 45N 85 15W
* 55 Mariano Machado 13 2S 14 40E
29 Marib 15 25N 45 20E
18 Maribor 46 36N 15 40E
61 Maricourt 61 36N 71 57W
75 Marie-Galante, I. 15 56N 61 16W
21 Mariehamn 60 5N 19 57E
56 Mariental 24 36S 18 0E
21 Mariestad 58 43N 13 50E
69 Marietta, Ga. 34 0N 84 30W
68 Marietta, Ohio 39 27N 81 27W
75 Marigot 15 32N 61 18W
24 Marniisk 56 10N 87 20E
79 Marília 22 0S 50 0W
13 Marin 42 23N 8 42W
35 Marinduque, I. 13 25N 122 0E
68 Marinette 45 4N 87 40W
80 Maringá 23 35S 51 50W
71 Marion, Ill. 37 45N 88 55W
68 Marion, Ind. 40 35N 85 40W
70 Marion, Iowa 42 2N 91 36W
68 Marion, Ohio 40 38N 83 8W
69 Marion, S.C. 34 11N 79 22W
69 Marion, Va. 36 51N 81 29W
19 Maritsa 42 1N 25 50E
31 Marjan 32 5N 68 20E
6 Market Drayton 52 55N 2 30W
7 Market Harborough 52 29N 0 55W
6 Market Rasen 53 24N 0 20W
22 Marks 51 45N 46 50E
42 Marlborough 22 46S 149 52E
47 Marlborough □ 41 45S 173 33E
7 Marlborough Downs 51 25N 1 55W
71 Marlin 31 25N 96 50W
32 Marmagao 15 25N 73 56E
30 Marmara Denizi, Sea 40 45N 28 15E
62 Marmora 44 28N 77 41W
12 Marne □ 49 0N 4 10E
12 Marne, R. 48 49N 2 24E
57 Maroantsetra 15 26S 49 44E
43 Maroochydore 26 35S 153 10W
53 Maroua 10 40N 14 20E
57 Marovoay 16 6S 46 39E
57 Marquard 28 40S 27 28E
2 Marquesas Is. 9 0S 139 30W
68 Marquette 46 30N 87 21W
51 Marra, J. 7 20N 27 35E
50 Marrakech 31 40N 8 0W
50 Marrakesh= Marrakech 31 40N 8 0W
42 Marrawah 40 56S 144 41E
43 Marree 29 39S 138 1E
51 Marsa Brega 30 30N 19 20E
51 Marsa Susa 32 52N 21 59E
52 Marsabit 2 18N 38 0E
18 Marsala 37 48N 12 25E
46 Marsden 33 47N 147 32E
12 Marseille 43 18N 5 23E
12 Marseilles= Marseille 43 18N 5 23E
70 Marshall, Minn. 44 25N 95 45W
70 Marshall, Mo. 39 8N 93 15W
71 Marshall, Tex. 32 29N 94 20W
3 Marshall Is. 9 0N 171 0E
70 Marshalltown 42 0N 93 0W
70 Marshfield 44 42N 90 10W
33 Martaban 16 30N 97 35E
33 Martaban, G. of 15 40N 96 30E
34 Martapura, Kalimantan 3 22S 114 56E
34 Martapura, Sumatera 4 19S 104 22E
53 Marte 12 23N 13 46E
43 Marthaguy Creek 30 16S 147 35E
68 Martha's Vineyard 41 25N 70 35W
14 Martigny 46 6N 7 3E
75 Martinique, I. 14 40N 61 0W
75 Martinique Pass. 15 15N 61 0W
68 Martins Ferry 40 5N 80 46W
68 Martinsburg 39 30N 77 57W
68 Martinsville, Ind. 39 29N 86 23W
69 Martinsville, Va. 36 41N 79 52W
47 Marton 40 4S 175 23E
13 Martos 37 44N 3 58W
53 Maru 12 22N 6 22E
36 Marugame 34 15N 133 55E
46 Marulan 34 43S 150 3E
52 Marungu Mts. 7 30S 30 0E
32 Marwar 25 43N 73 45E
24 Mary 37 40N 61 50E
42 Mary Kathleen 20 35S 139 48E
61 Mary River 70 30N 78 0W
43 Maryborough, Queens. 25 31S 152 37E
46 Maryborough, Vic. 37 0S 143 44E
68 Maryland □ 39 10N 76 40W
6 Maryport 54 43N 3 30W
63 Marystown 47 10N 55 10W
73 Marysvale 38 25N 112 17W
72 Marysville 39 14N 121 40W
69 Maryville 35 50N 84 0W
51 Marzūq 25 53N 14 10E
52 Masai Steppe 4 30S 36 30E
52 Masaka 0 21S 31 45E
53 Masakali 13 2N 12 32E
35 Masamba 2 30S 120 15E
38 Masan 35 11N 128 32E
31 Masandam, Ras. 26 30N 56 30E
52 Masasi 10 45S 38 52E
75 Masaya 12 0N 86 7W
53 Masba 10 35N 13 1E
35 Masbate 12 20N 123 30E
35 Masbate, I. 12 20N 123 30E
50 Mascara 35 26N 0 6E
56 Maseru 29 18S 27 30E
31 Mashhad 36 20N 59 35E
53 Mashi 13 0N 7 54E
62 Mashkode 47 2N 84 7W
57 Mashonaland West □ 16 30S 30 0E
57 Mashonaland East □ 18 0S 31 30E
52 Masindi 1 40N 41 43E
52 Masindi Port 1 43N 32 2E
52 Masisi 1 23S 28 49E
30 Masjed Soleyman 31 55N 49 25E
9 Mask, L. 53 36N 9 24W
57 Masoala, T. i. 15 59S 50 13E
70 Mason City 48 0N 119 0W
31 Masqat 23 37N 58 36E
18 Massa 44 2N 10 7E
68 Massachusetts □ 42 25N 72 0W
51 Massawa=Mitsiwa 15 35N 39 25E
68 Massena 44 52N 74 55W
64 Masset 54 0N 132 0W
12 Massif Central Reg. 45 30N 2 21E
68 Massillon 40 47N 81 30W
47 Masterton 40 56S 175 39E
32 Mastung 29 50N 66 42E
30 Mastura 23 7N 38 52E
36 Masuda 34 40N 131 51E
15 Masurian Lakes= Mazurski, Pojezierze 53 50N 21 0E
57 Matabeleland □ 20 0S 27 30E
35 Mataboor 1 41S 138 3E
62 Matachewan 47 50N 80 55W
38 Matad 47 12N 115 29E
54 Matadi 5 52S 13 31E
75 Matagalpa 13 10N 85 40W
62 Matagami 49 45N 77 34W
32 Matale 7 30N 80 44E
74 Matamoros 18 2N 98 17W
63 Matane 48 50N 67 33W
60 Matanuska 61 38N 149 0W
75 Matanzas 23 0N 81 40W
34 Mataram 8 41S 116 10E
44 Mataranka 14 55S 133 4E
13 Mataró 41 32N 2 29E
57 Matatiele 30 20S 28 49E
47 Mataura 46 11S 168 51E
74 Matehuala 23 40N 100 50W
57 Mateke Hills 21 48S 31 0E
18 Matera 40 40N 16 37E
32 Mathura 27 30N 77 48E
6 Matlock 53 8N 1 32W
50 Matmata 33 30N 9 59E
79 Mato Grosso □ 14 0S 54 0W
52 Matombo 7 3S 37 46E
48 Matopo 20 36S 28 20E
57 Matopo Hills 20 36S 28 20E
13 Matozinhos 41 11N 8 42W
31 Matrah 23 37N 58 30E
* 51 Matrûh 31 19N 27 9E
53 Matsena 13 5N 10 5E
39 Matsu, I. 26 9N 119 56E
36 Matsue 35 25N 133 10E
36 Matsumoto 36 15N 138 0E
36 Matsusaka 34 34N 136 32E
36 Matsuyama 33 45N 132 45E
32 Mattancheri 9 50N 76 15E
62 Mattawa 46 20N 78 45W
14 Matterhorn, Mt. 45 58N 7 39E
75 Matthew Town 20 57N 73 40W
70 Mattoon 39 30N 88 20W
34 Matua 2 58S 110 52E
78 Maturín 9 45N 63 11W
32 Mau Ranipur 25 16N 79 8E
78 Maués 3 20S 57 45W
66 Maui, I. 20 45N 156 20E
33 Maulamyaing 16 30N 97 40E
35 Maumere 8 38S 122 13E
56 Maun 20 0S 23 26E
66 Mauna Loa, Mt. 19 50N 155 28E
33 Maungmagan Is. 41 0S 97 48
52 Maungu 3 32S 38 42E
50 Mauritania ■ 20 50N 10 0W
49 Mauritius ■ 20 0S 57 0E
12 Maurienne, Reg. 45 15N 6 20E
28 Mavqi'im 31 38N 34 32E
33 Mawkmai 20 14N 97 50E
33 Mawlaik 23 40N 94 26E
42 Maxwelton 39 51S 174 49E
75 May Pen 17 58N 77 15W
74 Maya Mts. 16 30N 89 0W
75 Mayaguana I. 21 30N 72 44W
75 Mayagüez 18 12N 67 9W
45 Mayanup 33 58S 116 25E
42 Maydena 42 45S 146 39E
12 Mayenne 48 20N 0 38W
12 Mayenne □ 48 10N 0 40W
64 Mayerthorpe 53 57N 115 15W
69 Mayfield 36 45N 88 40W
23 Maykop 44 35N 40 25E
62 Maynooth, Canada 45 14N 77 56W
9 Maynooth, Eire 53 22N 6 38W
60 Mayo 63 38N 135 57W
9 Mayo □ 53 47N 9 7W
68 Maysville 38 43N 84 16W
54 Mayumba 3 25S 10 39E
25 Mayya 61 44N 130 18E
55 Mazabuka 15 52S 27 44E
79 Mazagão 0 20S 51 50W
64 Mazama 49 43N 120 8W
31 Mazan Deran □ 36 30N 53 30E
31 Mazar-i-Sharif 36 41N 67 0E
80 Mazarredo 47 10S 66 50W
13 Mazarrón 37 38N 1 19W
74 Mazatenango 14 35N 91 30W
74 Mazatlán 23 10N 106 30W
15 Mazurski, Pojezierze 53 50N 21 0E
57 Mbabane 26 18S 31 6E
54 M'Baiki 3 53N 18 1E
52 Mbala 8 46S 31 17E
52 Mbale 1 8N 34 12E
53 Mbalmayo 3 33N 11 33E
52 Mbamba Bay 11 13S 34 49E
54 Mbandaka 0 1S 18 18E
53 Mbanga 4 30N 9 33E
52 Mbarara 0 35S 30 25E
52 Mbeya 8 54S 33 29E
54 Mbuji-Mayi 6 9S 23 40E
52 Mbulamuti 0 57N 33 0E
52 Mbulu 3 45S 35 30E
52 Mchinja 9 46S 39 45E
55 Mchinji 13 47S 32 58E
18 Mdina 35 51N 14 25E
73 Mead, L. 36 10N 114 10W
45 Meadow 26 35S 114 30E
65 Meadow Lake 54 10N 108 10W
65 Meadow Lake Prov. Park 52 25N 109 0W
68 Meadville 41 39N 80 9W
62 Meaford 44 40N 80 36W
9 Meath □ 53 32N 6 40W
12 Meaux 48 58N 2 50E
30 Mecca=Makkah 21 30N 39 54E
11 Mechelen 51 2N 4 29E
14 Mecklenburger, B. 54 20N 11 40E
44 Meda P.O. 17 20S 123 59E
34 Medan 3 40N 98 38E
80 Medanosa, Pta. 48 0S 66 0W
50 Médéa 36 12N 2 50E
78 Medellín 6 15N 75 35W
50 Médenine 33 21N 10 30E
50 Mederdra 17 0N 15 38W
72 Medford 42 20N 122 52W
15 Mediaş 46 9N 24 22E
72 Medicine Bow 41 56N 106 11W
72 Medinine Bow Ra. 41 10N 106 25W
65 Medicine Hat 50 0N 110 45W
68 Medina 43 15N 78 27W
13 Medina del Campo 41 18N 4 55W
13 Medina-Sidonia 36 28N 5 57W
16 Mediterranean Sea 35 0N 15 0E
12 Médoc, Reg. 45 10N 0 56W
23 Medveditsa, R. 49 0N 43 58E
25 Medvezhi Oshova 71 0N 161 0E
22 Medvezhyegorsk 63 0N 34 25E
7 Medway, R. 51 27N 0 44E
45 Meeberrie 26 57S 116 0E
45 Meekatharra 26 32S 118 29E
32 Meerut 29 1N 77 50E
54 Mega 3 57N 38 30E
63 Mégantic 45 36N 70 56W
19 Mégara 37 58N 23 22E
33 Meghalaya □ 25 50N 91 0E
28 Megiddo 32 36N 15 11E
15 Mehadia 44 56N 22 23E
32 Mehsana 23 39N 72 26E
38 Meihokow 42 37N 125 46E
39 Meihsien 24 20N 116 0E
33 Meiktila 21 0N 96 0E
14 Meissen 51 10N 13 29E
80 Mejillones 23 10S 70 30W
51 Mekele 13 33N 39 30E
32 Mekhtar 30 33N 69 20E
50 Meknès 33 57N 5 33W
53 Meko 7 30N 3 0E
34 Mekong, R. 10 33N 105 24E
34 Melaka 2 15N 102 15E
34 Melalap 5 10N 116 5E
46 Melbourne 37 40S 145 0E
74 Melchor Múzquiz 27 50N 101 40W
22 Melekess= Dimitrovgrad 54 25N 49 33E
65 Melfort, Canada 52 50N 105 40W
57 Melfort, Rhod. 18 0S 31 25E
50 Melilla 35 21N 2 57W
28 Melilot 31 22N 34 37E
65 Melita 49 15N 101 5W
23 Melitopol 46 50N 35 22E
14 Melk 48 13N 15 20E
21 Mellerud 58 41N 12 28E
80 Melo 32 20S 54 10W
8 Melrose 55 35N 2 44W
6 Melton Mowbray 52 46N 0 52W
53 Melun 48 32N 2 39E
65 Melville 32 2S 115 48E
44 Melville, I., Australia 11 30S 131 0E
58 Melville, I., Canada 75 30N 111 0W
63 Melville, L. 53 45N 59 40W
61 Melville Pen. 68 0N 84 0W
57 Memel 27 38S 29 36E
22 Memel=Klaipeda 55 43N 21 10E
14 Memmingen 47 59N 10 12E
71 Memphis 35 7N 90 0W
6 Menai Str. 53 7N 4 20W
53 Ménaka 15 59N 2 18E
70 Menasha 44 13N 88 27W
34 Menate 0 12S 112 47E
39 Mencheng 33 27N 116 45E
12 Mende 44 31N 3 30E

* Renamed Ganda
† Renamed Marondera
* Renamed Marsá Maṭrûḥ

7 Mendip Hills 51 17N 2 40W
72 Mendocino 39 26N 123 50W
73 Mendota 36 46N 120 24W
80 Mendoza 32 50S 68 52W
78 Mene de Mauroa 10 45N 70 50W
78 Mene Grande 9 49N 70 56W
30 Menemen 38 36N 27 4E
11 Menen 50 47N 3 7E
18 Menfi 37 36N 12 57E
34 Menggala 4 20S 105 15E
37 Mengtz 23 20N 103 20E
46 Menindee 32 20N 142 25E
70 Menominee 45 9N 87 39W
70 Menomonie 44 50N 91 54W
13 Menor, Mar 37 40N 0 45W
13 Menorca, I. 40 0N 4 0E
34 Mentawai, Kep. 2 0S 99 0E
12 Menton 43 50N 7 29E
51 Menzel Temime 36 46N 11 0E
22 Menzelinsk 55 43N 53 8E
45 Menzies 29 40S 120 58E
28 Me'ona 33 1N 35 15E
11 Meppel 52 42N 6 12E
35 Merak 5 55S 106 1E
18 Merano 46 40N 11 10E
35 Merauke 8 29S 120 24E
29 Merca 1 48N 44 50E
32 Mercara 12 30N 75 45E
73 Merced 37 25N 120 30W
80 Mercedes, Buenos Aires 34 40S 59 30W
80 Mercedes, Corrientes 29 10S 58 5W
80 Mercedes, San Luis 33 40S 65 30W
80 Mercedes, Uruguay 33 12S 58 0W
80 Merceditas 28 20S 70 35W
47 Mercer 37 16S 175 5E
61 Mercy, C. 65 0N 62 30W
7 Mere 51 5N 2 16W
80 Meredith, C. 52 15S 60 40W
34 Mergui 12 30N 98 35E
34 Mergui Arch.= Myeik Kyunzu 11 0N 98 0E
74 Mérida, Mexico 20 50N 89 40W
13 Mérida, Sp. 38 55N 6 25W
78 Mérida, Ven. 8 36N 71 8W
68 Meriden 41 33N 72 47W
72 Meridian, Id. 43 41N 116 20W
71 Meridian, Miss. 32 20N 88 42W
79 Meriruma 1 15N 54 50W
11 Merksem 51 16N 4 25E
51 Merowe 18 29N 31 46E
45 Merredin 31 28S 118 18E
70 Merrill 45 11N 89 41W
64 Merritt 50 10N 120 45W
45 Merroe 27 53S 117 50E
54 Mersa Fatma 14 57N 40 17E
7 Mersea I. 51 48N 0 55E
14 Merseburg 51 20N 12 0E
6 Mersey, R. 53 25N 3 0W
6 Merseyside □ 53 25W 2 55W
30 Mersin 36 51N 34 36E
34 Mersing 2 25N 103 50E
7 Merthyr Tydfil 51 45N 3 23W
13 Mértola 37 40N 7 40E
71 Mertzon 31 17N 100 48W
52 Meru 0 3N 37 40E
52 Meru, Mt. 3 15S 36 46E
73 Mesa 33 20N 111 56W
31 Meshed=Mashhad 36 20N 59 35E
73 Mesilla 32 20N 107 0W
19 Mesolóngion 38 27N 21 28E
30 Mesopotamia, Reg.=Al Jazirah, Reg. 33 30N 44 0E
57 Messina, S.Africa 22 20S 30 12E
18 Messina, Str. di 38 5N 15 35E
19 Messíni 37 4N 22 1E
19 Messiniakós Kól. 36 45N 22 5E
19 Mesta, R. 40 41N 24 44E
78 Meta, R. 6 12N 67 28W
62 Metagama 47 0N 81 55W
80 Metán 25 30S 65 0W
47 Methven 43 38S 171 40E
64 Metlakatia 55 8N 131 35W
71 Metropolis 37 10N 88 47W
28 Metulla 33 17N 35 34E
12 Metz 49 8N 6 10E
34 Meulaboh 4 11N 96 3E
34 Meureudu 5 19N 96 10E
12 Meurthe-et-Moselle □ 48 52N 6 0E
12 Meuse □ 49 8N 5 25E
11 Meuse, R. 51 49N 5 1E
71 Mexia 31 38N 96 32W
79 Mexiana, I. 0 0 49 30W
74 Mexicali 32 40N 115 30W
74 Mexico, Mexico 19 20N 99 10W
70 Mexico, U.S.A. 39 10N 91 55W
74 Mexico ■ 20 0N 100 0W
74 México □ 19 20N 99 10W
22 Mezen, R. 66 11N 43 59E
22 Mezen 65 50N 44 20E
15 Mezökövesd 47 49N 20 35E
15 Mezötur 47 0N 20 41E
57 Mhlaba Hills 18 30S 30 30E
32 Mhow 22 33N 75 50E
74 Miahuatlán 16 21N 96 36W
69 Miami 25 52N 80 15W
69 Miami Beach 25 49N 80 6W
30 Miandowāb 37 0N 46 5E
57 Miandrivaso 19 31S 45 28E
30 Miāneh 37 30N 47 40E
32 Mianwali 32 38N 71 28E
39 Miaoli 24 34N 120 48E
24 Miass 54 59N 60 6E
60 Michelson, Mt. 69 19N 144 17W
68 Michigan □ 44 40N 85 40W
68 Michigan, L. 44 0N 87 0W
68 Michigan City 41 42N 86 56W
63 Michikamau L. 54 0N 6 0W
62 Michipicoten I. 47 55N 85 45W
62 Michipicoten River 47 50N 84 58W
74 Michoacán □ 19 0N 102 0W
22 Michurinsk 52 58N 40 27E
7 Mid Glamorgan □ 51 40N 3 25W
11 Middelburg, Neth. 51 30N 3 36E
57 Middelburg, C. Prov. 31 30S 25 0E
56 Middelburg, Trans. 25 49S 29 28E
56 Middelveld, Reg. 26 30S 26 0E
63 Middle Brook 48 40N 54 20W
68 Middlebury 44 0N 73 9W
69 Middlesboro 36 40N 83 40W
6 Middlesbrough 54 35N 1 14W
68 Middletown, Conn. 41 37N 72 40W
68 Middletown, N.Y. 41 28N 74 28W
68 Middletown, Ohio 39 29N 84 25W
63 Middleton 44 50N 65 5W
42 Middleton P.O. 22 22S 141 32E
12 Midi, Canal du 43 45N 1 21E
45 Midland, Australia 31 54S 115 59E
62 Midland, Canada 44 45N 79 50W
68 Midland, Mich. 43 37N 84 17W
71 Midland, Tex. 32 0N 102 3W
57 Midland □ 19 0S 29 30E
33 Midnapore 22 25N 87 21E
57 Midongy 23 35S 47 1E
2 Midway Is. 28 13N 177 22W
72 Midwest 43 27N 106 11W
36 Mie □ 34 20N 136 20E
14 Międzychod 52 35N 15 53E
15 Międzyrzec Podlaski 51 58N 22 45E
39 Mienyang 31 18N 104 26E
15 Miercurea Ciuc 46 21N 25 48E
13 Mieres 43 18N 5 48W
28 Migdal 32 51N 35 30E
28 Migdal Ha'Emeq 32 41N 35 14E
36 Mihara 34 25N 133 5E
52 Mikese 6 48S 37 55E
52 Mikindani 10 15S 40 2E
20 Mikkeli □ 61 56N 28 0E
22 Mikun 62 20N 50 0E
78 Milagro 2 0S 79 30W
18 Milan=Milano 45 28N 9 10E
43 Milang 35 20S 138 55E
18 Milano 45 28N 9 10E
18 Milazzo 38 13N 15 13E
7 Mildenhall 52 20N 0 30E
46 Mildura 34 13S 142 9E
43 Miles 26 37S 150 10E
70 Miles City 46 30N 105 50W
65 Milestone 50 0N 104 30W
59 Milford, Conn. 41 13N 73 4W
68 Milford, Del. 38 52N 75 26W
73 Milford, Utah 38 20N 113 0W
7 Milford Haven 51 43N 5 2W
45 Miling 30 30S 116 17E
12 Millau 44 8N 3 4E
63 Millertown Junction 48 49N 56 28W
43 Millicent 37 34S 140 21E
69 Millinocket 45 45N 68 45W
6 Millom 54 13N 3 16W
68 Millville 39 22N 74 0W
61 Milne Inlet 72 30N 80 0W
64 Milo 24 28N 103 23E
19 Mílos, I. 36 44N 24 25E
47 Milton, N.Z. 46 7S 169 59E
68 Milton, U.S.A. 41 0N 76 53W
7 Milton Keynes 52 3N 0 42W
9 Miltown Malbay 52 51N 9 25W
68 Milwaukee 43 9N 87 58W
72 Milwaukie 45 33N 122 39W
30 Minā al Ahmadi 29 5N 48 10E
30 Mina Saud 28 45N 48 20E
31 Mīnāb 27 10N 57 1E
36 Minamata 32 10N 130 30E
80 Minas 34 20S 55 15W
13 Minas de Rio Tinto 37 42N 6 22W
79 Minas Gerais □ 18 50S 46 0W
74 Minatitlán 17 58N 94 35W
33 Minbu 20 10N 95 0E
8 Minch, Little, Chan. 57 40N 6 50W
8 Minch, North, Chan. 58 0N 6 0W
35 Mindanao, I. 8 0N 125 0E
35 Mindanao Sea 9 0 124 0E
35 Mindanao Trench 8 0N 128 0E
14 Minden 52 18N 8 54E
71 Minden 32 40N 93 20W
35 Mindoro, I. 13 0N 121 0E
35 Mindoro Str. 12 30N 120 30E
7 Minehead 51 12N 3 29W
71 Mineral Wells 32 50N 98 5W
63 Mingan 50 20N 64 0W
23 Mingechaurskoye, Vdkhr. 40 56N 47 20E
42 Mingela 19 52S 146 38E
45 Mingenew 29 12S 115 21E
13 Minho, R. 41 52N 8 51W
13 Minho Reg. 41 40N 8 30W
39 Minhow=Foochow 26 5N 119 18E
45 Minilya 23 55S 114 0E
39 Min Kiang, R. 26 0N 119 30E
39 Minkiang 32 30N 114 10E
53 Minna 9 37N 6 30E
70 Minneapolis 44 58N 93 20W
65 Minnedosa 50 20N 99 50W
70 Minnesota □ 46 40N 94 0W
43 Minnipa 32 51S 135 9E
36 Mino 35 32N 136 55E
13 Minorca, I.= Menorca, I. 40 0N 4 0E
70 Minot 48 10N 101 15W
22 Minsk 53 52N 27 30E
15 Mińsk Mazowiecki 52 10N 21 33E
63 Minto 34 1S 150 51E
61 Minto, L. 48 0N 84 45W
72 Minturn 39 45N 106 25W
25 Minusinsk 53 50N 91 20E
33 Minutang 28 15N 96 30E
37 Minya Konka, Mt. 29 34N 101 53E
63 Miquelon, I. 47 8N 56 24W
32 Miraj 16 50N 74 45E
79 Miranda 20 10S 50 15W
13 Miranda de Ebro 42 41N 2 57W
13 Miranda do Douro 41 30N 6 16W
34 Miri 4 18N 114 0E
42 Miriam Vale 24 20S 151 39E
80 Mirim, L. 32 45S 52 50W
32 Mirpur Khas 25 30N 69 0E
33 Mirzapur 25 10N 82 45E
28 Mishan 45 31N 132 2E
68 Mishawaka 41 40N 86 8W
36 Mishima 35 10N 138 52E
28 Mishmar Alyalon 31 52N 34 57E
28 Mishmar Ha 'Emeq 32 37N 35 7E
28 Mishmar Ha Negev 31 22N 34 48E
28 Mishmar Ha Yarden 33 0N 35 56E
31 Miskīn 2344⅛ 56 52E
75 Miskitos, Cayos 14 26N 82 50W
15 Miskolc 48 7N 20 50E
35 Misool, I. 2 0S 130 0E
51 Misrātah 32 18N 15 3E
71 Mission 26 15N 98 30W
64 Mission City 49 10N 122 15W
71 Mississippi □ 33 0N 90 0W
71 Mississippi, R. 29 0N 89 15W
71 Mississippi, Delta of the 29 10N 89 15W
72 Missoula 47 0N 114 0W
70 Missouri □ 38 25N 92 30W
70 Missouri, Plat. du Coteau du 46 0N 99 30W
70 Missouri, R. 38 50N 90 8W
62 Mistassini, L. 51 0N 73 40W
43 Mitchell, Australia 26 29S 147 58E
70 Mitchell, U.S.A. 43 40N 98 0W
69 Mitchell, Mt. 35 40N 82 20W
9 Mitchelstown 52 16N 8 18W
19 Mitylene, I.= Lésvos, I. 39 0N 26 20E
19 Mitilíni 39 6N 26 35E
74 Mitla 16 55N 96 17W
36 Mito 36 20N 140 30E
57 Mitsinjo 16 1S 45 52E
51 Mitsiwa 15 35N 39 25E
46 Mittagong 34 28S 150 29E
46 Mittyack 35 8S 142 36E
54 Mitumba, Chaîne des 10 0S 26 20E
52 Mityana 0 24N 32 3E
36 Miyagi □ 38 15N 140 45E
36 Miyako 39 40N 141 75E
36 Miyakonojo 31 32N 131 5E
36 Miyazaki 31 56N 131 30E
36 Miyazaki 32 0N 131 30E
28 Miyet, Bahr el 31 30N 35 30E
36 Miyoshi 34 48N 132 32E
38 Miyun 40 22N 116 49E
9 Mizen Hd., Cork 51 27N 9 50W
9 Mizen Hd., Wicklow 52 52N 6 4W
33 Mizoram □ 23 0N 92 40E
28 Mizpe Ramon 20 36N 34 48E
52 Mjanji 0 17N 33 59E
21 Mjölby 58 20N 15 10E
21 Mjøsa, L. 60 45N 11 0E
52 Mkobela 10 57S 38 5E
55 Mkushi 14 20S 29 20E
52 Mkwaya 6 17S 35 40E
14 Mladá Boleslav 50 27N 14 53E
15 Mława 53 9N 20 25E
48 Mlanje, Mt. 16 2S 35 33E
53 Mme 6 18N 10 14E
20 Mo 66 15N 14 8E
35 Moa, I. 8 0S 128 0E
73 Moab 38 40N 109 35W
46 Moama 36 3S 144 45E
52 Moba 7 3S 29 47E
54 Mobaye 4 25N 21 5E
70 Moberly 39 25N 92 25W
62 Mobert 48 41N 85 40W
69 Mobile 30 41N 88 3W
52 Mobutu Sese Seko, L. 1 30N 31 0E
55 Moçambique 15 3S 40 42E
* 55 Moçâmedes 16 35S 12 30E
56 Mochudi 24 27S 26 7E
52 Moçimboa da Praia 11 25S 40 20E
78 Mocoa 1 15N 76 45W
74 Moctezuma, R. 21 59N 98 34W
55 Mocuba 16 54S 37 25E
12 Modane 45 12N 6 40E
56 Modderrivier 29 2S 24 38E
18 Módena 44 39N 10 55E
73 Modesto 37 43N 121 0W
18 Módica 36 52N 14 45E
46 Moe 38 12S 146 19E
79 Moengo 5 45N 54 20W
54 Moero, L. 9 0S 28 45E
8 Moffat 55 20N 3 27W
29 Mogadiscio 2 2N 45 25E
29 Mogadishu= Mogadiscio 2 2N 45 25E
50 Mogador= Essaouira 31 32N 9 42W
33 Mogaung 25 20N 97 0E
80 Mogi das Cruzes 23 45S 46 20W
79 Mogi Mirim 22 20S 47 0W
22 Mogilev 53 55N 30 18E
23 Mogilvev Podolskiy 48 20N 27 40E
25 Mogocha 53 40N 119 50E
73 Mogollon Mesa 43 40N 110 0W
45 Mogumber 31 2S 116 3E
15 Mohács 45 58N 18 41E
38 Moho 53 15N 122 27E
52 Mohoro 8 6S 39 8E
24 Mointy 47 40N 73 45E
73 Mojave 35 8N 118 8W
73 Mojave Des. 35 0N 117 30W
35 Mojokerto 7 29S 112 25E
47 Mokau, R. 38 42S 174 37E
39 Mokpo 34 50N 126 30E
53 Mokwa 9 18N 5 2E
11 Mol 51 11N 5 5E
6 Mold 53 10N 3 10W
23 Moldavian S.S.R. □ 47 0N 28 0E
20 Molde 62 46N 7 12E
56 Molepolole 24 28S 25 28E
18 Molfetta 41 12N 16 35E
70 Moline 41 30N 90 30W
18 Molise □ 41 45N 14 30E
78 Mollendo 17 0S 72 0W
21 Mölndal 57 40N 12 3E
66 Molokai, I. 21 8N 156 0W
46 Molong 33 5S 148 54E
56 Molopo, R. 28 30S 20 13E
56 Molteno 31 22S 26 22E
35 Molucca Sea 4 0S 124 0E

* Renamed Namibe

Moluccas, Is. = Maluku, Is. Mundo Novo

35 Moluccas, Is.= Maluku, Is. 1 0S 127 0E
57 Moma 16 47S 39 4E
52 Mombasa 4 2S 39 43E
52 Mombo 4 57S 38 20E
78 Mompos 9 14N 74 26W
21 Møn, I. 54 57N 12 15E
75 Mona, Pta. 9 37N 82 36W
75 Mona, I. 18 5N 67 54W
8 Monach Is. 57 32N 7 40W
12 Monaco ■ 43 46N 7 23E
8 Monadhliath Mts. 57 10N 4 4W
9 Monaghan 54 15N 6 58W
9 Monaghan □ 54 10N 7 0W
71 Monahans 31 35N 102 50W
51 Monastir 35 50N 10 49E
22 Monchegorsk 67 54N 32 58E
14 Mönchengladbach 51 12N 6 23E
13 Monchique 37 19N 8 38W
74 Monclava 26 50N 101 30W
63 Moncton 46 7N 64 51W
13 Mondego, R. 40 9N 8 52W
18 Mondovì 44 23N 7 56E
68 Monessen 40 9N 79 50W
62 Monet 48 10N 75 40W
13 Monforte de Lemos 42 31N 7 33W
33 Mong Kung 21 35N 97 35E
33 Mong Pan 20 19N 98 22E
33 Mong Pawk 22 4N 99 16E
33 Mong Ton 20 25N 98 45E
33 Mong Wa 21 26N 100 27E
33 Mong Yai 22 28N 98 3E
45 Monger, L. 29 25S 117 5E
33 Monghyr 25 23N 86 30E
51 Mongo 12 14N 18 43E
37 Mongolia ■ 47 0N 103 0E
53 Mongonu 12 40N 13 32E
55 Mongu 15 16S 23 12E
65 Monk 47 7N 69 59W
42 Monkira 24 46S 140 30E
7 Monmouth, U.K. 51 48N 2 43W
70 Monmouth, U.S.A. 40 50N 90 40W
75 Mono, Pta. del 12 0N 83 30W
18 Monópoli 40 57N 17 18E
71 Monroe, La. 32 32N 92 4W
68 Monroe, Mich. 41 55N 83 26W
69 Monroe, N.C. 35 2N 80 37W
70 Monroe, Wis. 42 38N 89 40W
50 Monrovia, Liberia 6 18N 10 47W
73 Monrovia, U.S.A. 34 7N 118 1W
11 Mons 50 27N 3 58E
64 Mont-Joli 48 37N 68 10W
62 Mont Laurier 46 35N 75 30W
12 Mont St-Michel 48 40N 1 30W
62 Mont Tremblant, Parc Prov. du 46 30N 74 30W
56 Montagu 33 45S 20 8E
63 Montague 46 10N 62 39W
74 Montague, I. 31 40N 144 46W
13 Montalbán 40 50N 0 45W
72 Montana □ 6 0S 73 0W
12 Montargis 48 0N 2 43E
12 Montauban 44 0N 1 21E
68 Montauk Pt. 41 4N 71 52W
12 Montbéliard 47 31N 6 48E
12 Mont-de-Marsan 43 54N 0 31W
79 Monte Alegre 2 0S 54 0W
79 Monte Azul 15 9S 42 53W
12 Monte Carlo 43 46N 7 23E
80 Monte Caseros 30 10S 57 50W
80 Monte Comán 34 40S 68 0W
18 Monte Sant 'Angelo 41 42N 15 59E
62 Montebello 45 40N 74 55W
78 Montecristi 1 0S 80 40W
75 Montego Bay 18 30N 78 0W
44 Montejinnie 16 40S 131 45E
12 Montélimar 44 33N 4 45E
74 Montemorelos 25 11N 99 42W
19 Montenegro□= Crna Gora 42 40N 19 20E
73 Monterey 36 35N 121 57W
78 Montería 8 46N 75 53W
74 Monterrey 25 40N 100 30W
79 Montes Claros 16 30S 43 50W
72 Montesano 47 0N 123 39W
80 Montevideo 34 50S 56 11W
7 Montgomery, U.K. 52 34N 3 9W
69 Montgomery, U.S.A. 32 20N 86 20W
32 Montgomery= Sahiwal 30 45N 73 8E
73 Monticello, Utah 37 55N 109 27W
13 Montijo 38 52N 6 39W
13 Montilla 37 36N 4 40W
70 Montivideo 44 55N 95 40W
12 Montluçon 46 22N 2 36E
63 Montmagny 46 58N 70 43E
63 Montmorency 46 53N 71 11W
42 Monto 24 52S 151 12E
13 Montoro 38 1N 4 27W
72 Montpelier, Id. 42 15N 11 29W
68 Montpelier, Vt. 44 15N 72 38W
12 Montpellier 43 37N 3 52E
62 Montreal 45 31N 73 34W
12 Montreuil 50 27N 1 45E
14 Montreux 46 26N 6 55E
8 Montrose, U.K. 56 43N 2 28W
73 Montrose, U.S.A. 38 30N 107 52W
75 Montserrat, I. 16 40N 62 10W
33 Monywa 22 7N 95 11E
57 Monze 16 17S 27 29E
32 Monze, C. 24 47N 66 37E
13 Monzón 41 52N 0 10E
45 Mooliabeenee 31 20S 116 2E
62 Moonbeam 49 20N 82 10W
43 Moonie 27 46S 150 20E
43 Moonta 34 6S 137 32E
45 Moora 30 37S 115 58E
42 Mooraberree 25 13S 140 54E
45 Moorarie 25 56S 117 35E
45 Moore, L. 29 50S 117 35E
45 Moore River 31 6S 115 32E
56 Moorreesburg 33 6S 18 38E
8 Moorfoot Hills 55 44N 3 8W
70 Moorhead 47 0N 97 0W
62 Moose, R. 43 37N 75 22W
62 Moose Factory 52 20N 80 40W
65 Moose Jaw 50 30N 105 30W
70 Moose Lake 46 27N 92 48W
65 Moosomin 50 9N 101 40W
62 Moosonee 51 25N 80 51W
55 Mopeia Velha 17 30S 35 40E
50 Mopti 14 30N 4 0W
78 Moquegua 17 15S 70 46W
21 Mora, Sweden 61 2N 14 38E
32 Moradabad 28 50N 78 50E
57 Moramanga 18 56S 48 12E
75 Morant Pt. 17 55N 76 12W
8 Morar, L. 56 57N 5 40W
32 Moratuwa 6 45N 79 55E
19 Morava, R. 48 10N 16 59E
45 Morawa 29 13S 116 0E
78 Morawhanna 8 30N 59 40W
8 Moray Firth 57 50N 3 30W
12 Morbihan □ 47 55N 2 50W
65 Morden 49 15N 98 10W
46 Mordialloc 38 1S 145 6E
22 Mordovian A.S.S.R. □ 54 20N 44 30E
20 Møre og Romsdal □ 63 0N 9 0E
6 Morecambe 54 5N 2 52W
6 Morecambe B. 54 7N 3 0W
43 Moree 29 28S 149 54E
69 Moorhead City 34 46N 76 44W
14 Moravian Hts.= Ceskomoravská V. 49 20N 15 30E
19 Morea□= Pelopónnisos 37 40N 22 15E
74 Morelia 19 40N 101 11W
42 Morella 23 0S 143 47E
74 Morelos □ 18 40N 99 10W
13 Morena, Sa. 38 20N 4 0W
73 Morenci 33 7N 109 20W
43 Moreton, I. 27 10S 153 25E
71 Morgan City 29 40N 91 15W
69 Morganton 35 46N 81 48W
68 Morgantown 39 39N 75 58W
57 Morgenzon 26 45S 29 36E
53 Moriki 12 52N 6 30E
64 Morinville 53 49N 113 41W
36 Morioka 39 45N 141 8E
12 Morlaix 48 36N 3 52W
42 Mornington, I., Australia 16 30S 139 30E
80 Mornington, I., Chile 49 50S 75 30W
35 Moro G. 6 30N 123 0E
50 Morocco ■ 32 0N 5 50W
52 Morogoro 6 50S 37 40E
74 Moroleón 20 8N 101 32W
57 Morombe 21 45S 43 22E
75 Morón 22 0N 78 30W
38 Mörön, R. 47 14N 110 37E
13 Morón de la Frontera 37 6N 5 28W
57 Morondavo 20 17S 44 27E
35 Morotai, I. 2 10N 128 30E
52 Moroto 2 28N 34 42E
52 Moroto, Mt. 2 30N 34 43E
6 Morpeth 55 11N 1 41W
71 Morrilton 35 10N 92 45W
79 Morrinhos 17 45S 49 10W
47 Morrinsville 37 40S 175 32E
65 Morris 49 25N 97 30W
45 Morris, Mt. 26 9S 131 4E
62 Morrisburg 44 55N 75 7W
69 Morristown, Tenn. 36 18N 83 20W
73 Morro Bay 35 27N 120 54W
78 Morrosquillo, G. de 9 35N 75 40W
22 Morshansk 53 28N 41 50E
80 Morteros 30 50S 62 0W
79 Mortes, R. 11 45S 50 44W
46 Mortlake 38 5S 142 50E
46 Morundah 34 57S 146 19E
43 Morven 26 22S 147 5E
8 Morvern, Reg. 56 38N 5 44W
46 Morwell 38 10S 146 22E
33 Moscos Is. 14 0N 97 45E
72 Moscow 46 45N 116 59W
22 Moscow=Moskva 55 45N 37 35E
14 Mosel, R. 50 22N 7 36E
12 Moselle, R. 50 22N 7 36E
12 Moselle □ 48 59N 6 33E
47 Mosgiel 45 53S 170 21E
52 Moshi 3 22S 37 18E
20 Mosjøen 65 51N 13 12E
22 Moskva 55 45N 27 35E
22 Moskva, R. 55 5N 38 50E
78 Mosquera 2 35N 78 30W
75 Mosquitos, G. de los 9 15N 81 0W
21 Moss 59 27N 10 40E
46 Moss Vale 34 32S 150 25E
65 Mossbank 50 0N 106 0W
47 Mossburn 45 41S 168 15E
56 Mosselbaai 34 11S 22 8E
54 Mossendjo 2 55S 12 42E
46 Mossgiel 33 15S 144 30E
42 Mossman 16 28S 145 23E
79 Mossoró 5 10S 37 15W
55 Mossuril 14 58S 40 42E
14 Most 50 31N 13 38E
18 Mosta 35 53N 14 26E
50 Mostaganem 35 54N 0 5E
19 Mostar 43 22N 17 50E
80 Mostardas 31 2S 50 51W
30 Mosul=Al Mawsil 36 20N 43 5E
21 Motala 58 32N 15 1E
8 Motherwell 55 48N 4 0W
33 Motihari 26 37N 85 1E
13 Motril 36 44N 3 37W
47 Motueka 41 7S 173 1E
54 Mouila 1 50S 11 0E
12 Moulins 46 35N 3 19¼
33 Moulmein= Maulamyaing 16 30N 97 40E
69 Moultrie 31 11N 83 47W
51 Moundou 8 40N 16 10E
68 Moundsville 39 53N 80 43W
69 Mount Airy 36 31N 80 37W
43 Mount Barker 34 38S 117 40E
68 Mount Carmel, Ill. 38 20N 87 48W
68 Mount Carmel, Pa. 40 46N 76 25W
42 Mount Coolon 21 25S 147 25E
55 Mount Darwin 16 47S 31 38E
42 Mount Douglas 21 35S 146 50E
47 Mount Eden 36 53S 174 46E
64 Mount Edgecumbe 57 3N 135 21W
44 Mount Elizabeth 16 0S 125 50E
62 Mount Forest 43 59N 80 43W
46 Mount Gambier 37 50S 140 46E
42 Mount Garnet 17 41S 145 7E
43 Mount Hope 34 7S 135 23E
42 Mount Isa 20 42S 139 26E
45 Mount Keith 27 15S 120 30E
42 Mount Larcom 23 48S 150 59E
32 Mount Lavinia 6 50N 79 50E
45 Mount Magnet 28 2S 117 47E
47 Mount Maunganui 37 40S 176 14E
42 Mount Molloy 16 42S 145 20E
42 Mount Morgan 23 40S 150 25E
45 Mount Narryer 26 30S 115 55E
44 Mount Newman 23 18S 119 45E
70 Mount Pleasant, Iowa 41 0N 91 35W
68 Mount Pleasant, Mich. 43 38N 84 46W
71 Mount Pleasant, Texas 33 5N 95 0W
72 Mount Pleasant, Utah 39 40N 111 29W
72 Mount Rainier Nat. Park 46 50N 121 20W
64 Mt. Revelstoke Nat. Park 51 6N 118 0W
64 Mount Robson 52 56N 119 15W
68 Mount Sterling 38 0N 84 0W
42 Mount Surprise 18 10S 144 17E
70 Mount Vernon, Ill. 38 19N 88 55W
68 Mount Vernon, N.Y. 40 57N 73 49W
68 Mount Vernon, Ohio 40 20N 82 30W
72 Mount Vernon, Wash. 48 27N 122 18W
43 Mount Willoughby 27 58S 134 8E
72 Mountain Home 43 3N 115 52W
64 Mountain Park 52 50N 117 15W
73 Mountain View 37 26N 122 5W
73 Mountainair 34 35N 106 15W
9 Mountmellick 53 7N 7 20W
42 Moura, Australia 24 35S 149 58E
78 Moura, Brazil 1 25S 61 45W
51 Mourdi, Depression du 18 10N 23 0E
53 Mouri 5 6N 1 14W
9 Mourne, Mts. 54 10N 6 0W
9 Mourne, R. 54 45N 7 25W
11 Mouscron 50 45N 3 12E
47 Moutohora 38 27S 177 32E
39 Mowming 21 50N 110 32E
38 Mowping 37 25N 121 34E
52 Moyale 3 30N 39 0E
9 Moyle □ 55 10N 6 15W
28 Moza 31 48N 35 8E
55 Mozambique ■ 19 0S 35 0E
48 Mozambique Chan. 20 0S 39 0E
22 Mozyr 52 0N 29 15E
52 Mpanda 6 23S 31 40E
55 Mpika 11 51S 31 25E
52 Mporokoso 9 25S 30 5E
52 Mpulungu 8 51S 31 5E
52 Mpwapwa 6 30S 36 30E
51 Msaken 35 49N 10 33E
55 Msoro 13 35S 31 50E
52 Mtito Andei 2 41S 38 12E
52 Mtwara 10 20S 40 20E
79 Muaná 1 25S 49 15W
37 Muang Chiang Rai 19 52N 99 50E
34 Muar=Bandar Maharani 2 3N 102 34E
34 Muarabungo 1 40S 101 10E
34 Muarakaman 0 2S 116 45E
34 Muaratembesi 1 42S 103 2E
34 Muaratewe 0 50S 115 0E
30 Mubairik 23 22N 39 8E
52 Mubende 0 33N 31 22E
53 Mubi 10 18N 13 16E
8 Muck, I. 56 50N 6 15W
79 Mucuri 18 0S 40 0W
52 Mueda 11 36S 39 28E
55 Mufulira 12 32S 28 15W
51 Muhammad Qol 20 53N 37 9E
52 Muheza 5 9S 38 48E
14 Mühlhausen 51 12N 10 29E
9 Muine Bheag 52 42N 6 59W
29 Mukalla 14 33N 49 2E
38 Mukden=Shenyang 41 48N 123 27E
29 Mukeiras 13 59N 45 52E
45 Mukinbudin 30 55S 118 5E
34 Mukomuko 2 20S 101 10E
52 Mukono 0 28N 32 37E
32 Muktsar 30 30N 74 30E
75 Mulatas, Arch. de las 6 51N 78 31W
80 Mulchén 37 45S 72 20W
14 Mulde, R., 51 10N 12 48E
52 Muleba 1 50S 31 37E
63 Mulgrave 45 38N 61 31W
13 Mulhacén, Mt. 37 4N 3 20W
14 Mülheim 51 26N 6 53W
12 Mulhouse 47 40N 7 20E
8 Mull of Galloway, Pt. 54 40N 4 55W
8 Mull of Kintyre, Pt. 55 20N 5 45W
8 Mull, I. 56 27N 6 0W
46 Mullengudgery 31 43S 147 29E
9 Mullet, Pen. 54 10N 10 2W
45 Mullewa 28 29S 115 30E
9 Mullingar 53 31N 7 20W
43 Mullumbimby 28 30S 153 30E
32 Multan 30 15N 71 30E
46 Mulwala 35 59S 146 0E
52 Mumias 0 20N 34 29E
34 Mun, R. 15 19N 105 31E
35 Muna, I. 5 0S 122 30E
32 Munabao 25 45N 70 17E
14 München 48 8N 11 33E
68 Muncie 40 10N 85 20W
14 Münden 51 25N 9 42E
44 Mundiwindi 23 47S 120 9E
79 Mundo Novo 11 50S 40 29W

45 Mundrabilla 31 52s 127 51 E
43 Mungallala 26 25s 147 34 E
42 Mungana 17 8s 144 27 E
43 Mungindi 28 58s 149 1 E
55 Munhango 12 9s 18 36 E
14 Munich= München 48 8N 11 33 E
80 Muñoz Gamero, Pen. 52 30s 73 5 E
9 Munster □ 52 20N 8 40W
14 Münster 51 58N 7 37 E
45 Muntadgin 31 48s 118 30 E
34 Muntok 2 5s 105 10 E
20 Muonio, R. 67 48N 23 25 E
14 Mur, R. 46 18N 16 53 E
80 Murallón, Mt. 49 55s 73 30W
52 Murangá 0 45s 37 9 E
52 Muranisgar Mts. 3 0N 35 0 E
22 Murashi 59 30N 49 0 E
46 Murchison, Australia 36 39s 145 14 E
47 Murchison, N.Z. 41 49s 172 21 E
45 Murchison, R. 26 1s 117 6 E
13 Murcia 38 2N 1 10W
13 Murcia, Reg. 38 35N 1 50W
15 Mureşul, R. 46 15N 20 13 E
69 Murfreesboro 35 50N 86 21W
24 Murgab 38 10N 73 59 E
43 Murgon 26 15s 151 54 E
14 Muritz See 53 25N 12 40 E
22 Murmansk 68 57N 33 10 E
22 Murom 55 35N 42 3 E
36 Muroran 42 25N 141 0 E
71 Murphysboro 37 50N 89 20W
69 Murray, Ky. 36 40N 88 20W
72 Murray, Utah 40 41N 111 58W
43 Murray, R. 35 22s 139 22 E
43 Murray Bridge 35 6s 139 14 E
56 Murraysburg 31 58s 23 47 E
46 Murrayville 35 16s 141 11 E
32 Murree 33 56N 73 28 E
45 Murrin Murrin 28 50s 121 45 E
46 Murrumbidgee, R. 34 43s 143 12 E
46 Murrurundi 31 42s 150 51 E
46 Murtoa 36 35s 142 28 E
47 Murupara 38 30s 178 40 E
33 Murwara 23 46N 80 28 E
43 Murwillumbah 28 18s 153 27 E
14 Mürzzuschlag 47 36N 15 41 E
19 Musala, Mt. 41 13N 23 27 E
31 Muscat=Masqat 23 37N 58 36 E
70 Muscatine 41 25N 91 5W
52 Mushao 2 2s 29 20 E
54 Mushie 2 56s 17 4 E
53 Mushin 6 32N 3 21 E
68 Muskegon 43 15N 86 17W
68 Muskegon Heights 43 12N 86 17W
71 Muskogee 35 50N 95 25W
51 Musmar 18 6N 35 40 E
52 Musoma 1 30s 33 48 E
8 Musselburgh 55 57N 3 3W
80 Musters, L. 45 20s 69 25W
46 Muswellbrook 32 16s 150 56 E
51 Mût 25 28N 28 58 E
38 Mutankiang 44 35N 129 30 E
42 Muttaburra 22 38s 144 29 E
63 Mutton Bay 50 50N 59 2W
25 Muya 56 27N 115 39 E
32 Muzaffarabad 34 25N 73 30 E
32 Muzaffarnagar 29 26N 77 40 E
32 Muzaffarpur 26 7N 85 32 E
24 Muzhi 65 25N 64 40 E
37 Muztagh, Mt. 36 30N 87 22 E
54 Mvadhi Ousye 1 13N 13 12 E
52 Mvomero 6 18s 37 28 E
52 Mwanza, Tanzania 2 30s 32 58 E
54 Mwanza, Zaire 7 55s 26 43 E
52 Mwaya 9 32s 33 55 E
54 Mweka 4 50s 21 40 E
54 Mweru, L. 9 0s 28 45 E
52 Mwirasandu 0 56s 30 22 E
34 My Tho 10 29N 106 23 E
33 Myanaung 18 25N 95 10 E
33 Myaungmya 16 30N 95 0 E
34 Myeik Kyunzu 11 0N 98 0 E
33 Myingyan 21 30N 95 30 E
33 Myitkyina 25 30N 97 26 E
33 Mymensingh= Nasirabad 24 42N 90 30 E
72 Myrtle Creek 43 0N 123 19W
72 Myrtle Point 43 0N 124 4W
32 Mysore 12 17N 76 41 E
20 Mývatn, L. 65 36N 17 0W
57 Mzimvubu, R. 31 30s 29 30 E

N

28 Na'an 31 53N 34 52 E
21 Naantali 60 27N 21 57 E
9 Naas 53 12N 6 40W
56 Nababeep 29 36s 17 46 E
33 Nabadwip 23 34N 88 20 E
51 Nabenl 36 30N 10 51 E
28 Nabi Rubin 31 56N 34 44 E
57 Naboomspruit 24 32s 28 40 E
28 Nābulus 32 14N 35 15 E
52 Nachingwea 10 49s 38 49 E
43 Nackara 32 48s 139 12 E
71 Nacogdoches 31 33N 95 30W
74 Nacozari 30 30N 109 50W
32 Nadiad 22 41N 72 56 E
31 Nadūshan 32 2N 53 35 E
22 Nadvoitsy 63 52N 34 15 E
24 Nadym 63 35N 72 42 E
53 Nafada 11 8N 11 20 E
33 Naga 13 38N 123 15 E
33 Nagaland □ 26 0N 95 0 E
36 Nagano 36 40N 138 10 E
36 Nagano □ 36 15N 138 0 E
36 Nagaoka 32 27N 138 51 E
32 Nagappattinam 10 46N 79 51 E
36 Nagasaki 32 47N 129 50 E
36 Nagasaki □ 3250⅛ 129 40 E
36 Nagato 36 15N 138 16 E
32 Nagaur 27 15N 73 45 E
32 Nagercoil 8 12N 77 33 E
25 Nagornyy 55 58N 124 57 E
36 Nagoya 35 10N 136 50 E
32 Nagpur 21 8N 79 10 E
14 Nagykanizsa 46 28N 17 0 E
15 Nagykörös 47 2N 19 48 E
39 Naha 26 12N 127 40 E
60 Nahannai Butte 61 5N 123 30W
28 Nahariyya 33 1N 35 5 E
30 Nahavand 34 10N 48 30 E
28 Nahf 32 56N 35 18 E
80 Nahuel Huapi, L. 41 0s 71 32W
65 Naicam 52 30N 104 30W
63 Nain 56 34N 61 40W
32 Nainpur 22 26N 80 6 E
8 Nairn 57 35N 3 54W
52 Nairobi 1 17s 36 48 E
52 Naivasha 0 40s 36 30 E
31 Najafābād 32 40N 51 15 E
30 Najd, Reg. 26 30N 42 0 E
32 Najibabad 29 40N 78 20 E
36 Nakamura 33 0N 133 0 E
52 Nakasongola 1 19N 32 28 E
30 Nakhi Mubarak 24 10N 38 10 E
23 Nakhichevan 39 14N 45 30 E
25 Nakhodka 43 10N 132 45 E
34 Nakhon Phanom 17 23N 104 43 E
34 Nakhon Ratchasima 14 59N 102 12 E
34 Nakhon Sawan 15 35N 100 12 E
34 Nakhon Si Thammarat 8 29N 100 0 E
62 Nakina 50 10N 86 40W
21 Nakskov 54 50N 11 8 E
52 Nakuru 0 15s 35 5 E
64 Nakusp 50 20N 117 45W
32 Nal, R. 26 2N 65 19 E
38 Nalayh 47 43N 107 22 E
23 Nalchik 43 30N 43 33 E
32 Nalgonda 17 6N 79 15 E
32 Nallamalai Hills 15 30N 78 50 E
51 Nālūt 31 54N 11 0 E
37 Nam Dinh 20 25N 106 5 E
34 Nam-Phan, Reg. 10 30N 106 0 E
34 Nam Tok 14 21N 99 0 E
37 Nam Tso, L. 30 40N 90 30 E
56 Namaland, Reg. 29 43s 19 5 E
24 Namangan 41 30N 71 30 E
55 Namapa 13 43s 39 50 E
52 Namasagali 1 2N 33 0 E
35 Namber 1 2s 134 57 E
43 Nambour 26 38s 152 49 E
43 Nambucca Heads 30 40s 152 48 E
37 Namcha Barwa, Mt. 29 30N 95 10 E
56 Namib Des.= Namibwoestyn 22 30s 15 0W
55 Namibia■= S.W. Africa ■ 22 0s 18 0 E
56 Namibwoestyn 22 30s 15 0W
35 Namlca 3 10s 127 5 E
72 Nampa 43 40N 116 40W
55 Nampula 15 6s 39 7 E
35 Namrole 3 46s 126 46 E
20 Namsen, R. 64 27N 11 28 E
20 Namsos 64 29N 11 30 E
33 Namtu 23 5N 97 28 E
11 Namur 50 27N 4 52 E
11 Namur □ 50 17N 5 0 E
55 Namutoni 18 49s 16 55 E
55 Namwala 15 44s 26 30 E
39 Namyung 25 15N 114 5 E
37 Nan 18 48N 100 46 E
37 Nan Shan, Mts. 38 0N 98 0 E
64 Nanaimo 49 10N 124 0W
43 Nanango 26 40s 152 0 E
36 Nanao 37 0N 137 0 E
39 Nanchang 28 34N 115 48 E
39 Nancheng 27 30N 116 28 E
39 Nancheng= Hanchung 33 10N 107 2 E
39 Nanching= Nanking 32 10N 118 50 E
39 Nanchung 30 47N 105 59 E
12 Nancy 48 42N 6 12 E
32 Nanda Devi, Mt. 30 30N 80 30 E
32 Nander 19 10N 77 20 E
47 Nandi 17 25s 176 50 E
32 Nandurbar 21 20N 74 15 E
32 Nandyal 15 30N 78 30 E
53 Nanga-Eboko 4 40N 12 26 E
32 Nanga Parbat, Mt. 35 10N 74 35 E
32 Nangal Dam 31 25N 76 38 E
31 Nangarhar □ 34 15N 70 30 E
39 Nankang 25 42N 114 35 E
39 Nanking 32 10N 118 50 E
36 Nankoku 33 39N 133 44 E
45 Nannine 26 51s 118 18 E
39 Nanning 22 51N 108 18 E
45 Nannup 33 59s 115 45 E
39 Nanping 26 45N 118 5 E
36 Nansei-Shotō, Is. 29 0N 129 0 E
45 Nanson 28 34s 114 46 E
39 Nantan 25 0N 107 35 E
12 Nantes 47 12N 1 33W
68 Nanticoke 41 12N 76 1W
64 Nanton 50 20N 113 50W
39 Nantou 23 57N 120 35 E
58 Nantucket I. 41 16N 70 3W
39 Nantung 32 0N 120 50 E
79 Nanuque 17 50s 40 21W
39 Nanyang 33 2N 112 35 E
38 Nanyuan 39 48N 116 23 E
52 Nanyuki 0 2N 37 4 E
13 Nao, C. de la 38 44N 0 14 E
36 Naoetsu 37 12N 138 10 E
72 Napa 38 18N 122 17W
62 Napanee 44 15N 77 0W
47 Napier 39 30s 176 56 E
44 Napier Broome, B. 14 0s 127 0 E
44 Napier Downs 16 20s 124 30 E
18 Naples= Nápoli 40 50N 14 5 E
78 Napo, R. 3 20s 72 40W
70 Napoleon 46 32N 99 49W
18 Nápoli 40 50N 14 5 E
36 Nara 34 40N 135 49 E
36 Nara □ 34 30N 136 0 E
46 Naracoorte 36 50s 140 44 E
33 Narasapur 16 26N 81 50 E
33 Narayanganj 23 31N 90 33 E
32 Narayanpet 16 45N 77 30 E
12 Narbonne 43 11N 3 0 E
45 Narembeen 32 4s 118 24 E
45 Naretha 31 0s 124 50 E
32 Narmada, R. 21 35N 72 35 E
52 Narok 1 20s 33 30 E
43 Narrabri 30 19s 149 46 E
43 Narran, R. 29 45s 147 20 E
46 Narrandera 34 42s 146 31 E
45 Narrogin 32 58s 117 14 E
46 Narromine 32 12s 148 12 E
32 Narsinghpur 22 54N 79 14 E
36 Naruto 35 36N 140 25 E
20 Narvik 68 28N 17 26 E
24 Narym 59 0N 81 58 E
24 Narymskoye 49 10N 84 15 E
24 Naryn 41 30N 76 10 E
50 Nasarawa 8 32N 7 41 E
51 Naser, Buheiret en 23 0N 32 30 E
72 Nashua, Mont. 48 10N 106 25W
68 Nashua, N.H. 42 50N 71 25W
69 Nashville 36 12N 86 46W
32 Nasik 20 2N 73 50 E
33 Nasirabad, Bangladesh 26 15N 74 45 E
32 Nasirabad, Pak. 28 25N 68 25 E
75 Nassau 25 0N 77 30W
80 Nassau, B. 55 20s 68 0W
51 Nasser, L.=Naser, Buheiret en 23 0N 32 30 E
21 Nässjö 57 38N 14 45 E
62 Nastapoka Is. 57 0N 77 0W
33 Nat Kyizio 14 55N 98 0 E
78 Natagaima 3 37N 75 6W
79 Natal, Brazil 5 47s 35 13W
34 Natal, Indonesia 0 35N 99 0 E
57 Natal □ 28 30s 30 30 E
63 Natashquan 50 14N 61 46W
63 Natashquan, R. 50 6N 61 49W
71 Natchez 31 35N 91 25W
71 Natchitoches 31 47N 93 4W
46 Natimuk 36 35s 141 59 E
53 Natitingou 10 20N 1 26 E
73 National City 32 45N 117 7W
79 Natividade 11 43s 47 47W
52 Natron, L. 2 20s 36 0 E
34 Natuna Besar, Kep. 4 0N 108 0 E
34 Natuna Selatan, Kep. 3 0N 109 55 E
14 Naumburg 51 10N 11 48 E
32 Naushahra 33 9N 74 15 E
33 Nautanwa 27 26N 83 25 E
73 Navajo Res. 36 55N 107 30W
13 Navalcarnero 40 17N 4 5W
9 Navan=An Uaimh 53 39N 6 40W
80 Navarino, I. 55 0s 67 30W
13 Navarra, Reg. 42 40N 1 40W
75 Navassa, I. 18 30N 75 0W
24 Navoi 40 9N 65 22 E
74 Navojoa 27 0N 109 30W
22 Navolok 62 33N 39 57 E
19 Návpaktos 38 23N 21 42 E
19 Navplion 37 33N 22 50 E
32 Navsari 20 57N 72 59 E
32 Nawabshah 26 15N 68 25 E
32 Nawalgarh 27 50N 75 15 E
19 Náxos, I. 37 5N 25 30 E
31 Nāy Band 27 20N 52 40 E
25 Nayakhan 62 10N 159 0 E
74 Nayarit □ 22 0N 105 0W
79 Nazaré, Brazil 13 0s 39 0W
28 Nazareth, Israel 32 42N 35 17 E
33 Nazir Hat 22 35N 91 55 E
52 Ndala 4 46s 33 16 E
54 Ndélé 8 25N 20 36 E
54 Ndendé 2 29s 10 46 E
51 Ndjamena 12 4N 15 8 E
55 Ndola 13 0s 28 34 E
52 Ndumbwe 10 14s 39 58 E
52 Ndungu 4 28s 38 4 E
9 Neagh, L. 54 35N 6 25W
60 Near Is. 53 0N 172 0W
7 Neath 51 39N 3 49W
42 Nebo 39 27N 90 47W
70 Nebraska □ 41 30N 100 0W
70 Nebraska City 40 40N 95 52W
18 Nebrodi, Monti 37 55N 14 35 E
14 Neckar, R. 49 31N 8 26 E
80 Necochea 38 30s 58 50W
73 Needles 34 50N 114 35W
32 Neemuch 24 30N 74 50 E
70 Neenah 44 10N 88 30W
65 Neepawa 50 20N 99 30W
50 Nefta 33 53N 7 58 E
23 Neftyannyye Kamni 40 20N 50 55 E
6 Nefyn 52 57N 4 31W
68 Negaunee 46 30N 87 36W
15 Negoiu, Mt. 45 48N 24 32 E
32 Negombo 7 12N 79 50 E
19 Negotin 44 16N 22 37 E
35 Negra Pt. 18 40N 120 50 E
78 Negra, Pta. 6 6s 81 10W
80 Negro, R., Arg. 41 2s 62 47W
78 Negro, R., Brazil 3 10s 59 58W
35 Negros, I. 10 0N 123 0 E
31 Nehbandān 31 35N 60 5 E
39 Neikiang 29 35N 105 10 E
14 Neisse, R. 52 4N 14 47 E
78 Neiva 2 56N 75 18W
51 Nekemte 9 4N 36 30 E
21 Neksø 55 4N 15 8 E
25 Nelkan 57 50N 136 15 E
32 Nellore 14 27N 79 59 E
25 Nelma 47 30N 139 0 E
64 Nelson, Canada 49 30N 117 20W
47 Nelson, N.Z. 41 18s 173 16 E
6 Nelson, U.K. 53 50N 2 14W
47 Nelson □ 42 11s 172 15 E
80 Nelson, Estrecho 51 30s 75 0W
65 Nelson, R. 55 30N 96 50W
64 Nelson Forks 59 30N 124 0W
57 Nelspruit 25 29s 30 59 E
50 Néma 16 40N 7 15W
36 Nemuro 43 20N 145 35 E
36 Nemuro-Kaikyō, Str. 43 30N 145 30 E
25 Nemuy 55 40N 135 55 E
9 Nenagh 52 52N 8 11W
60 Nenana 63 34N 149 7W
6 Nene, R. 52 48N 0 13 E
71 Neosho 35 59N 95 10W

Nepal ■ Northern Mid-Atlantic Ridge

33 Nepal ■ 28 0N 84 30 E
33 Nepalganj 28 0N 81 40 E
72 Nephi 39 43N 111 52W
25 Nerchinsk 52 0N 116 39 E
25 Nerchinskiyzavod 51 10N 119 30 E
13 Nerva 37 42N 6 30W
28 Nes Ziyyona 31 56N 34 48W
28 Nesher 32 45N 35 3 E
8 Ness, L. 57 15N 4 30W
21 Nesttun 60 19N 5 21 E
28 Netanya 32 20N 34 51 E
11 Netherlands ■ 52 0N 5 30 E
61 Nettilling L. 66 30N 71 0W
14 Neu Brandenburg 53 33N 13 17 E
14 Neuchâtel 47 0N 6 55 E
14 Neuchâtel, L. de 46 53N 6 50 E
14 Neumünster 54 4N 9 58 E
14 Neunkirchen 49 23N 7 6 E
80 Neuquén 38 0S 68 0 E
14 Neustrelitz 53 22N 13 4 E
71 Nevada 37 20N 94 40W
72 Nevada □ 39 20N 117 0W
13 Nevada, Sa. 37 3N 3 15W
78 Nevada de Sta. Marta, Sa. 10 55N 73 50W
25 Nevanka 56 45N 98 55 E
12 Nevers 47 0N 3 9 E
46 Nevertire 31 50S 147 44 E
75 Nevis, I. 17 0N 62 30W
68 New Albany 38 20N 85 50W
78 New Amsterdam 6 15N 57 30W
68 New Bedford 41 40N 70 52W
69 New Bern 35 8N 77 3W
71 New Braunfels 29 43N 98 9W
47 New Brighton 43 29S 172 43 E
68 New Britain 41 41N 72 47W
3 New Britain, I. 6 0S 151 0 E
68 New Brunswick 40 30N 74 28W
63 New Brunswick □ 46 50N 66 30W
53 New Bussa 9 55N 4 33 E
3 New Caledonia, I. 21 0S 165 0 E
13 New Castille= Castilla la Nueva 39 45N 3 20W
68 New Castle, Ind. 39 55N 85 23W
68 New Castle, Pa. 41 0N 80 20W
32 New Delhi 28 37N 77 13 E
64 New Denver 50 0N 117 25W
7 New Forest, Reg. 50 53N 1 40W
63 New Glasgow 45 35N 62 36W
41 New Guinea, I. 5 0S 141 0 E
68 New Hampshire □ 43 40N 71 40W
57 New Hanover 29 22S 30 31 E
68 New Haven 41 20N 72 54W
* 3 New Hebrides, Is. 15 0S 168 0 E
71 New Iberia 30 2N 91 54W
3 New Ireland, I. 3 0S 151 30 E
68 New Jersey □ 39 50N 74 10W
68 New Kensington 40 36N 79 43W
62 New Liskeard 47 31N 79 41W
68 New London 41 23N 72 8W
73 New Mexico □ 34 30N 106 0W
45 New Norcia 30 58S 116 13 E
42 New Norfolk 42 46S 147 2 E
71 New Orleans 30 0N 90 5W
68 New Philadelphia 40 29N 81 25W
47 New Plymouth 39 4S 174 5 E
75 New Providence I. 25 0N 77 30W
7 New Radnor 52 15N 3 10W
7 New Romney 50 59N 0 57 E
43 New South Wales □ 33 0S 146 0 E
70 New Ulm 44 15W 94 30W
63 New Waterford 46 13N 60 4W
64 New Westminster 49 10N 122 52W
68 New York 40 45N 74 0W
68 New York □ 42 40N 76 0W
47 New Zealand ■ 40 0S 173 0 E
52 Newala 10 58S 39 10 E
6 Newark, U.K. 53 6N 0 48W
68 Newark, N.J. 40 41N 74 12W
68 Newark, N.Y. 43 2N 77 10W
69 Newberry 46 20N 85 32W
68 Newburgh 41 30N 74 1W
7 Newbury 51 24N 1 19W
68 Newburyport 42 48N 70 50W
46 Newcastle, Australia 32 52S 151 49 E
63 Newcastle, Canada 47 1N 65 38W
9 Newcastle, Eire 52 27N 9 3W
57 Newcastle, S.Africa 27 45S 29 58 E
9 Newcastle, N. Ireland 54 13N 5 54W
6 Newcastle, Tyne and Tees 54 59N 1 37W
7 Newcastle Emlyn 52 2N 4 29W
42 Newcastle Waters 17 30S 133 28 E
6 Newcastle-under-Lyme 53 2N 2 15W
45 Newdegate 33 17N 118 58 E
28 Newe Etan 32 30N 35 32 E
28 Newe Sha'anan 32 47N 34 59 E
28 Newe Zohar 31 9N 35 21 E
60 Newenham, C. 58 37N 162 12W
63 Newfoundland □ 48 28N 56 0W
63 Newfoundland, I. 48 30N 56 0W
7 Newhaven 50 47N 0 4 E
44 Newman, Mt. 23 20S 119 34 E
9 Newmarket, Eire 52 13N 9 0W
7 Newmarket, U.K. 52 15N 0 23 E
69 Newnan 33 22N 84 48W
7 Newport, Gwent 51 35N 3 0W
7 Newport, I. of Wight 50 42N 1 18W
71 Newport, Ark. 35 38N 91 15W
68 Newport, Ky. 39 5N 84 23W
72 Newport, Oreg. 44 41N 124 2W
68 Newport, Rhode I. 41 30N 71 19W
68 Newport, Vt. 44 57N 72 17W
73 Newport Beach 33 40N 117 58W
68 Newport News 37 2N 76 54W
7 Newquay 50 24N 5 6W
9 Newry 54 10N 6 20W
9 Newry & Mourne □ 54 10W 6 20W
70 Newton, Iowa 41 40N 93 3W
71 Newton, Kans. 38 2N 97 30W
68 Newton, Mass. 42 21N 71 10W
68 Newton, N.J. 41 3N 74 46W
7 Newton Abbot 50 32N 3 37W
8 Newton Stewart 54 57N 4 30W
8 Newtonmore 57 4N 4 7W
46 Newtown, Australia 37 38S 143 40 E
7 Newtown, U.K. 52 31N 3 19W
9 Newtownabbey □ 54 40N 5 55W
9 Newtownards 54 37N 5 40W
22 Neya 58 21N 43 49 E
31 Neyshābūr 36 10N 58 20 E
23 Nezhin 51 5N 31 55 E
53 Ngala 12 15N 14 15 E
55 Ngami Depression 20 30S 22 46 E
57 Ngamo 19 3S 27 25 E
35 Nganjuk 7 32S 111 55 E
53 Ngaoundéré 7 15N 13 35 E
47 Ngapara 44 57S 170 46 E
35 Ngawi 7 24S 111 26 E
52 Ngerengere 6 47S 38 10 E
52 Ngomba 8 20S 32 53 E
52 Ngong 1 25S 36 39 E
37 Ngoring Nor, L. 34 50N 98 0 E
52 Ngorongoro Crater 3 11S 35 32 E
52 Ngudu 2 58S 33 25 E
53 Nguru 12 56N 10 29 E
52 Nguru Mts. 6 0S 37 30 E
34 Nha Trang 12 16N 109 10 E
46 Nhill 36 18S 141 40 E
62 Niagara Falls, Canada 43 7N 79 5W
68 Niagara Falls, U.S.A. 43 5N 79 0W
34 Niah 3 58S 113 46 E
53 Niamey 13 27N 2 6 E
54 Niangara 3 50N 27 50 E
34 Nias, I. 1 0N 97 40 E
75 Nicaragua ■ 11 40N 85 30W
18 Nicastro 39 0N 16 18 E
12 Nice 43 42N 7 14 E
36 Nichinan 31 28N 131 26 E
44 Nicholson Ra. 27 12S 116 40 E
27 Nicobar Is. 9 0N 93 0 E
64 Nicola 50 8N 120 40W
62 Nicolet 46 17N 72 35W
30 Nicosia=Levkosia, Cyprus 35 10N 33 25 E
75 Nicoya, G. de 10 0N 85 0W
75 Nicoya, Pen. de 9 45N 85 40W
6 Nidd, R. 54 1N 1 12W
14 Nieder-Osterreich □ 48 25N 15 40 E
14 Niedersachsen □ 52 45N 9 0 E
14 Nienburg 52 38N 9 15 E
79 Nieuw Amsterdam 5 53N 55 5W
79 Nieuw Nickerie 6 0N 57 10W
12 Nièvre □ 47 10N 3 40 E
30 Niğde 37 59N 34 42 E
57 Nigel 26 27S 28 25 E
50 Niger ■ 13 30N 10 0 E
53 Niger, R. 5 33N 6 33 E
53 Niger Delta 4 0N 5 30 E
53 Niger □ 10 0N 5 30 E
53 Nigeria ■ 8 30N 8 0 E
47 Nightcaps 45 57S 168 14 E
36 Niigata 37 58N 139 0 E
36 Niigata □ 37 15N 138 45 E
36 Niihama 33 55N 133 10 E
66 Niihau, I. 21 55N 160 10W
36 Niimi 34 59N 133 28 E
11 Nijkerk 52 13N 5 30 E
11 Nijmegen 51 50N 5 52 E
53 Nike 6 26N 7 29 E
35 Nikiniki 9 40S 124 30 E
53 Nikki 9 58N 3 21 E
23 Nikolayev 46 58N 32 7 E
23 Nikolayevsk 50 10N 45 35 E
25 Nikolayevskna-Am 53 40N 140 50 E
23 Nikopol 47 35N 34 25 E
51 Nîl, Nahr en, R. 30 10N 31 6 E
51 Nîl el Abyad, R. 15 40N 32 30 E
51 Nîl el Azraq, R. 11 40N 32 30 E
51 Nîl el Azraq □ 12 30N 34 30 E
73 Niland 33 16N 115 30W
51 Nile, R.= Nîl, Nahren, R. 30 10N 31 6 E
68 Niles 41 8N 80 40W
12 Nîmes 43 50N 4 23 E
46 Nimmitabel 36 29S 149 15 E
25 Nimneryskiy 58 0N 125 10 E
52 Nimule 3 32N 32 3 E
46 Ninety Mile Beach, The 38 30S 147 10 E
30 Nineveh 36 25N 43 10 E
39 Ningming 22 10N 107 59 E
39 Ningpo 29 50N 121 30 E
38 Ningsia Hui □ 37 45N 106 0 E
39 Ningteh 26 45N 120 0 E
38 Ningwu 39 2N 112 15 E
37 Ninh Binh 20 15N 105 55 E
11 Ninove 50 51N 4 2 E
70 Niobrara, R. 42 45N 98 0W
50 Nioro 13 40N 15 50W
12 Niort 46 19N 0 29W
65 Nipawin 53 20N 104 0W
65 Nipawin Prov. Park 54 0N 104 40W
62 Nipigon 49 0N 88 17W
62 Nipigon, L. 49 40N 88 30W
79 Niquelandia 14 27S 48 27W
36 Nirasaki 35 42N 138 27 E
19 Niš 43 19N 21 58 E
29 Nisab 14 25N 46 29 E
36 Nishinomiya 34 45N 135 20 E
79 Niterói 22 52S 43 0W
8 Nith, R. 55 0N 3 35W
15 Nitra 48 19N 18 4 E
15 Nitra, R. 47 46N 18 10 E
11 Nivelles 50 35N 4 20 E
12 Nivernais, Reg. 47 0N 3 40 E
32 Nizamabad 18 45N 78 7 E
33 Nizamghat 28 20N 95 45 E
25 Nizhne Kolymsk 68 40N 160 55 E
24 Nizhne-Vartovskoye 60 56N 76 38 E
25 Nizhneangarsk 56 0N 109 30 E
25 Nizhneudinsk 55 0N 99 20 E
24 Nizhniy Tagil 57 45N 60 0 E
30 Nizip 37 1N 37 46 E
15 Nizké Tatry, Mts. 48 55N 20 0 E
28 Nizzanim 31 42N 34 37 E
52 Njombe 9 0S 34 35 E
53 Nkambe 6 35N 10 40 E
53 Nkawkaw 6 36N 0 49W
52 Nkhata Bay 11 33S 34 16 E
55 Nkhota Kota 12 55S 34 15 E
52 Nkonge 0 15N 31 10 E
53 Nkongsamba 4 55N 9 55 E
33 Noakhali=Maijdi 22 48N 91 10 E
60 Noatak 67 34N 162 59W
36 Nobeoka 32 36N 131 41 E
18 Nocera Inferiore 40 45N 14 37 E
36 Noda 47 30N 142 5 E
74 Nogales, Mexico 31 36N 94 29W
73 Nogales, U.S.A. 31 33N 110 59W
36 Nōgata 33 48N 130 54 E
45 Noggerup 33 32S 116 5 E
25 Noginsk 55 50N 38 25 E
12 Noire, Mts. 48 11N 3 40W
12 Noirmoutier, Î. de 46 58N 2 10W
32 Nok Kundi 28 50N 62 45 E
25 Nokhhuysk 60 0N 117 45 E
60 Nome 64 30N 165 30W
42 Nonda 20 40S 142 28 E
34 Nong Khai 17 50N 102 46 E
44 Noonamah 12 38S 131 4 E
43 Noondoo 28 35S 148 30 E
11 Noord Beveland, I. 51 45N 3 50 E
11 Noord Brabant □ 51 40N 5 0 E
11 Noord Holland □ 52 30N 4 45 E
11 Noordoost-Polder 52 45N 5 45 E
11 Noordwijk 52 14N 4 26 E
64 Nootka I. 49 40N 126 50W
62 Noranda 48 20N 79 0 E
12 Nord □ 50 15N 3 30 E
14 Nord-Ostsee Kanal 54 5N 9 15 E
64 Nordegg 52 29N 116 5W
20 Nordkapp 71 11N 25 48 E
20 Nordland □ 65 40N 13 0 E
14 Nordrhein Westfalen □ 51 45N 7 30 E
25 Nordvik 73 40N 110 57 E
9 Nore, R. 52 25N 6 58W
70 Norfolk, Nebr. 42 3N 97 25W
68 Norfolk, Va. 36 52N 76 15W
6 Norfolk □ 52 39N 1 0 E
3 Norfolk I. 28 58S 168 3 E
25 Norilsk 69 20N 88 0 E
70 Normal 40 30N 89 0W
71 Norman 35 12N 97 30W
60 Norman Wells 65 40N 126 45W
12 Normandie, Reg. 48 45N 0 10 E
62 Normandin 48 49N 72 31W
12 Normandy, Reg.= Normandie, Reg. 48 45N 0 10 E
42 Normanton 17 40S 141 10 E
45 Nornalup 35 0S 116 49 E
80 Norquinco 41 51S 70 55W
20 Norrbotten □ 66 45N 23 0 E
21 Nørresundby 57 5N 9 52 E
68 Norristown 40 9N 75 15W
21 Norrköping 58 37N 16 11 E
20 Norrland, Reg. 64 25N 18 0 E
21 Norrtälje 59 46N 18 42 E
45 Norseman 32 8S 121 43 E
25 Norsk 52 30N 130 0 E
79 Norte, C. do 1 40N 49 55W
47 North, C. 34 23S 173 4 E
47 North I. 38 0S 176 0 E
68 North Adams 42 42N 73 6W
1 North America 45 0N 100 0W
65 North Battleford 52 50N 108 10W
62 North Bay 46 20N 79 30W
62 North Belcher Is. 56 30N 79 0W
64 North Bend, Canada 49 50N 121 35W
72 North Bend, Oreg. 43 28N 124 7W
8 North Berwick 56 4N 2 44W
34 North Borneo □= Sabah □ 6 0N 117 0 E
69 North Carolina □ 35 30N 80 0W
8 North Channel 55 0N 5 30W
68 North Chicago 42 19N 87 50W
70 North Dakota □ 47 30N 100 0W
45 North Dandalup 32 31S 115 58 E
9 North Down □ 54 40N 5 45W
7 North Downs 51 17N 0 30W
33 North East Frontier Agency= Arunachal Pradesh 28 0N 95 0 E
8 North Esk, R. 56 54N 2 38W
4 North European Plain 55 0N 25 0 E
7 North Foreland, Pt. 51 22N 1 28 E
52 North Horr 3 20N 37 8 E
64 North Kamloops 50 40N 120 25W
38 North Korea ■ 40 0N 127 0 E
33 North Lakhimpur 27 15N 94 10 E
2 North Magnetic Pole 76 5N 101 3W
8 North Minch 58 5N 5 55W
70 North Platte 41 10N 100 50W
8 North Ronaldsay, I. 59 20N 2 30W
65 North Saskatchewan, R. 53 15N 105 6W
4 North Sea 55 0N 5 0 E
63 North Sydney 46 12N 60 21W
68 North Tonawanda 43 5N 78 50W
20 N.-Trøndelag □ 64 30N 12 30 E
71 North Truchas Pk. 36 0N 105 30W
6 North Tyne, R. 54 59N 2 8W
8 North Uist, I. 57 40N 7 15W
64 North Vancouver 49 25N 123 20W
75 North Village 32 15N 64 45W
6 North Walsham 52 49N 1 22 E
44 North West, C. 21 45S 114 9 E
8 North West Highlands, Mts. 57 35N 5 2W
60 North West Territories □ 65 0N 100 0W
6 North York Moors 54 25N 0 50W
6 North Yorkshire □ 54 10N 1 25W
6 Northallerton 54 20N 1 26W
45 Northam 31 35S 116 42 E
45 Northampton, Australia 28 21S 114 33 E
7 Northampton, U.K. 52 14N 0 54W
68 Northampton, Mass. 42 22N 72 39W
7 Northampton □ 52 16N 0 55W
42 Northampton Downs 24 35S 145 48 E
45 Northcliffe 34 36S 116 7 E
53 Northern □ 9 0N 1 30W
33 Northern Circars, Reg. 17 30N 82 30 E
9 Northern Ireland ■ 54 45N 7 0W
1 Northern Mid-Atlantic Ridge 30 0N 40 0W

* *Renamed Vanuatu*

Northern Rhodesia ■ = Zambia — Opp

55 Northern Rhodesia ■ = Zambia ■ 15 0S 28 0E
40 Northern Territory □ 16 0S 133 0E
70 Northfield 44 37N 93 10W
6 Northumberland □ 55 12N 2 0W
42 Northumberland, Is. 21 45S 150 20E
63 Northumberland Str. 46 20N 64 0W
6 Northwich 53 16N 2 30W
57 Norton 17 52S 30 40E
60 Norton Sd. 64 0N 165 0W
68 Norwalk, Conn. 41 7N 73 27W
68 Norwalk, Ohio 41 15N 82 37W
20 Norway ■ 67 0N 11 0E
65 Norway House 53 55N 98 50W
3 Norwegian Dependency 75 0S 15 0E
4 Norwegian Sea 66 0N 1 0E
6 Norwich, U.K. 52 38N 1 17E
68 Norwich, N.Y. 42 32N 75 30W
24 Nosok 70 10N 82 20E
31 Nosratabad 29 55N 60 0E
8 Noss Hd. 58 29N 3 4W
56 Nossob, R. 26 55S 20 37E
57 Nosy Bé, I. 13 20S 48 15E
57 Nosy-Varika 20 35S 48 32E
14 Noteć R. 52 44N 15 26E
64 Notikewin 57 15N 117 5W
18 Noto 36 52N 15 4E
63 Notre Dame B. 49 45N 55 30W
61 Notre Dame de Koartac=Koartac 60 55N 69 40W
61 Notre Dame d'Ivugivik= Ivugivik 62 20N 78 0W
62 Nottawasaga B. 44 40N 80 30W
6 Nottingham 52 57N 1 10W
6 Nottinghamshire □ 53 10N 1 0W
50 Nouadhibou 21 0N 17 0W
50 Nouakchott 18 20N 15 50W
3 Nouméa 22 17S 166 30E
56 Noupoort 31 10S 24 57E
62 Nouveau Comptoir 53 2N 78 55W
79 Nova Cruz 6 28S 35 25W
79 Nova Friburgo 22 10S 42 30W
79 Nova Granada 20 29S 49 19W
79 Nova Lima 20 5S 44 0W
55 Nova Lisboa= Huambo 12 42S 15 54E
63 Nova Scotia □ 45 10N 63 0W
55 Nova Sofola 20 7S 34 48E
79 Nova Venecia 18 45S 40 24E
18 Novara 45 27N 8 36E
22 Novaya Ladoga 60 7N 32 16E
24 Novaya Lyalya 58 50N 60 35E
25 Novaya Sibir, Os. 75 10N 150 0E
24 Novaya Zemlya, I. 75 0N 56 0E
15 Nové Zámky 47 59N 18 11E
22 Novgorod 58 30N 31 25E
19 Novi-Sad 45 18N 19 52E
* **54** Novo Redondo 11 10S 13 48E
23 Novocherkassk 47 27N 40 5E
24 Novokazalinsk 45 40N 61 40E
22 Novokiybyshevsk 53 7N 49 58E
24 Novo-kuznetsk 54 0N 87 10E
22 Novomoskovsk 54 5N 38 15E
23 Novorossiyk 44 43N 37 52E
23 Novoshakhtinsk 47 39N 39 58E
24 Novosibirsk 55 0N 83 5E
25 Novosibirskiye Os. 75 0N 140 0E
22 Novotroitsk 51 10N 58 15E
23 Novouzensk 50 32N 48 17E
18 Novska 45 19N 17 0E
31 Now Shahr 36 40N 51 40E
46 Nowa Nowa 37 44S 148 3E
33 Nowgong 26 20N 92 50E
46 Nowra 34 53S 150 35E
15 Nowy Sącz 49 40N 20 41E
14 Nowy Tomyśl 52 19N 16 10E
12 Noyon 49 34N 3 0E
57 Nsanje 16 55S 35 12E
53 Nsawam 5 50N 0 24W
53 Nsukka 7 0N 7 50E
‡ **57** Nuanetsi 21 22S 30 45E
‡ **57** Nuanetsi, R. 22 40S 31 50E
† **53** Nuatja 7 0N 1 10E
48 Nubian Des. 21 30N 33 30E
51 Nûbîya, Es Sahrâ en 21 30N 33 30E
74 Nueva Rosita 28 0N 101 20W
80 Nueve de Julio 35 30S 60 50W
75 Nuevitas 21 30N 77 20W
80 Nuevo, G. 43 0S 64 30W
74 Nuevo Laredo 27 30N 99 40W
74 Nuevo León □ 25 0N 100 0W
47 Nuhaka 39 3S 177 45E
51 Nukheila 19 1N 26 21E
24 Nukus 42 20N 59 40E
60 Nulato 64 43N 158 6W
44 Nullagine 21 53S 120 6E
45 Nullarbor 31 26S 130 55E
45 Nullarbor Plain 31 20S 128 0E
53 Numan 9 29N 12 3E
36 Numata 36 38N 139 3E
36 Numazu 35 7N 138 51E
46 Numurkah 36 0S 145 26E
7 Nuneaton 52 32N 1 29W
60 Nunivak I. 60 0N 166 0W
38 Nunkiang 49 11N 125 12E
11 Nunspeet 52 21N 5 45E
18 Núoro 40 20N 9 20E
14 Nuremburg= Nürnberg 49 26N 11 5E
14 Nürnberg 49 26N 11 5E
34 Nusa Tenggara Barat 8 50S 117 30E
35 Nusa Tenggara Timur □ 9 30S 122 0E
32 Nushki 29 35N 65 59E
61 Nutak 57 30N 61 59W
56 Nuweveldberge 32 10S 21 45E
45 Nyabing 33 30S 118 7E
52 Nyahanga 2 20S 33 37E
52 Nyahua 5 25S 33 23E
52 Nyahururu 0 2N 36 27E
52 Nyakanazi 3 2S 31 10E
52 Nyakanyazi 1 10S 31 13E
53 Nyakrom 5 40N 0 50W
51 Nyâlâ 12 2N 24 58E
52 Nyalikungu 2 35S 33 27E
52 Nyanguge 2 30S 33 12E
52 Nyanza 2 20S 29 42E
55 Nyasa, L. 12 0S 34 30E
21 Nybro 56 44N 15 55E
24 Nyda 66 40N 73 10E
37 Nyenchen, Ra. 30 30N 95 0E
52 Nyeri 0 23S 36 56E
52 Nyika Plat. 10 30S 36 0E
15 Nyíregyháza 48 0N 21 47E
20 Nykarleby 63 32N 22 31E
21 Nykøbing 54 56N 11 52E
21 Nyköping 58 45N 17 0E
57 Nylstroom 24 42S 28 22E
21 Nynäshamn 58 54N 17 57E
46 Nyngan 31 30S 147 8E
53 Nyong, R. 3 17N 9 54E
46 Nyora 38 20S 145 41E
15 Nysa 50 40N 17 22E
14 Nysa, R. 52 4N 14 46E
25 Nyurba 63 17N 118 20E
52 Nzega 4 10S 33 12E
50 Nzérékoré 7 49N 8 48W

O

70 Oahe Dam 44 28N 100 25W
70 Oahe Res. 45 30N 100 15W
66 Oahu, I. 21 30N 158 0W
72 Oak Creek 40 15N 106 59W
68 Oak Park 41 55N 87 45W
69 Oak Ridge 36 1N 84 5W
71 Oakdale 30 50N 92 28W
6 Oakengates 52 42N 2 29W
72 Oakesdale 47 11N 117 9W
43 Oakey 27 25S 151 43E
6 Oakham 52 40N 0 43W
73 Oakland 37 50N 122 18W
46 Oakleigh 37 54S 145 6E
44 Oakover, R. 20 43S 120 33E
72 Oakridge 43 47N 122 31W
65 Oakville, Man. 49 56N 97 58W
47 Oamaru 45 6S 170 58E
74 Oaxaca □ 17 0N 97 0W
24 Ob, R. 62 40N 66 0E
62 Oba 49 4N 84 7W
8 Oban 56 25N 5 30W
64 Obed 53 30N 117 10W
14 Ober-Österreich □ 48 10N 14 0E
14 Oberhausen 51 28N 6 50E
53 Obiaruku 5 51N 6 9E
36 Obihiro 42 55N 143 10E
25 Obluchye 49 10N 130 50E
24 Obskaya Guba 70 0N 73 0E
53 Obuasi 6 17N 1 40W
53 Obudu 6 40N 9 10E
69 Ocala 29 11N 82 5W
78 Ocaña, Col. 8 15N 73 20W
13 Ocaña, Sp. 39 55N 3 30W
78 Occidental, Cord. 5 0N 76 0W
68 Ocean City 39 18N 74 34W
64 Ocean Falls 52 25N 127 40W
72 Oceanlake 45 0N 124 0W
73 Oceanside 33 13N 117 26W
8 Ochil Hills 56 14N 3 40W
70 Oconto 44 52N 87 53W
74 Ocatlán 20 21N 102 42W
78 Ocumare del Tuy 10 7N 66 46W
35 Ocussi 9 20S 124 30E
53 Ōda 5 50N 1 5W
20 Odáðahraun 65 5N 17 0W
36 Odawara 35 20N 139 6E
21 Odda 60 3N 6 35E
29 Oddur 4 0N 43 35E
30 Ödemiş 38 15N 28 0E
56 Odendaalsrus 27 48S 26 43E
21 Odense 55 22N 10 23E
14 Oder=Odra R. 53 33N 14 38E
14 Oder Haff 53 46N 14 14E
23 Odessa 46 30N 30 45E
71 Odessa 31 51N 102 23W
50 Odienné 9 30N 7 34W
14 Odra, R. 53 33N 14 38E
55 Odzi 18 58S 32 23E
79 Oeiras 7 0S 42 8W
70 Oelwein 42 39N 91 55W
44 Oenpelli 12 20S 133 4E
53 Offa 8 13N 4 42E
9 Offaly □ 53 20N 7 30W
14 Offenbach 50 6N 8 46E
13 Ofir 41 30N 8 52W
62 Ogahalla 50 6N 85 51W
36 Ōgaki 35 25N 136 35E
70 Ogallala 50 6N 85 51W
53 Ogbomosho 8 1N 3 29E
72 Ogden 41 13N 112 1W
68 Ogdensburg 44 40N 75 27W
18 Oglio, R. 45 15N 10 15E
42 Ogmore 22 37S 149 35E
53 Ogoja 6 38N 8 39E
62 Ogoki 51 35N 86 0W
54 Ogooué, R. 1 0S 10 0E
53 Ogun □ 6 55N 3 38E
53 Oguta 5 44N 6 44E
53 Ogwashi-Uku 6 15N 6 30E
80 O'Higgins, L. 49 0S 72 40W
47 Ohakune 39 24S 175 24E
71 Ohio, R. 38 0N 86 0W
68 Ohio □ 40 20N 83 0W
14 Ohre, R. 50 10N 12 30E
19 Ohrid 41 8N 20 52E
19 Ohrid, L.= Ohridsko, J. 41 8N 20 52E
19 Ohridsko, J. 41 8N 20 52E
57 Ohrigstad 24 41S 30 36E
79 Oiapoque 3 50N 51 50W
68 Oil City 41 26N 79 40W
12 Oise □ 49 28N 2 30E
36 Ōita 33 15N 131 36E
80 Ojos del Salado, Cerro, Mt. 27 0S 68 40W
56 Okahandja 22 0S 16 59E
72 Okanagan 48 24N 119 24W
47 Okarito 43 15S 170 9E
55 Okavango, R. 17 40S 19 30E
56 Okavango Swamps 19 30S 23 0E
36 Okaya 36 0N 138 10E
36 Okayama 34 40N 133 54E
36 Okayama □ 35 0N 133 50E
36 Okazaki 34 36N 137 0E
53 Oke-Iho 8 1N 3 18E
69 Okeechobee, L. 21 0N 80 50W
69 Okefenokee Swamp. 30 50N 82 15W
7 Okehampton 50 44N 4 1W
53 Okene 7 32N 6 11E
25 Okha 53 40N 143 0E
25 Okhotsk 59 20N 143 10E
25 Okhotsk, Sea of 55 0N 145 0E
25 Okhotskiy Perevoz 61 52N 135 35E
25 Oknotsko kolymskoy 63 0N 157 0E
36 Oki-Shotō 36 15N 133 15E
56 Okiep 29 39S 17 53E
53 Okigwi 5 52N 7 20E
53 Okija 5 54N 6 55E
39 Okinawa, I. 26 40N 128 0E
39 Okinawa-guntō, Is. 26 0N 127 30E
53 Okitipupa 6 31N 4 50E
71 Oklahoma □ 35 20N 97 30W
71 Oklahoma City 35 25N 97 30W
71 Okmulgee 35 38N 96 0W
53 Okrika 4 47N 7 4E
25 Oktyabriskoy Revolyutsii Os. 79 30N 97 0E
22 Oktyabrski 53 11N 48 40E
47 Okura 43 55S 168 55E
36 Okushiri-To, I. 42 15N 139 30E
53 Okuta 9 14N 3 12E
21 Öland, I. 56 45N 16 50E
43 Olary 32 17S 140 19E
70 Olathe 38 50N 94 50W
80 Olavarría 36 55S 60 20W
18 Ólbia 40 55N 9 30E
13 Old Castille= Castilla la Vieja 39 45N 3 20W
60 Old Crow 67 35N 139 50W
62 Old Factory 52 36N 78 43W
69 Old Town 45 0N 68 50W
9 Oldcastle 53 46N 7 10W
52 Oldeani 3 25S 35 35E
14 Oldenburg 53 10N 8 10E
11 Oldenzaal 52 19N 6 53E
64 Olds 51 50N 114 10W
68 Olean 42 8N 78 25W
25 Olekminsk 60 40N 120 30E
22 Olenegorsk 68 9N 33 15E
25 Olenek 68 20N 112 30E
12 Oléron, Î. d' 45 55N 1 15W
15 Oleśnica 51 13N 17 22E
25 Olga 43 50N 135 0E
45 Olga, Mt. 25 20S 130 40E
57 Olifants, R. 24 10S 32 40S
19 Olimbos, Oros 40 6N 22 23E
64 Oliver 49 20N 119 30W
78 Ollague 21 15S 68 10W
68 Olney 38 40N 88 0W
14 Olomouc 49 38N 17 12E
25 Olovyannaya 50 50N 115 10E
15 Olsztyn 53 48N 20 29E
15 Olt, R. 43 50N 24 40E
15 Oltenita 44 7N 26 42E
72 Olympia 47 0N 122 58W
72 Olympic Mts. 48 0N 124 0W
72 Olympic Nat. Park 47 35N 123 30W
72 Olympus Mt. 47 52N 123 40W
9 Omagh 54 36N 7 20W
9 Omagh □ 54 35N 7 20W
70 Omaha 41 15N 96 0W
72 Omak 48 25N 119 24W
29 Oman ■ 23 0N 58 0E
31 Oman, G. of 24 30N 58 30E
56 Omaruru 21 26S 16 0E
78 Omate 16 45S 71 0W
35 Ombai, Selat, Str 8 30S 124 50E
51 Omdurmân 15 40N 32 28E
28 Omez 32 22N 35 0E
36 Ōmiya 35 54N 139 38E
54 Omo, R. 8 48N 37 14E
24 Omsk 55 0N 73 38E
36 Ōmura 33 8N 130 0E
36 Ōmuta 33 0N 130 26E
13 Onda 39 55N 0 17W
55 Ondangua 17 57S 16 4E
53 Ondo 7 4N 4 47E
53 Ondo □ 7 0N 5 5E
38 Ondörhaan 47 22N 110 31E
22 Onega 64 0N 38 10E
22 Onega, R. 63 0N 39 0E
47 Onehunga 36 55N 174 30E
68 Oneida 43 5N 75 40W
70 O'Neill 42 30N 98 38W
68 Oneonta 42 26N 75 5W
22 Onezhskaya Guba 64 30N 37 0E
22 Onezhskoye, Oz 62 0N 35 30E
47 Ongarue 38 42S 175 19E
45 Ongerup 33 58S 118 29E
32 Ongole 15 33N 80 2E
57 Onilahy, R. 23 34S 43 45E
53 Onitsha 6 6N 6 42E
36 Onoda 34 2N 131 10E
44 Onslow 21 40S 115 0E
11 Onstwedde 52 2N 7 4E
36 Ontake-San, Mt. 35 50N 137 15E
73 Ontario 34 2N 117 40W
68 Ontario, L. 43 40N 78 0W
62 Ontario □ 52 0N 88 10W
43 Oodnadatta 27 33S 135 30E
45 Ooldea 30 27S 131 50E
42 Oorindi 20 40S 141 1E
11 Oostende 51 15N 2 50E
11 Oosterhout 51 38N 4 51E
11 Oosterschelde, R. 51 30N 4 0E
32 Ootacamund 11 30N 76 44E
25 Opala, U.S.S.R. 52 15N 156 15E
54 Opala, Zaïre 0 37S 24 21E
52 Opari 2 56N 32 0E
15 Opava 49 57N 17 58E
71 Opelousas 30 35N 92 0W
60 Ophir 63 10N 156 31W
53 Opi 6 36N 7 28E
53 Opobo 4 35N 7 34E
15 Opole 50 42N 17 58E
13 Oporto=Pôrto 41 8N 8 40W
47 Opotiki 38 1S 177 19E
69 Opp 31 19E 86 13W

* *Renamed Sumbe*
† *Notsé*
‡ *Renamed Mwenezi*

21 Oppland □ 61 15N 9 30 E
65 Optic Lake 54 46N 101 13W
47 Opua 35 19S 174 9 E
47 Opunake 39 26S 173 52 E
28 Or Yehuda 32 2N 34 50 E
15 Oradea 47 2N 21 58 E
20 Öraefajökull, Mt. 64 2N 16 15W
32 Orai 25 58N 79 30 E
80 Orán 23 10S 64 20W
50 Oran 35 37N 0 39W
46 Orange, Australia 33 15S 149 7 E
12 Orange, Fr. 44 8N 4 47 E
71 Orange, U.S.A. 30 0N 93 40W
55 Orange=Oranje, R. 28 30S 18 0 E
79 Orange, C. 4 20N 51 30W
56 Orange Free State □ 28 30S 27 0 E
74 Orange Walk 17 15N 88 47W
69 Orangeburg 33 27N 80 53W
62 Orangeville 43 55N 80 5W
14 Oranienburg 52 45N 13 15 E
56 Oranje, R. 28 41S 16 28 E
56 Oranje-Vrystaat □ 28 30S 27 0 E
55 Oranjemund 28 32S 16 29 E
55 Orapa 24 13S 25 25 E
18 Orbetello 42 26N 11 11 E
46 Orbost 37 40S 148 29 E
8 Orchy, Bridge of 56 30N 4 46W
44 Ord, Mt. 17 20S 125 34 E
44 Ord, R. 15 30S 128 21 E
8 Ord of Caithness 58 35N 3 37W
44 Ord River 17 23S 128 51 E
30 Ordu 40 55N 37 53 E
23 Ordzhonlkidze 43 0N 44 35 E
14 Ore Mts.= Erzgebirge 50 25N 13 0 E
21 Örebro 59 20N 15 18 E
21 Örebro □ 59 27N 15 0 E
72 Oregon □ 44 0N 120 0W
72 Oregon City 45 28N 122 35W
22 Orekhovo-Zuyevo 55 50N 38 55 E
22 Orel 52 59N 36 5 E
72 Orem 40 27N 111 45W
22 Orenburg 51 45N 55 6 E
13 Orense 42 19N 7 55W
47 Orepuki 46 19S 167 46 E
7 Orford Ness, C. 52 6N 1 31 E
62 Orient Bay 49 20N 88 10W
78 Oriental, Cord. 5 0N 74 0W
13 Orihuela 38 7N 0 55W
62 Orillia 44 40N 79 24W
78 Orinoco, R. 8 37N 62 15W
65 Orion 49 28N 110 49W
33 Orissa □ 21 0N 85 0 E
18 Oristano 39 54N 8 35 E
18 Oristano, G. di 39 50N 8 22 E
74 Orizaba 18 50N 97 10W
20 Orkanger 63 18N 9 52 E
20 Orkla, R. 63 18N 9 50 E
56 Orkney 26 42S 26 40 E
8 Orkney □ 59 0N 3 0W
72 Orland 39 46N 120 10W
69 Orlando 28 30N 81 25W
12 Orléanais, Reg. 48 0N 2 0 E
12 Orléans, Fr. 47 54N 1 52 E
63 Orleans, I. d' 46 54N 70 58W
50 Orléansville=El Asnam 36 10N 1 20 E
25 Orlik 52 30N 99 55 E
32 Ormara 25 16N 64 33 E
35 Ormoc 11 0N 124 37 E
47 Ormond 38 33S 177 56 E
6 Ormskirk 53 35N 2 54W
12 Orne □ 48 40N 0 0 E
20 Örnsköldsvik 63 17N 18 40 E
78 Orocué 4 48N 71 20W
53 Orodo 5 34N 7 4 E
63 Oromocto 45 54N 66 37W
28 Oron, Israel 30 55N 35 1 E
53 Oron, Nigeria 4 48N 8 14 E
79 Orós 6 15S 38 55W
72 Oroville 39 40N 121 30W
43 Orroroo 32 44S 138 37 E
22 Orsha 54 30N 30 25 E
22 Orsk 51 20N 58 34 E
15 Orşova 44 41N 22 25 E
13 Ortegal, C. 43 43N 7 52W
12 Orthez 43 29N 0 48W
13 Ortigueira 43 40N 7 50W
18 Ortles, Mt. 46 31N 10 33 E
18 Ortona 42 21N 14 24 E
78 Oruro 18 0S 67 19W
18 Orvieto 42 43N 12 8 E
7 Orwell, R. 51 57N 1 17 E
75 Osa, Pen. de 8 0N 84 0W
70 Osage, R. 38 35N 91 57W
36 Ōsaka 34 40N 135 30 E
36 Ōsaka □ 34 40N 135 30 E
70 Osborne 39 30N 98 45W
71 Osceola 35 40N 90 0W
62 Oshawa 43 50N 78 45W
56 Oshikango 17 9S 16 10 E
70 Oshkosh 44 3N 88 35W
53 Oshogbo 7 48N 4 37 E
19 Osijek 45 34N 18 41 E
23 Osipenko= Berdyansk 46 45N 36 49 E
70 Oskaloosa 41 18N 92 40W
21 Oskarshamn 57 15N 16 27 E
21 Oslo 59 55N 10 45 E
21 Oslofjorden 58 30N 10 0 E
30 Osmaniye 37 5N 36 10 E
14 Osnabrück 52 16N 8 2 E
80 Osorio 29 53S 50 17W
80 Osorno 40 25S 73 0W
11 Oss 51 46N 5 32 E
42 Ossa, Mt., Austral 41 54S 146 0 E
19 Ossa, Mt., Greece 39 47N 22 42 E
68 Ossining 41 9N 73 50W
11 Ostend=Oostende 51 15N 2 50 E
21 Österdalälven, R. 60 33N 15 8 E
21 Östergötlands □ 58 24N 15 34 E
20 Östersund 63 10N 14 38 E
21 Østfold □ 59 25N 11 25 E
14 Ostfriesische Is. 53 45N 7 15 E
18 Ostia 41 43N 12 17 E
15 Ostrava 49 51N 18 18 E
15 Ostróda 53 42N 19 58 E
15 Ostrołęka 53 4N 21 38 E
15 Ostrów Wielkopolski 51 39N 17 49 E
15 Ostrowiec-Swietokrzyski 50 57N 21 23 E
36 Ōsumi-Kaikyō, Str. 30 55N 131 0 E
36 Ōsumi-Shotō, Is. 30 30N 130 45 E
13 Osuna 37 14N 5 8W
68 Oswego 43 29N 76 30W
6 Oswestry 52 52N 3 3W
47 Otago □ 44 45S 169 10 E
36 Ōtake 34 27N 132 25 E
47 Otaki 40 45S 175 10 E
36 Otaru 43 13N 141 0 E
78 Otavalo 0 20N 78 20W
72 Othello 46 53N 119 8W
47 Otira Gorge 42 53S 171 33 E
56 Otjiwarongo 20 30S 16 33 E
47 Otorohanga 38 11S 175 12 E
19 Otranto 40 9N 18 28 E
19 Otranto, C. d' 40 7N 18 30 E
19 Otranto, Str. of 40 15N 18 40 E
36 Ōtsu 42 35N 143 40 E
62 Ottawa, Canada 45 27N 75 42W
70 Ottawa, Ill. 41 20N 88 55W
70 Ottawa, Kans 38 40N 95 10W
61 Ottawa Is. 59 50N 80 0W
62 Ottawa, R. 45 20N 73 58W
65 Otter Rapids 55 42N 104 46W
70 Ottumwa 41 0N 92 25W
53 Otu 8 14N 3 22 E
53 Otukpa 7 9N 7 41 E
53 Oturkpo 7 10N 8 15 E
80 Otway, B. 53 30S 74 0W
46 Otway, C. 38 52S 143 31 E
80 Otway, Seno de 53 5S 71 30W
15 Otwock 52 5N 21 20 E
53 Ouagadougou 12 25N 1 30W
53 Ouahigouya 13 40N 2 25W
50 Ouallene 24 41N 1 11 E
50 Ouargla 31 59N 5 25 E
50 Ouarzazate 30 55N 6 55W
54 Oubangi, R. 0 30S 17 42 E
11 Oudenaarde 50 50N 3 37 E
56 Oudtshoorn 33 35S 22 14 E
53 Oueme, R. 6 29N 2 32 E
12 Ouessant, I. d' 48 28N 5 6W
54 Ouesso 1 37N 16 5 E
50 Ouezzane 34 51N 5 42W
53 Ouidah 6 25N 2 0 E
50 Oujda 34 41N 1 45W
50 Ouled Djellal 34 28N 5 2 E
20 Oulu 65 1N 25 29 E
20 Oulu □ 64 36N 27 20 E
20 Oulujärvi, L. 64 25N 27 0 E
11 Our, R. 49 53N 6 18 E
79 Ouricuri 7 53S 40 5W
79 Ouro Prêto 20 20S 43 30W
42 Ouse 42 25S 146 42 E
7 Ouse, R., E. Sussex 50 47N 0 3 E
6 Ouse, R., N. Yorks 53 42N 0 41W
56 Outjo 20 5S 16 7 E
65 Outlook 51 30N 107 0W
46 Ouyen 35 1S 142 22 E
47 Ovalau, I. 17 40S 178 48 E
80 Ovalle 30 33S 71 18W
56 Ovamboland, Reg. 17 20S 16 30 E
13 Ovar 40 51N 8 40 E
11 Over Flakkee, I. 51 45N 4 5 E
11 Overijssel □ 52 25N 6 35 E
11 Overpelt 51 12N 5 20 E
13 Oviedo 43 25N 5 50W
47 Owaka 46 27S 169 40 E
36 Owase 34 7N 136 5 E
70 Owatonna 44 3N 93 17W
52 Owen Falls 0 30N 33 5 E
62 Owen Sound 44 35N 80 55W
54 Owendo 0 17N 9 30 E
68 Owensboro 37 40N 87 5W
53 Owerri 5 29N 7 0 E
53 Owo 7 18N 5 30 E
68 Owosso 43 0N 84 10W
21 Oxelösund 58 43N 17 15 E
7 Oxford, U.K. 51 45N 1 15W
69 Oxford, N.C. 36 19N 78 36W
7 Oxford □ 51 45N 1 15W
65 Oxford House 54 46N 95 16W
73 Oxnard 34 10N 119 14W
36 Oyama 36 18N 139 48 E
54 Oyem 1 37N 11 35 E
25 Oymyakon 63 25N 143 10 E
53 Oyo 7 46N 3 56 E
53 Oyo □ 8 0N 3 30 E
35 Ozamiz 8 15N 123 50 E
69 Ozark 31 29N 85 39W
58 Ozark Plat. 37 20N 91 40W
70 Ozarks, L. of the 38 10N 93 0W

P

34 Pa Sak, R. 15 30N 101 0 E
37 Paan 30 0N 99 3 E
33 Pa-an 16 45N 97 40 E
56 Paarl 33 45S 18 46 E
33 Pabna 24 1N 89 18 E
78 Pacaraima, Sa. 5 0N 63 0W
78 Pacasmayo 7 20S 79 35W
32 Pachpadra 25 57N 72 10 E
74 Pachuca 20 10N 98 40W
73 Pacific Groves 37 36N 121 58W
2 Pacific Ocean 10 0N 140 0W
35 Padalarang 7 50S 107 30 E
34 Padang 1 0S 100 20 E
65 Paddockwood 53 30N 105 30W
14 Paderborn 51 42N 8 44 E
60 Padlei 62 10N 97 5W
61 Padloping Island 67 0N 63 0W
18 Pádova 45 24N 11 52 E
7 Padstow 50 33N 4 57W
18 Padua=Pádova 45 24N 11 52 E
68 Paducah, Ky. 37 0N 88 40W
71 Paducah, Tes. 34 3N 100 16W
47 Paeroa 37 23S 175 41 E
18 Pag, I. 44 50N 15 0 E
35 Pagadian 7 55N 123 30 E
* 49 Pagalu, I. 1 35S 3 35 E
73 Page 47 11N 97 37W
31 Paghman 34 36N 68 57 E
47 Pago Pago 14 16S 170 43W
73 Pagosa Springs 37 16N 107 1W
32 Pagwa River 50 2N 85 14W
66 Pahala 20 25N 156 0W
47 Pahiatua 40 27S 175 50 E
38 Paicheng 45 40N 122 52 E
7 Paignton 50 26N 3 33W
68 Painesville 41 42N 81 18W
62 Paint Hills= Nouveau Comptoir 53 2N 78 55W
73 Painted Des. 36 40N 112 0W
8 Paisley 55 51N 4 27W
78 Paita 5 5S 81 0W
38 Paiyin 36 45N 104 4 E
34 Pak Phanang 8 21N 100 12 E
34 Pakanbaru 0 30N 101 15 E
39 Pakhoi 21 30N 109 10 E
32 Pakistan ■ 30 0N 70 0 E
33 Pakokku 21 30N 95 0 E
39 Pakongchow 23 50N 113 0 E
34 Pakse 15 5N 105 52 E
31 Paktya □ 33 0N 69 15 E
13 Palamós 41 50N 3 10 E
25 Palana 59 10N 160 10 E
34 Palangkaraya 2 16S 113 56 E
32 Palanpur 24 10N 72 25 E
56 Palapye 22 30S 27 7 E
69 Palatka 29 40N 81 40W
† 35 Palau Is. 7 30N 134 30 E
34 Palauk 13 10N 98 40 E
34 Palawan, I. 10 0N 119 0 E
34 Palawan Is. 10 0N 115 0 E
32 Palayancottai 8 45N 77 45 E
35 Paleleh 1 10N 121 50 E
34 Palembang 3 0S 104 50 E
13 Palencia 42 1N 4 34W
18 Palermo 38 8N 13 20 E
71 Palestine 31 42N 95 35W
33 Paletwa 21 30N 92 50 E
32 Palghat 10 46N 76 42 E
32 Pali 25 50N 73 20 E
* 53 Palimé 6 57N 0 37 E
70 Palisade 40 35N 101 10W
32 Palitana 21 32N 71 49 E
32 Palk B. 9 30N 79 30 E
32 Palk Str. 10 0N 80 0 E
42 Palm, Is. 18 40S 146 35 E
69 Palm Beach 26 46N 80 0W
73 Palm Springs 33 51N 116 35W
57 Palma, Moz. 10 46S 40 29 E
13 Palma, Spain 39 33N 2 39 E
75 Palma Soriano 20 15N 76 0W
79 Palmares 8 41S 35 36W
50 Palmas, C. 4 27N 7 46W
18 Palmas, G. di 39 0N 8 30 E
79 Palmeira dos Indios 9 25S 36 30W
60 Palmer 61 35N 149 10W
2 Palmer Ld. 73 0S 60 0W
47 Palmerston 45 29S 170 43 E
47 Palmerston North 40 21S 175 39 E
18 Palmi 38 21N 15 51 E
78 Palmira, Col. 3 32N 76 16W
2 Palmyra Is. 5 52N 162 5W
73 Palo Alto 37 25N 122 8W
35 Palopo 3 0S 120 16 E
13 Palos, C. de 37 38N 0 40W
30 Palu 38 45N 40 0 E
53 Pama 11 19N 0 44 E
35 Pamekason 7 10S 113 29 E
38 Pamiencheng 43 16N 124 4 E
24 Pamir, Mts. 38 0N 73 30 E
69 Pamlico Sd. 35 20N 76 0W
71 Pampa 35 35N 100 58W
35 Pampanua 4 22S 120 14 E
80 Pampas, Reg. 34 0S 64 0W
78 Pamplona, Col. 7 23N 72 39W
13 Pamplona, Spain 42 48N 1 38W
32 Panaji 15 25N 73 50 E
74 Panama 9 0N 79 25W
75 Panamá ■ 8 48N 79 55W
75 Panamá, B. de 8 50N 79 20W
75 Panamá, G. de 8 4N 79 20W
74 Panama Canal 9 10N 79 56W
69 Panama City 30 10N 105 41W
35 Panarukan 7 40S 113 52 E
35 Panay, I. 11 10N 122 30 E
35 Panay G. 11 0N 122 30 E
19 Pančevo 44 52N 20 41 E
32 Pandharpur 17 41N 75 20 E
24 Panfilov 44 30N 80 0 E
33 Pang-Long 23 11N 98 45 E
52 Pangani 5 25S 38 58 E
32 Panjinad Barr. 29 22N 71 15 E
39 Pangfou=Pengpu 33 0N 117 25 E
34 Pangkalanberandan 4 1N 98 20 E
34 Pangkalansusu 4 2N 98 42 E
61 Pangnirtung 66 8N 65 44W
73 Panguitch 37 52N 112 30W
33 Pangyang 22 10N 98 45 E
46 Panitya 35 15S 141 0 E
31 Panjao 34 21N 67 0 E
32 Panjgur 27 0N 64 5 E
32 Panjim=Panaji 15 25N 73 50 E
34 Pankalpinang 2 0S 106 0 E
53 Pankshin 9 25N 9 25 E
79 Panorama 21 21S 51 51W
38 Panshih 42 55N 126 3 E
18 Pantellaria, I. 36 52N 12 0 E
74 Pánuco 22 0N 98 25W
53 Panyam 9 27N 9 8 E
38 Paochang 41 46N 115 30 E
39 Paoki 34 25N 107 15 E
37 Paoshan 25 7N 99 9 E
38 Paoting 38 50N 115 30 E
38 Paotow 40 35N 110 3 E
39 Paoying 33 10N 119 20 E
15 Papá 47 22N 17 30 E
75 Papagayo, G. del 10 4N 85 50W
47 Papakura 37 45S 174 59 E
74 Papantla 20 45N 97 41W
34 Papar 5 45N 116 0 E
3 Papua New Guinea ■ 8 0S 145 0 E
79 Pará=Belém 1 20S 48 30W
79 Pará □ 3 20S 52 0W
79 Paracatú 17 10S 46 50W

* Renamed Annobon
† Renamed Belau

* Renamed Kpalimé

Parachilna Piedras Blancas Pt.

43 Parachilna 31 10s 138 21 E
72 Paradise 47 27N 114 54w
71 Paragould 36 5N 90 30w
78 Paraguaipoa 11 21N 71 57w
78 Paraguaná, Penide 12 0N 70 0w
80 Paraguari 25 36s 57 0w
80 Paraguay ■ 23 0s 57 0w
80 Paraguay, R. 27 18s 58 38w
79 Paraiba= João Pessoa 7 10s 34 52w
79 Paraiba □ 7 0s 36 0w
21 Parainen 60 18N 22 18 E
53 Parakou 9 25N 2 40 E
79 Paramaribo 5 50N 55 10w
80 Paraná, Arg. 32 0s 60 30w
79 Paraná, Brazil 12 30s 47 40w
80 Paraná, R. 33 43s 59 15w
80 Paraná □ 24 30s 51 0w
80 Paranaguá 25 30s 48 30w
79 Paranapanema, R. 22 40s 53 9w
80 Paranapiacaba, Sa. do 24 31s 48 35w
79 Paratinga 12 40s 43 10w
43 Paratoo 32 42s 139 22 E
32 Parbhani 19 8N 76 52 E
28 Pardes Hanna 32 28N 34 57 E
14 Pardubice 50 3N 15 45 E
35 Pare 7 43s 112 12 E
52 Pare Mts. 4 0s 37 45 E
25 Paren 62 45N 163 0 E
62 Parent 47 55N 74 35w
35 Parepare 4 0s 119 40 E
55 Parfuri 22 28s 31 17 E
22 Parguba 62 58N 34 25 E
75 Paria, G. de 10 20N 62 0w
78 Pariaguan 8 51N 64 43w
34 Pariaman 0 47s 100 11 E
35 Parigi 0 50s 120 5 E
78 Parika 6 50N 58 20w
15 Paringul-Mare, Mt. 45 20N 23 37 E
79 Parintins 2 40s 56 50w
62 Paris, Canada 43 20N 80 25w
12 Paris, Fr. 48 50N 2 20 E
69 Paris, Tenn. 36 20N 88 20w
71 Paris, Tex. 33 40N 95 30w
12 Paris □ 48 0N 2 20 E
72 Park City 40 42N 111 35w
72 Park Ra. 40 0N 106 30w
57 Park Rynie 30 25s 30 35 E
20 Parkano 62 5N 23 0 E
73 Parker, Ariz 34 8N 114 16w
70 Parker, S.D. 43 25N 97 7w
68 Parkersburg 39 18N 81 31w
65 Parkerview 51 28N 103 18w
46 Parkes 33 9s 148 11 E
64 Parksville 49 20N 124 21w
18 Parma, Italy 44 50N 10 20 E
72 Parma, U.S.A. 43 49N 116 59w
79 Parnaguá 10 10s 44 10w
79 Parnaíba, Piauí 3 0s 41 40w
79 Parnaiba, São Paulo 19 34s 51 14w
79 Parnaiba, R. 3 0s 41 50w
19 Parnassós, Mt. 38 17N 21 30 E
22 Pärnu 58 12N 24 33 E
19 Páros, I. 37 5N 25 12 E
73 Parowan 37 54N 112 56w
80 Parral 36 10s 72 0w
46 Parramatta 33 48s 151 1 E
74 Parras 25 30N 102 20w
7 Parrett, R. 51 13N 3 1w
63 Parrsboro 45 30N 64 10w
58 Parry Is. 77 0N 110 0w
62 Parry Sd. 42 20N 80 0w
71 Parsons 37 20N 95 10w
33 Parvatipuram 18 50N 83 25 E
31 Parwan □ 35 0N 69 0 E
57 Parys 26 52s 27 29 E
71 Pasadena, Calif. 34 5N 118 0w
73 Pasadena, Tex. 29 45N 95 14w
78 Pasaje 3 10s 79 40w
71 Pascagoula 30 30N 88 30w
72 Pasco 46 10N 119 0w
12 Pas-de-Calais □ 50 30N 2 30 E
34 Pasir Mas 6 2N 102 8 E
35 Pasirian 8 13s 113 8 E
45 Pasley, C. 33 52s 123 35 E
80 Paso de Indios 43 55s 69 0w
73 Paso Robles 35 40N 120 45w
63 Paspébiac 48 3N 65 17w
9 Passage West 51 52N 8 20w
14 Passau 48 34N 13 27 E
18 Passero, C. 36 42N 15 8 E
80 Passo Fundo 28 10s 52 30w
79 Passos 20 45s 46 29w
78 Pasto 1 13N 77 17w
35 Pasuruan 7 40s 112 53 E
76 Patagonia, Reg. 45 0s 69 0w
68 Patchogue 40 46N 73 1w
47 Patea 39 45s 174 30 E
53 Pategi 8 50N 5 45 E
56 Patensie 33 46s 24 49 E
18 Paterno 37 34N 14 53 E
68 Paterson 40 55N 74 10w
32 Pathankot 32 18N 75 45 E
72 Pathfinder Res. 42 0N 107 0w
32 Patan 23 52N 72 4 E
35 Patani 0 20N 128 50 E
38 Pataokiang 41 58N 126 30 E
32 Patiala 30 23N 76 26 E
33 Patkai Bum, Mts. 27 0N 95 30 E
19 Patmos, I. 37 21N 26 36 E
33 Patna 25 35N 85 18 E
80 Patos, L. dos 31 20s 51 0w
79 Patos de Minas 18 35s 46 32w
19 Pátrai 38 14N 21 47 E
19 Pátraikos Kól. 38 17N 21 30 E
79 Patrocínio 18 57s 47 0w
34 Pattani 6 48N 101 15 E
18 Patti 31 17N 74 54 E
75 Patuca, R. 15 50N 84 18w
74 Pátzcuaro 19 30N 101 40w
12 Pau 43 19N 0 25w
12 Pauillac 45 11N 0 46w
33 Pauk 21 55N 94 30 E
79 Paulistana 8 9s 41 9w
79 Paulo Afonso 9 21s 38 15w
57 Paulpietersburg 27 23s 30 50 E
71 Paul's Valley 34 40N 97 17w
18 Pavia 45 10N 9 10 E
24 Pavlodar 52 33N 77 0 E
23 Pavlograd 48 30N 35 52 E
22 Pavlovo, Gorkiy 55 58N 43 5 E
25 Pavlovo, Yakut A.S.S.R. 63 5N 115 25 E
23 Pavlovsk 50 26N 40 5 E
68 Pawtucket 41 51N 71 22w
34 Payakumbah 0 20s 100 35 E
72 Payette 44 0N 117 0w
61 Payne Bay=Bellin 60 0N 70 0w
61 Payne L. 59 30N 74 30w
45 Paynes Find 29 15s 117 42 E
80 Paysandú 32 19s 58 8w
72 Payson 40 8N 111 41w
19 Pazardzhik 42 12N 24 20 E
72 Pe Ell 46 30N 122 59w
65 Peace, R. 59 30N 111 30w
64 Peace River 56 15N 117 18w
64 Peace River, Res. 55 40N 123 40w
6 Peak, The., Mt. 53 24N 1 53w
42 Peak Downs Mine 22 17s 148 11 E
46 Peak Hill 32 39s 148 11 E
43 Peake 35 25s 140 0 E
66 Pearl City 21 21N 158 0w
66 Pearl Harbor 21 20N 158 0w
56 Pearston 32 33s 25 7 E
57 Pebane 17 10s 38 8 E
78 Pebas 3 10s 71 55w
19 Peć 42 40N 20 17 E
22 Pechenga 69 30N 31 25 E
22 Pechora 65 15N 57 0 E
22 Pechora, R. 68 13N 54 10 E
22 Pechorskaya Guba 68 40N 54 0 E
71 Pecos 31 25N 103 35w
71 Pecos, R. 29 42N 101 22w
15 Pécs 46 5N 18 15 E
79 Pedra Asul 16 1s 41 16w
75 Pedregal 8 22N 82 27w
79 Pedro Afonso 9 0s 48 10w
79 Pedro Juan Caballero 22 30s 55 40w
8 Peebles 55 40N 3 12w
68 Peekskill 41 18N 73 57w
6 Peel 54 14N 4 40w
60 Peel, R. 67 0N 135 0w
47 Pegasus, B. 43 20s 173 10 E
33 Pegu 17 20N 96 29 E
33 Pegu Yoma, Mts. 19 0N 96 0 E
39 Peh Kiang, R. 23 10N 113 10 E
38 Pehan 48 17N 120 31 E
39 Pehpei 29 44N 106 29 E
80 Pehuajó 36 0s 62 0w
38 Peiping 39 45N 116 25 E
79 Peixe 12 0s 48 40w
35 Pekalongan 6 53s 109 40 E
70 Pekin 40 35N 89 40w
38 Peking=Peiping 39 45N 116 25 E
35 Pelabuhan Ratu, Teluk, G. 7 0s 106 32 E
35 Pelabuhanratu 7 5s 106 30 E
15 Peleaga, Mt. 45 22N 22 55 E
35 Peleng, I. 1 20s 123 30 E
65 Pelican Narrows 55 12N 102 55 E
64 Pelican Portage 55 51N 113 0w
65 Pelican Rapids 52 38N 100 42 E
60 Pelly, R. 62 47N 137 19w
61 Pelly Bay 68 53N 89 51w
19 Peloponnese□= Pelopónnisos □ 37 40N 22 15 E
19 Pelopónnisos □ 37 40N 22 15 E
18 Peloro, C. 38 15N 15 40 E
47 Pelorus, Sd. 40 59s 173 59 E
80 Pelotas 31 42s 52 23w
12 Pelvoux, Massif du 44 52N 6 20 E
35 Pemalang 6 53s 109 23 E
34 Pematang 0 12s 102 4 E
34 Pematangsiantar 2 57N 99 5 E
55 Pemba 16 31s 27 22 E
52 Pemba I. 5 0s 39 45 E
45 Pemberton, Australia 34 30s 116 0 E
64 Pemberton, Canada 50 25N 122 50w
62 Pembroke, Canada 45 50N 77 15w
47 Pembroke, N.Z.= Wanaka 44 33s 169 9 E
7 Pembroke, U.K. 51 41N 4 57w
34 Penang□= Pinang □ 5 25N 100 15 E
79 Penápolis 21 24s 50 4w
13 Peñas, C. de 43 42N 5 52w
80 Penas, G. de 47 0s 75 0w
50 Pendembu 8 6N 10 45w
72 Pendleton 45 35N 118 50w
79 Penedo 10 15s 36 36w
62 Penetanguishene 44 50N 79 55w
32 Penganga, R. 19 53N 79 9 E
39 Penghu, I. 23 30N 119 30 E
38 Penglai 37 49N 120 47 E
39 Pengpu 33 0N 117 25 E
42 Penguin 41 8s 146 6 E
57 Penhalonga 18 54s 32 40 E
13 Peniche 39 19N 9 22w
8 Peniciuk 55 50N 3 14w
38 Penki 41 20N 132 50 E
68 Penn Yan 42 40N 77 3w
6 Pennine Ra. 54 50N 2 20w
68 Pennsylvania □ 40 50N 78 0w
64 Penny 53 58N 121 1w
69 Penobscot, R. 44 30N 68 50w
46 Penola 37 25s 140 47 E
75 Penonomé 8 37N 80 25w
2 Penrhyn Is. 9 0s 150 30w
46 Penrith, Australia 33 43s 150 38 E
6 Penrith, U.K. 54 40N 2 45w
69 Pensacola 30 30N 87 10w
64 Penticton 49 30N 119 30w
42 Pentland 20 32s 145 25 E
8 Pentland Firth 58 43N 3 10w
8 Pentland Hills 55 48N 3 25w
6 Pen-y-Ghent, Mt. 54 10N 2 15w
22 Penza 53 15N 45 5 E
7 Penzance 50 7N 5 32w
70 Peoria 40 40N 89 40w
34 Perabumilih 3 27s 104 15 E
12 Perche, Reg. 48 30N 1 0 E
44 Percival Lakes 21 25s 125 0 E
42 Percy, Is. 21 39s 150 16 E
12 Perdu, Mt. 42 40N 0 1 E
78 Pereira 4 49N 75 43w
23 Perekop 46 0N 33 0 E
45 Perenjori 29 26s 116 16 E
23 Pereyaslav khmelnitskiy 50 3N 31 28 E
74 Pérez, I. 22 40N 89 30w
80 Pergamino 33 52s 60 30w
63 Péribonca, R. 48 45N 72 5w
80 Perico 24 25s 65 10w
12 Perigord, Reg. 45 0N 0 40 E
12 Périgueux 45 10N 0 42 E
29 Perim, I. 12 39N 43 25 E
22 Perm 58 0N 57 10 E
79 Pernambuco= Recife 8 0s 35 0w
79 Pernambuco □ 8 0s 37 0w
19 Pernik 42 36N 23 2 E
45 Peron, C. 25 30s 113 30 E
12 Perpignan 42 42N 2 53 E
70 Perry, Iowa 41 48N 94 5w
71 Perry, Okla. 36 20N 97 20w
31 Persia=Iran ■ 35 0N 50 0 E
* 31 Persian G. 27 0N 50 0 E
45 Perth, Australia 31 57s 115 52 E
62 Perth, Canada 44 55N 76 20w
8 Perth, U.K. 56 24N 3 27w
68 Perth Amboy 40 31N 74 16w
78 Peru ■ 8 0s 75 0w
70 Peru, Ill. 41 18N 89 12w
68 Peru, Ind. 40 42N 86 0w
18 Perúgia 43 6N 12 24 E
23 Pervomaysk 48 5N 30 55 E
24 Pervouralsk 56 55N 60 0 E
18 Pésaro 43 55N 12 53 E
18 Pescara 42 28N 14 13 E
32 Peshawar 34 2N 71 37 E

* *Renamed The Gulf*

* 32 Peshawar □ 35 0N 72 50 E
79 Pesqueira 8 20s 36 42w
28 Petah Tiqwa 32 6N 34 53 E
72 Petuluma 38 13N 122 45w
11 Petange 49 33N 5 55 E
55 Petauke 14 14s 31 12 E
62 Petawawa 45 54N 77 17w
74 Petén Itzá, L. 16 58N 89 50w
62 Peterbell 48 36N 83 21w
43 Peterborough, Australia 32 58s 138 51 E
62 Peterborough, Can. 44 20N 78 20w
7 Peterborough, U.K. 52 35N 1 14w
8 Peterhead 57 30N 1 49w
6 Peterlee 54 45N 1 18w
64 Petersburg, Alas. 56 50N 133 0w
68 Petersburg, Va. 37 17N 77 26w
63 Petit Cap 48 58N 63 58w
75 Petit Goâve 18 27N 72 51w
12 Petit St. Bernard, Col du 45 41N 6 53 E
63 Petitcodiac 45 57N 65 11w
63 Petite Saguenay 47 59N 70 1w
32 Petlad 22 30N 72 45 E
47 Petone 41 13s 174 53 E
68 Petoskey 45 21N 84 55w
19 Petrich 41 24N 23 13 E
79 Petrolandia 9 5s 38 20w
62 Petrolia 52 54N 82 9w
79 Petrolina 9 24s 40 30w
24 Petropavlovsk 55 0N 69 0 E
25 Petropavlovsk-kamchatskiy 53 16N 159 0 E
79 Petrópolis 22 33s 43 9w
19 Petrovaradin 45 16N 19 55 E
22 Petrovsk 52 22N 45 19 E
25 Petrovsk-Zdbaykalskiy 51 17N 108 50 E
22 Petrozavodsk 61 41N 34 20 E
56 Petrusburg 29 8s 25 27 E
34 Peureulak 4 48N 97 45 E
25 Pevek 69 15N 171 0 E
14 Pforzheim 48 53N 8 43 E
32 Phagwara 31 13N 75 47 E
55 Phala 23 45s 26 50 E
32 Phalodi 27 12N 72 24 E
34 Phan Rang 11 34N 108 59 E
34 Phan Thiet 11 1N 108 9 E
34 Phangan, Ko 9 45N 100 4 E
34 Phangna 8 28N 98 30 E
34 Phanh Bho Ho Chi Minh 10 58N 106 40 E
37 Pharo Dzong 27 45N 89 14 E
34 Phatthalung 7 39N 100 6 E
69 Phenix City 32 30N 85 0w
34 Phetchabun 16 24N 101 11 E
34 Phetchaburi 16 25N 101 8 E
68 Philadelphia 40 0N 75 10w
19 Philippi 41 0N 24 19 E
35 Philippines ■ 12 0N 123 0 E
56 Philippolis 30 19s 25 13 E
56 Philipstown 30 26s 24 29 E
46 Phillip, I. 38 30s 145 12 E
43 Phillott 27 53s 145 50 E
72 Philomath 44 28N 123 21w
34 Phitsanulok 16 50N 100 12 E
34 Phnom Dangrek Ra. 14 15N 105 0 E
34 Phnom Penh 11 33N 104 55 E
73 Phoenix 33 30N 112 10w
2 Phoenix Is. 3 30s 172 0w
37 Phong Saly 21 41N 102 6 E
34 Phra Nakhon Si Ayutthaya 14 25N 100 30 E
34 Phu Quoc, I. 10 15N 104 0 E
34 Phuket 8 0N 98 28 E
34 Phuoc Le 10 30N 107 10 E
18 Piacenza 45 2N 9 42 E
43 Pialba 25 20s 152 45 E
43 Pian Creek 30 2s 148 12 E
15 Piatra Neamţ 46 56N 26 22 E
79 Piani □ 7 0s 43 0w
12 Picardie, Reg. 50 0N 2 15 E
12 Picardy, Reg.= Picardie, Reg. 50 0N 2 15 E
71 Picayune 30 40N 89 40w
80 Pichilemú 34 23s 72 2 E
6 Pickering 54 15N 0 46w
62 Pickle Crow 51 30N 90 0w
80 Pico Truncado 46 40s 68 10w
46 Picton, Australia 34 12s 150 34 E
62 Picton, Canada 44 1N 77 9w
47 Picton, N.Z. 41 18s 174 3 E
63 Pictou 45 41N 62 42w
64 Picture Butte 49 55N 112 45w
80 Picún Leufú 39 30s 69 5w
32 Pidurutalagala, Mt. 7 10N 80 50 E
73 Piedras Blancas Pt. 35 45N 121 18w

* *Now part of North West Frontier*

74 Piedras Negras 28 35N 100 35W
18 Piermonte □ 45 0N 7 30E
70 Pierre 44 23N 100 20W
57 Piet Retief 27 1S 30 50E
57 Pietermaritzburg 29 35S 30 25E
57 Pietersburg 23 54S 29 25E
15 Pietrosu, Mt. 47 8N 25 11E
15 Pietrosul, Mt. 47 36N 24 38E
62 Pigeon River 48 1N 89 42W
80 Pigüé 37 36S 62 25W
56 Piketberg 32 55S 18 40E
68 Pikeville 37 30N 82 30W
14 Piła 53 10N 16 48E
80 Pilar 26 50S 58 10W
79 Pilar 14 30S 49 45W
80 Pilcomayo, R. 25 21S 57 42W
32 Pilibhit 28 40N 78 50E
15 Pilica, R. 51 52N 21 17E
19 Pilos 36 55N 21 42E
14 Pilsen=Plzeń 49 45N 13 22E
14 Pilzen=Plzeń 49 45N 13 22E
73 Pima 32 54N 109 50W
43 Pimba 31 18S 136 46E
34 Pinang, I. 5 25N 100 15E
75 Pinar del Rio 22 26N 83 40W
65 Pinawa 50 15N 95 50W
64 Pincher Creek 49 30N 113 35W
15 Pinczów 50 32N 20 35E
45 Pindar 28 30S 115 47E
53 Pindiga 9 58N 10 53E
19 Pindos Óros 40 0N 21 0E
19 Pindus Mts.=
Pindos Óros 40 0N 21 0E
63 Pine, C. 46 37N 53 30W
71 Pine Bluff 34 10N 92 0W
44 Pine Creek 13 49S 131 49E
65 Pine Falls 50 51N 96 11W
64 Pine Point 60 50N 114 40W
22 Pinega, R. 64 8N 41 54E
42 Pinehill 23 38S 146 57E
18 Pinerolo 44 47N 7 21E
18 Pinetown 29 48S 30 54E
71 Pineville 31 22N 92 30W
34 Ping, R. 15 42N 100 9E
45 Pingaring 32 40S 118 32E
45 Pingelly 32 29S 116 59E
39 Pingkiang 28 45N 113 30E
38 Pingliang 35 32N 106 50E
39 Pingsiang 22 2N 106 55E
39 Pingtingshan 33 43N 113 28E
39 Pingtung 22 38N 120 30E
38 Pingyao 37 12N 112 10E
13 Pinhel 40 18N 7 0W
38 Pinhsien 35 10N 108 10E
19 Pinios, R. 39 54N 22 45E
45 Pinjarra 32 37S 115 52E
38 Pinkiang=
Harbin 45 46N 126 51E
46 Pinnaroo 35 13S 140 56E
75 Pinos, I. de 21 40N 82 40W
73 Pinos, Pt. 36 50N 121 57W
35 Pinrang 3 46S 119 34E
22 Pinsk 52 10N 26 8E
65 Pinto Butte, Mt. 49 22N 107 25W
45 Pintumba 31 50S 132 18E
39 Pinyang 23 12N 108 35E
22 Pinyug 60 5N 48 0E
73 Pioche 38 0N 114 35N
18 Piombino 42 54N 10 30E
15 Piotrków
Trybunalski 51 23N 19 43E
70 Pipestone 44 0N 96 20W
80 Pipinas 35 30N 57 19E
63 Pipmuacan,Rés. 49 40N 70 25W
44 Pippingarra 20 27S 118 42E
68 Piqua 40 10N 84 10W
79 Piracicaba 22 45S 47 30W
79 Piracuruca 3 50S 41 50W
19 Piraeus=
Piraiévs 37 57N 23 42E
19 Piraiévs 37 57N 23 42E
80 Pirané 25 44S 59 7W
19 Pírgos 37 40N 21 25E
79 Piripiri 4 15S 41 46W
35 Piru 3 3S 128 12E
18 Pisa 43 43N 10 23E
78 Pisagua 19 40S 70 15W
18 Pisciotta 40 7N 15 12E
78 Pisco 13 50S 76 5W
14 Pisek 49 19N 14 10E
18 Pistóia 43 57N 10 53E
2 Pitcairn I. 25 5S 130 5W
20 Pitea 65 20N 21 25E
15 Piteşti 44 52N 24 54E
33 Pithapuram 17 10N 82 15E
45 Pithara 30 20S 116 35E
8 Pitlochry 56 43N 3 43W
72 Pittsburg, Calif. 38 1N 121 50W
71 Pittsburg, Kans. 37 21N 94 43W
68 Pittsburgh, Pa. 40 25N 79 55W
71 Pittsburgh, Tex. 32 59N 94 58W
68 Pittsfield 42 28N 73 17W
68 Pittston 41 19N 75 50W
43 Pittsworth 27 41S 151 37E
78 Piura 5 5S 80 45W
18 Pizzo 38 44N 16 10E
63 Placentia 47 20N 54 0W
72 Placerville 38 47N 120 51W
75 Placetas 22 15N 79 44W
68 Plainfield 40 37N 74 28W
71 Plainview 34 10N 101 40W
71 Plaquemine 30 20N 91 15W
13 Plasencia 40 3N 6 8W
63 Plaster Rock 46 53N 67 22W
80 Plata, R. de la 34 45S 57 30W
80 Plate, R.=
Plata, R. de la 34 35S 57 30W
53 Plateau □ 8 30N 8 45E
78 Plato 9 47N 74 47W
70 Platte, R. 41 4N 95 53W
70 Platteville 40 18N 104 47W
68 Plattsburgh 44 41N 73 30W
70 Plattsmouth 41 0N 96 0W
14 Plauen 50 29N 12 9E
68 Pleasantville 39 25N 74 30W
47 Plenty, B. of 37 45S 177 0E
22 Plesetsk 62 40N 40 10E
63 Plessisville 46 14N 71 46W
19 Pleven 43 26N 24 37E
15 Płock 52 32N 19 40E
15 Ploieşti 44 57N 26 5E
19 Plovdiv 42 8N 24 44E
57 Plumtree 20 27S 27 55E
75 Plymouth,
Montserrat 16 42N 62 13W
7 Plymouth, U.K. 50 23N 4 9W
68 Plymouth, Ind. 41 20N 86 19W
14 Plzeň 49 45N 13 22E
53 Pô 11 10N 1 9W
18 Po, R. 44 57N 12 4E
38 Po Hai, G. 38 40N 119 0E
53 Pobé 6 58N 2 41E
25 Pobedino 49 51N 142 49E
72 Pocatello 42 50N 112 25W
79 Poços de
Caldas 21 50S 46 45W
25 Podkamenndya
Tunguska 61 50N 90 26E
22 Podolsk 55 30N 37 30E
22 Podporozhny 60 55N 34 2E
56 Pofadder 29 10S 19 22E
38 Pohang 36 8N 129 23E
62 Point Edward 43 10N 82 30W
54 Pointe-Noire 4 48S 12 0E
75 Pointe-à-Pitre 16 10N 61 30W
12 Poitiers 46 35N 0 20E
12 Poitou, Reg. 46 25N 0 15W
32 Pokaran 26 55N 71 55E
43 Pokataroo 29 30S 148 34E
54 Poko 3 7N 26 52E
38 Pokotu 48 46N 121 54E
25 Pokrovsk 61 29N 129 6E
73 Polacca 35 52N 110 25W
15 Poland ■ 52 0N 20 0E
80 Polcura 37 17S 71 43W
7 Polden Hills 51 7N 2 50W
38 Poli 8 34N 12 54E
35 Polillo Is. 14 56N 122 0E
19 Poljanovgrad 42 35N 26 58E
32 Pollachi 10 35N 77 0E
24 Polnovat 63 50N 66 5E
22 Polotsk 55 30N 28 50E
72 Polson 47 45N 114 12W
23 Poltava 49 35N 34 35E
22 Polyarny 69 8N 33 20E
79 Pombal, Brazil 6 55S 37 50W
13 Pombal, Port. 39 55N 8 40W
73 Pomona 34 2N 117 49W
69 Pompano 26 12N 80 6W
71 Ponca City 36 40N 97 5W
75 Ponce 18 1N 66 37W
61 Pond Inlet 72 30N 75 0W
32 Pondicherry 11 59N 79 50E
57 Pondoland 31 10S 29 30E
13 Ponferrada 42 32N 6 35W
33 Ponnyadaung, Mts. 22 0N 94 10E
22 Ponoi 67 0N 41 0E
64 Ponoka 52 35N 113 40W
35 Ponorogo 7 52S 111 29E
63 Pont Lafrance 47 40N 64 58W
80 Ponta Grossa 25 0S 50 10W
12 Pontarlier 46 54N 6 20E
71 Pontchartrain, L. 30 12N 90 0W
79 Ponte Nova 20 25S 42 54W
18 Pontedera 43 40N 10 37E
6 Pontefract 53 42N 1 19W
65 Ponteix 49 46N 107 29W
13 Pontevedra 42 26N 8 40W
70 Pontiac, Ill. 40 50N 88 40W
68 Pontiac, Mich. 42 40N 83 20W
34 Pontianak 0 3S 109 15E
30 Pontine Mts.=
Karadeniz
Dağlari, Mts. 41 30N 35 0E
7 Pontypool 51 42N 3 1W
7 Ponytpridd 51 36N 3 21S
18 Ponziane, Ís. 40 55N 13 0E
43 Poochera 32 43S 134 51E
7 Poole 50 42N 2 2W
32 Poona=Pune 18 29N 73 57E
78 Poopó, L. 18 30S 67 35W
45 Popanyinning 32 40S 117 2E
78 Popayán 2 27N 76 36W
11 Poperinge 50 51N 2 42E
25 Popigay 71 55N 110 47E
71 Poplar Bluff 36 45N 90 22W
74 Popocatepetl, Mt. 19 10N 98 40W
32 Porbandar 21 44N 69 43E
60 Porcupine, R. 66 35N 145 15W
21 Pori 61 29N 21 48E
20 Porjus 66 57N 19 50E
21 Porkkala 59 59N 24 26E
78 Porlamar 10 57N 63 51W
25 Poronaysk 49 20N 143 0E
43 Port Adelaide 34 46S 138 30E
64 Port Alberni 49 15N 124 50W
32 Port Albert
Victor 21 0N 71 30E
63 Port Alfred, Canada 48 18N 70 53W
56 Port Alfred, S. Afr. 33 6S 26 55E
64 Port Alice 50 25N 127 25W
68 Port Allegany 41 49N 78 17W
72 Port Angeles 48 0N 123 30W
62 Port Arthur,
Canada=
Thunder Bay 48 25N 89 10W
38 Port Arthur, China=
Lushun 38 48N 121 16E
71 Port Arthur,
U.S.A. 30 0N 94 0W
62 Port Arthur=
Thunder Bay 48 25N 89 10W
43 Port Augusta 32 30S 137 50E
63 Port aux Basques 47 32N 59 8W
57 Port-Bergé Vaovao 15 33S 47 40E
13 Port Bou 42 25N 3 9E
43 Port Broughton 33 37S 137 56E
33 Port Canning 22 18N 88 40E
63 Port Cartier 50 10N 66 50W
47 Port Chalmers 45 49S 170 30E
68 Port Chester 41 0N 73 41W
62 Port Colborne 42 50N 79 10W
64 Port Coquitlam 49 20N 122 45W
43 Port Darwin 12 18S 130 55E
75 Port de Paix 19 50N 72 50W
34 Port Dickson 2 30N 101 49E
42 Port Douglas 16 30S 145 30E
64 Port Edward 54 14N 130 18W
62 Port Elgin 44 25N 81 25W
56 Port Elizabeth 33 58S 25 40E
8 Port Ellen 55 39N 6 12W
6 Port Erin 54 5N 4 45W
50 Port Étienne=
Nouadhibou 21 0N 17 0W
46 Port Fairy 38 22S 142 12E
54 Port-Gentil 0 47S 8 40E
8 Port Glasgow 55 57N 4 40W
53 Port Harcourt 4 43N 7 5E
64 Port Hardy 50 41N 127 30W
61 Port Harrison=
Inoucdouac 58 25N 78 15W
44 Port Hedland 20 25S 118 35E
68 Port Henry 44 0N 73 30W
63 Port Hood 46 0N 61 32W
62 Port Hope 44 0N 78 20W
68 Port Jefferson 40 57N 73 4W
34 Port Kelang 3 0N 101 24E
46 Port Kembla 34 29S 150 56E
9 Port Laoise 53 2N 7 20W
71 Port Lavaca 28 38N 96 38W
43 Port Lincoln 34 42S 135 52E
50 Port-Lyautey=
Kenitra 34 15N 6 40W
43 Port Macquarie 31 25S 152 54E
63 Port Maitland 44 0N 66 2W
64 Port Mellon 49 32N 123 31W
63 Port Menier 49 51N 64 15W
60 Port Moller 00 00N 00 00W
3 Port Moresby 9 24S 147 8E
65 Port Nelson 57 5N 92 56W
56 Port Nolloth 29 17S 16 52E
61 Port Nouveau-
Quebec 58 30N 65 50W
75 Port of Spain 10 40N 61 20W
72 Port Orchard 47 31N 122 47W
62 Port Perry 44 6N 78 56W
43 Port Pirie 33 10S 137 58E
* 60 Port Radium 66 10N 117 40W
51 Port Said=
Bûr Saîd 31 16N 32 18E
57 Port St. Johns=
Umzimvubu 31 38S 29 33E
63 Port St. Servain 51 21N 58 0W
57 Port Shepstone 30 44S 30 28E
64 Port Simpson 54 30N 130 20W
62 Port Stanley 42 40N 81 10W
51 Port Sudan=
Bûr Sûdân 19 32N 37 9E
7 Port Talbot 51 35N 3 48W
72 Port Townsend 48 0N 122 50W
12 Port-Vendres 42 32N 3 8E
22 Port Vladimir 69 25N 33 6E
43 Port Wakefield 34 12S 138 10E
34 Port Weld 4 50N 100 38E
9 Portadown 54 27N 6 26W
70 Portage 43 31N 89 25W
65 Portage la Prairie 49 58N 98 18W
13 Portalegre 39 19N 7 25W
71 Portales 34 12N 103 25W
9 Portarlington 53 10N 7 10W
75 Port-au-Prince 18 40N 72 20W
56 Porterville, S. Afr. 33 0S 19 0E
73 Porterville, U.S.A. 36 5N 119 0W
7 Porthcawl 51 28N 3 42W
13 Portimão 37 8N 8 32W
46 Portland,
Australia 33 13S 149 59E
69 Portland, Me. 43 40N 70 15W
72 Portland, Oreg. 45 35N 122 30W
7 Portland Bill 50 31N 2 27W
7 Portland I. 50 32N 2 25W
61 Portland
Promontory 59 0N 78 0W
6 Portmadoc 52 51N 4 8W
63 Portneuf 46 43N 71 55W
13 Porto, Port. 41 8N 8 40W
80 Pôrto Alegre 30 5S 51 3W
55 Porto Amélia=
Pemba 12 58S 40 30E
79 Pôrto de Móz 1 41S 52 22W
18 Porto Empédocle 37 18N 13 30E
79 Porto Franco 9 45S 47 0W
79 Porto Grande 0 42N 51 24W
80 Pôrto Mendes 24 30S 54 15W
78 Pôrto Murtinho 21 45S 57 55W
79 Porto Nacional 10 40S 48 30W
53 Porto-Novo 6 23N 2 42E
79 Porto Seguro 16 20S 39 0W
18 Porto Torres 40 50N 8 23E
80 Porto União 26 10S 51 0W
12 Porto-Vecchio 41 35N 9 16E
78 Porto Velho 8 46S 63 54W
18 Portoferráio 42 50N 10 20E
72 Portola 39 49N 120 28W
18 Portoscuso 39 12N 8 22E
78 Portoviejo 1 0S 80 20W
8 Portpatrick 54 50N 5 7W
8 Portree 57 25N 6 11W
9 Portrush 55 13N 6 40W
7 Portsmouth, U.K. 50 48N 1 6W
68 Portsmouth, N.H. 43 5N 70 45W
68 Portsmouth, Ohio 38 45N 83 0W
68 Portsmouth, Va. 36 50N 76 50W
8 Portsoy 57 41N 2 41W
20 Porttipahta, I. 68 5N 26 40E
13 Portugal ■ 40 0N 7 0W
50 Portuguese
Guinea■=
Guinea Bissau ■ 12 0N 15 0W
9 Portumna 53 5N 8 12W
80 Porvenir 53 10S 70 30W
21 Provoo 60 27N 25 50E
80 Posadas 27 30S 56 0W
39 Poseh 23 50N 106 0E
38 Poshan=Tzepo 36 28N 117 58E
35 Poso 1 20S 120 55E
79 Posse 14 4S 46 18W
62 Poste de la Baleine 55 20N 77 40W
50 Poste Maurice
Cortier 22 14N 1 2E
56 Postmasburg 28 18S 23 5E
18 Postojna 45 46N 14 12E
56 Potchefstroom 26 41S 27 7E
18 Potenza 40 40N 15 50E
57 Potgietersrus 24 10S 29 3E
23 Poti 42 10N 41 38E
53 Potiskum 11 39N 11 2E
68 Potomac, R. 38 0N 76 20W
78 Potosí 19 38S 65 50W
35 Potatan 10 56N 122 38E
38 Potow 38 8N 116 31E
80 Potrerillos 26 26S 69 29W

* *Renamed Echo Bay*

Potsdam, E. Germany — Raglan, Australia

14 Potsdam, E. Germany 52 23N 13 4 E
68 Potsdam, U.S.A. 44 40N 74 59W
68 Pottstown 40 15N 75 38W
68 Pottsville 40 39N 76 12W
64 Pouce Coupe 55 40N 120 10W
68 Poughkeepsie 41 40N 73 57W
47 Poverty B. 38 43S 178 0 E
13 Póvoa de Varzim 41 25N 8 46W
22 Povenets 62 48N 35 0 E
62 Powassan 46 5N 79 25W
70 Powder, R. 46 44N 105 26W
72 Powder River 43 5N 107 0W
72 Powell 44 45N 108 45W
73 Powell, L. 37 25N 110 45W
64 Powell River 49 48N 125 20W
7 Powys □ 52 20N 3 30W
39 Poyang 28 59N 116 40 E
39 Poyang Hu, L. 29 10N 116 10 E
25 Poyarkovo 49 38N 128 45 E
19 Požarevac 44 35N 21 18 E
14 Poznań 52 25N 17 0 E
78 Pozo Almonte 20 10S 69 50W
53 Pra, R. 5 1N 1 37W
34 Prachuap Khiri Khan 11 48N 99 47 E
79 Prado 17 20S 39 20W
14 Prague=Praha 50 5N 14 22 E
14 Praha 50 5N 14 22 E
79 Prainha 1 45S 53 30W
42 Prairie 20 50S 144 35 E
72 Prairie City 45 27N 118 44W
70 Prairie du Chien 43 1N 91 9W
70 Prairies, Coteau des. 44 0N 97 0W
34 Praja 8 39S 116 37 E
79 Prata 19 25S 49 0W
18 Prato 43 5 11 5 E
71 Pratt 37 40N 98 45W
13 Pravia 43 30N 6 12W
65 Preeceville 52 0N 102 50W
64 Premier 56 4N 130 1W
14 Prenzlau 53 19N 13 51 E
19 Prepansko, J. 40 45N 21 0 E
15 Prerov 49 28N 17 27 E
62 Prescott, Canada 44 45N 75 30W
73 Prescott, U.S.A. 34 35N 112 30W
80 Presidencia Roque Saenz Peña 26 50S 60 30W
79 Presidente Epitácio 21 46S 52 6W
79 Presidente Prudente 15 45S 54 0W
15 Prešov 49 0N 21 15 E
69 Presque Isle 46 40N 68 0W
14 Pressburg= Bratislava 48 10N 17 7 E
53 Prestea 5 22N 2 7W
7 Presteign 52 17N 3 0W
6 Preston 53 46N 2 42W
8 Prestonpans 55 58N 3 0W
8 Prestwick 55 30N 4 38W
57 Pretoria 25 44S 28 12 E
19 Préveza 38 57N 20 47 E
60 Pribilov Is. 56 0N 170 0W
14 Příbram 49 41N 14 2 E
72 Price 39 40N 110 48W
56 Prieska 29 40S 22 42 E
23 Prikaspiyskaya Nizmennost 47 30N 50 0 E
* 23 Prikumsk 44 30N 44 10 E
19 Prilep 41 21N 21 37 E
23 Priluki 50 30N 32 15 E
65 Prince Albert 53 15N 105 50W
65 Prince Albert Nat. Park 54 0N 106 25W
60 Prince Albert Pen. 72 0N 116 0W
60 Prince Albert Sd. 70 25N 115 0W
61 Prince Charles I. 68 0N 76 0W
3 Prince Edward Is. 45 15S 39 0 E
63 Prince Edward I. □ 44 2N 77 20W
64 Prince George 53 50N 122 50W
58 Prince of Wales, C. 53 50N 131 30W
42 Prince of Wales, I., Australia 10 35S 142 0 E
60 Prince of Wales I., Canada 73 0N 99 0W
64 Prince of Wales I., U.S.A. 53 30N 131 30W
64 Prince Rupert 54 20N 130 20W
42 Princess Charlotte, B. 14 15S 144 0 E
64 Princeton, Canada 49 27N 120 30W
68 Princeton, Ind. 38 20N 87 35W
68 Princeton, Ky. 37 6N 87 55W
68 Princeton, W.Va. 37 21N 81 8W
49 Principé, I. 1 37N 7 25 E
56 Prins Albert 33 12S 22 2 E
22 Priozersk 61 2N 30 4 E
22 Pripet, R.= Pripyat, R. 51 20N 30 20 E
22 Pripyat, R. 51 20N 30 20 E
19 Priština 42 40N 21 13 E
69 Pritchard 30 47N 88 5W
35 Probolinggo 7 46S 113 13 E
32 Proddatur 14 45N 78 30 E
74 Progreso 21 20N 89 40W
24 Prokopyevsk 54 0N 87 3 E
33 Prome 18 45N 95 30 E
79 Propriá 10 13S 36 51W
42 Proserpine 20 21S 148 36 E
72 Prosser 46 11N 119 52W
14 Prostějov 49 30N 17 9 E
12 Provence, Reg. 43 40N 5 45 E
68 Providence 41 41N 71 15W
62 Providence Bay 45 41N 82 15W
75 Providencia, I. de 13 25N 81 26W
25 Provideniya 64 23N 173 18W
64 Provincial Cannery 51 33N 127 36W
12 Provins 48 33N 3 15 E
72 Provo 40 16N 111 37W
65 Provost 52 25N 110 20W
42 Prudhoe, I. 21 23S 149 45 E
60 Prudhoe Bay 70 10N 148 0W
65 Prudhomme 52 22N 105 47W
15 Pruszków 52 9N 20 49 E
23 Prut, R. 45 28N 28 12 E
15 Przemysl 49 50N 22 45 E
15 Przeworsk 50 6N 22 32 E
24 Przhevalsk 42 30N 78 20 E
22 Pskov 57 50N 28 25 E
80 Puán 37 30S 63 0W
78 Pucallpa 8 25S 74 30W
39 Puchi 29 42N 113 54 E
32 Pudukkottai 10 28N 78 47 E
74 Puebla 19 0N 98 10W
74 Puebla □ 18 30N 98 0W
70 Pueblo 38 20N 104 40W
80 Pueblo Hundido 26 20S 69 30W
13 Pueblonuevo 38 20N 5 15W
80 Puelches 38 5S 66 0W
80 Puente Alto 33 32S 70 35W
13 Puente Genil 37 22N 4 47W
37 Puerh 23 11N 100 56 E
75 Puerto Armuelles 8 20N 83 10W
78 Puerto Asís 0 30N 76 30W
78 Puerto Ayacucho 5 40N 67 35W
74 Puerto Barrios 15 40N 88 40W
78 Puerto Berrío 6 30N 74 30W
78 Puerto Bolívar 3 10S 79 55W
78 Puerto Cabello 10 28N 68 1W
75 Puerto Cabezas 14 0N 83 30W
78 Puerto Carreño 6 12N 67 22W
78 Puerto Casado 22 19S 57 56W
75 Puerto Cortes 15 51N 88 0W
74 Puerto Cortés 8 20N 82 20W
80 Puerto Coyle 50 54S 69 15W
78 Puerto Cumarebo 11 29N 69 21W
13 Puerto de Santa María 36 35N 6 15W
50 Puerto del Rosario 28 30N 13 52W
80 Puerto Deseado 47 45S 66 0W
78 Puerto Páez 6 13N 67 28W
78 Puerto Leguizamo 0 12S 74 46W
80 Puerto Lobos 42 0S 65 3W
80 Puerto Madryn 42 48S 65 4W
80 Puerto Montt 41 28S 72 57W
80 Puerto Natales 51 45S 72 25W
75 Puerto Padre 21 13N 76 35W
80 Puerto Pirámides 42 35S 64 20W
78 Puerto Piritu 10 5N 65 0W
75 Puerto Plata 19 40N 70 45W
35 Puerto Princesa 9 55N 118 50 E
80 Puerto Quellón 43 7S 73 37W
75 Puerto Rico, I. 18 15N 66 45W
80 Puerto Saavedra 38 47S 73 24W
78 Puerto Suárez 18 58S 57 52W
80 Puerto Varas 41 19S 72 59W
13 Puertollano 38 43N 4 7W
80 Pueyrredón, L. 47 20S 72 0W
22 Pugachev 52 0N 48 55 E
72 Puget Sd. 47 15N 123 30W
18 Puglia □ 41 0N 16 30 E
47 Pukaki, L. 44 5S 170 1 E
65 Pukatawagan 55 45N 101 20W
47 Pukekohe 37 12S 174 55 E
18 Pula 39 0N 9 0 E
78 Pulacayo 20 25S 66 41W
38 Pulantien 39 25N 122 0 E
68 Pulaski, N.Y. 43 32N 76 9W
69 Pulaski, Tenn. 35 10N 87 0W
68 Pulaski, Va. 37 4N 80 49W
15 Puławy 51 23N 21 59 E
32 Pulicat L. 13 40N 80 15 E
72 Pullman 46 49N 117 10W
34 Puloraja 4 55N 95 24 E
15 Pułtusk 52 43N 21 6 E
37 Puluntohai 47 2N 87 29 E
32 Punch 33 48N 74 4 E
32 Pune 18 29N 73 57 E
32 Punjab □ 31 0N 76 0 E
78 Puno 15 55S 70 3W
80 Punta Alta 38 53S 62 4W
80 Punta Arenas 53 0S 71 0W
80 Punta de Díaz 28 0S 70 45W
80 Punta Delgada 42 43S 63 38W
74 Punta Gorda 16 10N 88 45W
78 Punta Rieles 22 20S 59 40W
43 Puntabie 32 12S 134 5 E
75 Puntarenas 10 0N 84 50W
78 Punto Fijo 11 42N 70 13W
78 Purace, Mt. 2 21N 76 23W
7 Purbeck, I. of 50 40N 2 5W
33 Puri 19 50N 85 58 E
33 Purnea 25 45N 87 31 E
34 Pursat 12 34N 103 50 E
33 Purulia 23 17N 86 33 E
78 Purus, R. 3 42S 61 28W
35 Purwakarta 6 35S 107 29 E
35 Purwodadi, Jawa 7 7S 110 55 E
35 Purwodadi, Jawa 7 51S 110 0 E
35 Purwokerto 7 25S 109 14 E
35 Purworedjo 7 43S 110 2 E
38 Pusan 35 5N 129 0 E
25 Pushchino 54 20N 158 10 E
23 Pushkino 51 16N 47 9 E
33 Putao 27 28N 97 30 E
47 Putaruru 38 3S 175 47 E
38 Putehachi 48 4N 122 45 E
39 Putien 22 28N 119 0 E
32 Puttalam 8 4N 79 50 E
14 Puttgarden 54 28N 11 15 E
78 Putumayo, R. 3 7S 67 58 E
12 Puy de Dôme, Mt. 45 46N 2 57 E
72 Puyallup 47 10N 122 22W
12 Puy-de-Dôme □ 45 47N 3 0 E
52 Pweto 8 25S 28 51 E
23 Pyatigorsk 44 2N 43 0 E
33 Pyinmana 19 45N 96 20 E
38 Pyŏngyang 39 0N 125 30 E
4 Pyrenees, Mts. 42 45N 0 20 E
12 Pyrénées-Atlantiques □ 43 15N 0 45W
12 Pyrénées-Orientales □ 42 35N 2 25 E
33 Pyu 18 30N 96 35 E

Q

28 Qabatiya 32 25N 35 16 E
31 Qadam 32 55N 66 45 E
30 Qadhima 22 20N 39 13 E
30 Qal'at al Mu'azzam 27 43N 37 27 E
30 Qal'at Sālih 31 31N 47 16 E
30 Qal'at Sura 26 10N 38 40 E
31 Qala-i-Kirta 32 15N 63 0 E
31 Qala Nau 35 0N 63 5 E
28 Qalqīlya 32 12N 34 58 E
51 Qâra 29 38N 26 30 E
31 Qasr-e Qand 26 15N 60 45 E
51 Qasr Farâfra 27 0N 28 1 E
29 Qasr Hamam 21 5N 46 5 E
31 Qatar ■ 25 30N 51 15 E
51 Qattara Depression= Qattara, Munkhafed el 29 30N 27 30 E
51 Qattara, Munkhafed el 29 30N 27 30 E
30 Qazvin 36 15N 50 0 E
51 Qena 26 10N 32 43 E
28 Qesari 32 30N 34 53 E
31 Qeshm 26 55N 56 10 E
31 Qeshm, I. 26 50N 56 0 E
31 Qeys, Jazireh-ye 26 32N 53 56 E
28 Qezi'ot 30 52N 34 28 E
32 Qila Safed 29 0N 61 30 E
32 Qila Saifullah 30 45N 68 17 E
28 Qiryat Bialik 32 50N 35 5 E
28 Qiryat 'Eqron 31 52N 34 49 E
28 Qiryat Gat 31 36N 35 47 E
28 Qiryat Hayyim 32 49N 35 4 E
28 Qiryat Mal'akhi 31 44N 34 45 E
28 Qiryat Shemona 33 13N 35 35 E
28 Qiryat Tiv'om 32 43N 35 8 E
28 Qiryat Yam 32 51N 35 4 E
29 Qīzân 16 57N 42 3 E
31 Qom 34 40N 51 4 E
45 Quairading 32 0S 117 21 E
45 Qualeup 33 48S 116 48 E
34 Quan Long 9 7N 105 8 E
34 Quang Ngai 15 13N 108 58 E
34 Quang Tri 16 45N 107 13 E
7 Quantock Hills 51 8N 3 10W
80 Quaraí 30 15S 56 20W
31 Qūchān 37 10N 58 27 E
* 57 Que Que 18 58S 29 48 E
46 Queanbeyan 35 17S 149 14 E
63 Québec 46 52N 71 13W
63 Québec □ 50 0N 70 0W
64 Queen Charlotte 53 28N 132 2W
64 Queen Charlotte Is. 53 10N 132 0W
64 Queen Charlotte Str. 51 0N 128 0W
58 Queen Elizabeth Is. 75 0N 95 0W
60 Queen Maud G. 68 15N 102 0W
41 Queensland □ 15 0S 142 0 E
42 Queenstown, Australia 42 4S 145 35 E
47 Queenstown, N.Z. 45 1S 168 40 E
56 Queenstown, S.Africa 31 52S 26 52 E
79 Queimadas 11 0S 39 38W
54 Quela 9 10S 16 56 E
57 Quelimane 17 53S 36 58 E
39 Quemoy, I. = Kinmen, I. 24 25N 118 25 E
80 Quequén 38 30S 58 30W
74 Querêtaro 20 40N 100 23W
74 Querêtaro □ 20 30N 100 30W
64 Quesnel 53 5N 122 30W
62 Quetico 48 45N 90 55W
62 Quetico Prov. Park 48 15N 91 45W
32 Quetta 30 15N 66 55 E
† 32 Quetta □ 30 15N 68 30 E
74 Quezaltenango 14 40N 91 30W
35 Quezon City 14 38N 121 0 E
34 Qui Nhon 13 40N 109 13 E
78 Quibdo 5 42N 76 40W
12 Quiberon 47 29N 3 9W
80 Quilân, C. 43 15S 74 30W
55 Quilengues 14 12S 15 12 E
80 Quillota 32 54S 71 16W
32 Quilon 8 50N 76 38 E
43 Quilpie 26 35S 144 11 E
80 Quimilí 27 40S 62 30W
12 Quimper 48 0N 4 9W
12 Quimperlé 47 53N 3 33W
68 Quincy, Mass. 42 14N 71 0W
69 Quincy, Fla. 30 34N 84 34W
70 Quincy, Ill. 39 55N 91 20W
80 Quines 32 14S 65 48W
74 Quintana Roo □ 19 0 E 88 0W
13 Quintanar de la Orden 39 36N 3 5W
80 Quintero 32 45S 71 30W
78 Quito 0 15S 78 35W
79 Quixadá 4 55S 39 0W
28 Qumran 31 43N 35 27N
44 Quoin, I. 14 54S 129 32 E
43 Quorn 32 25S 138 0 E
37 Qurug-Tagh, Mts. 41 30N 90 0 E
51 Qûs 25 55N 32 50 E
51 Quseir 26 7N 34 16 E

R

28 Ra'anana 32 12N 34 52 E
20 Raane 64 40N 24 28 E
8 Raasay, I. 57 25N 6 4W
35 Raba 8 36S 118 55 E
52 Rabai 3 50S 39 31 E
50 Rabat 34 2N 6 48W
3 Rabaul 4 24S 152 18 E
30 Rabigh 22 50N 39 5 E
63 Race, C. 46 40N 53 18W
15 Racibórz 50 7N 18 18 E
68 Racine 42 41N 87 51W
68 Radford 37 8N 80 32W
15 Radom 51 23N 21 12 E
19 Radomir 42 37N 23 4 E
15 Radomsko 51 5N 19 28 E
7 Radstock 51 17N 2 25W
65 Radville 49 30N 104 15W
64 Rae 62 45N 115 50W
33 Rae Bareli 26 18N 81 20 E
61 Rae Isthmus 66 40N 87 30W
47 Raetihi 39 25S 175 17 E
80 Rafaela 31 10S 61 30W
30 Rafhā 29 35N 43 35 E
31 Rafsanjān 30 30N 56 5 E
51 Râgâ 8 28N 25 41 E
32 Ragama 7 0N 79 54 E
42 Raglan, Australia 23 42S 150 49 E

* *Renamed Budennovsk*

* *Renamed Kwekwe*

† *Now part of Baluchistan*

47 Raglan, N.Z. 37 55s 174 55 E
18 Ragusa 36 56N 14 42 E
51 Rahad el Bardi 11 20N 23 40 E
32 Raichur 16 10N 77 20 E
33 Raigarh 21 56N 83 25 E
42 Railton 41 25s 146 28 E
72 Rainier, Mt. 46 50N 121 50w
65 Rainy River 48 50N 94 30w
33 Raipur 21 17N 81 45 E
62 Raith 48 50N 90 0w
33 Raj Nandgaon 21 5N 81 5 E
33 Rajahmundry 17 1N 81 48 E
32 Rajapalaiyam 9 25N 77 35 E
32 Rajasthan □ 26 45N 73 30 E
32 Rajgarh 24 2N 76 45 E
32 Rajkot 22 15N 70 56 E
33 Rajshahi 24 22N 88 39 E
33 Rajshahi □ 25 0N 89 0 E
47 Rakaia 43 45s 172 1 E
47 Rakaia, R. 43 54s 172 12 E
35 Rakatau, P. 6 10s 105 20 E
65 Raleigh, Australia 30 27s 153 2 E
69 Raleigh, Canada 49 30N 92 5w
28 Rám Alláh 31 55N 35 10 E
46 Ram Head 37 47s 149 30 E
28 Rama 32 56N 35 21 E
32 Ramanathapuram 9 25N 78 55 E
28 Ramat Gan 32 4N 34 48 E
28 Ramat Ha Sharon 32 7N 34 50 E
28 Ramat Ha Shofet 32 36N 35 5 E
33 Rambre Kyun, I. 19 0N 94 0 E
35 Ramelau, Mt. 8 55s 126 22 E
33 Ramgarh 23 39N 85 31 E
30 Rāmhormoz 31 15N 49 35 E
52 Ramisi 4 35s 39 15 E
28 Ramla 31 55N 34 52 E
32 Ramnad 9 25N 78 55 E
73 Ramona 33 1N 116 56w
56 Ramoutsa 24 50s 25 52 E
60 Rampart 65 30N 150 10w
32 Rampur 23 25N 73 53 E
33 Rampur Hat 24 10N 87 50 E
62 Ramsey, Canada 47 25N 82 20w
6 Ramsey, U.K. 54 20N 4 21w
7 Ramsgate 51 20N 1 25 E
33 Ranaghat 23 15N 88 35 E
80 Rancagua 34 10s 70 50w
72 Ranchester 44 57N 107 12w
33 Ranchi 23 19N 85 27 E
80 Ranco, L. 40 15s 72 25w
21 Randers 56 29N 10 1 E
57 Randfontein 26 8s 27 45 E
68 Randolph 43 55N 72 39w
20 Råneå 65 53N 22 18 E
47 Rangaunu, B. 34 51s 173 15 E
33 Rangia 26 15N 91 20 E
47 Rangitaiki, R. 37 54s 176 53 E
47 Rangitata, R. 44 11s 171 30 E
35 Rangkasbitung 6 22s 106 16 E
33 Rangon= Rangoon 16 45N 96 20 E
33 Rangoon 16 45N 96 20 E
33 Rangpur 25 42N 89 22 E
33 Raniganj 23 40N 87 15 E
32 Raniwara 24 47N 72 10 E
60 Rankin Inlet 62 30N 93 0w
46 Rankins Springs 33 49s 146 14 E
8 Rannoch 56 41N 4 20w
8 Rannoch, L. 56 41N 4 20w
57 Ranohira 22 29s 45 24 E
34 Ranong 9 56N 98 40 E
34 Rantauprapat 2 15N 99 50 E
35 Rantemario, Mt. 3 15s 119 57 E
28 Rantis 32 4N 35 3 E
68 Rantoul 40 18N 88 10w
2 Rapa Iti, Is. 27 35s 144 20w
35 Rapang 3 45s 119 55 E
70 Rapid City 44 0N 103 0w
2 Rarotonga, I. 21 30s 160 0w
80 Rasa, Pte. 40 55s 63 20N
31 Ras al Khaima 25 50N 56 5 E
31 Ra's Al-Unuf 30 25N 18 15 E
30 Ra's al Tannurah 26 40N 50 10 E
51 Rashad 11 55N 31 0 E
51 Rashîd 31 21N 30 22 E
30 Rasht 37 20N 49 40 E
60 Rat Is. 51 50N 178 15 E
32 Ratangarh 28 5N 74 35 E
9 Rath Luirc 52 21N 8 40w
9 Rathdrum, Eire 52 57N 6 13w
72 Rathdrum, U.S.A 47 50N 116 58w
14 Rathenow 52 38N 12 23 E
9 Rathkeale 52 32N 8 57w
9 Rathlin, I. 55 18N 6 14w
14 Ratisbon= Regensburg 49 1N 12 7 E
32 Ratlam 23 20N 75 0 E
32 Ratnagiri 16 57N 73 18 E
71 Raton 37 0N 104 30w
8 Rattray Hd. 57 38N 1 50w
47 Raukumara, Ra. 38 5s 177 55 E
21 Rauma 61 10N 21 30 E
31 Ravar 31 20N 56 51 E
18 Ravenna 44 28N 12 15 E
14 Ravensburg 47 48N 9 38 E
42 Ravenshoe 17 37s 145 29 E
45 Ravensthorpe 33 35s 120 2 E
32 Ravi, R. 30 35N 71 38 E
52 Ravine 0 15N 36 15 E
32 Rawalpindi 33 38N 73 8 E
* 32 Rawalpindi □ 33 38N 73 8 E
62 Rawdon 46 3N 73 40w
47 Rawene 35 25s 173 32 E
45 Rawlinna 30 58s 125 28 E
72 Rawlins 41 50N 107 20w
80 Rawson 43 15s 65 0w
63 Ray, C. 47 33N 59 15w
33 Rayagada 19 15N 83 20 E
25 Raychikhinsk 49 46N 129 25 E
64 Raymond, Canada 49 30N 112 35w
72 Raymond, U.S.A. 46 45N 123 48w
71 Raymondville 26 30N 97 50w
65 Raymore 50 25N 104 31w
71 Rayne 30 16N 92 16w
12 Raz, Pte. du 48 2N 4 47w
12 Ré, I. de 46 12N 1 30w
7 Reading, U.K. 51 27N 0 57w
68 Reading, U.S.A. 40 20N 75 53w
80 Realicó 35 0s 64 15w
35 Rebi 5 30s 134 7 E
79 Recife 8 0s 35 0w
80 Reconquista 29 10s 59 45w
80 Recreo 29 25s 65 10w
71 Red, R. 48 10N 97 0w
72 Red Bluff 40 11N 122 11w
64 Red Deer 52 20N 113 50w
65 Red Lake 51 1N 94 1w
70 Red Oak 41 0N 95 10w
48 Red Sea 20 0N 39 0 E
70 Red Wing 44 32N 92 35w
7 Redbridge 51 35N 0 7 E
6 Redcar 54 37N 1 4w
65 Redcliff 50 10N 110 50w
43 Redcliffe 27 12s 153 0 E
46 Redcliffs 34 16s 142 10 E
72 Redding 40 30N 122 25w
7 Redditch 52 18N 1 57w
73 Redlands 34 0N 117 0w
45 Redmond, Australia 34 55s 117 40 E
72 Redmond, U.S.A. 44 19N 121 11w
75 Redonda, I. 16 58N 62 19w
13 Redondela 42 15N 8 38w
13 Redondo 38 39N 7 37w
73 Redondo Beach 33 52N 118 26w
7 Redruth 50 14N 5 14w
64 Redstone 52 8N 123 42w
65 Redvers 49 35N 101 40w
64 Redwater 53 55N 113 0w
73 Redwood City 37 30N 122 15w
9 Ree, L. 53 35N 8 0w
73 Reedley 34 40N 119 27w
72 Reedsport 43 45N 124 4w
47 Reefton 42 6s 171 51 E
28 Regavim 32 32N 35 2 E
14 Regensburg 49 1N 12 7 E
18 Reggio nell'Emilia 44 42N 10 38 E
18 Réggio di Calábria 38 7N 15 38 E
65 Regina 50 30N 104 35w
31 Registan, Reg. 30 15N 65 0 E
56 Rehoboth 17 55s 15 5 E
28 Rehovot 31 54N 34 48 E
14 Reichenbach 50 36N 12 19 E
45 Reid 35 17s 149 8 E
42 Reid River 19 40s 146 48 E
69 Reidsville 36 21N 79 40w
7 Reigate 51 14N 0 11w
12 Reims 49 15N 4 0 E
28 Reina 32 43N 35 18 E
80 Reina Adelaida, Arch. 52 20s 74 0w
65 Reindeer L. 57 20N 102 20w
47 Reinga, C. 34 25s 172 43 E
13 Reinosa 43 2N 4 15w
14 Reisengebirge 50 40N 15 45 E
57 Reitz 27 48s 28 29 E
25 Rekinniki 60 38N 163 50 E
79 Remanso 9 41s 42 4w
35 Rembang 6 42s 111 21 E
31 Remeshk 26 55N 58 50 E
14 Remscheid 51 11N 7 12 E
14 Rendsburg 54 18N 9 41 E
25 Rene 66 2N 179 25w
62 Renfrew, Canada 45 30N 76 40w
8 Renfrew, U.K. 55 52N 4 24w
34 Rengat 0 30s 102 45 E
51 Renk 11 47N 32 49 E
11 Renkum 51 58N 5 43 E
43 Renmark 34 11s 140 43 E
12 Rennes 48 7N 1 41w
72 Reno 39 30N 119 0w
72 Renton 47 30N 122 9w
70 Republican, R. 39 3N 96 48w
61 Repulse Bay 66 30N 86 30w
65 Reserve 33 50N 108 54w
80 Resistencia 27 30s 59 0w
15 Reşiţa 45 18N 21 53 E
61 Resolution I., Canada 61 30N 65 0w
47 Resolution, I., N.Z. 45 40s 166 40 E
57 Ressano Garcia 25 25s 32 0 E
74 Retalhulen 14 33N 91 46w
19 Réthímnon 35 15N 24 40 E
49 Réunion, Î. 22 0s 56 0 E
13 Reus 41 10N 1 5 E
14 Reutlingen 48 28N 9 13 E
64 Revelstoke 51 0N 118 0w
2 Revilla Gigedo Is. 18 40N 112 0w
33 Rewa 24 33N 81 25 E
32 Rewari 28 15N 76 40 E
72 Rexburg 43 45N 111 50w
53 Rey Malabo 3 45N 8 50 E
20 Reykanes, Pen. 63 48N 22 40w
20 Reykjavik 64 10N 21 57 E
74 Reynosa 26 5N 98 18w
‡ 30 Reza'iyeh 37 40N 45 0 E
7 Rhayader 52 19N 3 30w
11 Rheden 52 0N 6 3 E
14 Rhein, R. 51 42N 6 20 E
14 Rhein-Donau-Kanal 49 45N 11 0 E
14 Rheine 52 17N 7 25 E
14 Rheinland-Pfalz □ 50 50N 7 0 E
14 Rhine, R. = Rhein, R. 51 42N 6 20 E
70 Rhinelander 45 38N 89 29w
50 Rhir, C. 30 38N 9 54w
68 Rhode Island □ 41 38N 71 37w
19 Rhodes, I.= Ródhos, I. 36 15N 28 10 E
* 57 Rhodesia ■ 20 0s 28 30 E
19 Rhodope, Mts. = Rhodopi Planina 41 40N 24 20 E
19 Rhodopi Planina 41 40N 24 20 E
14 Rhön, Mts. 50 25N 10 0 E
7 Rhondda 51 39N 3 30w
12 Rhône □ 45 54N 4 35 E
12 Rhône, R. 43 28N 4 42 E
8 Rhum, I. 57 0N 6 20w
6 Rhyl 53 19N 3 29w
79 Riachão 7 20s 46 37w
34 Riau □ 1 0N 102 35 E
34 Riau, Kep. 0 30N 104 20 E
13 Ribadeo 43 35N 7 5w
79 Ribas do Rio Pardo 20 27s 53 46w
13 Ribatejo, Reg. 39 15N 8 30w
6 Ribble, R. 54 13N 2 20w
21 Ribe 55 19N 8 44 E
79 Ribeirão Prêto 21 10s 47 50w
47 Riccarton 43 32s 172 37 E
70 Rice Lake 44 10N 78 10w
55 Richards B. 28 48s 32 6 E
63 Richibucto 46 42N 64 54w
72 Richland 44 49N 117 9w
42 Richmond, Australia 20 43s 143 8 E
47 Richmond, N.Z. 41 4s 173 12 E
56 Richmond, C. Prov 31 23s 23 56 E
57 Richmond, Natal S. Africa 29 54s 30 8 E
7 Richmond, Surrey 51 28N 0 18w
6 Richmond, Yorks. 54 24N 1 43w
72 Richmond, Calif. 38 0N 122 30w
68 Richmond, Ind. 39 50N 84 50w
68 Richmond, Ky. 37 40N 84 20w
72 Richmond, Utah 41 55N 111 48w
68 Richmond, Va. 37 33N 77 27w
† 62 Richmond Gulf 56 20N 75 50w
68 Richwood 38 17N 80 32w
65 Ridgedale 53 0N 104 10w
62 Ridgetown 42 26N 81 52w
68 Ridgway 41 25N 78 43w
65 Riding Mountain Nat. Park 50 55N 100 25w
14 Ried 48 14N 13 30 E
56 Riet, R. 29 0s 23 54 E
18 Rieti 42 23N 12 50 E
72 Rifle 39 40N 107 50w
22 Riga 56 53N 24 8 E
63 Rigolet 54 10N 58 23w
53 Rijau 11 7N 5 14 E
18 Rijeka 45 20N 14 21 E
11 Rijssen 52 19N 6 30 E
11 Rijswijk 52 4N 4 22 E
72 Riley 39 18N 96 50w
53 Rima, R. 13 10N 5 15 E
53 Rimi 12 58N 7 43 E
18 Rímini 44 3N 12 33 E
15 Rîmnicu Sărat 45 26N 27 3 E
15 Rîmnicu Vîlcea 45 9N 24 21 E
63 Rimouski 48 27N 68 30w
9 Rineanna 52 42N 85 7w
53 Ringim 12 8N 9 10 E
21 Ringkøbing 56 5N 8 15 E
79 Rio Amazonas, Estuario do 1 0N 49 0w
78 Rio Branco, Brazil 9 58s 67 49w
80 Rio Branco, Uruguay 32 34s 53 25w
75 Rio Claro 10 20N 61 25w
80 Rio Cuarto 33 10s 64 25w
79 Rio de Janeiro 23 0s 43 12w
79 Rio de Janeiro □ 22 50s 43 0w
80 Rio do Sul 27 95s 49 37w
80 Rio Gallegos 51 35s 69 15w
80 Rio Grande 32 0s 52 20w
66 Rio Grande, R. 37 47N 106 15w
79 Rio Grande do Norte □ 5 45s 36 0w
80 Rio Grande do Sul □ 30 0s 54 0w
79 Rio Largo 9 28s 35 50w
78 Rio Mulatos 19 40s 66 50w
54 Rio Muni □ 1 30N 10 0 E
80 Rio Negro 26 0s 50 0w
79 Rio Verde, Brazil 17 43s 50 56w
74 Río Verde, Mexico 21 56N 99 59w
72 Rio Vista 38 11N 121 44w
78 Riobamba 1 50s 78 45w
78 Ríohacha 11 33N 72 55w
78 Ríosucio 5 30N 75 40w
78 Rioscio 7 27N 77 7w
6 Ripon, U.K. 54 8N 1 31w
70 Ripon, U.S.A. 43 51N 88 50w
28 Rishon Le Zion 31 58N 34 48 E
28 Rishpon 32 12N 34 49 E
21 Risør 58 43N 9 13 E
53 Riti 7 57N 9 41 E
72 Ritzville 47 10N 118 21w
18 Riva 45 53N 10 50 E
80 Rivadavia, Arg. 24 5s 63 0w
80 Rivadavia, Chile 29 50s 70 35w
75 Rivas 11 30N 85 50w
80 Rivera 31 0s 55 50w
68 Riverhead 40 53N 72 40w
65 Riverhurst 50 55N 106 50w
53 Rivers □ 5 0N 6 30 E
56 Riversdale 34 7s 21 15 E
73 Riverside, Calif. 34 0N 117 15w
72 Riverside, Wyo. 41 12N 106 57w
43 Riverton, Australia 34 10s 138 46 E
65 Riverton, Canada 51 5N 97 0w
47 Riverton, N.Z. 46 21s 168 0 E
72 Riverton, U.S.A. 43 1N 108 27w
18 Riviera di Levante 44 23N 9 15 E
18 Riviera di Ponente 43 50N 7 58 E
63 Rivière Bleue 47 26N 69 2w
63 Rivière-du-Loup 47 50N 69 30w
63 Rivière-Pentecôte 49 57N 67 1w
30 Riyadh = Ar Riyád 24 41N 46 42 E
30 Rize 41 0N 40 30 E
21 Rjukan 59 54N 8 33 E
12 Roanne 46 3N 4 4 E
69 Roanoke, Ala. 33 9N 85 23w
68 Roanoke, Va 37 19N 79 55w
69 Roanoke Rapids 36 36N 77 42w
75 Roatán, I. de 16 23N 86 26w
56 Robertson 33 46s 19 50 E
62 Roberval 48 32N 72 15w
65 Roblin 51 21N 101 25w
64 Robson, Mt. 53 10N 119 10w
71 Robstown 27 47N 97 40w
13 Roca, C. da 38 40N 9 31w
* 56 Rocadas 16 45s 15 0 E
79 Rocas, Is. 4 0s 34 1w
80 Rocha 34 30s 54 25w
6 Rochdale 53 36N 2 10w
12 Rochefort 45 56N 0 57w
70 Rochelle 41 55N 89 5w
64 Rocher River 61 12N 114 0w
46 Rochester, Australia 36 22s 144 41 E
7 Rochester, U.K. 51 22N 0 30 E
70 Rochester, Minn. 44 1N 92 28w
68 Rochester, N.H. 43 19N 70 57w
68 Rochester, N.Y. 43 10N 77 40w
69 Rock Hill 34 55N 81 2w
70 Rock Island 41 30N 90 35w
75 Rock Sound 24 54N 76 12w
72 Rock Springs 46 55N 106 11w
4 Rockall, I. 57 37N 13 42w
70 Rockford, Ill. 42 20N 89 0w

* Now part of Punjab

* Renamed Zimbabwe
† French nameform Guillaume Delisle, L.
‡ Renamed Orūmīyeh

* Renamed Xangongo

70	Rockford, Mich.	43 7N	85 33W
42	Rockhampton	23 22S	150 32E
45	Rockingham	32 15S	115 38E
69	Rockland, Mass.	44 6N	69 8W
68	Rockville, Md.	39 7N	77 10W
45	Rocky Gully	34 30S	117 0E
69	Rocky Mount	35 55N	77 48W
64	Rocky Mountain House	52 22N	114 55W
58	Rocky Mts.	48 0N	113 0W
64	Rockyford	51 13N	113 8W
21	Rødbyhavn	54 39N	11 22E
63	Roddickton	50 51N	56 8W
12	Rodez	44 21N	2 33E
19	Ródhos	36 15N	28 10E
19	Ródhos, I.	36 15N	28 10E
47	Rodney, C.	36 17S	174 50E
3	Rodriguez, I.	20 0S	65 0E
44	Roebourne	20 44S	117 9E
44	Roebuck, B.	18 5S	122 20E
44	Roebuck Plains P.O.	17 56S	122 28E
11	Roermond	51 12N	6 0E
61	Roes Welcome Sd.	65 0N	87 0W
11	Roeselare	50 57N	3 7E
21	Rogaland □	59 12N	6 20E
71	Rogers	36 20N	94 0W
62	Roggan River	54 24N	78 5W
56	Roggeveldberge	32 10S	20 10E
32	Rohri	27 45N	68 51E
32	Rohtak	28 55N	76 43E
80	Rolândia	23 5S	52 0W
71	Rolla	38 0N	91 42W
42	Rollingstone	19 2S	146 24E
42	Rolleston	43 35S	172 24E
75	Rolleville	23 41N	76 0W
43	Roma, Australia	26 32S	148 49E
18	Roma, Italy	41 54N	12 30E
21	Roma, Sweden	57 32N	18 28E
15	Roman	43 8N	23 54E
15	Romania■ = Rumania ■	46 0N	25 0E
60	Romanzof, C.	61 49N	165 56W
18	Rome, Italy = Roma	41 54N	12 30E
69	Rome, Ga.	34 20N	85 0W
68	Rome, N.Y.	43 14N	75 29W
7	Romney Marsh	51 0N	1 0E
12	Romorantin-Lanthenay	47 21N	1 45E
20	Romsdalen, R.	62 25N	7 50E
8	Ronaldsay, North I.	59 23N	2 26W
8	Ronaldsay, South I.	58 47N	2 56W
79	Roncador, S. do	12 30S	52 30W
13	Roncevoux	43 0N	1 23W
13	Ronda	36 46N	5 12W
78	Rondônia □	11 0S	63 0W
79	Rondonópolis	16 28S	54 38W
52	Rongai	0 10S	35 51E
21	Rønne	55 6N	14 44E
45	Ronsard, C.	24 46S	113 10E
11	Ronse	50 45N	3 35E
55	Roodepoort-Maraisburg	26 11S	27 54E
32	Roorkee	29 52N	77 59E
11	Roosendaal	51 32N	4 29E
73	Roosevelt Res.	33 46N	111 0W
42	Roper, R.	14 43S	135 27E
78	Roraima □	2 0N	61 30W
78	Roraima, Mt.	5 10N	60 40W
14	Rosa, Mte.	45 57N	7 53E
80	Rosario, Arg.	33 0S	60 50W
79	Rosário, Brazil	3 0S	44 15W
74	Rosario, Mexico	23 0S	105 52W
80	Rosario de la Frontera	25 50S	65 0W
80	Rosário do Sul	30 15S	54 55W
13	Rosas	42 19N	3 10E
13	Rosas, G. de	42 10N	3 15E
9	Roscommon	53 38N	8 11W
9	Roscommon □	53 40N	8 15W
9	Roscrea	52 57N	7 47W
63	Rose Blanche	47 38N	58 45W
64	Rose Harbour	52 15N	131 10W
65	Rose Valley	52 19N	103 49W
75	Roseau	48 56N	96 0W
71	Rosenberg	29 30N	95 48W
72	Rosebud	31 5N	97 0W
72	Roseburg	43 10N	123 10W
46	Rosedale	38 11S	146 48E
65	Rosetown	57 33N	108 0E
51	Rosetta = Rashîd	31 21N	30 22E
72	Roseville	38 46N	121 41W
43	Rosewood	35 38S	147 52E
28	Rosh Ha'Ayin	32 5N	34 47E
28	Rosh Pinna	32 58N	35 32E
78	Rosignol	6 15N	57 30W
21	Roskilde	55 38N	12 3E
22	Roslavl	53 57N	32 55E
47	Ross, N.Z.	42 53S	170 49E
7	Ross, U.K.	51 55N	2 34W
9	Ross □	70 0S	170 5W
2	Ross Dependency □	70 0S	170 0W
3	Ross Sea	74 0S	178 0E
64	Rossland	49 6N	117 50W
9	Rosslare	52 17N	6 23W
50	Rosso	16 30N	15 49W
23	Rossosh	50 15N	39 20E
65	Rosthern	52 40N	106 20W
14	Rostock	54 4N	12 9E
23	Rostov	47 15N	39 45E
71	Roswell	33 26N	104 32W
8	Rosyth	56 2N	3 26W
7	Rother, R.	50 59N	0 40W
6	Rotherham	53 26N	1 21W
8	Rothes	57 31N	3 12W
8	Rothesay	55 50N	5 3W
35	Roti, I.	10 50S	123 0E
46	Roto	33 0S	145 30E
47	Rotorua	38 9S	176 16E
47	Rotorua, L.	38 5S	176 18E
11	Rotterdam	51 55N	4 30E
45	Rottnest, I.	32 0S	115 27E
14	Rottweil	48 9N	8 38E
3	Rotuma, I.	12 25S	177 5E
12	Roubaix	50 40N	3 10E
12	Rouen	49 27N	1 4E
12	Rouergue, Reg.	44 20N	2 20E
15	Roumania■ = Rumania ■	46 0N	25 0E
43	Round, Mt.	30 26S	152 16E
72	Roundup	46 25N	108 35W
8	Rousay, I.	59 10N	3 2W
12	Roussillon, Reg.	45 24N	4 49E
56	Rouxville	30 11S	26 50E
62	Rouyn	48 20N	79 0W
20	Rovaniemi	66 29N	25 41E
18	Rovereto	45 53N	11 3E
18	Rovigo	45 4N	11 48E
18	Rovinj	45 18N	13 40E
23	Rovno	50 40N	26 10E
35	Roxas	11 36N	122 49E
47	Roxburgh	45 33S	169 19E
44	Roy Hill	22 37S	119 58E
68	Royal Oak	42 30N	83 5W
70	Royale, I.	48 0N	89 0W
12	Royan	45 37N	1 2W
22	Rtishchevo	52 35N	43 50E
47	Ruapehu, Mt.	39 18S	175 35E
52	Rubeho Mts.	6 50S	36 25E
78	Rubio	7 43N	72 22W
24	Rubtsovsk	51 30N	80 50E
60	Ruby	38 27S	145 55E
43	Rudall	33 43S	136 17E
22	Rudnichny	59 38N	52 26E
25	Rudnogorsk	57 15N	103 42E
24	Rudnyy	52 57N	63 7E
52	Rudolf, L. = Turkana, L.	4 10N	36 10E
51	Rufa'a	14 44N	33 32E
52	Rufiji, R.	8 0S	39 20E
80	Rufino	34 20S	62 50W
50	Rufisque	14 43N	17 17W
7	Rugby, U.K.	52 23N	1 16W
70	Rugby, U.S.A.	48 21N	100 0W
14	Rügen, I.	54 22N	13 25E
28	Ruhâma	31 31N	34 43E
52	Ruhengeri	1 30S	29 36E
14	Ruhr, R.	51 27N	6 44E
54	Ruki, R.	0 5N	18 17E
52	Rukungiri	0 53S	29 58E
52	Rukwa, L.	7 50S	32 10E
44	Rum Jungle	13 0S	130 59E
15	Rumania ■	46 0N	25 0E
42	Rumbalara	25 20S	134 29E
68	Rumford	44 30N	70 30W
36	Rumoi	43 56N	141 39W
52	Rumuruti	0 17N	36 32E
47	Runanga	42 25S	171 15E
6	Runcorn	53 20N	2 44W
52	Rungwa	6 55S	33 32E
52	Rungwe, Mt.	9 11S	33 32E
53	Runka	12 28N	7 20E
34	Rupat, I.	1 45N	101 40E
62	Rupert House = Fort Rupert	51 30N	78 40W
57	Rusape	18 35S	32 8E
19	Ruse	43 48N	25 59E
7	Rushden	52 17N	0 37W
68	Rushville	39 38N	85 22W
46	Rushworth	36 32S	145 1E
79	Russas	4 56S	37 58W
65	Russell, Canada	50 50N	101 20W
70	Russell, U.S.A.	38 56N	98 55W
69	Russellville, Ala.	34 30N	87 44W
71	Russellville, Ark.	35 15N	93 0W
* **24**	Russian Soviet Federal Socialist Rep.	60 0N	80 0E
24	Russkaya Polyana	53 47N	73 53E
56	Rustenburg	25 41S	27 14E
71	Ruston	32 30N	92 40W
35	Ruteng	8 26S	120 30E
72	Ruth	39 15N	115 1W
46	Rutherglen, Australia	36 5S	146 29E
8	Rutherglen, U.K.	55 50N	4 11W
68	Rutland	43 38N	73 0W
52	Rutshuru	1 13S	29 25E
52	Ruvu	6 49S	38 43E
52	Ruvuma, R.	10 29S	40 28E
52	Ruwenzori, Mts.	0 30N	29 55E
15	Ruzomberok	49 3N	19 17E
52	Rwanda ■	2 0S	30 0E
8	Ryan, L.	55 0N	5 2W
22	Ryazan	54 38N	39 44E
22	Ryazhsk	53 40N	40 7E
24	Rybache	46 40N	81 20E
22	Rybachiy Pol.	69 43N	32 0E
† **22**	Rybinsk	58 3N	38 52E
22	Rybinskoye, Vdkhr.	58 30N	38 25E
7	Ryde	50 44N	1 9W
7	Rye	50 57N	0 46E
6	Rye, R.	54 12N	0 53W
15	Rypin	53 3N	19 32E
39	Ryūkyū, Is.	26 0N	128 0E
15	Rzeszów	50 5N	21 58E
22	Rzhev	56 15N	34 18E

S

28	Sa'ad	31 28N	34 33E
31	Sa'ādatābād	30 10N	53 5E
14	Saale, R.	51 57N	11 55E
14	Saar, R.	49 20N	6 45E
14	Saarbrücken	49 15N	6 58E
22	Saaremaa, I.	58 30N	22 30E
14	Saarland □	49 20N	0 75E
75	Saba, I.	17 30N	63 10W
13	Sabadell	41 28N	2 7E
34	Sabah □	6 0N	117 0E
30	Sabalan, Kuhha-ye	38 15N	47 49E
78	Sabanalargo	10 38N	74 55W
34	Sabang	5 50N	95 15E
79	Sabará	19 55S	43 55W
28	Sabastiya	32 17N	35 12E
18	Sabáudia	41 17N	13 2E
51	Sabhah	27 9N	14 29E
57	Sabie	25 4S	30 48E
74	Sabinas	27 50N	101 10W
74	Sabinas Hidalgo	26 40N	100 10W
71	Sabine, R.	30 0N	93 45W
59	Sable, C., Canada	43 29N	65 38W
63	Sable, C., U.S.A.	25 5N	81 0W
63	Sable I.	44 0N	60 0W
53	Sabou	12 1N	2 28W
31	Sabzevār	36 15N	57 40E
31	Sabzvāran	28 45N	57 50E
69	Saco	43 29N	70 28W
72	Sacramento	38 39N	121 30E
72	Sacramento, R.	38 3N	121 56W
73	Sacramento Mts.	32 30N	105 30W
13	Sádaba	2 19N	1 12W
51	Sadd el Aali	24 5N	32 54E
53	Sade	11 22N	10 45E
36	Sado, I.	38 15N	138 30E
30	Safaniya	28 5N	48 42E
31	Safed Koh	34 15N	64 0E
73	Safford	32 54N	109 52W
7	Saffron Walden	52 5N	0 15E
50	Safi	32 20N	9 17W
35	Saga, Indonesia	2 40S	132 55E
36	Saga, Japan	33 15N	130 18E
36	Saga □	33 15N	130 20E
33	Sagaing	22 0N	96 0E
32	Sagar	23 50N	78 50E
37	Sagil	50 15N	91 15E
68	Saginaw	43 26N	83 55W
68	Saginaw B.	43 50N	83 40W
61	Saglouc	62 30N	74 15W
13	Sagres	37 0N	8 58W
75	Sagua la Grande	22 50N	80 10W
73	Saguache	38 10N	106 4W
63	Saguenay, R.	48 10N	69 45W
13	Sagunto	39 42N	0 18W
13	Sahagun	42 18N	5 2W
50	Sahara	23 0N	5 0W
32	Saharanpur	29 58N	77 33E
32	Sahiwal	30 45N	73 8E
31	Sa'idābād	29 30N	55 45E
32	Saidapet	13 0N	80 15E
32	Saidu	34 50N	72 15E
31	Saighan	35 10N	67 55E
34	Saigon = Phanh Bho Ho Chi Minh	10 58N	106 40E
29	Saihut	15 12N	51 10E
36	Saijo	34 0N	133 5E
36	Saiki	32 35N	131 50E
8	St. Abbs Hd.	55 55N	2 10W
7	St. Albans, U.K.	51 46N	0 21W
68	St. Albans, U.S.A.	44 49N	73 5W
7	St. Albans Hd.	50 34N	2 3W
57	St. André, T.	16 10S	44 27E
8	St. Andrews	56 20N	2 48W
46	St. Arnaud	36 32S	143 16E
6	St. Asaph	53 15N	3 27W
† **63**	St-Augustin	51 19N	58 48W
69	St. Augustine	29 52N	81 20W
7	St. Austell	50 20N	4 48W
75	St. Barthelémy, I.	17 50N	62 50W
6	St. Bees Hd.	54 30N	3 38E
65	St. Boniface	49 50N	97 10W
7	St. Bride's B.	51 48N	5 15W
12	St-Brieuc	48 30N	2 46W
7	St. Catherine's Pt.	50 34N	1 18W
70	St. Charles	38 46N	90 30W
75	St. Christopher, I.	17 20N	62 40W
62	St. Clair, L.	42 30N	82 45W
65	St. Claude	49 40N	98 22W
70	St. Cloud	45 30N	94 11W
63	St-Cœur de Marie	48 39N	71 43W
45	St. Cricq, C.	25 17S	113 6E
75	St. Croix, I.	17 30N	64 40W
7	St. Davids	51 54N	5 16W
7	St. David's Hd.	51 54N	5 16W
75	St. David's I.	32 22N	64 39W
12	St-Denis	48 56N	2 22E
60	St. Elias, Mt.	60 20N	141 59W
12	St-Étienne	45 27N	4 22E
62	St-Félicien	48 40N	72 25W
63	St. Fintan's	48 10N	58 50W
12	St Flour	45 2N	3 6E
56	St. Francis, C.	34 14S	24 49E
62	St-Gabriel de Brandon	46 17N	73 24W
14	St. Gallen	47 25N	9 23E
43	St. George, Australia	28 1S	148 41E
75	St. George, Bermuda	32 24N	64 42W
63	St. George, Canada	45 11N	66 57W
73	St. George, U.S.A.	37 10N	113 35W
69	St. George, C.	29 36N	85 2W
46	St. George Hd.	35 11S	150 45E
65	St. George West	50 33N	96 7W
11	St. Georges, Belgium	50 37N	4 20E
62	St-Georges, Canada	46 42N	72 35W
79	St. George's, Fr. Guiana	4 0N	52 0W
75	St. Georges, Grenada	12 5N	61 43W
63	St. George's B.	48 20N	59 0W
10	St. George's Chan.	52 0N	6 0W
75	St. George's I.	32 22N	64 40W
49	St. Helena, I.	15 55S	5 44W
56	St. Helenabaai	32 40S	18 10E
42	St. Helens, Australia	41 20S	148 15E
6	St. Helens, U.K.	53 28N	2 44W
72	St. Helens, U.S.A.	45 55N	122 50W
62	St-Hyacinthe	45 40N	72 58W
7	St. Ives, Cambridge	52 20N	0 5W
7	St. Ives, Cornwall	50 13N	5 29W
62	St-Jean	45 20N	73 50W
65	St. Jean Baptiste	49 15N	97 20W
62	St-Jérôme	45 55N	74 0W
63	St. John	45 20N	66 8W
* **63**	St. John, L.	48 40N	72 0W
75	St. John's, Antigua	17 6N	61 51W
63	St. John's, Canada	47 35N	52 40W
68	St. Johnsbury	44 25N	72 1W
68	St. Joseph, Mich.	42 6N	86 29W
70	St. Joseph, Mo.	39 46N	94 51W
62	St-Jovite	46 8N	74 38W
47	St. Kilda	45 53S	170 31E
10	St. Kilda, I.	57 50N	8 40W
75	St. Kitts, I. = St. Christopher, I.	17 20N	62 40W
65	St. Laurent	50 25N	97 58W
63	St. Lawrence	46 54N	55 23W
63	St. Lawrence, G. of	48 25N	62 0W
60	St. Lawrence, I.	63 0N	170 0W

* *Renamed Russian Soviet Federative Socialist Republic*
† *Renamed Andropov*

* *French nameform St-Jean, L.*
† *Renamed Anatsogno*

St. Lawrence, R. Sanlúcar-la-Mayor

63 St. Lawrence, R. 49 15N 67 0W
63 St. Leonard 47 12N 67 58W
62 St-Lin 45 44N 73 46W
12 St-Lô 49 7N 1 5W
12 St. Louis, France 47 35N 7 34E
50 St. Louis, Senegal 16 8N 16 27W
70 St. Louis, U.S.A. 38 40N 90 20W
57 St. Lucia, C. 28 32S 32 29E
75 St. Lucia, I. 14 0N 60 50W
57 St. Lucia, L. 28 5S 32 30E
75 St. Lucia Chan. 14 15N 61 0W
75 St. Maarten, I. 18 0N 63 5W
12 St-Malo 48 39N 2 1W
75 St. Marc 19 10N 72 5W
72 St. Maries 47 17N 116 34W
75 St. Martin, I. 18 0N 63 0W
63 St. Martins 45 22N 65 38W
42 St. Marys, Australia 41 32S 148 11E
68 St. Marys, U.S.A. 41 30N 78 33W
7 St. Marys, I. 49 55N 6 17W
60 St. Matthew I. 60 30N 172 45W
7 St. Michael's Mt. 50 7N 5 30W
14 St. Moritz 46 30N 9 50E
12 St-Nazaire 47 17N 2 12W
7 St. Neots 52 14N 0 16W
11 St. Niklaas 51 10N 4 8E
12 St-Omer 50 45N 2 15E
63 St-Pacôme 47 24N 69 58W
63 St-Pamphile 46 58N 69 48W
63 St-Pascal 47 32N 69 48W
64 St. Paul, Canada 51 34N 57 47W
70 St. Paul, U.S.A. 44 54N 93 5W
2 St. Paul, I., Atlantic Oc. 0 50N 31 40W
3 St. Paul, I., Indian Oc. 30 40S 77 34E
70 St. Peter 44 15N 93 57W
7 St. Peter Port 49 27N 2 31W
69 St. Petersburg 27 45N 82 40W
63 St-Pierre 46 40N 56 0W
62 St-Pierre, L. 46 10N 72 50W
63 St-Pierre et Miquelon □ 46 49N 56 15W
12 St-Quentin 49 50N 3 16E
63 St-Siméon 47 51N 69 54W
63 St. Stephen 45 16N 67 17W
62 St. Thomas, Canada 42 47N 81 12W
75 St. Thomas, Virgin Is. 18 21N 64 56W
62 St-Tite 46 45N 72 40W
12 St-Tropez 43 17N 6 38E
11 St. Troud 50 48N 5 10E
12 St-Valéry 50 10N 1 38E
75 St. Vincent, I. 13 10N 61 10W
75 St. Vincent Pass. 13 30N 61 0W
65 St. Walburg 53 39N 109 12W
63 Ste-Anne de Beaupré 47 2N 70 58W
63 Ste. Cecile 47 56N 64 34W
75 Ste. Marie 14 48N 61 1W
* **57** Ste. Marie, C. 25 36S 45 8E
63 Ste-Marie de la Madeleine 46 26N 71 0W
75 Ste. Rose 16 20N 61 45W
65 Ste. Rose du lac 51 10N 99 30W
12 Saintes 45 45N 0 37W
12 Saintonge, Reg. 45 40N 0 50W
33 Sairang 23 50N 92 45E
36 Saitama □ 36 25N 137 0E
78 Sajama, Mt. 18 6S 68 54W
52 Saka 0 11S 39 30E
36 Sakai 34 30N 135 30E
36 Sakaide 34 32N 133 50E
36 Sakaiminato 35 33N 133 15E
36 Sakata 38 55N 139 56E
53 Sakété 6 40N 2 32E
25 Sakhalin 51 0N 143 0E
28 Sakhnin 32 52N 35 12E
39 Sakishima-gunto, Is. 24 30N 124 0E
55 Sakrivier 30 54S 20 28E
21 Sala 59 58N 16 35E
2 Sala-y-Gomez, I. 26 28S 105 28W
80 Saladillo 35 40S 59 55W
80 Salado, R., Buenos Aires 36 0S 57 30W
80 Salado, R., Sta. Fe. 31 40S 60 41W
50 Salaga 8 31N 0 31W
80 Salamanca, Chile 32 0S 71 25W
13 Salamanca, Sp. 40 58N 5 39W
68 Salamanca, U.S.A. 42 10N 78 42W
19 Salamis 37 56N 23 30E
35 Salatiga 7 19S 110 30E
22 Salavat 53 21N 55 55E
78 Salaverry 8 15S 79 0W
35 Salawati, I. 1 7S 130 54E
† **54** Salazar 9 18S 14 54E
56 Saldanha 33 0S 17 58E
46 Sale, Australia 38 7S 147 0E
6 Sale, U.K. 53 26N 2 19W
50 Salé 34 3N 6 48W
24 Salekhard 66 30N 66 25E
32 Salem, India 11 40N 78 11E
68 Salem, Mass. 42 29N 70 53W
68 Salem, Ohio 40 52N 80 50W
72 Salem, Oreg. 45 0N 123 0W
68 Salem, Va. 37 19N 80 8W
21 Sälen 64 41N 11 27E
18 Salerno 40 40N 14 44E
6 Salford 53 30N 2 17W
30 Salihli 38 29N 28 9E
55 Salima 13 47S 34 26E
70 Salina 38 50N 97 40W
18 Salina I. 38 35N 14 50E
74 Salina Cruz 16 10N 95 10W
79 Salinas, Brazil 16 20S 42 10W
73 Salinas, U.S.A. 36 40N 121 38W
75 Salinas, B. de 11 4N 85 45W
80 Salinas Grandes 29 30S 65 0W
79 Salinópolis 0 40S 47 20W
43 Salisbury, Australia 34 46S 138 38E
* **57** Salisbury, Zimbabwe 17 50S 31 2E
7 Salisbury, U.K. 51 4N 1 48W
68 Salisbury, Md. 38 20N 75 38W
69 Salisbury, N.C. 35 42N 80 29W
7 Salisbury Plain 51 13N 2 0W
72 Salmon 45 12N 113 56W
72 Salmon, R. 45 51N 116 46W
64 Salmon Arm 50 40N 119 15W
45 Salmon Gums 32 59S 121 38E
72 Salmon River Mts. 45 0N 114 30W
21 Salo 60 22N 23 3E
19 Salonica= Thessaloniki 40 38N 23 0E
15 Salonta 46 49N 21 42E
7 Salop □ 52 36N 2 45W
23 Salsk 46 28N 41 30E
72 Salt Lake City 40 45N 111 58W
80 Salta 24 47S 65 25W
8 Saltcoats 55 38N 4 47W
74 Saltillo 25 30N 100 57W
80 Salto 31 20S 58 10W
73 Salton Sea 33 20N 116 0W
53 Saltpond 5 15N 1 3W
64 Saltspring 48 54N 123 37W
51 Salûm 31 31N 25 7E
33 Salur 18 27N 83 18E
18 Saluzzo 44 39N 7 29E
79 Salvador, Brazil 13 0S 38 30W
65 Salvador, Canada 52 20N 109 25W
74 Salvador ■ 13 50N 89 0W
33 Salween, R. 16 31N 97 37E
14 Salzburg 47 48N 13 2E
14 Salzburg □ 47 25N 13 15E
14 Salzgitter 52 2N 10 22E
71 Sam Rayburn Res. 31 15N 94 20W
24 Sama 60 10N 60 15E
25 Samagaltai 50 36N 95 3E
31 Samangan □ 36 15N 67 40E
35 Samar, I. 12 0N 125 0E
28 Samaria, Reg.= Shomron, Reg. 32 15N 35 13E
34 Samarinda 0 30S 117 9E
24 Samarkand 39 40N 67 0E
33 Sambalpur 21 28N 83 58E
32 Sambhal 28 35N 78 37E
32 Sambhar 26 52N 75 5E
18 Sambiase 38 57N 16 17E
11 Sambre, R. 50 28N 4 52E
38 Samchŏk 37 27N 129 10E
52 Same 4 2S 37 38E
47 Samoa Is. 14 0S 171 0W
19 Sámos, I. 37 45N 26 50E
19 Samothráki, I. 40 28N 25 38E
80 Sampacho 33 20S 64 50W
35 Sampang 7 11S 113 13E
34 Sampit 2 20S 113 0E
39 Samshui 23 7N 112 58E
30 Samsun 41 15N 36 15E
34 Samui, Ko 9 30N 100 0E
34 Samut Prakan 13 32N 100 40E
34 Samut Songkhram 13 24N 100 1E
50 San 13 15N 4 45W
34 San, R., Cambodia 13 32N 105 57E
15 San, R., Poland 50 45N 21 51E
2 San Ambrosio, I. 26 21S 79 52W
75 San Andrés, I. de 12 42N 81 46W
74 San Andrés Tuxtla 18 30N 95 20W
71 San Angelo 31 30N 100 30W
80 San Antonio, Chile 33 40S 71 40W
13 San Antonio, Sp. 38 58N 1 27E
71 San Antonio, U.S.A. 29 30N 98 30W
80 San Antonio, C., Arg. 36 15S 56 40W
75 San Antonio, C., Cuba 21 50N 84 57W
75 San Antonio de los Banos 22 54N 82 31W
80 San Antonio Oeste 40 40S 65 0W
18 San Benedetto 45 2N 10 57E
71 San Benito 26 5N 97 32W
73 San Bernardino 34 7N 117 18W
35 San Bernardino Str. 12 37N 124 12E
80 San Bernardo 33 40S 70 50W
78 San Bernardo, I. de 9 45N 75 50W
75 San Blas, Cord. de 9 15N 78 30W
80 San Carlos, Arg. 33 50S 69 0W
35 San Carlos, Philippines 10 29N 123 25E
80 San Carlos, Uruguay 34 46S 54 58W
78 San Carlos, Ven. 1 55N 67 4W
78 San Carlos, Ven. 9 40N 68 36W
80 San Carlos de Bariloche 41 10S 71 25W
78 San Carlos del Zulía 9 1N 71 55W
73 San Carlos L. 33 13N 110 24W
73 San Clemente, U.S.A. 33 29N 117 45W
73 San Clemente I. 33 0N 118 30W
75 San Cristóbal, Dom. Rep. 18 25N 70 6W
80 San Cristóbal, Arg. 30 20S 61 10W
78 San Cristóbal, Ven. 7 46N 72 14W
74 San Cristóbal de las Casas 16 50N 92 33W
73 San Diego 32 50N 117 10W
80 San Diego, C. 54 40S 65 10W
80 San Felipe, Chile 32 43S 70 50W
78 San Felipe, Ven. 10 20N 68 44W
13 San Felíu de Guíxals 41 45N 3 1E
77 San Felix, I. 26 30S 80 0W
35 San Fernando, Philippines 15 5N 120 37E
35 San Fernando, Philippines 16 40N 120 23E
13 San Fernando, Sp. 36 22N 6 17W
75 San Fernando, Trinidad 10 20N 61 30W
73 San Fernando, U.S.A. 34 15N 118 29W
78 San Fernando de Apure 7 54N 67 28W
78 San Fernando de Atabapo 4 3N 67 42W
80 San Francisco, Arg. 31 30S 62 5W
73 San Francisco, U.S.A. 37 35N 122 30W
73 San Francisco, R. 32 59N 109 22W
75 San Francisco de Macoris 19 19N 70 15W
80 San Francisco de Monte del Oro 32 36S 66 8W
74 San Francisco del Oro 26 52N 105 50W
78 San Gil 6 33N 73 8W
14 San Gottardo, P. del 46 33N 8 33E
80 San Ignacio 26 52S 57 3W
72 San Joaquin, R. 36 43N 121 50W
80 San Jorge, G. de, Arg. 46 0S 66 0W
75 San José, Costa Rica 10 0N 83 57W
74 San José, Guatemala 14 0N 90 50W
35 San Jose, Philippines 15 45N 120 55E
35 San Jose, Philippines 10 50N 122 5E
73 San Jose, U.S.A. 37 20N 122 0W
80 San José, G. 42 20S 64 20W
80 San José de Jáchal 30 5S 69 0W
80 San José de Mayo 34 27S 56 27W
78 San José de Ocune 4 15N 70 20W
80 San José del Boquerón 26 5S 63 38W
74 San José del Cabo 23 0N 109 50W
78 San José del Guaviare 2 35N 72 38W
79 San José do Rio Prêto 21 0S 49 30W
80 San Juan, Arg. 31 30S 68 30W
75 San Juan, Dom. Rep. 18 49N 71 12W
74 San Juan, Mexico 21 20N 102 50W
75 San Juan, Puerto Rico 18 40N 66 11W
73 San Juan, R. 37 18N 110 28W
73 San Juan Capistrano 33 29N 117 46W
78 San Juan de los Morros 9 55N 67 21W
75 San Juan del Norte, B. de 11 30N 83 40W
73 San Juan Mts. 38 30N 108 30W
80 San Julián 49 15S 68 0W
80 San Justo 30 55S 60 30W
73 San Leandro 37 40N 122 6W
78 San Lorenzo, Ecuador 1 15N 78 50W
80 San Lorenzo, Mt. 47 40S 72 20W
74 San Lucas, C. de 22 50N 110 0W
80 San Luis 33 20S 66 20W
74 San Luis de la Paz 21 18N 100 31W
73 San Luis Obispo 35 17N 120 40W
74 San Luis Potosí 22 9N 100 59W
74 San Luis Potosí □ 22 30N 100 30W
74 San Marcos, Guatemala 14 59N 91 52W
71 San Marcos, U.S.A. 29 53N 98 0W
18 San Marino 43 56N 12 25E
18 San Marino ■ 43 56N 12 25E
73 San Mateo 37 32N 122 25W
80 San Matías, G. 41 30S 64 0W
74 San Miguel, Salvador 13 30N 88 12W
80 San Miguel de Tucumán 26 50S 65 20W
80 San Nicolás de los Arroyas 33 17S 60 10W
80 San Pedro, Arg. 24 10S 57 15W
75 San Pedro, Dom. Rep. 18 30N 69 18W
74 San Pedro de las Colonias 25 50N 102 59W
80 San Pedro del Paraná 26 43S 56 13W
74 San Pedro Sula 15 30N 88 0W
35 San Quintin 16 1N 120 56E
80 San Rafael 34 40S 68 30W
18 San Remo 43 48N 7 47E
80 San Roque 28 15S 58 45W
80 San Rosendo 37 10S 72 50W
74 San Salvador 13 40N 89 20W
75 San Salvador, I. 24 0N 74 40W
80 San Salvador de Jujuy 23 30S 65 40W
80 San Sebastián, Arg. 53 10S 68 30W
13 San Sabastián, Spain 43 17N 1 58W
18 San Severo 41 41N 15 23E
73 San Simon 32 14N 109 16W
80 San Valentín, Mt. 46 30S 73 30W
13 San Vicente de la Barquera 43 30N 4 29W
29 Sana 15 27N 44 12E
18 Sana, R. 45 3N 16 23E
53 Sanaga, R. 3 35N 9 38E
35 Sanana 2 5S 125 50E
30 Sanandaj 35 25N 47 7E
75 Sancti Spíritus 21 52N 79 33W
62 Sand Lake 47 46N 84 31W
71 Sand Springs 36 12N 96 5W
34 Sandakan 5 53N 118 10E
8 Sanday, I. 59 14N 2 30W
73 Sanders 35 12N 109 25W
43 Sandgate 27 20S 153 5E
30 Sandikli 38 30N 30 20E
21 Sandnes 58 50N 5 45E
15 Sandomierz 50 40N 21 43E
33 Sandoway 18 20N 94 30E
72 Sandpoint 48 20N 116 40W
6 Sandringham 52 50N 0 30E
45 Sandstone 28 0S 119 15E
68 Sandusky 41 25N 82 40W
56 Sandveld 32 0S 18 15E
21 Sandviken 60 38N 16 46E
33 Sandwip Chan. 22 35N 91 35E
42 Sandy, C. 24 41S 153 8E
69 Sanford, Fla. 28 45N 81 20W
69 Sanford, N.C. 35 30N 79 10W
60 Sanford, Mt. 62 30N 143 0W
73 Sanger 36 47N 119 35W
34 Sanggau 0 5N 110 30E
35 Sangihe, Pulau 3 45N 125 30E
32 Sangli 16 55N 74 33E
54 Sangmelina 2 57N 12 1E
13 Sangonera, R. 37 59N 1 4W
71 Sangre de Cristo Mts. 37 0N 105 0W
37 Sangsang 29 30N 86 0E
54 Sangwa 5 30S 26 0E
13 Sanlucar de Barrameda 36 47N 6 21W
13 Sanlúcar-la-Mayor 37 26N 6 18W

* *Renamed Vohimena, T.'i*
† *Renamed Ndalatando*

* *Renamed Harare*

39 Sanmenhsia 34 46N 111 30 E
15 Sanok 49 35N 22 10 E
8 Sanquhar 55 21N 3 56W
* 53 Sansanné-Mango 10 20N 0 30 E
78 Santa Ana, Ecuador 1 10S 80 20W
74 Santa Ana, Mexico 30 31N 111 8W
74 Santa Ana, Salvador 14 0N 89 40W
73 Santa Ana, U.S.A. 33 48N 117 55W
74 Santa Barbara, Mexico 26 48N 105 50W
73 Santa Bárbara, U.S.A. 34 25N 119 40W
73 Santa Catalina, G. of 33 0N 118 0W
73 Santa Catalina I. 33 20N 118 30W
80 Santa Catarina □ 27 25S 48 30W
75 Santa Clara, Cuba 22 20N 80 0W
73 Santa Clara, U.S.A. 37 21N 122 0W
80 Santa Cruz, Arg. 50 0S 68 50W
50 Santa Cruz, Canary Is. 28 29N 16 26W
75 Santa Cruz, Costa Rica 10 15N 85 41W
35 Santa Cruz, Philippines 14 20N 121 30 E
73 Santa Cruz, Calif. 36 55N 122 10W
73 Santa Cruz, N. Mex. 35 59N 106 1W
3 Santa Cruz, I. 0 38S 90 23W
80 Santa Cruz, R. 50 10S 68 20W
80 Santa Cruz do Sul 29 42S 52 25W
80 Santa Fe, Arg. 31 35S 60 41W
73 Sante Fe, U.S.A. 35 40N 106 0W
79 Santa Filomena 9 0S 45 50W
80 Santa Inés, I. 54 0S 73 0W
80 Santa Isabel 36 10S 67 0W
73 Santa Lucia Ra. 36 0N 121 30W
74 Santa Margarita, I. 24 30N 112 0W
80 Santa Mariá, Brazil 29 40S 53 40W
73 Santa Maria, U.S.A. 34 58N 120 29W
79 Santa Maria de Vitória 13 24S 44 12W
19 Santa Maria di Leuca, C. 39 48N 18 20 E
78 Santa Marta 11 15N 74 13W
73 Santa Monica 34 0N 118 30W
73 Santa Paula 34 20N 119 2W
80 Santa Rosa, Arg. 36 40S 64 30W
80 Santa Rosa, Brazil 27 52S 54 29W
74 Santa Rosa, Honduras 14 40N 89 0W
72 Santa Rosa, Calif. 38 20N 122 50W
71 Santa Rosa, N. Mex. 34 58N 104 40W
73 Santa Rosa I. 34 0N 120 15W
74 Santa Rosalía 27 20N 112 30W
80 Santa Vitória do Palmar 33 32S 53 25W
39 Santai 31 10N 105 2 E
80 Santana do Livramento 30 55S 55 30W
13 Santander 43 27N 3 51W
72 Santaquin 40 0N 111 51W
79 Santarem, Brazil 2 25S 54 42W
13 Santarém, Port. 39 12N 8 42W
80 Santiago, Brazil 29 11S 54 52W
80 Santiago, Chile 33 24S 70 50W
75 Santiago, Dom. Rep. 19 30N 70 40W
75 Santiago, Panama 8 0N 81 0W
13 Santiago de Compostela 42 52N 8 37W
75 Santiago de Cuba 20 0N 75 49W
80 Santiago del Estero 27 50S 64 15W
74 Santiago Ixcuintla 21 50N 105 11W
79 Santo Amaro 12 30S 38 50W
80 Santo Ângelo 28 15S 54 15W
75 Santo Domingo 18 30N 70 0W
80 Santo Tomé 28 40S 56 5W
13 Santoña 43 29N 3 20W
80 Santos 24 0S 46 20W
39 Santu 25 59N 113 3 E

* Renamed Mango

39 Santuaho 26 36N 119 42 E
28 Sanur 32 22N 35 15 E
39 Sanyuan 34 35N 108 54 E
80 São Borja 28 45S 56 0W
79 São Carlos 22 0S 47 50W
79 São Cristóvão 11 15S 37 15W
79 São Domingos 13 25S 46 10W
79 São Francisco 16 0S 44 50W
79 São Francisco, R. 10 30S 36 24W
80 São Francisco do Sul 26 15S 48 36W
80 São Gabriel 30 10S 54 30W
80 São João del Rei 21 8S 44 15W
79 São João do Araguaia 5 23S 48 46W
79 São João do Piaui 8 10S 42 15W
80 São Leopoldo 29 50S 51 10W
79 São Lourenço 16 30S 55 5W
79 São Luís 2 39S 44 15W
79 São Marcos, B. de 2 0S 44 0W
79 São Mateus 18 44S 39 50W
80 São Paulo 23 40S 56 50W
79 São Paulo □ 22 0S 49 0W
79 São Roque, C. de 5 30S 35 10W
† 54 São Salvador do Congo 6 18S 14 16 E
80 São Sebastião, I. de 23 50S 45 18W
49 São Tomé, I. 0 10N 7 0 E
13 São Vicente, C. de 37 0N 9 0W
12 Saône, R. 45 44N 4 50 E
12 Saône-et-Loire □ 46 25N 4 50 E
53 Sapele 5 50N 5 40 E
78 Saposoa 6 55S 76 30W
36 Sapporo 43 0N 141 15 E
71 Sapulpa 36 0N 96 40W
30 Saqqez 36 15N 46 20 E
13 Saragossa= Zaragoza 41 39N 0 53W
19 Sarajevo 43 52N 18 26 E
68 Saranac Lake 44 20N 74 10W
52 Saranda 5 45S 34 59 E
80 Sarandí del Yi 33 21S 55 58W
35 Sarangani B. 6 0N 125 13 E
22 Saransk 54 10N 45 10 E
22 Sarapul 56 28N 53 48 E
69 Sarasota 27 10N 82 30W
68 Saratoga Springs 43 5N 73 47W
22 Saratov 51 30N 46 2 E
34 Saravane 15 42N 106 3 E
34 Sarawak □ 2 0S 113 0 E
31 Sarbāz 26 38N 61 19 E
31 Sarbisheh 32 30N 59 40 E
33 Sarda, R. 27 22N 81 23 E
32 Sardarshahr 28 30N 74 29 E
18 Sardegna, I. 39 57N 9 0 E
18 Sardinia, I.= Sardegna, I. 39 57N 9 0 E
32 Sargodha 32 10N 72 40 E
* 32 Sargodha □ 31 45N 72 0 E
51 Sarh 9 5N 18 23 E
31 Sarī 36 30N 53 11 E
30 Sarikamiş 40 22N 42 35 E
34 Sarikei 2 8N 111 30 E
42 Sarina 21 22S 149 13 E
38 Sariwon 38 31N 125 44 E
7 Sark, I. 49 25N 2 20W
12 Sarlat-la-Canéda 44 54N 1 13 E
80 Sarmiento 45 35S 69 5W
62 Sarnia 42 58N 82 29W
22 Sarny 51 17N 26 40 E
19 Saronikós Kól. 37 45N 23 45 E
21 Sarpsborg 59 16N 11 12 E
12 Sarthe □ 47 58N 0 10 E
12 Sarthe, R. 47 30N 0 32W
24 Sartynya 63 30N 62 50 E
31 Sarur 23 17N 58 4 E
24 Sary Tash 39 45N 73 40 E
24 Saryshagan 46 12N 73 48 E
29 Sasabeneh 7 59N 44 43 E
33 Sasaram 24 57N 84 5 E
36 Sasebo 33 15N 129 50 E
65 Saskatchewan □ 53 40N 103 30W
65 Saskatchewan, R. 53 12N 99 16W
65 Saskatoon 52 10N 106 45W
25 Saskylakh 71 55N 114 1 E
57 Sasolburg 26 46S 27 49 E
22 Sasovo 54 25N 41 55 E
50 Sassandra 5 0N 6 8W
50 Sassandra, R. 4 58N 6 5W
18 Sássari 40 44N 8 33 E
14 Sassnitz 54 29N 13 39 E
32 Satara 17 44N 73 58 E
22 Satka 55 3N 59 1 E

* Now part of Punjab
† Renamed Mbanza Congo

32 Satmala Hills 20 15N 74 40 E
33 Satna 24 35N 80 50 E
15 Sátoraljaújhely 48 25N 21 41 E
32 Satpura Ra. 21 40N 75 0 E
15 Satu Mare 47 48N 22 53 E
34 Satun 6 43N 100 2 E
21 Sauda 59 38N 6 21 E
20 Sauđarkrókur 65 45N 19 40W
29 Saudi Arabia ■ 26 0N 44 0 E
62 Sault Ste. Marie, Canada 46 30N 84 20W
68 Saulte Ste. Marie, U.S.A. 46 27N 84 22W
12 Saumur 47 15N 0 5W
20 Saurbaer 64 24N 21 35W
53 Sauri 11 30N 6 35 E
19 Sava, R. 44 50N 20 26 E
47 Savaii, I. 13 35S 172 25W
53 Savalou 7 57N 2 4 E
70 Savanna 42 5N 90 10W
69 Savannah 32 4N 81 4W
69 Savannah, R. 32 2N 80 53W
34 Savannakhet 16 30N 104 49 E
62 Savant Lake 50 20N 90 40W
53 Savé 8 2N 2 17 E
57 Save, R. 43 47N 1 17 E
30 Sāveh 35 2N 50 20 E
53 Savelugu 9 38N 0 54W
12 Savoie □ 45 26N 6 35 E
12 Savoie, Reg. 45 30N 5 20 E
18 Savona 44 19N 8 29 E
35 Sawai 3 0S 129 5 E
34 Sawankhalok 17 19N 99 54 E
73 Sawatch Mts. 38 30N 106 30W
51 Sawknah 29 4N 15 47 E
55 Sawmills 19 30S 28 2 E
35 Sawu Sea 9 30S 121 50 E
53 Saya 9 30N 3 18 E
63 Sayabec 38 35N 67 41W
30 Sayda 33 35N 35 25 E
38 Saynshand 44 55N 110 11 E
68 Sayre 42 0N 76 30W
32 Sazin 35 35N 73 30 E
6 Sca Fell, Mt 54 27N 3 14W
4 Scandinavia, Reg. 65 0N 15 0 E
8 Scapa Flow 58 52N 3 0W
6 Scarborough 54 17N 0 24W
14 Schaffhausen 47 42N 8 36 E
63 Schefferville 54 50N 66 40W
11 Schelde, R. 51 22N 4 15 E
68 Schenectady 42 50N 73 58W
11 Scheveningen 52 6N 4 18 E
11 Schiedam 51 55N 4 25 E
18 Schío 45 42N 11 21 E
14 Schleswig-Holstein □ 54 10N 9 40 E
35 Schouten, Kep. 1 0S 136 0 E
62 Schreiber 48 45N 87 20W
62 Schumacher 48 30N 81 16W
72 Schurz 38 59N 118 57W
14 Schwäbische Alb, Mts. 48 30N 9 30 E
38 Schwangcheng 45 27N 126 27 E
38 Schwangyashan 46 35N 131 15 E
56 Schwarzrand, Mts. 26 0S 17 0 E
14 Schwarzwald 48 0N 8 0 E
14 Schweinfurt 50 3N 10 12 E
56 Schweizer-Reneke 27 11S 25 18 E
14 Schwerin 53 37N 11 22 E
14 Schwyz 47 2N 8 39 E
18 Sciacca 37 30N 13 3 E
18 Scilla 38 15N 15 44 E
29 Scillave 6 22N 44 32 E
7 Scilly Is. 49 55N 6 15W
70 Scobey 48 47N 105 30W
46 Scone, Australia 32 0S 150 52 E
8 Scone, U.K. 56 25N 3 26W
2 Scotia Sea 56 5S 56 0W
8 Scotland ■ 57 0N 4 0W
70 Scott City 38 30N 100 52W
70 Scottsbluff 41 55N 103 35W
57 Scottsburgh 30 15S 30 47 E
42 Scottsdale 41 9S 147 31 E
68 Scranton 41 22N 75 41W
6 Scunthorpe 53 35N 0 38W
46 Sea Lake 35 28S 142 55 E
62 Seaforth 43 35N 81 25W
65 Seal, R. 59 4N 94 48W
73 Searchlight 35 31N 111 57W
71 Searcy 35 15N 91 45W
72 Seattle 47 41N 122 15W
74 Sebastián Vizcaíno, B. 28 0N 114 0W
72 Sebastopol 38 16N 122 56W
69 Sebring 27 36N 81 47W
47 Secretary, I. 45 15S 166 56 E
32 Secunderabad 17 28N 78 30 E
70 Sedalia 38 40N 93 18W

12 Sedan 49 43N 4 57 E
47 Seddon 41 40S 174 7 E
47 Seddonville 41 33 E 172 1 E
28 Sede Ya'aqov 32 43N 35 7 E
64 Sedgewick 52 48N 111 41W
28 Sedom 31 5N 35 20 E
72 Sedro Woolley 48 30N 122 15W
56 Seeheim 26 32S 17 52 E
34 Segamat 2 30N 102 50 E
50 Ségou 13 30N 6 10W
13 Segovia 40 57N 4 10W
13 Segre, R. 41 40N 0 43 E
50 Séguéla 7 57N 6 40W
71 Seguin 29 34N 97 58W
13 Segura, R. 38 6N 0 54W
31 Sehkonj, Kuh-e 30 0N 57 30 E
32 Sehore 23 10N 77 5 E
12 Seille, R. 49 7N 6 11 E
20 Seinäjoki 62 47N 22 50 E
12 Seine, R. 49 30N 0 20 E
12 Seine-et-Marne □ 48 45N 3 0 E
12 Seine-Maritime □ 49 40N 1 0 E
12 Seine-St -Denis □ 48 55N 2 28 E
52 Seke 3 20S 33 31 E
52 Sekenke 4 18S 34 11 E
53 Sekondi-Takoradi 5 2N 1 48W
34 Selatan □, Kalimantan 3 0S 115 0 E
35 Selatan □, Sulawesi 3 0S 120 0 E
34 Selatan □, Sumatera 3 0S 105 0 E
6 Selby 53 47N 1 5W
60 Seldovia 59 27N 151 43W
55 Selebi-Pikwe 22 0S 27 45 E
38 Selenge 49 25N 103 59 E
50 Sélibaby 15 20N 12 15W
65 Selkirk, Canada 50 10N 97 20W
8 Selkirk, U.K. 55 33N 2 50W
64 Selkirk Mts. 51 0N 117 10W
69 Selma, Ala. 32 30N 87 0W
73 Selma, Calif. 36 39N 119 30W
7 Selsey Bill 50 43N 0 48W
† 57 Selukwe 19 40S 30 0 E
80 Selva 29 50S 62 0W
35 Semarang 7 0S 110 26 E
35 Semeru, Mt. 8 4S 113 3 E
72 Seminoe Res. 42 0N 107 0W
71 Seminole, Okla. 35 15N 96 45W
71 Seminole, Tex. 32 41N 102 38W
24 Semiozernoye 52 35N 64 0 E
24 Semipalatinsk 50 30N 80 10 E
31 Semnān 35 55N 53 25 E
31 Semnān □ 36 0N 54 0 E
35 Semporna 4 30N 118 33 E
78 Sena Madureira 9 5S 68 45W
79 Senador Pompeu 5 40S 39 20W
55 Senanga 16 2S 23 14 E
36 Sendai, Kagoshima 31 50N 130 20 E
36 Sendai, Miyagi 38 15N 141 0 E
72 Seneca 44 10N 119 2W
68 Seneca Falls 42 55N 76 50W
50 Senegal ■ 14 30N 14 30W
50 Senegal, R. 16 30N 15 30W
48 Senegambia, Reg. 14 0N 14 0W
57 Senekal 28 18S 27 36 E
79 Senhor-do Bonfim 10 30S 40 10W
18 Senj 45 0N 14 58 E
12 Senlis 49 13N 2 35 E
51 Sennâr 13 30N 33 35 E
62 Senneterre 48 25N 77 15W
12 Sens 48 11N 3 15 E
35 Sentolo 7 55S 110 13 E
53 Senya Beraku 5 28N 0 31W
13 Seo de Urgel 42 22N 1 23 E
38 Seoul=Soul 37 20N 126 15 E
63 Separation Pt. 53 40N 57 16W
63 Sept-Îles 50 13N 66 22W
72 Sequim 48 3N 123 9W
73 Sequoia Nat. Park 36 20N 118 30W
11 Seraing 50 35N 5 32 E
35 Seram, I. 3 10S 129 0 E
35 Seram Sea 3 0S 130 0 E
33 Serampore 22 44N 88 30 E
35 Serang 6 8S 106 10 E
19 Serbia □ 43 30N 21 0 E
22 Serdobsk 52 28N 44 10 E
34 Seremban 2 43N 101 53 E
52 Serengeti Nat. Park 2 40S 35 0 E
55 Serenje 13 11S 30 52 E
79 Sergipe □ 10 30S 37 30W
34 Seria 4 37N 114 30 E
34 Serian 1 10N 110 40 E
19 Sérifos 37 8N 24 34 E
24 Serov 59 40N 60 20 E
56 Serowe 22 25S 26 43 E
* 55 Serpa Pinto 14 48S 17 52 E
45 Serpentine 32 22S 115 59 E

* Renamed Menongue
† Renamed Shurugwi

22 Serpukhov 54 55N 37 28 E
19 Sérrai 41 5N 23 32 E
80 Serrezuela 30 40 S 65 20W
79 Serrinha 11 39 E 39 0W
79 Sertania 8 5 S 37 20W
55 Serule 21 57 S 27 11 E
52 Sese Is. 0 30 S 32 30 E
56 Sesheke 17 29 S 24 13 E
13 Sestao 43 18N 3 0W
12 Sète 43 25N 3 42 E
79 Sete Lagôas 19 27 S 44 16W
50 Sétif 36 9N 5 26 E
36 Seto 35 14N 137 6 E
36 Setonaikai 34 10N 133 10 E
50 Settat 33 0N 7 40W
54 Setté Cama 2 32 S 9 57 E
6 Settle 54 5N 2 18W
13 Setúbal 38 30N 8 58W
13 Setúbal, B. de 38 40N 8 56W
34 Seulimeum 5 27N 95 15 E
23 Sevan L.
23 Sevastopol 44 35N 33 30 E
62 Severn, R., Canada 56 2N 87 36W
7 Severn, R., U.K. 51 25N 3 0W
25 Severnaya Zemlya, I. 79 0N 100 0 E
22 Severnyye Uvaly, Reg. 58 0N 48 0 E
22 Severodvinsk 64 27N 39 58 E
13 Sevilla 37 23N 6 0W
13 Seville=Sevilla 37 23N 6 0W
60 Seward 60 0N 149 40W
60 Seward Pen. 65 0N 164 0W
27 Seychelles, Is. 5 0 S 56 0 E
20 Seyđisfjörđur 65 16N 14 0W
46 Seymour, Australia 36 58 S 145 10 E
68 Seymour, U.S.A. 39 0N 85 50W
51 Sfax 34 49N 10 48 E
15 Sfintu-Gheorghe 45 52N 25 48 E
11 's-Gravenhage 52 7N 4 17 E
49 Shaba, Reg. 8 30 S 25 0 E
† 57 Shabani 20 17 S 30 2 E
54 Shabunda 2 40 S 27 16 E
24 Shadrinsk 56 5N 63 38 E
53 Shaffa 10 30N 12 6 E
7 Shaftesbury 51 0N 2 12W
53 Shagamu 6 51N 3 39 E
‡ 31 Sháhábád 37 40N 56 50 E
• 30 Shāhbād 34 10N 46 30 E
38 Shahcheng 40 18N 115 27 E
31 Shahdād 30 30N 57 40 E
32 Shahdadkot 27 50N 67 55 E
51 Shahhat 32 40N 21 35 E
** 31 Shāhī 36 30N 52 55 E
†† 30 Shāhpūr 38 12N 44 45 E
‡‡ 31 Shahrezā 32 0N 51 55 E
32 Shahrig 30 15N 67 40 E
* 31 Shāhrūd 36 30N 55 0 E
•• 31 Shahsavar 36 45N 51 12 E
31 Shaikhabad 34 0N 68 45 E
32 Shajapur 23 20N 76 15 E
23 Shakhty 47 40N 40 10 E
22 Shakhunya 57 40N 47 0 E
53 Shaki 8 41N 3 21 E
39 Shalu 24 24N 120 26 E
31 Sham, Jabal ash 23 10N 57 5 E
53 Shama 5 1N 1 42W
31 Shamil 29 32N 77 18 E
54 Shamo, L. 5 45N 37 30 E
68 Shamokin 40 47N 76 33W
55 Shamva 17 18 S 31 34 E
33 Shan □ 21 30N 98 30 E
38 Schanchengtze 42 2N 123 47 E
50 Shanga 9 1N 5 2 E
55 Shangani, R. 18 41 S 27 10 E
38 Shangchih 45 10N 127 59 E
39 Schangchwan Shan, I. 21 35N 112 45 E
39 Shanghai 31 10N 121 25 E
39 Shangjao 28 25N 117 25 E
39 Shangkiu 34 28N 115 42 E
39 Shangshui 33 42N 115 4 E
38 Shanh 47 5N 103 5 E
53 Shani 10 14N 12 2 E
47 Shannon 40 33 S 17 25 E
9 Shannon, R. 52 30N 9 53W
38 Shansi □ 37 0N 113 0 E
39 Shantou= Shantow 23 25N 116 40 E
39 Shantow 23 25N 116 40 E
38 Shantung □ 37 0N 118 0 E
39 Shanyang 33 39N 110 2 E
39 Shaohing 30 0N 120 32 E
39 Shaowu 27 25N 117 30 E
39 Shaoyang 27 10N 111 30 E
8 Shapinsay, I. 59 2N 2 50W
30 Shaqra 25 15N 45 16 E
38 Sharin Gol 49 12N 106 27 E
31 Sharjah 25 23N 55 26 E
45 Shark, B. 25 15 S 133 20 E
68 Sharon 41 14N 80 31W
22 Sharya 58 12N 45 40 E
55 Shashi 21 40 S 28 40 E
57 Shashi, R. 22 14 S 29 20 E
39 Shasi 30 16N 112 20 E
72 Shasta, Mt. 41 45N 122 0W
72 Shasta Res. 40 50N 122 15W
65 Shaunavon 49 35N 108 40W
70 Shawano 44 45N 88 38W
62 Shawinigan 46 35N 72 50W
71 Shawnee 35 15N 97 0W
29 Shebele, Wabi 2 0N 44 0 E
68 Sheboygan 43 46N 87 45W
53 Shebshi Mts. 8 30N 12 0 E
63 Shediac 46 14N 64 32W
7 Sheerness 51 26N 0 47 E
28 Shefar'am 32 48N 35 10 E
6 Sheffield 53 23N 1 28W
32 Shekhupura 31 42N 73 58 E
39 Shekki 22 30N 113 15 E
39 Sheklung 23 5N 113 55 E
63 Shelburne, Nova Scotia 43 47N 65 20W
62 Shelburne, Ont. 44 4N 80 15W
72 Shelby, Mont. 48 30N 111 59W
69 Shelby, N.C. 35 18N 81 34W
68 Shelbyville, Ind. 39 30N 85 42W
69 Shelbyville, Tenn. 35 30N 86 25W
63 Sheldrake 50 20N 64 51W
25 Shelikhova Zaliv 59 30N 157 0 E
65 Shell Lake 53 19N 107 6W
65 Shellbrook 53 13N 106 24W
63 Shelter Bay 50 30N 67 20W
60 Shelton, Alaska 55 20N 105 0W
72 Shelton, Wash. 47 15N 123 6W
23 Shemakha 40 50N 48 28 E
70 Shenandoah, Iowa 40 50N 95 25W
68 Shenandoah, Pa. 40 49N 76 13W
68 Shenandoah, R. 39 19N 77 44W
53 Shendam 9 10N 9 30 E
51 Shendî 16 46N 33 33 E
38 Shensi □ 35 0N 109 0 E
38 Shenyang 41 35N 123 30 E
46 Shepparton 36 18 S 145 25 E
7 Sherborne 50 56N 2 31W
50 Sherbro I. 7 30N 12 40W
63 Sherbrooke 45 24N 71 57W
72 Sheridan 44 50N 107 0W
71 Sherman 33 40N 96 35W
65 Sherridon 55 10N 101 5W
11 s'Hertogenbosch 51 41N 5 19 E
6 Sherwood Forest 53 5N 1 5W
55 Shesheke 17 50 S 24 0 E
8 Shetland □ 60 30N 1 30W
24 Shevchenko 44 25N 51 20 E
28 Shevut'Am 32 19N 34 55 E
29 Shibam 16 0N 48 36 E
31 Shibarghan 36 40N 65 48 E
36 Shibushi 31 25N 131 0 E
* 63 Shickshock Mts. 48 40N 66 30W
8 Shiel, L. 56 48N 5 32W
36 Shiga □ 35 20N 136 0 E
37 Shigatse 29 10N 89 0 E
38 Shihchiachuangi= Shihkiachwang 38 0N 114 32 E
38 Shihkiachwang 38 0N 114 32 E
39 Shihpu 29 12N 121 58 E
38 Shihwei 51 28N 119 59 E
32 Shikarpur 27 57N 68 39 E
36 Shikoku, I. 33 45N 133 30 E
36 Shikoku □ 33 30N 133 30 E
9 Shillelagh 52 46N 6 32W
25 Shilka 52 0N 115 55 E
33 Shillong 25 30N 92 0 E
36 Shimada 34 49N 138 19 E
36 Shimane □ 35 0N 132 30 E
25 Shimanovsk 52 15N 127 30 E
36 Shimizu 35 0N 138 30 E
36 Shimodate 36 20N 139 55 E
32 Shimoga 13 57N 75 32 E
36 Shimonoseki 33 58N 131 0 E
24 Shimpek 44 50N 74 10 E
8 Shin, L. 58 7N 4 30W
31 Shin Dand 33 12N 62 8 E
36 Shingú 33 40N 135 33 E
52 Shinyanga 3 45 S 33 27 E
63 Shippegan 47 45N 64 45W
36 Shirane-San, Mt. 35 40N 138 15 E
31 Shiráz 29 42N 52 30 E
55 Shire, R. 17 42 S 35 19 E
39 Shiukwan 24 58N 113 3 E
32 Shivpuri 25 18N 77 42 E
36 Shizuoka 35 0N 138 30 E
36 Shizuoka □ 35 15N 138 40 E
19 Shkodra 42 6N 19 20 E
65 Shoal Lake 50 30N 100 35W
7 Shoeburyness 51 13N 0 49 E
38 Shohsien 39 30N 112 25 E
32 Sholapur 17 43N 75 56 E
25 Shologontsy 66 13N 114 14 E
28 Shomera 33 4N 35 17 E
28 Shómrón, Reg. 32 15N 35 13 E
72 Shoshone 43 0N 114 27W
55 Shoshong 22 0 S 26 30 E
73 Show Low 34 16N 110 0W
71 Shreveport 32 30N 93 50W
6 Shrewsbury 52 42N 2 45W
39 Shucheng 31 25N 117 2 E
39 Shuikiahu 32 14N 117 4 E
60 Shumagin Is. 55 0N 159 0W
24 Shumikha 55 15N 63 30 E
28 Shunat Nimran 31 54N 35 37 E
39 Shunchang 26 52N 117 48 E
60 Shungnak 66 53N 157 2W
29 Shuqra 13 22N 45 34 E
31 Shúsf 31 50N 60 5 E
30 Shushtar 32 0N 48 50 E
28 Shuweika 32 20N 35 1 E
38 Shwangliano 43 39N 123 40 E
33 Shwebo 22 30N 95 45 E
33 Shwegu 24 15N 96 50 E
32 Shyok 34 15N 78 5 E
32 Shyok, R. 35 13N 75 53 E
34 Si Racha 13 20N 101 10 E
32 Siahan Ra. 27 30N 64 40 E
37 Siakwan 25 45N 100 10 E
32 Sialkot 32 32N 74 30 E
34 Siam=Thailand ■ 15 0N 100 0 E
* 34 Siam, G. of 11 30N 101 0 E
39 Sian 34 2N 109 0 E
39 Sian Kiang, R. 22 30N 110 10 E
39 Siangfan 32 15N 112 2 E
39 Siangtan 28 0N 112 55 E
39 Siangyang 32 18N 111 0 E
38 Siao Hingan Ling, Mts. 49 0N 127 0 E
35 Siargao, I. 9 52N 126 3 E
22 Siauhai 55 56N 23 15 E
65 Sibbald 51 24N 110 10W
18 Sibenik 43 48N 15 54 E
3 Siberia, Reg. 66 0N 120 0 E
34 Siberut, I. 1 30 S 99 0 E
32 Sibi 29 30N 67 48 E
54 Sibiti 3 38 S 13 19 E
15 Sibiu 45 45N 24 9 E
34 Sibolga 1 50N 98 45 E
33 Sibsagar 27 0N 94 36 E
34 Sibu 2 19N 111 51 E
35 Sibutu Pass. 4 50N 120 0 E
35 Sibuyan, I. 12 25N 122 40 E
35 Sibuyan Sea 12 50N 122 20 E
37 Sichang 28 0N 102 10 E
18 Sicilia □ 37 30N 14 30 E
18 Sicilia, I. 37 30N 14 30 E
78 Sicuani 14 10 S 71 10W
51 Sidi Barrâni 31 32N 25 58 E
50 Sidi bel Abbès 35 13N 0 10W
50 Sidi Ifni 29 29N 10 3W
8 Sidlaw Hills 56 32N 3 10W
7 Sidmouth 50 40N 3 13W
64 Sidney, Canada 48 39N 123 24W
68 Sidney, U.S.A. 40 18N 84 6W
35 Sidoardjo 7 30 S 112 46 E
15 Siedlce 52 10N 22 20 E
14 Siegen 50 52N 8 2 E
34 Siem Reap 13 20N 103 52 E
18 Siena 43 20N 11 20 E
39 Sieyang 34 20N 108 48 E
78 Sierra Gorda 23 0 S 69 15W
50 Sierra Leone ■ 9 0N 12 0W
72 Sierra Nevada, Mts. 40 0N 121 0W
19 Sifnos, I. 37 0N 24 45 E
15 Sighet 47 57N 23 32 E
15 Sighisoara 46 12N 24 50 E
34 Sigli 5 25N 96 0 E
20 Siglufjörđur 66 12N 18 55W
78 Sigsig 3 0 S 78 50W
21 Sigtuna 59 36N 17 44 E
13 Sigüenza 41 3N 2 40W
50 Siguiri 11 31N 9 10W
73 Sigurd 38 57N 112 0W
34 Sihanoukville = Kompong Som 10 40N 103 30 E
39 Sihsien 29 55N 118 23 E
30 Siirt 37 57N 41 55 E
39 Si Kiang, R. 22 0N 114 0 E
39 Sikandarabad 28 30N 77 39 E
32 Sikar 27 39N 75 10 E
50 Sikasso 11 7N 5 35W
71 Sikeston 36 52N 89 35W
25 Sikhote Alin Khrebet 46 0N 136 0 E
33 Sikkim □ 27 50N 88 50 E
13 Sil, R. 42 27N 7 43W
38 Silamulun, R. 43 20N 121 0 E
28 Sîlat adh Dhahr 32 19N 35 11 E
14 Silesia, Reg.= Slask, Reg. 51 0N 16 45 E
33 Silghat 26 35N 93 0 E
33 Siliguri 26 45N 88 25 E
19 Silistra 44 6N 27 19 E
21 Siljan, L. 60 55N 14 45 E
21 Silkeborg 56 10N 9 32 E
* 55 Silva Porto 12 22 S 16 55 E
73 Silver City, Panama Canal Zone 9 21N 79 53W
73 Silver City, U.S.A. 32 50N 108 18W
68 Silver Creek 42 33N 79 9W
28 Silwan 31 59N 35 15 E
34 Simanggang 1 15N 111 25 E
52 Simba 2 11 S 37 35 E
62 Simcoe, Canada 42 50N 80 20W
62 Simcoe, L. 44 20N 79 20W
25 Simenga 62 50N 107 55 E
15 Simeria 45 51N 23 1 E
34 Simeulue, I. 2 45N 95 45 E
23 Simferopol 44 55N 34 3 E
32 Simla 31 2N 77 15
65 Simmie 49 56N 108 6W
14 Simplonpass 46 15N 8 0 E
42 Simpson, Des. 25 0 S 137 0 E
51 Sinâ', Gebel el Tih Es 29 0N 33 30 E
51 Sinai = Es Sinâ' 29 0N 34 0 E
74 Sinaloa □ 25 50N 108 20W
78 Sincelejo 9 18N 75 24W
39 Sincheng 34 25N 113 56W
79 Sincorá, Sa. do 13 30 S 41 0W
32 Sind Sagar Doab 32 0N 71 30 E
35 Sindangbarang 7 27 S 107 9 E
13 Sines 37 56N 8 51 E
39 Sinfeng 26 59N 106 55 E
51 Singa 13 10N 33 57 E
35 Singaparna 7 23 S 108 4 E
34 Singapore ■ 1 17N 103 51 E
52 Singida 4 49 S 34 48 E
19 Singitikós Kól. 40 6N 24 0 E
33 Singkling Hkamti 26 0N 95 45 E
34 Singkawang 1 0N 109 5 E
34 Singkep 0 30 S 140 20 E
34 Singora=Songkhla 7 13N 100 37 E
38 Singtai 37 2N 114 30 E
39 Singtze 29 30N 116 4 E
39 Sinhailien 34 31N 119 0 E
38 Sinhsien 38 25N 112 45 E
39 Sinhwa 27 36N 111 6 E
37 Sining 36 35N 101 50 E
30 Sinjār 36 19N 41 52 E
28 Sinjil 32 3N 35 15 E
51 Sinkat 18 55N 36 49 E
38 Sinkiang 35 35N 111 25 E
37 Sinkiang-Uigur □ 42 0N 85 0 E
38 Sinkin 39 30N 122 29 E
79 Sinnamary 5 23N 52 57W
51 Sinnûris 29 26N 30 31 E
† 57 Sinoia 17 20 S 30 8 E
30 Sinop 42 1N 35 11 E
39 Sinsiang 35 15N 113 55 E
34 Sintang 0 5N 111 35 E
13 Sintra 38 47N 9 25W
38 Sinuiju 40 5N 124 24 E
39 Sinyang 32 6N 114 2 E
14 Sion 46 14N 7 20 E
70 Sioux City 42 32N 96 25W
70 Sioux Falls 43 35N 96 40W
62 Sioux Lookout 50 10N 91 50W
75 Siparia 10 15N 61 30W
39 Siping 33 25N 114 10 E
75 Siquia, R. 12 30N 84 30W
31 Sir Bani Yas, I. 24 20N 54 0 E
42 Sir Edward Pellew Group, Is. 15 40 S 137 10 E
60 Sir James McBrien, Mt. 62 7N 127 41W
18 Siracusa 37 4N 15 17 E
33 Sirajganj 24 25N 89 47 E
15 Siret, R. 47 55N 26 5 E
19 Síros 37 28N 24 56 E
32 Sirsa 29 33N 75 4 E
18 Sisak 45 30N 16 21 E
34 Sisaket 15 8N 104 23 E
34 Sisophon 13 31N 102 59 E
31 Sistan Baluchistan □ 27 0N 62 0 E
33 Sitapur 27 38N 80 45 E
13 Sitges 41 17N 1 47 E
64 Sitka 57 9N 134 58W
33 Sittang Myit, R. 18 20N 96 45 E
11 Sittard 51 0N 5 52 E
35 Situbondo 7 45 S 114 0 E
31 Sivand 30 5N 52 55 E

* Renamed Emāmrud
† Renamed Zvishavane
‡ Renamed Ashkhāneh
• Renamed Eslāmābād-e Gharb

* French nameform Chic-Chocs, Mts.

** Renamed Qā'emshahr
†† Renamed Salmās

* Thailand, G. of

‡‡ Renamed Qomsheh
•• Renamed Tonekābon

* Renamed Kuito
† Renamed Chinhoyi

30 Sivas 39 43N 36 58E
30 Siverek 37 50N 39 25E
51 Siwa 29 11N 25 31E
33 Siwalik Ra. 28 0N 83 0E
7 Sizewell 52 13N 1 38E
21 Sjaelland, I. 55 30N 11 30E
19 Skadarsko, Jezero, L. 42 10N 19 15E
21 Skagen 57 43N 10 35E
21 Skagerrak, Str. 57 30N 9 0E
64 Skagway 59 30N 135 20W
21 Skara 58 25N 13 30E
21 Skaraborg □ 58 20N 13 30E
32 Skardu 35 20N 73 35E
64 Skeena, R. 54 15N 130 5W
64 Skenna Mts. 56 40N 128 0W
6 Skegnwss 53 9N 0 20E
78 Skeldon 6 0N 57 20W
20 Skellefteå 64 45N 20 59E
20 Skelleftehamn 64 41N 21 14E
9 Skibbereen 51 33N 9 16W
6 Skiddaw, Mt. 54 39N 3 9W
21 Skien 59 12N 9 35E
15 Skierniewice 51 58N 20 19E
50 Skikda 36 50N 6 58E
6 Skipton 53 57N 2 1W
19 Skíros, I. 38 55N 24 34E
21 Skive 56 33N 9 2E
21 Skoghall 59 20N 13 30E
19 Skopje 42 1N 21 32E
19 Skoplje=Skopje 42 1N 21 32E
21 Skövde 58 24N 13 50E
25 Skovorodino 53 59N 123 55E
69 Skowhegan 44 49N 69 40W
21 Skudeneshavn 59 10N 5 10E
9 Skull 51 32N 9 40W
14 Skwierzyna 52 46N 15 30E
8 Skye, I. 57 15N 6 10W
9 Slaney, R. 52 52N 6 45W
14 Slask, Reg. 51 0N 16 45E
15 Slatina 44 28N 24 22E
71 Slaton 33 27N 101 38W
53 Slave Coast 6 0N 2 30E
64 Slave Lake 55 25N 114 50W
24 Slavgorod 53 10N 78 50E
23 Slavyansk 45 15N 38 11E
6 Sleaford 53 0N 0 22W
8 Sleat, Sd. of 57 5N 5 47W
11 Sliedrecht 51 50N 4 45E
18 Sliema 35 55N 14 29E
9 Sligo 54 17N 8 28W
9 Sligo □ 54 10N 8 40W
21 Slite 57 42N 18 45E
22 Slobodskoy 58 40N 50 6E
7 Slough 51 30N 0 35W
18 Slovenia□= Slovenija 45 58N 14 30E
18 Slovenija □ 45 58N 14 30E
15 Slovenské Rudohorie, Mts. 50 25N 13 0E
14 Słupsk 54 28N 17 1E
25 Slyudyanka 51 40N 103 30E
65 Smeaton 53 30N 105 49W
19 Smederevo 44 40N 20 57E
64 Smith 55 10N 114 0W
60 Smith Arm, B. 66 30N 123 0W
64 Smithers 54 45N 127 10W
56 Smithfield, S. Afr 30 13S 26 32E
69 Smithfield, U.S.A. 35 31N 78 16W
62 Smiths Falls 44 55N 76 0W
42 Smithton 40 53S 145 6E
62 Smoky Falls 50 10N 82 10W
70 Smoky Hill, R. 39 3N 96 48W
22 Smolensk 54 45N 32 0E
19 Smolikas, Mt. 40 9N 20 58E
62 Smooth Rock Falls 49 17N 81 37W
6 Snaefell, Mt. 54 18N 4 26W
20 Snaefellsjökull.Mt. 64 50N 23 49W
72 Snake, R. 46 12N 119 2W
72 Snake River Plain 43 13N 113 0W
11 Sneek 53 2N 5 40E
56 Sneeuberg 31 46S 24 20E
14 Sněžka, Mt. 50 41N 14 55E
20 Snøhetta, Mt. 62 19N 9 16E
65 Snow Lake 54 53N 101 2W
6 Snowdon, Mt. 53 4N 4 8W
73 Snowflake 34 30N 110 4W
72 Snowshoe Pk. 48 13N 115 41W
46 Snowy, Mts. 36 15S 148 20E
71 Snyder 32 45N 100 57W
57 Soalala 16 6S 45 20E
72 Soap Lake 47 29N 119 31W
79 Sobral 3 50S 40 30W
37 Soche 38 24N 77 20E
23 Sochi 43 35N 39 40E
2 Society Is. 17 0S 151 0W
78 Socorro, Col. 6 29N 73 16W
73 Socorro, U.S.A. 34 3N 106 58W
29 Socotra, I. 12 30N 54 0E
64 Soda Creek 52 25N 122 10W
72 Soda Springs 42 4N 111 40W
21 Söderhamn 61 18N 17 10E
21 Söderköping 58 31N 16 35E
21 Södermanlands □ 59 10N 16 30E
21 Södertälje 59 12N 17 50E
54 Sodo 7 0N 37 57E
57 Soekmekaar 23 30S 29 55E
11 Soest, Neth. 52 9N 5 19E
55 Sofala = Beira 19 50S 34 52E
19 Sofia=Sofiya 42 45N 23 20E
19 Sofiya 42 45N 23 20E
78 Sogamoso 5 43N 72 56W
21 Sogn og Fjordane □ 61 40N 6 0E
51 Sohâg 26 27N 31 43E
11 Soignes 50 35N 4 5E
12 Soissons 49 25N 3 19E
30 Soke 37 48N 27 28E
53 Sokodé 9 0N 1 11E
22 Sokol 59 30N 40 5E
15 Sokólka 53 25N 23 30E
53 Sokoto 13 2N 5 16E
53 Sokoto, R. 11 20N 4 10E
53 Sokoto □ 11 40N 5 15E
52 Solai 0 2N 36 12E
35 Solano 16 25N 121 15E
78 Soledad, Col. 10 55N 74 46W
73 Soledad, U.S.A. 36 27N 121 16W
78 Soledad, Ven. 8 10N 63 34W
7 Solent 50 45N 1 25W
22 Soligalich 59 5N 42 10E
22 Solikamsk 59 38N 56 50E
20 Sollefteå 63 10N 17 20E
13 Sóller 39 43N 2 45E
12 Sologne, Reg. 47 40N 2 0E
34 Solok 0 55S 100 40E
74 Sololá 14 49N 91 10E
3 Solomon Is. 8 0S 159 0E
14 Solothurn 47 13N 7 32E
31 Soltānābād 36 29N 58 5E
* 30 Soltāniyeh 36 20N 48 55E
21 Sölvesborg 56 5N 14 35E
22 Solvychegodsk 61 21N 46 52E
55 Solwezi 12 20S 26 26E
8 Solway Firth 54 45N 3 38W
† 57 Somabula 19 40S 29 38E
29 Somali Rep. ■ 7 0N 47 0E
75 Somerset, Bermuda 32 20N 64 55W
68 Somerset, Ky. 37 5N 84 40W
7 Somerset □ 51 9N 3 0W
56 Somerset East 32 42S 25 35E
56 Somerset West 34 8S 18 50E
75 Somerset I., Bermuda 32 20N 64 55W
60 Somerset I., Canada 73 30N 93 0W
15 Someş, R. 47 9N 23 55E
12 Somme □ 40 0N 2 15E
12 Somme, R. 50 11N 1 39E
19 Somovit 43 45N 24 48E
13 Somport, Pto. de 42 48N 0 31W
56 Sondags, R. 33 44S 25 51E
21 Sønderborg 54 55N 9 49E
2 Søndre Strømfjord 66 30N 50 52W
32 Sonepat 29 0N 77 5E
33 Sonepur 20 55N 83 50E
52 Songea 10 40S 35 40E
21 Songefjorden 61 10N 5 30E
34 Songkhla 7 13N 100 37E
32 Sonmiani 25 25N 66 40E
71 Sonora 30 33N 100 37W
74 Sonora □ 37 59N 120 27W
74 Sonsonate 13 45N 89 45W
39 Soochow 31 18N 120 41E
15 Sopot 54 27N 18 31E
14 Sopron 47 41N 16 37E
63 Sop's Arm 49 46N 56 56W
20 Sør Trøndelag □ 63 0N 11 0E
78 Sorata 15 50S 68 50W
62 Sorel 46 0N 73 10W
18 Sorgono 40 1N 9 7E
13 Soria 41 43N 2 32W
31 Sorkh, Kuh-e 35 40N 58 30E
80 Sorocaba 23 31S 47 35W
35 Sorong 0 55S 131 15E
52 Soroti 1 43N 33 35E
20 Sørøya, I. 70 35N 22 45E
18 Sorrento 40 38N 14 23E
20 Sorsele 65 31N 17 30E
22 Sortavala 61 42N 30 41E
22 Sosnogorsk 63 37N 53 51E
25 Sosnovka 54 9N 109 35E
15 Sosnowiec 50 20N 19 10E
54 Souanke 2 10N 14 10E
19 Soúdas, Kol. 35 28N 24 10E
38 Soul 37 33N 126 58E
57 Sources, Mt. aux 28 45S 28 50E
79 Soure 0 35S 48 30W
65 Souris 49 40N 100 20W
65 Souris, R. 49 39N 99 34W
79 Sousa 7 0S 38 10W
79 Sousel 2 38S 52 29W
51 Sousse 35 50N 10 33E
56 South Africa ■ 30 0S 25 0E
1 South America 10 0S 60 0W
40 South Australia □ 32 0S 139 0E
68 South Bend, Ind. U.S.A. 41 38N 86 20W
72 South Bend, Wash. 46 44N 123 52W
69 South Boston 36 42N 78 58W
69 South Carolina □ 33 45N 81 0W
68 South Charleston 38 20N 81 40W
26 South China Sea 10 0N 111 0E
70 South Dakota □ 45 0N 100 0W
9 South Esk, R. 56 40N 2 40W
2 South Georgia, I. 54 30S 37 0W
7 South Glamorgan □ 51 28N 3 26W
43 South Grafton 42 11S 71 42W
68 South Haven 42 22N 86 20W
52 South Horr 2 12N 36 56E
47 South Invercargill 46 26S 168 23E
47 South Island 43 50S 171 0E
38 South Korea ■ 36 0N 128 0E
3 South Magnetic Pole 66 30S 139 30E
68 South Milwaukee 42 50N 87 52W
2 South Orkney Is. 63 0S 45 0W
70 South Platte, R. 41 7N 100 42W
62 South Porcupine 48 30N 81 12W
62 South River 45 52N 79 21W
2 South Sandwich Is. 57 0S 27 0W
65 South Saskatchewan, R. 53 15N 105 5W
2 South Shetland Is. 62 0S 59 0W
6 South Shields 54 59N 1 26W
70 South Sioux City 42 30N 96 30W
6 South Tyne, R. 54 59N 2 8W
9 South Uist, I. 57 10N 7 10W
* 56 South West Africa ■ 22 0S 18 0E
29 South Yemen ■ 15 0N 48 0E
6 South Yorkshire □ 52 45N 1 25W
62 Southampton, Canada 44 30N 81 25W
7 Southampton, U.K. 50 54N 1 23W
68 Southampton, U.S.A. 40 54N 72 22W
61 Southampton I. 64 30N 84 0W
7 Southend 51 32N 0 43E
47 Southern Alps, Mts. 43 41S 170 11E
45 Southern Cross 31 12S 119 15E
1 Southern Mid-Atlantic Ridge 30 0S 15 0W
3 Southern Ocean 62 0S 160 0W
8 Southern Uplands, Mts. 55 30N 4 0W
43 Southport, Australia 28 0S 153 25E
6 Southport, U.K. 53 38N 3 1W
7 Southwold 52 19N 1 41E
57 Soutpansberge 22 55S 29 30E
22 Sovetsk 57 38N 48 53E
25 Sovetskaya Gavan 48 50N 140 0E
13 Spain ■ 40 0N 5 0W
6 Spalding 52 47N 0 9W
14 Spandau 52 32N 13 13E
63 Spaniard's Bay 47 38N 53 20W
72 Spanish Fork 40 10N 111 37W
75 Spanish Pt. 32 12N 64 45W
75 Spanish Town 18 0N 77 20W
72 Sparks 39 30N 119 45W
70 Sparta 43 55N 91 10W
69 Spartanburg 35 0N 82 0W
19 Spárti 37 5N 22 25E
18 Spartivento, C., Italy 37 56N 16 4E
18 Spartivento, C., Sardinia 38 52N 8 50E
25 Spassk-Dal'niy 44 40N 132 40E
19 Spátha, Ákra 35 42N 23 43E
70 Spearfish 44 32N 103 52W
46 Speed 35 21S 142 27E
75 Speightstown 13 18N 59 30W
52 Speke G. 2 20S 32 50E
60 Spenard 61 0N 149 50W
60 Spence Bay 69 32N 93 31W
70 Spencer 43 5N 95 3W
43 Spencer, G. 34 30S 137 0E
47 Spenser, Mts. 42 15S 172 45E
9 Sperrin Mts. 54 50N 7 0W
8 Spey, R. 57 40N 3 6W
14 Speyer 49 19N 8 26E
18 Spezia=La Spezia 44 8N 9 50E
18 Spinazzola 40 58N 16 5E
64 Spirit River 55 45N 119 0W
7 Spithead 50 46N 1 12W
18 Split 43 31N 16 26E
72 Spokane 47 45N 117 25W
18 Spoleto 42 44N 12 44E
19 Sporades, Is.= Sporádhes, Voríai 39 15N 23 30E
19 Sporádhes, Voríai 39 15N 23 30E
14 Spree, R. 52 32N 13 13E
56 Springbok 29 42S 17 54E
47 Springburn 43 40S 171 32E
63 Springdale, Canada 49 30N 56 6W
71 Springdale, U.S.A. 36 10N 94 5W
73 Springerville 34 10N 109 16W
47 Springfield, N.Z. 43 19S 171 56E
70 Springfield, Ill. 39 58N 89 40W
68 Springfield, Mass. 42 8N 72 37W
71 Springfield, Mo. 37 15N 93 20W
68 Springfield, Ohio 39 50N 83 48W
72 Springfield, Ore. 44 2N 123 0W
69 Springfield, Tenn. 36 35N 86 55W
56 Springfontein 30 15S 25 40E
63 Springhill 45 40N 64 4W
57 Springs 26 13S 28 25E
42 Springsure 24 8S 148 6E
42 Springvale, Queens. 23 33S 140 42E
44 Springvale, W.Australia 17 48S 127 41E
68 Springville, N.Y. 42 31N 78 41W
72 Springville, Utah 40 14N 111 35W
6 Spurn Hd. 53 34N 0 8W
64 Squamish 49 45N 123 10W
18 Squillace 38 45N 16 28E
35 Sragen 7 28S 110 59E
25 Sredinnyy Khrebet 57 0N 160 0E
25 Sredne Tamborskoye 50 55N 137 45E
25 Srednekolymsk 67 20N 154 40E
25 Srednevilyuysk 63 50N 123 5E
19 Sremska Mitrovica 44 58N 19 37E
34 Srépok, R. 13 33N 106 16E
25 Sretensk 52 10N 117 40E
32 Sri Lanka ■ 7 30N 80 50E
33 Srikakulam 18 14N 84 4E
32 Srinagar 34 12N 74 50E
18 Srnetica 44 25N 16 33E
8 Staffa, I. 56 26N 6 21W
6 Stafford 52 49N 2 9W
6 Stafford □ 52 53N 2 10W
7 Staines 51 26N 0 30W
23 Stalingrad = Volgograd 48 40N 44 25E
6 Stalybridge 53 29N 2 2W
42 Stamford, Australia 21 15S 143 46E
7 Stamford, U.K. 52 39N 0 29W
68 Stamford, Conn. 41 5N 73 30W
71 Stamford, Tex. 32 58N 99 50W
57 Standerton 26 55S 29 13E
57 Stanger 29 18S 31 21E
19 Stanke Dimitrov 42 27N 23 9E
42 Stanley, Australia 40 46S 145 19E
80 Stanley, Falkland Is. 51 40S 58 0W
72 Stanley, U.S.A. 44 10N 114 59W
48 Stanley Falls = Chutes Boyoma 0 12N 25 25E
54 Stanleyville = Kisangani 0 41N 52 11E
* 74 Stann Creek 17 0N 88 20W
25 Stanovoy Khrebet 55 0N 130 0E
43 Stanthorpe 28 36S 151 59E
60 Stanton 69 45N 128 52W
19 Stara Planina 43 15N 23 0E
19 Stara Zagora 42 26N 25 39E
22 Staraya Russa 57 58N 31 10E
2 Starbuck I. 5 37S 155 55W
14 Stargard Szczecinski 53 20N 15 0E
71 Starkville 37 10N 104 31W
7 Start Pt. 50 13N 3 38W
25 Staryy Keydzhan 60 0N 144 50E
68 State College 40 47N 77 49W
69 Statesboro 32 26N 81 46W
69 Statesville 35 48N 80 51W
68 Staunton 38 7N 79 4W
21 Stavanger 58 57N 5 40E
23 Stavrapol 45 2N 41 59E
46 Stawell 36 58S 142 47E
72 Steamboat Springs 40 30N 106 58W
68 Steelton 40 17N 76 50W
64 Steen River 59 40N 117 12W
45 Steep, Pt. 26 8S 113 8E
54 Stefanie, L. = Chew Bahir 4 40N 30 50E
14 Steiermark □ 47 26N 15 0E
56 Steilrandberg 17 30S 13 0E
65 Steinbach 49 32N 96 40W
20 Steinkjer 63 59N 11 31E
56 Stellaland 26 45S 24 50E

* *Renamed Sa'īdiyah*
† *Renamed Somabhula*

* *Renamed Namibia*

* *Renamed Dangriga*

63 Stellarton 45 34N 62 40W
56 Stellenbosch 33 58S 18 50E
18 Stelvio, P. de 46 32N 10 27E
14 Stendal 52 36N 11 50E
23 Stepanakert 40 0N 46 25E
70 Stephen 48 30N 96 53W
46 Stephens Creek 31 50S 141 30E
63 Stephenville, Canada 48 31N 58 30W
71 Stephenville, U.S.A. 32 12N 98 12W
23 Stepnoi = Elista 46 25N 44 17E
19 Stereá Ellas □ 38 55N 22 0E
56 Sterkstroom 31 32S 26 32E
70 Sterling, Colo. 40 40N 103 15W
70 Sterling, Ill. 41 45N 89 45W
22 Sterlitamak 53 40N 56 0E
15 Stettin=Szczecin 53 27N 14 27E
64 Stettler 52 25N 112 40W
68 Steubenville 40 21N 80 39W
70 Stevens Point 44 32N 89 34W
80 Stewart, I., Chile 54 50S 71 30W
47 Stewart, I., N.Z. 46 58S 167 54E
60 Stewart River 63 25N 139 30W
56 Steynsburg 31 15S 25 49E
14 Steyr 48 3N 14 25E
56 Steytlerville 33 17S 24 19E
64 Stikine, R. 56 40N 132 30W
56 Stilfontein 26 50S 26 50E
70 Stillwater, Minn. 45 3N 92 47W
71 Stillwater, Okla. 36 5N 97 3W
72 Stillwater Mts. 39 45N 118 6W
19 Štip 41 42N 22 10E
8 Stirling 56 17N 3 57W
14 Stockerau 48 24N 16 12E
21 Stockholm 59 17N 18 3E
21 Stockholms □ 59 40N 18 45E
6 Stockport 53 25N 2 11W
46 Stockton, Australia 32 56S 151 47E
6 Stockton, U.K. 54 34N 1 20W
73 Stockton, U.S.A. 38 0N 121 20W
6 Stoke-on-Trent 53 1N 2 11W
62 Stokes Bay 45 0N 81 22W
25 Stolbovaya 64 50N 153 50E
42 Stonehenge, Australia 24 22S 143 17E
7 Stonehenge, U.K. 51 9N 1 45W
8 Stonehaven 56 58N 2 11W
65 Stonewall 50 10N 96 50W
20 Storavan, L. 65 45N 18 10E
21 Store Baelt 55 28N 11 0E
20 Støren 63 3N 10 18E
70 Storm Lake 42 35N 95 5W
56 Stormberg 31 16S 26 17E
8 Stornoway 58 12N 6 23W
20 Storsjön, L. 60 35N 16 45E
65 Stoughton 49 40N 103 0W
7 Stour, R., Dorset 50 43N 1 46W
7 Stour, R., Hereford and Worcester 52 20N 2 15W
7 Stour, R., Kent 51 18N 1 22E
7 Stour, R., Suffolk 51 52N 1 16E
7 Stourbridge 52 28N 2 8W
7 Stowmarket 52 11N 1 0E
9 Strabane 54 50N 7 28W
9 Strabane □ 54 50N 7 28W
42 Strahan 42 8S 145 24E
14 Stralsund 54 17N 13 5E
56 Strand 34 9S 18 48E
9 Strangford, L. 54 30N 5 37W
8 Stranraer 54 54N 5 0W
65 Strasbourg, Canada 51 10N 104 55W
12 Strasbourg, Fr. 48 35N 7 42E
46 Stratford, Australia 37 59S 147 5E
62 Stratford, Canada 43 23N 81 0W
47 Stratford, N.Z. 39 20S 174 19E
7 Stratford-on-Avon 52 12N 1 42W
8 Strath Spey 57 15N 3 40W
43 Strathalbyn 35 13S 138 53E
8 Strathclyde □ 55 30N 5 0W
64 Strathmore 51 5N 113 25W
8 Strathmore, Reg. 58 23N 4 40W
62 Strathroy 42 58N 81 38W
8 Strathy, Pt. 58 35N 4 0W
43 Streaky Bay 32 51S 134 18E
70 Streator 41 9N 88 52W
25 Strelka 58 5N 93 10E
24 Strezhevoy 60 42N 77 34E
18 Strómboli, I. 38 48N 15 12E
8 Stromeferry 57 20N 5 33W
21 Strömstad 58 55N 11 15E
8 Stronsay, I. 59 8N 2 38W
7 Stroud 51 44N 2 12W
21 Struer 56 30N 8 35E
19 Struma, R. 40 47N 23 51E
68 Struthers 41 6N 80 38W
34 Stung Treng 13 26N 106 0E
68 Sturgeon Bay 44 52N 87 20W
62 Sturgeon Falls 46 25N 79 57W
44 Sturt Cr. 20 8S 127 24E
56 Stutterheim 32 33S 27 28E
71 Stuttgart, U.S.A. 34 30N 91 33W
14 Stuttgart, W.Germany 48 46N 9 10E
22 Styr, R. 52 7N 26 35E
51 Suakin 19 0N 37 20E
39 Suancheng 30 58N 118 57E
38 Suanhwa 40 35N 115 0E
39 Suao 24 32N 121 42E
35 Subang 7 30S 107 45E
19 Subotica 46 6N 19 29E
74 Suchitato 13 56N 89 0W
39 Suchou=Soochow 31 18N 120 41E
39 Suchow 34 10N 117 20E
9 Suck, R. 53 16N 8 3W
78 Sucre 19 0S 65 15W
51 Sudan ■ 15 0N 30 0E
62 Sudbury 46 30N 81 0W
51 Sûdd 8 20N 29 30E
14 Sudetes, Mts.= Sudety, Mts. 50 20N 16 45E
14 Sudety, Mts. 50 20N 16 45E
35 Sudirman, Pengunungan, Ra. 4 30S 137 0E
13 Sueca 39 12N 0 21W
51 Suez = El Suweis 28 40N 33 0E
68 Suffolk 36 47N 76 33W
68 Suffolk □ 52 16N 1 0E
37 Sufu 39 44N 75 53E
61 Sugluk = Saglouc 62 10N 75 40W
31 Suhar 24 20N 56 40E
38 Suhbaatar 50 17N 106 10E
39 Suhsien 33 28N 117 54E
38 Suichung 40 45N 120 46E
39 Suichwan 26 26N 114 32E
38 Suihwa 46 40N 126 57E
39 Suikhai 21 17N 110 19E
39 Suiping 33 15N 114 6E
9 Suir, R. 52 15N 7 0W
35 Sukabumi 6 56S 106 57E
34 Sukadana 1 10S 110 0E
23 Sukhumi 43 0N 41 0E
32 Sukkur 27 50N 68 46E
32 Sulaiman Ra. 30 30N 69 50E
28 Sulam Tsor 33 4N 35 6E
35 Sulawesi, I. 2 0S 120 0E
15 Sulina 45 10N 29 40E
20 Sulitälma 67 17N 17 28E
20 Sulitjelma 61 7N 16 8E
78 Sullana 5 0S 80 45W
68 Sullivan 39 5N 87 26W
71 Sulphur 30 20N 93 22W
71 Sulphur Springs 33 5N 95 30W
33 Sultanpur 26 18N 82 10E
35 Sulu Arch. 6 0N 121 0E
35 Sulu Sea 8 0N 120 0E
51 Suluq 31 44N 20 14E
35 Sumalata 1 0N 122 37E
34 Sumatera □ 0 40N 100 20E
34 Sumatera, I. 0 40N 100 20E
72 Sumatra 46 45N 107 37W
34 Sumatra, I. = Sumatera, I. 0 40N 100 20E
35 Sumba, Selat, Str. 9 0S 118 40E
35 Sumba, I. 9 45S 119 35E
35 Sumbawa, I. 8 34S 117 17E
34 Sumbawa Besar 8 30S 117 26E
52 Sumbawanga 7 57S 31 35E
38 Sümber 46 40N 108 50E
35 Sumbing, Mt. 7 19S 110 3E
35 Sumedang 6 49S 107 56E
35 Sumenep 7 3S 113 51E
63 Summerside 46 29N 63 41W
62 Summit 47 50N 72 20W
64 Summit Lake 54 20N 122 40W
73 Summit Pk. 37 20N 106 48W
36 Sumoto 34 21N 134 54E
14 Sumperk 49 59N 17 0E
69 Sumter 33 55N 80 10W
23 Sumy 50 57N 34 50E
8 Sunart, L. 56 42N 5 35W
68 Sunbury 40 50N 76 46W
39 Sunchon 34 52N 127 31E
34 Sunda, Selat 6 0S 105 45E
33 Sundarbans, Reg. 22 0N 89 0E
6 Sunderland 54 54N 1 22W
62 Sundridge 45 45N 79 25W
20 Sundsvall 62 23N 17 17E
34 Sungaigerung 4 58S 105 7E
34 Sungaipakning 1 19N 102 0E
34 Sungaipenuh 2 1S 101 20E
34 Sungaitiram 0 45S 117 8E
38 Sungari, R. 47 30N 132 30E
35 Sungguminasa 5 17S 119 30E
39 Sungkiang 31 0N 121 20E
37 Sungpan 32 50N 103 20E
39 Sungtzu Hu, L. 30 10N 111 45E
72 Sunnyside 46 24N 120 2W
46 Sunshine 37 48S 144 52E
53 Sunyani 7 21N 2 22W
33 Supaul 26 10N 86 40E
73 Superior, Ariz. 33 19N 111 9W
70 Superior, Wis. 46 45N 92 0W
62 Superior, L. 47 40N 87 0W
39 Supu 27 57N 110 15E
30 Sūr, Lebanon 33 19N 35 16E
31 Sūr, Oman 22 34N 59 32E
22 Sura, R. 56 6N 46 0E
35 Surabaya 7 17S 112 45E
35 Surakarta 7 35S 110 48E
32 Surat 21 12N 72 55E
34 Surat Thani 9 3N 99 28E
32 Suratgarh 29 18N 73 55E
24 Surgut 61 20N 73 28E
33 Suri 23 50N 87 34E
28 Surif 31 40N 35 4E
77 Surinam ■ 4 0N 56 15W
7 Surrey □ 51 16N 0 30W
51 Surt 31 11N 16 46E
51 Surt, Khalij
20 Surtsey, I. 63 27N 20 15W
36 Suruga-Wan, G. 34 45N 138 30E
18 Susa 45 8N 7 3E
36 Susaki 33 22N 133 17E
25 Susanino 52 50N 140 14E
72 Susanville 40 28N 120 40W
68 Susquehanna, R. 39 33N 76 5W
80 Susques 23 35S 66 25W
63 Sussex 45 45N 65 37W
25 Susuman 62 47N 148 10E
65 Sutherland, Canada 52 15N 106 40W
56 Sutherland, S. Africa 32 33S 20 40E
32 Sutlej, R. 29 23N 71 2E
6 Sutton-in-Ashfield 52 8N 1 16W
47 Suva 17 40S 178 8E
15 Suwałki 54 8N 22 59E
69 Suwannee, R. 29 18N 83 9W
36 Suwanose-Jima, I. 29 26N 129 30E
2 Suwarrow Is. 13 15S 163 5W
28 Suweilih 32 2N 35 50E
51 Suweis, Kalig es 28 40N 33 0E
39 Suwen 20 27N 110 2E
38 Suwôn 37 17N 127 1E
22 Suzdal 56 29N 40 26E
36 Suzu 37 25N 137 17E
36 Suzuka 34 55N 136 36E
3 Svalbard, Is. 78 0N 17 0E
20 Svappavaara 67 40N 21 3E
20 Svartisen, Mt. 66 40N 14 16E
21 Svealand, Reg. 60 0N 15 0E
21 Sveg 62 2N 14 21E
21 Svendborg 55 4N 10 35E
24 Sverdlovks 56 50N 60 30E
58 Sverdrup Is. 79 0N 97 0W
19 Svishtov 43 36N 25 23E
25 Svobodnyy 51 20N 128 0E
20 Svolvaer 68 15N 14 34E
14 Swabian Mts.= Scwäbische Alb., Mts. 48 30N 9 30E
56 Swakop, R. 22 38S 14 36E
56 Swakopmund 22 37S 14 30E
6 Swale, R. 54 6N 1 20W
46 Swan Hill 35 15S 143 31E
64 Swan Hills 54 42N 115 49W
75 Swan Is. 17 22N 83 57W
65 Swan River 52 10N 101 25W
7 Swanage 50 36N 1 59W
46 Swansea, Australia 33 3S 151 35E
7 Swansea, U.K. 51 37N 3 57W
56 Swartberge 30 15S 29 23E
56 Swartruggens 25 39S 26 42E
39 Swatow = Shantow 23 25N 116 40E
57 Swaziland ■ 26 30S 31 30E
20 Sweden ■ 67 0N 15 0E
53 Swedru 5 32N 0 41W
71 Sweetwater 32 30N 100 28W
56 Swellendam 34 1S 20 26E
14 Swidnica 50 50N 16 30E
14 Swiebodzin 52 15N 15 37E
65 Swift Current 50 20N 107 45W
7 Swindon 51 33N 1 47W
14 Swinoujście 53 54N 14 16E
14 Switzerland ■ 46 30N 8 0E
9 Swords 53 27N 6 15W
46 Sydney, Australia 33 53S 151 10E
63 Sydney, Canada 46 7N 60 7W
63 Sydney Mines 46 18N 60 15W
22 Syktyvkar 61 45N 50 40E
69 Sylacauga 33 10N 86 15W
33 Sylhet 24 43N 91 55E
64 Sylvan Lake 52 20N 114 10W
24 Sym 60 20N 87 50E
24 Syr Darya, R. 46 3N 61 0E
68 Syracuse 38 0N 101 40W
30 Syria ■ 35 0N 38 0E
25 Syul'dzhyukyor 63 25N 113 40E
22 Syzran 53 12N 48 30E
14 Szczecin 53 27N 14 27E
39 Szechwan □ 30 15N 103 15E
15 Szeged 46 16N 20 10E
15 Székesfehérvár 47 15N 18 25E
15 Szekszárd 46 22N 18 42E
37 Szemao 22 50N 101 0E
39 Szengen 24 50N 108 0E
15 Szentes 46 39N 20 21E
38 Szeping 43 10N 124 18E
15 Szolnok 47 10N 20 15E
14 Szombathely 47 14N 16 38E

T

38 Ta Hingan Ling, Mts. 48 0N 120 0E
37 Ta Liang Shan, Mts. 28 0N 103 0E
80 Tabacal 23 15S 64 15W
53 Tabagné 7 53N 3 7W
8 Tabasco □ 17 45N 93 30W
64 Taber 49 48N 111 5W
35 Tablas, I. 12 20N 122 10E
56 Table Mt. 34 0S 18 22E
44 Tableland 17 16S 126 51E
42 Tabletop, Mt. 23 30S 147 0E
14 Tábor 49 25N 14 39E
52 Tabora 5 2S 32 57E
50 Tabou 4 30N 7 20W
30 Tabriz 38 7N 56 20E
30 Tabuk 28 30N 36 25E
78 Tachira 8 7N 72 21W
35 Tacloban 11 1N 125 0E
78 Tacna 18 0S 70 20W
72 Tacoma 47 15N 122 30W
80 Tacuarembó 31 45S 56 0W
50 Tademait, Plateau du 28 30N 2 30E
29 Tadjoura 11 50N 44 55E
47 Tadmor, N.Z. 41 27S 172 45E
30 Tadmor, Syria 34 30N 37 55E
63 Tadoussac 48 11N 69 42W
24 Tadzhik S.S.R. □ 35 30N 70 0E
38 Taegu 35 50N 128 25E
38 Taejon 35 30N 127 22E
13 Tafalla 42 30N 1 41W
56 Tafelbaai 33 35S 18 25E
7 Taff, R. 51 27N 3 9W
31 Taftan, Kūh-e, Mt. 28 36N 61 6E
23 Taganrog 47 12N 38 50E
35 Tagbilaran 9 42N 124 3E
18 Tagliamento, R. 45 38N 13 6E
79 Taguatinga 12 26S 45 40W
47 Tahakopa 46 30S 169 23E
34 Tahan, Gunong 4 38N 102 14E
37 Tahcheng 46 50N 83 1E
2 Tahiti, I. 17 45S 149 30W
72 Tahoe, L. 39 6N 120 0W
53 Tahoua 14 57N 5 16E
39 Tahsien 31 12N 108 13E
51 Tahta 26 44N 31 32E
39 Tai Hu 31 10N 120 0E
39 Taichow 32 30N 119 50E
39 Taichung 24 10N 120 35E
38 Taihan Shan, Mts. 36 0N 114 0E
47 Taihape 39 41S 175 48E
39 Taiho 26 50N 114 54E
38 Taiku 37 46N 112 28E
38 Tailai 46 28N 123 18E
43 Tailem Bend 35 12S 139 29E
30 Taima 27 35N 38 45E
8 Tain 57 49N 4 4W
39 Tainan 23 0N 120 15E
19 Taínaron, Ákra 36 22N 22 27E
39 Taipei 25 2N 121 30E
34 Taiping 4 50N 100 43E
80 Taitao, Pen. de 46 30S 75 0W
39 Taitung 22 43N 121 4E
39 Taiwan ■ 23 30N 121 0E
28 Taiyiba, Israel 32 36N 35 27E
28 Taiyiba, Jordan 31 55N 35 17E
38 Taiyuan 38 0N 112 30E
29 Ta'izz 13 38N 44 4E
13 Tajo, R. 38 40N 9 24W
51 Tājūra 32 51N 13 27E
34 Tak 17 0N 99 10E

36 Takachiho 32 42N 131 18 E
36 Takada 37 7N 138 15 E
47 Takaka 40 51S 172 50 E
36 Takamatsu 34 20N 134 5 E
36 Takaoka 36 40N 137 0 E
47 Takapuna 36 47S 174 47 E
36 Takasaki 36 20N 139 0 E
36 Takatsuki 34 40N 135 37 E
52 Takaungu 3 38S 39 52 E
36 Takayama 36 10N 137 5 E
36 Takefu 35 50N 136 10 E
31 Takhar □ 36 30N 69 30 E
37 Takla Makan, Reg. 39 40N 85 0 E
53 Takoradi 4 58N 1 55W
53 Takum 7 18N 10 0 E
78 Talara 4 30S 81 10W
53 Talata Mafara 12 35N 6 2 E
35 Talaud, Kep. 4 30N 127 10 E
13 Talavera de la Reina 39 55N 4 46W
80 Talca 35 20S 71 46W
80 Talcahuano 36 40S 73 10W
24 Taldy Kurgan 45 10N 78 45 E
28 Talfit 32 5N 35 17 E
32 Talguppa 14 11N 74 51 E
39 Tali, Shensi 34 48N 109 48 E
37 Tali, Yunnan 25 50N 100 0 E
35 Taliabu, I. 1 45S 125 0 E
38 Talien 38 53N 121 35 E
34 Taliwang 8 50S 116 55 E
60 Talkeetna 62 20N 149 50W
69 Talladega 33 28N 86 2W
69 Tallahassee 30 25N 84 15W
46 Tallangatta 36 10S 147 14 E
22 Tallinn 59 29N 24 58 E
71 Tallulah 32 25N 91 12W
28 Talluza 32 17N 35 18 E
80 Taltal 25 23S 70 40W
43 Talwood 28 27S 149 20 E
53 Tamale 9 22N 0 50W
36 Tamano 34 35N 133 59 E
50 Tamanrasset 22 56N 5 30 E
7 Tamar, R. 50 22N 4 10W
36 Tamashima 34 27N 133 18 E
53 Tamaské 14 55N 5 40 E
* 57 Tamatave 18 10S 49 25 E
* 57 Tamatave □ 18 0S 49 0 E
74 Tamaulipas □ 24 0N 99 0W
50 Tambacounda 13 55N 13 45W
45 Tambellup 34 4S 117 37 E
42 Tambo 24 54S 146 14 E
34 Tambora, I. 8 14S 117 55 E
22 Tambov 52 45N 41 20 E
50 Tamchaket 17 25N 10 40W
74 Tamiahua, Laguna de 21 30N 97 30W
32 Tamil Nadu □ 11 0N 77 0 E
38 Taming 36 20N 115 10 E
28 Tammun 32 18N 35 23 E
69 Tampa 27 57N 82 30W
21 Tampere 61 30N 23 50 E
74 Tampico 22 20N 97 50W
29 Tamra 32 51N 35 12 E
38 Tamsagbulag 47 15N 117 5 E
43 Tamworth, Australia 31 0S 150 58 E
7 Tamworth, U.K. 52 38N 1 2W
20 Tana 70 23N 28 13 E
51 Tana, L. 12 0N 37 20 E
52 Tana, R. 2 32S 40 31 E
36 Tanabe 33 44N 135 22 E
60 Tanacross 63 40N 143 30W
34 Tanahgrogot 1 55S 116 15 E
35 Tanahmeroh 6 0S 140 7 E
44 Tanami, Des. 23 15S 132 20 E
60 Tanana 65 10N 152 15W
60 Tanana, R. 64 25N 145 30W
57 Tananarive = Antananarivo 18 55S 47 31 E
57 Tananarive □ 19 0S 47 0 E
18 Tánaro, R. 44 9N 7 50 E
53 Tanda 7 48N 3 10W
80 Tandil 37 15S 59 6W
32 Tando Adam 25 45N 48 40 E
47 Taneatua 38 4S 177 1 E
36 Tane-ga-Shima, I. 30 30N 131 0 E
33 Tanen Tong Dan, Mts. 19 40N 99 0 E
50 Tanezrouft 23 9N 0 11 E
52 Tanga 5 5S 39 2 E
52 Tanganyika■ = Tanzania ■ 6 40S 34 0 E
52 Tanganyika, L. 6 40S 30 0 E
50 Tanger 35 50N 5 49W
35 Tangerang 6 12S 106 39 E
37 Tanghla Shan, Mts. 33 10N 90 0 E
50 Tangiers=Tanger 35 50N 5 49W
39 Tangshan, Anhwei 34 23N 116 34 E
38 Tangshan, Hopei 39 40N 118 10 E
39 Tangtu 31 37N 118 39 E
53 Tanguiéta 10 37N 1 16 E
39 Tangyang 30 50N 111 45 E
35 Tanimbar, Kep. 7 30S 131 30 E
34 Tanjung 2 10S 115 25 E
34 Tanjungbalai 2 55N 99 44 E
34 Tanjungkarang 5 25S 105 16 E
34 Tanjungpandan 2 45S 107 39 E
34 Tanjungredeb 2 12N 117 35 E
34 Tanjungselor 2 55N 117 25 E
62 Tannin 49 40N 91 0 E
53 Tanout 14 58N 8 53 E
51 Tanta 30 45N 30 57 E
43 Tanunda 34 30S 139 0 E
52 Tanzania ■ 6 40S 34 0 E
38 Taonan 45 30N 122 20 E
39 Taoyuan 25 0N 121 4 E
39 Tapa Shan, Mts. 31 45N 109 30 E
74 Tapachula 14 54N 92 17W
34 Tapah 4 10N 101 17 E
34 Tapaktuan 3 30N 97 10 E
47 Tapanui 45 56N 169 18 E
32 Tapti, R. 21 5N 72 40 E
47 Tapuaenuka, Mt. 41 55S 173 50 E
24 Tara 56 55N 74 30 E
24 Tara, R. 56 42N 74 36 E
25 Tarabagatay, Khrebet, Mts. 47 30N 84 0 E
30 Tarābulus, Lebanon 34 31N 35 52 E
51 Tarābulus, Libya 32 49N 13 7 E
46 Tarago 35 6S 149 39 E
34 Tarakan 3 20N 117 35 E
47 Taranaki □ 39 5S 174 51 E
32 Taranga Hill 24 0N 72 40 E
18 Táranto 40 30N 17 11 E
18 Táranto, G. di 40 0N 17 15 E
78 Tarapaca 2 56S 69 46W
78 Tarapoto 6 30S 76 20W
47 Tarawera 39 2S 176 36 E
47 Tarawera, L. 38 13S 176 27 E
8 Tarbat Ness 57 52N 3 48W
32 Tarbela Dam 34 0N 72 52 E
8 Tarbert 57 54N 6 49W
12 Tarbes 43 15N 0 3 E
46 Taree 31 50S 152 30 E
13 Tarifa 36 1N 5 36W
78 Tarija 21 30S 64 40W
37 Tarim, R. 41 5N 86 40 E
56 Tarkastad 32 0S 26 16 E
23 Tarkhankut, Mys. 45 25N 32 30 E
24 Tarko Sale 64 55N 77 50 E
53 Tarkwa 5 20N 2 0W
35 Tarlac 15 30N 120 25 E
42 Tarlton Downs 22 40S 136 45 E
12 Tarn, R. 44 5N 1 6 E
12 Tarn □ 43 50N 2 8 E
12 Tarn-et-Garonne □ 44 8N 1 20 E
15 Tarnobrzeg 50 35N 21 41 E
15 Tarnów 50 3N 21 0 E
15 Tarnowskie Góry 50 27N 18 54 E
31 Tarom 28 11N 55 42 E
13 Tarragona 41 5N 1 17 E
13 Tarrasa 41 26N 2 1 E
51 Tarso Emissi 21 27N 18 36 E
30 Tarsus 36 58N 34 55 E
78 Tartagal 22 30S 63 50W
22 Tartu 58 25N 26 58 E
30 Tartūs 34 55N 35 55 E
34 Tarutung 2 0N 99 0 E
51 Tasāwah 26 0N 13 37 E
62 Tashereau 48 40N 78 40W
24 Tashauz 42 0N 59 20 E
37 Tashigong 33 0N 79 30 E
24 Tashkent 41 20N 69 10 E
37 Tashkurgan 37 51N 74 57 E
31 Tashkurghan 36 45N 67 40 E
24 Tashtagol 52 47N 87 53 E
35 Tasikmalaya 7 18S 108 12 E
25 Taskan 63 5N 150 5 E
47 Tasman, B. 40 59S 173 25 E
47 Tasman Glacier 43 45S 170 20 E
3 Tasman Sea 42 30S 168 0 E
42 Tasmania, I. □ 49 0S 146 30 E
15 Tatabánya 47 32N 18 25 E
22 Tatar A.S.S.R. □ 55 30N 51 30 E
24 Tatarsk 55 50N 75 20 E
36 Tateyama 35 0N 139 50 E
39 Tatien 25 45N 118 0 E
15 Tatra Mts. = Tatry, Mts. 49 20N 20 0 E
15 Tatry, Mts. 49 20N 20 0 E
37 Tatsaitan 37 55N 95 0 E
80 Tatui 23 25S 48 0W
38 Tatung 40 10N 113 10 E
38 Tatungkow 39 55N 124 10 E
80 Taubaté 23 5S 45 30W
47 Taumarunui 38 53S 175 15 E
78 Taumaturgo 9 0S 73 50W
56 Taung 27 33S 24 47 E
33 Taungdwingyi 20 1N 95 40 E
33 Taunggyi 20 50N 97 0 E
33 Taungup Taunggya 18 20N 93 40 E
7 Taunton, U.K. 51 1N 3 7W
68 Taunton, U.S.A. 41 54N 71 6W
14 Taunus, Mts. 50 15N 8 20 E
47 Taupo 38 41S 176 7 E
47 Taupo, L. 38 46S 175 55 E
47 Tauranga 37 35S 176 11 E
30 Taurus Mts. = Toros Daglari 37 0N 35 0 E
39 Tava Wan, G. 22 40N 114 40 E
60 Tavani 62 10N 93 30W
24 Tavda 58 7N 65 8W
24 Tavda, R. 57 47N 67 16 E
52 Taveta 3 31N 37 37 E
47 Taveuni, I. 16 51S 179 58W
13 Tavira 37 8N 7 40W
7 Tavistock 50 33N 4 9W
33 Tavoy 14 7N 98 18 E
7 Taw, R. 51 4N 4 11W
35 Tawitawi, I. 5 2N 120 0 E
8 Tay, Firth of 56 25N 3 8W
8 Tay, L. 56 30N 4 10W
8 Tay, R. 56 37N 3 58W
78 Tayabamba 8 15S 77 10 E
71 Taylor 30 30N 97 30W
73 Taylor, Mt. 35 16N 107 50W
70 Taylorville 39 32N 29 20W
25 Taymyr Pol. 75 0N 100 0 E
8 Tayport 56 27N 2 52W
25 Tayshet 55 58N 97 25 E
8 Tayside □ 56 30N 3 35W
35 Taytay 10 45N 119 30 E
39 Tayu 25 38N 114 9 E
37 Tayulehsze 29 15N 98 1 E
50 Taza 34 10N 4 0W
24 Tazovskiy 67 28N 78 42 E
23 Tbilisi 41 50N 44 50 E
51 Tchad ■ 12 30N 17 15 E
53 Tchad, L. 13 30N 14 30 E
54 Tchibanga 2 45S 11 12 E
47 Te Anau, L. 45 15S 167 45 E
47 Te Aroha 37 32S 175 44 E
47 Te Awamutu 38 1S 175 20 E
47 Te Horo 40 48S 175 6 E
47 Te Kuiti 38 20S 175 11 E
47 Te Puke 37 46S 176 22 E
50 Tébessa 35 28N 8 9 E
34 Tebingtinggi 3 38S 102 1 E
74 Tecuala 22 24N 105 30W
15 Tecuci 45 51N 27 27 E
24 Tedzhen 37 23N 60 31 E
6 Tees, R. 54 34N 1 16W
6 Teesside 54 37N 1 13W
78 Tefé 3 25S 64 50W
35 Tegal 6 52S 109 8 E
11 Tegelen 51 20N 6 9 E
53 Tegina 10 5N 6 14 E
75 Tegucigalpa 14 10N 87 0W
38 Tehchow 37 28N 116 18 E
31 Tehrān 35 44N 51 30 E
31 Tehrān □ 35 30N 51 0 E
37 Tehtsin 28 45N 98 58 E
74 Tehuacán 18 20N 97 30W
74 Tehuantepec 16 10N 95 19W
74 Tehuntepec, Istmo de 17 0N 94 30W
7 Teifi, R. 52 7N 4 42W
7 Teign, R. 50 33N 3 29W
7 Teignmouth 50 33N 3 30W
* 55 Teixeira da Silva 12 12S 15 52 E
† 54 Teixeira de Sousa 10 42S 22 12 E
13 Tejo, R. 38 40N 9 24W
47 Tekapo, L. 43 48S 170 32 E
74 Tekax 20 20N 89 30W
24 Tekeli 44 50N 79 0 E
30 Tekirdag 40 58N 27 30 E
33 Tekkali 18 43N 84 24 E
28 Tel Aviv-Yafo 32 4N 34 48 E
28 Tel Mond 32 15N 34 56 E
74 Tela 15 40N 87 28W
34 Telanaipura = Jambi 1 38S 103 30 E
23 Telavi 42 0N 45 30 E
64 Telegraph Creek 58 0N 131 10W
21 Telemark □ 59 30N 8 30 E
6 Telford 52 42N 2 29W
38 Telisze 39 50N 112 0 E
64 Telkwa 54 41N 126 56W
68 Tell City 38 0N 86 44W
32 Tellicherry 11 45N 75 30 E
34 Telok Anson 4 0N 101 10 E
80 Telsen 42 30S 66 50W
34 Telukbetung 5 29S 105 17 E
34 Telukbutun 4 5N 108 7 E
34 Telukdalem 0 45N 97 50 E
53 Tema 5 41N 0 .0 E
35 Temanggung 7 18S 110 10 E
57 Tembuland 31 30S 28 20 E
7 Teme, R. 52 9N 2 18W
34 Temerloh 3 27N 102 25 E
24 Temir 49 8N 57 6 E
24 Temirtou 53 10N 87 20 E
62 Temiskaming 46 44N 79 5W
46 Temora 34 30S 147 30 E
73 Tempe 33 26N 111 59W
34 Tempino 1 55S 103 23 E
71 Temple 31 5N 97 28W
9 Templemore 52 48N 7 50W
80 Temuco 38 50S 72 50W
47 Temuka 44 14S 171 17 E
53 Tenado 12 6N 2 38 E
32 Tenali 16 15N 80 35 E
74 Tenancingo 18 98N 99 33W
74 Tenango 19 0N 99 40W
34 Tenasserim 12 6N 99 3 E
7 Tenby 51 40N 4 42W
12 Tenda, Col di 44 9N 7 34 E
12 Tende 44 5N 7 34 E
50 Tenerife, I. 28 20N 16 40W
35 Tengah□, Java 7 0S 110 0 E
34 Tengah□, Kalimantan 2 20S 113 0 E
37 Tengchung 24 58N 98 30 E
39 Tenghsien 35 10N 117 10 E
24 Tengiz, Oz. 50 30N 69 0 E
32 Tenkasi 8 55N 77 20 E
53 Tenkodogo 11 55N 0 20W
42 Tennant Creek 19 30S 134 0 E
69 Tennessee, R. 37 0N 88 20W
69 Tennessee □ 36 0N 86 30W
36 Tenryū-Gawa, R. 34 39N 137 47 E
43 Tenterfield 29 0S 152 0 E
79 Teófilo Otoni 17 15S 41 30W
74 Teotihuacan 19 44N 98 50W
74 Tepic 21 30N 104 54W
14 Teplice 50 39N 13 48 E
13 Ter, R. 42 1N 3 12 E
53 Téra 14 1N 0 50 E
46 Terang 38 3S 142 59 E
23 Terek, R. 43 44N 46 33 E
79 Teresina 5 2S 42 45W
24 Termez 37 0N 67 15 E
18 Términi Imerese 37 59N 13 51 E
74 Términos, L. de 18 35N 91 30W
18 Térmoli 42 0N 15 0 E
35 Ternate 0 45N 127 25 E
11 Terneuzen 51 20N 3 50 E
18 Terni 42 34N 12 38 E
43 Terowie 38 10S 138 50 E
64 Terrace 54 30N 128 35W
18 Terracina 41 17N 13 12 E
18 Terralba 39 43N 8 37 E
3 Terre Adélie 67 0S 140 0 E
68 Terre Haute 46 30N 75 13W
71 Terrell 32 44N 96 19W
11 Terschelling, I. 53 25N 5 20 E
13 Teruel 40 22N 1 8W
20 Tervola 66 6N 24 59 E
50 Tessalit 20 12N 1 0 E
53 Tessaoua 13 45N 8 0 E
7 Test, R. 51 7N 1 30W
80 Tetas, Pta. 22 28S 70 38W
57 Tete 16 13S 33 33 E
57 Tete □ 16 20S 32 30 E
50 Tetouan 35 30N 5 25W
25 Tetyukhe = Dalnergorsk 44 40N 135 50 E
80 Teuco, R. 25 35S 60 11W
65 Teulon 50 30N 97 20W
14 Teutoburger Wald 52 5N 8 15 E
18 Tevere, R. 41 44N 12 14 E
8 Teviot, R. 55 36N 2 26W
43 Tewantin 26 27S 153 3 E
7 Tewkesbury 51 59N 2 8W
71 Texarkana, Ark. 33 25N 94 0W
71 Texarkana, Tex. 33 25N 94 0W
43 Texas 28 49S 151 15 E
71 Texas □ 31 30N 98 30W
71 Texas City 27 20N 95 20W
11 Texel, I. 53 5N 4 50 E
74 Teziutlán 19 50N 97 30W
33 Tezpur 26 40N 92 45 E
57 Thabana Ntlenyana 29 30S 29 9 E
56 Thabazimbi 24 40S 26 4 E
34 Thailand ■ 16 0N 101 0 E
34 Thakhek 17 25 104 45 E
32 Thal 33 28N 70 33 E
32 Thal Desert 31 0N 71 30 E
43 Thallon 28 30S 148 57 E
7 Thame, R. 51 52N 0 47W
47 Thames 37 7S 175 34 E
62 Thames, R., Canada 42 19N 82 28W
7 Thames, R., U.K. 51 28N 0 43 E

* *Renamed Toamasina*

* *Renamed Bailundo*
† *Renamed Luau*

37 Than Hoa 19 48N 105 46 E
32 Thana 19 12N 72 59 E
7 Thanet, I. 51 21N 1 20 E
44 Thangoo P.O. 18 10s 122 22 E
42 Thangool 24 29s 150 35 E
32 Thanjavur 10 48N 79 12 E
32 Thar Des.= Gt. Indian Des. 28 25N 72 0 E
43 Thargomindah 27 58s 143 46 E
33 Tharrawaddy 17 30N 96 0 E
19 Thásos, I. 40 40N 24 40 E
73 Thatcher 32 54N 109 46w
33 Thaton 17 0N 97 39 E
33 Thaungdut 24 30N 94 30 E
33 Thayetmyo 19 19N 95 11 E
33 Thazi 21 0N 96 5 E
75 The Bight 24 19N 75 24w
72 The Dalles 45 40N 121 11w
75 The Flatts 32 19N 64 45w
38 The Great Wall of China 37 30N 109 0 E
75 The Grenadines 12 40N 61 15w
11 The Hague = s'Gravenhage 52 7N 7 14 E
45 The Johnston Lakes 32 25s 120 30 E
65 The Pas 53 45N 101 15w
43 Theebine 26 0s 152 30 E
42 Theodore 24 55s 150 3 E
19 Thermaikós Kól. 40 15N 22 45 E
72 Thermopolis 43 14N 108 10 E
19 Thermopílai Giona, Mt. 38 48N 22 45 E
19 Thessalía □ 39 30N 22 0 E
62 Thessalon 46 20N 83 30w
19 Thessaloníki 40 38N 23 0 E
7 Thetford 52 25N 0 44 E
19 Thessaly□= Thessalía □ 39 30N 22 0 E
63 Thetford Mines 46 8N 71 18w
43 Thevenard 32 9s 133 38 E
71 Thibodaux 29 48N 90 49w
65 Thicket Portage 55 25N 97 45w
70 Thief River Falls 48 15N 96 10w
50 Thiès 14 50N 16 51w
52 Thika 1 1s 37 5 E
12 Thionville 49 20N 6 10 E
19 Thíra, I. 36 23N 25 27 E
6 Thirsk 54 15N 1 20w
21 Thisted 56 57N 8 42 E
19 Thíval 38 19N 23 19 E
69 Thomasville, Ala. 31 55N 87 42w
69 Thomasville, Fla. 30 50N 84 0w
69 Thomasville, N.C. 35 5N 80 4w
65 Thompson 55 50N 97 34w
14 Thonon 46 22N 6 29 E
33 Thori 27 20N 84 40 E
6 Thornaby on Tees 54 36N 1 19w
19 Thráki □ 41 9N 25 30 E
72 Three Forks 45 5N 111 40w
64 Three Hills 51 43N 113 15w
53 Three Points C. 4 42N 2 6w
2 Thule 76 0N 68 0w
14 Thun 46 45N 7 38 E
62 Thunder Bay 48 25N 89 10 E
64 Thunder River 52 13N 119 20w
34 Thung Song 8 10N 99 40 E
14 Thüringer Wald 50 35N 11 0 E
14 Thuringian Forest= Thüringer Wald 50 35N 11 0 E
9 Thurles 52 40N 7 53w
41 Thursday I. 10 59s 142 12 E
62 Thurso, Canada 45 36N 75 15w
8 Thurso, U.K. 58 34N 3 31w
2 Thurston I. 72 0s 100 0w
38 Tianjin=Tientsin 39 10N 117 0 E
50 Tiaret 35 28N 1 21 E
50 Tiassalé 5 58N 4 57w
53 Tibati 6 22N 12 30 E
18 Tiber, R.= Tevere, R. 41 44N 12 14 E
28 Tiberias 32 47N 35 32 E
51 Tibesti 21 0N 17 30 E
37 Tibet □ 32 30N 86 0 E
26 Tibet, Plateau of 35 0N 90 0 E
43 Tibooburra 29 26s 142 1 E
74 Tiburón, I. 29 0N 112 30w
18 Ticino, R. 45 9N 9 14 E
74 Ticul 20 20N 89 50w
50 Tidjikdja 18 4N 11 35w
38 Tiehling 42 25N 123 51 E
11 Tiel 51 54N 5 5 E
11 Tielt 51 0N 3 20 E
26 Tien Shan, Mts. 42 0N 80 0 E
38 T'ienching= Tientsin 39 10N 117 0 E
11 Tienen 50 48N 4 57 E
39 Tienshui 34 30N 105 34 E
38 Tientsin 39 10N 117 0 E
39 Tientung 23 47N 107 2 E
13 Tierra de Campos 42 5N 4 45w
80 Tierra del Fuego, I. 54 0s 69 0w
13 Tiétar, R. 39 55N 5 50w
68 Tiffin 41 8N 83 10w
28 Tifrah 31 19N 34 42 E
69 Tifton 31 28N 83 32w
35 Tifu 3 39s 126 18 E
63 Tignish 46 58N 63 57w
30 Tigris, R. = Dijlah, Nahr 31 0N 47 25 E
25 Tigu 29 48N 91 38 E
33 Tigyaing 23 45N 96 10 E
73 Tijuana 32 30N 117 10w
74 Tikal 17 2N 89 35w
23 Tikhoretsk 45 56N 40 5 E
53 Tiko 4 4N 9 20 E
25 Tiksi 71 50N 129 0 E
11 Tilburg 51 31N 5 6 E
62 Tilbury, Canada 42 17N 84 23 E
7 Tilbury, U.K. 51 27N 0 24 E
25 Tilichiki 61 0N 166 5 E
53 Tillabéri 14 10N 1 30 E
62 Tillsonburg 42 53N 80 55w
19 Tílos, I. 36 27N 27 27 E
43 Tilpa 30 58s 144 30 E
22 Timanskiy Kryazh 65 58N 50 5 E
47 Timaru 44 23s 171 14 E
53 Timbuktu = Tombouctou 16 50N 3 0w
15 Timişoara 4543 1 21 15 E
62 Timmins 48 28N 81 25w
19 Timok, R. 44 13N 22 40 E
79 Timon 5 8s 42 52w
35 Timor, I. 9 0s 125 0 E
44 Timor, Sea 10 0s 127 0 E
50 Timris, C. 19 15N 16 30w
35 Timur□, Java 7 20s 112 0 E
34 Timur□, Kalimantan 1 15N 117 0 E
50 Tindouf 27 50N 8 4w
45 Tinkurrin 33 0s 117 38 E
21 Tinnoset 59 45N 9 3 E
80 Tinogasta 28 0s 67 40w
19 Tínos, I. 37 33N 25 8 E
39 Tinpak 21 40N 111 15 E
43 Tintinara 35 48s 140 2 E
34 Tioman, Pulau 2 50N 104 10 E
33 Tipongpani 27 20N 95 55 E
9 Tipperary 52 28N 8 10w
9 Tipperary □ 52 37N 7 55w
7 Tipton 52 32N 2 4w
28 Tira 32 14N 34 56 E
31 Tirān 32 45N 51 0 E
19 Tirana 41 18N 19 49 E
23 Tiraspol 46 55N 29 35 E
28 Tirat Karmel 32 46N 34 58 E
28 Tirat Tsevi 32 26N 35 51 E
28 Tirat Yehuda 32 1N 34 56 E
30 Tire 38 5N 27 50 E
30 Tirebolu 40 58N 38 45 E
8 Tiree, I. 56 31N 6 49w
15 Tîrgovişte 44 55N 25 27 E
15 Tîrgu-Jiu 45 5N 23 19 E
15 Tîrgu-Mureş 46 31N 24 38 E
32 Tirich Mir, Mt. 36 15N 71 35 E
14 Tirol, Reg. 46 50N 11 40 E
14 Tirol □ 47 3N 10 43 E
32 Tiruchchirappalli 10 45N 78 45 E
32 Tirunelveli 8 45N 77 45 E
32 Tirupati 13 45N 79 30 E
15 Tisa, R. 45 15N 20 17 E
65 Tisdale 52 50N 104 0w
25 Tit-Ary 71 58N 127 1 E
78 Titicaca, L. 15 30s 69 30w
53 Titiwa 12 14N 12 53 E
33 Titlagarh 20 15N 83 5 E
19 Titograd 42 30N 19 19 E
19 Titov Veles 41 46N 21 47 E
19 Titovo Uzice 43 55N 19 50 E
54 Titule 3 15N 25 31 E
68 Titusville 41 35N 79 39w
7 Tiverton 50 54N 3 30w
18 Tívoli 41 58N 12 45 E
31 Tiwi 22 45N 59 12 E
50 Tizi-Ouzou 36 48N 4 2 E
74 Tizimín 21 0N 88 1w
74 Tlaxcala □ 19 30N 98 20w
74 Tlaxiaco 17 10N 97 40w
50 Tlemcen 34 52N 1 15w
80 Toay 36 50s 64 30w
32 Toba Kakar Ra. 31 30N 69 0 E
75 Tobago, I. 11 10N 60 30w
35 Tobelo 1 25N 127 56 E
42 Tobermorey, Australia 22 12s 138 0 E
62 Tobermory, Canada 45 12N 81 40w
8 Tobermory, U.K. 56 37N 6 4w
24 Tobolsk 58 0N 68 10 E
51 Tobruk = Tubruq 32 7N 23 55 E
79 Tocantinopolis 6 20s 47 25w
79 Tocantins, R. 1 45s 49 10w
69 Toccoa 34 35N 83 19w
36 Tochigi 36 25N 139 45 E
36 Tochigi □ 36 45N 139 45 E
78 Tocopilla 22 5s 70 10w
46 Tocumwal 35 45s 145 31 E
79 Todos os Santos, B. de 12 45s 38 40w
22 Togliatti 53 37N 49 18 E
53 Togo ■ 6 15N 1 35 E
36 Tohoku □ 38 40N 142 0 E
15 Tokaj 48 8N 21 27 E
36 Tōkamachi 37 8N 138 43 E
51 Tokar 18 27N 37 43 E
36 Tokara Kaikyō, Str. 30 0N 130 0 E
36 Tokara-Shima, I. 29 0N 129 0 E
47 Tokarahi 44 56s 170 39 E
30 Tokat 40 22N 36 35 E
2 Tokelau Is. 9 0s 172 0w
24 Tokmak 47 16N 35 42 E
53 Tokombere 11 18N 3 30 E
36 Toku-no-Shima, I. 27 50N 129 2 E
36 Tokushima 34 0N 134 45 E
36 Tokushima □ 35 50N 134 50 E
36 Tokuyama 34 0N 131 50 E
36 Tōkyō 35 45N 139 45 E
36 Tōkyō □ 35 40N 139 30 E
47 Tolaga 38 21s 178 20 E
19 Tolbukhin 43 37N 27 49 E
13 Toledo, Sp. 39 50N 4 2w
68 Toledo, U.S.A. 41 37N 83 33w
13 Toledo, Mts. de 39 30N 4 30w
78 Tolima, Mt. 4 40N 75 19w
35 Tolitoli 1 5N 120 50 E
73 Tolleson 33 29N 112 10w
35 Tolo, Teluk, G. 2 20s 122 10 E
13 Tolosa 43 8N 2 5w
74 Toluca 19 20N 99 50w
38 Tolun 42 22N 116 30 E
44 Tom Price 22 50s 117 40 E
13 Tomar 39 36N 8 25w
69 Tombigbee, R. 32 0N 88 6 E
53 Tombouctou 16 50N 3 0w
73 Tombstone 31 40N 110 4w
35 Tomini, Teluk, G. 0 10s 122 0 E
8 Tomintoul 57 15N 3 22w
25 Tommot 58 50N 126 30 E
24 Tomsk 56 30N 85 12 E
74 Tonalá 16 8N 93 41w
78 Tonantins 2 45s 67 45w
68 Tonawanda 43 0N 78 54w
7 Tonbridge 51 12N 0 18 E
47 Tonga ■ 20 0s 173 0w
57 Tongaat 29 33s 31 9 E
47 Tongatapu, I. 20 0s 174 0w
11 Tongeren 50 47N 5 28 E
39 Tonghing 21 30N 108 0 E
37 Tongking, G. of 20 0N 108 0 E
80 Tongoy 30 25s 71 40w
8 Tongue 58 29N 4 25w
51 Tonj 7 20N 28 44 E
32 Tonk 26 6N 75 54 E
34 Tonlé Sap, L. 13 0N 104 0 E
73 Tonopah 38 4N 117 12w
21 Tønsberg 59 19N 11 3 E
72 Tooele 40 30N 112 20w
43 Toompine 27 15s 144 19 E
43 Toowoomba 27 32s 151 56 E
22 Top, Oz. 65 35N 32 0 E
70 Topeka 39 3N 95 40 E
24 Topki 55 25N 85 20 E
64 Topley 54 32N 126 5w
72 Toppenish 46 27N 120 16w
78 Torata 17 3s 70 1w
31 Torbat-e Heydariyeh 35 15N 59 12w
63 Torbay, Canada 47 40N 52 42w
7 Torbay, U.K. 50 26N 3 31w
13 Tordesillas 41 30N 5 0w
14 Torgau 51 32N 13 0 E
11 Torhout 51 5N 3 7 E
18 Torino 45 4N 7 40 E
20 Torne, R. 65 48N 24 8 E
20 Torneträsk, L. 68 20N 19 10 E
20 Tornio 65 57N 24 12 E
80 Tornquist 38 0s 62 15w
80 Toro, Cerro del 29 0s 69 50w
19 Toronaíos Kól. 40 5N 23 30 E
68 Toronto, Canada 43 39N 79 20w
68 Toronto, U.S.A. 40 27N 80 36w
52 Tororo 0 45N 34 12 E
30 Toros Dăglari, Mts. 37 0N 35 0 E
7 Torquay 50 27N 3 31w
18 Torre Annunziata 40 45N 14 26 E
13 Tôrre de Moncorvo 41 12N 7 8w
13 Torrelavega 43 20N 4 5w
13 Torremolinos 36 38N 4 30w
43 Torrens, L. 31 0s 137 45 E
74 Torreon 25 33N 103 25w
41 Torres Str. 10 0s 142 0 E
13 Torres Veldras 39 5N 9 15w
13 Torrevieja 37 59N 0 42w
7 Torridge, R. 51 3N 4 11w
8 Torridon, L. 57 35N 5 50w
68 Torrington 41 50N 73 9w
75 Tortola, I. 18 19N 65 0w
13 Tortosa 40 49N 0 31 E
13 Tortosa, C. 40 41N 0 52 E
15 Toruń 53 3N 18 39 E
36 Tosa-Wan, G. 33 15N 133 30 E
18 Toscana □ 43 30N 11 5 E
80 Tostado 29 15s 61 50w
55 Toteng 20 22s 22 58 E
22 Totma 60 0N 42 40 E
7 Totnes 50 26N 3 41w
79 Totness 5 53N 56 19w
74 Totonicapán 14 50N 91 20w
36 Tottori 35 30N 134 15 E
36 Tottori □ 35 30N 134 12 E
50 Toubkal, Djebel, Mt. 31 0N 8 0w
50 Touggourt 33 10N 6 0 E
50 Tougué 11 25N 11 50w
12 Toul 48 40N 5 53 E
12 Toulon 43 10N 5 55 E
12 Toulouse 43 37N 1 28 E
51 Toummo 22 45N 14 8 E
33 Toungoa 19 0N 96 30 E
12 Touraine, Reg. 47 20N 0 30 E
34 Tourane = Da Nang 16 10N 108 7 E
12 Tourcoing 50 42N 3 10 E
11 Tournai 50 35N 3 25 E
12 Tournon 45 5N 4 50 E
12 Tours 47 22N 0 40 E
56 Touwsrivier 33 20s 20 0 E
33 Towang 27 33N 91 56 E
46 Townsend, Mt. 36 25s 148 16 E
42 Townsville 19 15s 146 45 E
68 Towson 39 26N 76 34w
7 Towyn 52 37N 4 8w
36 Toyama 36 40N 137 15 E
36 Toyama □ 36 45N 137 30 E
36 Toyama-Wan, G. 37 0N 137 30 E
36 Toyohashi 34 45N 137 25 E
36 Toyokawa 34 48N 137 27 E
36 Toyonaka 34 50N 135 35 E
36 Toyooka 35 35N 135 55 E
36 Toyota 35 5N 137 9 E
50 Tozeur 33 54N 8 4 E
30 Trabzon 41 0N 39 45 E
73 Tracy 44 12N 95 3w
37 Tradom 30 0N 83 59 E
46 Trafalgar 38 14s 146 12 E
13 Trafalgar, C. 36 10N 6 2w
80 Traiguén 38 12s 72 40w
64 Trail 49 5N 117 40w
9 Tralee 52 16N 9 42w
9 Tramore 52 10N 7 10w
21 Tranås 58 3N 14 59 E
80 Trancas 26 11s 65 20w
34 Trang 7 33N 99 38 E
35 Trangan, I. 6 40s 134 20 E
18 Trani 41 17N 16 24 E
57 Tranoroa 24 42s 45 4 E
65 Transcona 49 50N 97 0w
15 Transilvania, Reg.= Transylvania, Reg. 46 20N 25 0 E
57 Transkei □ 32 15s 28 15 E
57 Transvaal □ 25 0s 29 0 E
15 Transylvania, Reg. 46 20N 25 0 E
4 Transylvanian Alps, Mts. 45 30N 25 0 E
18 Trápani 38 1N 12 30 E
46 Traralgon 38 6s 146 31 E
13 Tras os Montes Alto Douro, Reg. 41 30N 7 5w
18 Trasimeno, L. 43 30N 12 5 E
68 Traverse City 44 45N 85 39w
19 Travnik 44 17N 17 39 E
45 Trayning 31 8s 117 42 E
14 Třebíč 49 13N 15 53 E
19 Trebinje 42 44N 18 22 E
14 Třeboň 48 59N 14 48 E
7 Tredegar 51 47N 3 16w
7 Tregaron 52 14N 3 56w
80 Treinta y Tres 33 10s 54 50w
56 Trekveld 30 35s 19 45 E
80 Trelew 43 10s 65 20w
21 Trelleborg 55 20N 13 5 E
72 Tremonton 41 45N 112 10w
35 Trenggalek 8 5s 111 44 E

80 Trenque Lauquen . 36 0s 62 45w
6 Trent, R. 53 40N 0 40w
18 Trentino-Alto Adige □ 46 5N 11 0E
18 Trento 46 5N 11 8E
62 Trenton, Canada 44 10N 77 40w
68 Trenton, U.S.A. 40 15N 74 41w
63 Trepassey 46 43N 53 25w
80 Tres Arroyos 38 20s 60 20w
79 Três Corações 21 30s 45 30s
79 Três Lagoas 20 50s 51 50w
80 Tres Montes, C. 47 0s 75 35w
80 Tres Puentes 27 50s 70 15w
80 Tres Puntas, C. 47 0s 66 0w
79 Três Rios 22 20s 43 30w
21 Treungen 58 55N 8 27E
18 Treviso 45 40N 12 15E
42 Triabunna 42 28s 148 0E
32 Trichinopoly= Tiruchchirappalli 10 45N 78 45E
32 Trichur 10 20N 76 18E
14 Trier 49 45N 6 37E
18 Trieste 45 39N 13 45E
18 Triglav, Mt. 46 30N 13 45E
19 Tríkkala 39 34N 21 47E
35 Trikora, Puncak, Mt. 4 11s 138 0E
9 Trim 53 34N 6 48w
32 Trincomalee 8 38N 81 15E
2 Trindade, I. 20 20s 29 50w
78 Trinidad, Bolivia 14 54s 64 50w
75 Trinidad, Cuba 21 40N 80 0w
71 Trinidad, U.S.A. 37 15N 104 30w
80 Trinidad, Uruguay 33 30s 56 50w
80 Trinidad I., Arg. 39 10s 62 0w
75 Trinidad I., Trinidad & Tobago 10 30N 61 20w
75 Trinidad & Tobago ■ 10 30N 61 20w
71 Trinity, R. 29 47N 94 42w
60 Trinity Is. 56 33N 154 25w
30 Tripoli, Lebanon= Tarābulus 34 34N 35 52E
51 Tripoli, Libya= Tarābulus 32 49N 13 7E
19 Trípolis 37 31N 22 25E
33 Tripura □ 24 0N 92 0E
2 Tristan de Cunha, I. 37 6s 12 20w
32 Trivandrum 8 31N 77 0E
15 Trnava 48 23N 17 35E
63 Trois Pistoles 48 5N 69 10w
62 Trois Rivières 46 25N 72 40w
24 Troitsk 54 10N 61 35E
22 Troitsko Pechorsk 62 40N 56 10E
21 Trollhättan 58 17N 12 20E
56 Trompsburg 30 2s 25 5E
20 Troms □ 69 19N 19 0E
20 Tromsø 69 40N 19 0E
80 Tronador, Mt. 41 53s 71 0w
20 Trondheim 63 25N 10 25E
20 Trondheims, Fd. 63 40N 10 45E
30 Tróodos, Mt. 34 58N 32 55E
8 Troon 55 33N 4 40w
8 Trossachs, Reg. 56 14N 4 24w
8 Trotternish, Reg. 57 32N 6 15w
12 Trouville 49 21N 0 54E
7 Trowbridge 51 18N 2 12w
69 Troy, Ala. 31 50N 85 58w
68 Troy, N.Y. 42 45N 73 39w
68 Troy, Ohio 40 0N 84 10w
12 Troyes 48 19N 4 3E
72 Truckee 39 29N 120 12w
75 Trujillo, Honduras 16 0N 86 0w
78 Trujillo, Peru 8 0s 79 0w
13 Trujillo, Sp. 39 28N 5 55w
78 Trujillo, Ven. 9 22N 70 26w
3 Truk, I. 7 25N 151 46E
34 Trung-Phan, Reg. 16 0N 108 0E
63 Truro, Canada 45 21N 63 14w
7 Truro, U.K. 50 17N 5 2w
45 Truslove 33 20s 121 45E
73 Truth or Consequences 33 9N 107 16w
37 Tsaidam, Reg. 37 0N 95 0E
38 Tsanghsien 38 24N 116 57E
37 Tsangpo, R. 29 40N 89 0E
39 Tsaochwang 35 11N 115 28E
57 Tsaratanana 16 47s 47 39E
57 Tsaratanana, Mt. de 14 0s 49 0E
37 Tsaring Nor, L. 35 0N 97 0E
55 Tsau 20 12s 22 22E
52 Tsavo 3 0s 38 27E
24 Tselinograd 51 10N 71 30E
38 Tsetserleg 47 46N 101 32E
53 Tsévié 6 25N 1 13E
55 Tshabong 26 2s 22 29E
55 Tshane 24 5s 21 54E
55 Tshwane 22 24s 22 1N
39 Tsiaotso 35 11N 113 37E
57 Tsihombe 25 18s 45 29E
23 Tsimlyanskoye, Vdkhr. 47 45N 42 0E
39 Tsin Ling Shan, Mts. 34 0N 107 30E
38 Tsinan 34 50N 105 40E
38 Tsincheng 35 30N 113 0E
38 Tsinghai 38 56N 116 52E
37 Tsinghai □ 35 10N 96 0E
39 Tsingkiang, Kiangsi 27 50N 114 38E
39 Tsingkiang, Kiangsu 33 30N 119 2E
38 Tsingning 35 25N 105 50E
39 Tsingshih 29 43N 112 13E
38 Tsingtao 36 0N 120 25E
39 Tsining, Inner Mongolia 40 59N 112 59E
38 Tsining, Shantung 35 30N 116 35E
39 Tsinyang 35 2N 112 59E
57 Tsiroanomandidy 18 46s 46 2E
38 Tsitsihar 47 20N 124 0E
57 Tsivory 24 4s 46 5E
23 Tskhinvali 42 14N 44 1E
22 Tsna, R. 54 32N 42 5E
36 Tsu 34 45N 136 25E
36 Tsuchiura 36 12N 140 15E
36 Tsugaru-Kaikyo, Str. 41 30N 140 30E
38 Tsuiluan 47 58N 28 27E
56 Tsumeb 19 9s 17 44E
39 Tsungfa 23 35N 113 35E
39 Tsungtso 22 20N 107 25E
39 Tsunyi 27 40N 107 0E
36 Tsuruga 35 35N 136 0E
39 Tsushima-Kaikyō, Str. 34 20N 130 0E
36 Tsuyama 35 0N 134 0E
57 Tswana □ 24 0s 27 50E
35 Tual 5 30s 132 50E
9 Tuam 53 30N 8 50w
2 Tuamotu Arch. 17 0s 144 0w
23 Tuapse 44 5N 39 10E
47 Tuatapere 48 7s 167 43E
73 Tubac 31 45N 111 2w
35 Tuban 6 57s 112 4E
80 Tubarão 28 30s 49 0w
28 Tubas 32 20N 35 22E
30 Tubayq, Jabal at 29 40N 37 30E
14 Tübingen 48 31N 9 4E
53 Tubo, R. 10 25N 7 10E
51 Tubruq 32 7N 23 55E
2 Tubuai Is. 23 20s 151 0w
78 Tucacas 10 48N 68 19w
45 Tuckanarra 27 8s 118 1E
75 Tucker's Town 32 19N 64 43w
73 Tucson 32 14N 110 59w
71 Tucumcari 35 12N 103 45w
78 Tucupita 9 4N 62 0w
79 Tucurui 3 45s 49 48w
13 Tudela 42 4N 1 39w
57 Tugela, R. 29 14s 31 30E
35 Tuguegarao 17 35N 121 42E
35 Tugur 53 50N 136 45E
39 Tuhshan 25 40N 107 30E
60 Tuktoyaktuk 69 15N 133 0w
52 Tukuyu 9 17s 33 35E
53 Tula, Nigeria 9 51N 11 27E
22 Tula, U.S.S.R. 54 13N 37 32E
37 Tulan 37 24N 98 1E
73 Tulare 36 15N 119 26w
73 Tularosa 33 4N 106 1w
55 Tulbagh 33 16s 19 6E
78 Tulcán 0 48N 77 43w
15 Tulcea 45 13N 28 46E
* 57 Tuléar 23 21s 43 40E
* 57 Tuléar □ 21 0s 45 0E
55 Tuli 1 24s 122 26E
28 Tülkarm 32 19N 35 10E
69 Tullahoma 35 23N 86 12w
9 Tullamore 53 17N 7 30w
12 Tulle 45 16N 1 47E
9 Tullow 52 48N 6 45w
42 Tully 17 30s 141 0E
51 Tulymaythah 32 40N 20 55E
71 Tulsa 36 10N 96 0w
73 Tulua 4 6N 76 11w
25 Tulun 54 40N 100 10E
35 Tulungagung 8 5s 111 54E
75 Tuma, R. 13 6N 84 35w
78 Tumaco 1 50N 78 45w
78 Tumatumari 5 20N 58 55w
54 Tumba, L. 0 50s 18 0E
78 Tumbes 3 30s 80 20w
43 Tumby Bay 34 21s 136 8E
38 Tumen 42 46N 129 59E
78 Tumeremo 7 18N 61 30w
32 Tumkur 13 18N 77 12w

* Renamed Toliara

8 Tummel, L. 56 43N 3 55w
32 Tump 26 7N 62 16E
34 Tumpat 6 11N 102 10E
79 Tumucumaque South 2 0N 55 0w
46 Tumut 35 16s 148 13E
7 Tunbridge Wells 51 7N 0 16E
52 Tunduma 9 20s 32 48E
52 Tunduru 11 0s 37 25E
19 Tundzha, R. 41 40N 26 34E
32 Tungabhadra, R. 15 57N 78 15E
39 Tungcheng 31 0N 117 3E
38 Tungchow 39 58N 116 50E
39 Tungchuan 35 4N 109 2E
39 Tungfanghsien 18 50N 108 33E
38 Tunghwa 41 46N 126 0E
38 Tungkiang 47 40N 132 30E
39 Tungkwanshan 31 0N 117 45E
38 Tungliao 43 42N 122 11E
39 Tunglu 29 50N 119 35E
38 Tungping 35 50N 116 20E
39 Tungshan 29 36N 144 28E
39 Tungshan, I. 23 40N 117 31E
64 Tungsten 61 52N 128 1w
39 Tungtai 32 55N 120 15E
39 Tungting Hu, L. 28 30N 112 30E
39 Tungtze 27 59N 106 56E
38 Tunhwa 43 27N 128 16E
37 Tunhwang 40 5N 94 46E
50 Tunis 36 50N 10 11E
50 Tunisia ■ 33 30N 9 0E
78 Tunja 5 40N 73 25E
25 Tuoy-khaya 62 30N 111 0w
69 Tupelo 34 15N 88 42w
25 Tupik 54 26N 119 57E
78 Tupiza 21 30s 65 40w
68 Tupper Lake 44 18N 74 30w
80 Tupungato, Mt. 33 15s 69 50w
78 Túquerres 1 5N 77 37w
28 Tur 31 47N 35 14E
33 Tura, India 25 30N 90 16E
52 Tura, Tanz. 5 15s 33 48E
30 Turayf 31 45N 38 30E
78 Turbaco 10 20N 75 25w
78 Turbo 8 6N 76 43E
15 Turda 46 35N 23 48E
15 Turek 52 3N 18 30E
37 Turfan 43 6N 89 24E
37 Turfan Depression 43 0N 88 0E
19 Turgovishte 43 17N 26 38E
30 Turgutlu 38 30N 27 48E
30 Turhal 40 24N 36 19E
13 Turia, R. 39 27N 0 19w
79 Turiaçu 1 40s 45 28w
18 Turin=Torino 45 3N 7 40E
52 Turkana, L. 4 10N 36 10E
24 Turkestan 43 10N 68 10E
30 Turkey ■ 39 0N 36 0E
44 Turkey Creek P.O. 17 2s 128 12E
24 Turkmen S.S.R. 39 0N 59 0E
75 Turks Is. 21 20N 71 20w
21 Turku 60 27N 22 14E
73 Turlock 37 30N 122 55w
74 Turneffe Is. 17 20N 87 50w
11 Turnhout 51 19N 4 57w
19 Tûrnovo 43 5N 25 41E
15 Turnu Măgurele 43 46N 24 56E
15 Turnu-Severin 44 39N 22 41E
8 Turriff 57 32N 2 58w
65 Turtle 48 52N 92 40w
65 Turtleford 53 30N 108 50w
30 Turūbah 28 20N 43 15E
21 Turun ja Pori □ 61 0N 22 30E
69 Tuscaloosa 33 13N 87 31w
69 Tuskegee 32 26N 85 42w
79 Tutoja 2 45s 42 20w
14 Tuttlingen 47 59N 8 50E
35 Tutuala 8 25s 127 15E
2 Tutuila, I. 14 19s 170 50w
25 Turukhansk 65 55N 88 5E
25 Tuva, A.S.S.R. 52 0N 95 0E
3 Tuvalu ■ 8 0s 176 0E
30 Tuwaiq, Jabal 23 0N 46 0E
74 Tuxpan 20 50N 97 30w
74 Tuxtla Gutiérrez 16 50N 93 10w
13 Tuy 42 3N 8 39w
39 Tuyun 26 5N 107 20E
30 Tuz Gölü 38 45N 33 30E
30 Tuz Khurmātu 34 50N 44 45E
6 Tweed, R. 55 46N 2 0w
64 Tweedsmuir Prov. Park 52 55N 126 5w
57 Tweeling 27 38s 28 30E
72 Twin Falls 42 30N 114 30w
68 Two Rivers 44 10N 87 31w
71 Tyler 32 20N 95 15w
25 Tyndinskiy 55 10N 124 43E
6 Tyne, R. 55 1N 1 26w
6 Tyne & Wear □ 54 55N 1 35w
6 Tynemouth 55 1N 1 27w
30 Tyre =Sur 33 19N 35 16E
46 Tyrendarra 38 12s 141 50E
21 Tyrifjorden 60 2N 10 3E
14 Tyrol, Reg.= Tirol, Reg. 46 50N 11 40E
18 Tyrrhenian Sea 40 0N 12 30E
24 Tyumen 57 0N 65 18E
7 Tywi, R. 51 46N 4 22w
57 Tzaneen 23 47s 30 9E
39 Tzeki 27 40N 117 5E
39 Tzekung 29 25N 104 30E
39 Tzekwei 31 0N 110 46E
38 Tzepo 36 28N 117 58E
38 Tzeyang 32 47N 108 58E

U

29 Uarsciek 2 28N 45 55E
78 Uaupés 0 8s 67 5w
79 Ubá 21 0s 43 0w
79 Ubaitaba 14 18s 39 20w
36 Ube 34 6N 131 20E
13 Ubeda 38 3N 3 23w
79 Uberaba 19 50s 48 0w
79 Uberlândia 19 0s 48 20w
53 Ubiaja 6 40N 6 20E
34 Ubon Ratchathani 15 15N 104 50E
54 Ubundu 0 22s 25 30E
78 Ucayali, R. 4 30s 73 30w
65 Uchi Lake 51 10N 92 40w
36 Uchiura-Wan, G. 42 25N 140 40E
64 Ucluelet 48 57N 125 32w
32 Udaipur 24 36N 73 44E
21 Uddevalla 58 21N 11 55E
20 Uddjaur, L. 65 55N 17 50E
53 Udi 6 23N 7 21E
18 Údine 46 5N 13 10E
32 Udipi 13 25N 74 42E
22 Udmurt A.S.S.R. □ 57 30N 52 30E
34 Udon Thani 17 29N 102 46E
52 Udzungwa Ra. 8 30s 35 30E
36 Ueda 36 30N 138 10E
25 Uelen 66 10N 170 0w
14 Uelzen 53 0N 10 33E
54 Uere, R. 3 42N 25 24E
22 Ufa 54 45N 55 55E
52 Uganda ■ 2 0N 32 0E
60 Ugashik Lakes 57 0N 157 0w
53 Ugep 5 50N 8 1E
25 Uglegorsk 49 10N 142 5E
56 Uitenhage 33 40s 25 28E
52 Ujiji=Kigoma-Ujiji 4 57s 29 40E
32 Ujjain 23 9N 75 43E
15 Ujpest 47 33N 19 6E
35 Ujung Pandang 5 10s 119 0E
25 Uka 57 50N 162 0E
52 Ukerewe I. 2 0s 33 0E
33 Ukhrul 25 10N 94 25E
22 Ukhta 63 55N 54 0E
72 Ukiah 39 10N 123 9w
23 Ukrainian S.S.R. □ 48 0N 35 0E
38 Ulaanbaatar 48 0N 107 0E
38 Ulan Bator = Ulaanbaatar 48 0N 107 0E
25 Ulan Ude 52 0N 107 30E
38 Ulanhot 46 5N 122 1E
32 Ulhasnagar 19 15N 73 10E
46 Ulladulla 35 21s 150 29E
8 Ullapool 57 54N 5 10w
6 Ullswater, L. 54 35N 2 52w
14 Ulm 48 23N 10 0E
21 Ulricehamn 57 46N 13 26E
68 Ulrichsville 40 27N 81 30w
9 Ulster □ 54 45N 6 30w
52 Uluguru Mts. 7 15s 37 30E
6 Ulverston 54 13N 3 7w
42 Ulverstone 41 11s 146 11E
22 Ulyanovsk 54 25N 48 25E
23 Uman 48 40N 30 12E
33 Umaria 23 31N 80 40E
18 Umbria □ 42 53N 12 30E
20 Umeå 63 45N 20 20E
57 Umfuli, R. 17 50s 29 40E
57 Umkomaas 30 13s 30 48E
31 Umm al Qaiwain 25 30N 55 35E
28 Umm el Fahm 32 31N 35 9E
51 Umm Keddada 13 36N 26 42E
30 Umm Lajj 25 0N 37 23E
60 Umnak I. 53 0N 168 0w
57 Umniati, R. 17 30s 29 23E
* 57 Umtali 18 58s 32 38E

* Renamed Mutare

Umtata Vila Cabral = Lichinga

57 Umtata 31 36s 28 49e
53 Umuahia 5 33n 7 29e
* 57 Umvuma 19 16s 30 30e
57 Umzimvubu 31 38s 29 33e
57 Umzinto 30 15s 30 45e
18 Unac, R. 44 30n 16 9e
60 Unalakleet 63 53n 160 50w
60 Unalaska I. 54 0n 164 30w
73 Uncompahgre Pk. 38 5n 107 32w
46 Underbool 35 10s 141 51e
46 Ungarie 33 38s 146 56e
61 Ungava B. 59 30n 67 0w
61 Ungava Pen. 60 0n 75 0w
79 União 4 50s 37 50w
80 União da Vitoría 26 5s 51 0w
60 Unimak I. 54 30n 164 30w
69 Union 34 49n 81 39w
68 Union City, Pa. 41 53n 79 50w
71 Union City, Tenn. 36 35n 89 0w
72 Union Gap 46 38n 120 29w
27 Union of Soviet Socialist Republics ■ 60 0n 60 0e
56 Uniondale 33 39s 23 7e
68 Uniontown 39 54n 79 45w
31 United Arab Emirates ■ 24 0n 54 30e
10 United Kingdom ■ 55 0n 3 0w
66 United States of America ■ 37 0n 96 0w
65 Unity 52 30n 109 5w
8 Unst, I. 60 50n 0 55w
30 Ünye 41 5n 37 15e
36 Uozu 36 48n 137 24e
78 Upata 8 1n 62 24w
56 Upington 28 25s 21 15e
47 Upolu, I. 13 58s 172 0w
53 Upper □ 10 40n 2 0w
47 Upper Hutt 41 8s 175 5e
63 Upper Musquodoboit 45 10n 62 58w
† 53 Upper Volta ■ 12 0n 0 30w
21 Uppsala 59 53n 17 42e
21 Uppsala □ 60 0n 17 30e
30 Ur 30 55n 46 25e
78 Uracará 2 20s 57 50w
46 Ural, Mt. 33 21s 146 12e
22 Ural Mts. = Uralskie Gory 60 0n 59 0e
24 Ural, R. 47 0n 51 48e
43 Uralla 30 37s 151 29e
24 Uralsk 51 20n 51 20e
22 Uralskie Gory 60 0n 59 0e
42 Urandangi 21 32s 138 14e
65 Uranium City 59 28n 108 40w
36 Urawa 35 50n 139 40e
24 Uray 60 5n 65 15e
70 Urbana, Ill. 40 7n 88 12w
68 Urbana, Ohio 40 9n 83 44w
18 Urbino 43 43n 12 38e
6 Ure, R. 54 1n 1 12w
24 Urengoy 66 0n 78 0e
30 Urfa 37 12n 38 50e
14 Urfahr 48 19n 14 17e
24 Urgench 41 40n 60 30e
78 Uribia 11 43n 72 16w
28 Urim 31 18n 34 32e
30 Urmia, L. = Daryâcheh-ye Reza'iyeh 37 30n 45 30e
79 Uruaca 14 35s 49 16w
74 Uruapán 19 30n 102 0w
79 Uruçui 7 20s 44 28w
80 Uruguay ■ 32 30s 55 30w
80 Uruguay, R. 34 0s 58 30w
80 Uruguaiana 29 50s 57 0w
37 Urumchi= Wulumuchi 43 40n 87 50e
37 Urungu, R. 46 30n 88 50e
31 Uruzgan □ 33 30n 66 0e
22 Usa, R. 65 57n 56 55e
30 Uşak 38 43n 29 28e
56 Usakos 22 0s 15 31e
52 Usambara Mts. 4 50s 38 20e
14 Usedom, I. 53 50n 13 55e
30 Usfan 21 58n 39 27e
24 Ush-Tobe 45 16n 78 0e
12 Ushant, I.= Ouessant, I. d' 48 28n 5 6w
80 Ushuaia 54 50s 68 23w
25 Ushuman 52 47n 126 32e
7 Usk, R. 51 36n 2 58w
30 Üsküdar 41 0n 29 5e
22 Usman 52 5n 39 48e
52 Usoke 5 8s 32 24e
25 Usolye Sibirskoye 52 40n 103 40e
53 Usoro 5 34n 6 13e
80 Uspallata, P. 32 30s 69 28w
24 Uspenskiy 48 50n 72 55e
25 Ussuriysk 43 40n 131 50e
25 Ust-Ilga 55 5n 104 55e
25 Ust-Ilimsk 58 3n 102 39e
24 Ust Ishim 57 45n 71 10e
25 Ust-Kamchatsk 56 10n 162 0e
24 Ust Kamenogorsk 50 0n 82 20e
25 Ust-Kut 56 50n 105 10e
25 Ust Kuyga 70 1n 135 36e
25 Ust Maya 60 30n 134 20e
25 Ust Olenck 73 0n 120 10e
24 Ust Post 70 0n 84 10e
22 Ust Tsilma 65 25n 52 0e
25 Ust-Tungir 55 25n 120 15e
22 Ust Usa 66 0n 56 30e
25 Ustchaun 68 47n 170 30e
14 Ustí nad Labem 50 41n 14 3e
18 Ustica, I. 38 42n 13 10e
25 Ustye 55 30n 97 30e
74 Usulután 13 25n 88 28w
72 Utah □ 39 30n 111 30w
35 Utara □, Sulawesi 1 0n 120 3e
34 Utara □, Sumatera 2 0n 99 0e
52 Utete 7 59s 38 47e
30 Uthmaniya 25 5n 49 6e
68 Utica 43 5n 75 18w
11 Utrecht, Neth. 52 3n 5 8e
11 Utrecht, Neth. □ 52 6n 5 7e
57 Utrecht, S. Africa 27 38s 30 20e
13 Utrera 37 12n 5 48w
36 Utsunomiya 36 30n 139 50e
33 Uttar Pradesh □ 27 0n 80 0e
34 Uttaradit 17 36n 100 5e
6 Uttoxeter 52 53n 1 50w
21 Uudenmaa □ 60 25n 23 0e
38 Uuldza 49 8n 112 10e
21 Uusikaupunki 60 47n 21 28e
71 Uvalde 29 15n 99 48w
24 Uvat 59 5n 68 50e
52 Uvinza 5 5s 30 24e
54 Uvira 3 22s 29 3e
37 Uvs Nuur, L. 50 20n 92 30e
36 Uwajima 33 10n 132 35e
74 Uxmal 20 22n 89 46w
53 Uyo 5 1n 7 53e
78 Uyuni 20 35s 66 55w
24 Uzbek S.S.R. 40 5n 65 0e

V

56 Vaal, R. 29 4s 23 38e
20 Vaasa 63 10n 21 35e
20 Vaasa □ 63 6n 23 0e
15 Vác 47 49n 19 10e
32 Vadodara 22 20n 73 10e
20 Vadsø 70 3n 29 50e
15 Váh, R. 47 55n 18 0e
24 Vaigach 70 10n 59 0e
62 Val-d'Or 48 7n 77 47w
65 Val Marie 49 15n 107 45w
15 Valahia, Reg. 44 35n 25 0e
80 Valchete 40 40s 66 20w
12 Val-d'Oise □ 49 5n 2 0e
12 Val-de-Marne □ 48 45n 2 28e
22 Valdayskaya Vozvyshennost 57 0n 33 40e
13 Valdepeṇas, Ciudad Real 38 43n 3 25w
80 Valdés, Pen. 42 30s 63 45w
60 Valdez 61 14n 146 10w
80 Valdivia 39 50s 73 14w
69 Valdosta 30 50n 83 48w
79 Valença, Brazil 13 20s 39 5w
79 Valença do Piaui 6 20s 41 45w
12 Valence 44 57n 4 54e
13 Valencia, Sp. 39 27n 0 23w
78 Valencia, Ven. 10 11n 68 0w
13 Valencia, G. de 39 30n 0 20e
13 Valencia, Reg. 39 25n 0 45w
13 Valencia de Alcantara 39 25n 7 14w
12 Valenciennes 50 20n 3 34e
9 Valentia, I. 51 54n 10 22w
70 Valentine 42 50n 100 35w
78 Valera 9 19n 70 37w
11 Valkenswaard 51 21n 5 29e
74 Valladolid, Mexico 20 30n 88 20w
13 Valladolid, Sp. 41 38n 4 43w
18 Valle d'Aosta □ 45 45n 7 22e
78 Valle de la Pascua 9 13n 66 0w
74 Valle de Santiago 20 25n 101 15w
13 Vallecas 40 23n 3 41w
72 Vallejo 38 12n 122 15w
80 Vallenar 28 30s 70 50w
18 Valletta 35 54n 14 30e
70 Valley City 46 57n 98 0w
62 Valleyfield 45 15n 74 8w
64 Valleyview 55 5n 117 25w
13 Valls 41 18n 1 15e
12 Valognes 49 30n 1 28w
80 Valparaíso 33 2s 71 40w
56 Valsbaai 34 15s 18 40e
13 Valverde del Camino 37 35n 6 47w
71 Van Buren, Ark. 35 28n 94 18w
63 Van Buren, Me. 47 10n 68 1w
44 Van Diemen, C. 16 30s 139 46e
44 Van Diemen, G. 12 0s 132 0e
30 Van Gölü 38 30n 43 0e
68 Van Wert 40 52n 84 31w
64 Vancouver, Canada 49 20n 123 10w
72 Vancouver, U.S.A. 45 44n 122 41w
64 Vancouver I. 49 50n 126 30w
70 Vandalia 38 57n 89 4w
57 Vanderbijlpark 26 42s 27 54e
64 Vanderhoof 54 0n 124 0w
42 Vandyke 24 8s 142 45e
21 Vänern, L. 58 47n 13 50e
21 Vänersborg 58 26n 12 27e
54 Vanga 4 35s 39 12e
57 Vangaindrano 23 21s 47 36e
25 Vankarem 67 51n 175 50w
62 Vankleek Hill 45 32n 74 40w
20 Vännäs 63 58n 19 48e
12 Vannes 47 40n 2 47w
56 Vanrhynsdorp 31 36s 18 44e
21 Vansbro 60 32n 14 15e
47 Vanua Levu, I. 15 45s 179 10e
12 Var □ 43 27n 6 18e
33 Varanasi 25 22n 83 8e
18 Varaždin 46 20n 16 20e
21 Varberg 57 17n 12 20e
19 Vardar, R. 40 35n 22 50e
18 Varese 45 49n 8 50e
21 Värmlands □ 59 45n 13 0e
19 Varna 43 13n 27 56e
21 Värnamo 57 10n 14 3e
13 Vascongadas, Reg. 42 50n 2 45w
15 Vaslui 46 38n 27 42e
21 Västerås 59 37n 16 38e
20 Västerbotten □ 64 58n 18 0e
21 Västerdalälven, R. 60 33n 15 8e
20 Västernorrlands □ 63 30n 17 40e
21 Västervik 57 43n 16 43e
21 Västmanlands □ 89 5n 16 20e
18 Vasto 42 8n 14 40e
20 Vatnajökull 64 30n 16 30w
57 Vatomandry 19 20s 48 59e
15 Vatra-Dornei 47 22n 25 22e
21 Vättern, L. 58 25n 14 30e
12 Vaucluse □ 44 3n 5 10e
73 Vaughan 34 37n 105 12w
64 Vauxhall 50 5n 112 9w
21 Växjö 56 52n 14 50e
24 Vaygach, Os. 70 0n 60 0e
11 Vechte, R. 52 35n 6 5e
15 Vedea, R. 43 53n 25 59e
11 Veendam 53 5n 6 25e
11 Veenendaal 52 2n 5 34e
20 Vefsna, R. 65 50n 13 12e
20 Vegafjord 65 37n 12 0e
64 Vegreville 53 30n 112 5w
13 Vejer de la Frontera 36 15n 5 59w
21 Vejle 55 47n 9 30e
12 Velay, Mts. du 45 0n 3 40e
56 Velddrif 32 42s 18 11e
18 Velebit Planina, Mts. 44 50n 15 20e
78 Vélez 6 2n 73 43w
13 Vélez Málaga 36 48n 4 5w
13 Vélez Rubio 37 41n 2 5w
22 Velikiy Ustyug 60 47n 46 20e
22 Velikiye Luki 56 25n 30 32e
32 Velikonda Ra. 14 45n 79 10e
18 Velletri 41 43n 12 43e
32 Vellore 12 57n 79 10e
11 Velsen 52 27n 4 40e
22 Velsk 61 10n 42 5e
80 Venado Tuerto 33 50s 62 0w
12 Vendée □ 46 40n 1 20w
18 Veneto □ 45 30n 12 0e
18 Venézia 45 27n 12 20e
18 Venézia, G. di 45 20n 13 0e
78 Venezuela ■ 8 0n 65 0w
78 Venezuela, G. de 11 30n 71 0w
32 Vengurla 15 53n 73 45e
18 Venice=Venézia 45 27n 12 20e
11 Venlo 51 22n 6 11e
11 Venraij 51 31n 6 0e
7 Ventnor 50 35n 1 12w
22 Ventspils 57 25n 21 32e
73 Ventura 34 16n 119 25w
80 Vera, Arg. 29 30s 60 20w
13 Vera, Sp. 37 15n 1 15w
74 Veracruz 19 10n 96 10w
74 Veracruz □ 19 0n 96 15w
32 Veraval 20 53n 70 27e
18 Vercelli 45 19n 8 25e
80 Verde, R. 41 56s 65 5w
14 Verden 52 56n 9 15e
12 Verdun 49 12n 5 24e
57 Vereeniging 26 38s 27 57e
23 Verkhniy Baskunchak 48 5n 46 50e
25 Verkhoyansk 67 50n 133 50e
25 Verkhoyanskiy Khrebet 66 0n 129 0e
65 Vermilion 53 20n 110 50w
65 Vermilion, R. 53 44n 110 18w
65 Vermilion Bay 49 50n 93 20w
70 Vermillion 42 50n 96 56w
68 Vermont □ 43 40n 72 50w
72 Vernal 40 28n 109 35w
62 Verner 46 25n 80 8w
64 Vernon, Canada 50 20n 119 15w
71 Vernon, U.S.A. 34 0n 99 15w
18 Verona 45 27n 11 0e
12 Versailles 48 48n 2 8e
50 Verte, C. 14 45n 17 30w
57 Verulam 29 38s 31 2e
11 Verviers 50 37n 5 52e
23 Veselovskoye, Vdkhr. 47 0n 41 0e
12 Vesoul 60 40n 6 11e
21 Vest-Agde □ 58 30n 7 0e
21 Vestfold □ 59 15n 10 0e
20 Vestmannaejar, Is. 63 27n 20 15w
18 Vesuvio, Mt. 40 50n 14 22e
18 Vesuvius, Mt.= Vesuvio, Mt. 40 50n 14 22e
15 Veszprém 47 8n 17 57e
21 Vetlanda 57 24n 15 3e
12 Vexin, Reg. 49 20n 1 30e
78 Viacha 16 30s 68 5w
79 Viana 3 0s 44 40w
13 Viana do Castelo 41 42n 8 50w
79 Vianopolis 16 40s 48 35w
21 Viborg 56 27n 9 23e
18 Vicenza 45 32n 11 31e
13 Vich 41 58n 2 19e
12 Vichy 46 9n 3 26e
71 Vicksburg 32 22n 90 56w
79 Vicosa 9 28s 36 25w
43 Victor Harbour 35 30s 138 37e
41 Victoria, Australia 21 16s 149 3e
* 53 Victoria, Cameroon 4 1n 9 10e
64 Victoria, Canada 48 30n 123 25w
80 Victoria, Chile 38 22s 72 29w
39 Victoria, Hong Kong 22 25n 114 15e
34 Victoria, Malaysia 5 20n 115 20e
18 Victoria, Malta 36 2n 14 14e
71 Victoria, U.S.A. 28 50n 97 0w
52 Victoria, L. 1 0s 33 0e
44 Victoria, R. 15 12s 129 43e
† 57 Victoria □ 20 55s 31 50e
65 Victoria Beach 50 45n 96 32w
75 Victoria de las Tunas 20 58n 76 59w
56 Victoria Falls 17 58s 25 45e
60 Victoria I. 71 0n 11 0w
9 Victoria Ld. 75 0s 160 0e
52 Victoria Nile, R. 2 14n 31 26e
33 Victoria Taungdeik, Mt. 21 15n 93 55e
56 Victoria West 31 25s 23 4e
63 Victoriaville 46 4n 71 56w
80 Victorica 36 15s 65 30w
73 Victorville 34 32n 117 18w
80 Vicuña 30 2s 70 44w
69 Vidalia 32 13n 82 25w
19 Vidin 43 59n 22 52e
80 Viedma 40 50s 63 0w
80 Viedma, L. 49 30s 72 30w
14 Vienna = Wien 48 12n 16 22e
12 Vienne 45 31n 4 53e
12 Vienne, R. 47 13n 0 5e
12 Vienne □ 45 53n 0 42e
27 Vientiane 18 7n 102 35e
12 Vierzon 47 13n 2 5e
34 Vietnam ■ 16 0n 108 0e
35 Vigan 17 35n 120 28e
79 Vigia 0 50s 48 5w
13 Vigo 42 12n 8 41w
33 Vijayawada 16 31n 80 39e
24 Vikulovo 56 50n 70 40e
55 Vila Cabral = Lichinga 13 13s 35 11e

* *Renamed Mvuma*
† *Renamed Burkina Faso*

* *Renamed Limbe*
† *Renamed Masvingo*

57 Vila da Maganja 17 18S 37 30E
57 Vila de Manica 18 58S 32 58E
13 Vila Franca de Xira 38 57N 8 59W
55 Vila Machado 19 15S 34 14E
13 Vila Real 41 17N 7 48W
13 Vila Real de Sto. António 37 10N 7 28W
12 Vilaine, R. 47 30N 2 27W
25 Viliga 60 2N 156 56E
80 Villa Ángela 27 34S 60 45W
50 Villa Cisneros = Dakhla 23 50N 15 53W
80 Villa Colón 31 38S 68 20W
80 Villa Hayes 25 0S 57 20W
75 Villa Julia Molina 19 5N 69 45W
80 Villa María 32 20S 63 10W
80 Villa Mazán 28 40S 66 10W
80 Villa Ocampo 28 30S 59 20W
14 Villach 46 37N 13 51E
80 Villa de Maria 29 55S 63 45W
13 Villagarcia de Arosa 42 34N 8 46W
80 Villaguay 32 0S 58 45W
74 Villahermosa, Mexico 17 45N 92 50W
13 Villalba 40 36N 3 59W
73 Villanueva 35 16N 105 31W
13 Villanueva de la Serena 38 59N 5 50W
13 Villarreal 39 55N 0 3W
80 Villarrica 39 15S 72 30W
78 Villavicencio 4 9N 73 37W
13 Villaviciosa 43 32N 5 27W
78 Villazón 22 0S 65 35W
62 Ville Marie 47 20N 79 30W
71 Ville Platte 30 45N 92 17W
13 Villena 38 39N 0 52W
57 Villiers 27 2S 28 36E
64 Vilna 54 7N 111 55W
22 Vilnius 54 38N 25 25E
11 Vilvoorde 50 56N 4 26E
25 Vilyuysk 63 40N 121 20E
80 Viña del Mar 33 0S 71 30W
13 Vinaroz 40 30N 0 27E
68 Vincennes 38 42N 87 29W
32 Vindhya Ra. 22 50N 77 0E
37 Vinh 18 45N 105 38E
34 Vinh Loi 17 4N 107 2E
71 Vinita 36 40N 95 12W
19 Vinkovci 45 19N 18 48E
23 Vinnitsa 49 15N 28 30E
46 Violet Town 36 19S 145 37E
35 Viqueque 8 42S 126 30E
32 Viramgam 23 5N 72 0E
65 Virden 49 50N 101 0W
80 Vírgenes, C. 52 19S 68 21W
75 Virgin Gorda, I. 18 45N 64 26W
75 Virgin Is., Br. 18 40N 64 30W
75 Virgin Is., U.S. 18 20N 64 50W
56 Virginia, S. Afr. 28 8S 26 55E
70 Virginia, U.S.A. 47 30N 92 32W
68 Virginia □ 37 45N 78 0W
68 Virginia Beach 36 54N 75 58W
72 Virginia City 45 25N 111 58W
11 Virton 49 35N 5 32E
32 Virudunagar 9 30N 78 0E
18 Vis, I. 43 0N 16 10E
73 Visalia 36 25N 119 18W
35 Visayan Sea 11 30N 123 30E
21 Visby 57 37N 18 18E
58 Viscount Melville Sd. 78 0N 108 0W
11 Visé 50 44N 5 41E
79 Viseu, Brazil 1 10S 46 20W
13 Viseu, Port. 40 40N 7 55W
33 Vishakhapatnam 17 45N 83 20E
56 Visrivier 31 45S 25 20E
15 Vistula, R.= Wisła, R. 54 22N 18 55E
18 Viso, Mte. 44 40N 7 7E
22 Vitebsk 55 10N 30 15E
18 Viterbo 42 25N 12 8E
47 Viti Levu, I. 17 30S 177 30E
25 Vitim 59 45N 112 25E
25 Vitim, R. 59 26N 112 34E
79 Vitoria, Brazil 20 20S 40 22W
13 Vitória, Sp. 42 50N 2 41W
79 Vitória da Conquista 14 51S 40 51W
79 Vitoria de Santo Antão 8 10S 37 20W
18 Vittória 36 58N 14 30E
18 Vittório Véneto 45 59N 12 18E
13 Vivero 43 39N 7 38W
33 Vizianagaram 18 6N 83 10E
11 Vlaardingen 51 55N 4 21E
22 Vladimir 56 0N 40 30E
25 Vladivostok 43 10N 131 53E
11 Vlissingen 51 26N 3 34E
19 Vlóra 40 32N 19 28E
35 Vogelkop, Mt.= Doberai, Djazirah 1 25S 133 0E
57 Vohimarina 13 25S 50 0E
57 Vohipeno 22 22S 47 51E
52 Voi 3 25S 38 32E
23 Volga, R. 45 55N 47 52E
23 Volga Heights, Mts. 51 0N 46 0E
23 Volgograd 48 40N 44 25E
23 Volgogradskoye, Vdkhr. 50 0N 45 20E
57 Volksrust 27 24S 29 53E
11 Vollenhove 52 40N 5 58E
25 Volochanka 71 0N 94 28E
22 Vologda 59 25N 40 0E
19 Vólos 39 24N 22 59E
22 Volsk 52 5N 47 28E
53 Volta, L. 7 30N 0 15E
53 Volta, R. 5 46N 0 41E
50 Volta Noire, R. 8 41N 1 33W
79 Volta Redonda 22 31S 44 5W
18 Volterra 43 24N 10 50E
23 Volzhskiy 48 56N 44 46E
57 Vondrozo 22 49S 47 20E
11 Voorburg 52 5N 4 24E
14 Vor-Arlberg □ 47 15N 9 55E
22 Vorkuta 67 48N 64 20E
22 Voronezh 51 40N 39 10E
23 Voroshilovgrad 48 38N 39 15E
12 Vosges, Mts. 48 20N 7 10E
12 Vosges □ 48 12N 6 20E
21 Voss 60 38N 6 26E
25 Vostochnyy Sayan 54 0N 96 0E
2 Vostok, I. 10 5S 152 23W
22 Votkinsk 57 0N 53 55E
22 Votkinskoye, Vdkhr. 57 30N 55 0E
22 Vozhe, Oz. 60 45N 39 0E
25 Voznesenka 46 51N 35 26E
23 Voznesensk 47 35N 31 15E
22 Voznesenye 61 0N 35 45E
25 Vrangelya, Os. 71 0N 180 0E
19 Vranje 42 34N 21 54E
19 Vratsa 43 13N 23 30E
57 Vrede 27 30S 29 6E
56 Vredefort 27 5S 27 16E
55 Vredenburg 32 51S 18 0E
56 Vredendal 31 41S 18 35E
19 Vršac 45 8N 21 18E
56 Vryburg 26 55S 24 45E
57 Vryheid 27 54S 30 47E
11 Vught 51 38N 5 20E
64 Vulcan 50 25N 113 15W
18 Vulcano, I. 38 27N 14 58E
22 Vyatskiye 56 5N 51 0E
22 Vyazma 55 10N 34 15E
22 Vyborg 60 42N 28 45E
15 Vychodné Beskydy 49 30N 22 0E
22 Vyg, Oz. 63 30N 34 0E
6 Vyrnwy, L. 52 48N 3 30W
22 Vyshniy Volochek 57 30N 34 30E
22 Vytegra 61 15N 36 40E

W

53 Wa 10 7N 2 25W
11 Waal, R. 51 55N 4 30E
63 Wabana 47 40N 53 0W
68 Wabash 40 48N 85 46W
68 Wabash, R. 37 46N 88 2W
65 Wabowden 54 55N 98 35W
15 Wabrzeźno 53 16N 18 57E
63 Wabush City 52 40N 67 0W
71 Waco 31 33N 97 5W
51 Wad Banda 13 10N 27 50E
51 Wad Hamid 16 20N 32 45E
51 Wâd Medanî 14 28N 33 30E
36 Wadayama 35 19N 134 52E
11 Waddeniladen, Is. 53 30N 5 30E
11 Waddenzee 53 15N 5 15E
45 Wadderin Hill 32 0S 118 25E
64 Waddington, Mt. 51 10N 125 20W
65 Wadena, Canada 52 0N 103 50W
70 Wadena, U.S.A. 46 25N 95 2W
51 Wadi Halfa 21 53N 31 19E
11 Wageningen 51 58N 5 40E
61 Wager Bay 66 0N 91 0W
46 Wagga Wagga 35 7S 147 24E
45 Wagin, Austral 33 17S 117 25E
53 Wagin, Nigeria 12 45N 7 8E
35 Wahai 2 48S 129 35E
70 Wahpeton 46 20N 96 35W
47 Waiau 42 39S 173 5E
47 Waiau, R. 42 46S 173 23E
35 Waigeo, I. 0 20S 130 40E
47 Waihi 37 23S 175 52E
47 Waihou, R. 37 10S 175 32E
47 Waikaremoana, L. 38 49S 177 9E
47 Waikari 42 58S 72 41E
47 Waikato, R. 37 23S 174 43E
47 Waikerie 34 9S 140 0E
47 Waikokopu 39 3S 177 52E
47 Waikouaiti 45 36S 170 41E
47 Waimakariri, R. 43 24S 172 42E
47 Waimarino 40 40S 175 20E
47 Waimate 44 53S 171 3E
32 Wainganga, R. 18 50N 79 55E
35 Waingapu 9 35S 120 11E
65 Wainwright 52 50N 110 50W
47 Waiouru 39 29S 175 40E
47 Waipara 43 3N 172 46E
47 Waipawa 39 56S 176 38E
47 Waipiro 38 2S 176 22E
47 Waipu 35 59S 174 29E
47 Waipukurau 40 1S 176 33E
47 Wairakei 38 37S 176 6E
47 Wairau, R. 41 32S 174 7E
47 Wairoa 39 3S 177 25E
47 Waitaki, R. 44 56S 171 7E
47 Waitara 38 59S 174 15E
47 Waiuku 37 15S 174 45E
39 Waiyeung 23 12N 11432E
36 Wajima 37 30N 137 0E
52 Wajir 1 42N 40 20E
36 Wakasa 35 20N 134 24E
36 Wakasa-Wan 34 45N 135 30E
47 Wakatipu, L. 45 6S 168 30E
65 Wakaw 52 39N 105 44W
36 Wakayama 34 15N 135 15E
36 Wakayama □ 34 50N 135 30E
3 Wake, I. 19 18N 166 36E
6 Wakefield, U.K. 53 41N 1 31W
47 Wakefield, N.Z. 41 24S 173 5E
61 Wakeham Bay = Maricourt 61 36N 71 57W
36 Wakkanai 45 28N 141 35E
57 Wakkerstroom 27 24S 30 10E
35 Wakre 0 30S 131 5E
15 Walachia, Reg.= Valahia, Reg. 44 35N 25 0E
14 Walbrzych 50 45N 16 18E
7 Walbury Hill 51 22N 1 28W
43 Walcha 30 55S 151 31E
11 Walcheren, I. 51 30N 3 35E
72 Walden 40 47N 106 20W
65 Waldron 50 53N 102 35W
45 Walebing 30 40S 116 15E
10 Wales ■ 52 30N 3 30W
43 Walgett 30 0S 148 5E
45 Walkaway 28 59S 114 48W
62 Walkerton 44 10N 81 10W
72 Walla Walla 46 3N 118 25W
72 Wallace 47 30N 116 0W
62 Wallaceburg 42 40N 82 30W
43 Wallal 26 32S 146 7E
44 Wallal Downs 19 47S 120 40E
43 Wallaroo 33 56S 137 39E
6 Wallasey 3 26S 3 2W
46 Wallerawang 33 25S 150 4E
42 Wallahallow 17 50S 135 50E
72 Wallowa 45 40N 117 35W
6 Wallsend 54 59N 1 30W
43 Wallumbilla 26 33S 149 9E
56 Walmer 33 57S 25 35E
6 Walney, I 54 5N 3 15W
46 Walpeup 35 10S 142 2E
7 Walsall 52 36N 1 59W
71 Walsenburg 37 42N 104 45W
62 Waltham 45 57N 76 57W
56 Walvisbaai 23 0S 14 28E
56 Walvis Bay = Walvisbaai 23 0S 14 28E
53 Wamba 2 10N 27 57E
47 Wanaka, L. 44 33S 169 7E
35 Wanapiri 4 30S 135 50E
43 Wanbi 34 46S 140 17E
57 Wanderer 19 37S 29 59E
43 Wandoan 26 5S 149 55E
47 Wanganui 39 35S 175 3E
46 Wangaratta 36 21S 146 19E
46 Wangary 34 33S 135 29E
38 Wangtu 38 42N 115 4E
39 Wanhsien 30 45N 108 20E
* 56 Wankie 18 18S 26 30E
65 Wanless 54 11N 101 21W
39 Wanning 18 45N 110 28E
39 Wantsai 28 1N 114 5E
39 Wanyang Shan, Mts. 26 30N 113 30E

* *Renamed Hwange*

39 Wanyuan 32 3N 108 16E
72 Wapato 46 30N 120 25W
29 Warandab 7 20N 44 2E
32 Warangal 17 58N 79 45E
47 Ward 41 49S 174 11E
31 Wardak □ 34 15N 68 0E
57 Warden 27 56S 29 0E
32 Wardha 20 45N 78 39E
43 Warialda 29 29S 150 33E
35 Warkopi 1 12S 134 9E
47 Warkworth 36 24S 174 41E
7 Warley 52 30N 2 0W
65 Warman 52 25N 106 30W
57 Warmbad 24 51S 28 19E
55 Warmbad, S.W. Africa 28 25S 18 42E
55 Warmbad, S.W. Africa 19 14S 13 51E
46 Warncoort 38 30S 143 45E
14 Warnemünde 54 9N 12 5E
72 Warner Ra. 41 30S 120 20W
69 Warner Robins 32 41N 83 36W
45 Waroona 32 50S 115 55E
46 Warracknabeal 36 9S 142 26E
46 Warragul 38 10S 145 58E
43 Warrego, R. 30 24S 145 21E
46 Warren, Australia 31 42S 147 51E
68 Warren, Ohio 41 18N 80 52W
68 Warren, Pa. 41 52N 79 10W
71 Warren 33 35N 92 3W
9 Warrenpoint 54 7N 6 15W
70 Warrensburg 38 45N 93 45W
56 Warrenton, S. Africa 28 9S 24 47E
72 Warrenton, U.S.A. 46 11N 123 59W
53 Warri 5 30N 5 41E
6 Warrington, U.K. 53 25N 2 38W
69 Warrington, U.S.A. 30 22N 87 16W
46 Warrnambool 38 25S 142 30E
32 Warsak Dam 34 10N 71 25E
68 Warsaw 41 14N 85 50W
15 Warsaw=Warszawa 52 13N 21 0E
15 Warszawa 52 13N 21 0E
15 Warta, R. 52 35N 14 39E
7 Warwick □ 52 20N 1 30W
43 Warwick, Australia 28 10S 152 1E
7 Warwick, U.K. 52 17N 1 36W
68 Warwick, U.S.A. 41 43N 71 25W
64 Wasa 49 45N 115 50W
58 Wasatch Mts. 40 30N 111 15W
57 Wasbank 28 15S 30 9E
73 Wasco, Calif. 35 37N 119 16W
73 Wasco, Oreg. 45 45N 120 46W
70 Waseca 44 3N 93 31W
6 Wash, The 52 58N 0 20W
72 Washington □ 47 45N 120 30W
68 Washington, D.C. 38 52N 77 0W
68 Washington, Ind. 38 40N 87 8W
70 Washington, Iowa 41 20N 91 45W
70 Washington, Mo. 38 33N 91 1W
69 Washington, N.C. 35 35N 77 1W
68 Washington, Ohio 39 34N 83 26W
68 Washington, Pa. 40 10N 80 20W
68 Washington, Mt. 44 15N 71 18W
11 Wassenaar 52 8N 4 24E
62 Waswanipi 49 30N 77 0W
35 Watangpon 4 29S 120 25E
57 Waterberg 24 14S 28 0E
68 Waterbury 41 32N 73 0W
9 Waterford 52 16N 7 8W
9 Waterford □ 51 10N 7 40W
11 Waterloo, Belgium 50 43N 4 25E
62 Waterloo, Canada 43 30N 80 32W
70 Waterloo, Iowa 42 27N 92 20W
68 Watertown, N.Y. 43 58N 75 57W
70 Watertown, S.D. 44 57N 97 5W
70 Watertown, Wis. 43 15N 88 45W
57 Waterval-Boven 25 40S 30 18E
69 Waterville 44 35N 69 40W
68 Watervliet 42 46N 73 43W
35 Wates 7 53S 110 6E
7 Watford 51 38N 0 23W
45 Watheroo 30 15S 116 0W
68 Watkins Glen 42 25N 76 55E
75 Watling, I. 24 0N 74 30W
65 Watrous 51 40N 105 25W
52 Watsa 3 4N 29 30E
45 Watson 30 19S 131 41E
64 Watson Lake 60 12N 129 0W
73 Watsonville 37 58N 121 49W
46 Waubra 37 21S 143 39E
46 Wauchope 31 28S 152 45E
65 Waugh 49 40N 95 20W
68 Waukegan 42 22N 87 54W
70 Waukesha 43 0N 88 15W
70 Waupun 43 38N 88 44W
70 Wausau 44 57N 89 40W
68 Wauwatosa 43 6N 87 59W

44 Wave Hill 17 32N 131 0E
7 Waveney, R. 52 28N 1 45E
47 Waverley 39 46S 174 37E
70 Waverly 42 40N 92 30W
11 Wavre 50 43N 4 38E
51 Wâw 7 45N 28 1E
71 Waxahachie 32 22N 96 53W
42 Wayatinah 42 19S 146 27E
69 Waycross 31 12N 82 25W
68 Waynesboro, Pa. 39 46N 77 32W
68 Waynesboro, Va. 38 4N 78 57W
69 Waynesville 35 31N 83 0W
31 Wazirabad, Afghanistan 36 44N 66 47E
32 Wazirabad, Pak. 32 30N 74 8E
7 Weald, The 51 7N 0 9E
6 Wear, R. 54 55N 1 22W
71 Weatherford 32 45N 97 48W
70 Webster City 42 30N 93 50W
70 Webster Green 38 38N 90 20W
35 Weda 0 30N 127 50E
80 Weddell I. 51 50S 61 0W
2 Weddell Sea 72 30S 40 0W
46 Wedderburn 36 20S 143 33E
63 Wedgeport 43 44N 65 59W
43 Wee Waa 30 11S 149 26E
72 Weed 41 29N 122 22W
57 Weenen 28 57S 30 3E
11 Weert 51 15N 5 43E
39 Wei Ho, R. 35 45N 114 30E
38 Weifang 36 47N 119 10E
38 Weihai 37 30N 122 10E
14 Weimar 51 0N 11 20E
39 Weinan 34 30N 109 35E
42 Weipa 12 24S 141 50E
65 Weir River 57 0N 94 10W
72 Weiser 44 10N 117 0W
15 Wejherow 54 35N 18 12E
65 Wekusko 54 45N 99 45W
68 Welch 37 29N 81 36W
56 Welkom 28 0S 26 50E
62 Welland 43 0N 79 10W
6 Welland, R. 52 53N 0 2E
42 Wellesley, Is. 17 20S 139 30E
7 Wellingborough 52 18N 0 41W
46 Wellington, Australia 32 30S 149 0E
62 Wellington, Canada 43 57N 77 20W
47 Wellington, N.Z. 41 19S 174 46E
6 Wellington, U.K. 52 42N 2 31W
71 Wellington, U.S.A. 37 15N 97 25W
47 Wellington □ 40 8S 175 36E
80 Wellington, I. 49 30S 75 0W
6 Wells, Norfolk 52 57N 0 51E
7 Wells, Somerset 51 12N 2 39W
72 Wells, U.S.A. 41 8N 115 0W
45 Wells, L. 26 44S 123 15W
68 Wellsboro 41 45N 77 16W
68 Wellsville, N.Y. 42 9N 77 57W
68 Wellsville, Ohio 40 36N 80 40W
14 Wels 48 9N 14 1E
46 Welshpool, Australia 38 42S 146 26E
7 Welshpool, U.K. 52 40N 3 9W
6 Wem 52 52N 2 45W
72 Wenatchee 47 30N 120 17W
39 Wenchang 19 38N 110 42E
53 Wenchi 7 46N 2 8W
39 Wenchou= Wenchow 28 0N 120 35E
39 Wenchow 28 0N 120 35E
72 Wendell 42 50N 114 51W
39 Wensiang 34 35N 110 40E
6 Wensleydale 54 20N 2 0W
37 Wensu 41 15N 80 14E
38 Wenteng 25 15S 23 16E
46 Wentworth 34 2S 141 54E
56 Wepener 29 42S 27 3E
55 Werda 25 15S 23 16E
14 Werra, R. 51 26N 9 39E
46 Werribee 37 54S 144 40E
46 Werris Creek 31 8S 150 38E
14 Weser, R. 53 32N 8 34E
63 Wesleyville 49 8N 53 36W
42 Wessel, Is. 11 10S 136 45E
68 West Bend 43 25N 88 10W
33 West Bengal □ 25 0N 90 0E
7 West Bromwich 52 32N 2 1W
70 West Des Moines 41 30N 93 45W
80 West Falkland, I. 51 30S 60 0W
70 West Frankfort 37 56N 89 0W
14 West Germany ■ 51 0N 9 0E
7 West Glamorgan □ 51 40N 3 55W
71 West Helena 34 30N 90 40W
2 West Indies 20 0N 65 0W
71 West Memphis 35 5N 90 3W
7 West Midlands □ 52 30N 2 0W
71 West Monroe 32 32N 92 7W
69 West Palm Beach 26 44N 80 3W
75 West Pt. 18 14N 78 30W
71 West Point, Miss. 33 36N 88 38W
68 West Point, Va. 37 35N 76 47W
7 West Sussex □ 50 55N 0 30W
68 West Virginia □ 39 0N 18 0W
46 West Wyalong 33 56S 147 10E
6 West Yorkshire □ 53 45N 1 40W
69 Westbrook 43 41N 70 21W
42 Westbury 41 30S 146 51E
53 Western □ 6 0N 2 20W
40 Western Australia □ 25 0S 118 0E
32 Western Ghats, Mts. 15 30N 74 30E
8 Western Isles □ 57 30N 7 10W
47 Western Samoa ■ 14 0S 172 0W
11 Westerschelde, R. 51 25N 4 0E
14 Westerwald, Mts. 50 39N 8 0E
47 Westland □ 43 33S 169 59E
64 Westlock 54 20N 113 55W
9 Westmeath □ 53 30N 7 30W
68 Westminster 39 34S 77 1W
73 Westmorland 33 2N 115 42W
34 Weston, Malaysia 5 10N 115 35E
68 Weston, U.S.A. 39 3N 80 29W
7 Weston-super-Mare 51 20N 2 59W
15 Westphalia □ = Nordrhein-Westfalen □ 51 45N 7 30E
9 Westport, Eire 53 44N 9 31W
47 Westport, N.Z. 41 46S 171 37E
8 Westray, I. 59 18N 3 0W
64 Westview 49 50N 124 31W
72 Westwood 40 26N 121 0W
35 Wetar, I. 7 30S 126 30E
64 Wetaskiwin 52 55N 113 24W
11 Wetteren 51 0N 3 53E
14 Wetzlar 50 33N 8 30E
71 Wewaka 35 10N 96 35W
9 Wexford 52 20N 6 28W
9 Wexford □ 52 20N 6 40W
65 Weyburn 49 40N 103 50W
7 Weymouth, U.K. 50 36N 2 28W
47 Whakatane 37 57S 177 1E
61 Whale, R. 57 40N 67 0W
65 Whale Cove 62 10N 93 0W
8 Whalsay, I. 60 22N 1 0W
47 Whangamomona 39 8S 174 44E
47 Whangarei 35 43S 174 21E
47 Whangaroa, Harbour 35 4S 173 46E
6 Wharfe, R. 53 51N 1 7W
70 Wheatland 42 4N 105 58W
73 Wheeler Pk. 38 57N 114 15W
68 Wheeling 40 2N 80 41W
6 Whernside, Mt. 54 14N 2 24W
6 Whitby 54 29N 0 37W
68 White, R., Ind. 38 25N 87 44W
71 White, R., Ark. 33 53N 91 3W
43 White Cliffs 30 50S 143 10E
7 White Horse, Vale of 51 37N 1 30W
51 White Nile, R. = Nîl el Abyad 9 30N 31 40E
62 White River, Canada 48 35N 85 20W
57 White River, S. Afr. 25 20S 31 0E
22 White Sea= Beloye More 66 30N 38 0E
72 White Sulphur Springs 46 35N 111 0W
57 White Volta, R. 9 10N 1 15W
47 Whitecliffs 43 26S 171 55E
72 Whitefish 48 25N 114 22W
72 Whitehall, Wis. 44 20N 91 19W
6 Whitehaven 54 33N 3 35W
64 Whitehorse 60 45N 135 10W
65 Whiteshell Prov. Park 50 0N 95 25W
42 Whitewood 21 28S 143 30E
65 Whitewood 50 20N 102 20W
8 Whithorn 54 55N 4 25W
47 Whitianga 36 47S 175 41E
73 Whitney, Mt. 36 35N 118 14W
7 Whitstable 51 21N 1 2E
42 Whitsunday, I. 20 15S 149 4E
60 Whittier 60 46N 148 48W
43 Whittle, C. 50 11N 60 8W
43 Whyalla 33 2S 137 30E
62 Wiarton 44 50N 81 10W
53 Wiawso 6 12N 2 29W
71 Wichita 37 40N 97 29W
71 Wichita Falls 33 57N 98 30W
8 Wick 58 26N 3 5W
73 Wickenburg 33 58N 112 45W
45 Wickepin 32 50S 117 30E
9 Wicklow 53 0N 6 2W
9 Wicklow □ 52 59N 6 25W
9 Wicklow Mts. 53 0N 6 30W
45 Widgiemooltha 31 30S 121 34E
6 Widnes 53 22N 2 44W
15 Wieliczka 50 0N 20 5E
15 Wieluń 51 15N 18 40E
14 Wien 48 12N 16 22E
14 Wiener Neustadt 47 49N 16 16E
11 Wierden 52 22N 6 35E
14 Wiesbaden 50 7N 8 17E
6 Wigan 53 33N 2 38W
8 Wigtown 54 52N 4 27W
8 Wigtown B. 54 46N 4 15W
46 Wilcannia 31 30S 143 26E
68 Wildwood 39 5N 74 46W
14 Wilhelmshaven 53 30N 8 9E
68 Wilkes-Barre 41 15N 75 52W
3 Wilkes Ld. 69 0S 120 0E
65 Wilkie 52 27N 108 42W
73 Willcox 32 13N 109 53W
75 Willemstad 12 5N 69 0W
44 Willeroo 15 14S 131 37E
43 William Creek 28 58S 136 22E
45 Williams, Australia 33 0S 117 0E
73 Williams, U.S.A. 35 16N 112 11W
64 Williams Lake 52 20N 122 10W
68 Williamsburg 37 17N 76 44W
68 Williamson 37 46N 82 17W
68 Williamsport 41 18N 77 1W
46 Williamstown, Australia 37 46S 144 58E
56 Williston, S. Afr. 31 20S 20 53E
70 Williston, U.S.A. 48 10N 103 35W
72 Willits 39 28N 123 17W
70 Willmar 45 5N 95 0W
46 Willow Tree 31 40S 150 45E
56 Willowmore 33 15S 23 30E
42 Willows, Australia 23 45S 147 25E
72 Willows, U.S.A. 39 30N 122 10W
68 Wilmette 42 6N 87 44W
68 Wilmington, Del. 39 45N 75 32W
69 Wilmington, N.C. 34 14N 77 54W
68 Wilmington, Ohio 39 29N 83 46W
69 Wilson 35 44N 77 54W
73 Wilson, Mt. 37 55N 105 3W
46 Wilson's Promontory 39 5S 146 28E
7 Wilton 51 5N 1 52W
7 Wiltshire □ 51 20N 2 0W
45 Wiluna 26 40S 120 25E
56 Winburg 28 30S 27 2E
7 Winchester, U.K. 51 4N 1 19W
68 Winchester, Ind. 40 10N 84 56W
68 Winchester, Ky. 38 0N 84 8W
68 Winchester, Va. 39 14N 78 8W
68 Windber 40 14N 78 50W
6 Windermere, L. 54 20N 2 57W
56 Windhoek 22 35S 17 4E
42 Windorah 25 24S 142 36E
7 Windrush, R. 51 42N 1 25W
46 Windsor, Australia 33 34S 150 44E
63 Windsor, Nova Scotia 44 59N 64 5W
62 Windsor, Ont. 42 25N 83 0W
7 Windsor, U.K. 51 28N 0 36W
68 Windsor, U.S.A. 43 30N 72 25W
75 Windward Is. 13 0N 63 0W
64 Winfield, Canada 52 58N 114 26W
71 Winfield, U.S.A. 37 15N 97 0W
46 Wingen 31 50S 150 58E
62 Wingham 43 55N 81 25W
62 Winisk, R. 55 17N 85 5W
65 Winkler 49 15N 98 0W
53 Winneba 5 25N 0 36W
72 Winnemucca 41 0N 117 45W
65 Winnepegosis, L. 52 40N 100 0W
68 Winnetka 42 8N 87 46W
71 Winnfield 31 57N 92 38W
44 Winning 23 9S 114 32E
65 Winnipeg 49 50N 97 15W
65 Winnipeg, L. 52 30N 98 0W
65 Winnipegosis 52 40N 100 0W
70 Winona 44 2N 91 45W
68 Winooski 44 31N 73 11W
11 Winschoten 53 9N 7 3E
73 Winslow 35 2N 110 41W
69 Winston-Salem 36 7N 80 15W
69 Winter Haven 28 0N 81 42W
69 Winter Park 28 34N 81 19W
56 Winterhoek, Mt. 33 5S 19 35E
14 Winterthur 47 30N 8 44E
42 Winton 22 21S 143 0E
47 Winton 46 8S 168 20E
43 Wirrulla 32 24S 134 31E
6 Wisbech 52 39N 0 10E
70 Wisconsin □ 44 30N 90 0W
70 Wisconsin Rapids 44 25N 89 50W
8 Wishaw 55 46N 3 55W
15 Wisła, R. 54 22N 18 55E
14 Wismar 53 53N 11 23E
57 Witbank 25 51S 29 14E
6 Witham, R. 52 56N 0 4E
6 Withernsea 53 43N 0 2W
7 Witney 51 47N 1 29W
55 Witsand 34 24S 20 50E
14 Wittenberg 51 51N 12 39E
14 Wittenberge 53 0N 11 44E
44 Wittenoom 22 15S 118 20E
52 Witu 2 23S 40 26E
35 Wlingi 8 5S 112 25E
15 Włocławek 52 39 19 2E
15 Włodawa 51 34N 23 32E
46 Wodonga 36 5S 146 50E
35 Wokam, I. 5 45S 134 28E
62 Wolfe I. 44 7N 76 27E
14 Wolin, I. 53 55N 14 31E
80 Wollaston, Is. 55 40S 67 30W
65 Wollaston L. 58 20N 103 30W
60 Wollaston Pen. 69 30N 113 0W
46 Wollongong 34 25S 150 54E
56 Wolmaransstad 27 12S 26 13E
65 Wolseley, Canada 50 25N 103 15W
56 Wolseley, S. Afr. 33 26S 19 12E
58 Wolstenholme, C. 62 50N 78 0W
7 Wolverhampton 52 35N 2 6W
42 Wonarah P.O. 19 55S 136 20E
43 Wondai 26 20S 151 49E
45 Wongan Hills 30 53S 116 42E
38 Wŏnju 37 30N 127 59E
38 Wŏnsan 39 20N 127 25E
46 Wonthaggi 38 29S 145 31E
64 Wood Buffalo Nat. Park 59 30N 113 0W
45 Woodanilling 33 31S 117 24E
46 Woodend 37 20N 144 33E
72 Woodland 38 40N 121 50W
65 Woodridge 49 20N 96 20W
45 Woodroffe, Mt. 26 20S 131 45E
65 Woods, L. of the 49 30N 94 30W
42 Woodstock, Australia 19 22S 142 45E
62 Woodstock, Ont. 43 10N 80 45W
63 Woodstock, N.B. 46 11N 67 37W
7 Woodstock, U.K. 51 51N 1 20W
70 Woodstock, Ill. 42 17N 88 30W
47 Woodville 40 20S 175 53E
71 Woodward 36 24N 99 28W
45 Woolgangie 31 12S 120 35E
43 Woolgoolga 30 7S 153 12E
43 Woombye 26 40S 152 55E
46 Woomelang 35 37S 142 40E
43 Woomera 31 9S 136 56E
46 Woonona 34 32S 150 49E
68 Woonsocket 42 0N 71 30W
70 Woonsockett 44 5N 98 15W
45 Wooramel 25 45S 114 40E
45 Wooramel, R. 25 47S 114 10E
45 Wooroloo 31 45S 116 25E
68 Wooster 40 38N 81 55W
56 Worcester, S. Africa 33 39S 19 27E
7 Worcester, U.K. 52 12N 2 12W
68 Worcester, U.S.A. 42 14N 71 49W
6 Workington 54 39N 3 34W
6 Worksop 53 19N 1 9W
72 Worland 44 0N 107 59W
14 Worms 49 37N 8 21E
45 Worsley 33 15S 116 2E
7 Worthing 50 49N 0 21W
70 Worthington 43 35N 95 30W
35 Wosi 0 15S 128 0E
64 Wrangell 56 30N 132 25W
60 Wrangell Mts. 61 40N 143 30W
8 Wrath, C. 58 38N 5 0W
6 Wrekin, The, Mt. 52 41N 2 35W
6 Wrexham 53 5N 3 0W
64 Wright, Canada 51 45N 121 30W
35 Wright, Philippines 11 42N 125 2E
60 Wrigley 63 0N 123 30W
14 Wrocław 51 5N 17 5E
15 Września 52 21N 17 36E
45 Wubin 30 8S 116 30E
38 Wuchang, Heilungkiang 44 51N 127 10E
39 Wuchang, Hupei 30 34N 114 25E
39 Wuchow 23 26N 111 19E
38 Wuchung 38 4N 106 12E
39 Wuhan 30 32N 114 22E
39 Wuhsi=Wusih 31 30N 120 30E
39 Wuhu 31 21N 118 30E
53 Wukari 7 57N 9 42E
37 Wulumuchi 43 40N 87 50E
53 Wum 6 23N 10 4E
32 Wun 19 59N 78 52E
33 Wuntho 23 55N 95 45E

14 Wuppertal 51 15N 7 8 E
45 Wurarga 28 15S 116 12 E
14 Würzburg 49 46N 9 55 E
39 Wusih 31 30N 120 30 E
37 Wusu 44 10N 84 55 E
38 Wutai Shan 39 4N 113 35 E
37 Wutunghliao 29 25N 104 0 E
37 Wuwei 38 0N 102 30 E
39 Wuyi Shan, Mts. 26 40N 116 30 E
38 Wuying 48 10N 129 20 E
53 Wuyo 10 25N 11 50 E
38 Wuyuan 41 45N 108 30 E
45 Wyalkatchem 31 8S 117 22 E
68 Wyandotte 42 14N 83 13W
43 Wyandra 27 12S 145 56 E
46 Wycheproot 36 0N 143 17 E
7 Wye, R. 51 37N 2 39W
7 Wymondham 52 34N 1 7 E
56 Wynberg 34 0S 18 30 E
44 Wyndham 15 33S 128 3 E
43 Wynnum 27 29S 152 58 E
43 Wynyard, Australia 40 59S 145 45 E
65 Wynyard, Canada 51 45N 104 10W
72 Wyoming □ 42 48N 109 0W
46 Wyong 33 14S 151 24 E
68 Wytheville 37 0N 81 3W

X

19 Xánthi 41 10N 24 58 E
68 Xenia 39 42N 83 57W
39 Xi'an=Sian 34 2N 109 0 E
37 Xieng Khouang 19 17N 103 25 E
55 Xinavane 25 2S 32 47 E
79 Xingu, R. 1 30S 51 53W
79 Xique-Xique 10 40S 42 40W

Y

42 Yaamba 23 8S 150 22 E
37 Yaan 30 0N 102 59 E
53 Yabassi 4 32N 10 2 E
25 Yablonovy Khrebet 53 0N 114 0 E
28 Ya'Bud 32 27N 35 10 E
78 Yacuiba 22 0S 63 25W
32 Yadgir 16 45N 77 5 E
28 Yagur 32 45N 35 4 E
39 Yaicheng 18 14N 109 7 E
53 Yajua 11 25N 12 50 E
72 Yakima 46 42N 120 30W
53 Yako 13 2N 2 15W
38 Yakoshih 49 13N 120 35 E
36 Yaku-Shima, I. 30 20N 130 30 E
52 Yakuluku 4 22N 28 45 E
25 Yakut A.S.S.R. □ 66 0N 125 0 E
60 Yakutat 59 50N 139 44W
25 Yakutsk 62 5N 129 40 E
34 Yala 6 45N 101 15 E
42 Yalboroo 20 50S 148 30 E
45 Yalgoo 23 16S 116 39 E
74 Yalkubul, Pta. 21 32N 88 37W
46 Yallourn 38 10S 146 18 E
23 Yalta 44 30N 34 10 E
38 Yalu, R. 47 30N 123 30 E
37 Yalung Kiang, R. 32 0N 100 0 E
24 Yalutorovsk 56 30N 65 40 E
36 Yamagata 37 55N 140 20 E
36 Yamagata □ 38 30N 140 0 E
36 Yamaguchi 34 10N 131 32 E
36 Yamaguchi □ 34 20N 131 40 E
24 Yamal Pol. 71 0N 70 0 E
30 Yamama 24 5N 47 30 E
36 Yamanashi □ 35 40N 138 40 E
46 Yamba 29 30S 153 22 E
35 Yamdena, I. 7 45S 131 20 E
33 Yamethin 20 26N 96 9 E
53 Yamil 12 55N 8 5 E
44 Yampi, Sd. 15 15S 123 30 E
39 Yamhsien 21 45N 108 31 E
53 Yamrat 10 10N 9 55 E
28 Yamun 32 29N 35 14 E
33 Yamuna, R. 27 0N 78 30 E
53 Yan 10 5N 12 15 E
36 Yanai 33 58N 132 7 E
22 Yanaul 56 25N 55 0 E
53 Yanda Bayo 11 30N 10 55 E
45 Yandanooka 29 18S 115 29 E
33 Yandoon 17 2N 95 39 E
54 Yangambi 0 47N 24 20 E
39 Yangchow 32 25N 119 25 E
38 Yangchuan 38 0N 113 29 E
24 Yangi-Yer 40 17N 68 48 E
39 Yangtze Kiang, R. 31 40N 122 0 E
70 Yankton 42 55N 97 25W
43 Yanna 26 58S 146 0 E
39 Yanping 22 25N 112 0 E
39 Yao Shan, Mts. 24 0N 110 0 E
53 Yaoundé 3 50N 1 35 E
35 Yap Is. 9 30N 138 10 E
35 Yapen, I. 1 50S 136 0 E
35 Yapen, Teluk, G. 1 30S 136 0 E
42 Yaraka 24 53S 144 3 E
22 Yaransk 57 13N 47 56 E
7 Yare, R. 52 40N 1 45 E
22 Yarensk 61 10N 49 8 E
37 Yarkand= Soche 38 24N 77 20 E
32 Yarkhun, R. 36 30N 72 45 E
63 Yarmouth 43 53N 65 45W
22 Yaroslavl 57 35N 39 55 E
45 Yarra Yarra Lakes 29 12S 115 45 E
44 Yarraloola 21 34S 115 52 E
43 Yarraman 26 46S 152 1 E
24 Yar-Sale 66 50N 70 50 E
25 Yartsevo 60 20N 90 0 E
78 Yarumal 6 58N 75 24W
47 Yasawa Is. 17 0S 177 23 E
53 Yashi 12 25N 7 58 E
46 Yass 34 50S 149 0 E
28 Yas'ur 32 54N 35 10 E
60 Yathkyed, L. 63 0N 98 0W
36 Yatsushiro 32 30N 130 40 E
28 Yattah 31 27N 35 6 E
28 Yavne 31 52N 34 45 E
36 Yawatehama 33 27N 132 24 E
31 Yazd 31 55N 54 27 E
31 Yazdan 33 30N 60 50 E
71 Yazoo City 32 48N 90 28W
33 Ye 15 15N 97 51 E
45 Yealering 32 35S 117 30 E
33 Yebyu 14 15N 98 13 E
80 Yegros 26 20S 56 25W
38 Yehsien 37 12N 119 58 E
25 Yelanskoye 61 25N 128 0 E
43 Yelarbon 28 33S 150 49 E
22 Yelets 52 40N 38 30 E
8 Yell, I. 46 42N 2 20W
38 Yellow, R.= Hwang Ho, R. 37 32N 118 19 E
26 Yellow Sea 35 0N 124 0 E
45 Yellowdine 31 18S 119 39 E
64 Yellowhead P. 53 0N 118 30W
64 Yellowknife 62 30N 114 10W
60 Yellowknife, R. 63 30N 113 30W
72 Yellowstone Nat. Park 44 35N 110 0W
72 Yellowtail Res. 45 6N 108 8W
42 Yelvertoft 20 13S 138 53 E
53 Yelwa 10 50N 4 50 E
29 Yemen ■ 15 0N 44 0 E
33 Yenangyaung 20 30N 95 0 E
39 Yencheng 36 44N 110 2 E
53 Yendi 9 17N 0 22 E
25 Yeniseysk 58 39N 92 4 E
24 Yenisey, R. 68 0N 86 30 E
24 Yeniseyskiy Zaliv 72 20N 81 0 E
38 Yenki 43 12N 129 30 E
38 Yentai 37 30N 121 22 E
25 Yenyuka 58 20N 121 30 E
7 Yeo, R. 51 1N 2 46W
32 Yeola 20 0N 74 30 E
32 Yeotmal 20 20N 78 15 E
7 Yeovil 50 57N 2 38W
42 Yeppoon 23 5S 150 47 E
23 Yerevan 40 10N 44 20 E
25 Yermakovo 52 35N 126 20 E
25 Yerofey Pavlovich 54 0N 122 0 E
28 Yeroham 30 59N 34 55 E
23 Yershov 51 15N 48 27 E
28 Yerushalayim= Jerusalem 31 47N 35 10 E
7 Yes Tor 50 41N 3 59 E
12 Yeu, Î.d' 46 42N 2 20W
39 Yeungchun 22 15N 111 40 E
39 Yeungkong 21 55N 112 0 E
23 Yeysk Stavo 46 40N 38 12 E
19 Yiannitsa 40 46N 22 24 E
31 Yibal 22 10N 56 8 E
39 Yilan 24 47N 121 44 E
38 Yin Shan, Mts. 41 0N 111 0 E
38 Yinchwan 38 30N 106 20 E
39 Yingcheng 31 0N 113 44 E
38 Yingkow 40 38N 122 30 E
39 Yingtan 28 12N 117 0 E
54 Yirga Alem 6 34N 38 29 E
19 Yíthion 36 46N 22 34 E
38 Yitu 36 40N 118 24 E
39 Yiyang 28 45N 112 16 E
28 Yizre'el 32 34N 35 19 E
20 Ylivieska 64 4N 24 28 E
71 Yoakum 29 20N 97 10W
53 Yobe, R. 13 0N 13 45 E
35 Yogyakarta 7 49S 110 22 E
36 Yokkaichi 35 0N 136 30 E
36 Yokohama 35 30N 139 32 E
36 Yokosuka 35 20N 139 40 E
53 Yola 9 10N 12 25 E
34 Yom, R. 16 40N 100 14 E
36 Yonago 35 25N 133 19 E
38 Yongchon 35 55N 138 55 E
68 Yonkers 40 57N 73 51W
12 Yonne □ 47 50N 3 40 E
12 Yonne, R. 48 23N 2 58 E
28 Yoqne'am 32 39N 35 7 E
45 York, Australia 31 52S 116 47 E
6 York, U.K. 53 38N 1 7W
70 York, Nebr. 40 55N 97 35W
68 York, Pa. 39 57N 76 43W
42 York, C. 75 55N 66 25W
44 York, Sd. 14 30S 125 0 E
65 York Factory 57 0N 92 30W
6 York Wolds 54 0N 0 30W
43 Yorke, Pen. 34 40S 137 35 E
65 Yorkton 51 11N 102 28W
45 Yornup 34 2S 116 10 E
73 Yosemite Nat. Park 31 50N 119 30W
22 Yoshkar Ola 56 49N 47 10 E
39 Yosu 34 47N 127 45 E
28 Yotvata 29 53N 35 2 E
9 Youghal 51 58N 7 51W
46 Young 34 19S 148 18 E
43 Younghusband, Pen. 34 45S 139 15 E
68 Youngstown 43 16N 79 2W
45 Yoweragabbie 28 10S 117 30 E
39 Yoyang 29 27N 113 10 E
68 Ypsilanti 42 18N 83 40W
72 Yreka 41 44N 122 40W
21 Ystad 55 26N 13 50 E
8 Ythan, R. 57 26N 1 12W
25 Ytyk-kel 62 20N 133 28 E
39 Yu Shan, Mt. 23 30N 121 0 E
39 Yuan Kiang, R. 28 40N 110 30 E
39 Yuanling 28 30N 110 5 E
37 Yuanyang 23 10N 102 58 E
72 Yuba City 39 12N 121 45W
74 Yucatán □ 21 30N 86 30W
75 Yucatán, Canal de 22 0N 86 30W
73 Yucca 34 56N 114 6W
24 Yudino 55 10N 67 55 E
44 Yuendumu 22 16S 131 49 E
19 Yugoslavia ■ 44 0N 20 0 E
39 Yukikow 31 29N 118 17 E
60 Yukon Territory □ 63 0N 135 0W
60 Yukon, R. 65 30N 150 0W
25 Yukti 63 20N 105 0 E
39 Yülin, Hainan 18 10N 109 31 E
39 Yülin Kwangsi-Chuang 22 30N 110 50 E
73 Yuma, Ariz. 32 45N 114 45W
70 Yuma, Colo. 40 10N 102 43W
37 Yumen 41 13N 96 55 E
45 Yuna 28 20S 115 0 E
45 Yunndaga 29 45S 121 0 E
39 Yungan 25 50N 117 25 E
39 Yungchun 25 20N 118 15 E
39 Yungfu 24 59N 109 59 E
39 Yungshun 29 3N 109 50 E
39 Yungtsi 34 50N 110 25 E
39 Yunlin 23 45N 120 30 E
37 Yunnan □ 25 0N 102 30 E
39 Yunsiao 24 0N 117 20 E
43 Yunta 32 35S 139 33 E
24 Yurga 55 42N 84 51 E
24 Yuribei 71 20N 76 30 E
78 Yurimaguas 5 55S 76 0W
39 Yütu 5 0N 115 24 E
38 Yutze 37 45N 112 45 E
39 Yuyang 28 44N 108 46 E
39 Yuyao 30 0N 121 20 E
25 Yuzhno-Sakhalinsk 47 5N 142 5 E
12 Yvelines □ 48 40N 1 45 E
12 Yvetot 49 37N 0 44 E

Z

11 Zaandam 52 26N 4 49 E
25 Zabaykalskiy 49 40N 117 10 E
29 Zabid 14 10N 43 17 E
31 Zabol 31 0N 61 25 E
31 Zāboli 27 10N 61 35 E
15 Zabrzé 50 24N 18 50 E
31 Zabul □ 32 0N 67 15 E
74 Zacapa 14 59N 89 31W
74 Zacatecas 22 49N 102 34W
74 Zacatecas □ 23 30N 103 0W
74 Zacatecoluca 13 29N 88 51W
18 Zadar 44 8N 15 8 E
53 Zadawa 11 30N 10 22 E
34 Zadetkyi Kyun, I. 10 0N 98 25 E
13 Zafra 38 26N 6 30W
14 Zagań 51 39N 15 22 E
51 Zagazig 30 40N 31 12 E
53 Zagnanado 7 15N 2 15 E
18 Zagreb 45 50N 16 0 E
30 Zagros, Kudhā-ye 33 45N 47 0 E
28 Zahala 32 8N 34 49 E
31 Zāhedān 29 30N 60 50 E
30 Zahlah 33 52N 35 50 E
54 Zaïre ■ 3 0S 23 0 E
54 Zaïre, R. 6 4S 12 24 E
25 Zakamensk 50 23N 103 17 E
23 Zakavkazye 42 0N 44 0 E
30 Zākhū 37 10N 42 50 E
19 Zákinthos 37 47N 20 54 E
19 Zákinthos, I. 37 45N 27 45 E
51 Zalingei 13 5N 23 10 E
57 Zambeze, R. 18 46S 36 16 E
57 Zambézia □ 16 15S 37 30 E
55 Zambia ■ 15 0S 28 0W
35 Zamboanga 6 59N 122 3 E
74 Zamora, Mexico 20 0N 102 21W
13 Zamora, Sp. 41 30N 5 45W
15 Zamość 50 50N 23 22 E
11 Zandvoort 52 22N 4 32 E
68 Zanesville 39 56N 82 2W
30 Zanjan 36 40N 48 35 E
19 Zante, I.= Zákinthos, I. 37 47N 20 54 E
45 Zanthus 30 55S 123 29 E
52 Zanzibar 6 12S 39 12 E
52 Zanzibar, I. 6 12S 39 12 E
50 Zaouiet Reggane 26 32N 0 3 E
15 Západné Beskydy, Mts. 49 30N 19 0 E
25 Zapadnyy Sayan 53 0N 94 0 E
80 Zapala 39 0S 70 5W
22 Zapolyarnyy 69 26N 30 48 E
23 Zaporozhye 47 50N 35 10 E
13 Zaragoza 41 39N 0 53W
31 Zarand 30 46N 56 34 E
78 Zaraza 9 21N 65 19W
53 Zari 13 5N 12 44 E
53 Zaria 11 0N 7 40W
78 Zaruma 3 40S 79 30W
14 Żary 51 37N 15 10 E
51 Zarzis 33 31N 11 2 E
25 Zashiversk 67 25N 142 40 E
32 Zaskar Mts. 33 15N 77 30 E
56 Zastron 30 18S 27 7 E
31 Zavareh 33 35N 52 28 E
25 Zavitinsk 50 10N 129 20 E
15 Zawiercie 50 30N 19 13 E
25 Zayarsk 56 20N 102 55 E
24 Zaysan, Oz. 48 0N 83 0 E
15 Zduńska Wola 51 37N 18 59 E
21 Zealand= Sjaelland 55 30N 11 30 E
64 Zeballos 49 49N 126 50W
11 Zeebrugge 51 19N 3 12 E
42 Zeehan 41 52S 145 25 E
11 Zeeland □ 51 30N 3 50 E
56 Zeerust 25 33S 26 6 E
28 Zefat 32 58N 35 29 E
29 Zeila 11 15N 43 30 E
11 Zeist 52 5N 5 15 E
28 Zeita 32 23N 35 2 E
19 Zemun 44 51N 20 23 E
14 Zerbst 51 59N 12 8 E
25 Zeya 54 2N 127 20 E
13 Zêzere, R. 40 0N 7 55W
24 Zhanatas 43 11N 81 18 E
23 Zhdanov 47 5N 37 31 E
25 Zheleznogorsk-Ilimskiy 56 34N 104 8 E
25 Zhigansk 66 35N 124 10 E
23 Zhitomir 50 20N 28 40 E
22 Zhlobin 52 55N 30 0 E
25 Zhupanovo 51 59N 15 9 E
14 Zielona Góra 51 57N 15 31 E
50 Ziguinchor 12 25N 16 20W
28 Zikhron Ya'aqov 32 34N 34 56 E
30 Zile 40 15N 36 0 E
15 Žilina 49 12N 18 42 E
51 Zillah 28 40N 17 41 E
37 Zilling Tso, L. 31 40N 89 0 E
25 Zima 54 0N 102 5 E

57 Zimbabwe■ (Rhodesia) ..... 20 0s 28 30 E
15 Zimnicea .... 43 39N 25 21 E
53 Zinder .... 13 48N 9 0 E
53 Ziniaré 12 35N 1 18w
29 Zinjibar .... 13 5N 46 0 E
73 Zion Nat. Park 37 25N 112 50w
78 Zipaquira 5 0N 74 0w
28 Zippori .... 32 64N 35 16 E
31 Zirko, I. .... 25 0N 53 30 E
74 Zitácuaro 19 20N 100 30w
22 Zlatoust .... 55 10N 59 30 E
51 Zlitan .... 32 25N 14 35 E
14 Znojmo .... 48 50N 16 2 E
56 Zoar .... 33 30s 21 58 E
28 Zohar .... 31 36N 34 42 E
55 Zomba .... 15 30s 35 19 E
30 Zonguldak .... 41 28N 31 50 E
53 Zorgo 12 15N 0 36w
78 Zorritos 3 50s 80 40w
50 Zouérate 22 35N 12 30w
19 Zrenjanin .... 45 22N 20 23 E
53 Zuba .... 9 5N 7 10 E
51 Zuetina .... 30 58N 20 7 E
29 Zufar, Reg. .... 17 40N 54 0 E
14 Zug .... 47 10N 8 31 E
11 Zuid Holland □ ... 52 0N 4 35 E
11 Zuider Zee= Ijsselmeer, L. ... 52 45N 5 20 E
54 Zula .... 15 17N 39 40 E
57 Zululand .... 28 15s 31 45 E
55 Zumbo .... 15 35s 30 26 E
14 Zürich .... 47 22N 8 32 E
53 Zuru .... 11 25N 5 12 E
11 Zutphen .... 52 9N 6 12 E
51 Zuwarah .... 32 58N 12 1 E
24 Zverinogolovskoye 55 0N 62 30 E
14 Zwettl .... 48 35N 15 9 E
14 Zwickau .... 50 43N 12 30 E
11 Zwolle .... 52 31N 6 6 E
25 Zyryanka .... 65 45N 150 51 E
24 Zyryanovsk .... 49 43N 84 20 E
15 Zyrardów .... 52 3N 20 35 E

Recent Place-Name Changes

The following place-name changes have recently occurred in Angola, Iran, Madagascar and Zimbabwe. The new names are given on the maps but the former names are in the index.

Angola

Former Name	*New Name*
Bié	Kuito
Dolisie	Loubomo
Luso	Luena
Malange	Malanje
Mariano Machado	Ganda
Moçâmedes	Namibe
Nova Redondo	Sumbe
Roçadas	Xangongo
Salazar	Ndalatando
Sao Salvador do Congo	Mbanza Congo
Serpa Pinta	Menongue
Teixeira da Silva	Bailundo
Teixeira de Sousa	Luau

Madagascar

Former Name	*New Name*
Ambre, C. de	Bobaomby, Tanjon'i
Ambre, Mt. d'	Ambohitra
Brickaville	Vohibinany
Diégo Suarez	Antsirañana
Fénérive	Fenoarivo Atsinanana
Fort-Dauphin	Faradofay
Hell-Ville	Andoany
Majunga	Mahajanga
St. Augustin	Anatsogno
Ste. Marie, C.	Vohimena, T.'i
Ste. Marie, I.	Boraha, Nosy
Tamatave	Toamasina
Tuléar	Toliara

Iran

Former Name	*New Name*
Bandar-e Pahlavi	Bandar-e Anzalī
Bandar-e Shah	Bandar-e Torkeman
Bandar-e Shahpur	Bandar-e Khomeynī
Dezh Shahpur	Marīvan
Gach Sārān	Gachsāran
Herowābād	Khalkhāl
Kermanshah	Bakhtāran
Reza'iyeh	Orūmīyeh
Reza'iyeh, Daryacheh-ye	Orūmīyeh, Daryācheh-ye
Shāhābād	Ashkhāneh
Shāhābād	Eslāmābād-e Gharb
Shāhī	Qā'emshahr
Shahpur	Salmās
Shahreza	Qomsheh
Shāhrud	Emāmrūd
Shahsavar	Tonekābon
Soltaniyeh	Sa'īdīyeh

Zimbabwe

Former Name	*New Name*
Chipinga	Chipinge
Enkeldoorn	Chivhu
Fort Victoria	Masvingo
Gatooma	Kadoma
Gwelo	Gweru
Hartley	Chegutu
Marandellas	Marondera
Nuanetsi	Mwenezi
Que Que	Kwekwe
Salisbury	Harare
Selukwe	Shurugwi
Shabani	Zvishavane
Sinoia	Chinhoyi
Somabula	Somabhula
Umtali	Mutare
Umvuma	Mvuma
Wankie	Hwange

Climatic Statistics – 1

These four pages give temperature and precipitation statistics for over 80 stations, which are arranged by listing the continents and the places within each continent in alphabetical order. The elevation of each station, in metres above mean sea level, is stated beneath its name. The average monthly temperature, in degrees Celsius, and the average monthly precipitation, in millimetres, are given. To the right, the average yearly rainfall, the average yearly temperature, and the annual range of temperature (the difference between the warmest and the coldest months) are also stated.

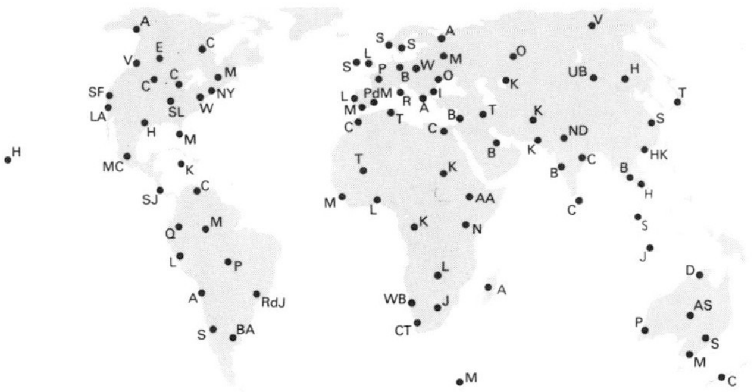

AFRICA

Station		*Jan.*	*Feb.*	*Mar.*	*Apr.*	*May*	*June*	*July*	*Aug.*	*Sept.*	*Oct.*	*Nov.*	*Dec.*	*Year*	*Annual Range*
Addis Ababa, Ethiopia															
	Precipitation	201	206	239	102	28	< 3	0	< 3	3	25	135	213	1 151	
2 450 m	*Temperature*	19	20	20	20	19	18	18	19	21	22	21	20	20	4
Cairo, Egypt															
	Precipitation	5	5	5	3	3	< 3	0	0	< 3	< 3	3	5	28	
116 m	*Temperature*	13	15	18	21	25	28	28	28	26	24	20	15	22	15
Cape Town, South Africa															
	Precipitation	15	8	18	48	79	84	89	66	43	31	18	10	508	
17 m	*Temperature*	21	21	20	17	14	13	12	13	14	16	18	19	17	9
Casablanca, Morocco															
	Precipitation	53	48	56	36	23	5	0	< 3	8	38	66	71	404	
50 m	*Temperature*	13	13	14	16	18	20	22	23	22	19	16	13	18	10
Johannesburg, South Africa															
	Precipitation	114	109	89	38	25	8	8	8	23	56	107	125	709	
1 665 m	*Temperature*	20	20	18	16	13	10	11	13	16	18	19	20	16	10
Khartoum, Sudan															
	Precipitation	< 3	< 3	< 3	< 3	3	8	53	71	18	5	< 3	0	158	
390 m	*Temperature*	24	25	28	31	33	34	32	31	32	32	28	25	29	9
Kinshasa, Zaïre															
	Precipitation	135	145	196	196	158	8	3	3	31	119	221	142	1 354	
325 m	*Temperature*	26	26	27	27	26	24	23	24	25	26	26	26	25	4
Lagos, Nigeria															
	Precipitation	28	46	102	150	269	460	279	64	140	206	69	25	1 836	
3 m	*Temperature*	27	28	29	28	28	26	26	25	26	26	28	28	27	4
Lusaka, Zambia															
	Precipitation	231	191	142	18	3	< 3	< 3	0	< 3	10	91	150	836	
1 277 m	*Temperature*	21	22	21	21	19	16	16	18	22	24	23	22	21	8
Monrovia, Liberia															
	Precipitation	31	56	97	216	516	973	996	373	744	772	236	130	5 138	
23 m	*Temperature*	26	26	27	27	26	25	24	25	25	25	26	26	26	3
Nairobi, Kenya															
	Precipitation	38	64	125	211	158	46	15	23	31	53	109	86	958	
1 820 m	*Temperature*	19	19	19	19	18	16	16	16	18	19	18	18	18	3
Antananarivo, Madagascar															
	Precipitation	300	279	178	53	18	8	8	10	18	61	135	287	1 356	
1 372 m	*Temperature*	21	21	21	19	18	15	14	15	17	19	21	21	19	7
Timbuktu, Mali															
	Precipitation	< 3	< 3	3	< 3	5	23	79	81	38	3	< 3	< 3	231	
301 m	*Temperature*	22	24	28	32	34	35	32	30	32	31	28	23	29	13
Tunis, Tunisia															
	Precipitation	64	51	41	36	18	8	3	8	33	51	48	61	419	
66 m	*Temperature*	10	11	13	16	19	23	26	27	25	20	16	11	18	17
Walvis Bay, South Africa															
	Precipitation	< 3	5	8	3	3	< 3	< 3	3	< 3	< 3	< 3	< 3	23	
7 m	*Temperature*	19	19	19	18	17	16	15	14	14	15	17	18	18	5

AMERICA, NORTH

Station		*Jan.*	*Feb.*	*Mar.*	*Apr.*	*May*	*June*	*July*	*Aug.*	*Sept.*	*Oct.*	*Nov.*	*Dec.*	*Year*	*Annual Range*
Anchorage, Alaska, U.S.A.															
	Precipitation	20	18	15	10	13	18	41	66	66	56	25	23	371	
40 m	*Temperature*	–11	–8	–5	2	7	12	14	13	9	2	–5	–11	2	25
Cheyenne, Wyo., U.S.A.															
	Precipitation	10	15	25	48	61	41	53	41	31	25	13	13	376	
1 871 m	*Temperature*	–4	–3	1	5	10	16	19	19	14	7	1	–2	7	23
Chicago, Ill., U.S.A.															
	Precipitation	51	51	66	71	86	89	84	81	79	66	61	51	836	
251 m	*Temperature*	–4	–3	2	9	14	20	23	22	19	12	5	–1	10	27
Churchill, Man., Canada															
	Precipitation	13	15	23	23	23	48	56	69	58	36	28	18	406	
13 m	*Temperature*	–28	–27	–21	–10	–1	6	12	11	5	–3	–15	–24	–8	40

		Jan.	Feb.	Mar.	Apr.	May	June	July	Aug.	Sept.	Oct.	Nov.	Dec.	Year	Annual range
Edmonton, Alta., Canada															
	Precipitation	23	15	20	23	46	78	84	58	33	18	18	20	439	
676 m	*Temperature*	–15	–11	–5	4	11	14	16	15	10	5	–4	–11	3	31
Honolulu, Hawaii, U.S.A.															
	Precipitation	104	66	79	48	25	18	23	28	36	48	64	104	643	
12 m	*Temperature*	23	18	19	20	22	24	25	26	26	24	22	19	22	8
Houston, Tex., U.S.A.															
	Precipitation	89	76	84	91	119	117	99	99	104	94	89	109	1 171	
12 m	*Temperature*	12	13	17	21	24	27	28	29	26	22	16	12	21	17
Kingston, Jamaica															
	Precipitation	23	15	23	31	102	89	38	91	99	180	74	36	800	
34 m	*Temperature*	25	25	25	26	26	28	28	28	27	27	26	26	26	3
Los Angeles, Calif., U.S.A.															
	Precipitation	79	76	71	25	10	3	< 3	< 3	5	15	31	66	381	
95 m	*Temperature*	13	14	14	16	17	19	21	22	21	18	16	14	17	9
Mexico City, Mexico															
	Precipitation	13	5	10	20	53	119	170	152	130	51	18	8	747	
2 309 m	*Temperature*	12	13	16	18	19	19	17	18	18	16	14	13	16	7
Miami, Fla., U.S.A.															
	Precipitation	71	53	64	81	173	178	155	160	203	234	71	51	1 516	
8 m	*Temperature*	20	20	22	23	25	27	28	28	27	25	22	21	24	8
Montreal, Que., Canada															
	Precipitation	97	76	89	66	79	86	94	89	94	86	89	91	1 036	
57 m	*Temperature*	–10	–9	–3	5	13	19	21	19	15	8	1	–7	6	31
New York, N.Y., U.S.A.															
	Precipitation	94	97	91	81	81	84	107	109	86	89	76	91	1 092	
96 m	*Temperature*	–1	–1	3	10	16	20	23	23	21	15	7	2	8	24
St. Louis, Mo., U.S.A.															
	Precipitation	58	64	89	97	114	114	89	86	81	74	71	64	1 001	
173 m	*Temperature*	0	1	7	13	19	24	26	26	22	15	8	2	14	26
San Francisco, Calif., U.S.A.															
	Precipitation	119	97	79	38	18	3	< 3	< 3	8	25	64	112	561	
16 m	*Temperature*	10	12	13	13	14	15	15	15	17	16	14	11	14	7
San José, Costa Rica															
	Precipitation	15	5	20	46	229	241	211	241	305	300	145	41	1 798	
1 146 m	*Temperature*	19	19	21	21	22	21	21	21	21	20	20	19	20	2
Vancouver, B.C., Canada															
	Precipitation	218	147	127	84	71	64	31	43	91	147	211	224	1 458	
14 m	*Temperature*	3	4	6	9	13	16	18	18	14	10	6	4	10	15
Washington, D.C., U.S.A.															
	Precipitation	86	76	91	84	94	99	112	109	94	74	66	79	1 064	
22 m	*Temperature*	1	2	7	12	18	23	25	24	20	14	8	3	13	24

AMERICA, SOUTH

		Jan.	Feb.	Mar.	Apr.	May	June	July	Aug.	Sept.	Oct.	Nov.	Dec.	Year	Annual range
Antofagasta, Chile															
	Precipitation	0	0	0	< 3	< 3	3	5	3	< 3	3	< 3	0	13	
94 m	*Temperature*	21	21	20	18	16	15	14	14	15	16	18	19	17	7
Buenos Aires, Argentina															
	Precipitation	79	71	109	89	76	61	56	61	79	86	84	99	950	
27 m	*Temperature*	23	23	21	17	13	9	10	11	13	15	19	22	16	14
Caracas, Venezuela															
	Precipitation	23	10	15	33	79	102	109	109	107	109	94	46	836	
1 042 m	*Temperature*	19	19	20	21	22	21	21	21	21	21	20	20	21	3
Lima, Peru															
	Precipitation	3	< 3	< 3	< 3	5	5	8	8	8	3	3	< 3	41	
120 m	*Temperature*	23	24	24	22	19	17	17	16	17	18	19	21	20	8
Manaus, Brazil															
	Precipitation	249	231	262	221	170	84	58	38	46	107	142	203	1 811	
44 m	*Temperature*	28	28	28	27	28	28	28	28	29	29	29	28	28	2
Paraná, Brazil															
	Precipitation	287	236	239	102	13	< 3	3	5	28	127	231	310	1 582	
260 m	*Temperature*	23	23	23	23	23	21	21	22	24	24	24	23	23	3
Quito, Ecuador															
	Precipitation	99	112	142	175	137	43	20	31	69	112	97	79	1 115	
2 879 m	*Temperature*	15	15	15	15	15	14	14	15	15	15	15	15	15	1
Rio de Janeiro, Brazil															
	Precipitation	125	122	130	107	79	53	41	43	66	79	104	137	1 082	
61 m	*Temperature*	26	26	25	24	22	21	21	21	21	22	23	25	23	5
Santiago, Chile															
	Precipitation	3	3	5	13	64	84	76	56	31	15	8	5	358	
520 m	*Temperature*	21	20	18	15	12	9	9	10	12	15	17	19	15	12

Climatic Statistics – 2

ASIA

		Jan.	Feb.	Mar.	Apr.	May	June	July	Aug.	Sept.	Oct.	Nov.	Dec.	Year	Annual range
Bahrain															
	Precipitation	8	18	13	8	< 3	0	0	0	0	0	18	18	81	
5 m	*Temperature*	17	18	21	25	29	32	33	34	31	28	24	19	26	16
Bangkok, Thailand															
	Precipitation	8	20	36	58	198	160	160	175	305	206	66	5	1 397	
2 m	*Temperature*	26	28	29	30	29	29	28	28	28	28	26	25	28	5
Beirut, Lebanon															
	Precipitation	191	158	94	53	18	3	< 3	< 3	5	51	132	185	892	
34 m	*Temperature*	14	14	16	18	22	24	27	28	26	24	19	16	21	14
Bombay, India															
	Precipitation	3	3	3	< 3	18	485	617	340	264	64	13	3	1 809	
11 m	*Temperature*	24	24	26	28	30	29	27	27	27	28	27	26	27	6
Calcutta, India															
	Precipitation	10	31	36	43	140	297	325	328	252	114	20	5	1 600	
6 m	*Temperature*	20	22	27	30	30	30	29	29	29	28	23	19	26	11
Colombo, Sri Lanka															
	Precipitation	89	69	147	231	371	224	135	109	160	348	315	147	2 365	
7 m	*Temperature*	26	26	27	28	28	27	27	27	27	27	26	26	27	2
Jakarta, Indonesia															
	Precipitation	300	300	211	147	114	97	64	43	66	112	142	203	1 798	
8 m	*Temperature*	26	26	27	27	27	27	27	27	27	27	27	26	27	1
Harbin, China															
	Precipitation	5	5	10	23	43	94	112	104	46	33	8	5	488	
160 m	*Temperature*	–18	–15	–5	6	13	19	22	21	14	4	–6	–16	3	40
Hong Kong															
	Precipitation	33	46	74	137	292	394	381	361	257	114	43	31	2 162	
33 m	*Temperature*	16	15	18	22	26	28	28	28	27	25	21	18	23	13
Kabul, Afghanistan															
	Precipitation	31	36	94	102	20	5	3	3	< 3	15	20	10	338	
1 815 m	*Temperature*	–3	–1	6	13	18	22	25	24	20	14	7	3	12	28
Karachi, Pakistan															
	Precipitation	13	10	8	3	3	18	81	41	13	< 3	3	5	196	
4 m	*Temperature*	19	20	24	28	30	31	30	29	28	28	24	20	26	12
New Delhi, India															
	Precipitation	23	18	13	8	13	74	180	172	117	10	3	10	640	
218 m	*Temperature*	14	17	23	28	33	34	31	30	29	26	20	15	25	20
Ho Chi Minh City, Vietnam															
	Precipitation	15	3	13	43	221	330	315	269	335	269	114	56	1 984	
9 m	*Temperature*	26	27	29	30	29	28	28	28	27	27	27	26	28	4
Shanghai, China															
	Precipitation	48	58	84	94	94	180	147	142	130	71	51	36	1 135	
7 m	*Temperature*	4	5	9	14	20	24	28	28	23	19	12	7	16	24
Singapore															
	Precipitation	252	173	193	188	173	173	170	196	178	208	254	257	2 413	
10 m	*Temperature*	26	27	28	28	28	28	28	27	27	27	27	27	27	2
Tehran, Iran															
	Precipitation	46	38	46	36	13	3	3	3	3	8	20	31	246	
1 220 m	*Temperature*	2	5	9	16	21	26	30	29	25	18	12	6	17	28
Tokyo, Japan															
	Precipitation	48	74	107	135	147	165	142	152	234	208	97	56	1 565	
6 m	*Temperature*	3	4	7	13	17	21	25	26	23	17	11	6	14	23
Ulan Bator, Mongolia															
	Precipitation	< 3	< 3	3	5	10	28	76	51	23	5	5	3	208	
1 325 m	*Temperature*	–26	–21	–13	–1	6	14	16	14	8	–1	–13	–22	–3	42

AUSTRALIA, NEW ZEALAND and ANTARCTICA

		Jan.	Feb.	Mar.	Apr.	May	June	July	Aug.	Sept.	Oct.	Nov.	Dec.	Year	Annual range
Alice Springs, Australia															
	Precipitation	43	33	28	10	15	13	8	8	8	18	31	38	252	
579 m	*Temperature*	29	28	25	20	15	12	12	14	18	23	26	28	21	17
Christchurch, New Zealand															
	Precipitation	56	43	48	48	66	66	69	48	46	43	48	56	638	
10 m	*Temperature*	16	16	14	12	9	6	6	7	9	12	14	16	11	10
Darwin, Australia															
	Precipitation	386	312	254	97	15	3	< 3	3	13	51	119	239	1 491	
30 m	*Temperature*	29	29	29	29	28	26	25	26	28	29	30	29	28	5
Mawson, Antarctica															
	Precipitation	11	30	20	10	44	180	4	40	3	20	0	0	362	
14 m	*Temperature*	0	–5	–10	–14	–15	–16	–18	–18	–19	–13	–5	–1	–11	18

		Jan.	Feb.	Mar.	Apr.	May	June	July	Aug.	Sept.	Oct.	Nov.	Dec.	Year	Annual Range
Melbourne, Australia															
	Precipitation	48	46	56	58	53	53	48	48	58	66	58	58	653	
35 m	*Temperature*	20	20	18	15	13	10	9	11	13	14	16	18	15	11
Perth, Australia															
	Precipitation	8	10	20	43	130	180	170	149	86	56	20	13	881	
60 m	*Temperature*	23	23	22	19	16	14	13	13	15	16	19	22	18	10
Sydney, Australia															
	Precipitation	89	102	127	135	127	117	117	76	73	71	73	73	1 181	
42 m	*Temperature*	22	22	21	18	15	13	12	13	15	18	19	21	17	10

EUROPE and U.S.S.R.

		Jan.	Feb.	Mar.	Apr.	May	June	July	Aug.	Sept.	Oct.	Nov.	Dec.	Year	Annual Range
Archangel, U.S.S.R.															
	Precipitation	31	19	25	29	42	52	62	56	63	63	47	41	530	
13 m	*Temperature*	–16	–14	–9	0	7	12	15	14	8	2	–4	–11	0	31
Athens, Greece															
	Precipitation	62	37	37	23	23	14	6	7	15	51	56	71	402	
107 m	*Temperature*	10	10	12	16	20	25	28	28	24	20	15	11	18	18
Berlin, Germany															
	Precipitation	46	40	33	42	49	65	73	69	48	49	46	43	603	
55 m	*Temperature*	–1	0	4	9	14	17	19	18	15	9	5	1	9	20
Istanbul, Turkey															
	Precipitation	109	92	72	46	38	34	34	30	58	81	103	119	816	
114 m	*Temperature*	5	6	7	11	16	20	23	23	20	16	12	8	14	18
Kazalinsk, U.S.S.R.															
	Precipitation	10	10	13	13	15	5	5	8	8	10	13	15	125	
63 m	*Temperature*	–12	–11	–3	6	18	23	25	23	16	8	–1	–7	7	37
Lisbon, Portugal															
	Precipitation	111	76	109	54	44	16	3	4	33	62	93	103	708	
77 m	*Temperature*	11	12	14	16	17	20	22	23	21	18	14	12	17	12
London, U.K.															
	Precipitation	54	40	37	37	46	45	57	59	49	57	64	48	593	
5 m	*Temperature*	4	5	7	9	12	16	18	17	15	11	8	5	11	14
Málaga, Spain															
	Precipitation	61	51	62	46	26	5	1	3	29	64	64	62	474	
33 m	*Temperature*	12	13	15	17	19	29	25	26	23	20	16	13	18	17
Moscow, U.S.S.R.															
	Precipitation	39	38	36	37	53	58	88	71	58	45	47	54	624	
156 m	*Temperature*	–13	–10	–4	6	13	16	18	17	12	6	–1	–7	4	31
Odessa, U.S.S.R.															
	Precipitation	57	62	30	21	34	34	42	37	37	13	35	71	473	
64 m	*Temperature*	–3	–1	2	9	15	20	22	22	18	12	9	1	10	25
Omsk, U.S.S.R.															
	Precipitation	15	8	8	13	31	51	51	51	28	25	18	20	318	
85 m	*Temperature*	–22	–19	–12	–1	10	16	18	16	10	1	–11	–18	–1	40
Palma de Mallorca, Spain															
	Precipitation	39	34	51	32	29	17	3	25	55	77	47	40	449	
10 m	*Temperature*	10	11	12	15	17	21	24	25	23	18	14	11	17	15
Paris, France															
	Precipitation	56	46	35	42	57	54	59	64	55	50	51	50	619	
75 m	*Temperature*	3	4	8	11	15	18	20	19	17	12	7	4	12	17
Rome, Italy															
	Precipitation	71	62	57	51	46	37	15	21	63	99	129	93	744	
17 m	*Temperature*	8	9	11	14	18	22	25	25	22	17	13	10	16	17
Shannon, Irish Republic															
	Precipitation	94	67	56	53	61	57	77	79	86	86	96	117	929	
2 m	*Temperature*	5	5	7	9	12	14	16	16	14	11	8	6	10	11
Stavanger, Norway															
	Precipitation	93	56	45	70	49	84	93	118	142	129	125	126	1 130	
85 m	*Temperature*	1	1	3	6	10	13	15	15	13	9	6	3	8	14
Stockholm, Sweden															
	Precipitation	43	30	25	31	34	45	61	76	60	48	53	48	554	
44 m	*Temperature*	–3	–3	–1	5	10	15	18	17	12	7	3	0	7	21
Verkhoyansk, U.S.S.R.															
	Precipitation	5	5	3	5	8	23	28	25	13	8	8	5	134	
100 m	*Temperature*	–50	–45	–32	–15	0	12	14	9	2	–15	–38	–48	–17	64
Warsaw, Poland															
	Precipitation	27	32	27	37	46	69	96	65	43	38	31	44	555	
110 m	*Temperature*	–3	–3	2	7	14	17	19	18	14	9	3	0	8	22

Population of Cities

The population figures used are from censuses or more recent estimates and are given in thousands for towns and cities over 200 000 (over 500 000 in China and India and 250 000 in Brazil, Japan, United States and U.S.S.R.). Where possible the population of the metropolitan areas is given e.g. Greater London. Greater New York, etc.

AFRICA

ALGERIA (1974)
- Algiers 1 503
- Oran 485
- Constantine 350
- Annaba 313
- Tizi-Ouzou 224

ANGOLA (1970)
- Luanda 475

CAMEROON (1976)
- Douala 458
- Yaoundé 314

CANARY ISLANDS (1981)
- Las Palmas 360

CONGO (1980)
- Brazzaville 422

EGYPT (1976)
- Cairo 5 074
- Alexandria 2 318
- El Giza 1 230
- Shubra el Kheima 394
- El Mahalla el Kubra 292
- Tanta 285
- Port Said 263
- El Mansura 259
- Asyut 214
- Zagazig 203

ETHIOPIA (1980)
- Addis Abeba 1 277
- Asmera 443

GABON (1976)
- Libreville 186

GHANA (1970)
- Accra 738
- Kumasi 345

GUINEA (1972)
- Conakry 526

IVORY COAST (1976)
- Abidjan 850
- Bouaké 318

KENYA (1979)
- Nairobi 835
- Mombasa 312

LIBYA (1973)
- Tripoli 551
- Benghazi 282

MADAGASCAR (1978)
- Antananarivo 400

MALAWI (1977)
- Blantyre 229

MALI (1976)
- Bamako 419

MOROCCO (1973)
- Casablanca 1 753
- Rabat-Salé 596
- Marrakesh 436
- Fès 426
- Meknès 403
- Oujda 349
- Kénitra 341
- Tétouan 308
- Safi 215
- Tanger 208

MOZAMBIQUE (1970)
- Maputo 384

NIGERIA (1975)
- Lagos 1 477
- Ibadan 847
- Ogbomosho 432
- Kano 399
- Oshogbo 282
- Ilorin 282
- Abeokuta 253
- Port Harcourt 242
- Zaria 224
- Ilesha 224
- Onitsha 220
- Iwo 214
- Ado-Ekiti 213
- Kaduna 202

SENEGAL (1976)
- Dakar 799

SIERRA LEONE (1974)
- Freetown 214

SOMALI REP. (1980)
- Mogadishu 400

SOUTH AFRICA (1970)
- Johannesburg 1 441
- Cape Town 1 107
- Durban 851
- Pretoria 563
- Port Elizabeth 476
- Germiston 222

SUDAN (1980)
- Khartoum 561
- Omdurman 454
- Khartoum North 249
- Port Sudan 205

TANZANIA (1978)
- Dar-es-Salaam 757

TUNISIA (1976)
- Tunis 944
- Sfax 475
- Sousse 255

UGANDA (1975)
- Kampala 332

ZAIRE (1975)
- Kinshasa 2 242
- Lubumbashi 481
- Kananga 377
- Kisangani 298
- Mbuji Mayi 283

ZAMBIA (1980)
- Lusaka 641
- Kitwe 341
- Ndola 323

ZIMBABWE (1981)
- Harare 686
- Bulawayo 400

ASIA

AFGHANISTAN (1979)
- Kabul 913

BANGLADESH (1982)
- Dhaka 3 459
- Chittagong 1 388
- Khulna 623
- Narayanganj 298

BURMA (1977)
- Rangoon 2 276
- Mandalay 458
- Kanbe 254

CAMBODIA (1981)
- Phnom Penh 400

CHINA (1970)
- Shanghai 11 860
- Peking 9 231
- Tientsin 7 764
- Shenyang 2 800
- Wuhan 2 560
- Canton 2 500
- Chungking 2 400
- Nanking 1 750
- Harbin 1 670
- Luta 1 650
- Sian 1 600
- Lanchow 1 450
- Taiyuan 1 350
- Tsingtao 1 300
- Chengtu 1 250
- Changchun 1 200
- Kunming 1 100
- Tsinan 1 100
- Fushun 1 080
- Anshan 1 050
- Chengchow 1 050
- Hangchow 960
- Tangshan 950
- Paotow 920
- Tzepo 850
- Changsha 825
- Shihkiachwang 800
- Tsitsihar 760
- Soochow 730
- Kirin 720
- Suchow 700
- Foochow 680
- Nanchang 675
- Kweiyang 660
- Wusih 650
- Hofei 630
- Hwainan 600
- Penki 600
- Loyang 580
- Nanning 550
- Huhehot 530
- Sining 500
- Wulumuchi 500

HONG KONG (1981)
- Kowloon 2 450
- Hong Kong 1 184
- Tsuen Wan 599

INDIA (1981)
- Calcutta 9 194
- Bombay 8 243
- Delhi 5 729
- Madras 4 289
- Bangalore 2 922
- Ahmedabad 2 548
- Hyderabad 2 546
- Pune 1 686
- Kanpur 1 639
- Nagpur 1 302
- Jaipur 1 015
- Lucknow 1 008
- Coimbatore 920
- Patna 919
- Surat 914
- Madurai 908
- Indore 829
- Varanasi 797
- Jabalpur 757
- Agra 747
- Vadodara 744
- Cochin 686
- Dhanbad 678
- Bhopal 671
- Jamshedpur 670
- Allahabad 650
- Ulhasnagar 649
- Tiruchchirapalli 610
- Ludhiana 606
- Srinagar 606
- Vishakhapatnam 604
- Amritsar 595
- Gwalior 556
- Calicut 546
- Vijawada 543
- Meerut 537
- Dharwad 527
- Trivandrum 520
- Salem 519
- Solapur 515
- Jodhpur 506
- Ranchi 503

INDONESIA (1971)
- Jakarta 4 576
- Surabaya 1 556
- Bandung 1 202
- Semarang 647
- Medan 636
- Palembang 583
- Ujung Pandang 435
- Malang 422
- Surakarta 414
- Yogyakarta 342
- Banjarmasin 282
- Pontianak 218

IRAN (1976)
- Tehran 4 496
- Esfahan 672
- Mashhad 670
- Tabriz 599
- Shiraz 416
- Ahvaz 329
- Abadan 296
- Bakhtāran 291
- Qom 247

IRAQ (1970)
- Baghdad 2 969
- Basra 371
- Mosul 293
- Kirkuk 208

ISRAEL (1981)
- Jerusalem 407
- Tel Aviv-Jaffa 335
- Haifa 230

JAPAN (1980)
- Tokyo 8 349
- Yokohama 2 774
- Osaka 2 648
- Nagoya 2 088
- Kyoto 1 473
- Sapporo 1 402
- Kobe 1 367
- Fukuoka 1 089
- Kitakyushu 1 065
- Kawasaki 1 041
- Hiroshima 899
- Sakai 810
- Chiba 746
- Sendai 665
- Okayama 546
- Kumamoto 526
- Amagasaki 524
- Higashiosaka 522
- Kagoshima 505
- Hamamatsu 491
- Funabashi 479
- Niigata 458
- Shizuoka 458
- Nagasaki 447
- Himeji 446
- Sagamihara 439
- Yokosuka 421
- Kanazawa 418
- Gifu 410
- Nishinoyama 410
- Kurashiki 404
- Toyonaka 403
- Matsuyama 402
- Matsudo 401
- Wakayama 401
- Hachioji 387
- Kawaguchi 379
- Utsunomiya 378
- Ichikawa 364
- Oita 360
- Urawa 358
- Omiya 354
- Asahikawa 353
- Hirakata 353
- Fukuyama 346
- Iwaki 342
- Takatsuki 341
- Suita 332
- Nagano 324
- Hakodate 320
- Takamatsu 317
- Toyama 305
- Toyohashi 304
- Kochi 301
- Fujisawa 300
- Nara 298
- Naha 296
- Machida 295
- Aomori 288
- Koriyama 286
- Akita 285
- Toyota 282
- Yao 273
- Shimonoseki 269
- Maebashi 265
- Miyazaki 265
- Fukushima 263
- Okazaki 262
- Kawagoe 259
- Neyagawa 256
- Akashi 255
- Yokkaichi 255
- Ichinomiya 253
- Sasebo 251

JORDAN (1979)
- Amman 649
- Az Zarqa 216

KOREA, NORTH (1967-70)
- Pyongyang 1 500
- Chongjin 265

KOREA, SOUTH (1980)
- Seoul 8 367
- Pusan 3 160
- Taegu 1 607
- Inchon 1 085
- Kwangju 728
- Taejon 652
- Masan 387
- Seongnam 376
- Chonju 367
- Suweon 311
- Ulsan 253

KUWAIT (1975)
- Kuwait 775

LEBANON (1980)
- Beirut 702

MACAU (1981)
- Macau 250

MALAYSIA (1980)
- Kuala Lumpur 938
- Ipoh 301
- Georgetown 251

MONGOLIA (1980)
- Ulan Bator 419

NEPAL (1971)
- Katmandu 210

PAKISTAN (1972)
- Karachi 3 499
- Lahore 2 165
- Faisalabad 822
- Hyderabad 628
- Rawalpindi 615
- Multan 542
- Gujranwala 360
- Peshawar 268
- Sialkot 204
- Sargodha 201

PHILIPPINES (1975)
- Manila 1 479
- Quezon City 957
- Davao 485
- Cebu 413
- Caloocan 397
- Iloilo 265
- Pasay 255
- Zamboanga 227

SAUDI ARABIA (1974)
- Riyadh 667
- Jedda 561
- Mecca 367
- Taif 205

SINGAPORE (1981)
- Singapore 2 443

SRI LANKA (1981)
- Colombo 1 412

SYRIA (1979)
- Damascus 1 156
- Aleppo 919
- Homs 326
- Latakia 204

TAIWAN (1981)
- Taipei 2 271
- Kaohsiung 1 227
- Taichung 607
- Tainan 595
- Chilung 348
- Sanchung 335
- Chiai 252
- Hsinchu 243

THAILAND (1979)
- Bangkok 4 871

TURKEY (1980)
- Istanbul 2 854
- Ankara 2 204
- Izmir 754
- Adana 569
- Bursa 466
- Gaziantep 371
- Konya 326
- Eskisehir 309
- Kayseri 273

UNITED ARAB EMIRATES (1980)
- Abu Dhabi 449
- Dubai 278

VIETNAM (1973-79)
- Ho Chi Minh City 3 420
- Hanoi 2 571
- Haiphong 1 279
- Da-Nang 492
- Nha-trang 216
- Qui-Nhon 214
- Hue 209

YEMEN, SOUTH (1977)
- Aden 285

AUSTRALASIA

AUSTRALIA (1981)
- Sydney 3 205
- Melbourne 2 723
- Brisbane 1 029
- Adelaide 932
- Perth 899
- Newcastle 389
- Wollongong 223
- Canberra 220

NEW ZEALAND (1981)
- Auckland 770
- Wellington 321
- Christchurch 290

EUROPE

AUSTRIA (1981)
- Vienna 1 516
- Graz 243

BELGIUM (1983)
- Brussels 989
- Gent 237
- Charleroi 216
- Liège 207

BULGARIA (1980)
- Sofia 1 052
- Plovdiv 346
- Varna 289

CZECHOSLOVAKIA (1982)
- Prague 1 184
- Bratislava 392
- Brno 377
- Ostrava 323
- Kosice 209

DENMARK (1981)
- Copenhagen 1 382

FINLAND (1981)
- Helsinki 483

FRANCE (1975)
- Paris 9 863
- Lyon 1 152
- Marseille 1 004
- Lille 929
- Bordeaux 591
- Toulouse 495
- Nantes 438
- Nice 433
- Rouen 389
- Grenoble 389
- Toulon 379
- Strasbourg 355
- St-Etienne 335
- Lens 313
- Nancy 279
- Le Havre 264
- Grasse-Cannes 255
- Tours 235
- Clermont-Ferrand 225
- Valenciennes 224
- Mulhouse 219
- Rennes 213
- Montpellier 205
- Orléans 205
- Dijon 203
- Douai 203

GERMANY, EAST (1981)
- East Berlin 1 158
- Leipzig 562
- Dresden 517
- Karl-Marx-Stadt 318
- Magdeburg 289
- Rostock 234
- Halle 232
- Erfurt 212

GERMANY, WEST (1980)
- West Berlin 1 896
- Hamburg 1 645
- München 1 299
- Cologne 977
- Essen 648
- Frankfurt am Main 629
- Dortmund 608
- Düsseldorf 590
- Stuttgart 581
- Duisburg 558

Bremen 555
Hannover 535
Nürnberg 484
Bochum 401
Wuppertal 393
Bielefeld 313
Gelsenkirchen 304
Mannheim 304
Bonn 288
Wiesbaden 274
Karlsruhe 272
Münster 270
Braunschweig 261
Mönchengladbach 258
Kiel 250
Augsburg 248
Aachen 244
Oberhausen 229
Krefeld 224
Lübeck 221
Hagen 219

GREECE (1981)
Athens 3 027
Thessaloniki 706

HUNGARY (1980)
Budapest 2 060
Miskolc 207

IRISH REPUBLIC (1981)
Dublin 525

ITALY (1981)
Rome 2 831
Milano 1 635
Napoli 1 211
Torino 1 104
Genova 760
Palermo 700
Bologna 456
Firenze 453
Catánia 379
Bari 371
Venézia 333
Verona 261
Messina 256
Trieste 251
Táranto 243
Cágliari 233
Padova 231
Bréscia 206

NETHERLANDS (1983)
Rotterdam 1 025
Amsterdam 936
s'Gravenhage 674
Utrecht 499
Eindhoven 374
Arnhem 291
Heerlen-Kerkrade 265
Enschede-Hengelo 248
Nijmegen 229
Tilburg 221
Haarlem 219
Groningen 206

NORWAY (1980)
Oslo 624
Bergen 208

POLAND (1981)
Warsaw 1 612
Lódz 843
Kraków 723
Wroclaw 622
Poznań 558
Gdańsk 459
Szczecin 390
Katowice 364
Bydgoszcz 352
Lublin 309
Sosnowiec 252
Bytom 238
Czestochowa 238
Gdynia 237
Bialystok 230
Gliwice 202

PORTUGAL (1981)
Lisbon 818
Oporto 330

ROMANIA (1980)
Bucharest 2 090
Brasov 305
Timisoara 287
Cluj 284
Constanta 284
Iasi 271
Galati 261
Craiova 227
Braila 215
Ploiesti 212

SPAIN (1981)
Madrid 3 159
Barcelona 1 753
Valencia 745
Sevilla 646
Zaragoza 572
Málaga 502
Bilbao 433
Valladolid 320
Hospitalet 295
Palma de Mallorca 290
Murcia 285
Córdoba 279
Vigo 261
Gijón 256
Granada 247
Alicante 246
La Coruña 232
Badalona 230

SWEDEN (1980)
Stockholm 1 387
Göteborg 693
Malmö 453

SWITZERLAND (1982)
Zürich 705
Basel 363
Genève 339
Berne 289
Lausanne 226

U.S.S.R. (1981)
Moskva 8 203
Leningrad 4 676
Kiyev 2 248
Tashkent 1 858
Kharkov 1 485
Gorkiy 1 367
Novosibirsk 1 343
Minsk 1 333
Sverdlovsk 1 239
Kuybyshev 1 238
Dnepropetrovsk 1 100
Tbilisi 1 095
Odessa 1 072
Chelyabinsk 1 055
Yerevan 1055
Baku 1 046
Omsk 1 044
Donetsk 1 040
Perm 1 018
Kazan 1 011
Ufa 1 009
Alma-Ata 975
Rostov 957
Volgograd 948
Saratov 873
Riga 850
Krasnoyarsk 820
Zaporozhye 812
Voronezh 809
Lvov 688
Krivoy Rog 663
Yaroslavl 608
Karaganda 583
Krasnodar 581
Novokuznetsk 581
Ustinov 574
Irkutsk 568
Vladivostok 565
Frunze 552
Barnaul 549
Khabarovsk 545
Kishinev 539
Togliatti 533
Tula 521
Zhdanov 511
Dushanbe 510
Vilnius 503
Penza 500
Samarkand 489
Kemerovo 486
Ulyanovsk 485
Orenburg 482
Voroshilovgrad 474
Ivanovo 470
Astrakhan 470
Ryazan 470
Nikolayev 458
Makeyevka 442
Tallinn 442
Tomsk 439
Kalinin 422
Lipetsk 415
Magnitogorsk 413
Bryansk 407
Gomel 405
Nizhniy Tagil 404
Kirov 396
Murmansk 394
Arkhangelsk 391
Kursk 390
Kaunas 383
Groznyy 379
Tyumen 378
Kaliningrad (Kaliningrad region) 366
Brezhnev 346
Cheboksary 340
Gorlovka 338
Chimkent 334
Vinnitsa 332
Kherson 329
Ashkhabad 325
Kurgan 322
Orel 315
Chita 315
Sevastopol 315
Simferopol 314
Smolensk 311
Ulan Ude 310
Vitebsk 310
Mogilev 308
Vladimir 307
Sochi 295
Semipalatinsk 291
Pavlodar 288
Ordzhonikidze 287
Ust-Kamenogorsk 286
Poltava 284
Taganrog 281
Saransk 280
Cherepovets 279
Tambov 277
Dzhambul 277
Kaluga 276
Komsomolsk-na-Amur 274
Stavropol 271
Makhachkala 269
Prokopyevsk 267
Dzerzhinsk 263
Kostroma 259
Dneprodzerzhinsk 257
Belgorod 255
Orsk 254
Zhitomir 254
Chernigov 252

UNITED KINGDOM (1981)
London 6 696
Birmingham 920
Glasgow 762
Liverpool 510
Sheffield 477
Leeds 449
Manchester 449
Edinburgh 419
Bristol 388
Belfast 374
Coventry 314
Bradford 281
Leicester 280
Cardiff 274
Nottingham 271
Hull 268
Wolverhampton 252
Stoke-on-Trent 252
Plymouth 244
Derby 216
Southampton 204

YUGOSLAVIA (1971)
Belgrade 775
Zagreb 602
Skopje 388
Sarajevo 271
Ljubljana 213

NORTH AMERICA

CANADA (1981)
Toronto 2 999
Montréal 2 828
Vancouver 1 268
Ottawa 718
Edmonton 657
Calgary 593
Winnipeg 585
Québec 576
Hamilton 542
St. Catherines 304
Kitchener 288
London 284
Halifax 278
Windsor 246
Victoria 233

COSTA RICA (1982)
San José 265

CUBA (1981)
Havana 1 924
Santiago de Cuba 345
Camagüey 345

DOMINICAN REPUBLIC (1978)
Santo Domingo 1 103
Santiago de los Caballeros 242

EL SALVADOR (1974)
San Salvador 366

GUATEMALA (1979)
Guatemala City 793

HAITI (1982)
Port-au-Prince 888

HONDURAS (1980)
Tegucigalpa 473
San Pedro Sula 343

JAMAICA (1980)
Kingston 671

MEXICO (1979)
Mexico City 14 750
Guadalajara 2 468
Netzahualcóyotl 2 331
Monterrey 2 019
Puebla de Zaragoza 711
Ciudad Juárez 625
León de los Aldamas 625
Tijuana 566
Acapulco 462
Torreón 407
Tampico 390
Chihuahua 386
Mexicali 349
San Luis Potosi 327
Culiacán 324
Hermosillo 319
Veracruz Llave 307
Mérida 270
Saltillo 258
Aguascalientes 257
Morelia 251
Toluca 242
Cuernavaca 241
Reynosa 231
Durango 229
Nuevo Laredo 224
Jalapa 201

NICARAGUA (1979)
Managua 608

PANAMA (1981)
Panama 655

PUERTO RICO (1980)
San Juan 1 086
Ponce 253
Bayamón 209

UNITED STATES (1980)
New York 16 121
Los Angeles 11 498
Chicago 7 870
Philadelphia 5 548
San Francisco 5 180
Detroit 4 618
Boston 3 448
Houston 3 101
Washington 3 061
Dallas 2 975
Cleveland 2 834
Miami 2 644
St. Louis 2 356
Pittsburgh 2 264
Baltimore 2 174
Minneapolis-St Paul 2 114
Seattle 2 093
Atlanta 2 030
San Diego 1 817
Cincinnati 1 660
Denver 1 621
Milwaukee 1 570
Tampa 1 569
Phoenix 1 509
Kansas City 1 327
Indianapolis 1 306
Portland 1 243
Buffalo 1 243
New Orleans 1 187
Providence 1 096
Columbus 1 093
San Antonio 1 072
Sacramento 1 014
Dayton 1 014
Rochester 971
Salt Lake City 936
Memphis 913
Louisville 906
Nashville 851
Birmingham 847
Oklahoma 834
Greensboro 827
Norfolk 807
Albany 795
Toledo 792
Honolulu 763
Jacksonville 738
Hartford 726
Orlando 700
Tulsa 689
Syracuse 643
Scranton 640
Charlotte 637
Allentown 635
Richmond 632
Grand Rapids 602
Omaha 570
Greenville 569
West Palm Beach 577
Austin 537
Tucson 531
Springfield 531
Youngstown 531
Raleigh 531
Flint 522
Fresno 515
Baton Rouge 494
El Paso 480
Knoxville 477
Lansing 472
Las Vegas 463
Albuquerque 454
Harrisburg 447
Mobile 444
Johnson City 434
Charleston (S.C.) 430
Chattanooga 427
New Haven 418
Wichita 411
Columbia 410
Canton 404
Bakersfield 403
Bridgeport 395
Little Rock 394
Davenport 384
Fort Wayne 383
York 381
Shreveport 377
Beaumont 375
Worcester 373
Peoria 366
Newport News 364
Lancaster 362
Stockton 347
Spokane 342
Des Moines 338
Augusta 327
Corpus Christi 326
Madison 324
Lakeland 322
Jackson 320
Utica 320
Lexington-Fayette 318
Colorado Springs 317
Reading 313
Huntingdon 311
Huntsville 309
Evansville 309
Binghamton 301
Santa Barbara 299
Santa Rosa 292
Appleton 291
Salinas 290
Pensacola 290
McAllen 283
South Bend 281
Erie 280
Rockford 280
Kalamazoo 279
Eugene 275
Montgomery 273
Melbourne 273
Charleston (W. Va.) 270
Duluth 267
Modesto 266
Johnstown 265
Newburgh 260
Daytona Beach 259
Macon 254
Salem 250

SOUTH AMERICA

ARGENTINA (1980)
Buenos Aires 9 927
Córdoba 982
Rosario 955
Mendoza 597
La Plata 560
San Miguel de Tucuman 497
Mar del Plata 407
San Juan 290
Santa Fé 287
Salta 260
Bahía Blanca 221
Resistencia 218

BOLIVIA (1980)
La Paz 720
Santa Cruz 255
Cochabamba 205

BRAZIL (1980)
São Paulo 8 732
Rio de Janeiro 5 539
Belo Horizonte 1 937
Salvador 1 502
Recife 1 433
Fortaleza 1 307
Brasilia 1 306
Pôrto Alegre 1 221
Nova Iguaçu 1 184
Curitiba 943
Belém 934
Goiânia 680
Duque de Caxias 666
São Gonçalo 660
Santo André 634
Campinas 587
Osasco 492
Manaus 483
Santos 453
Sào João de Meriti 442
Niterói 433
São Luiz 405
Guarulhos 404
Natal 401
Maceió 390
Campos 357
Londrina 349
Teresina 349
São Bernardo do Campo 348
Juiz de Fora 334
João Pessoa 332
Jaboatao 321
Ribeirão Preto 309
Olinda 308
Feira de Santana 274
Aracaju 273
Campina Grande 266
Pelotas 256

CHILE (1982)
Santiago 3 831
Viña del Mar 306
Valparaiso 272
Concepción 245
Talcahuano 233

COLOMBIA (1973)
Bogotá 2 855
Medellin 1 159
Cali 990
Barranquilla 692
Cartagena 355
Bucaramanga 323
Cucuta 279
Manizales 232
Pereira 227
Ibagué 223

ECUADOR (1981)
Guayaquil 1 169
Quito 844

PARAGUAY (1978)
Asunción 602

PERU (1981)
Lima 4 601
Arequipa 447
Callao 441
Trujillo 355
Chiclayo 280
Chimbote 216

URUGUAY (1975)
Montevideo 1 173

VENEZUELA (1979)
Caracas 2 849
Maracaibo 874
Valencia 488
Barquisimeto 474
Maracay 333
Barcelona-Puerto La Cruz 267
San Cristóbal 264

Population of Countries

Country	Area in thousands of square km	Population in thousands	Density of population per sq. km.	Capital Population in thousands
Afghanistan	647	16 786	26	Kabul (1036)
Albania	29	2 858	99	Tiranë (198)
Algeria	2 382	20 293	9	Algiers (1 503)
Angola	1 247	7 452	6	Luanda (475)
Argentina	2 767	28 432	10	Buenos Aires (9 927)
Australia	7 687	15 175	2	Canberra (220)
Austria	84	7 571	90	Vienna (1 516)
Bangladesh	144	92 619	643	Dacca (3 459)
Belgium	31	9 845	318	Brussels (995)
Belize	23	171	7	Belmopan (3)
Benin	113	3 618	32	Porto-Novo (132)
Bhutan	47	1 355	29	Thimphu (60)
Bolivia	1 099	5 916	5	Sucre (63) La Paz (635)
Botswana	600	859	1	Gaborone (60)
Brazil	8 512	126 806	15	Brasilia (1 306)
Brunei	6	250	42	Bandar Seri Begawan (58)
Bulgaria	111	9 107	82	Sofia (1 052)
Burma	677	37 065	55	Rangoon (2 276)
Burundi	28	4 460	159	Bujumbura (157)
Cambodia	181	6 981	39	Phnom Penh (400)
Cameroon	475	8 865	19	Yaoundé (314)
Canada	9 976	24 625	2	Ottawa (718)
Central African Rep.	623	2 405	4	Bangui (302)
Chad	1 284	4 643	4	Ndjamena (303)
Chile	757	11 487	15	Santiago (3 831)
China	9 597	1 020 673	106	Peking (9 231)
Colombia	1 139	28 776	25	Bogota (2 855)
Congo	342	1 621	5	Brazzaville (422)
Costa Rica	51	2 324	46	San José (265)
Cuba	115	9 782	85	Havana (1 924)
Cyprus	9	645	72	Nicosia (161)
Czechoslovakia	128	15 369	120	Prague (1 184)
Denmark	43	5 118	119	Copenhagen (1 382)
Djibouti	22	332	15	Djibouti (150)
Dominican Republic	49	5 744	117	Santo Domingo (1 103)
Ecuador	284	8 945	31	Quito (844)
Egypt	1 001	44 673	45	Cairo (5 074)
El Salvador	21	4 999	238	San Salvador (366)
Equatorial Guinea	28	381	14	Rey Malabo (37)
Ethiopia	1 222	32 775	27	Addis Abeba (1 277)
Fiji	18	658	37	Suva (68)
Finland	337	4 824	14	Helsinki (483)
France	547	54 221	99	Paris (9 863)
French Guiana	91	64	1	Cayenne (39)
Gabon	268	563	2	Libréville (186)
Gambia	11	635	58	Banjul (109)
Germany, East	108	16 864	156	East Berlin (1 158)
Germany, West	249	61 638	248	Bonn (288)
Ghana	239	12 244	51	Accra (738)
Greece	132	9 793	74	Athens (3 027)
Greenland	2 176	52	0.02	Godthåb (10)
Guatemala	109	7 699	71	Guatemala (793)
Guinea	246	5 285	21	Conakry (526)
Guinea-Bissau	36	594	17	Bissau (109)
Guyana	215	922	4	Georgetown (187)
Haiti	28	5 201	186	Port-au-Prince (888)
Honduras	112	3 955	35	Tegucigalpa (473)
Hong Kong	1	5 233	5 233	Hong Kong (1 184)
Hungary	93	10 702	115	Budapest (2 060)
Iceland	103	236	2	Reykjavik (84)
India	3 288	711 664	216	Delhi (5 729)
Indonesia	2 027	153 032	75	Jakarta (4 576)
Iran	1 648	40 240	24	Tehran (4 496)
Iraq	435	13 997	32	Baghdad (2 969)
Irish Republic	70	3 483	50	Dublin (525)
Israel	21	4 022	192	Jerusalem (407)
Italy	301	56 276	187	Rome (2 831)
Ivory Coast	322	8 568	27	Abidjan (850)
Jamaica	11	2 253	205	Kingston (671)
Japan	372	118 449	318	Tokyo (8 349)
Jordan	98	3 489	36	Amman (649)
Kenya	583	17 864	31	Nairobi (835)
Korea, North	121	18 747	155	Pyongyang (1 500)
Korea, South	98	39 331	401	Seoul (8 367)
Kuwait	18	1 562	87	Kuwait (775)
Laos	237	3 902	16	Vientiane (90)
Lebanon	10	2 739	274	Beirut (702)
Lesotho	30	1 409	47	Maseru (45)
Liberia	111	2 113	19	Monrovia (204)
Libya	1 760	3 224	2	Tripoli (551)
Luxembourg	3	357	119	Luxembourg (79)
Madagascar	587	9 233	16	Antananarivo (400)
Malawi	118	6 267	53	Lilongwe (103)
Malaysia	330	14 765	45	Kuala Lumpur (938)
Mali	1 240	7 342	6	Bamako (419)
Malta	0.3	360	1 200	Valletta (14)
Mauritania	1 031	1 730	2	Nouakchott (135)
Mauritius	2	983	492	Port Louis (146)
Mexico	1 973	73 011	37	Mexico (14 750)
Mongolia	1 565	1 764	1	Ulan Bator (419)
Morocco	447	21 667	48	Rabat (597)
Mozambique	783	11 052	14	Maputo (384)
Namibia	824	852	1	Windhoek (61)
Nepal	141	15 020	107	Katmandu (210)
Netherlands	41	14 310	349	Amsterdam (936)
New Zealand	269	3 158	12	Wellington (321)
Nicaragua	130	2 918	22	Managua (608)
Niger	1 267	5 646	4	Niamey (130)
Nigeria	924	82 392	89	Lagos (1 477)
Norway	324	4 115	13	Oslo (624)
Oman	212	948	4	Muscat (25)
Pakistan	804	87 125	108	Islamabad (77)
Panama	76	2 043	27	Panama (655)
Papua New Guinea	462	3 094	7	Port Moresby (123)
Paraguay	407	3 370	8	Asunción (602)
Peru	1 285	18 790	15	Lima (4 601)
Philippines	300	50 740	169	Manila (1 479)
Poland	313	36 227	116	Warsaw (1 612)
Portugal	92	10 056	109	Lisbon (818)
Puerto Rico	9	3 952	439	San Juan (1 086)
Romania	238	22 638	95	Bucharest (2 090)
Rwanda	26	5 276	203	Kigali (90)
Saudi Arabia	2 150	9 684	5	Riyadh (667)
Senegal	196	5 968	30	Dakar (799)
Sierra Leone	72	3 672	51	Freetown (214)
Singapore	0.6	2 472	4 120	Singapore (2 443)
Somali Republic	638	5 116	8	Mogadishu (400)
South Africa	1 221	31 008	25	Pretoria (563) Cape Town (1 107)
Spain	505	37 935	75	Madrid (3 159)
Sri Lanka	66	15 189	230	Colombo (1 412)
Sudan	2 506	19 451	8	Khartoum (561)
Surinam	163	407	2	Paramaribo (151)
Swaziland	17	585	34	Mbabane (23)
Sweden	450	8 325	19	Stockholm (1 387)
Switzerland	41	6 478	158	Berne (289)
Syria	185	9 660	52	Damascus (1 156)
Taiwan	36	18 458	513	Taipei (2 271)
Tanzania	945	19 111	20	Dar-es-Salaam (757)
Thailand	514	48 450	94	Bangkok (4 871)
Togo	56	2 747	49	Lomé (247)
Trinidad and Tobago	5	1 202	240	Port of Spain (66)
Tunisia	164	6 672	41	Tunis (944)
Turkey	781	46 312	59	Ankara (2 204)
Uganda	236	14 057	60	Kampala (332)
United Arab Emirates	84	790	9	Abu Dhabi (449)
U.S.S.R.	22 402	269 994	12	Moscow (8 203)
United Kingdom	245	55 782	228	London (6 696)
United States	9 363	232 057	25	Washington (3 061)
***Upper Volta**	274	6 360	23	Ouagadougou (173)
Uruguay	178	2 947	17	Montevideo (1 173)
Venezuela	912	14 714	16	Caracas (2 849)
Vietnam	330	56 205	170	Hanoi (2 571)
Western Samoa	3	159	53	Apia (32)
Yemen, North	195	6 077	31	Sana (448)
Yemen, South	288	2 093	7	Aden (285)
Yugoslavia	256	22 646	88	Belgrade (775)
Zaïre	2 345	26 377	11	Kinshasa (2 242)
Zambia	753	6 163	8	Lusaka (641)
Zimbabwe	391	7 540	19	Harare (686)

Renamed Burkina Faso

Philips'

World Atlas